Third Edition

Generalist Social Work Practice

An Empowering Approach

Karla Krogsrud Miley
Black Hawk College

Michael O'Melia
St. Ambrose University

Brenda DuBois
St. Ambrose University

Allyn and Bacon
Boston • London • Toronto • Sydney • Tokyo • Singapore

Senior Editor, Social Work and Family Therapy: Judy Fifer
Editor in Chief, Social Sciences: Karen Hanson
Editorial Assistant: Alyssa Pratt
Executive Marketing Manager: Lisa Kimball
Marketing Manager: Jackie Aaron
Editorial Production Service: Chestnut Hill Enterprises, Inc.
Manufacturing Buyer: Megan Cochran
Cover Administrator: Linda Knowles
Electronic Composition: Omegatype Typography, Inc.

Copyright © 2001, 1998, 1995 by Allyn & Bacon
A Pearson Education Company
160 Gould Street
Needham Heights, MA 02494

Internet: www.abacon.com

Between the time Website information is gathered and published, some sites may have closed. Also, the transcription of URLs can result in typographical errors. The publisher would appreciate notification where these occur so that they may be corrected in subsequent editions.

Library of Congress Cataloging-in-Publication Data
Miley, Karla Krogsrud, 1942–
    Generalist social work practice : an empowering approach / Karla Krogsrud Miley,
Michael O'Melia, Brenda DuBois.—3rd ed.
      p.   cm.
    Includes bibliographical references and index.
    ISBN 0-205-31951-3
    1. Social service. 2. Social case work. I. O'Melia, Michael. II. DuBois, Brenda, 1949–
III. Title.
HV40 .M5223 2000
361.3'2—dc21   00-026662

Printed in the United States of America
10 9 8 7 6 5 4 3 2 1   05 04 03 02 01 00

Photo Credits: Chapter 1: Courtesy of the National Association of Social Workers; Chapter 2: Michael Dwyer/Stock Boston; Chapters 3, 5–7, 9–15: Robert Harbison; Chapter 4: Jim Pickerell; Chapters 8, 9: Will Hart; Chapter 16: Linwood J. Albarado

Contents

Preface

In the preface to the first edition of *Generalist Social Work Practice* we wrote:

> *The approach to social work practice presented in this text acknowledges our interdependence and celebrates the resources that collaboration creates. It maintains a broad-based view of human functioning and explores processes for activating resources in people and their environments. Moreover, it specifically focuses on the nature of the helping relationship itself as a resource for both workers and clients. Collaboration is the heart of this empowering approach. We believe in the creative synergy of collaborative processes. It's how we wrote this book.*

This passage still applies, although it means something more to us now. We continue to find new ways to collaborate—with our students, our colleagues, social workers in our local community, readers and reviewers of the first, second, and third editions, and social work professionals who contribute to the knowledge base of the profession through articles, books, and presentations. We appreciate all the astute feedback we've received, especially the people who noticed what we did right.

This book develops and describes an empowerment-based generalist approach to social work practice. The practice process presented accomplishes three goals:

1. It articulates processes for a general approach to social work practice that readily apply to enhancing human system functioning at any level, including individual, couple, family, group, organization, community, and society.
2. It describes these generalist processes purposefully, using language to create an empowering practice reality of client strengths, resource possibilities, and continual progress.
3. It actuates a social work, value-centered approach that respects human dignity, advocates social justice, and meets social work's dual challenge to enhance human functioning and create responsive environments.

We continue to update our thinking and refine our approach with new research and perspectives. For this third edition, we have integrated over two hundred new resources concentrating on generalist practice, empowerment, the strengths perspective, and multicultural competence. We have added a new feature that appears at the ends of Chapters 1 through 15 called "Reflecting Back." This section singles out chapter-related issues and questions for critical reflection.

Other key additions are also evident. We have more fully articulated the theoretical foundation of an empowerment practice method with new attention to social constructionism and feminism (Chapter 2). We have honed our discussion of multiculturally competent practice to differentiate the knowledge, values, and skill base for competence, and added a section on status and privilege (Chapter 3). There is new information on the dialogue skills of proactive responding (Chapter 7) and additional specification on working with involuntary clients, a new section on elder abuse, and major revisions in the sections on child abuse and intimate partner violence (Chapter 8). Updates to the sections on ethnic and cultural groups and a new section on women of color enhance Chapter 9.

New tools for assessment include frameworks for discovering resources within groups, organizations, and communities (Chapter 10). Descriptions of participatory research and evaluation as an empowerment strategy show the influence of empowerment on research and evaluation (Chapter 15). Special issues related to grief and to closure with larger client systems receive additional attention (Chapter 16). Throughout the book we continue to refine the description of empowering processes with example applications at all levels of practice.

Plan of the Book

This book organizes material into four parts. Part One creates a perspective for empowerment-oriented generalist social work practice. Parts Two, Three, and Four describe and explain empowering processes that generalist social workers apply with clients at the micro-, mid-, and macrolevels of practice.

Part 1, "Social Work Practice Perspectives," describes how generalist social workers using an empowerment-based approach can meet the purposes of social work to enhance human functioning and promote social justice.

Chapter 1—Generalist Social Work Practice: overviews the profession of social work including its value base and purpose. This chapter defines generalist social work, describes roles for generalist practitioners, and introduces the empowering approach to generalist practice featured throughout this text.

Chapter 2—The Ecosystems Perspective: considers the importance of theoretical frameworks for practice, notes the influence of the key perspectives of feminism and social constructionism, describes the ecosystems view and related concepts about human systems, and proposes an ecosystems framework to apply these perspectives in practice.

Chapter 3—Values and Multiultural Competence: explores the various filters through which we experience the world including expectations, values, and culture. It describes how practitioners can infuse professional values and cultural competence into their practice.

Chapter 4—Strengths and Empowerment: introduces the strengths perspective, describes the principles of empowerment, and discusses the implications of these orientations for practice.

Chapter 5—An Empowering Approach to Generalist Practice: integrates the perspectives offered in Part 1 into an empowerment-based generalist practice model and applies it to examples at the micro-, mid-, and macrolevels of practice.

Part 2, "The Dialogue Phase," describes the practice processes related to constructing and maintaining empowering client system–worker relationships, communicating effectively with diverse clients about their situations, and defining a purpose for the work.

Chapter 6—Forming Partnerships: examines the social worker/client system relationship and the qualities necessary for building professional partnerships. Also, this chapter discusses how to relate with clients who are culturally different, oppressed, or reluctant to participate.

Chapter 7—Articulating Situations: discusses dialogue skills. It emphasizes how social workers respond proactively to clients in ways that clarify their challenges and leave them in charge of the direction of the work.

Chapter 8—Defining Directions: explains how workers reorient clients away from describing what is wrong toward creating a vision of how they would like things to be. It also discusses how to increase client motivation, collaborate with clients who resist, partner with involuntary clients, and take priority actions in response to crisis situations.

Part 3, "The Discovery Phase," presents solution-oriented processes for identifying client system strengths and environmental resources and using them in planning.

Chapter 9—Identifying Strengths: describes how workers can orient their conversations with clients to uncover strengths and potential solutions. Specifically, this chapter helps workers locate strengths through solution-focused dialogue, in clients' cultural memberships, and in how clients have responded to adversity.

Chapter 10—Assessing Resource Capabilities: offers processes and tools for social workers and clients at all system levels to explore their resources and the resources of their environments.

Chapter 11—Framing Solutions: describes planning processes in which clients and social workers collaborate to look at situations, determine what is useful, set concrete goals and objectives, and generate possible strategies for change.

Part 4, "The Development Phase," features generalist social work skills for implementing, evaluating, and stabilizing change efforts.

Chapter 12—Activating Resources: describes intervention activities to empower client systems with their own resources and increase their access to the resources of their environments. Workers implement processes to enhance interaction, develop power, change perspectives, manage resources, and educate clients.

Chapter 13—Creating Alliances: explores ways to initiate alliances to support client systems in their change efforts. New relationships formed among clients such as in the examples of empowerment groups, natural support networks, and service delivery alliances all have potential benefits.

Chapter 14—Expanding Opportunities: examines possibilities for resource expansion through social reform, policy development, legislative advocacy, and community change. These activities fulfill the professional mandate to ensure a just distribution of societal resources.

Chapter 15—Recognizing Success: discusses how to monitor the success of the social work effort in order to maintain client motivation, determine effective strategies, and recognize successful outcomes. Specifically, this chapter describes practice evaluation, research, the use of single-system designs, and the influence of empowerment on research processes.

Chapter 16—Integrating Gains: focuses on closure processes. Workers use skills to complete contracts with clients, make necessary referrals, stabilize the progress achieved, and resolve the emotional elements of the relationship. Endings with larger client systems receive special attention.

Ancillary material includes an Instructor's Manual and Internet-based resources. The manual contains chapter outlines, teaching ideas, test items, discussion questions, worksheets, ideas for class exercises, and a full-length generalist-focused case study that coordinates with each of the four parts of this book. An extensive annotated bibliography on empowerment-based social work practice prepared by Miley and DuBois is available in the web gallery on the Allyn and Bacon web site (http://www.abacon.com).

Acknowledgments

We are thankful for the encouragement and support offered by our colleagues, friends, and families. We especially thank David, Jane, and Jim! We are grateful for the technical assistance provided by the River Bend Library System and Black Hawk College librarian, Charlet Key. We also express appreciation to Karen Hanson for her unwavering commitment to this project; to Judy Fifer for her thoughtful direction and support; and to both for their diligent work during various stages of production. We also thank the reviewers who offered thoughtful comments on the first two editions of this book: Edward W. Ihle, Syracuse University; Betty J. Kramer, University of Wisconsin–Madison; Stephen C. Anderson, University of Oklahoma; Thomas J. Blakely, Western Michigan University; M. Jenise Comer, Central Missouri State University; Mark W. Lusk, University of Montana; Robert Madden, Saint Joseph College; Mary Harris Pegram, Bowling Green State University; and Eleanor Reardon Tolson, The University of Illinois at Chicago. The following reviewers also made helpful comments in preparation for the third edition: Robert H. Keefe, Syracuse University, and Doman Lum, California State University, Sacramento.

Part 1

Social Work Practice Perspectives

Social workers strive to create order and enhance opportunities for people in an increasingly complex world. The social work profession charges its members with the responsibility of promoting competent human functioning and fashioning a responsive and just society. To achieve these goals, social workers require a clear understanding of the way things are and a positive view of the way things could be. Social work practitioners fine-tune their vision by incorporating into it professional perspectives on human behavior, cultural diversity, social environments, and approaches to change.

Part 1 describes the knowledge, values, and skills that social workers apply in practice. Specifically, it defines generalist social work, an approach in which practitioners work with a variety of human systems, including individuals, families, groups, organizations, and communities. The chapters in this section discuss generalist social workers and the theoretical frameworks, professional values, and practice orientations that support their work. These perspectives guide generalist practitioners to an empowering practice approach that views human behavior in context, builds on the inherent strengths and potential capabilities of human systems, and respects cultural differences.

Chapter 1

Generalist Social Work Practice

"What's working well that you would like to see continue?" With this question, Andrea Barry, a family preservation worker, shifts focus in her work with the Clemens family. She carefully studies the reactions to her question on the faces of the family members who are gathered with her around their kitchen table. She reads caution, apprehension, maybe even a little anger, and yes, there it is, a growing sense of surprise, of intrigue with her approach. As a social worker with the family preservation program of Northside Family Services, Andrea has seen this before. Preparing to fend off the blame of abuse or neglect, families involved with the program are often taken off guard by the careful, nonjudgmental phrasing of her questions. With the question, "What's working well?" Andrea recognizes family strengths and looks toward the future, toward things families can still do something about. In other words, she sets the stage for empowering families by focusing on their strengths and promoting their competence.

Andrea's question embodies her view of how families might find themselves in this predicament. To continue to focus on "What are your problems?" doesn't make sense to Andrea who sees family difficulties arising from the challenge of scarce resources rather than resulting from something that the family is doing wrong. In fact, as reflected in her question, Andrea believes that even those families referred by the Child Protective Unit for work with the family preservation program are actually doing a lot right. She regards families as doing the best they can with currently available resources. So, of course, in trying to overcome their present difficulties, the subsequent question becomes, "What can we do to build on your strengths?" rather than "What else is wrong?" Her approach presumes that all families have strengths and are capable of making changes; it prompts them into collaborating with her as partners in the change process.

Andrea has learned from experience that different families benefit from different constellations of resources for optimal functioning. Some family members need to understand themselves and each other better. Others need information about how to cope with the inevitable and also the unexpected changes that occur throughout their lives. Often, isolated families benefit from connections to the support of interpersonal relationships. Still other families need to access resources from within the community. Andrea teams with families to manage a network of social services, selecting among possibilities ranging from housing assistance to job training to crisis child care to child abuse prevention.

Andrea also recognizes the need to broaden her focus, to look beyond the needs of individual families in order to serve their best interests. Many times, families, confined by forces they consider are beyond their personal control, seek a professional voice to speak out for them at the levels of government, policy, and resource allocation. They certainly need power and resources to take charge of their own directions in a world that has grown complex and confusing.

As Andrea provides opportunities for the Clemens family members to respond to her question, she reminds herself that this family is unique. She knows to attend to the ways that her clients are similar as well as to the ways they are different. As an African American woman, Andrea herself is sensitive to the confinement of prejudgments. The strengths the Clemens family members have to offer and the challenges they face are particular to their own situation. Demonstrating her cultural competence, Andrea thoughtfully examines the assumptions she makes about people based on their obvious similarities in order not to ignore their inevitable differences.

Clients have taught Andrea that individual differences themselves can be the keys to solutions. Social work practitioners accept the challenge to enable each client system to access its own unique capabilities and the resources of its particular context. Andrea's role in the professional relationship is that of partner in order to *empower* families with their own strengths, not *overpower* families with her own considerable practice knowledge and skills. Andrea has learned to depend on each family system's special competencies to guide her in this empowering process.

Even though Andrea considers the Clemens family as a whole, she will not neglect her professional mandate to act in the best interest of the Clemens children. Ethical considerations and legal obligations compel Andrea to protect the children in this family. However, family service social workers simultaneously focus on the preservation of families and the protection of children. Andrea sees the needs of families and children as convergent. What benefits the family will help the children in their development. What benefits the children will contribute to the cohesiveness of the family. Theoretically, she sees the whole family system as her client and knows that any change in the family system will create changes for individual family members.

Andrea's work with the Clemens family reinforces her opinion that social policy which aims to keep families together is good policy. She always feels best when implementing a policy that reflects a professional philosophy that so neatly fits her own values. The policy of family preservation makes sense in Andrea's practice experience, as well. She has observed the trauma for families and children when children at-risk are removed from their own homes. And, reuniting them, even after positive changes occur, always seems to be a difficult transition. Research in the field of child welfare confirms Andrea's practice observations and lends support for the current policy of family preservation. Andrea believes that keeping families together makes good economic sense, too. She suspects that economic considerations are a major force motivating the development of policies that favor family preservation.

"What's working well that you'd like to see continue?" A simple question, yet it reflects Andrea Barry's empowerment orientation toward social work practice. Andrea has learned that even simple questions can have dramatic effects. Simple questions set the tone, bond relationships, and lead to successful solutions.

This chapter provides an overview of social work practice. It describes the underlying values, purposes, and perspectives that contribute to the empowering approach that Andrea Barry uses and explains what generalist social workers do. Specifically, this chapter:

- Explores the value base and purpose of the social work profession
- Defines the integrated elements of generalist social work including practice, policy, and research
- Discusses the activities of social workers at each system level of practice
- Offers a comprehensive framework explaining the multiple functions and roles of generalist social workers
- Introduces the foundations for empowering social work practice including an ecosystemic view of human behavior, sensitivity to human diversity, and a strengths orientation to change

The outcome is a foundation on which to build an understanding of social work practice from a generalist perspective.

Social Work Values and Purpose

Andrea Barry practices in family services—one of many fields of social work. Other practice arenas include school social work, medical social work, probation and other criminal justice services, mental health, youth services, child welfare, housing and urban development, to name a few. All social work practitioners, regardless of their particular field of practice, share a common professional identity and work toward similar purposes. The National Association of Social Workers (NASW), in its *Code of Ethics* (National, 2000), defines this unifying purpose, or mission, of all social work as "to enhance human well-being and help meet the basic human needs of all people, with particular attention to the needs and empowerment of people who are vulnerable, oppressed, and living in poverty" (Preamble). To meet this purpose, social workers develop a dual focus on changing both persons and social conditions. As Schwartz (1974) says:

> There can be no "choice"—or even a division of labor—between serving individual needs and dealing with social problems, if we understand that a private trouble is simply a specific example of a public issue, and that a public issue is made up of many private troubles. (p. 95)

Social workers strive to strengthen human functioning and promote the effectiveness of societal structures. This simultaneous focus on persons and their environments permeates all social work practice. As a social worker, Andrea Barry works with the Clemens family to facilitate the adaptive functioning of their family and preserve their unity. She also works to create a resource-rich and responsive environment which will contribute to the development and stability of the Clemens family. Both of these activities reflect Andrea's integration of the fundamental values of the social work profession. The overarching values of *human dignity and worth* and *social justice* shape her attitudes; the purpose of the profession directs her actions.

Human Dignity and Worth

Valuing the inherent human dignity and worth of all people reflects a particular view of humankind. This view "implies that human beings have a right to be respected and that social workers should not discriminate among individuals based on considerations such as those related to race, ethnicity, gender, sexual preference, or socioeconomic status" (Reamer, 1987, p. 801). The NASW *Code of Ethics* (2000) charges social workers to "treat each person in a caring and respectful fashion, mindful of individual differences and cultural and ethnic diversity,"…"promote clients' socially responsible self-determination,"…"enhance clients' capacity and opportunity to change and to address their own needs,"… and "resolve conflicts between clients' interests and the broader society's interests in a socially responsible manner" (Preamble). Respectful interaction with others affirms their sense of dignity and worth. Effective social workers treat people with consideration, respect their uniqueness, appreciate the validity of their perspectives, and listen carefully to what they have to say. Ultimately, according people dignity and worth affords them the opportunities and resources of a just society.

Social Justice

Social justice refers to the manner in which society distributes resources among its members. Social justice is an "ideal condition in which all members of a society have the same basic rights, protection, opportunities, obligations, and social benefits" (Barker, 1999, p. 451). Saleebey (1990) details the fabric of social justice:

(a) *Social resources are distributed on the principle of need with the clear understanding that such resources underlie the development of personal resources, with the proviso that entitlement to such resources is one of the gifts of citizenship.*

(b) *Opportunities for personal and social development are open to all with the understanding that those who have been unfairly hampered through no fault of their own will be appropriately compensated.*

(c) *The establishment, at all levels of society, of agenda and policies that have human development and the enriching of human experience as their essential goal and are understood to take precedence over other agenda and policies is essential.*

(d) *The arbitrary exercise of social and political power is forsaken.*

(e) *Oppression as a means for establishing priorities, for developing social and natural resources and distributing them, and resolving social problems is forsworn. (p. 37)*

Social injustice prevails when society infringes on human rights, holds prejudicial attitudes toward some of its members, and institutionalizes inequality by discriminating against segments of its citizenry. Encroachments on human and civil rights deny equal access to opportunities and resources, limiting full participation in society. Collectively, the injustices enacted by advantaged groups create conditions of discrimination and oppression for disadvantaged groups. Personally, members of oppressed groups often experience dehumanization and victimization. Social workers understand the consequences of injustice and intervene to achieve individual and collective social and economic justice.

Social workers actualize the social justice ideal by expanding the opportunities and resources provided by social institutions—adequate education, political participation, economic self-sufficiency, and health and well-being. They promote just social and economic policies in the areas of health, education, employment, and social welfare and organize the social service delivery network in such a way that all persons can access its benefits. Ensuring people equal access affirms human dignity and worth and defines a society as just.

Translating Values into Practice

Expanding on the foundational values of human dignity and social justice, the professional values of social work set the standards for what is desirable in practice. The Council on Social Work Education (CSWE), which accredits undergraduate and graduate social work programs, lists professional values that guide professional practice:

- *Social workers' professional relationships are built on regard for individual worth and dignity and are furthered by mutual participation, acceptance, confidentiality, honesty, and responsible handling of conflict.*

- *Social workers respect people's right to make independent decisions and to participate actively in the helping process.*
- *Social workers are committed to assisting client systems to obtain needed resources.*
- *Social workers strive to make social institutions more humane and responsive to human needs.*
- *Social workers demonstrate respect for and acceptance of the unique characteristics of diverse populations.*
- *Social workers are responsible for their own ethical conduct, the quality of their practice, and seeking continuous growth in the knowledge and skills of their profession. (Council on Social Work Education, 1992, p. 6)*

Achieving the Purpose of Social Work

Social work focuses on *releasing human power* in individuals to reach their potential and contribute to the collective good of society; and it emphasizes *releasing social power* to create changes in society, social institutions, and social policy which in turn create opportunities for individuals (Smalley, 1967). This view conceptualizes the purpose of social work in relation to both individual and collective resources. The trademark of the social work profession is this simultaneous focus on persons and their impinging social and physical environments.

To this end, practitioners work with people in ways that strengthen their sense of competence, link them with needed resources, and promote organizational and institutional change so that the structures of society respond to the needs of all societal members (National, 1981). Social workers also engage in research to contribute to social work theory and evaluate practice methods (Council, 1992). To achieve this purpose, social workers engage in a variety of activities.

First, workers strive to "enhance the problem-solving, coping, and developmental capacities of people" (National, 1981, p. 12). They work with clients to assess challenges in social functioning, process information in ways that enhance their ability to discover solutions, develop skills to resolve problems in living, and create support for change.

Second, social workers link people with resources and services, a vital strategy in any change effort. More than simply connecting people with services, workers advocate optimal benefits, develop networks of communication among organizations in the social service delivery network, and establish access to resources. When necessary resources do not exist, practitioners generate new opportunities, programs, and services.

Third, the NASW charges practitioners to work toward a humane and adequate social service delivery system. To accomplish this, social workers champion the planning of pertinent programs by advocating client-centeredness, coordination, effectiveness, and efficiency in the delivery of services. Importantly, they strengthen lines of accountability and ensure the application of professional standards, ethics, and values in service delivery.

Fourth, social workers participate in social policy development. In the arena of social policy, workers analyze social problems for policy ramifications, develop new policies, and retire those that are no longer productive. They also translate statutes, policies, and regulations into responsive programs and services that meet individual and collective needs.

Finally, practitioners engage in research to further the knowledge and skill base of social work. Effective and ethical social work depends on practitioners using research-based theory and methods as well as contributing to the knowledge base of the professional through their own research and evaluation activities.

Generalist Social Work

Generalist social work provides an integrated and multileveled approach for meeting the purposes of social work. Generalist practitioners acknowledge the interplay of personal and collective issues, prompting them to work with a variety of human systems—societies, communities, neighborhoods, complex organizations, formal groups, families, and individuals—to create changes which maximize human system functioning. This means that generalist social workers work directly with client systems at all levels, connect clients to available resources, intervene with organizations to enhance the responsiveness of resource systems, advocate just social policies to ensure the equitable distribution of resources, and research all aspects of social work practice (Figure 1.1).

The generalist approach to social work practice rests on four major premises. First, human behavior is inextricably connected to the social and physical environment. Second, based on this linkage among persons and environments, opportunities for enhancing the functioning of any human system include changing the system itself, modifying its interactions with the

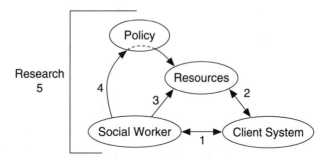

FIGURE 1.1 **Generalist: Practice, Policy, and Research. Generalist social workers:**
(1) **Work directly with client systems—individuals, families, groups, organizations, and communities**
(2) **Connect client systems to resources**
(3) **Enhance the responsiveness of resource systems**
(4) **Advocate just social policies to ensure equitable resource distribution**
(5) **Research all aspects of the process**

From "Skills for Protecting Children While Preserving Families" by M. O'Melia (May, 1995). Used with permission of the author.

environment, and altering other systems within its environment. Generalist practitioners implement multilevel assessments and multimethod interventions in response to these possible avenues for change. Third, work with any level of human system—from individual to society—uses similar social work processes. Social work intervention with all human systems requires an exchange of information through some form of dialogue, a process of discovery to locate resources for change, and a phase of development to accomplish the purposes of the work. Finally, generalist practitioners have responsibilities beyond direct practice to work toward just social policies as well as to conduct and apply research.

Levels of Intervention in Generalist Practice

Generalist social workers look at issues in context and find solutions within the interactions between people and their environments. The generalist approach moves beyond the confines of individually focused practice to the expansive sphere of intervention at multiple system levels (Figure 1.2). The multilevel nature of generalist social work practice consists of:

> *assisting individuals, families, small groups, and larger social systems to work on change which promotes the best possible relationship between people and their environment. In this process, all social work methods—traditional and innovative— are utilized, singly or in combination, to meet reality needs and to alleviate stresses in ways that enhance or strengthen the inherent capacities of client systems. Generalist practice is addressed to the solution and/or prevention of problems at all levels of intervention: intrapersonal, familial, interpersonal, organizational, community, institutional, and societal. (Brown, 1982, p. 123)*

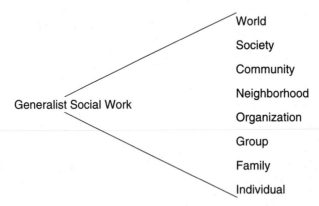

FIGURE 1.2   Generalist Social Work. Generalist social work involves intervention with a variety of social systems. These systems may be the "client system" or they may be the target system for change.

In generalist social work, the nature of presenting situations, the particular systems involved, and potential solutions shape interventions rather than a social worker's adherence to a particular method.

The view of generalist social work is like the view through a wide-angle lens of a camera. It takes in the whole even when focusing on an individual part. Workers assess people in the backdrop of their settings and interventions unfold with an eye to outcomes at all system levels. Visualize potential clients and agents for change on a continuum ranging from micro- to mid- to macrolevel interventions, small systems to large systems, including the system of the social work profession itself (Figure 1.3). Generalist social workers view problems in context, combine practice techniques to fit the situation, and implement skills to intervene at multiple system levels.

Working with Microlevel Systems

Microlevel intervention focuses on work with people individually, in families, or in small groups to foster changes within personal functioning, in social relationships, and in the ways people interact with social and institutional resources. Social workers draw on the knowledge and skills of clinical practice, including strategies such as crisis intervention, family therapy, linkage and referral, and the use of group process. For instance, in this chapter's introductory example, Andrea Barry could work with Mr. and Mrs. Clemens to improve their parenting skills or refer them to a parent support group.

Although microlevel interventions create changes in individual functioning, social workers do not necessarily direct all efforts at changing individuals themselves. Often, workers target changes in other systems, including changes in the social and physical environments, to facilitate improvement in an individual's or family's social functioning. These activities involve work with systems at other levels.

Working with Midlevel Systems

Midlevel intervention creates changes in task groups, teams, organizations, and the network of service delivery. In other words, the locus for change is within organizations and formal

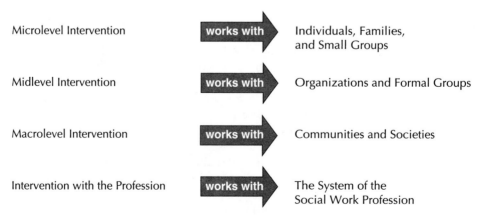

	works with	
Microlevel Intervention		Individuals, Families, and Small Groups
Midlevel Intervention		Organizations and Formal Groups
Macrolevel Intervention		Communities and Societies
Intervention with the Profession		The System of the Social Work Profession

FIGURE 1.3   System Levels for Social Work Intervention

groups including their structures, goals, or functions. For example, if in working with the Clemens children, Andrea learns of their embarrassment at receiving lunch subsidies because the school physically segregates the "free lunch" students from the "full pay" students in the cafeteria, she can help them and other families who report similar concerns by working directly on the school's policy. Andrea's work with the school to address this demeaning and discriminatory practice represents a midlevel intervention. Effecting change in organizations requires an understanding of group dynamics, skills in facilitating decision-making, and a proficiency in organizational planning. Working with agency structures and the social service delivery network is essential for developing quality resources and services.

Working with Macrolevel Systems

Macrolevel intervention facilitates social change through work with neighborhoods, communities, and society. At this level, generalist practitioners work to achieve social change through neighborhood organizing, community planning, locality development, public education, and social action. A worker's testimony at a legislative hearing reflects a macrolevel strategy to support a comprehensive national family welfare policy. Working with neighborhood groups to lobby for increased city spending on police protection, street repair, and park maintenance is another example of a macrolevel intervention. Social policy formulation and community development lead to macrosystem change.

Working with the Social Work Profession

Finally, generalist practitioners address issues within the *system* of the social work profession itself. These activities define professional relationships with social work and interdisciplinary colleagues, reorient priorities within the social work profession, or reorganize the system of service delivery. For instance, by supporting social work licensure and the legal regulation of practice, practitioners use their collective influence to ensure the competence of those persons who become social workers. Standard-setting and accountability call for social workers to be actively involved in the system of the social work profession.

Policy and Generalist Practice

Generalist social workers recognize the implications of social policy. Reflecting societal values and traditions, social policy determines how a society distributes its resources among its members to promote well-being. Social policies direct the delivery of health and human services. Policies particularly relevant to social work include government plans and programs in the areas of social welfare, economic security, education, criminal justice, and health care, among others (Barker, 1999). Social workers press for fair and responsive social policies that benefit all persons and advocate changes in policies affecting disenfranchised and oppressed groups whose dignity has been diminished by injustice.

Policy considerations characterize all social work practice (Schorr, 1985). First, value-based policies implicitly guide how we orient social workers to the profession, the ways we train workers for practice, and the choices we make to define the dimensions of practice activities. Second, policy shapes bureaucracy and the structure of agency practice—a culture which ultimately defines who gets services and what services they get. And, finally, in their own practice activities, social workers unavoidably make policy judgments by attending to or overlooking constantly changing social realities. To this list, Specht (1983) adds other major policy decisions that arise in the sociopolitical context of social work practice. These policy choices determine eligibility requirements, the array of programs and services offered, the structure of the social service delivery system, financing for health and human services, the form and substance of educating social work practitioners, and the regulation of social work activities.

To understand the impact of social policies on social work practice, consider how policy affects all aspects of Andrea Barry's practice in family preservation. Social policies, framed at the legislative level in the amendments to the Social Security Act and implemented through state administrative procedures, define the goals and processes that Andrea implements in family preservation. Agency-level policy to design programs and services consistent with empowering principles and a strengths perspective further refines Andrea's approach to working with families. And, as a professional social worker, Andrea's direct practice with families falls within the policy guidelines established by the NASW's standards for child protection. Policy choices at many levels—federal, state, agency, and worker—influence the day-to-day practice of social work.

Research in Generalist Practice

Research is a method of systematic investigation or experimentation, the results of which can enrich theory and refine practice applications. Research informs social work practice in several ways. It contributes to the theoretical base for understanding human behavior and change. Further, research is a tool for designing intervention strategies, measuring intervention effectiveness, and evaluating practice. And, research is essential for program development and policy analysis. Aware of the integral relationship between theory and practice, generalist social workers utilize research-based knowledge to support practice activities and directly conduct their own research and analysis.

Research enhances social work effectiveness as illustrated in the example of Andrea Barry's work with clients in family preservation. Her course work on empowerment-based practice, theories about families, and the dynamics of child abuse and neglect—all information rooted in decades of social work research—informs Andrea each time she interacts with her clients. Andrea regularly reads professional journals, especially *Social Work, Child Welfare,* the *Journal of Multicultural Social Work,* and *Families in Society,* to keep up with practice innovations. She also uses evaluation and research techniques to monitor her clients' progress toward goals and assess her own practice effectiveness. Additionally, Andrea's work presents opportunities to add to the knowledge base of the profession as she and other family preservation workers carefully document the results of a new intervention program piloted by her agency. Research supports practice and practitioners conduct research.

Advantages of a Multifaceted Approach

Social workers realize many advantages from their generalist practice approach. Inevitably, changes in one system ripple through other interrelated systems as well. In other words, a significant improvement in a client or environmental system might go a long way toward initiating other beneficial changes. Or, a policy change may have far-reaching benefits for an entire society. And, research demonstrating effective change strategies in one situation may lead to broader implementations to assist others in similar situations. For any given problem, the generalist uncovers more than one possible solution.

Generalist social workers see many possible angles from which to approach any solution. They analyze the many dimensions of any challenging situation to discover entry points for change. They also align the motivations and efforts of client systems with systems in their environments, synchronizing the movements of all involved toward achieving the desired outcome. Generalist social work frames a way of thinking about both problems and solutions in context, and it describes a way of working with clients at a variety of system levels.

Social Work Functions and Roles

Generalists work with systems at many levels, but what does that actually mean in their daily practice of social work? As a family preservation worker, Andrea Barry intervenes directly with individuals and families. She provides them with education, counseling, and linkage to needed community resources—activities associated with roles at the microlevel. Yet, Andrea's work encompasses more than microlevel intervention. In her position, Andrea identifies gaps in the social service delivery network when resources families need are not available. As a result, she works with other professionals in child welfare to address social service delivery issues—a midlevel intervention. She and her interdisciplinary colleagues are developing a community education plan to promote effective parenting—a macrolevel strategy. Finally, Andrea systematically evaluates the effectiveness of her work and keeps abreast of child welfare policy initiatives. In doing so, Andrea demonstrates the integration of research, policy, and multilevel intervention that characterizes generalist social work practice.

Activities of generalist social work practice fall broadly into three related functions—consultancy, resource management, and education (Tracy & DuBois, 1987; DuBois & Miley, 1999). (See Figure 1.4.) Within each function are associated roles that explicate the nature of the interaction between clients and social workers at various system levels. These roles define responsibilities for both client systems and practitioners. Interventions designed within this model cover the range of issues presented to generalist social workers by clients at all system levels.

Consultancy

Through consultancy, social workers seek to find solutions for challenges in social functioning with individuals, families, groups, organizations, and communities. Within the roles of the consultancy function of social work, workers and clients confer and deliberate together to develop plans for change. Practitioners and clients share their expertise with one another for the purpose of resolving personal, family, organizational, and societal problems. Consultancy acknowledges that both social workers and client systems bring information and resources, actual and potential, which are vital for resolving the issue at hand.

As a collaborative process, consultancy draws upon the knowledge, values, and skills of social workers and clients to clarify issues, recognize strengths, discuss options, and identify potential courses of action. As consultants, social workers empower clients by re-

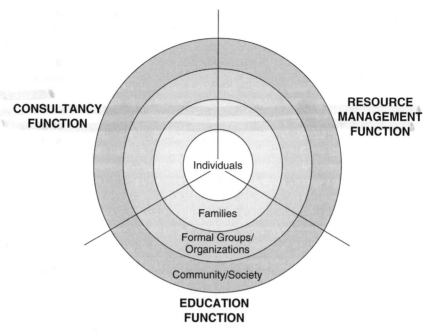

FIGURE 1.4 **Social Work Functions. Three functions—consultancy, resource management, and education—broadly categorize social work activities at all system levels.**

specting their competence, drawing upon their strengths, and working with them collaboratively to discover solutions. These consultancy activities cast workers into the roles of enabler, facilitator, planner, and colleague (Table 1.1).

Enabler Role

As enablers, social workers engage individuals, families and small groups in counseling processes. An enabler encourages action by helping "people identify their needs, clarify their problems, and develop the capacity to deal with them effectively" (Brieland, Costin, &

TABLE 1.1 **Consultancy Roles**

Level	Role	Strategy
Micro-	Enabler	Empower clients in *finding solutions*
Mid-	Facilitator	Foster *organizational development*
Macro-	Planner	Coordinate program and policy development through *research and planning*
Social Work System	Colleague/Monitor	Mentor, guide, and support *professional acculturation*

Adapted with permission of the authors from *Information Model for Generalist Social Work Practice,* p. 2, by B. C. Tracy and B. DuBois, 1987. All rights reserved.

Atherton, 1985, p. 159). In other words, enablers are change agents who "use varying approaches in order to provide the conditions necessary for clients to achieve their purposes, meet life challenges, engage in their natural life development processes, and carry out their tasks" (Maluccio, 1981, p. 19). In the context of work with groups, social workers as enablers help "the group develop a supportive culture in which members can count on one another for mutual aid in overcoming problems" (Toseland & Rivas, 1998, p. 254). As enablers, practitioners consult with individual and family client systems to improve social functioning by modifying behaviors, relationship patterns, and social and physical environments.

Facilitator Role
Facilitators activate the participation of organizational members in change efforts. By facilitating group processes, social workers encourage competent group functioning, stimulate intra-group support, observe group interaction, offer constructive feedback, and share information about group dynamics. As facilitators, social workers enhance linkages within organizations and help them counteract apathy and disorganization (Pincus & Minahan, 1973). In this role, practitioners may even target their own agency settings to increase the cooperation of staff and ensure the effectiveness of social service delivery.

Planner Role
Effective planners "need to understand the social fabric of society, community sociology, social problems, community psychology, social planning and social policy" (Brieland, Costin, & Atherton, 1985, p. 163). Social planners use research and planning strategies to collect data systematically, explore alternative courses of action, and recommend changes to community leaders (Barker, 1999). Techniques for planning include needs assessments, service inventories, community profiles, community inventories, environmental scans, and field research to understand social problems and develop innovative solutions at the macrolevel.

Colleague and Monitor Roles
Through their colleague and monitor roles, social workers uphold expectations for the ethical conduct of members of their profession. Consultative relationships among social work practitioners lead to sound practice and professional development. As colleagues, social workers develop working partnerships with other practitioners through their participation in professional organizations such as the NASW and its local membership groups, and through their everyday contacts with other professionals. The *Code of Ethics* (National, 2000) specifically casts social workers as monitors, charging them to review the professional activities of peers to ensure quality and maintain professional standards.

Resource Management

In the resource management function, social workers stimulate exchanges with resources that client systems already use to some extent, access available resources that client systems are not using, and develop resources that are not currently available. Resources are sources of power and provide the impetus for change at any system level. Resources are found within individuals, in relationships, and in social institutions.

Resources are not gifts bestowed by social workers. Instead, both social workers and clients play active roles in managing resources. Clients, as resource managers, take action to explore existing opportunities, activate dormant supports, and assert their rights to services. Social workers bring the resources of professional practice—the value imperative of equitable access to societal resources, the broad knowledge of the availability of resources, and a repertoire of skills to access and develop resources. Resource management is empowering when it increases the client system's own resourcefulness through coordinating, systematizing, and integrating rather than through controlling or directing. Social workers as resource managers function in the roles of broker, advocate, convener, mediator, activist, and catalyst (Table 1.2).

Broker and Advocate Roles

The professional mandate of the social work profession, "to help people obtain resources," lays the foundation for the roles of broker and advocate. As brokers, social workers link clients with available resources by providing information about resource options and making appropriate referrals (McPheeters, 1971). Competent brokers assess situations, provide clients with choices among alternative resources, facilitate clients' connections with referral agencies, and follow-up to evaluate their efforts.

As advocates, social workers act as intermediaries between clients and other systems to protect clients' rights. Frequently, advocates function as spokespersons for clients in the bureaucratic maze of governmental structures. Advocates plead causes on behalf of clients to secure "a needed resource or service or obtain a policy change or concession from a resistant, disinterested, or unresponsive system" (Pincus & Minahan, 1973, p. 113). Circumstances often press social workers to take on advocacy roles because social welfare history "has been fraught with attempts to deprive potential recipients of their rights to the service for a host of usually moralistic excuses" (Federico, 1983, p. 244).

Convener and Mediator Roles

Social workers often serve as conveners and mediators with formal groups and organizations to coordinate resource distribution and development. Conveners promote interagency

TABLE 1.2   Resource Management Roles

Level	Role	Strategy
Micro-	Broker/Advocate	Link clients with resources through *case management*
Mid-	Convener/Mediator	Assemble groups and organizations to *network* for resource development
Macro-	Activist	Initiate and sustain social change through *social action*
Social Work System	Catalyst	Stimulate *community service* through interdisciplinary activities

Adapted with permission of the authors from *Information Model for Generalist Social Work Practice*, p. 2, by B. C. Tracy and B. DuBois, 1987. All rights reserved.

discussion and planning, mobilize coordinated networks for effective service delivery, and advocate policies that promise equitable funding and just service provisions. As conveners, social workers use networking strategies to bring together diverse representatives to address collective goals such as in the examples of community task groups, interagency committees, and United Way panels. When controversy or conflicts of interest arise, social workers as mediators use their skills for negotiating differences and resolving conflicts. Conveners–mediators ally service providers in identifying service delivery gaps and encouraging proactive interagency planning, activities that are central to prevention efforts in social work.

Activist Role

Generalist social workers are in positions to identify societal conditions detrimental to the well-being of clients—a view which informs the social worker as activist. According to Barker (1999), social activists alert the general public about social problems or injustices and garner support to alleviate these conditions. Social activists mobilize resources, build coalitions, take legal actions, and lobby for legislation. They create just social policies as well as initiate new funding or funding reallocations which address their identified priority issues. Engendering community support, activists empower community-based efforts to resolve community issues, redress social injustice, and generate social reform.

Catalyst Role

As catalysts for change, social workers team with other professionals to develop humane service delivery, advocate just social and environmental policy, and support a world view acknowledging global interdependence. Through professional organizations, social workers lobby at the state and federal levels and provide expert testimony. As catalysts, social workers initiate, foster, and sustain interdisciplinary cooperation to highlight client, local, national, and international issues.

Education

The social work function of education requires an empowering information exchange between a client system and a social work practitioner. Mutual sharing of knowledge and ideas are central to the educational function. In fact, educational processes at all system levels reflect partnerships of co-learners and co-teachers. Freire (1993) supports dialogue as the most effective educational tool. Collaborative learning presumes that client systems are self-directing, possess reservoirs of experiences and resources on which to base educational experiences, and desire immediate applications of new learning. The education function of social work respects the knowledge and experience that all parties contribute. Functioning as educators involves social workers in the activities of teaching, training, outreach, and research and scholarship (Table 1.3).

Teacher Role

The teaching role in social work empowers client systems with information to stimulate "effective mastery of life tasks, role performance and control over one's life" (Freud, 1987, p. 115). Through teaching strategies, social workers strengthen clients with information to resolve current issues and to prevent other difficulties from emerging. As an educator, a

TABLE 1.3   Education Roles

Level	Role	Strategy
Micro-	Teacher	Facilitate *information processing* and provide educational programming
Mid-	Trainer	Instruct through *staff development*
Macro-	Outreach	Convey public information about social issues and social services through *community education*
Social Work System	Researcher/Scholar	Engage in discovery for *knowledge development*

worker "presents new information to help resolve [clients'] concerns; demonstrates and models new or improved behaviors; and suggests role plays, simulations, and in-vivo activities to help [clients] practice new or different ways of behaving in problematic situations" (Toseland & Rivas, 1998, p. 256). To affirm clients' existing knowledge and skills, social workers select collaborative learning strategies to implement educational activities. Educational exchanges may occur in structured client–worker conferences, in formalized instructional settings, or in experiential exercises such as role plays.

Trainer Role

As educational resource specialists for formal groups, trainers make presentations, serve as panelists at public forums, and conduct workshop sessions. Sometimes, trainers are organizational employees; other times, organizations contract with social workers to provide specific training experiences. Effective trainers select methods and resource materials based on research about adult education, attitude change, and learning modalities. Successful training strategies require a careful assessment of staff development needs, clear goals of what the organization seeks, the ability to convey information through appropriate training formats, and a concrete evaluation process.

Outreach Role

In outreach roles, social workers inform a variety of audiences about social problems, describe social injustices, and suggest services and policies to address these issues. Workers disseminate information to inform the community about public and private social service organizations, thereby enhancing service accessibility. At the macrosystem level of community and society, the outreach role supports the prevention of problems. Increasing awareness of such issues as poverty, health care, disease control, stress, suicide, infant mortality, substance abuse, and family violence leads to early intervention and stimulates support for preventive actions. Using mass media, distributing posters and leaflets, conducting mailings, staffing information booths, and public speaking all bolster community members' awareness about programs and services. Sensitive to the unique needs of potential clients, outreach social workers provide multilingual, signed, braille, and large print announcements.

TABLE 1.4   Family Service Interventions—Case Example: Andrea Barry

	Microlevel	Midlevel	Macrolevel	Social Work Profession
Consultancy	Counseling with families	Facilitating organizational change to prevent burnout in child protective workers	Participating in child welfare community planning	Addressing ethical and legal issues in mandatory reporting of child abuse and neglect
Resource Management	Linking families with additional community resources	Coordinating service delivery planning among local agencies	Developing a stable funding base for child welfare services	Stimulating interdisciplinary cooperation to develop resources
Education	Providing opportunities for learning anger control and positive parenting	Leading staff development training on mandatory reporting at local day care centers	Initiating public education regarding child protective resources	Presenting family preservation research at a regional conference

Researcher and Scholar Roles

The social work *Code of Ethics* (National, 2000) specifically describes how professional knowledge and scientific research form the basis for practice. The *Code of Ethics* obligates social workers to contribute to the profession by conducting their own empirical research and sharing their findings with colleagues. Professionals also critically examine the social work literature to integrate research findings with their practice. Social workers contribute to and draw upon research related to human behavior and the social environment, service delivery, social welfare policy, and intervention methods.

Integrating Generalist Functions

In practice, social workers interweave the functions of consultancy, resource management, and education. For example, in addition to counseling, consultancy may involve linking clients with resources and teaching them new skills. Similarly, even though education is identified as a separate function, educational processes are inherent in all other social work activities as well. Rather than compartmentalizing these roles, this trilogy of social work functions provides an organizing schema for generalist social workers to construct and integrate multifaceted interventions. Table 1.4 offers examples of how family service worker Andrea Barry engages in consultancy, resource management, and educational interventions at all system levels.

Reflecting Back

Generalist social work is a multifaced approach to helping people overcome the challenges in their lives. Generalist social workers play many practice roles, contribute to social work research, and improve social policy in their efforts to promote human dignity and ensure social justice—the core values of social work. It is these core values that call people to social work. Adhering to these values becomes the litmus test for determining one's fit with the profession. What do these core values mean to you? Specifically consider the notions of *inherent* dignity and worth and rights of *all* persons to social justice.

Looking Forward

Proficiency as a social worker requires a coherent practice framework, resourceful ways to look at human and social system functioning, and dynamic processes for change. This book explains the perspectives and processes that are essential for the effective practice of an empowerment-oriented method of generalist social work. Chapter 2 discusses social work theory in practice and articulates how various views, such as the ecosystems perspective and social constructionism, support an empowering generalist approach. Chapter 3 describes how values, expectations, and diverse cultural and ethnic influences filter our perceptions and affect our work. Chapter 4 explains the strengths perspective and empowerment and discusses their implications for generalist practice.

Chapter 5 introduces this empowering method of social work practice framed within three concurrent phases—dialogue, discovery, and development—each explicated by discrete practice processes. Through *dialogue,* workers and clients develop and maintain collaborative partnerships, exchange relevant information, and define the purposes of the work. In *discovery,* practitioners and clients locate resources on which to construct plans for change. Through *development,* workers and clients activate resources, forge alliances with others, and create new opportunities to distribute the resources of a just society. Chapters 6 through 16 delineate these phases, examine each process in full detail, and offer applications at the micro-, mid-, and macrosystem levels.

Chapter *2*

The Ecosystems Perspective

In the deserts of the Southwestern United States, plants develop various ways to survive in the face of harsh, dry, and hot conditions. The creosote bush, for example, sends down a tap root 30 feet to drink from the water table. Other plants send out a network of fine roots just under the soil to capture every available drop of surface moisture. Still others have roots that emit toxins to choke out all available competition for scarce water. Each plant also has its own unique way to hang on to the precious moisture it captures. Some have tiny leaves that minimize evaporation, while others grow waxy and spiny surfaces that ward off those who seek to drink from its reserves. In the same environment, each different plant adapts uniquely.

In the mountains of New England, a beaver builds a dam to meet its own unique needs. But this change in the environment has ramifications beyond the beaver's life. The pond which results is not only a resource to the beaver but also to other creatures, such as frogs, fish, birds, and deer. When any organism modifies its environment, other organisms within the same ecosystem are affected and may benefit as well.

These examples from the field of ecology show the reciprocal connection between organisms and their environments. In addition, they illustrate the uniqueness and interconnectedness among living things. Human beings are more complex than desert plants or beavers, but they show similar patterns of relationship and adaptation. Consider the following example describing how Grady, a person who is unable to read, adapts to life in a literate world.

Grady is unclear about why he never learned to read. Sometimes he thinks it's because his family moved around so much and he was always either out of school or way behind everyone else. Maybe, it's because his father died when he was twelve and he stopped going to school altogether to work on his aunt's farm. Or maybe, Grady thinks, he just wasn't smart enough. One thing he has learned for sure—when you don't read, you keep it to yourself. People never give you a chance when they find that out. Besides, Grady is a proud man and even the sound of the word "illiterate" leaves him feeling ashamed.

Not knowing how to read never stops Grady, though. He can get around on the bus—the routes are color-coded. He rides the red line to work and the green line to go to the grocery store. At the grocery store, he buys items that he can see directly or those that have pictures on them. There are aisles that have cheaper food in them—generic products—but Grady seldom takes a chance with them because those boxes all look alike. Once he got some kind of box mix instead of the cereal he thought he was buying and he couldn't read the directions to figure out how to make it. Grady can't make that kind of mistake very often. Money is too scarce for that.

One thing Grady does everyday is buy a newspaper. He carries it, tucked under his arm, wherever he goes. No one would ever suspect he can't read then. He pulls it out on his break at work, chuckles to himself, and shares news items with his coworkers. The truth is, he listens to the news and sports every morning and evening on his radio so he can join in the conversations at work. Grady especially doesn't want the people at work to know he can't read; employers don't hire you if they figure out you can't read. Grady remembers how he pretended to forget his glasses when he picked up the job application, so he could take it with him and get help from his friend at the coffee shop to fill it out.

Grady has worked as a field hand at the local nursery for the last five years. It's a minimum wage job, but it pays the bills at least part of the year. His boss and coworkers tease him about living "the good life" since Grady heads south each winter when the nursery shuts down. Grady smiles broadly when he talks about his sister's winter place right on the beach. In reality, he wanders homeless from place to place. He buys food with the money he earns doing odd jobs and panhandling. Sometimes, when he runs short of cash, he goes for days without eating.

Grady's coworkers cope with their winter layoff by signing up for unemployment benefits, food stamps, and temporary jobs through the local temporary employment office, but Grady doesn't see this as an option for him. There is no way to get any of those benefits without filling out the forms right there in the office. That means reading, and that is out of the question for Grady. Sometimes Grady doesn't like the limited choices he has, but he has found ways to adapt to his situation.

In all professional practice settings, social workers meet people like Grady who have developed their own adaptive styles of coping with their particular sets of circumstances. All people, including social work clients, evolve to maintain their own unique "ecological fit" with their environments. Comprehending this interface of persons with their environments and understanding the human diversity that results constitute essential knowledge for social workers. Social work incorporates concepts from the science of ecology to help explain our behavior, our environment, and our incredible diversity.

Ecology is one of the many disciplines that enrich the knowledge base of social work and guide practice activities. This chapter explains concepts from ecology and other theoretical perspectives to create an "ecosystems framework" for generalist social work practice. Specifically, this chapter:

- Considers the diverse theoretical perspectives that support generalist practice
- Presents characteristics of the ecosystems perspective
- Details related concepts from social systems theory
- Develops an ecosystemic framework as a tool for generalist practice

The result is a dynamic view of human system behavior in the context of the social environment. Generalist social workers maintain this broad view throughout each phase of the practice process.

The Knowledge Base of Generalist Practice

Just as purpose and values orient social work practice, knowledge nourishes and guides our work. By definition, generalist social work requires extensive knowledge about the functioning of many types of human systems, necessitating a multidisciplinary preparation for practice. "The dual goals of improving societal institutions and assisting clients within their social and cultural milieu have led to the mining of concepts from different disciplines" (Greene & Ephross, 1991, p. 10). Areas of study most relevant to social work include biology, sociology, linguistics, psychology, ethology, communication, anthropology, economics, political science, history, and ecology (Table 2.1).

Theoretical Frameworks for Practice

The diversity of client systems prompts social workers to draw from many different theoretical perspectives "to explain why people behave as they do, to better understand how the environment affects behavior, to guide interventive behavior, and to predict what is likely

TABLE 2.1   Disciplines Contributing to Social Work Knowledge

Discipline	Research Domains
Anthropology	Culture and values Cross-cultural sensitivity Cultural and religious diversity Linguistics
Biological Sciences	Health and wellness Illness Chemical dependency Physical development, aging, and death Ecology Genetics Nutrition Physical environment
Economics	Distribution of goods and services Capitalism Socialism International finance Labor and trade Consumerism Welfare economics Employment theories Governmental fiscal policies
Psychology	Personality dynamics Gender roles Developmental issues Problem solving Perception Learning Memory Interpersonal relationships
Sociology	Structure and function of groups, organizations, and society Small group behavior Social stratification Discrimination and the "'isms" Deviance Role theory Demographics Social change theory Family dynamics

to be the result of a particular social work intervention" (Greene & Ephross, 1991, p. 5). Workers apply theoretical frameworks to organize their perceptions of clients' situations and to facilitate processes for change.

Social work theories, perspectives, models, and orientations comprise the knowledge base of generalist practice. Although some use these terms interchangeably, most consider theories more firmly grounded in research than the other concepts listed. A *theory* represents a plausible explanation about the relationship of a set of facts or circumstances and "offers both an explanation of certain behaviors or situations and broad guidelines about how those behaviors or situations can be changed" (Sheafor, Horejsi, & Horejsi, 1997, p. 51). In contrast, perspectives, models, and orientations are more descriptive yet still useful for conceptualizing human system behavior and processes for change. Social workers commonly integrate concepts from many theories and perspectives about human system functioning with theories and models of change to create frameworks for practice (Table 2.2).

Theories and Perspectives about Human Systems

Theories about human systems—including theories about communication, group process, social structures, power, and diversity—inform practitioners. Derived primarily from the social and behavioral sciences, theories about human systems provide a cogent understanding of how biological, psychological, social, cultural, economic, and political systems affect and are affected by human behavior and social structures. This knowledge base orients social workers to the complexity of human behavior, the interactional dynamics of multiperson systems, and the nature and impact of conditions in the social environment.

In practice, generalists sometimes use theories specific to the level of the client system. Examples include family life cycle theory to assess issues in family development and conflict theory to describe group dynamics. Other times, social workers use more general the-

TABLE 2.2   Selected Theories and Models for Social Work Practice

Addictions model	Learning theory
Behavioral theory	Locality development model
Bureaucratic theory	Management theory
Case management model	Mediating structures model
Cognitive-behavioral theory	Natural helping network theory
Communication theory	Person-centered theory
Constructivism	Problem solving model
Crisis intervention model	Psychodynamic theory
Developmental theory	Psychosocial approach
Ecological–Life Model	Reality therapy
Ecosystems perspective	Remedial model
Ethnic sensitive perspective	Self-help model
Existential theory	Small group theories
Family centered practice model	Social action model
Family preservation model	Social constructionism
Family structural therapy	Social planning model
Family systems approach	Solution-focused therapy
Feminist perspectives	Strategic family therapy
General systems theory	Strengths perspective
Generalist approach	Structural model
Gestalt therapy	Symbolic interactionism
Human relations theory	Task-centered model
Humanist theory	Teamwork model
Integrative model	Value clarification model
Interactional model	

oretical perspectives that apply to all system levels. For example, the general systems perspective offers principles that apply to the functioning of all human systems—individuals, social groups, communities, and even complex bureaucracies. Combining the general systems perspective with concepts from the field of ecology forms the universally applicable ecosystems framework that supports this book's approach to generalist practice.

Theories and Models of Change

Knowledge about how change occurs in sociopolitical, organizational, community, group, family, and individual systems influences social work processes—the ways that workers approach practice. These theories and models of change define the interaction between the social worker and the client system, influence which change strategies the social worker selects, and describe "who should do what" to create the changes desired. Various practice models, including the empowering approach to generalist practice featured in this book, emerge from an understanding of the dynamics of change and its implications for the professional helping relationship.

Developing a Practice Framework

No one practice framework clearly represents "the social work view." A survey of social workers reveals tremendous diversity in perspectives guiding social work practice (Norlin & Chess, 1997). Practitioners in this study said they applied psychosocial and social systems theories most frequently, but many respondents also reported using principles from the psychoanalytic, behavioral, humanistic, and ecological perspectives. Significantly, a large proportion of these social workers do not implement a single theory in isolation but, instead, integrate concepts from several perspectives to construct an eclectic approach. Another study showed that experienced social workers each applied an average of eight distinct theories in their practice (Timberlake, Sabatino, & Martin, 1997).

All social workers develop frameworks for practice. A comprehensive framework for generalist practice interweaves personal and social work values, theoretical perspectives on human behavior, and orientations to change. Beginning practitioners launch their professional careers by adopting established models for practice. Over time, workers modify and update their approaches to match their own experience of what works, to incorporate feedback received from clients and colleagues, and to assimilate new theories, knowledge, and research.

Analyzing Theoretical Perspectives

Having many useful theories, perspectives, orientations, models, and approaches available forces social workers to make choices about what theoretical constructs to apply. To evaluate a theory's utility in practice, workers examine its knowledge base, description of change, role expectations for practitioners and clients, definition of problems, significant areas of focus, specific intervention methods, consistency with social work ethics and values, and effectiveness in application as substantiated by research. Questions to address in assessing a theory's appropriateness include:

- What is the main focus of the theory? Is it relevant to the situation?
- To what system level does the theory apply?

- Does the theory apply widely to diverse situations or narrowly to particular cases?
- Does the theory further the worker's understanding of human system behavior or guide the worker's efforts in change activities?
- What research supports the theory? Are the samples in the research studies representative of diverse groups or particular segments of the population?
- Is the theory congruent with the professional value base of social work?
- What assumptions does the theory make about clients, including their power, expertise, and roles?

The choices social workers make about theory determine whether they function as agents of social control or, in contrast, empower clients to make changes in themselves, their situation, and social structures. These choices demonstrate an adherence to either traditional or alternative paradigms (Schriver, 1998). The traditional paradigm builds on scientific and quantitative knowledge; reflects a masculine, patriarchal, and "white" perspective; and values competition and privilege. On the other hand, the alternative paradigm incorporates subjective, intuitive, and qualitative information; reflects feminism and diversity; and recognizes the interconnections among all human beings.

Key Perspectives for Empowering Practice

The ecosystems perspective represents the current way many generalist social workers frame their practice. This view conceptualizes the exchanges between people and their physical and social environments (Germain, 1979, 1983; Siporin, 1980; Germain & Gitterman, 1995, 1996). Other perspectives fit well with the ecosystems framework to support an empowering approach to generalist practice. Constructivism and social constructionism are two views that focus on how people understand themselves and interpret what is happening in their lives. The feminist perspective advocates a political stance and drives a social worker's efforts to fashion a just society.

Ecosystems

The ecosystems view combines key concepts from ecology and general systems theory. Ecology "focuses specifically on how things fit together, how they adapt to one another" (Greif, 1986, p. 225). In ecological terms, adaptation is "a dynamic process between people and their environments as people grow, achieve competence, and make contributions to others" (p. 225). General systems theory "reduces highly complex social realities to manageable constructs [and] extends our knowledge about the diversity of human behavior" (Schafer, 1969, p. 26). It offers principles about how human systems operate and interact with one another. Together, ecology and systems theory describe the configuration and functioning of human systems in their social and physical environments.

In the ecosystems view, persons and environments are not separate but exist in ongoing transactions with each other. We cannot simply add an understanding of persons to an understanding of environments. Instead, we must also examine the reciprocal interactions or transactions between the two. Siporin (1980) describes this relationship, saying: "People and their physical–social–cultural environment are understood to interact in processes of mutual reciprocity and complementary exchanges of resources" (p. 509). In other words, the ecosystems perspective provides a framework for viewing the ways that environments affect people and the ways people affect their environments. The ecosystems view is compatible with various theories of human behavior, making it particular useful as an organizational tool for synthesizing the many perspectives that social workers apply in practice.

Constructivism

Constructivism questions the belief in a concrete and objective reality. A constructivist view postulates that events occurring in people's lives come to have meaning only as they are interpreted by the people who experience them. Unlike objectivism, with its focus on an ultimate reality, "constructivism maintains that there are multiple realities" (Fisher, 1991, p. 4). Two people can experience the same event very differently because each constructs a personalized, idiosyncratic view of what has occurred. The "reality" each person constructs is not consciously and deliberately chosen. Instead, it is actively created in interaction based on that particular person's history, expectations, sense of self, and perception of the situation at hand. Each of us selectively attends to, interprets, and acts on our beliefs about ourselves and the world around us. We operate within our own individually constructed frame of reference (Fisher, 1991; Held, 1995).

The relevance of constructivism for empowering practice is readily apparent. People feel empowered when they create experiences and interpret events in ways that accentuate their competencies and cultivate feelings of power and control. Operating within the constructivist view, a social worker's task is to recognize and reinforce constructions of reality that boost the experience of power and help clients reinterpret those situations that deflate a sense of self-esteem or erode feelings of personal control.

Social Constructionism

Social constructionism refocuses the constructivist view to emphasize the impact of the social and cultural environment. Similar to constructivism, social constructionism centers on how people construct meaning in their lives, but social constructionism shifts the emphasis from individual perceptions to the social elements of meaning generated through language, cultural beliefs, and social interaction (Gergen, 1994). "Knowledge is created, not discovered, and context is all important" (Dean & Rhodes, 1998, p. 3). People do not choose interpretations within a vacuum. Each person determines meaning as it is filtered through the "ecosystemic" layers of the social and cultural environment. "People construct some 'reality' or nonreality in groups as a function of their common/consensual linguistic constructions" (Held, 1995, p. 310).

Your cultural identity and social position influence the person you believe yourself to be and therefore the way you interpret the events in your life. The privilege of membership in an advantaged group offers a sense of fit with the world and tilts individual perception toward interpretations that reinforce efficacy and feelings of control. In contrast, members of cultural groups disadvantaged by oppression, prejudice, and stereotypes are likely to be encumbered by dominant cultural views. To counter any perceived threats to their power, those holding dominant views tend to devalue the unique characteristics of groups in the minority (Greene, Jensen, & Jones, 1996). "Consequently, a person from an ethnic group in the minority may construct a sense of self that is influenced by this devaluation, lack of power, and discrimination in the societal context" (p. 2). Furthermore, "to the extent that our linguistic terrain is defined by others, our discourse will reproduce their realities and interests" (Witkin, 1999, p. 6).

Applying the social constructionist view, social workers can intervene at two different points in a client's interpretive process. First, workers can interfere with the internalization of disempowering beliefs by collaborating with clients to question socially generated "truths" and their relevance for the particular client. For example, the practitioner who questions how a female client's love of another woman can be "wrong" and validates the experience as "maybe something to celebrate" is working to disable the heterosexist bias that undermines the client's emotional experience.

Second, workers can advocate for social and political changes to liberate disadvantaged groups from oppressive environmental conditions and belief systems that delimit individual experience. Such would be the case if the worker in the previous example fought to legalize same-sex marriages, thus providing societal support for the client's loving feelings. Both the intervention at the individual and societal level apply social constructionist thinking by operating to overturn the socially generated "truth" that undermines the client's experience and inhibits free choice.

Social Constructivism

Key similarities link constructivism and social constructionism. Each theory "questions the view of knowledge as something 'built up' within the mind through dispassionate observation" (Gergen, 1994), favoring instead the idea of each individual's creation of a unique reality. Both also view this reality as socially constructed and maintained through language (Lee & Greene, 1999). In social work literature, the terms constructivism and social constructionism are frequently used interchangeably, most recently leading to the coining of *social constructivism*, a term that unites the two perspectives (Lee & Greene, 1999).

Feminism

Feminism offers another essential perspective for social workers striving to achieve a just society (Bricker-Jenkins, Hooyman, & Gottlieb, 1991; Saulnier, 1996; Baines, 1997; Gutiérrez & Lewis, 1998). Consistent with the ecosystemic perspective, a feminist view concretely links individual experiences with social forces. Gender is the organizing concept for interactions at all levels of society.

In feminist practice, the personal is political. The subjugation of women is embedded in society and reflected in interpersonal relationships and interactions. To ignore this social reality is to participate in it. Both workers and clients exist in this oppressive milieu and should examine situations and solutions for gender bias. Feminism forces workers from a stance of neutrality into a position of advocacy for gender equality.

There is no singular feminist view, but rather a set of perspectives that have a core consistency. Key elements of feminist practice include:

• Developing collaborative, nonhierarchical relationships with clients that recognize client expertise

- Refraining from applying stigmatizing labels to clients
- Self-disclosure by the worker to humanize relationships
- Deliberately introducing gender as a topic as essential to the consideration of any issue in focus
- Actively promoting egalitarian relationships within client systems
- Working toward the goal of empowerment by exploring unique options, even those out of the norm
- Recognizing traditionally assigned "feminine" traits as strengths (Whipple, 1996)

In some ways, feminism fits with social constructionist theory, proposing that the oppressed position of women in our society is a patriarchal construction of reality. Disempowering views held toward women are rooted in the constructions of dominant groups who ignore the perspectives and experiences of those who are disadvantaged. The feminist practitioner believes that "rejecting the notion of an objective reality in favor of a view of socially negotiated interpretations encourages us to attend to many voices" (Akamatsu, Basham, & Olson, 1998, p. 23). The social worker's task becomes one of "deconstructing" a disempowering reality for women and "reconstructing" a new one that is sensitive to diversity and honors unique experiences.

Feminist ideology, likewise, is compatible with an ecological framework. Bricker-Jenkins (1991) says that "feminist practitioners lead with an assumption that individual and collective pain and problems of living always have a political and/or cultural dimension. That is, they reflect and express ideologies, relations, structures of power and privileges, or other salient features of the cultural milieu" (p. 279). A feminist perspective that focuses on the relationship between the personal and the political augments the ecological systems approach of social work practice.

The Ecosystems Perspective

We emphasize the ecosystems view as a way to frame the many theories and perspectives that support generalist social work practice. There are three good reasons for adopting the ecosystems view. First, because of its integrative nature, the ecosystems view draws on the strengths of many other helpful theories to describe human behavior in all of its complexity. Second, it considers the behaviors of individuals, families, groups, organizations, communities, and their interconnected relationships—making this an ideal perspective to support generalist social work practice. Third, the ecosystems view clearly focuses on how people and their environments fit, rather than forcing workers to place blame on either one for problems that arise (Germain & Gitterman, 1996). This accepting view of human behavior is consistent with the value base of social work; it allows workers and clients to join forces against the problematic fit of client and situation rather than assume that clients themselves are inherently deficient.

The ecosystems perspective informs generalist practice. It conceptualizes and explains human system functioning. Specifically, it:

- Presents a dynamic view of human beings as systems interacting in context
- Emphasizes the significance of human system transactions
- Traces how human behavior and interaction develop over time in response to internal and external forces
- Describes current behavior as an adaptive fit of "persons in situations"

- Conceptualizes all interaction as adaptive or logical in context
- Reveals multiple options for change within persons, their social groups, and in their social and physical environments

Humans in Context

The ecosystems perspective describes humans as very complex. We are biological, psychological, spiritual, social, and cultural beings with thoughts, feelings, and observable behaviors. We are initiators within our environments as well as responders to those same environments. We create our own traditions and legacies just as we inherit and respond to our cultural and ethnic heritage. The ecosystems view acknowledges that we react consciously and intentionally but also act unconsciously and spontaneously. We are complex wholes with internal parts and, at the same time, we are parts or members of larger groups. We are "actively adapting to our changing environments: we shape our surroundings at the same time as our surroundings shape us" (Brower, 1988, p. 413). In the ecosystemic view, humans are neither completely powerful nor powerless. Instead, humans play an active role in creating events which shape their lives, a role tempered by environmental forces and conditions.

Focus on Transactions

Humans and their environments evolve in continuously accommodating responses to one another (Brower, 1988). Notice this two-way influence when you visualize the connection of a person interacting with the environment. This connection is called a transaction. Transactions are reciprocal interactions, "the processes by which people continually shape their environments and are shaped by them over time" (Germain, 1983, p. 115). The phrase "person:environment" symbolizes this mutual relationship (Germain & Gitterman, 1995). The colon emphasizes the dynamic, interrelatedness of people in transaction with their social and physical environments (Figure 2.1).

Each of us takes part in innumerable transactions every day. When we talk with friends, have dinner with family members, or buy groceries, we are interacting with people around us. We are also part of larger systems which engage in transactions. Examples of larger system transactions include a social agency that trains a group of volunteers, sends staff members to a conference, or runs public service announcements on a local television station. Transactions are the means by which people and systems exchange resources with their environments. Therefore, productive transactions serve as sources of energy to sustain a system's functioning and fuel change. Deficient transactions inhibit growth and possibly even threaten basic sustenance.

The concept of transaction reaffirms social work's focus on social functioning—"people coping with life situations [or the] balance between demands of the social environment and people's coping efforts" (Bartlett, 1970, p. 130). This definition describes flexible people adapting to their demanding environments. An empowerment-based view of transaction increases the emphasis on the reciprocal dimension of social functioning, the notion that both people and environments can change. Not only do people respond to environmental demands, but environments must also adapt to the demands of people (Figure 2.2).

In addition, transactions are more complicated than simple connections of people with environments. Transactions encompass interactions which are imbedded in and influenced

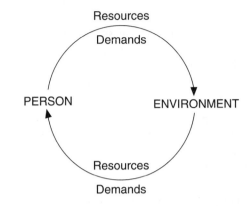

FIGURE 2.1   Person:Environment. The interaction between any given system and its environment is a dynamic, reciprocal interchange of demands and resources. People affect their environments and, likewise, the social and physical environment affects people.

by other interactions in the situation as well (Johnson, 1998). For example, any person's behavior that we observe arises from the ongoing interaction of the individual's internal life combined with the continuous interaction among environmental events. It is at this intersection or point of transaction that we observe human behavior.

Development as Evolutionary Change

The ecosystems perspective views human development as evolutionary. It describes how individuals and other human systems change and stabilize in response to internal and external

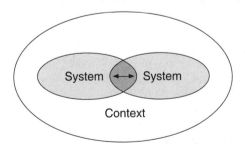

FIGURE 2.2   Transactions between Systems. Embedded in the context of other exchanges, social structures, and culture, transactions are interchanges between systems.

forces. As humans grow physically, emotionally, and intellectually, their behaviors reveal and respond to these internal changes. But, changes within systems are not the only determinants of human behavior. Instead, these internal experiences themselves affect and respond to contextual events.

Contextual Influences

Individuals develop in a context where other systems are evolving too. Social groups, organizations, and institutions—entities that humans themselves help create—seem to take on lives of their own as they also grow and develop. These social systems act upon and respond to individuals' behaviors. The effects are mutual. Neither the external nor internal world has total responsibility for causing any particular human behavior. Instead, both internal and external experiences influence each other. We create our world just as our world creates us.

When explaining human growth and development, certain contexts merit special note. Cultural identities powerfully influence how we view ourselves and how others view us. Race, ethnicity, culture, and socioeconomic and gender contexts can be stepping stones to success for the power elite; however, they may function as roadblocks for those who are oppressed. Burdening individual development with stereotypic expectations denies overwhelming evidence of in-group diversity and ignores other environmental influences. Humans develop in societies that congregate individuals into categories and value certain group memberships over others. Though not unchangeable, these prejudices persist. Assumptions and expectations arising from social group membership influence self-perceptions, the course of development, and interactions with others.

Goodness-of-Fit

The ecosystems perspective explains behavior in terms of adapting to a situation. All individual and social systems try to match what they need and have to offer with the resources and demands of their worlds. "Our specific actions are best understood as our attempts to competently respond to the situations we encounter; we do the best we can given what we know about ourselves and what is needed in the situation" (Brower, 1988, p. 413). How we interact at any specific time arises from a synthesis of what is happening in the world within us, what is happening in the world around us, and how we interpret those events.

Various theorists characterize the nature of these transactions as an adaptive balance between persons and environments. Germain (1979) refers to this as "goodness-of-fit." Brower (1988) defines the concept of "niche," a comfortable and unique place where an individual exists interdependently with the environment. However described, we seek to behave in ways that fit ourselves and our situations best.

View of Dysfunction

In the ecosystems view, the terms "maladaptive" and "dysfunctional" don't really apply. After all, if behaviors are adaptations to meet internal needs and the demands of environments, how can any behaviors be maladaptive? Even a ten-year-old child who carries a gun to the neighborhood playground is displaying a behavior understandable in the threatening environment of a violence-plagued community. While behaviors like these are unacceptable and have negative consequences, all behaviors make sense in context.

In contrast, describing a client's behavior as dysfunctional or maladaptive leaves the client with labels such as "deviant, emotionally disturbed, or behaviorally troubled" (Pardeck, 1988, p. 95). This linear perspective blames clients and neglects the reciprocal responsibility of environments for human behavior. Proposing a transactional view of dysfunction, Pardeck shifts the focus from individual pathology to the possibility of malfunctioning ecosystems. He suggests thinking in terms of maladaptive patterns of interaction, viewing problems in social functioning "as stemming from an interactive, reciprocal, and dynamic set of forces operating between the person and the ecosystem" (p. 95). Thus, the ecosystems view removes the blame from clients in favor of describing problems as transactional—a "fit" in context.

How Problems Arise

Human beings never have the luxury of taking life "one transaction at a time." No behavior occurs in isolation from other events. Rather, humans respond to multiple internal and environmental events simultaneously. In the world of gloves, we may be able to find that "one size fits all." However, in human behavior, we often find that a behavior that may be perfectly adaptive in one specific person:environment configuration is a mismatch in another. The third-grade boy who finds that swearing on the playground elevates his status among his peers will experience the ill fit of this behavior when the principal overhears him. Although the swearing may lead to this boy's identification as having a school behavior problem, careful examination of his behavior and the situation shows clearly that it is not deviant per se but, rather, understandable in context. A focus on the interaction within the peer group leads to the alternative conclusion that he is socially astute.

Environmental Resources and Demands

Whether difficulties tend to arise when people encounter physical, intellectual, psychological, emotional, or situational challenges depends on the responsiveness of the environment and the strengths of the particular human system. A nurturing and supportive environment often compensates for a system's limitations, enabling the system to achieve the goodness-of-fit that characterizes the ecosystemic view of health.

Consider the following examples. Given access to appropriate resources, such as a seeing eye dog, modern technology, and a supportive social network, a person who is unable to see can construct a way to visualize and maneuver in a seeing world. Given direct payment to meet basic human needs for food and shelter, unemployed persons can concentrate on improving their employment situations, rather than resorting to crime or lapsing into depression. With social policies and legislation sensitive to human diversity, persons with disabilities have better access to the community at large. An example is the Americans with Disabilities Act of 1990 that mandates removal of architectural barriers in private businesses. A resource-rich, responsive environment transforms persons who may be labelled dysfunctional into contributors who can further enrich their environments.

On the other hand, even persons who are gifted in every conceivable way encounter demanding environments that would immobilize the most well-prepared among us. Perfectly functional people become overwhelmed in times of great stress such as war, grief, physical illness, or crises, and in the face of discrimination and oppression. Clearly, difficulties don't reside in persons or environments alone. Instead, gaps in the fit between persons and their environments determine whether both can contribute to and benefit from the functioning of the other.

By considering the responsibility of environments, the ecosystems view precludes labeling individuals or social systems as dysfunctional or pathological. There is simply no goodness-of-fit. That which the system lacks, the environment isn't providing. For that which the environment isn't providing, the system is unable to compensate with its own resources. Even a good adaptation in one particular transaction may not work effectively in other simultaneous transactions. Moreover, the ecosystems view concludes that dysfunctional behavior is transitory, changeable, and related to the responsiveness of the environment.

Implications for Change

How we work with people and their situations logically follows from how we perceive human behavior. If we believe the ecosystems model cogently explains how people develop strengths and vulnerabilities, then the choices we make in supporting growth and change will reflect this perspective. Ecosystemically oriented social work practice centers on changing and maintaining both client and environmental systems.

> *On the one hand, the environmental emphasis of the ecological view supports environmentally oriented interventions directed toward strengthening or establishing networks of social support. On the other hand, the transactional emphasis of the ecological perspective fosters individually oriented interventions directed toward promoting personal competencies for dealing with institutional or environmental blocks to achieving personal objectives. (Holahan, Wilcox, Spearly, & Campbell, 1979, p. 6)*

Multiple Possibilities for Change

This complex description of human behavior has the potential to immobilize any social work practitioner trying to influence the multiplicity of forces affecting clients and their situations. Indeed, it is probably this sense of immensity and subsequent powerlessness that bogs down clients as they work to master challenges. But there is good news! Just as each element in these complex transactions contributes to the challenging nature of human functioning, these very same elements hold multiple possibilities for resolutions.

A fundamental principle of ecosystems theory states that a change in one part of the system creates a change in another part of the system which, in turn, changes the functioning of the entire system (von Bertalanffy, 1968). In other words, altering one part of any person:environment transaction affects the other transactional elements. For example, when social worker Jan Kim encourages Dorothy, a disgruntled resident of Northside Care Center, to organize a resident's council, a variety of related changes occur. Dorothy's mood improves as she directs her energy toward relating with the other residents. Once the council forms, they take charge of planning recreational and social events that match their own interests. They also lobby members of the management team to change policies regarding visiting hours and roommate assignments. Dorothy's son even comments about her remarkable adjustment to living at the care center. Count all of the positive changes! Prompting one productive change initiates a cycle that may have subsequent benefits throughout the entire transactional system.

Focus on Strengths

Although the ecosystems perspective offers many intervention possibilities, social workers move cautiously to initiate change. Since human beings naturally evolve to work in harmony with their environments, it is likely that client systems are actually doing a lot right. One ecosystemic practice principle mandates social workers "to respect the balances and processes through which people and environments have adapted to each other's needs, while attempting to improve transactional patterns that are maladaptive" (Siporin, 1980, p. 517). This challenges us to build on the strengths and competencies clients already have available. A strengths orientation (described fully in Chapter 4) is an essential tool for successfully applying an ecosystemic perspective.

Human Systems

The systems with which practitioners work may be as small as a single element of the internal processes of one individual or as large as the entire human population. Generalist social workers need to develop skills to comprehend, support, and change behaviors of many kinds of human systems, since systems at all levels are potential clients and targets for change.

System Defined

Technically speaking, a system is "an organized whole made up of components that interact in a way distinct from their interaction with other entities and which endures over some period of time" (Anderson, Carter, & Lowe, 1999, p. 294). More simply, a social system is a "structure of interacting and interdependent people" (Greene & Ephross, 1991, p. 259). Groups of people are identified as systems because they interact with each other in some definable way or are associated with each other because of shared attributes. In other words, a pattern of relationships or shared characteristics separates one group from other groups in the environment. This definition of system encompasses groups as different as a street gang, a Girl Scout troop, residents of a nursing home, employees of a corporation, and social work professionals. These and all other social systems, small and large, share common features.

Systems as Holons

All social systems are *holons*. This means that each system is a part of a larger system while, at the same time, it is composed of smaller systems (Anderson, Carter, & Lowe, 1999). A family is a social system that is only one part of the neighborhood suprasystem in which the family resides. Children and parents within this family are also systems themselves within the context of the larger family system. All of these systems—the children, the parents, the family, and the neighborhood—are holons which share systemic properties.

Subsystems and Environments

To clarify the idea of systems within systems, we define two important concepts: *subsystem* and *environment*. The smaller systems within every system are subsystems. Children and parents make up subsystems of the larger family system. Similarly, each individual within a family is actually a subsystem. Conversely, the larger system which encompasses a social system is that system's environment. The environment influences and provides the context for the systems functioning within it. The neighborhood is one example of the social environment for a family system. Broadening the focus to an even larger picture, the community is the social environment for both neighborhoods and families (Figure 2.3).

All systems have subsystems and environments. In fact, all systems are also subsystems while, at the same time, they are environments. For example, the family is a system itself, but, in switching the focus, this same family is also the environment of the children within it. Another perspective shift leads us to describe this family as a subsystem of the neighborhood in which it lives. Whether we label a system a "subsystem," "system," or an "environment" is relative and changes as we shift our point of focus.

Dimensions of Systems

The complex behavior of human systems gives rise to several helpful ways for viewing them, including the system's structure, interaction, biopsychosocial dimensions, and cultural elements. *Structure* refers to the organization of the system at a point in time. *Interac-*

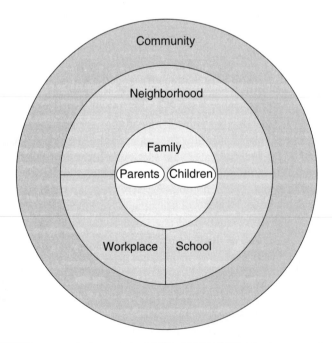

FIGURE 2.3   Subsystems and Environments. Whether social workers define a particular system as an environment or a subsystem depends on which system they identify as the focal system.

tion puts this organization into motion and shows how the system operates as its components respond to and affect each other. *Biopsychosocial* dimensions feature the biological, cognitive, and affective characteristics of persons. The *cultural* view appraises the influences of ethnicity and culture on human functioning. Each dimension helps social workers conceptualize human behavior in productive ways and suggests creative possibilities for change (Figure 2.4).

A Structural View of Systems

How individuals and subsystems within a system arrange themselves is the structure of the system. Structure is not actually visible; we discern it by observing two variables that characterize the structural arrangements of any system—*closeness* and *power*. Closeness refers to the closed or open nature of system boundaries; whereas, the distribution of power aligns the system hierarchy. When we ask, "How close or distant are members?" we discover the boundaries of a system. When we ask, "Who's in charge?" we uncover the hierarchy for distributing power within a system. Considering both boundaries and hierarchies offers a complete picture of a system's structure.

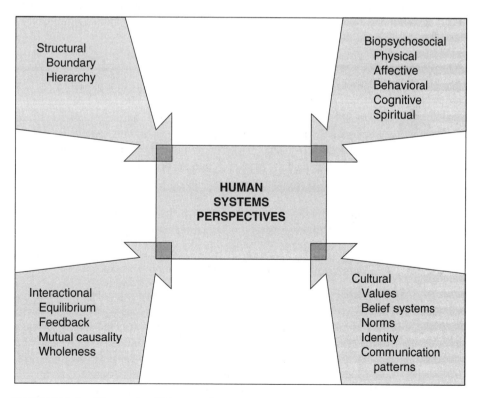

FIGURE 2.4   Elements of Human Systems

Boundaries

Boundaries define systems. In other words, boundaries distinguish the interior of the system from its environment. Human systems' boundaries are not visible like boundaries that mark real estate properties. We deduce their location and characteristics by observing how the system operates (Anderson, Carter, & Lowe, 1999).

Boundaries vary in permeability or in how many transactions they allow between systems. Consider the analogy of a fence. If the fence is short and full of gates, the system and its boundary are "open." Open systems interact frequently and exchange resources with their environments. If the fence is a high stone wall with no entry or exit, the system and boundary are "closed." Having no access to the environment, closed systems must meet all of their needs by drawing on resources from within their own systems. With such limited access to additional resources, closed systems have the potential for depleting their resource supplies.

Boundaries also differentiate people within a given system. Internal boundaries, which exist around various individuals and subgroups within a larger system, define subsystems. For example, for most social agencies, boundaries define administrative, supervisory, and direct service subsystems. Particular agencies may also distinguish other subsystems such as "experts" and "novices"; professionals, paraprofessionals, and clerical staff; or direct and indirect service providers. These internal boundaries have different degrees of permeability. Like boundaries that define systems, subsystems boundaries vary on a continuum from open to closed. The level of closeness within a system is a significant element in understanding the system's structure.

Hierarchy

Hierarchy indicates which individuals and subsystems in a particular system have status, privileges, and power. Typically, hierarchy describes who is in charge in business or formal organizational systems. By looking at organizational charts, formalized procedures, and position titles such as president, director, or supervisor, you can clearly define hierarchy in formal organizational systems. Describing hierarchy in other systems may be more difficult. Although titles such as "mother," "father," or "ringleader" may give clues about power and control within the system, these titles may not match the system's actual distribution of power. Observing who makes decisions and who initiates actions provides a more accurate picture of hierarchy. Examining the power distribution and the boundary construction in any given system offers structural information about that system.

An Interactional View of Systems

The interactional view examines the way in which people relate within a system and with their environments. In contrast to structure which offers a static look at systems, interaction puts the structure in motion. The interactional view traces the activity of the various members of the system and their environment as they communicate with each other. Communication includes all verbal and nonverbal interpersonal behavior. Any message sent through the system, whether a clear verbal statement or a subtle nonverbal expression, affects the system's functioning. The interactional perspective focuses on the ways systems respond to these exchanges of information.

Equilibrium

The tendency of a system to interact in ways that maintain its balance or equilibrium is a key concept in the interactional view. Events that temporarily knock a system out of balance leave it scrambling to regain its previous equilibrium or lead it quickly toward establishing a new one. For example, funding cuts require a social service provider's immediate response. It is likely that the agency's first action is an attempt to maintain the status quo by locating new funds. If this isn't possible, the agency may look internally, cutting staff positions and redistributing the workload to ensure survival and maintain system balance. Rebalancing can also occur if this agency system changes its relationship to the environment. The agency may cut back on the services it offers to the community, thereby reaching a new balance without overloading the remaining staff. Whatever the agency does to regain equilibrium, one thing is clear—changes in funding, staffing, or programming create other changes in the internal functioning of the system as well as in its ability to work with clients.

Repetitive interactions provide evidence of a system's current equilibrium. "When one is observing people who have a history and a future together, one sees that they follow organized ways of behaving with one another" (Haley, 1976, p. 102). Identifying, reinforcing, and modifying various patterns is one way to change a system. Social workers attempt to stabilize productive patterns while interrupting patterns in which difficulties reside. As an example, consider a social worker who suggests that a father allow his teenager more privileges, attempting to interrupt the pattern of restriction and rebellion which has characterized the parent–child relationship. As the teen responds responsibly and the father reinforces the change through increased privileges, the worker encourages this new, more productive pattern.

Feedback

Feedback provides a continuous flow of information. Some information fits neatly with the system's existing way of doing things. The system assimilates this feedback, reinforcing the current pattern. On the other hand, incompatible information forces the system to change in order to accommodate the discrepancy. In other words, there are two forms of feedback—information that maintains the existing equilibrium and information that induces change toward a new equilibrium.

Social workers provide both kinds of feedback. They offer reinforcing feedback to maintain the existing strengths. An example is when a social worker facilitating a group comments on the group members' acceptance of diverse views. In contrast, workers also introduce system altering feedback to disrupt problematic patterns, clearing the way for new possibilities. When a social worker confronts a citizen's advisory committee with its inequitable distribution of community development funds, this worker provides feedback to disrupt the status quo and seek a new, more equitable pattern of distributing funds. Social workers select feedback carefully to work toward desired goals.

Mutual Causality

The principle of mutual or circular causality states that a person's behavior is mutually determined in interaction with others (Watzlawick, Bavelas, & Jackson, 1967). Human systems influence their environments and are influenced by them. In other words, one person does not cause the behavior of any other; people participating in a particular interaction mutually work out how they will relate to each other. For example, social workers who constantly instruct and advise clients on how to change their lives bear some responsibility for their clients' lack of initiative. Likewise, clients' withdrawn and dependent behavior contributes to overfunctioning by social workers.

While, theoretically, all members of a system have some degree of power and share some responsibility for the behavior of the system, there is an important note of caution here! Social workers remain particularly vigilant when considering the principle of mutuality in relationships characterized by large discrepancies in power. Clearly, social work ethics does not allow the conclusion that persons who are victimized are to blame for the acts of others. The principle of mutual causality does not free those who abuse others from responsibility for their own behaviors or blame victims for having no access to power.

Wholeness

Closely related to mutual causality, wholeness describes how "every part of a system is so related to its fellow parts that a change in one part will cause a change in all of them and in the total system" (Watzlawick, Bavelas, & Jackson, 1967, p. 123). This rule extends beyond the system's boundary to describe how a system changes in response to its environment as well as how an environment responds to changes in those systems within it. Consider the previous example of the agency and its funding cuts. A change in the environment, which, in this case, takes the form of reduced funding, has ramifications throughout the agency system and subsequently reemerges to affect the environment in terms of the agency's ability to serve its clients.

This interactional perspective on systems fits neatly into an ecosystems view. Concepts from ecology describe the ongoing balancing act of systems with their environments. The evolution to reach the "goodness-of-fit" necessitates that systems continue to change and stabilize in response to feedback. To keep a comfortable balance, a system must at times resist change and at other times go with the flow. Likewise, the environment responds to the feedback sent out of the system. The interactional perspective complements the structural view and gives social work practitioners yet another way to conceptualize their work with client systems.

Biopsychosocial Dimensions

All social systems have distinctive human qualities based on the biopsychosocial characteristics of their individual members. Similar to social systems, individual human beings are multidimensional. Longres (1995) identifies two domains of individual functioning, the biophysical and the psychological. He further divides the psychological into cognitive, affective, and behavioral components. Others add spiritual dimensions to this list (Canda, 1988; Krill, 1988). The mutual impact of these internal subsystems on one another reflects the same principles that apply to larger social systems.

This biopsychosocial view of systems holds special significance for change processes. As thinking and feeling beings, we have options and to some extent the power to choose our responses to what is happening in our lives. These options may be limited by individual and environmental conditions; but, within a reasonable range, we are able to make choices about how we view ourselves and interpret the events around us.

Events are not mandates for human behavior. Each of us may respond to the "same" events in different ways. The way we see ourselves and others, our previous experiences, and our current feelings and thoughts all influence our responses. Regardless of the "reality" of the situation, we react based on our own subjective interpretations; our responses are idiosyncratic. The constructivist view says that changes in thoughts or feelings alter our experiences with the world. If we believe we can accomplish something, our beliefs are resources for reaching our goals.

A biopsychosocial view applies to more than individual functioning. Multiperson systems, composed of thinking and feeling individual members, also have cognitive and affective dimensions which can lead to change. The neighborhood whose residents "believe" that a neighborhood watch program can ensure personal safety and property rights will activate and participate in such a program. Families who "feel" pride in their reputation and accomplishments will risk activities that have the potential to add to their accomplishments, further contributing to a greater sense of pride. This psychosocial view of social systems expands the options for social workers and clients. Workers can help clients construct new ways of perceiving and responding to events.

Cultural Influences

Every individual and social system exists within a web of other interlocking and overlapping human systems. These contextual systems vary with respect to size, type, and degree of influence. Each of us carries the imprints of those systems of which we are a part. As members of the human race we have universal similarities. As members of different racial, ethnic, gender, religious, cohort, community, and other groups we also develop differences. The particular configuration and relative influence of each of these systems contributes to the diversity which characterizes individual human identities and behaviors.

The concept of culture speaks to the influence that these various external system memberships exert on human behavior.

> *Culture is not an easy concept to define, but it generally incorporates all the symbolic meanings—the beliefs, values, norms, and traditions—that are shared in a community and govern social interactions among community members or between members and outsiders. The values and norms of the various social classes, of religious denominations, of gays and lesbians, of ethnic and racial groups constitute their cultures. (Longres, 1995, p. 74)*

Every human system has cultural dimensions. Social groups at every system level have unique ways of interacting and patterns of understanding (Anderson, Carter, & Lowe, 1999). Each of us incorporates influences from the multiple cultures in which we participate.

Every human being identifies cultural memberships in a seemingly endless list of larger contextual systems. Race, ethnicity, gender, socioeconomic class, religion, sexual orientation, age group, geographic location, political affiliation, occupation, and lifestyle are several of the cultural dimensions that influence human behavior. Cultural influences are profound. Not only do we build our own identities around the various groups of which we are members, frequently others view us more in terms of our general cultural attributes than our own unique identities.

Cultural Influences on Systems

Our cultural memberships affect the way others treat us. Human societies do not afford the same status and privileges across cultural categories. Privileged groups sometimes disenfranchise members of other cultural groups. For example, in the United States, someone identified culturally as male, white, and heterosexual simply has more opportunities and fewer constraints than someone whose cultural group memberships include female, African American, and lesbian.

Generalizations based on memberships in cultural systems also obscure individual differences. Although membership in a particular cultural group usually indicates certain similarities among group members, individual members hold other cultural group memberships as well. Add these multicultural influences to each person's unique physical, cognitive, and affective attributes and the result is diversity among members within even the most influential of cultural groups. Simply put, no two people are alike! The multiple influences of simultaneous cultural contexts individuate even members of the same family. Think about your own family if you're not convinced. Can you identify cultural differences among family members? Every human system internalizes elements of the multiple contexts in which it exists. Each and every one of us is a virtual "melting pot" of cultural influences.

Ecosystems: A Conceptual Framework for Practice

The ecosystems perspective provides a way to comprehend human diversity and the relationships between humans and their environments. The views of human systems as structural, interactional, biopsychosocial, and cultural entities offer boundless possibilities on which to build understanding and change. A simple, yet comprehensive, way to organize the ecosystems perspective into a user-friendly framework for generalist social work practice involves a five-point schema (O'Melia, 1991):

- *Identify the focal system.*
- *What's happening inside the system?*
- *What's happening outside the system?*
- *How do the inside and outside connect?*
- *How does the system move through time?*

A closer look reveals the universality and usefulness of this simple framework (Table 2.3 and Figure 2.5).

Identify the Focal System

All aspects of generalist practice involve human systems. Social workers practice within systems such as agencies, departments, institutions, and various other organizations. Social workers interact with client systems, including individuals, couples, families, groups, orga-

TABLE 2.3   Ecosystems: Conceptual Practice Framework

Questions	Description
What's the focal system?	Identifies the system on which the ecosystems analysis will focus—can be an individual, family, group, organization, or community.
What's inside the system?	Explores the structure, interaction, biopsycho-social dimensions, and cultural features within the focal system.
What's outside the system?	Delineates the network of other systems and resources in the focal system's environmental context.
How do the inside and outside connect?	Examines the transactions between the focal system and systems in its context.
How does the system move through time?	Observes adaptation and changes occurring in the process of the focal system's development.

From *Generalist Perspectives in Case Coordination* by M. O'Melia (May, 1991). Used with permission of the author.

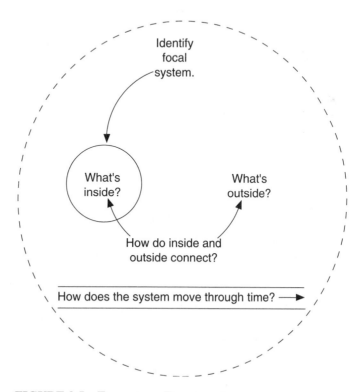

FIGURE 2.5   Ecosystems Framework

nizations, and communities. Social workers also target changes in environmental systems to benefit their clients. Practitioners themselves are systems who exist in a network of personal and professional systems that may support or inhibit their work. For effective generalist practice, workers need to understand the functioning of and resources within each of these systems, including their settings, their clients, their communities, and themselves.

The ecosystems view recognizes the complex configuration of these nested and interlocking systems. To ignore the multiple influences present in any situation is to offer only a partial account of why things are the way they are, what resources exist, and how things might change. Acknowledging these influences requires a step-by-step analysis that begins with a well-defined reference point which we call the focal system.

What we determine to be the focal system depends on our purpose or activity. If we are trying to increase our self-understanding, we may focus on ourselves including our own thoughts, feelings, and interactions with others. If we are beginning work with a new client, the developing professional relationship requires attention and becomes the focal system. If we are assessing a client system's functioning in its own ecological context, the client is the focal system. If we are implementing intervention strategies, we may identify a system in the client's environment as the focal system. In generalist social work practice, the system in focus may vary during the process.

What's Happening Inside the System?

Determining the focal system allows us to apply our understanding of human systems to the task at hand. A structural perspective offers information about the system's membership, boundaries, and hierarchies. Highlighting the interactional view provides information about how system members communicate, the patterns they develop, and the ways they maintain balance. Exploring biopsychosocial dimensions provides information about system members' physical health, thoughts, and feelings. Considering the cultural influences of values, beliefs, attitudes, communication patterns, and norms adds to our understanding of functioning inside the focal system.

What's Happening Outside the System?

Exploring the focal system's context is essential to understanding any situation. All systems exist as part of an *ecosystem*—a set of interconnected, interdependent, and interactive systems that affect one another. Examining what's outside the system begins to identify important environmental influences accounting for the focal system's behavior and reveals possible targets for intervention. Since ecosystems are also systems, workers can describe and analyze ecosystems by applying the same perspectives for describing any system—structural, interactional, biopsychosocial, and sociocultural.

Though many systems share aspects of the same environments, the particular ecosystem of any one system is a unique configuration, idiosyncratic to the focal system. Consider the following examples of the ecosystems of potential client systems. For one eight-year-old child, relevant environmental systems may be the child's immediate family, extended family, peer group, neighborhood, school, and church. For a different eight-year-old child placed in foster care, relevant environments include the child's biological family, foster family, social worker, case management team, foster children's support group, and the family court system. On another level, significant contextual systems for a public housing project include the community, city government, local social agencies, and federal housing departments, to name a few. The ecosystem varies depending on the specific focal system and the changing experience of that system as it evolves and adapts.

How Do the Inside and Outside Connect?

The viability of any human system depends on its success in interacting with its environment. Social workers need personal and professional backing. Clients need information, resources, and support. This interface of the system with the environment—the system:environment transaction—is a major target for assessment and intervention.

To illustrate how this relates to professional practice, consider the example of Tony Marelli. As a social worker for the Northside Addictions Recovery Center, Tony is experiencing feelings of burnout. There are significant events in Tony's connections to his environment contributing to this situation. The Addiction Recovery Center's loss of a state grant has forced layoffs and a redistribution of work to remaining staff. Tony's workload has increased from 25 to 35 clients as a result. Normally, the agency has a supportive collegial and supervisory system with whom Tony exchanges ideas about his experiences with clients, but the overload has sent everyone scrambling. Consequently, the workers hardly even have time to talk to one another.

Look closely at the changes in Tony's connections to the world around him. The previous balance of Tony (the inside) with his clients and coworkers (the outside) is now skewed. His boundaries have opened wide to clients and have closed with respect to his professional support network. For Tony, more resources are going out and fewer are coming in, obviously contributing to his burnout. This ecosystemic analysis also points the way toward what might be done to ease Tony's situation. Changes in Tony's workload or his relationships with colleagues may be solutions. Analyzing any system's transactions with its environment offers insights into what is currently happening and stimulates thinking about the possibilities for change.

How Does the System Move Through Time?

The ecosystems perspective emphasizes the evolutionary nature of human systems. Systems at every level, from individual to society, move along their developmental paths in response to expected and unexpected events. Both kinds of events, predictable and surprising, affect systems. How systems negotiate these changes as they move through the context of time merits careful review. Social workers incorporate historical and developmental contexts by gathering enough information about the focal system to understand the system's evolution.

Many evolutionary changes occur naturally, including physical maturation and other developmental transitions. Erikson (1963) describes expected stages of psychosocial development for individuals. Carter and McGoldrick (1989) expand this notion of developmental change to families and examine the mutual influences of individual and family life cycles. Another theorist describes the natural path of group development as sequential, passing through stages of forming, storming, norming, performing, and adjourning (Tuckman, 1965, cited in Anderson, Carter, & Lowe, 1999). Systems at all levels evolve in predictable and adaptable ways.

Nodal Events

Other changes are unexpected and can create temporary havoc in systems as they struggle to regain equilibrium. Consider how the sudden death of a child in a family system imme-diately disrupts the family's sense of how things should be and requires extensive adjust-ment in the way the family operates. These unexpected changes, called *nodal events*, have a dramatic effect on a system's development (Carter & McGoldrick, 1989). The addition or loss of a member or a significant change in a member's role profoundly affects the system as a whole. Such is the case in birth, marriage, death, and serious illness. Examples of nodal events in larger systems are organizational expansion and downsizing. In a community, nodal events can include a change in leadership, plant closings, or the receipt of federal grants. Nodal events can improve a system's functioning or challenge its capabilities.

Applying the Ecosystems Framework

This ecosystems framework provides ways for social workers to organize information about "what is" in a way that hints at "what might be." Specifically, this framework guides practitioners as they build effective relationships with clients, assess client functioning, and implement change activities.

Building Relationships with Client Systems

By identifying the professional relationship as the focal system, workers can develop and monitor how they relate to clients. The structural perspective allows workers to question is-sues of power and closeness: Does the client system have sufficient power in the relation-ship with the worker to ensure feelings of control, an experience of competence, and a guarantee of self-determination? Is the relationship sufficiently close to encourage an open and honest sharing of information yet distant enough to ensure professional integrity and encourage independence? By applying this framework, workers can construct empowering and respectful relationships with client systems.

This framework also helps workers monitor the effects of outside forces on their work with clients. Obviously, the relationships of social workers and clients respond to influ-ences in their respective ecosystems. Cultural contexts are particularly important. Analyz-ing cultural dimensions can help workers recognize and confront their own biases and sensitize them to relate to clients in culturally appropriate ways.

Assessing Functioning

The ecosystems framework offers a concrete approach for assessing a client's situation re-gardless of the particular level of client system. Observing a system from structural, inter-actional, biopsychosocial, and cultural points of view offers comprehensive information for understanding individuals, families, groups, and communities. Assessing the client sys-tem's progress as it evolves through time contributes additional clues about important his-toric events, the system's ability to adapt, and its future direction.

Planning and Implementing Change

Knowing the specific ways that systems function reveals entry points for social workers and clients to initiate change. Altering internal aspects of a system's functioning, changing environments, or modifying the connections between the two all hold potential for creating change. Social workers and clients carefully analyze these possibilities to construct plans and carry out activities to create changes in the direction of goals. Workers and clients use this framework to plan and implement actions to enhance client competence, activate environmental supports, create alliances, and expand opportunities.

Reflecting Back

Conventional wisdom says that theory is essential in organizing and justifying actions that social workers take. Current debate questions whether theory supported by empirical research is really so necessary for effective practice. A social constructionist might say that a professional's theoretical explanation of events is only one construction of reality and contains no more "truth" than the explanation offered by the client system. In fact, favoring the professional view over the client's perspective may be oppressive and contrary to the social work values of acceptance and client self-determination. Consider how theory fits into your practice and how you will choose among conflicting conceptualizations of what is going on and how it might change.

Looking Forward

The ecosystems perspective is an adaptable framework for social work practice. It broadens our view of human behavior and suggests ways for practitioners to conceptualize, plan, and evaluate their work. Social workers apply the ecosystems perspective flexibly in ways that fit their styles and the characteristics of client systems. Identifying the focal system is the first step, since all subsequent steps relate to the system social workers and clients designate as the focal system. From there, social workers and clients proceed to examine other aspects of the system:environment configuration. Possibilities for understanding and change are present in every element of the ecological milieu.

The ecosystems perspective offers a way of thinking about human systems and their functioning. Feminism, social constructionism, and constuctivism provide additional lenses to filter our perceptions. Chapter 3 describes how attitudes, expectations, professional and personal values, and cultural identities influence professional practice. Social workers must inventory their own values and cultural backgrounds to prepare for value-based, culturally competent practice.

Values and Multicultural Competence

By the first time social workers and clients actually talk together, both have already been formulating their expectations about each other and the work ahead. Both bring values, attitudes, and assumptions that will undeniably influence their interaction with each other. Effective social workers acknowledge these existing frames of reference.

To create empowering experiences, practitioners examine their value base, develop their cultural competence, and even take it one step further by purposefully constructing a set of presuppositions about clients that will influence their work productively. This chapter explores the ways that social workers prepare themselves both professionally and personally for relationships with clients, particularly in the areas of values and diversity. Specifically, this chapter:

- Describes how expectations and personal perspectives influence our perceptions, interactions, and relationships
- Delineates the values and principles of social work practice that guide workers to build ethical relationships with clients
- Considers the influences of a social worker's personal resources and self-awareness on professional practice
- Explores cultural diversity and discusses ways to increase multicultural competence
- Articulates a generalist view of cultural competence

Value-prepared, culturally competent social workers prepare to form relationships that activate clients' resources, respect their contributions, and maintain professional integrity.

Frames of Reference

Have you ever "misread" an examination question, answered it in the context of your reading error, and, upon reviewing your test, wondered how you could have missed something so obvious? Your experience is likely to illustrate an important point: The way we perceive questions influences how we process information and develop solutions.

To experience the effect of assumptions firsthand, try the nine dot problem in Figure 3.1. Record your attempts and then review your results. What strategies did you use? How did your assumptions limit your choices? Did you eventually look up the solution? Does the solution seem obvious now that you redefined the boundaries of the task? Our assumptions create frames of reference which filter information about tasks and limit our ideas for solutions. Assumptions are powerful forces; they affect how we process information, construct interpretations, and determine actions.

Now identify the following items using words ending with an "oak" sound:

A tree which produces acorns	(oak)
A popular soft drink	(coke)
A riddle with a punch line	(joke)
A family kinship group	(folk)
The white of an egg	?

FIGURE 3.1   Nine-Dot Problem. Connect all the dots by drawing four lines without lifting your pencil, doubling over any line, or crossing any line more than once. Find the solution in Figure 3.2 at the end of the chapter.

In all honesty, did you say that the *white* of an egg is a yolk? Is this response accurate? Are you certain that the white of an egg is a yolk? Try this exercise with your friends. It's likely that their responses will reveal that most people become so locked into their patterned responses that they fail to recognize the obvious solution. Clearly, mental sets or frames of reference powerfully influence our thinking and construct our reality!

Research documents that what people expect to happen influences how they respond, a phenomenon called the "placebo" effect. Experiments repeatedly demonstrate how positive changes in behavior result from participants' expectations that improvements will occur. Commenting on the placebo effect, Wylie (1996) says: "This benign mutual collaboration in belief and hope is a powerful curative agent in its own right (an estimated 10 to 90 percent improvement in medical conditions are due to placebo)" (p. 37). Our expectations are influential in shaping how we understand experiences and in swaying our responses.

What others expect of us influences our responses, too. In a classic educational study, Rosenthal and Jacobson (1968) found that a diverse group of children randomly labeled "bloomers" lived up to their teacher's expectations. You can imagine the results if those same children had been labeled difficult or slow. Whether preconceived notions are positive or negative, their effects are often dramatic. What we expect powerfully shapes our sense of self, influences our behavior, and constructs the reality in which we interpret events.

Our values, culture, and patterns of thinking as well as our expectations of situations and others' expectations of us all contribute to our frames of reference. These factors serve as filters through which we view, interpret, and respond to our situations. For example, several people can witness the same incident yet each perceives or explains the situation differently. Our actions and reactions to others reveal our frames of reference.

Your Frame of Reference Shows

Fundamentally, all social work activities, at any system level and in any field of practice, have a common core. Social work depends on interaction and communication with others. As social workers, we purposefully and spontaneously interact with clients. Within this interaction, our communication unavoidably and automatically reveals our frame of reference. Two facets of communication—its constancy and its influence on relationships—deserve careful attention in preparing for empowerment-based social work practice.

Communication Is Constant

Since assumptions influence outcomes, social workers should interact in ways that demonstrate positive expectations. They should only communicate messages that help clients accomplish their goals. This sounds simple enough, but the very nature of communication makes communicating productively a challenging task. Watzlawick, Bavelas, and Jackson (1967) describe this inherent difficulty succinctly when they say, "one cannot not communicate. Activity or inactivity, words or silence all have message value" (p. 42). Think about the implications of this simple concept. We are always communicating. In the way we look, the way we sit, the words we select, the information we choose to notice, and in countless other ways, we automatically send messages to one another. There is no way to avoid it. In the presence of another human being, "one cannot not behave, not relate, not mean" (Keeney & Ross, 1985, p. 6).

Communication Defines Relationships

Messages are more than simple bits of information. Communication theorists believe that every message communicated has two sides: content and relationship (Watzlawick, Bavelas, & Jackson, 1967). This means that a message both provides information and defines something about the relationship of the communicators. The relationship aspect of communication says, "This is how I see myself…this is how I see you…this is how I see you seeing me" (p. 52).

Communicating in Empowering Ways

What social workers truly feel and sincerely believe about themselves and about clients emerges in social work interactions. Professionally constructed relationships are not merely role plays. On the contrary, they are genuine relationships in which the values, beliefs, and opinions of social workers and clients show through. Perceptive social workers acknowledge the complex, continuous, and unavoidable nature of communication. They understand that "words serve as lenses that have the power to shape, to filter, or indeed even to 'create' what it is we see in front of us" (Laird, 1990, p. 213).

If a worker's implicit or explicit messages reflect little confidence in a client or judgments about a client's culture, these messages undermine empowerment and countermand goals for promoting competence. On the other hand, to the extent that social workers implicitly and explicitly relay messages of confidence, acceptance, and respect for diversity, their communication empowers.

Professional Values and Practice Principles

Personal and professional values are a significant component of a social worker's frame of reference. "Values abstractly shape social workers' ways of thinking and concretely direct their actions through principles for social work practice" (DuBois & Miley, 1999, p. 124). These principles guide the day-to-day practice of social work (Table 3.1). They include

TABLE 3.1   Social Work Practice Principles

Acceptance	Conveys positive regard for clients' strengths and potential for growth
Individualization	Affirms each client's unique and distinctive characteristics
Nonjudgmentalism	Maintains nonblaming attitudes toward clients
Objectivity	Promotes professional caring, concern, and commitment in working with clients
Self-determination	Upholds clients' rights to exercise their own decision-making
Access to services	Promotes and fosters access to resources and opportunities
Confidentiality	Respects clients' rights to privacy
Accountability	Ensures competent professional conduct and comportment

acceptance, individualization, nonjudgmentalism, objectivity, self-determination, access to resources, confidentiality, and accountability (Biestek, 1957; Goldstein, 1973; Levy, 1976; Perlman, 1976; Piccard, 1988; Reamer, 1994a; Kadushin & Kadushin, 1997; Hepworth, Rooney, & Larsen, 1997; Morales & Sheafor, 1998; Compton & Galaway, 1999; DuBois & Miley, 1999).

Acceptance

The principle of acceptance charges social workers to go beyond merely tolerating clients to regarding clients positively (Plant, 1970; Siporin, 1985; Barker, 1999). Social workers demonstrate acceptance when they affirm clients' perspectives and value what clients contribute to the work. Accepting workers treat clients with respect and dignity, realizing that clients have unique strengths and resources to offer.

According to Tillich (1962), an existentialist theologian who wrote about the philosophy of social work, the type of love shown in acceptance is different from charity, as charity makes no critical demands. Instead, he associates acceptance with *agape* or *caritas,* the Greek and Latin words for love. The regard for others shown in *agape* or *caritas* "is critical as well as accepting, and it is able to transform what it loves" (p. 15). Social workers whose practice reflects acceptance authenticate the worth and dignity of client systems, expect clients to utilize their capacities for growth, and build on their strengths.

Individualization

Valuing individualization means recognizing that all humans have a right "to be individuals and to be treated not just as a human being but as this human being with personal differences" (Biestek, 1957, p. 25). Although practitioners do rely upon general information about human behavior gleaned from research, they carefully differentiate the distinctive qualities and circumstances of each client system. Social workers' sensitivity toward diversity prevents them from deducing too much about clients from background information, knowing that any cultural characteristic is only one of several individual and group identities clients hold. Individual members of any cultural group have distinctive stories to tell.

Oppression and discrimination seriously impede individualization:

*Cutting to basics, racism, sexism, ageism, and other attitudinal bases for discrim-
ination, exploitation, and oppression have at their core the stereotyping of people
on the basis of real or perceived traits. There is little effort to view people as unique,
and when exceptions to the stereotype are encountered, the signifiers view this as
an unusual case or outlier to their schematic. (Sullivan & Rapp, 1994, pp. 87–88)*

The principle of individualization prompts social workers to customize their generalized
view to accommodate individual differences. A social worker who individualizes clients,
their situations, and their diversity resists applying labels or employing stereotypes. Individualizing also means "eschew[ing] pre-conceived plans and solutions" (Nosko & Breton,
1997–98, p. 57). To focus on each client's unique characteristics, workers treat clients as
persons with rights and dignity rather than "objects," "cases," or "the next appointment."

Nonjudgmentalism

Think for a moment about conversations in which you feel blamed, evaluated, or con-
demned. Do you try to justify your behavior? Are you so aggravated that you stop listening?
Do you feel as if the person with whom you are talking isn't really listening to you or
understanding your situation? Judgmental attitudes and behaviors tend to shut down communication processes, create barriers to relationships, and cast doubts about abilities. Nonjudgmental social workers neither blame clients nor evaluate them as good or bad. Instead,
the worker lets clients make their own value decisions.

Being nonjudgmental does not mean social workers never make judgments about what
clients are doing. Social workers inevitably filter what they learn about clients through their
own professional and personal value screens, as "there is no relationship that is free of values" (Loewenberg & Dolgoff, 1996, p. 116). However, an ethical social worker is careful
to help clients examine the value issues of their decisions through their own value screens,
not the worker's. It is an ethical obligation "that the social worker's own value judgment
never become the sole criterion for making a decision" (p. 116).

"One reason for suspending value judgments, according to many, is that in our plural-
istic society there is no longer any absolute *right* or *wrong*" (Loewenberg & Dolgoff, 1996,
p. 112). A social worker applying an ecosystemic perspective readily recognizes that diversity of choices is a natural result of the many influences which create human behavior. Culturally competent practice requires workers to avoid applying their own values and suspend
making judgments in favor of learning the client's world view—a perspective in which the
client's behavior makes sense. Nonjudgmental practitioners recognize circumstances that
provoke judgment and blame, acknowledge that their personal values and beliefs are not
likely to apply to the circumstances of others, and work to set aside their personal opinions.

Objectivity

Objectivity, individualization, and nonjudgmentalism are all closely related. Objective practitioners separate their own personal feelings from a client's situation. They listen openly to
avoid distorting a client's story with their own biases and refrain from prejudicially labeling

the client. Objective social workers avoid the pitfalls of extreme reactions, responding neutrally with neither cold detachment nor emotional overidentification. Taken to an extreme, objectivity can mean being aloof, dispassionate, or indifferent; however, objective social workers demonstrate caring and concern for clients.

Empathy expresses the objective caring and commitment that competent social work practice requires. A social worker's honest feedback which *describes rather than evaluates* a client's behavior reflects objectivity, too. Self-awareness helps sort out the worker's personal perspective and provides insight on which to draw for empathy with the client's situation. In keeping with the principle of objectivity, social workers invest themselves in their work with clients, yet maintain a professional perspective.

Self-Determination

The NASW *Code of Ethics* (National, 2000) upholds clients' rights to make their own decisions. This freedom to choose and decide reflects the principle of self-determination (Biestek, 1957). Self-determination relates to freedom and self-growth:

> *For this growth from within to occur there must be freedom—freedom to think, freedom to choose, freedom from condemnation, freedom from coercion, freedom to make mistakes as well as to act wisely. Strength to understand and to act upon one's understanding comes only as one actually experiences and exercises the freedom to direct one's owns thoughts and behaviors—and that is what we mean by self-determination. (Hollis, 1967, p. 26)*

Simply, self-determination is the freedom to make choices. But, actualizing this freedom to choose depends on the presence of options and resources. Scarce resources limit opportunities for choice and, therefore, limit a client's potential for self-determination. Empowerment-based social work practice creates opportunities for clients to exercise choice and helps clients recognize their privilege to decide. Involving social service consumers at all levels of decision-making quells potential encroachments on self-determination: "If practitioners align themselves with the interests of consumers, including consumer input and control, the result will be greater self-determination among clients and less ethical discord regarding paternalism within the helping professions" (Tower, 1994, p. 196).

Self-determination also presupposes freedom from coercion (Abramson, 1985). When social workers impose solutions, give direct advice, assume the role of expert, treat clients as subordinates, or in other ways control decisions, they thwart client self-determination. On the other hand, upholding self-determination doesn't mean abandoning clients, abdicating responsibility, or failing to provide direction. Social workers committed to client self-determination actively guide rather than coercively direct the helping process (Solomon, 1983). Social workers who advocate self-determination foster collaboration, affirm client strengths, activate resources, and expand opportunities.

Access to Resources

Without choices and resources, people lack power. Honoring dignity and self-determination hinges on clients having access to resources (Hopps, Pinderhughes, & Shankar, 2000). Guaranteeing clients access to alternatives and opportunities is a fundamental practice principle and requisite of empowerment. The profession's *Code of Ethics* (National, 2000) mandates social workers to advocate the development of opportunities for oppressed and disadvantaged populations and to promote policy changes that improve social conditions. These efforts reveal workers' commitment to social justice and uphold client self-determination by providing rightful access to the resources that society offers.

To promote access to resources, social workers ensure that their practice settings demonstrate sensitivity to diversity. Workers urge their agencies to incorporate multicultural illustrations into their brochures, to provide multilingual staff and literature, to create information forms that are sensitive to lifestyle diversity, and to design office spaces that are comfortable and accessible to people with disabilities. Access to services is only a reality when clients can see that the agency is adapting to their styles and needs.

Confidentiality

All clients have a right to privacy, a right to have what they share held in confidence by the practitioner and protected by the agency. "This information includes the identity of the client, content of overt verbalizations, professional opinions about the client, and material from records" (Barker, 1999, p. 97). As an ethical principle, confidentiality guides professional behavior and forms the basis for trustworthy professional relationships. Workers make exceptions only if clients give their express consent to disclose information or if laws compel workers to reveal information. Respecting privacy by maintaining confidentiality builds trust and demonstrates respect for client systems, two essential ingredients for developing collaborative partnerships.

Accountability

Our identities as social workers leave us accountable for our personal and professional conduct. Accountability requires that practitioners be proficient in the performance of professional practice. It means that workers regard the service obligation of social work as primary and, thus, prevent discriminatory and inhumane practices. Accountable social workers act with professional integrity and impartiality, and they utilize sound protocols in practice and research (National, 2000). The *Code of Ethics* clarifies professional roles and relationships at various levels of responsibility in relation to clients, colleagues, employers, employing organizations, the social work profession, and society (See Appendix A). Ethical social workers study the code to understand its implications for their practice of social work.

To meet the standards of accountability, social workers must know relevant laws and their implications for social work practice. There is a continuum of legal technicalities—from the program and procedural requirements of policy initiatives to federal and state laws to the specifics of case law—that apply to particular fields of social work practice. Judicious social workers increase their professional accountability when they familiarize themselves with laws related to the general practice of social work as well as those related to their specific fields of practice.

Value Conflicts in Practice: An Example

Values and principles guide professional behavior, yet making the most ethical choice is not always easy in practice. Hingsburger (1990) relates the story of Sylvia, a client with mental retardation, placed as a volunteer in a nursing home. Difficulties developed when Sylvia did her job so effectively that visitors to the facility would sometimes mistake her for a nurse, a situation that upset the professional staff and led to a meeting with Sylvia's employment counselor and the nursing home manager.

> *The manager had come to the meeting with a compromise. Sylvia could come back to work if she wore a tag that said, "Retarded Volunteer." This was unquestionably unacceptable. Negotiation occurred and the employment counsellor offered the alternative of having Sylvia wear a tag that said, "Volunteer." It made sense that in a medical establishment one be able to quickly identify medical staff for emergencies.*
>
> *A week or two of calm went by and the second call came. Sylvia was to be fired. Again the counsellor pleaded for a meeting and got an audience with the manager. Sylvia had become a problem. Some of the nurses didn't like her and didn't want anything to do with her. The only compromise that could be reached was stunning. The employment counsellor was told that Sylvia could come to work if, and only if, she followed the following rules. First, she would speak to no staff except for the head nurse on duty. Second, she would take her breaks early in the cafeteria by herself. Third, she would clean up after herself after breaks. Fourth, she would come to work fifteen minutes late so as not to arrive with any of the other staff. These conditions were brought to a meeting.*
>
> *We all sat there and discussed this. Sylvia and her mother were very quiet and we basically said that the placement was over. We needed to find another place. I asked Sylvia if she understood. She looked at me and said, "I'm going back to work. I'm going to do what they say." This was unacceptable and Sylvia was being unreasonable. "No Sylvia, they want me to teach you to never be with or speak to any staff there. I can't do that." Sylvia didn't care what I could or could not do. She said something that no other client before or since has ever said. "You work for me. Teach me."…*
>
> *I taught her.*
>
> *We put staff back in and reinforced her for solitary behaviour. She was taught how to clean up in the cafeteria and when to contact the head nurse. I hated doing this. A month later I arrived at the group home to find Sylvia waiting at the door for me, "Guess what!!!" Sylvia's excitement knew no bounds. "What?" I asked. "One of the nurses said good morning to me." I listened to her voice and looked in her eyes. I saw the eyes of every liberationist who has ever known victory. I saw courage. I saw strength. I saw faith. (pp. 119–121)*

In this example, the worker's acceptance and respect for Sylvia made it difficult to recognize Sylvia's right to make her own choices. Value conflicts such as this are frequent in social work, especially in practice with clients like Sylvia whom workers may feel the need to protect. When social workers experience ethical conflicts, they apply theories and principles for ethical decision making (Reamer, 1993, 1995); consult clients, colleagues, supervisors, and ethics committees; and sometimes obtain legal advice to make informed choices about their actions.

Personal Values and Resources

The personal values and resources of social workers support the professional helping process. A singular emphasis on having professional knowledge, techniques, and skills denies the importance of the "person" of the social worker. Personal attributes of warmth, honesty, genuineness, openness, creativity, sensitivity, commitment, and optimism are all assets for workers in engaging clients and building relationships.

Use of Self in Social Work

A repertoire of intervention techniques without positive personal qualities makes us merely technicians, not social workers, featuring the "science" of worker in our title rather than emphasizing the "art" of the social.

> *The social worker's self is very much involved in the process of helping others. One of the commonly accepted goals in learning social work is the "conscious use of self," which requires self-discipline. Self-discipline necessitates knowledge of the self. There can be no escaping this aspect of the involvement of the self in the social work process, particularly in direct practice. To deny it is simply not to recognize its presence. Social workers are often aware of what is called personal style in their work. The expression of personal style really says, in effect, that this is how I can best use who I am in the social work relationship with this other person. (Imre, 1982, p. 93)*

Personal styles of practitioners are resources for working with clients. Reflective social workers inventory their personal values and resources as a way of preparing to work with clients.

Increasing Self-Awareness

Since so much of our personhood finds its way into practice, self-awareness is an essential quality for every social work practitioner:

> *Those who are real, genuine, and congruent in a helping relationship are ones who know themselves, are unafraid of what they see in themselves, and are comfortable with who they are. They can enter a helping relationship without anything to prove or protect; thus, they are unafraid of others' emotions. (Compton & Galaway, 1999, p. 181)*

To prepare for practice, we identify and accept our own strengths and areas for growth. To heighten our self-awareness, we examine a broad range of personal characteristics such as our lifestyle, moral codes, values, family roots, manner of meeting personal needs, attitude toward change, response to various life circumstances, as well as the personal biases and stereotypes we hold (Johnson, 1998). In addition, understanding our own cultural history and identity is a prerequisite for culturally sensitive social work. As practicing professionals, social workers refine their self-awareness through feedback from supervision, reviews by peers, team consultations, interactions with clients, and educational opportunities.

The Benefits of Self-Awareness

Our knowledge of "self" allows us to discern our inner core, our needs, thoughts, commitments, and values and, at the same time, to observe ourselves. The very fact of "who we are affects what we see in our clients and the ways that we hear and tell their stories" (Dean, 1989, p. 121). Therefore, perceptive social workers learn to know themselves—their personal stories that reveal their attitudes, values, and beliefs—and step back and observe themselves in order to use themselves most effectively in the helping process. Responsible social workers "always return to the need to be self-aware and self-knowing, for authentic dialogue with and true understanding of our clients, as well as for effective helping" (Siporin, 1985, p. 214).

When social workers are aware of their own perspectives, thoughts, and aspirations, they carry a supportive base of personal resources into each new relationship with a client. Effective social workers acknowledge their own needs and actively pursue their own goals in their personal lives. In this way, social workers are able to enter and endure professional relationships in which their own needs are contained in order to work to benefit others.

Values and Principles in Action: A Practice Example

Personal qualities develop over a lifetime of relating, communicating, and reflecting. Expanding self-awareness of personal qualities blends with professional values, knowledge, and skills as social workers prepare to interact with clients. In the example that follows, note how Paul Quillin reflects on his own readiness as he anticipates his work with a new client system. Follow Paul's thinking as he applies the professional practice principles of acceptance, individuation, nonjudgmentalism, objectivity, and self-determination while still maintaining his own personal values. Notice also how he uses his self-awareness as a tool for empathy and as a way to build positive expectations about his clients.

Paul Quillin is one of several social workers at Northside Family Services (NFS) who gather weekly to share ideas and strategize new ways to deliver agency programs and services. The discussion at the last team meeting revealed that several gay and lesbian clients had expressed common concerns about parenting issues. In some ways, their issues include the usual parenting challenges; however, for these parents, the usual translates into complex realities made more difficult by the societal context of prejudice and discrimination. The workers concur that they and their clients have no easy answers for gays and lesbians in a homophobic society.

Brainstorming possible strategies, the workers report many examples of their clients' assertive, creative, and effective responses to the difficult situations. It seems only logical that these clients might benefit from the mutual support that group meetings could offer. When the social workers subsequently poll potential group members to determine their interest in a support group, they discover an enthusiastic, affirmative response. This sets the stage for Paul's work with the new support group for gay and lesbian parents.

Using Self-Awareness

Now, as Paul reads through the referrals, he anticipates who the group's members might be and what he himself has to offer. Paul reflects on what he knows about people who are gay or lesbian. Narrow definitions of homosexuality lead to limited descriptions of sexuality. Understood more broadly in the context of social oppression, being gay or lesbian has dramatic implications. Paul realizes that each prospective group member is likely to experience the stress, anxiety, and fear that often accompany people's awareness that their sexual orientation evokes unpredictable responses from others. These responses range from acceptance to ignorance and misunderstanding, to imposing labels of pathology, to antagonistic acts of rejection, ridicule, and violence.

Paul's own identity as gay allows him to empathize with the struggles that are likely to characterize the life experiences of the support group members. Paul recognizes the strengths that he develops as he accepts and asserts his identity in the face of discrimination. Paul recounts that his own process of coming out has increased his self-awareness, respect for human diversity, and ability to assert himself even when others disagree with his point of view. While Paul knows that his own personal experiences will be helpful in his work with the support group, he tempers his thinking with the realization that his life doesn't actually match the lives of others. Similar sexual orientations do not mean that Paul and the support group members are all the same. Paul fully expects that group members have also accumulated a unique wealth of knowledge and developed many distinctive personal strengths as a result of confronting the array of challenges in their own lives.

Respecting What Clients Bring

Consider the diverse array of resources that clients can offer to each other as the support group convenes. Members of the group will include Rita and Stephanie who have been partners for 10 years. They met in graduate school when they were members of a lesbian activist group. They remain politically active. Both women have supportive extended families and friends. Rita's two children, Thomas who is 11 and Ursala who is 13, have always regarded Stephanie as a parent. They have grown up accepting their parents' lifestyle but now find themselves in uncomfortable struggles with their friends about their family. Previously, both parents had assertively intervened when the children reported incidents of discrimination against them. But lately, Ursala resists their assistance and keeps to herself. Both parents would like to reinitiate the support that was previously accepted by their daughter.

Vince has been a single parent to 8-year-old William since his wife abandoned the family shortly after William was born. Vince is quite accomplished as a single parent, balancing his job as an attorney with an active social life and responsible parenting. He has received much support and assistance from his family and friends in the care of his son. Currently, Vince is considering moving in with Andrew with whom he has been in a committed relationship for two years. Although he is comfortable with this move for himself, he wonders about its effect on William. The three of them have fun together, but William isn't quite sure where Andrew fits into his dad's life. Vince wants to maintain an atmosphere of openness and honesty with his son, but doesn't quite know what and how much to say. Vince is apprehensive about how to explain his decision to William, wonders about how to include Andrew in their daily family life, and is uncertain about the reactions of other family members and friends.

Barb teaches Language Arts and coordinates the reading program at the local middle school. Her divorce was a difficult one, finalized just a little more than a year ago after an extensive battle for custody of 6-year-old Carissa. Barb has come to understand and accept her sexual orientation gradually. At this time, she is only open with a few close friends. She has expressed many concerns about the consequences of others finding out that she is a lesbian. She worries about questions like: What about the custody of her daughter? Could her ex-husband use this against her? What about her job? The school district's policies are unclear about protection for employees and her experiences with some of the parents make her cringe at the thought that they would find out about her sexuality. Barb is looking forward to discussing these issues with other group members, but she is cautious with concerns about privacy and confidentiality.

Each person offers considerable resources which may be useful to the group and its members. Rita and Stephanie have successfully negotiated a working relationship as partners and parents. Vince may benefit from learning about their experiences. As an attorney, Vince has relevant knowledge for Barb. He may be able to inform her decisions about the risks involved in her coming out, the implications for her custody of Carissa and her employment as a teacher. Rita and Stephanie's openness about their sexuality may offer an experiential model for the transitions happening in Barb's life. Even Barb herself, although tentative in her decision to come out, clearly has important resources for the other group members. She brings a first-hand view of adolescence from her training and years of experience as a middle school teacher. Barb's insight into teenagers and their relationships may enlighten Rita and Stephanie as they struggle to cope with the changes in their parenting of 13-year-old Ursala. This list of potential resources is only a beginning. As the support group works together, its members will reveal again and again that they possess distinctive knowledge which is a reservoir of resources upon which they can draw.

How Values Influence Practice

Paul's intensive consideration of the support group members offers little help in anticipating the exact value system that each new group member will bring. Being parents and gay or lesbian does not prescribe common beliefs or values. In fact, differences within a group are often as striking as differences between groups. For example, members will likely have differing views on whether asserting one's identity as gay or lesbian is a personal or political matter. Each probably maintains different views on parenting, what is important for children to know, and how involved parents should be in their children's lives. Regardless of their particular beliefs, each has valid perceptions to support the way that he or she feels.

When the group convenes, Paul Quillin will consciously avoid imposing his values on the group. Instead, he will identify and validate the value perspectives held by group members and encourage members to assert their unique views. Paul will help group members sort through and accept value differences as they form relationships, describe their perspectives, and develop solutions to their challenges.

Forming Relationships

Values influence the formation of professional relationships. Values often bond social workers with client systems when their respective value systems are similar. On the other hand, differing values may distinguish social workers from client systems. Differences test a worker's ability to demonstrate acceptance and affirm client self-determination. If Paul imposes his own values on the group, members will likely withdraw and fail to invest their resources in the group's efforts.

Also consider the interaction within the support group. Similar values among members will probably lead to cohesion, mutual respect, and congruent goals. Discrepant values among members may lead to disagreements and stalemates unless members can develop an atmosphere of acceptance and curiosity in which they question and enhance their own belief systems by incorporating the perspectives of other group members. The existing values of the support group members will intermingle to create group norms, which ultimately affect the behavior of each group member.

Viewing Situations

The way clients view their situations reveals their longstanding, deeply held beliefs and values. Often, the issues at hand are value laden, charged with conflicts and ethical dilemmas (Goldstein, 1987; Siporin, 1983, 1985). Frequently signaled by the word "should"—"What *should* I do?"—or denoted as a quandary about determining the right answer, these moral dilemmas are fraught with inner turmoil, intrapersonal conflict, and, sometimes, labels of immorality (Goldstein, 1987). Consider the support group members. Rita and Stephanie question how they *should* parent Thomas and Ursala. Vince is trying to decide how he *should* incorporate his partner Andrew into his family life. Barb is grappling with whether she *should* be open about her sexual identity. These issues all raise questions that have value issues at their core. Clients respond to challenges and solutions within the context of their values and beliefs.

Screening Possible Solutions

Clients screen options for change through the values they hold. What may be a viable solution for one may conflict with the values of another. Clients most readily apply change strategies that are congruent with their existing belief systems. An ethical social worker suggests options that are a good fit with clients' values or, as an alternative, guides clients to reconsider their value systems and broaden the range of acceptable solutions.

Values can change when people are exposed to different views. The dissonance that new information and perspectives creates can alter beliefs and lead to behavioral changes. For example, a father's newly acquired understanding of sexual orientation may change his perspective on whether he should welcome his gay son's life partner as a member of the family. Whatever beliefs currently guide a client system's behavior, perceptive social workers recognize that these beliefs inform a client's perspective, prescribe the dimensions of possible solutions, and influence the social worker–client relationship.

Values and Diversity

Values are not random; they develop over a lifetime. Each of us demonstrates values molded by family, friends, ethnic group, cohort group, neighborhood, region, and a host of other cultural influences. Recognizing and accepting a client's values requires social workers to be informed about human diversity.

Multicultural Competence

Social work values and principles are essential to working successfully with diverse clients, but good values alone are not sufficient for competent multicultural social work practice.

Without ongoing efforts to develop capabilities in cross-cultural practice, even accepting, well-intentioned, and professionally principled practitioners make significant errors in relating to culturally diverse clients. Putting social work values into practice requires knowledge of the dynamics of diversity and skills for working with diverse populations.

Many factors contribute to the movement toward a multicultural approach to social work practice. Dungee-Anderson and Beckett (1995) describe three important reasons including: (1) traditional approaches fail to meet the needs of persons of color and other diverse people, (2) the CSWE and the NASW now emphasize cultural competence in their revised practice and policy standards, and (3) demographic projections indicate that more than 25 percent of the U.S. population will be persons of color—an accelerating trend when considering birth rates and immigration patterns. These population trends in racial and ethnic groups previously described as "minorities" and the aging of the U.S. population as a whole virtually assure that clients and practitioners will notice many cultural differences in each other (Murdock & Michael, 1996).

"Culture is the means by which we receive, organize, rationalize, and understand our particular experiences in the world" (Saleebey, 1994, p. 352). So, differences in cultural background significantly affect partnerships between social workers and clients. Coming from different worlds can lead to misunderstandings and leave workers and clients feeling alienated from one another—the antithesis of collaborative partnerships that characterize empowerment-oriented social work. Although both workers and clients experience difficulties in cross-cultural relationships, adjusting to those cultural differences is the responsibility of social work practitioners.

Cultural Diversity Defined

Cultural diversity, in its broadest sense, describes the phenomena of human differences as generated by membership in various identifiable human groups. Pinderhughes (1995) describes culturally diverse populations as including all who differ from the white middle class norm "by ethnicity and/or race as well as those who are socially different, such as people in poverty, gay men and lesbians, and people who are physically or developmentally challenged" (p. 132). The Curriculum Policy Statement of the CSWE (Council, 1992) mandates content on diverse populations, including "groups distinguished by race, ethnicity, culture, class, gender, sexual orientation, religion, physical or mental ability, age, and national origin" (p. 101).

Sometimes, social workers apply the term diversity more specifically to emphasize differences in race or ethnicity. Race refers to physical characteristics, with special attention to skin color and facial features, whereas ethnic group members share common cultural attributes such as language, ancestry, or religion (Sheafor, Horejsi, & Horejsi, 1997). In a society that categorizes, segregates, and discriminates based on race and ethnicity, these differences may be especially difficult for social workers and clients to bridge. Frequently, "the professional faces a formidable challenge—the development of a relationship qualitatively different than either party may have previously experienced with a racially dissimilar other" (Proctor & Davis, 1994, p. 315).

None of us, regardless of our primary cultural identity, is monocultural. Our own cultural uniqueness derives from membership in multiple cultures such as cultures associated with gender, occupations, clubs and organizations, geographic regions, ethnicity, and religion, to name a few. Members of a group generally share some values or rules of behavior for participation and/or membership in that group. However, individual members of the same group also possess many qualities and behaviors that differentiate them from each other. "Variations within groups are often great, depending upon the effects of socioeconomic status, education, family history, identification with ethnic group, and time since and cause of immigration" (Rounds, Weil, & Bishop, 1994, p. 7). If we consider this multitude of sociocultural variables affecting both workers and clients, we can unequivocally conclude that most social work relationships are, in fact, multicultural.

Proficient Multicultural Practice

Citing the works of others, Lee and Greene (1999) distinguish between culturally competent and culturally sensitive approaches to multicultural practice. *Cultural competence* targets social worker knowledge for development, focusing "on a particular cultural group, with the purpose of developing culture-specific concepts, knowledge, and techniques within the specific context" (p. 23). In contrast, achieving *cultural sensitivity* is more value-centered. Implementing a culturally sensitive approach requires a worker's genuine appreciation of the client's uniqueness and universalistic respect for the client's humanness. A third possibility for success in multicultural practice is a skill-based approach we describe as *cultural responsiveness*. To be culturally responsive, social workers use dialogue skills that place the client's construction of reality at the center of the conversation. Clients take the role of cultural expert, leaving the worker as an inquisitive and respectful learner. A competent, sensitive, and responsive approach to multicultural practice is rooted in the knowledge, values, and skills of generalist social work; it is cultivated through years of experience interacting with those who are culturally different.

Cultural Competence

Cultural competence requires an infusion of ethnocultural knowledge, beliefs, and culturally competent helping behaviors into all phases of the practice process (Chau, 1995). It "denotes the ability to transform knowledge and cultural awareness into…interventions that support and sustain healthy client-system functioning within the appropriate cultural context" (McPhatter, 1997, p. 261). "Culturally competent professionals recognize similarities and differences in the values, norms, customs, history, and institutions of groups of people that vary by ethnicity, gender, and sexual orientation" (Poole, 1998, p. 163). And, they tailor this knowledge to fit the particular client situation at hand. These workers are able to identify their own cultural lenses, see clients for who they really are, drop assumptions and misperceptions in response to conflicting information, and demonstrate appreciation for the cultural attributes of each client (Pinderhughes, 1995).

To be culturally competent, a worker should build a base of cultural knowledge and individualize clients within their own cultural contexts. In doing so, practitioners must also recognize the power differentials that characterize intergroup relationships (Green, 1999). Differences in power and privilege as associated with cultural identity have a significant impact on workers' efforts to collaborate as partners with clients. Thus, self-awareness and knowledge of one's own culture are prerequisites for cultural competence (Pinderhughes, 1989, 1995, 1997; Dungee–Anderson & Beckett, 1995; Devore & Schlesinger, 1999).

Cultural Sensitivity

Culturally sensitive practice shifts the emphasis from acquiring extensive knowledge about various cultural groups toward developing the worker's attitude of acceptance, respect, and appreciation for each client's cultural uniqueness. Practitioners who are culturally sensitive demonstrate social work values in action and display a willingness to learn about the cultural worlds of their clients. In maintaining an open and inquisitive style, workers become lifelong learners about human diversity, defining multicultural competence as a process of becoming rather than an achievement or end product (Castex, 1994a; Green, 1999; Sue & Sue, 1999). "Cultural sensitivity implies an awareness of the influences of other isolated or multiple factors that can impact and shape the priorities and perspectives of individuals and families in our society" (Dennis & Giangreco, 1996).

Cultural Responsiveness

A culturally responsive approach accentuates key practice skills as a method to achieve multicultural competence. Extensive knowledge about a client's culture is not the key. Rather, the answer lies in the worker's abilities to frame the conversation without overriding the client's perspective. "The worker's expertise lies in applying the skills necessary to access the client's cultural expertise. The ability to elicit and accept client stories without imposing the worker's assumptions, biases, or interpretations is the starting point" (O'Melia, 1998). This approach suggests that "one way to learn about a culture is from the client" using attitudes of "cultural naivete and respectful curiosity" (Dyche & Zayas, 1995, p. 389). By applying client-centered responding skills, workers initiate "a discovery procedure, a way of accessing and learning about the world of people different from ourselves" (Green, 1999, p. 82).

A Generalist View of Cultural Competence

Social workers do not function in isolation, but, rather, in a professional context that includes colleagues, agencies, and the community in which they work. What happens in these contextual systems influences the capability of workers to practice in culturally sensitive ways. Cultural competence requires a systemic effort—the synchronization of values, knowledge, skills, and attitudes at the worker, agency, and service network levels—as well as the incorporation of these attributes into practices, policies, services, institutions, and community functioning (Rounds, Weil, & Bishop, 1994; Smith, 1996; Green, 1999). Culturally competent practice begins at the personal level of the worker and must be supported by both the agency and the community to sustain an ongoing and successful effort.

Practitioner-Level Cultural Competence

Workers themselves bear primary responsibility for developing competence in multicultural social work. Key elements of this personal level of competence include (1) self-awareness, both in terms of values and cultural background, (2) knowledge of other cultures coupled with the skill to adapt general knowledge to specific clients, and (3) the ability to identify and articulate the power and privilege differentials that characterize intercultural relationships (Rounds, Weil, & Bishop, 1994; Dungee–Anderson & Beckett, 1995; Pinderhughes, 1995; Green, 1999).

Self-Awareness

To truly know others, you must first know yourself. The abilities of workers to sort out differences among values and cultural dimensions begins with an intensive review and articulation of their own personal values and cultural heritage. Multiculturally competent practitioners "are aware of cultural values and patterns that motivate their own and their clients' behaviors. They are sensitive to differences and do not project their own internalized cultural responses onto practice situations" (Dungee–Anderson & Beckett, 1995, p. 465).

Culturally competent social workers continuously refine their self-awareness. They acknowledge the way their own biases influence their professional practice. Effective practitioners determine how similarities as well as differences between themselves and clients affect their perceptions and professional judgments. An extensive consideration of our own cultural identities is a requisite for developing a culturally competent repertoire of practices. "Stated simply: 'we' must learn about our own culture before 'we' can learn about 'other' cultures" (Nakanishi & Rittner, 1992, p. 29). Complete the cultural self-inventory in Table 3.2 as a way to begin to envision the cultural lens through which you perceive the world and the clients with whom you will work.

Earlier, this chapter described the pervasive influence of values and principles in social work practice. No where are value differences and conflicts more evident than in cross-cultural social work. In this context, certain values are pivotal, such as one's position on assimilation and cultural pluralism (Devore & Schlesinger, 1999). Assimilation is the process by which cultural minorities absorb characteristics of the dominant culture, whereas pluralism refers to respecting and maintaining cultural distinctions among different groups (Green, 1999). Questions to ask yourself to sort out your view on this issue include:

- As a worker, do you help maintain the cultural integrity of the people with whom you work or do expect them to adapt to the dominant norm?
- Which do you see as more beneficial—cultural assimilation or cultural pluralism?
- Which more closely matches your views of what society should be?
- Which is easier for you to implement in practice?
- How is your perspective similar or different from those of your clients?

Awareness of Others

None of us enters any relationship without expectations about the cultures of those with whom we are about to relate. These presuppositions have many sources. Our knowledge of other cultures develops throughout our lives, influenced by our families, our neighborhoods, the media, and our own history of experiences with others. Some of us have had extensive contact with people who are culturally different from ourselves, while others of us have been isolated in more secluded monocultural worlds. Whether diverse or narrow, our experiences leave us with preconceived notions, stereotypes, and prejudices which taint our views even when, as students of social work, we accumulate knowledge about others through academic preparation, volunteer work, and field experiences.

TABLE 3.2   Cultural Self-Inventory

Personal Identity
- What are your ethnic identities?
- Of which other cultural groups are you a member?
- Which cultural memberships are most influential in the way you define yourself?
- What characteristics or behaviors do you display that indicate the influences of these cultural identities?
- What values are associated with these cultural memberships?
- Do you feel positively or negatively about these identities?
- Have you ever experienced discrimination based on your cultural memberships?
- What privileges do your cultural memberships afford you?

Spiritual Beliefs
- What are your spiritual beliefs?
- What led you to these beliefs?
- How important are spiritual beliefs in your daily life?
- How do these beliefs influence the way you perceive others who hold different beliefs?

Knowledge of Others
- What other cultural groups are present in your community?
- What do you know about the beliefs, values, and customs of members of these other cultural groups?
- What is the source of this knowledge?
- Have your interactions with people from these cultures reinforced or altered this knowledge base?
- What stereotypes or prejudices do you hold about other cultural groups?
- What is the source of your biases?
- What are you doing to increase your knowledge about people who are culturally different from you?

Cross-Cultural Skills
- Are you currently involved in relationships or activities in which you have ongoing interactions with people from other cultures?
- What is your comfort level while interacting with people who are culturally different from you?
- Are you able to talk with people who are culturally different from you about these differences?
- What languages do you speak other than your own primary language?
- What words, phrases, or nonverbal behaviors do you know that have different meanings in different cultures?

Identifying our views about others combined with acquiring more formal knowledge begins to build a more realistic understanding of cultural differences. The more we articulate and question our preconceived notions as we examine various cultures, the more we experience alternative ways of knowing, feeling, and behaving. However, no single practitioner can know all that is relevant to know about every cultural group. Instead, workers should develop specific "knowledge and understanding of the cultural and community context of the population they serve" (Rounds, Weil, & Bishop, 1994, p. 9). To do so, workers can initiate interactions with others in the community while systematically monitoring what they observe and how they react to their experiences.

Studying Cultural Groups.   Multicultural competence requires processes by which practitioners can continue to educate themselves about the particular groups and individuals with whom they work.

One way workers might increase their awareness of diverse cultural groups is to employ the anthropological approach of naturalistic observation. Green (1999) says:

> *The route to greater appreciation of the role of culture in human behavior requires direct observation and participation in naturalistic settings, away from the confines of offices and their imposing routines. For instance, the practitioner who has failed to attend a black church service or talked with a black minister might not understand black clients as well as he or she could. The worker serving American-Indian clients who has not spent enough time in an Indian home seeing how extended families take care of their children and their elderly, or how ritual practices are used for preserving traditional ways, really doesn't know enough about Indian clients. (p. 97)*

By observing people interacting within their cultural contexts, workers can identify those values, resources, skills, and supports indigenous to their communities of practice. Green (1999) suggests three concrete steps:

1. *Preparing to enter an unfamiliar community.* Social workers first review the literature about the particular ethnic group, including research studies, statistical information, and ethnic literature and poetry. They can also study the particular community through social mapping.
2. *Using key respondents as cultural guides.* In this step, workers identify resourceful indigenous people who are willing to articulate what they know to an outsider, develop trusting relationships with them, and learn about their lives in the ethnic community.
3. *Observing while participating.* Finally, workers utilize their relationships with key community members to become involved in the ethnic community's activities. Informed by a research orientation and directed by clear-cut goals, this observation focuses on important attributes of the ethnic community's functioning, placing special emphasis on available leadership, resources, and preferred methods for solving problems.

Experientially generated knowledge of the cultural groups with whom practitioners will work placed in the context of the dominant cultural perspectives to which these various cultural groups must respond are essential supplements to the "textbook overviews" by which most practitioners begin their journey to cultural sensitivity.

Status and Privilege

Cultural group membership means more than differences of values, attitudes, and behaviors. Membership in some culture groups also confers differences in status and privilege. A socially and economically stratified society such as the United States does not afford all groups equal status or privileges. Many of us have the luxury to ignore this fact. "Power differences are less apparent to the privileged, who can more readily accept a view of American society as classless and color-blind—the myth of the 'level playing field'" (Akamatsu, 1998, p. 129).

To develop collaborative cross-cultural relationships, both workers and clients need to neutralize the impact of the wider society as to whom society has granted greater status. To do so, practitioners must understand "the dynamics of power and powerlessness and how these forces operate in human functioning. Moreover, practitioners must be able and willing to apply such knowledge to themselves as well as clients" (Pinderhughes, 1995, p. 133). For example, do you recognize the privileges or restrictions that society assigns you based on your own cultural identity? How might these privileges affect your practice with people from other cultures?

Certain cultural characteristics—such as race, gender, and economic class—are weighted more heavily in determining social privilege and ranking societal status. Most Whites are oblivious to white privilege and the underlying racist ideologies incultured in the institutional structures of society (McIntosh, 1998). "Keeping most people unaware that freedom of confident action is there for just a small number of people props up those in power, and serves to keep power in the hands of the same groups that have most of it already" (p. 152). White privilege is particularly insidious: "Because of the embeddedness of racism in our society, White skin privilege is a camouflage for those who are not targeted. Not perceiving themselves as unknowing, they may never think, or may feel vaguely reluctant, to ask for information" (Akamatsu, 1998, p. 131). Commenting on the interactions between race and economic status found in their research, Davis and Gelsomino (1994) conclude:

> *Both white and minority practitioners may need to be more cognizant of their class biases in their perceptions and subsequent treatment of client difficulties. In particular, both groups may need to pay greater attention to how socioeconomic factors may interact with race. This consideration seems to be especially relevant for their practice with low-income white clients who may be ascribed greater responsibility for their misfortunes than is warranted by their social realities and life opportunities. (p. 122)*

History reveals a plethora of instances of gender stereotyping, gender bias, and discrimination based on sex. "Hidden assumptions about sex and gender remain embedded in cultural discourses, social institutions, and individual psyches that invisibly and systematically reproduce male power in generation after generation" (Bem, 1993, p. 2). Bem calls the sexist assumptions of androcentrism (men are human and women are "other"), gender polarization (men are masculine and women are feminine), and biological essentialism (biological destiny) the lenses of gender. "Not only do these lenses shape how people perceive, conceive, and discuss social reality, but because they are embedded in social institutions, they also shape the more material things—like unequal pay and inadequate day care—that constitute social reality itself" (p. 2).

Sexism interacts with other types of oppression and exploitation, such as racism, heterosexism, and classism. Women of color face the double jeopardy of racism and sexism. Lesbians must deal with the patriarchy inherent in sexism as well as in heterosexism and its corollary, homophobia. And classism multiplies the oppression and discrimination experienced by the expanding ranks of women who are poor. Sexism can "neither be fully understood nor overcome apart from all other manifestations of injustice" (Gil, 1994, p. 249).

Becoming a Competent Cross-Cultural Social Worker
In summary, learning to be a competent cross-cultural practitioner is an evolutionary process that begins with awareness and increases with each interaction with clients. Workers

first attempt to understand their own cultural filters. Next, they build a knowledge base of other perspectives through literature reviews and field research. Third, workers analyze the impact of cultural identities on the power dynamics of the worker–client partnership. Finally, practitioners continue to fine tune their cultural sensitivity through their ongoing practice experiences with unique client systems.

Agency-Level Cultural Competence

The agency setting is crucial in supporting workers' attempts to deliver culturally sensitive services. A culturally competent agency prepares its workers with the necessary training and skills for diversity-sensitive practice, and it promotes multicultural awareness and functioning in all aspects of its organizational structure and program delivery. Specifically, culturally competent agencies infuse multicultural influences into their policies, orientations to practice, structures, resource networks, and physical environments.

Agency Policies

Organizational policies guide an agency's operations, including hiring and training staff, evaluating program effectiveness, and defining criteria for eligibility for services. Reflected in these policies are cultural attitudes and assumptions. Agency policies may simply ignore diversity issues, adopting a dominant cultural perspective by omission. Or, these policies may reflect sensitivity to the cultural elements inherent in all human interaction.

Multiculturally sensitive administrators actively seek to employ a staff that reflects the cultural and social diversity of the community (Gutiérrez & Nagda, 1996). This means hiring diverse staff at all levels of the agency including administrative, supervisory, direct service, clerical, and maintenance personnel. Ideally, hiring policies and procedures will ensure processes for actively recruiting culturally diverse staff members. Interviewers will incorporate interview questions that evaluate the cultural sensitivity of prospective employees. And ongoing training will provide opportunities for all agency personnel to develop the specific cultural knowledge and skills that are relevant to the community.

Eligibility guidelines can either enhance or restrict access to services. Culturally competent policies ensure the accessibility of services to all potential clients. Culturally sensitive agencies recognize the difficulty that many people, particularly those who have been historically disenfranchised, have in connecting to traditionally delivered social services. In response, an agency develops inclusive policies to promote access to diverse clients through the creative design of service delivery—such as locating services in various neighborhoods and offering concrete, pragmatic aid as part of its program (Lum, 1996).

Culturally aware agencies also structure their program evaluation methods for maximum participation by the consumers of their services. Evaluation procedures are most effective when they request input from clients through consumer satisfaction surveys, seek direct feedback from clients in other forums, and ask clients to provide specific information regarding their perceptions of the cultural sensitivity of the agency's practices.

Orientation toward Practice

An agency's theoretical orientation affects the ways that workers view clients and their situations. In social constructionist terms, workers construct the world in which they interact with clients by selecting which theories and perspective to apply. Not all these choices are equal in terms of cultural sensitivity. For example, an agency that implements an intrapsychic approach may overlook the social etiology and ramifications of the client's situation. Multicultural competence at the agency-level means choosing theories that place clients in cultural and social contexts.

Gutiérrez and Nagda (1996) recommend that organizations adopt an ethnoconscious approach to enhance their level of cultural competence. This approach "combines an ethnic-sensitive orientation and an empowerment perspective on practice" (p. 205). It requires a generalist perspective which defines problems and works toward creating change at all system levels, rather than remediating individual clients (Gutiérrez, 1992). "At its center is a concern with power and confronting social inequality through work with individuals, families, groups, organizations, and communities" (Gutiérrez & Nagda, p. 205). Others agree that even when agencies primarily serve clients on the individual and family level, addressing macrolevel issues—including policy, social inequity, and the distribution of resources—is an essential ingredient of multiculturally sensitive practice (Rounds, Weil, & Bishop, 1994; Pinderhughes, 1995; Smith, 1996).

Additionally, in a culturally competent approach, "the process of helping is that of partnership, participation, and advocacy" (Gutiérrez & Nagda, 1996, p. 205). The agency's orientation toward practice encourages workers to describe clients' challenges as transactional, resulting from limited options for coping with the environment, rather than to conclude that problems are inherent deficits of the clients themselves. Competent agencies develop programs and procedures that focus on client strengths, employ culturally sensitive assessment instruments, consider culture a resource, and make use of ethnically-oriented, indigenous helping networks.

Structures

The way in which an agency organizes itself affords opportunities to facilitate cultural competence, particularly in determining the roles that clients play. At its best, an agency can structure "client collaboration and partnerships in organizational governance, program development, staffing and evaluation" (Gutiérrez & Nagda, 1996, p. 207). Involving diverse clients in agency operations ensures synergistic multicultural interchanges in all aspects of agency functioning. It prods the agency to keep pace with the current issues of its various cultural constituencies.

The distribution of power within the agency is an important structural component. Traditional organizations maintain rigid vertical lines of authority, hierarchial structures which likely mirror the inequities of the larger society (Bailey, 1994). In contrast, a flatter organizational structure encourages the sharing of power through consensus-based decision-making. It also enhances opportunities for mutual influence among management, direct service, and support staff. When the agency's organizational structure allows workers to have greater control over their practice, workers, in turn, are more likely to respond similarly with their clients, encouraging them to participate more fully in planning, evaluating, and developing services (Adams & Krauth, 1994). When clients have a greater influence on services, agencies meet clients' needs more consistently regardless of the variations in culture they represent.

Physical Environment

The culturally competent agency is accessible in every way. This means that it is physically accessible to persons with disabilities. It is verbally accessible to those who speak languages other than English. It also is conveniently located in neighborhoods where clients live, has offices on major public transit routes, offers clients transportation, or provides outreach services.

Even the ways that an agency decorates and furnishes its offices and promotes its programs affects whether clients will perceive the agency as culturally open or as an agent of majority control. See Table 3.3 for a list of questions to evaluate the degree of an agency's cultural competence. These expressions of an agency's perspective can be critical to helping clients feel comfortable or they can edge clients toward a more guarded mode of interaction.

Resource Networks

All social work organizations connect to a network of services both to refer clients to services and to receive referrals from other agencies. For an agency to be considered culturally competent, this continuum must include "more than the network of community agencies and referral services. It includes institutions, individuals, and customs for resolving problems that are indigenous to the client's own community" (Green, 1999, p. 92). Examples of indigenous resources include churches, schools, clubs, local healers, neighborhood leaders, and culturally oriented media.

Culturally competent agencies are also active participants in their larger environments. Agencies need to connect with legislative bodies to advocate clients' rights and social justice reforms (Gutiérrez & Nagda, 1996). Agencies should also work to build coalitions with other community groups and organizations working toward social change.

Community-Level Cultural Competence

Both workers and clients respond to the same community context. In some ways each cross-cultural practice relationship is a microcosm of the status of similar relationships in the

---

TABLE 3.3   Cultural Inventory for Agencies

- Can persons with disabilities access the agency readily? Consider those with difficulties in walking, hearing, and seeing as well as those with intellectual and emotional challenges.
- Does the agency display art work that is culturally diverse?
- Is the reading material available in waiting areas of interest to a variety of cultural groups?
- Do story books, games, dolls, and other toys appeal to both boys and girls as well as children from various cultural backgrounds?
- Are brochures and orienting information multilingual and do they contain pictures which reflect the diversity of the agency's clients? Are forms and brochures available in large print format?
- Are agency materials nonracist, nonsexist, and nonheterosexist?
- Do agency materials define concepts inclusively? For example, does its literature on family life define family to include blended families, extended families, and families with same-sex parents?
- Does the agency staff represent diverse cultural groups?

community. A community which discriminates in housing, segregates its schools, and maintains separateness in cultural events fixes distinct boundaries between cultural groups—a chasm which workers and clients must bridge to form working partnerships. On the other hand, a community that values pluralism, celebrates its diversity, promotes cross-cultural interactions, and works toward social justice facilitates the work of social workers and clients. Even practitioners working at the individual and family level can, in generalist fashion, play an activist role in the community-at-large to encourage cross-cultural interactions, awareness, and respect.

Reflecting Back

Professional practice principles, personal values, cultural attributes, individual belief systems, and expectations permeate the relationships of social workers and clients. The social worker–client relationship is potentially a complex web of personal–professional–relational transactions. Social workers must resolve conflicts between their personal values and professional obligations, between their cultural backgrounds and those of clients, between their own perspectives and clients' perspectives, and between the values of social work and those of society. What issues and ethical dilemmas are inherent in these areas of conflict? What principles should guide the resolution of these conflicts? Consider, for example, clients' rights in service delivery, social work values and ethics, and the purpose of the social work profession.

Looking Forward

Workers' expectations that develop from personal and professional preparation and anticipation of what clients will bring to the process will influence the relationship. A positive view of clients, appreciation of cultural diversity, understanding of ethical principles, and heightened self-awareness prepare social workers to construct effective relationships with clients. But these are not the only filters through which workers view clients and their situations. Chapter 4 discusses the strengths perspective and empowerment which also orient a worker's views and approach to practice.

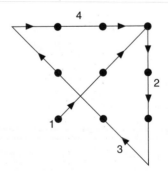

FIGURE 3.2   Nine-Dot Solution

Strengths and Empowerment

A good conference can be energizing and this one, "Empowerment and the Strengths Perspective," is giving Mark Nogales a real boost. Mark's eight years as an outreach worker in the Community Support Program of the County Mental Health Center sometimes leaves him in need of professional revitalization. Facilitating the community integrated living arrangements for persons with chronic mental illnesses has its challenges. But today's conference is crystallizing something for Mark that he has been sensing for some time now. People's lives get better when you focus on what they *can* do rather than on what they *can't*. Mark has learned that his clients, often identified more by their pathological labels and diagnoses than as the unique individuals that Mark knows them to be, bring considerable talents and skills to the challenges in their lives. Mark openly acknowledges and celebrates the diverse resources each client reveals. And now, this conference on the strengths perspective clearly says that the very process of activating client strengths is the quickest and most empowering path toward increasing client competence.

Mark's undergraduate study of social work taught him to implement a process focused on solving problems. "Good social work practice," the words of his first social work professor still echo, "has a beginning, a middle, and an end." More specifically, Mark knew this professor was talking about a well-organized social work process that begins with a concrete definition of problems. Mark built his early practice using this framework offered by experts in the field.

But, as a practicing social worker, Mark is learning from other experts in the field—his clients. These experts are teaching him to look beyond their presenting problems, to shift the attention of the work from solving problems per se to developing strengths and finding solutions. This gradual transition has been a natural evolution for Mark and his clients, a subtle, yet significant, shift in Mark's orientation toward practice.

Simply put, Mark sees the impossibility of trying to solve the problems of chronic mental illness which are, by definition, unchangeable and lifelong. Besides, working closely with the people defined as his clients, Mark has discovered that the various labels of mental illness assigned to them hold little meaning to the relationships he forms with them. Each of his clients is unique. Mark's work with them reflects his awareness that diversity in approach is a natural response to a clientele so distinct in lifestyle, personality, and aspirations as to defy the deficiencies implied in the categories by which they are grouped.

The common message to Mark from his clients is consistent and clear. They respond in positive ways when Mark accepts their challenges and accentuates their talents. Mark is learning it. His clients are proving it. His practice experience is validating it. And now, at this conference, the "experts" in the social work field are promoting it. Practice processes which focus on client strengths rather than deficits actualize empowerment.

Mark's orientation to strengths reveals his respect for his clients. He affirms their capacity and creativity to discover ways to manage their own challenges. When trying to accomplish something, it only makes sense to make use of all the resources available. Building on resources reflects the growing trend in social work to practice from a strengths perspective. When social workers incorporate the strengths perspective, their orientation simply represents *"good, basic social work practice"* (Saleebey, 1992b, p. 43).

Adopting a strengths perspective influences the ways that social workers view client systems and involve them in the change process. This chapter discusses the strengths perspective and empowerment as the foundation for an empowering approach to generalist social work practice. In detail, this chapter:

- Describes the strengths perspective and examines the implications of this view for practice
- Introduces the concept of empowerment as a social work process and desirable goal
- Explores how an orientation toward strengths and empowerment shapes social work practice

Understanding the strengths perspective and empowerment prepares social workers to implement an empowering approach with clients that emphasizes their abilities and ensures their active participation in change processes.

Strengths Perspective

Client strengths are resources in working for change and the focus of a contemporary approach to social work practice. The strengths perspective subscribes

> *to the notion that people have untapped, undetermined reservoirs of mental, physical, emotional, social, and spiritual abilities that can be expressed. The presence of this capacity for continued growth and heightened well-being means that people must be accorded the respect that this power deserves. This capacity acknowledges both the being and the becoming aspects of life. (Weick, Rapp, Sullivan, & Kisthardt, 1989, p. 352)*

All people have a natural power within themselves that can be released (Weick, 1992). When social workers support this inherent power, they enhance the probability for positive growth. People strive toward the development of their potential, mastery, and self-actualization (Maluccio, 1981). This humanistic view leads social workers to recognize "each person's multipotentialities—that is actual as well as latent resources, strengths, and creativity" (p. 11).

The strengths perspective is consonant with social work's fundamental values regarding human worth and social justice. In fact, a focus on strengths is essential to operationalizing social work's professional value base:

> *Focusing and building on client strengths is not only a counterweight to the prevalent deficit model. It is an imperative of the several values that govern our work and the operation of a democratic and pluralistic society including distributive justice, equality, respect for the dignity of the individual, and the search for maximum autonomy within maximum community. (Saleebey, 1992c, p. 169)*

By adopting a strengths perspective, workers infuse values into their practice. "The social work values of promoting human dignity, worth, and self-determination implicitly recognize clients' innate potentialities, capacities, and strengths" (Cowger, 1992, p. 139). A strengths orientation is "more responsive to the humanistic, ethical, and political consider-ations that characterize the helping process" (Goldstein, 1990, p. 267). Simply stated, ap-plying a strengths perspective creates an atmosphere which accords client systems dignity and support.

Practice Assumptions

Currently, the strengths perspective encompasses a "collation of principles, ideas, and tech-niques" which promote the "resources and resourcefulness of clients" (Saleebey, 1992a, p. 15). Strengths-oriented social workers believe that the strengths of all client systems—individual, familial, group, organizational, and societal—are resources to initiate, energize, and sustain change processes (see Table 4.1). Workers draw upon the resources available, both within client systems and in their environmental contexts, to promote more effective functioning.

Key Transitions

Words construct the meaning of our experiences. The particular words we use to describe social work, the metaphors we select to elaborate the process, and the labels we assign to categorize information are extremely significant. Words influence how we think, interpret situations, envision possibilities, and conduct day-to-day activities. The evolution of social work practice from "expert treatment" to a practice process which promotes strengths com-pels us to enrich our professional language to reflect these changes. Rappaport (1985) sup-ports a shift in language, advocating "a language for helping that is steeped in symbols that communicate the powerful force for change contained within ourselves, our significant oth-ers, and our communities" (p. 16). Social work that focuses on strengths and emphasizes col-laboration transforms the way that professionals conceptualize their practice of social work.

To apply the strengths perspective, practitioners need to reexamine their orientation to practice, their views of client systems, and their interpretation of the issues clients present. Practicing from a strengths perspective prompts social workers to examine three key

---

TABLE 4.1   Assumptions of a Strengths Perspective

Social workers who subscribe to the strengths perspective:

- Acknowledge that clients have existing reservoirs of resources and competencies to draw upon.
- Recognize that each client has a distinct capacity for growth and change.
- Define problems as occurring within the transactions between systems rather than residing in deficient system functioning.
- Hold that collaboration augments existing strengths to build new resources.
- Affirm that clients know their situations best and, given options, can determine the best solu-tions for their challenges.
- Maintain that positive change builds on a vision of future possibilities.
- Support a process to magnify mastery and competence rather than correct deficits.

transitions—the transitions from problems to challenges, from pathology to strengths, and from a preoccupation with the past to an orientation toward the future.

Problems or Challenges?

Problems have long been the focus of social work intervention. Typically, clients engage social service delivery systems because they are having difficulties which they or others consider problematic or damaging. Thus, a focus on solving problems emerged as the logical framework for social work intervention. But, does this preoccupation with "problems" enhance or inhibit a client's discovery of solutions?

Think for a moment about the "problems" in your life. What thoughts and feelings does this focus on problems engender? Recounting problems identifies our failures, overwhelms us with impossibilities, engulfs us with hopelessness, and generalizes our view so that the stigma of problems invades our identity. A social work process that focuses solely on problems has the same effect on clients. Fundamentally, a social worker who is preoccupied with detecting problems "empowers the problem and disempowers the person" (Graber & Nice, 1991, p. 3). The term, "problem," sidetracks the helping process. Problems carry with them shame, blame, and guilt; they lead to one-down positions. Social workers using an approach which overemphasizes problems may inadvertently increase those very difficulties that clients are working to overcome.

Wolin and Wolin (1993) direct strengths-oriented practitioners to move from a "damage" model to a "challenge" model for professional practice. Viewing problems as challenges, turning points, or opportunities for growth shifts the perspectives of social workers and clients. Consider the implications of the word "challenge." Can you imagine "meeting the challenge" or "overcoming the challenge?" Do you visualize an invigorating pursuit, a pulling together of your resources and strengths to persevere, striving to attain your goal? Reconceptualizing problems as challenges is more than just a clever turn of a phrase. It is a new way of *thinking* that leads to a new way of *doing* social work.

Pathology or Strength?

Social workers who focus on strengths do not ignore the difficulties that clients bring. The point is not whether problems are part of the helping process; they are. But, when social workers orient their view of clients toward strengths, they question the centrality of focusing on pathology. Narrowly focusing on problems and pathology blocks the ability to uncover strengths. Negative frames of reference obscure the unique capabilities of client systems (Pray, 1991). For example, the problem of "a half glass of water" is that the glass is half empty. But, if we fail to recognize that the glass is half full, we may go thirsty because of our oversight.

There were good reasons for social work's long-standing focus on pathology. Following World War I, the social work profession ushered in an era of practice based primarily on the psychoanalytic perspective and the medical model. This approach, replete with its own language set, served the profession well. Widely accepted, the model helped social work achieve professional status, gain society's sanction by providing psychiatric services to veterans and their families, and establish a definitive theoretical and technical base for practice. As its title implies, the medical model adopts the medical practice of predicating any prescriptive treatment on a diagnosis. Transposed to the arena of social work, the medical model views presenting problems as "pathology" which require "diagnosis" by a social work "expert" in order to recommend and carry out the proper course of "treatment." Though helpful as an organizing framework for practice, the medical model falls short of acknowledging the reciprocal nature of human interaction in environmental context. Instead, the medical model presumes individual fault, failure, personal inadequacy, and deficiency (Weick, 1983).

Diagnosing "pathology" does more than obscure people's strengths. It creates labels that conveniently describe the presenting "pathological" behaviors. This may prompt social workers to move from the construct of a "person with a pathology" to the stigmatizing conceptualization of a "pathological person." Clients, whose behavior society judges immoral—those involved in child abuse, domestic violence, incest, or other criminal acts—are themselves labeled immoral (Goldstein, 1987). Clients who have been victimized, and, thus, called "victims," begin to take on the diminished, impotent persona of the victim role. When careless social workers belittle their clients by evoking labels such as "welfare cases," "those people," "the handicapped," or "run-down communities," even their images of clients become depersonalized and dehumanized.

Maligning clients with unfavorable and impersonal labels generates images of stagnation with no potential for regeneration, renewal, or change. The labels social workers use influence their sense of a client's worth and even shape their ideas about what needs to be done. Pathological labels establish negative expectations that diminish the chances for positive change. Collectively, pejorative labels and stereotypes assign categorical meanings, block visions of potential, and constrict plans for service delivery and social policy. When social work practitioners shift their orientations to strengths, they escape the many pitfalls of focusing on pathology.

Past or Future?

The shift in perspective from problems to challenges also refocuses our view from a look at the past to an eye on the future. An intervention process based on the medical model searches the past to detect when, why, and how client systems went wrong. In contrast, strengths-oriented social workers explore the present to discover the resources that clients currently have which they can use to take charge of the future. Take careful note of this shift—*from the past to the future*. This change *from what was* to *what can and will be* reorients our thinking about the entire process of social work practice.

Life doesn't stand still. No matter how stuck we may feel, we have little choice but to go on as life continues to present its challenges and possibilities. Clients have all gone on and are continuing on despite previous events which may have stretched their capabilities. The ecosystems perspective describes the ongoing evolution of human systems as they adapt to difficult circumstances in productive ways or even as they cope in ways that further complicate their situations. Regardless of its positive or negative direction, change is always occurring. When clients and social workers begin their work together, they can only influence the current situation and the direction of future evolution; they cannot alter past events. What's done is done. What's yet to come is still in question.

None of us can stop the clock or reverse time to rewrite an episode in our past. Our lives just keep happening. If we become mired in looking backward, we are likely to be blindsided to presently occurring events. As an alternative, if we face toward the future, we have opportunities to review what we currently know, apply skills we have developed, and determine what additional resources are available to meet upcoming challenges. There are no rules that say all past problems must be uncovered and resolved or all deficits erased in order to move forward. Consider a new approach that permits cutting loose and forging ahead to a more promising future in which past difficulties fade in the light of success.

Applying a Strengths Perspective

By dwelling on a client system's problems and how they developed, practitioners have difficulty moving from a preoccupation with what went wrong in the past. To apply a strengths perspective, practitioners need a clear understanding of how to focus on the present and to incorporate a vision of the future. Consider the example of how Olivia Adams builds on her present strengths to construct a workable future.

Olivia, a 24-year-old client of Mark Nogales, resides in a supportive living arrangement and attends a work activity program sponsored by the County Mental Health Center where Mark is employed. Olivia presents herself as withdrawn and socially awkward and seldom interacts with others at the center. While she is very capable of performing her assigned tasks, she isolates herself. Mark could dwell on the etiology of Olivia's timorous behavior, but instead Mark uses a forward looking perspective that considers what *is,* not what *was.*

Mark believes the unique way that Olivia copes is a potential resource for directing the future. In withdrawing from social situations, Olivia shifts her attention away from others toward solitary activities. Olivia is gifted with incredible memory skills, especially remembering dates. Fascinated with holidays and celebrations, she can easily recite dates for every U.S., Mexican, and Canadian holiday and religious observance. Her interest also extends to significant dates in the lives of persons with whom she is acquainted. Olivia recalls birthdays and wedding anniversaries of everyone in her extended family. And, she reminds Mark on a weekly basis of the upcoming birthdays of clients and staff associated with the work activity program. Mark recognizes this significant strength in Olivia.

One of Olivia's goals is to develop her social support network. As a first step, Mark and Olivia plan a way to increase Olivia's contacts with friends at the center by building on Olivia's unique capacity for remembering dates. The work activity program has a policy of granting paid leave for both clients and staff on their birthdays. Olivia's new job will be to acknowledge each individual's birthday by personally delivering the agency's birthday greeting and the letter granting paid leave. One can easily imagine the positive exchange that accompanies this interaction. As Olivia uses her talents productively, she becomes more confident in interpersonal relationships and develops friendships through her contacts with coworkers.

In viewing client systems as resourceful, social work practitioners demonstrate their respect for what clients have to offer. Mark Nogales discovers and activates the strengths present in his clients' current situations and in their previous adaptations to life events. Mark and his clients draw upon these strengths as well as the resources available in the community network to achieve their goals. This orientation toward client strengths and environmental resources is an essential backdrop for implementing practice processes which empower change.

Empowerment

Social work pioneers in the settlement house movement planted the seeds of empowerment. However, the problem-focused, medical genre of social casework practice overshadowed empowerment as a practice process in the decades following World War I. Today, the integration of empowerment into practice mandates social workers to move beyond diagnosing deficits toward emphasizing strengths, and to create solutions that incorporate elements of social action.

Empowerment is a complex concept that has personal and political implications. On a *perrsonal level* empowerment refers to a subjective state of mind, feeling competent and experiencing a sense of control; on a *political level,* it refers to the objective reality of opportunities in societal structures and the reallocation of power through a modification of social structures (Swift & Levin, 1987). "Empowerment involves the process of increasing personal, interpersonal, or political power so that individuals, families, and communities can take action to improve their situations" (Gutiérrez, 1994, p. 202). Empowerment has personal, interpersonal, and structural dimensions which apply to social systems at all levels (Rappaport, 1987). (See Table 4.2.)

Personal Dimensions of Empowerment

Personal empowerment embodies our own sense of competence, mastery, strength, and ability to effect change.

> *[Empowerment] suggests a sense of control over one's life in personality, cognition, and motivation. It expresses itself at the level of feelings, at the level of ideas about self-worth, at the level of being able to make a difference in the world around us, and*

TABLE 4.2   Dimensions of Empowerment

As a Concept	As a Process
Personal	Actualizing
Competence	Becoming
Mastery	Collaborating
Feelings of Control	Respecting
Esteem	Consciousness-Raising
Goodness-of-Fit	Discovering
Interpersonal	Acknowledging
Interdependence	Enhancing
Sense of Influence	Strengthening
Partnership	Developing
Social Support	Activating
Respected Status	Connecting
Sociopolitical	Creating
Privilege	Constructing
Citizens' Rights	Expanding
Control of Resources	Integrating
Access to Opportunities	
Social Justice	

even at the level of something more akin to the spiritual. It is a process ability that we all have, but which needs to be released, similar to the way our bodies can be self-healing when endorphins are released. We all have it as a potential. It does not need to be purchased, nor is it a scarce commodity. (Rappaport, 1985, p. 17)

Essentially, people who experience personal power perceive themselves as competent (Gutiérrez, 1991). Competence is the ability of any human system to fulfill its function of taking care of itself, to draw resources from effective interaction with other systems, and to contribute to the resource pool of the social and physical environment.

A Transactional View of Competence

On the surface, words used to describe human competence such as efficacy, mastery, and accomplishment seem like self-appraisals. Without looking beyond individuals, we are left wondering, "Effective in what way?" "Mastery over what?" or "Accomplished in what endeavor?" Rather than being individually derived, feelings of competence arise from the goodness-of-fit between systems and their environments. In contrast, a sense of helplessness, ineffectiveness, or inadequacy results from the lack of fit between systems and their social and physical environments. You may be a master at swatting flies but feel utterly helpless standing before a grizzly bear with fly swatter in hand. It is not the system alone, but, rather, the system in the context of the environment that defines the competence.

From a transactional view, personal empowerment and competence result from the interplay between a system's assets and needs and the environment's resources and demands. A sense of power results from a good fit between a system and its environment, a fit that offers support, security, protection, and resources (Hopps, Pinderhughes, & Shankar, 1995). "Competence is not a fixed attribute of the person. It is the outcome of the transaction between (1) the person's capacities, skills, and motivation and (2) environmental qualities, such as the resources of social networks, social supports, and the demands, obstacles, and deficits in one's ecological context" (Maluccio & Libassi, 1984, p. 52). A transactional view of human competence highlights the interdependence of individual, interpersonal, and environmental factors in competent system functioning.

Personal Competence in a Political Context

A transactional understanding of competence "facilitates the design of empowerment-oriented strategies that deal simultaneously with internal and external blockages, increasing the probability that empowerment both as a process and as a goal will be achieved" (Breton, 1993, p. 32). However, competence is a necessary but not sufficient condition for empowerment: "When personal competence is isolated from the interpersonal, social and structural contexts in which it manifests, and when individual rights are not coupled with responsibilities towards others' rights, the outcome can be nefarious as often as it can be benign" (p. 31). Personal competence coupled with personal responsibility is not enough. Empowerment requires access to societal resources.

Interpersonal Dimensions of Empowerment

Although we may experience empowerment as a feeling within, it emerges from our interactions with others. *Interpersonal empowerment* refers to our ability to influence others

(Gutiérrez & Ortega, 1991). Our successful interaction with others and the regard others hold for us contribute to our sense of interpersonal empowerment.

The social power of positions, roles, communication skills, knowledge, and appearance contribute to a person's feelings of interpersonal empowerment (Gutiérrez, 1991). Therefore, interpersonal power comes from two sources. The first source is power based on social status—for example, power based on race, gender, and class. The second is power achieved through learning new skills and securing new positions, key features of empowerment. Both reshaping the societal ascription of power and enhancing personal skills expand our experience of interpersonal power.

Sociopolitical Dimensions of Empowerment

Empowerment also has *structural dimensions,* meaning that it involves our relationships to social and political structures. "[People] are empowered because the result of their interactions with the environment has been a gain in access and control of resources" (Rappaport, Reischl, & Zimmerman, 1992, p. 86). Having access to resources and opportunities develops individual strengths and accentuates interpersonal competence.

All human systems require an ongoing, expansive set of resource options to keep pace with constantly changing conditions. The more options available, the more likely systems can master their challenges. The fewer the options, the greater the vulnerability of systems. In regard to communities, "the better the resources that have been developed, the more successful the community will be in developing effective responses to problems it encounters; e.g., crime, unemployment, housing problems" (Solomon,1976, pp. 19–20). Competent social systems contribute to the effective functioning of their members and likewise function as opportunity structures for other systems in their environments.

Blocks to Sociopolitical Power

Power blocks at three levels deny access to opportunities and thereby undermine competent functioning (Solomon, 1976, 1987). First, power blocks deny "access to resources needed to develop some critical personal resource" (1987, p. 81); inadequate health care is a barrier to good health. A second power block barricades sources for learning technical and interpersonal skills; people fail to qualify for jobs or promotions as a consequence of inadequate educational opportunities. The third power block denies a valued social role; "discriminatory employment practices may prevent a father from obtaining a job adequate to support the family" (p. 81). In groups and communities, these blocks can produce powerlessness resulting in "the inability to use resources to achieve collective goals" (1976, p. 19). Powerlessness usurps a system's energy and blocks access to a sufficient mix of personal, interpersonal, and contextual strengths, resources, and support to achieve empowerment.

To expect individuals to seek a higher "empowered state" without considering whether they have a minimum level of resources needed to even exercise choice "is simply a mockery of empowerment" (Clark, 1989, p. 271). However, even having access to resources is insufficient for empowerment, as people also need opportunities to contribute to their communities as respected citizens to fully experience empowerment (Breton, 1993). The goal of empowerment should include "the creation of structural conditions under which people can choose to 'give to' their community as well as 'take from' their community" (p. 29).

People are more likely to overcome barriers to power by making structural changes in political and social institutions than by changing themselves (Solomon, 1976). Achieving structural changes creates new opportunities to redistribute resources equitably and to give and take within a competent society.

Power

Having power means having access to information, choosing actions from many possibilities, and acting on one's choices. Power is "the ability to get what one needs; the ability to influence how others think, feel, act, or believe; and the ability to influence the distribution of resources in a social system such as a family, organization, community, or society" (Gutiérrez, 1991, pp. 201–202). The personal, interpersonal, and sociopolitical dimensions of power intertwine. The experience of power within one realm contributes resources for accessing power in another.

Powerlessness

Like power, powerlessness is multidimensional. Personal, social, and political factors all "play into the cyclical nature of powerlessness which keeps certain individuals and groups oppressed, impairing individual functioning and the functioning of family and community systems" (Dodd & Gutiérrez, 1990, p. 65). Blocks to power at one level can impede access to power at another.

Powerlessness combines "an attitude of self-blame, a sense of generalized distrust, a feeling of alienation from resources for social influence, an experience of disenfranchisement and economic vulnerability, and a sense of hopelessness in sociopolitical struggle" (Kieffer, 1984, p. 16). However, there is hope. Someone who feels powerless is not empty of resources, as "competencies are already present or at least possible, given niches and opportunities…[and] that what you see as poor functioning is a result of social structure and lack of resources which make it impossible for the existing competencies to operate" (Rappaport, 1981, p. 16).

Oppression

Powerlessness and oppression go hand-in-hand. Oppression refers to "relations of domination and exploitation—economic, social, and psychological—between individuals; between groups and classes within and beyond societies; and, globally, between entire societies" (Gil, 1994, p. 233). Oppression is the injustice that results from the domination and control of resources and opportunities that entitles favored groups and disenfranchises others (DuBois & Miley, 1999).

Oppression results in injustice or "discriminatory, dehumanizing, and development-inhibiting conditions of living (e.g., unemployment, poverty, homelessness, and lack of health care), imposed by oppressors upon dominated and exploited individuals, social groups, classes, and peoples" (Gil, 1994, p. 233). By imposing categorical judgments, dominant groups in society classify other groups as less worthy, affording them little prestige, few possibilities, and limited resources. Racism, classism, ableism, heterosexism, regionalism, sexism, ethnocentrism, and ageism are all interrelated expressions of oppression, exploitation, and injustice (Table 4.3).

TABLE 4.3   Prejudicial Attitudes Contributing to Oppression

Racism	Ideology often based on negative stereotyping that perpetuates individual and institutional discrimination against members of racial groups
Sexism	Based on sex role stereotyping and cultural beliefs that one sex is superior to the other
Classism	Elitist attitudes about persons based on their socioeconomic status or class
Heterosexism	Prejudice and discrimination directed against persons who are homosexual
Ableism	Prejudicial attitudes and behaviors that result in unequal regard for persons because of their physical or mental disability
Ageism	Negative stereotyping of persons based on their age
Regionalism	Generalizations about the character of individuals or population groups based on the geographic region of their origin or residence
Ethnocentrism	Condescending belief that one's own ethnic group, culture, or nation is superior to others

Victim Blaming

Victim blaming compounds the insidious experience of oppression. According to Ryan (1976) in his book, *Blaming the Victim,* victim blaming occurs in two different ways. One way labels victims as inferior, genetically defective, or unfit. The other casts blame for inferiority on environmental circumstances. Victim blaming is "a brilliant ideology for justifying a perverse form of social action designed to change, not society, as one might expect, but rather society's victim" (p. 78). Specifically, Ryan says:

> *All of this happens so smoothly that it seems down right rational. First, identify a social problem. Second, study those affected by the problem and discover in what ways they are different from the rest of us as a consequence of deprivation and injustice. Third, define the differences as the cause of the social problem itself. Finally, of course, assign a government bureaucrat to invent a humanitarian action program to correct the differences. (pp. 8–9)*

Although "do-good" helpers recognize the impact of social problems, they probe those who "have the problem," designate them different from others, and label them "incapable," "unskilled," "ignorant," and "subhuman." People who subscribe to this view believe that changing "those people" is requisite to solving social problems (Ryan, 1976). They unjustly blame those who experience the effects of social problems, rather than recognizing that these difficulties result from oppression, discrimination, and injustice. These are sociopolitical issues that require sociopolitical solutions.

Persons who experience blame, shame, and stigma often assimilate this negativity into their self-images (Patten, Gatz, Jones, & Thomas, 1989). Self-blame may lead people to feel incompetent, dependent, and rejected (Janis & Rodin, 1980). Ironically, people who feel victimized may identify with the oppressors, conclude these charges are accurate, and apply the derogatory labels to themselves. In general, feelings of powerlessness increase, often resulting in low self-esteem, alienation, and despair.

Social Work Clients and Oppression

Social work clients often find themselves trapped by powerlessness and oppression. In today's world, social workers likely deal with clients who are "profoundly vulnerable …overwhelmed by oppressive lives, and by circumstances and events they [feel] powerless to control" (Gitterman, 1991, p. 1). Simon (1994) links powerlessness and oppression to empowerment-based social work practice:

> *Client empowerment presupposes an existing condition of client disempowerment and marginality. Fitting subjects, therefore, of empowerment social work are socially despised persons, families, and groups. They may be poor in a county that values economic success, black in a culture that privileges white skin, chronically ill in a nation that equates health with productivity and productivity with merit, or old in a land that cherishes the vigor of youth and shuns symbolic and material reminders of human mortality. (pp. 24–25)*

Oppression, discrimination, injustice, and experiences of powerlessness are the very circumstances that call for the application of empowerment-based social work practice (Solomon, 1976; Gutiérrez, 1994; Simon, 1994; Lee, 1994). Mullender (1996b) charges social workers to "challenge all forms of oppression, whether by reason of race, gender, sexual orientation, age, class, disability, or any other form of social differentiation upon which spurious notions of superiority and inferiority are developed and kept in place by the exercise of power" (p. 188).

Empowerment as a Concept and a Process

To address these issues of oppression, injustice, and powerlessness, strengths-oriented social work practice incorporates empowerment as both a concept and a process. Empowerment as a *concept,* "helps organize thoughts or develop a framework within which one can identify the circumstances of individuals and groups in society" (Nystrom, 1989, p. 161). Empowerment offers a perspective to assess the interconnections between personal and political realities.

As a *process,* empowerment describes how practitioners actually do their work. "As a process, empowerment enables people to develop and implement organized responses to circumstances that affect their lives" (Nystrom, 1989, p. 161). In other words, the process of empowerment represents the way by which systems gain control—the way that "people, organizations, and communities gain mastery over their lives" (Rappaport, 1984, p. 3). Empowerment is a "process through which clients obtain resources—personal, organizational, and community—that enable them to gain greater control over their environment and to attain their aspirations" (Hasenfeld, 1987, pp. 478–479).

The process of acquiring power does not necessitate a struggle or relinquishment of power by one group in favor of another. Empowerment is geometrically expansive rather than a zero sum commodity. Empowering—the process of empowerment—means recognizing, facilitating, and promoting a system's capacity for competent functioning. Empowering also implies taking actions that respond to the linkages among the personal, interpersonal, and sociopolitical dimensions of empowerment.

Empowerment-Based Practice

Working toward the goal of empowerment significantly affects the way social workers practice. First, workers apply an ecosystems perspective and a strengths orientation in practice. This means that workers consider client situations in context, search for client strengths and environmental resources, and describe needs in terms of transitory challenges rather than fixed problems. Second, as generalists, social workers draw on skills for resolving issues at many social system levels and respond to the interconnections between personal troubles and public issues. Instead of dwelling on vulnerabilities, empowerment-based practice accentuates resiliencies. An empowering approach liberates client systems from the encumbrances of eliminating problems to the promises of generating solutions. Empowerment-based practitioners join with clients as partners and rely on clients' expertise and participation in change processes. They discern the interconnections between client empowerment and social change. These changes are not trivial! They redirect every phase of the practice process.

The Paradox of an Empowering Process

Social workers empower clients toward feelings of competence and control of resources. Take note, however, as the idea of empowering others is a fundamental paradox (Gruber & Trickett, 1987). Social workers cannot give empowerment away. They cannot bestow it on other systems from star-tipped wands.

> *The one function that social workers, or for that matter, anyone else cannot perform for another person is that of empowerment. Empowerment is a reflexive activity, a process capable of being initiated and sustained only by the agent or subject who seeks power or self-determination. Others can only aid and abet in this empowerment process. They do so by providing a climate, a relationship, resources, and procedural means through which people can enhance their own lives. (Simon, 1990, p. 32)*

Even if one could bestow power, bestowing power, in itself, would be disempowering! Empowerment-based social workers actively involve client-partners in collaborative processes to release the resources of change. "Empowerment insists on the primacy of the target population's participation in any intervention affecting its welfare. It is the antithesis of paternalism" (Swift, 1984, p. xiv). Rather than given away, empowerment draws upon both internal and external resources; it generates from within systems and their environments.

Collaboration and Partnership

"We should not seek to do for others what they must do for themselves. We should not focus so much on designing programs 'on behalf of' others; rather, we must strive to collaborate *with* others in developing the emotional and practical resources they require" (Kieffer, 1984, p. 28). An orientation toward strengths and empowerment compels social workers to redefine their relationships to embrace the notion of collaboration and partnership. Without this redefinition, overzealous social workers assume responsibility for solutions and often ascribe responsibility for failures to clients.

> *The role of the expert supported by a socialization process of revering authority fig-*
> *ures and teaching that the expert is in charge has the unintended side effect of as-*
> *cribing to the professional an unrealistic amount of responsibility for the solution of*
> *the client's problems.... Then, when they do not succeed, they tend to rationalize in*
> *terms of the mysteries of scientific expertise and/or to blame the clients and call for*
> *more thorough compliance with their decisions. (Lenrow & Burch, 1981, p. 243)*

Empowerment liberates social workers from an elevated status and functions as an antidote to burnout, since it shifts the burden of the work to a sense of mutual responsibility.

For clients, collaboration is a resource for power. Rollo May (1972) in his book, *Power and Innocence,* identifies nutrient power or "power for the other" and integrative power or "power with the other" as positive manifestations of power. "Both of these positive expressions of power suggest collaboration in a common enterprise in which cooperation becomes a form of power" (Weick, 1980, p. 183). In other words, social workers who share power with clients, free clients to access their own power; the cooperation within the professional relationship itself becomes a new source of power. Collaboration is the hallmark of empowerment (Figure 4.1).

Clients or Consumers?

The terms social workers use to describe their clients shape the expectations for their roles and define the nature of professional relationships. Over the years, practitioners have assigned many different labels to persons or groups who use social services including "supplicants," "patients," and "those receiving help." Each of these labels characterizes clients as "people who need fixing." Furthermore, these labels imply that professionals are experts who have the knowledge, power, and authority necessary to supply, heal, or treat, leaving receivers of services as "have-nots" who passively acquire supplies, healing, or treatment.

Some use the term "consumer" to emphasize a client's active role (Gummer, 1983). Viewed as consumers, social work clients seek information, make choices, and contract for what they need from public or private organizations or corporations through fees, vouchers, or citizens' rights (Tracy & DuBois, 1987). "Consumerism offers a way that, in combination with other strategies for equalizing power and control between givers and receivers of services, can revitalize and relegitimate our social welfare institution" (Gummer, 1983, p. 934). Tower (1994) elaborates, stating that:

> *the basic doctrine of consumerism within human services systems is that individ-*
> *uals who have direct experience with a particular life condition (for example, ag-*
> *ing, disability, mental illness) are more knowledgeable about their own needs and*
> *interests than are their professional counterparts. When individuals redefine their*
> *role from that of patient, client, or recipient of goods and services to that of con-*
> *sumer, their sense of control over their own lives is elevated. (p. 192)*

Others criticize the term, "consumer," as conveying passive, compliant consumption. And, on the receiving end, those labeled consumers may believe they need to be on guard

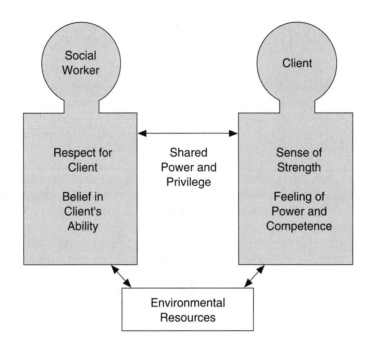

FIGURE 4.1   Elements of Empowerment in the Social Worker–Client Relationship. An empowering social worker–client relationship has personal, interpersonal, and sociopolitical elements.

as "buyers must beware." Consumer may also imply a consumer market strategy of rationing services rather than an empowerment model of service-user involvement (Barnes & Walker, 1996; Adams, 1997). In its most empowering construction, the concept of consumer conveys the idea that a person or other social system seeking services has both rights and responsibilities, yet negative connotations about consumerism restrain widespread use of this term in social work.

The most widely accepted term for those utilizing social services is "client" (Aho El Nasr, 1989). In fact, usage of the term "client" predominates social work literature, codes of ethics, and international documents. Numerous other professional groups apply the term client when referring to those who engage their services. Critics contend that client suggests a subservient position to the professional expert, thus lending too much power to the "expert" professional. However, in general usage, the term client affords dignity. Consider the example of an international business client or the client of a corporate attorney. Only in relation to social work does "client" seem to take on negative connotations. Perhaps, it's not the word "client" that conjures negative images, but society's view of social work itself that taints any term we choose.

Today, several different terms are in vogue, depending on the context. Some alternatives used in agency practice include neighbors, participants, residents, parents, members, students, and citizens. Writers vary among the use of the term "client," which reflects a professional relationship, "client system," which broadens the concept beyond individuals to include multiperson systems, and "consumers of social services," which emphasizes active participation and rights.

Carefully chosen words embody a sense of reciprocity. Any term chosen should clearly recognize that clients are people first and our relationships with them should encompass the dignity and respect of collaborative partnerships. In this text, we use the terms "client" along with "client systems" to emphasize the various system levels in generalist social work and "partners" to acknowledge their collaborative participation. We will also, without apology, refer to practitioners as social workers!

Empowerment-Oriented Strategies

Empowerment-oriented social workers assume that a client's issues reflect a lack of congruence between the system's capacities and environmental demands. They acknowledge the imbalance between the pool of personal, interpersonal, and societal resources and the system's need for these resources to meet the challenge. They select multilevel strategies that heighten the availability of personal, interpersonal, and sociopolitical resources. In the tradition of empowerment-based practice, this means selecting strategies that increase self-efficacy, develop skills, discern connections between personal difficulties and public troubles, enhance collectivity, and take actions to create sociopolitical changes (Cox & Parsons, 1993; Gutiérrez, 1994; Lee, 1994; Simon, 1994).

Using Group Modalities

Many practitioners conclude that working with clients in groups enhances their experiences of empowerment (Hirayama & Hirayama, 1988; Simon, 1990, 1994; Ward & Mullender, 1991; Breton, 1993, 1999; Lee, 1994, 1997; Gutiérrez, 1994; Mullender, 1996a, 1996b; McInnis-Dittrich, 1997; Nosko & Breton, 1997–98; Home, 1999). Work in small groups "is the perfect environment for raising consciousness, engaging in mutual aid, developing skills, problem solving, and experiencing one's own effectiveness in influencing others" (Dodd & Gutiérrez, 1990, p. 71).

Hearing others tell stories similar to one's own has a dramatic effect, particularly for those who have experienced oppression. "The collective view of experiences tends to reduce self-blame, increase the tendency to look for causes other than personal failure, and bring about a sense of shared fate and consciousness raising" (Cox & Parsons, 1993, p. 37). In addition, group work "provides an opportunity for support, mutual aid, and collective action on behalf of the whole" (Parsons, 1991, p. 12).

Developing a Critical Consciousness

Developing a critical consciousness about the interconnections of the personal and political is another essential component of empowerment-oriented practice (Moreau, 1990; Simon, 1994; Parsons, 1991; Breton, 1993; Lee, 1994; Gutiérrez, 1994). Critical reflection leads to understanding the social origins of individual actions and recognition that institutional forms are changeable (Young, 1994). Social workers need to restore consciousness-raising to center stage, as it contextualizes experiences, reduces self-blame, and "helps group members to take account of the nature and impact of their own choices and actions and to take responsibility for them" (Simon, 1990, p. 35). Furthermore, when this dialogue occurs in the context of a group, group members form a solidarity that can lead to collective actions. (See Figure 4.2.)

Reflecting and Acting: Praxis

Building on strengths, social workers and clients collaborate on change at many levels. They form partnerships to increase the client's competence, while simultaneously they

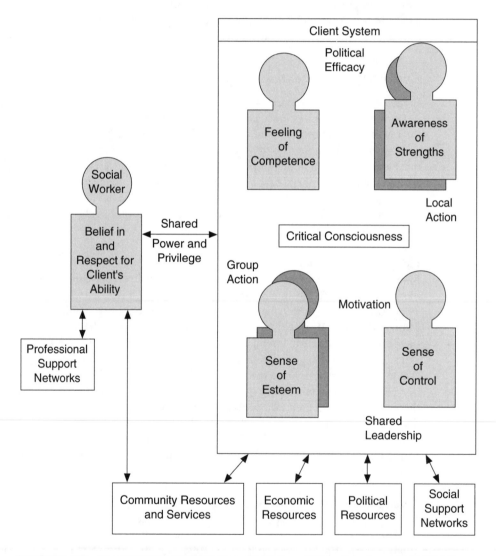

FIGURE 4.2   Developing a Critical Consciousness. Alliances among individuals create opportunities for developing social bonds, enhancing personal competence and political efficacy, and achieving a critical consciousness as requisites to collective social action.

work to redress social injustice and create networks of resources that are more responsive to the client's needs. Social workers and clients take actions, then pause to observe and reflect to guide the next step. As the work unfolds, reflection and action intertwine in praxis (Dodd & Gutiérrez, 1990). "As clients are actively involved in change, they are also reflecting upon and analyzing their experiences. The result of this analysis is then integrated into the development of future efforts" (p. 70).

Taking Social Action

Social action is the key to sociopolitical empowerment and a legacy of the social work profession (Belcher & Hegar, 1991; Cox, 1991; Ward & Mullender, 1991; Simon, 1994; Hanna & Robinson, 1994; Boes & VanWormer, 1997; Ping-Kwong, 1997; Wilson & Anderson, 1997). Collective action strives to reallocate sociopolitical power so that disenfranchised citizens can access the opportunities and resources of society and, in turn, find meaningful ways to contribute to society as valued citizens.

Social action is not exclusively the domain of the macropractitioner. Generalist practitioners working primarily with microlevel clients also make efforts to improve conditions in communities, bureaucracies, and society. For example, they may act as advocates to speak out with clients at the institutional and political level to influence changes in social policies. In these ways, practitioners work in collaboration with clients to create social and political change.

Tenets for Empowerment-Based Social Work Practice

To guide practitioners' in their work with clients to facilitate personal, interpersonal, and sociopolitical empowerment, DuBois and Miley (1999) propose the following tenets for social work practice:

1. *Empower people, individually and collectively, to utilize their own problem-solving and coping capabilities more effectively.*
2. *Support a proactive position in regard to social and economic policy development, to prevent problems for individuals and society from occurring.*
3. *Uphold the integrity of the profession in all aspects of social work practice.*
4. *Establish linkages between people and societal resources to further social functioning and enhance the quality of life.*
5. *Develop cooperative networks within the institutional resource system.*
6. *Facilitate the responsiveness of institutional resource systems to meet health and human service needs.*
7. *Promote social justice and equality of all people in regard to full participation in society.*
8. *Contribute to the development of knowledge for the social work profession through research and evaluation.*
9. *Encourage an information exchange in those institutional systems in which both problems and resource opportunities are produced.*
10. *Enhance communication through an appreciation of diversity and in ethnically sensitive, nonsexist social work practice.*
11. *Employ educational strategies for the prevention and resolution of problems.*
12. *Embrace a worldview of human issues and solutions to problems. (pp. 56–57)*

Reflecting Back

Understanding diversity involves a process of critical questioning about issues of powerless, oppression, and discrimination. This approach goes beyond merely examining the demographic differences of diverse population groups to exploring the commonality of the experience of victimization and exploitation. Only in this way can social work practitioners step outside of their own perspectives into clients' worldviews. What is the process of critical reflection that social workers need to experience to learn about diversity and oppression? Consider how critical reflection changes social work intervention from solutions focused on personal adaptation to those that consider the ramifications of political, institutional, and structural dynamics inherent in an oppressive society.

Looking Forward

When social workers view clients through the perspective of strengths and competence, they discover and appreciate the uniqueness and diversity inherent in all human systems. They affirm that client systems already have potential—knowledge, experiences, and resources—upon which to draw. When social workers magnify client strengths, they heighten motivation and involvement as collaborative partners. When clients get in touch with their own strengths, they discover solutions in the personal, interpersonal, and sociopolitical dimensions of their situations.

An orientation to strengths and empowerment is essential to implement an empowering approach to generalist practice. Chapter 5 describes how social workers transform these perspectives on practice into a coherent approach which empowers clients at all system levels.

Chapter 5

An Empowering Approach to Generalist Practice

An empowerment orientation has profound implications for the processes that guide social workers. Empowering processes move clients to center stage—positioning them as the authors of their stories as well as the directors and producers of the action. This leaves workers in the roles of accentuating clients' "unique coping and adaptive patterns, mobilizing their actual or potential strengths, emphasizing the role of natural helping networks, and using environmental resources" (Maluccio & Libassi, 1984, p. 52). Changes accomplished by clients through such processes are likely to endure, since they are "funded by the coin of their capabilities, knowledge, and skills" (Saleebey, 1992a, p. 6).

The method of generalist practice described here empowers clients. Consistently, it demonstrates confidence in the abilities of client systems, builds solutions on their capabilities, and acknowledges the essential role of social and political change in empowerment. This approach also recognizes the incredible diversity in the strengths that various client systems present. It acknowledges that there is no single way to live a life or solve a problem; instead, there are a multitude of potential solutions available given the unique capabilities of client systems. This shift helps social workers view clients as resources, "as human beings with assets and potentialities that can be mobilized on their own behalf, and also to help clients to see themselves as resources" (Maluccio, 1981, p. 15).

This chapter presents an overview of this text's empowering approach to generalist social work practice. Specifically, it:

- Summarizes the perspectives which support an empowering approach to generalist practice
- Describes phases of dialogue, discovery, and development which orient activities of the social work process
- Details processes and skills for each phase of this empowering approach
- Offers examples applying this generalist model with clients at the micro-, mid-, and macrolevels of practice
- Discusses the flexibility of this approach to fit the particular situation

When generalist practitioners use an empowerment approach, they work with clients to rediscover their own strengths and to access resources from their environments.

Elements of an Empowering Generalist Approach

This approach to generalist social work draws on the practice perspectives presented thus far. It applies the ecosystemic perspective, reflects the multiple dimensions of empowerment, and actualizes the strengths orientation through its assumptions of client expertise and consistent emphasis on collaborative roles for both clients and practitioners.

Infusing an Ecosystems Perspective

The ecosystems perspective examines the interplay of human systems with their environments to understand what is happening and to develop strategies for initiating change. Consistent with the ecosystems perspective, this empowering practice approach guides social workers and clients to view challenges and strengths in context, to identify the many possible paths to solutions, and to recognize that change in any given system reverberates through other system levels. Each phase of this approach accommodates the transactional nature of social work by considering the interaction of client systems and their environments. Informed by an ecosystemic perspective, workers are able to locate resources for change present in the entire ecosystem in which their relationships with clients exist.

Reflecting a Social Justice Commitment

All social work practice is political. Social workers participate in defining whether a society is just. If social workers impose dominant cultural views about human behavior, function to control deviance as defined by majority values, and offer expert solutions to client problems, they reinforce and perpetuate oppression. In contrast, if social workers align with client worldviews, define problems transactionally, and seek solutions in social and political change, they nudge society in the direction of social justice. Processes within this empowerment-oriented approach consistently reveal the requisite client-centeredness and focus on environmental conditions necessary to meet social work's commitment to social and economic justice.

Applying a Strengths Orientation

As a lens for viewing clients, the strengths perspective shifts the view of clients from one of pathology toward one of potential. The fundamental question switches from "what is wrong" to "what is available" within clients and their environments to achieve desired changes. Strength-oriented social work processes describe methods for clients to discover what might be useful in the present for constructing a more positive future. Cultivating client strengths and resources throughout all phases of the practice process is essential for implementing an empowerment-based approach to social work practice. However, adopting a strengths perspective is insufficient in many situations. Activating client strengths is most effective in a socially and economically just environment in which opportunities are accessible to all.

Collaborating with Clients

An orientation toward strengths redefines the social worker–client relationship and reconstructs the social work process. Recognizing client expertise, social workers work in partnership with clients. Workers and clients collaborate to create a vision of what they hope to accomplish, then concentrate their efforts to search the present situation for resources to reach that goal. Collaboration entrusts clients with rights and responsibilities in each phase of practice. This kind of participation encourages clients to discover their own solutions and remain in charge of their own changes. "Clients, by contrast, who empower themselves in collaborative 'alliance' with social workers, to use Bertha Reynolds' conception, have retained crucial control of the purpose, pace, and direction of the work" (Simon, 1990, pp. 32–33). In an empowerment-focused approach, clients feel their own sense of power in the social work process and carry these feelings of competence and control beyond the boundaries of their relationships with social workers.

Constructing an Empowering Reality

Consistent with a social constructionist perspective, research demonstrates that a professional's prehelping attitudes and beliefs (Dunst, 1993) and the helpgiving practices of social service programs (Trivette, Dunst, Boyd, & Hamby, 1995; Dunst, Trivette, & Hamby, 1996; Trivette, Dunst & Hamby, 1996) influence a client's experience of empowerment. This research also affirms that positive attributions and program orientations make a difference in a social worker's effectiveness. The empowerment method of practice introduced in this chapter consistently describes social work processes in language that frames a future-oriented, solution-saturated, and client-validating reality.

Effective social workers purposefully construct an empowering "practice reality" by orienting themselves toward client strengths, empowerment, and collaboration. They develop productive assumptions about clients and the practice process, including:

Assumptions about Human Systems

- All people deserve acceptance and respect.
- Clients know their situations best.
- All human system behavior makes sense in context.
- All human system behavior is motivated.
- Challenges emerge from transactions between human systems and their physical and social environments rather than reside in clients themselves.
- Strengths are diverse including personal feelings of worth, cultural pride, successful relationships, and resourceful interdependence within a community

Assumptions about Change

- Change is not only possible, it is inevitable.
- A small change in one part of the ecosystem may initiate a chain of beneficial changes.
- Challenges are likely to have many solutions.
- You don't have to solve a problem to find a solution.
- Enduring change builds on strengths.
- Strengths and the potential for growth characterize all human systems.
- Given niches and opportunities, human systems cultivate competencies.
- Collaborative relationships stimulate feelings of power and lead to actions.
- Cultural differences are resources offering broader perspectives, additional options, and possibilities of synergistic solutions.

When social workers believe that clients have the rights to their own beliefs, that they have made choices and can make new choices, and that they have the potential to achieve their goals, these expectations prepare workers to implement an empowering practice process.

Phases and Processes of Empowering Practice

This empowering approach is organized and deliberate, yet dynamic and flexible, as social workers guide clients through phases of dialogue, discovery, and development. Specific processes guide social workers' activities within each of these phases of practice. These processes distinguish essential components for implementing an empowering approach. Table 5.1 describes the processes that comprise the dialogue, discovery, and development phases.

The Dialogue Phase

Successful social work requires conversation, an ongoing dialogue with clients about their situations, goals, and strengths. Through this exchange, practitioners define their relationships

TABLE 5.1   An Empowering Approach to Generalist Practice

Phase	Process	Activities
Dialogue	Forming Partnerships	Building empowering social worker–client relationships that acknowledge clients' privileges and respect their uniqueness
	Articulating Situations	Assessing challenging situations by responding to validate clients' experiences, add transactional dimensions, and look toward goals
	Defining Directions	Determining a preliminary purpose for the relationship to activate client motivation and guide the exploration for relevant resources
Discovery	Identifying Strengths	Searching for client strengths in general functioning, coping with challenging situations, cultural identities, and overcoming adversity
	Assessing Resource Capabilities	Exploring resources in clients' transactions with the environment including connections to family, social groups, organizations, and community institutions
	Framing Solutions	Constructing an achievable plan of action that utilizes client and environmental resources and leads toward desired goals
Development	Activating Resources	Implementing the action plan by mobilizing available resources through consultancy, resource management, and education
	Creating Alliances	Forging empowering alliances among clients, within clients' natural support networks, and within the service delivery system
	Expanding Opportunities	Developing new opportunities and resources through program development, community organizing, and social action
	Recognizing Success	Evaluating the success of the change efforts to recognize achievements and inform continuing actions
	Integrating Gains	Wrapping up the change process in ways that resolve the relationship, celebrate success, and stabilize positive changes

with clients as a collaborative partnership to which both will contribute. In this phase social workers and clients clarify the purpose of their relationship and define a preliminary focus for their work together. In the dialogue phase, practitioners and clients collaborate to:

- Build partnerships based on acceptance, respect, and trust
- Define their respective roles
- Discuss clients' experiences with challenging situations
- Define the purpose of their work together
- Activate client motivation for change
- Address crisis needs

In the dialogue phase, workers and clients talk with one another to assess what is happening and develop a preliminary vision of the way clients would like things to be. These processes require open and respectful exchanges of information between practitioners and clients. Specific processes associated with this phase include forming partnerships, articulating challenges, and defining directions.

Forming Partnerships

Forming partnerships is the process whereby a worker and client system define their working relationship in ways which reflect the purposes of social work and standards of ethical codes (Chapter 6). For the process to be empowering, social workers and client systems resolve power and authority dilemmas by defining their relationship in an egalitarian way, maximizing their respective contributions. Social workers and clients are collaborators, working together to understand situations and accomplish change.

Articulating Situations

In the process of *articulating situations,* workers and clients develop a mutual understanding of what prompts clients to seek social work assistance (Chapter 7). To do so, social workers actively listen to what clients say and respond to both the information and feelings within these messages. Skillful social workers employ both verbal and nonverbal techniques and recognize cultural variations inherent in communication processes.

Defining Directions

In *defining directions,* practitioners and clients orient their work together toward a specific purpose (Chapter 8). This concrete sense of direction brings relevance to the challenges that clients face and determines which of their resources and strengths are useful in constructing solutions. Defining directions incorporates a sense of purpose and motivates clients to participate. While clients are describing their situations and the outcomes they seek, alert social workers screen for issues requiring immediate attention such as trauma, homelessness, family violence, child abuse and neglect, substance abuse, and the threat of suicide.

The Discovery Phase

During the discovery phase, clients and social workers continue to assess, systematically exploring resources on which to build solutions. These resources may be present within client systems or outside in their social and physical environments. Working as partners, social workers and clients also organize the information gathered to develop plans for change. Specifically, they:

- Explore clients' strengths as resources for change
- Implement a transactional view by examining resource possibilities in clients' environments
- Collect relevant information from collateral sources
- Assess capabilities of available resource systems
- Specify outcome goals and concrete objectives
- Construct a plan of action
- Negotiate a contract for change

In this phase, client systems and practitioners explore personal and institutional resource systems in order to set goals and contract for change. Universally applicable to clients at all social system levels, discovery processes include identifying strengths, assessing resource capabilities, and framing solutions.

Identifying Strengths

The process, *identifying strengths,* presumes that client strengths are cornerstones for change and, therefore, should be noted early and often (Chapter 9). Exclusively focusing on problems traps workers and clients into thinking that everything is in disarray. Scanning for strengths allows them to search for exceptions and discover possibilities. Workers also set a positive tone and convey expectations of success when they invite clients to share what is working in addition to what is not. Listening to clients describe their challenges with an ear for strengths leads workers to discover clients' abilities, resourcefulness, and creativity as well as strengths found in interpersonal relationships, culture, organizational networks, and community connections. When workers accentuate strengths, clients feel empowered to contribute as full partners and experience hope that they have access to the capabilities and resources they need to succeed.

Assessing Resource Capabilities

The process of *assessing resource capabilities* adds transactional dimensions to the understanding of clients' situations (Chapter 10). Workers and clients jointly assess personal, interpersonal, familial, group, organizational, community, societal, and political systems to detail a positive, broad-based view of the client system in transaction with its environment. Through this strength-oriented assessment, workers and clients discover what might contribute to the change effort and speculate on what resource systems they might activate to reach the outcomes they seek.

Framing Solutions

The discovery phase culminates in *framing solutions,* a process in which social workers and clients develop plans for action (Chapter 11). Action plans contain explicit statements about what clients hope to achieve as well as concrete strategies for achieving their goals and objectives. Developing this comprehensive plan signals the transition from understanding what is happening to acting on this information to make the changes that clients desire. A detailed action plan guides activities throughout the development phase.

The Development Phase

In the development phase, practitioners and clients intervene to activate interpersonal and institutional resources, create alliances with other systems, and expand opportunities through resource development. This approach empowers clients with their own abilities and the resource of their environments. It also stabilizes the changes made in client systems and their environments. Together, workers and clients:

- Operationalize the plan of action
- Increase the experience of power within client systems
- Access resources necessary to achieve goals
- Create alliances among persons and organizations to accomplish the plan
- Enhance opportunities and choices by creating additional resources
- Evaluate ongoing progress and outcomes
- Identify and generalize achievements and gains
- Wrap up the professional relationship

Major activities in the development phase are to organize and expand resources, reach outcome goals, measure achievements, and conclude the formal intervention process. This implementation phase includes the processes of activating resources, creating alliances, expanding opportunities, recognizing success, and integrating gains.

Activating Resources

In *activating resources,* workers and clients collaborate to put the agreed-upon plan into action (Chapter 12). Clients make connections with necessary interpersonal and institutional resources, experiment with new behaviors and interactions, and carry out the tasks developed in their meetings with workers. Social workers organize and monitor intervention activities, motivate clients to participate in the plan, facilitate cooperative efforts in multiperson client systems, detail options and choices, and provide helpful feedback to clients. Workers play a variety of roles as they consult on strategies, work with clients to manage resources, and oversee educational activities.

Creating Alliances

Alliances generate new resources to fuel change. By *creating alliances,* social workers and clients align the efforts of clients in empowerment groups, strengthen the functioning of clients within their natural support networks, and organize the service delivery network (Chapter 13). These alliances bring emotional support to clients and build bases of power for their efforts at social change. Social workers also benefit from alliances through their collaboration with colleagues, supervisors, and professional organizations. Social workers who feel supported and experience their own power are most likely to engender these same feelings in their clients.

Expanding Opportunities

Generalist social workers understand the need to develop resources at all system levels. They join with clients to expand societal resources and develop new opportunities. Through the process, *expanding opportunities,* workers and clients team to create resources that redress social injustice (Chapter 14). Possibilities for change in the service delivery network include refining access to existing social services and creating new programs. Practitioners and clients work to develop just social policy at the agency, local, state, and national levels; they use community organizing and social action strategies to inspire political reforms and legislative changes.

Recognizing Success

All effective plans of action include procedures for evaluation. The process, *recognizing success,* highlights the numerous ways to measure the achievement of goals and evaluate service effectiveness (Chapter 15). Evaluating outcomes guarantees a worker's accountability to client systems and practice settings, credits clients with their contributions to the success, and functions as part of the process to bring closure to professional relationships. Measuring success gives clients and social workers a sense of their accomplishments and helps both clients and social workers generalize the success of a particular endeavor to cope with other situations that each will confront. Formal research increases the knowledge base and contributes to the development of the social work profession.

Integrating Gains

The final process of *integrating gains* emphasizes that clients grow, develop, and change even after their efforts with social workers end (Chapter 16). The ultimate measure of the success of any social work endeavor is whether clients can independently continue their progress initiated within the professional relationship. To encourage independence and continued success, workers facilitate a closure process which helps clients review the work, express their thoughts and feelings about ending, and recognize the transferability of the strategies implemented to managing other events.

From Solving Problems to Promoting Competence

This model for empowerment-based practice draws its organizational framework from the problem-solving model. Like problem-solving, empowerment-based practice guides workers through activities of building relationships, defining purposes, assessing situations, planning, and implementing change. The empowering approach presented in this text refines traditional problem-solving with language and concepts that emphasize strengths, empowerment, and working in partnerships with clients at all system levels to promote competence (Table 5.2).

This approach emphasizes strengths rather than deficits, solution-seeking rather than problem-detecting, competence promotion rather than prescriptive directives, and collaborative partnerships rather than professional expertise. It sets a different tone from deficit-based practice and reflects the contemporary paradigm shift in social work practice to empowerment. Empowerment influences *assessment*—how we describe the client system, *intervention*—what we do to create change, and the *underlying process*—the way we gather

TABLE 5.2   **Empowering Processes and Traditional Problem-Solving**

Problem-Solving	Empowering Processes
Engagement	Forming Partnerships
Problem Identification and Assessment	Articulating Situations Defining Directions Identifying Strengths Assessing Resource Capabilities
Goal Setting and Planning	Framing Solutions
Implementation	Activating Resources Creating Alliances Expanding Opportunities
Evaluation	Recognizing Success
Termination	Integrating Gains

information, organize our work, and implement strategies for change. An empowering approach consistently operates on the presumption that clients have strengths, that environments hold potential resources, that social structures can change as well as client systems, and that clients should participate as full partners in all aspects of change processes.

Processes in Action: Practice Examples

As a way to begin to understand this generalist practice approach, read the following examples carefully. Examine the actions of the social workers to discover the underlying theories, perspectives, competencies, and values which support their work. Specifically, look for generalist thinking, an ecosystemic perspective, respect for cultural diversity, and an orientation to strengths. Notice how the same processes apply at various client system levels, demonstrating the generalist application of this approach.

An Example at the Microlevel

On her way to the intake appointment, Kay Landon recalls her conversation with Helen Ingersoll. Helen sounded desperate when she made the appointment. Kay could hear the feelings of helplessness as Helen described events leading to her call. Helen's husband Jack is recovering from a work-related head injury that occurred six months ago. Things are not going well. Helen is overwhelmed. Jack's progress is slow, and the doctors are talking about "permanent disability." Helen is out of energy and nearly out of hope.

Kay empathizes, but she feels anything but hopeless. From Kay's experiences with other clients in Northside Prevention Services' Family Support Program, she knows that situations like these feel stressful. But, paradoxically, these challenges also bring out capabilities in clients they may not realize they have. Helen Ingersoll has been coping with this traumatic situation for six months with little assistance. She obviously has a great deal of strength. And, Kay is not willing to count Jack out either. The concept of "permanent disability" is one that Kay cannot quite grasp. Maybe Jack is not capable of things that he used to be able to do, but Kay will look for what he still can do. Kay has observed it so often that she assumes it: All clients bring strengths to the social work process.

Dialogue

When Kay arrives, she doesn't have to knock. Helen greets her at the door. Helen is clearly motivated. Once they are seated in the living room, Kay introduces herself and asks to meet Jack. Helen is unsure whether Jack should join them since he can be "unpredictable." Kay's response, "I guess we're all somewhat unpredictable at times," puts Helen at ease; and she leads Jack into the room. Kay begins the meeting by clarifying who she is, what the Family Support Program has to offer, and answers the couple's questions about the services.

Next, it's the Ingersolls turn to talk. Kay allows them to lead the way, responding attentively to encourage them to keep talking. She clarifies information that confuses her and reassures them that she understands what they say. Kay learns much as Helen and Jack describe their situation in their own way.

Only a few months ago, Helen and Jack Ingersoll were experiencing the kind of life which they had planned. Having launched the second of their two children, they were settling into the "good life," relaxing with friends, pursuing individual interests, enjoying time together, and looking ahead to early retirement and travel. Jack was working at the power company and had only three years remaining to retire with full benefits. Helen worked part-time as a substitute teacher.

Then, the unexpected happened. Helen was stunned to receive the call about Jack's accident. He had slipped from a utility pole and fallen to the ground. The head and back injuries Jack sustained left him with numerous problems. Even now, his mobility remains limited, he requires assistance in many activities of daily living, and he has trouble remembering things. His condition requires Helen's constant care. This event reverberates throughout every aspect of the couple's lives.

As Kay gathers information, she readily identifies Helen's stress. The months of adjustment have taken their toll. Helen reels off a list of complicated issues. Tending Jack's needs leaves her exhausted. Even though she provides loving care, she endures Jack's frequent criticism and resistance, so uncharacteristic of his "old self." Helen doesn't understand Jack's angry outbursts and seeming lack of motivation to do things for himself. She feels confined to the house and socially isolated. She is frustrated by her inability to return to work, watching their bills pile up as their income decreases. Jack describes his feelings of depression and anger at his helplessness. He admits that he is sometimes difficult and that conflicts interrupt their previously tranquil relationship. For Jack and Helen, these problems seem insurmountable.

As Helen and Jack complete their story, Kay responds, "What resilience! How have you been able to make it this far?" At first, Helen and Jack hesitate. Then each begins to describe what has gotten them through the last few months. Helen talks about the emotional support that her children offer even though they live out of state. She mentions a friend from church who stops by weekly with a covered dish. Jack credits Helen for her support and endurance. And he admits that occasionally there are good days; in fact, today is one of them. Sometimes, he believes that he just might get "back to normal." Both see their caring relationship as a source of strength throughout the entire ordeal. As the Ingersolls describe what is working, Kay notices a lightening of the mood and the looks of affection the couple exchange with each other.

When Kay asks, "So, what are you looking for from me?" Helen takes the lead. She explains that even though she knows things will never be the same, she still wants them back to the way they were. When Kay asks Helen to be more specific, Helen explains that she would like to be able to do some things on her own again. And, she wants greater financial stability, maybe even to return to work. Jack states he would like to take care of himself better so that Helen can get out more. Kay believes these are workable goals and agrees to work with the Ingersolls to achieve them.

Discovery

With a direction in mind, Kay continues her exploration to assess what resources the Ingersolls have to facilitate this effort. Having identified the Ingersoll couple as the *focal system,* she seeks additional information to discover *what is happening inside the system.* Previously, the Ingersolls enjoyed times together as well as maintaining their separate interests. Now, Jack's health care needs throw them together intensively around-the-clock. This circumstance blurs the boundaries that define them as distinct individuals. Consequently, each suffers a loss of independence and identity. The sense of equality and partnership previously characteristic of their marriage is disrupted. Jack feels dependent on Helen; and Helen feels trapped by the care Jack needs. Kay observes that both are held hostage by the challenge of Jack's physical condition. To Kay, the couple's depression and conflicts make sense in terms of their feelings of powerlessness. Kay also recognizes that in spite of their difficulties they show genuine concern and caring for each other.

What is happening outside of the system also influences this couple's experience. At first, the Ingersoll's family and friends showed support. However, as time passes, their attention dwindles. The couple's children are concerned, but they live out of state and can offer only long-distance support. Early on, numerous friends stopped by and called. Now, only one friend visits regularly. Kay notes that the potential for natural support exists but is not fully activated. Kay knows of several community programs assisting people in this situation. Yet, Helen and Jack have sought no other outside help. Finally, Kay discovers what contributes to the couple's financial instability. Disagreement over liability among the Ingersoll's insurance company, the manufacturer of the utility tower, and Jack's employer have stalled any kind of settlement for the injury.

How does the inside connect to the outside? Kay identifies that Jack's accident has initiated a sequence of events, isolating this couple from the resources of their environment. Before, the Ingersolls were free to work, interact with friends, and pursue individual interests. Now, Jack's injuries confine them to a shrinking world just as their needs for outside support increase. The pressure builds for Jack and Helen as they run out of reserves.

The information Kay gathers shows that, in the past, the Ingersolls had been artful in negotiating life's expected transitions. Not every family system *progresses through time* with the success evident in this couple's affection, achievements, and accomplishments. Kay sees this adaptability as a strength the couple has yet to rediscover.

Together, Kay and the Ingersolls analyze this information. They identify the power that Jack's health holds over the couple. They recognize the financial bind imposed by Helen's lack of opportunity to work and the unresolved insurance claim. They acknowledge the significance of the disruptions in their relationships with family and friends. And, they note the absence of helpful social services. All agree these are issues for focus as they plan a strategy for change.

Building on this analysis, Kay helps Helen and Jack set concrete goals to guide their work together. They decide to stabilize their financial situation by resolving the insurance claim and freeing up Helen to return to work. They also will access community services to relieve Helen's responsibilities, giving her more time to spend with friends and for herself. Finally, they will coordinate a network of health related services to improve Jack's physiological functioning. As they articulate each phase of this plan, Kay works with Helen and Jack to generate specific objectives and activities to pursue each of these goals.

Development

Kay and the Ingersolls collaborate to get things moving. Kay provides information about available resources and the Ingersolls take charge of contacting and organizing the services they select. They access in-home physical therapy. A respite worker comes one full day each week, allowing Helen time for her own pursuits. Helen uses part of this time to attend a Northside Hospital "mini-course" on caring for persons with head injuries. She talks with others having similar experiences and learns about people recovering from head trauma. Helen also spends time with friends; she comes home with renewed energy and more patience for Jack. As Helen feels better, Jack's mood improves. He no longer feels stuck. He participates in rehabilitation activities and a support group for persons with head injuries. He develops new skills in self-sufficiency which restore some feelings of control and reduce Helen's caregiving duties.

The goal of financial stability requires Kay to seek additional help. She locates a trained legal advocate, Quyen Nguyen of the Center for Citizens' Rights, who works to resolve the intersystem conflict over liability for John's accident. Quyen facilitates the flow of information among Jack's doctors, the insurance company, Jack's employer, the manufacturer of the utility tower, and the Ingersolls. Through advocacy and mediation, Quyen influences the participants to negotiate an acceptable settlement and avoid a lengthy court process.

Kay encounters obstacles in her efforts to assist Helen back to work. She finds no respite services providing care on short notice to match Helen's unpredictable work schedule as a substitute teacher. The only respite care in Northside has few openings and limits regularly scheduled care to a maximum of one day a week. Kay reports this gap in service to the Northside Network, a consortium of social service providers in the Northside community, to encourage resource development efforts to increase respite services.

While implementing the plan, Kay and the Ingersolls monitor the progress they are making. Kay emphasizes the success the Ingersolls are achieving. The Ingersolls have regained their momentum. In meetings with Kay, they now report their progress rather than request assistance. Kay realizes that the Ingersolls are planning a future again rather than looking back at what they have lost. While their lives have changed course, they have overcome many hurdles and have the power to continue on their own. Kay wraps up her work with Helen and Jack by reviewing their success and celebrating their collaborative achievements.

An Example at the Midlevel

Midlevel practice focuses on change within organizations and formal groups. Social worker Effie Mako works toward organizational change in her role as Employee Assistance Counselor with Northside Human Resource Center's Employee Assistance Program (EAP). One of Effie's clients is Environmental Industries (EI), a recycling plant employing 150 people. Effie's client is the company itself. Her role is to assist the company to create a positive work environment that encourages health, satisfaction, and efficiency.

A midlevel social work client system benefits from processes similar to those used with all other clients. Note how Effie, like Kay Landon in the previous example, guides her client through phases of dialogue, discovery, and development to achieve the outcomes the company seeks.

Dialogue

Effie begins her work with the company through a dialogue in which she defines her relationship with the company and articulates its challenges in order to define a direction for the work. Effie uses several forms of dialogue to establish working partnerships at various levels within the company including management, supervisory, and worker.

Initially, Effie develops a working partnership with EI's management team; she clarifies her role and devises an acceptable strategy for talking with other company employees. Through these meetings, Effie discovers that EI managers believe that satisfying working conditions are good for company productivity. They are willing to work to achieve these conditions in cost effective ways. Effie arranges to continue to meet with the management team on a weekly basis and then moves on to talk with other organizational employees.

To connect to other employees, Effie addresses the workers during a morning break. She introduces herself, explains the services of the EAP, and describes the company's purpose in hiring her social work services. She fields questions from employees to clarify her role and describes the part that employees can play. Effie also establishes a regular set of "office hours" at the plant so employees can drop in to discuss their issues.

These informal conversations generate energy and ideas from company employees but establish no clear direction for organizational change. So, Effie uses other dialogue processes to ensure widespread input by employees as they define the focus of these efforts. For example, she uses a nominal group technique—an efficient collaborative decision-making process that guarantees each participant opportunities to contribute to the conversation and to influence the outcome of the discussion.

To accommodate the large number of employees, Effie facilitates 20 small groups. She organizes separate groups for employees at each level of the company so that workers feel free to talk outside of the presence of their supervisors. Workers select the particular group to attend, so they participate with whom they feel most comfortable.

When Effie compiles the results of these meetings she uncovers two key concerns—employees want to get along with each other better and they want the company to support their family lives more effectively. Having defined these two directions, Effie and the company move to the discovery phase in order to assess the company's functioning and uncover strengths and resources for meeting their defined purposes.

Discovery

A company is a human system composed of people who interact with one another. More than that, a company organization has structures, functions, and policies which affect the nature of these interactions. A company also develops its own particular culture, and this culture less formally prescribes the relationships among employees and across divisions. Effie must assess each of these aspects of functioning to understand the company's challenges and to find resources for change. By exploring each area of interaction, Effie answers the question *what's happening inside the system?*

To look for strengths within the organization Effie uses a multifaceted approach. She works with the management team to examine the company's policies and practices. Effie also meets with managers, supervisors, and workers; she helps employees discuss what might enhance or inhibit their interrelationships at work and describe the ways in which the company currently supports their family lives.

During these conversations, Effie uses solution-focused dialogue skills to look for "exceptions," times when employees felt that they were working together well, when people were getting along, and when the company seemed to acknowledge that they were people with families as well as workers. Effie allows all persons to tell their stories in their own words. She uses her responding skills to clarify information and maintains a solution-focused orientation to lead the conversation toward areas of success.

Implementing these discovery processes reveals that the company has strengths and areas of need in order to achieve better working relationships. Effie discovers that the company's new employee orientation emphasizes cooperation and a team spirit, yet the company doesn't ask people about teaming skills during the hiring process and doesn't train people in teaming after they are hired. Moreover, in the daily operation of the company, only the management and supervisory units actually function in teams; plant workers have little access to the "company team." The company shows strengths in its teamwork philosophy and its management functioning, but needs to incorporate this philosophy more fully into actual operations.

During these conversations, certain supervisors and employees surface as "natural team players"—key leaders who have the abilities to elicit cooperation. Effie notes that these key leaders are important internal system resources that the company can activate to improve teaming. Effie also discovers an additional challenge, the challenge of accepting cultural differences. Distinctive subgroups have developed among workers, groups separated by differences in age, race, culture, and gender.

Considering the second preliminary purpose—the desire for a more family-friendly atmosphere—Effie finds more challenges than strengths. Effie notes that company policies have little flexibility in time off to care for family members or to attend special family events. The family leave policy provides only the federally guaranteed minimum time off. Effie also notices the absence of "domestic partner language," suggesting a heterosexist bias in regard to sick time and insurance benefits. Her conversations with employees at all levels of the operation lead her to the same conclusion—many company practices interfere with family commitments. Employees want flexible scheduling, on-site day care facilities, and easier access to community services during the work day. However, workers generally feel powerless to assert their ideas under the company's current operating scheme. Effie notices workers, supervisors, and managers all report similar concerns.

The company's internal functioning is not the only place to search for resources. As with all human systems, EI does not function in isolation of its environment. Effie also examines *what's happening outside the system* and *how the inside connects to the outside* to understand more about the company's challenges and strengths. EI is well connected to the community in regard to its recycling operation, but it is removed from the community in other ways. Health Care Associates, the managed care company supplying health care benefits to employees, is the only community resource other than Effie's EAP that EI consistently uses. EI's boundaries are relatively closed.

Tracking another important aspect of system functioning—*changes over time,* Effie notices two important evolutions in EI's work force. First, the work force is getting younger. Retiring older workers are replaced with young adults, many are parents with young children. Effie also discovers that the ethnic composition of employees shows a trend toward increasing diversity. Currently, Spanish is the language of choice within many workers' conversations.

To develop a concrete plan of action, Effie works with the company's management to convene a small team of managers, supervisors, and workers for an information analysis and planning session. Participants in this meeting agree about the need to improve the working relationships among employees and to develop a more family-friendly form of functioning. However, group members also conclude that the employees' current inability to work together will undermine any efforts to improve policies and procedures affecting family life. To organize the intervention in the most effective way, the group decides to work first toward increasing the cooperation among all company employees.

The team chooses to improve employee relationships before working to support family life for two reasons. First, the company has several resources for creating a cooperative work environment—their express philosophy preferring a team approach, the successful teamwork at the management and supervisory levels, and the natural team-building talents exhibited by some employees. These resources are readily accessible and quickly activated for creating a solution.

Second, to increase the family-friendly functioning of the company will require a blending of very different perspectives—increased skills in teaming, and widespread acceptance of diversity. To negotiate policies affecting families will be a more readily achievable goal after the company is functioning in a more team-oriented fashion.

To reach the goal of improved employee relationships, the group establishes two separate objectives: (1) to increase the use of teams in company planning and (2) to increase acceptance of cultural diversity in employee interactions. Achieving these objectives will give employees greater opportunities to interact and the tools to relate successfully, leading to improved employee relationships.

Development

Within the development phase, social workers and clients collaborate to implement the action plan. Effie and her "company" client launch a multifaceted strategy to reach the stated objectives.

To increase the use of teams, Effie consults with managers to test the team approach in several areas of the company's functioning. Members on these teams will represent the company's diverse employees including people from all three levels of hierarchy as well as those from the various cultural groups within the company's work force.

Effie also functions as an educator; she works with each newly established team to develop skills in leadership, communication techniques including listening and responding, and consensus decision-making. To help with the empolyees' understanding of and sensitivity to diversity, Effie arranges for services from the Northside Civil Rights Commission, which offers training for cultural competence. Effie activates resources from within and also from the outside of her client system to work toward goals.

Finally, Effie works with the company's personnel department to access those employees identified as "talented teamers." They will function as company experts, offering team training to the remaining agency employees, orienting new hires toward teamwork, and functioning as resources in the daily operations of EI.

As she sees the new teams develop and observes more interactions among diverse employees, Effie believes that the interventions are producing the desired results. New alliances also develop across hierarchical lines. Comments like "I never really knew how much I had in common with the people I work with" indicate success. But, Effie must implement more formal evaluation procedures in order to demonstrate the achievement of goals.

Effie's evaluation confirms the success of the interventions. Institutionalizing of functioning teams at the company and involving the talents of indigenous workers within the organization will stabilize these changes. Effie moves to wrap up this phase of her work. She sponsors employee discussion groups to report the results of their efforts, to poll employees' views about the strategies implemented and the changes made, and to urge them forward toward their next goal.

An Example at the Macrolevel

Leon Casey's job as a community prevention specialist at the Neighborhood Development Association (NDA) prompts him to keep abreast of community issues. At first, the neighborhood conflict between a Caucasian resident and his new African American neighbor seemed to Leon like an isolated incident. But when subsequent events occur—the fights between groups of Latino and Caucasian students at the high school, the charge of police brutality by an Asian American claiming racial discrimination, and now a cross burning on the front lawn of Northside's only synagogue—a trend emerges. After the civil rights commission contacts Leon with the same concerns, Leon directs his efforts toward the simmering ethnic and intercultural tensions in his client system—the Northside community.

Dialogue

Leon quickly convenes a meeting of relevant community members to function as key informants about this challenging issue. Participants include the community liaison from the Police Department, the chairperson of the Civil Rights Commission, the current president of the Ecumenical Council, the director of the Gay and Lesbian Alliance, a representative from United Way, the chairperson of a neighborhood action council, and the rabbi from the site of the cross burning. Each participant can offer additional examples of cultural intolerance, and the group members agree that the Northside community must promote a greater acceptance of diversity.

Participants agree to work together to reduce intercultural tension, and they form themselves into a steering committee in order to assess the situation further and develop a strategy for change. Leon facilitates this committee, exploring ways to articulate this challenge in more detail. Members agree to host community forums at their respective sites to encourage citizen participation in the assessment process. Leon's role is to coordinate the scheduling of these events. He will use the outreach capabilities of NDA to announce these forums to the public. Leon also trains forum observers to record information offered by citizens at the various meetings and to compile the results for the steering committee's consideration.

Discovery

Leon facilitates the community steering group's assessment processes, helping them complete a strengths-oriented ecosystemic assessment. This means Leon guides the group to look for strengths and resources within the community rather than focusing solely on its challenges. And, Leon will also orient group members to consider the community's interactions with its environment as potential resources for change.

The community forums help Leon understand *what is happening inside the system.* Citizens report additional acts of racial and cultural hatred. Observers note several angry interchanges at the forums among citizens from different cultural groups. On the positive side, citizens describe several exceptions to these problems—successful cross-cultural community events and acts of kindness and friendships among diverse people counteracting the trend toward intolerance. Those attending the forums want the community to respond quickly before the incidents "get out of hand" or "somebody really gets hurt."

Leon leads the steering group to consider *what's happening outside the system* and *how the inside is connecting to the outside.* Group members are all too familiar with national events that create a context of racial and cultural divisiveness. An anti-immigration sentiment pervades national opinion; homophobia leads to regressive social policies and laws; white supremacy groups grow in popularity; and movements promoting English as the only language evidence the trend away from cultural pluralism.

On the other hand, not all that is happening in the environment of the Northside community is bleak. Other cities, responding to the same pressures, have begun efforts to increase cultural acceptance in their communities. In a phone survey of similar-sized municipalities, Leon learns of several strategies used in other areas that are yielding positive results. He carefully records the information and asks these municipalities to send pamphlets, brochures, newspaper articles, program evaluation results, and other written information about their efforts.

Compiling the information obtained from the community forums and the telephone survey, steering committee members work together to construct a plan of action. They confirm their original purpose by setting a goal to increase acceptance of cultural diversity in the Northside community. To meet this goal they articulate two objectives including (1) to form a Quick Response Team to deal with hate crimes and (2) to establish a Mediation Center. These objectives are concrete steps toward the goal of cultural tolerance.

Development

Steering group members divide up their efforts in order to achieve both objectives simultaneously. Some members complete activities to form the Quick Response Team. After studying the composition of such teams in other locations, steering group members determine criteria for team membership. Qualifications include skills in crisis response, conflict resolution, bilingualism, and cultural competence. Subsequently, steering committee members poll social service agencies and other community organizations to see whether they have qualified personnel and whether they are willing to donate their resources.

In response to these inquiries, the Quick Response Team begins to take shape. A large pool of team members will be assembled. Each individual response team will include at least one representative from the police department, a person skilled in mediation and conflict resolution, and a person or persons fluent in the languages and familiar with the cultures of the citizens involved. Other members from the larger pool of volunteers will join an individual team as necessary in specific situations.

Leon's own agency takes a coordinating role with the team. The Northside Development Association uses its resources to supply office space and an emergency phone line. NDA will also serve as the center for the ongoing recruitment and training of the response team members.

Other steering committee members work on the second objective. They secure a site for the Northside Mediation Center when the rabbi volunteers space at the synagogue. They also visit other mediation centers in nearby communities to gather ideas for how to organize the Mediation Center. Once they develop a tentative plan for the center, the steering committee holds a public meeting at the proposed site to elicit additional input.

The steering committee integrates the information gathered from other mediation centers, adds the perspectives from the citizen's forum, incorporates its own ideas, and then proposes a model for organizing and operating the Mediation Center. Members vote to approve the proposal, and then focus their efforts on launching the new program. Steering group members use their community networks to locate both private and public sources of support including technical expertise, funding, and volunteer mediators.

Finally, steering committee members working on both objectives combine their efforts to determine the interface between these two projects. Clearly, the Quick Response Team and the Mediation Center have complementary roles. Committee members negotiate a service agreement by which the Quick Response Team focuses on crisis situations and refers citizens to the Mediation Center for more lasting solutions to their conflicts.

Once the team and the center are operational, the committee begins to wrap up its work and seek ways to ensure their achievements are established as ongoing programs in the community. The Quick Response Team will continue to function as part of the Northside Development Association. The Mediation Center will remain at the synagogue and be governed by a board of directors that includes some members from the original steering committee and other volunteers recruited from the community.

The steering committee also agrees to follow up on its work. In six-month intervals, they will review evaluations of the two new programs and examine police reports to assess whether cultural tolerance is increasing.

A Process for All Human Systems

Generalist practitioners can use the approach presented in this text to work with client systems at all levels. In addition, these same processes apply to other systems affecting clients as well, including a neighborhood system which affects a family client, a social service delivery network in the case of an agency client, or a state bureaucracy for a community client, to name a few examples. All these target systems respond to the same practice strategies used with clients. Workers establish a relationship with the target system, assess its functioning, identify its resources and strengths, and work collaboratively to implement strategies for change. Successful intervention with any system, client or otherwise, depends on a flexible application of dialogue, discovery, and development processes.

Maintaining Flexibility in Application

Although this approach provides a structure for intervention, a perceptive worker is aware of its dynamic and flexible nature. Rather than rigid and sequential, these processes are recurring and often simultaneous in their implementation. Social workers adjust this approach to match the unique qualities of client systems. They also use the phases of this approach to structure individual meetings with clients.

The Recurring Nature of Social Work Processes

Configuring this approach as three phases involving several processes gives the illusion that components are distinct and arranged in sequential steps. You might expect that you first complete one process and follow it with the next and so on. However, in practice, these phases and processes overlap and interconnect. Workers interweave processes and move freely among phases as the situation warrants.

Consider the ways in which the phases of dialogue, discovery, and development interrelate. As strength-focused practitioners build relationships with clients, a dialogue phase process, they unavoidably notice strengths, a process described as part of the discovery phase. While workers and clients implement strategies for change, a development phase process, they continue to search for additional resources, a discovery phase activity. In effective applications of this approach, social workers move freely among various phases of practice over the course of the professional relationship and even within the same meeting with any client system. Change in human systems is not likely to proceed in a step-by-step fashion. Social workers match what clients need by implementing empowering processes flexibly.

Structuring Sessions

The eleven processes of this empowering approach to practice suggest an overall framework for working with clients at any system level, but social workers can also use this framework of processes to organize individual sessions. By doing so, social workers ensure that each particular encounter provides clients with opportunities for dialogue, discovery, and development—to reconnect with the worker and other group, family, team, or organizational members, to share recent information, to evaluate progress, to discover resources, to plan new activities in pursuit of goals, and to leave each meeting with a clear idea about what will happen next. Visualize particular sessions or the whole group of sessions as proceeding through a diamond-shape structure that incorporates all the processes of dialogue, discovery, and development (see Figure 5.1).

Reflecting Back

The approach to generalist practice presented in this chapter provides a framework for working with clients at all system levels. These processes incorporate a contextual view of

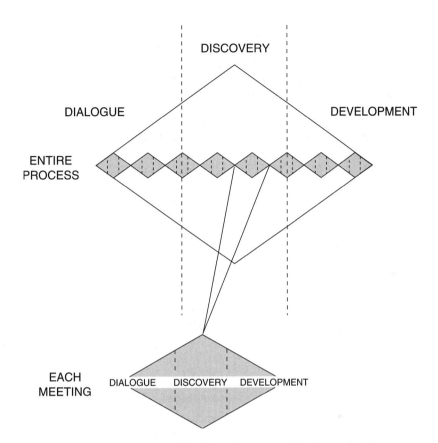

FIGURE 5.1   Flexibility in Applying Processes. Each meeting between social worker and client system can be structured as a "mini" model of the entire process including elements of dialogue, discovery, and development.

situations, a partnership view of the social worker–client relationship, and a solution-focused view of outcomes. In what ways does this approach actualize the values of the profession and the principles of empowerment? Consider such factors as language, the distribution of power, and the integration of the personal and political.

Looking Forward

Theoretical orientations to human behavior and change combined with social work values and skills prepare social workers for practice. The ecosystems perspective in unison with a strengths orientation provides the foundation for the empowering approach to generalist social work practice. This paradigm frames practice within dialogue, discovery, and development phases and distinguishes empowering processes to implement in each. Practitioners use this approach to structure their work with clients, while maintaining flexibility in its implementation to fit the unique circumstances of each client system accounting for the level of the system, cultural diversity, and the particulars of clients' situations.

The remaining chapters fully describe this approach to generalist social work practice. These chapters explore the conceptual base, delineate collaborative roles for workers and clients, consider cultural diversity, apply skills to all levels of human systems, and highlight ethics for each empowering process. Chapter 6, "Forming Partnerships," describes the social worker–client relationship and offers specific guidelines for translating positive expectations and assumptions about clients into empowering partnerships with them.

Part 2

The Dialogue Phase: Building Relationships and Describing Situations

A respectful, collaborative relationship between worker and client system is the core of any social work endeavor. Whether client systems are individuals or larger groups, social workers must establish an atmosphere of trust and a sense of purpose to ensure an open sharing of relevant information. Social workers move quickly to engage clients in a focused dialogue which clarifies challenging issues and defines the purpose of their work together. The success of this dialogue depends on the worker's professional skills and interpersonal qualities.

The *dialogue phase* begins the assessment process. Assessment clarifies "what is the matter" and leads to decisions about courses of action to undertake (Meyer, 1993). Importantly, the assessment process also defines the nature of the working relationship between client and practitioner. Even when clients look for workers to take charge, empowering practitioners move to establish an equal partnership as they gather information and define the direction for change. As Bricker-Jenkins (1991) says, "the practitioner takes responsibility for restructuring the working relationship as people gradually claim their rights to define the conditions of work" (p. 290). Within the dialogue phase, workers construct empowering relationships with clients as they mutually assess the situation at hand and determine where the relationship is going.

C h a p t e r **6**

Forming Partnerships

Relationships between social workers and clients are fundamentally relationships between human beings. Whether working with an individual or a whole community system, social workers are connecting with other humans to achieve mutual purposes. The relationships formed by social workers and clients differ from social relationships. Although they are friendly, social workers and clients are not friends. Although these relationships are genuine, they have designated purposes and defined endings. In addition to being spontaneous and personable, social work relationships are deliberate and professional. Successful professional partnerships are complex and directed toward goals. Social workers and clients carefully construct and monitor their relationships to ensure that they meet the purposes for which they exist.

Within the helping relationship, participants establish trust, sort out their respective roles and responsibilities, and develop patterns of interaction necessary to engage in a process for change. To the extent that this relationship nurtures and encourages mutual participation, it is empowering. Practitioners and clients work together as collaborative partners, with each serving as a resource for the other.

When the social work relationship is a partnership, the relationship, itself, is an empowering resource for change. "Partnering" with clients means:

> *basing the helping relationship on collaboration, trust, and shared power; accepting the client's definition of the problem; identifying and building upon the client's strengths; actively involving the client in the change process; experiencing a sense of personal power within the helping relationship. (Gutiérrez, 1989, p. 7)*

To meet the purposes of this collaborative partnership, practitioners need a conceptual understanding of the relationship, effective communication and interpersonal skills, abilities to relate cross-culturally, and social work ethics and values to guide their transactions. This chapter discusses how workers develop relationships with clients that are collaborative and empowering. In detail, this chapter:

- Describes the nature of the collaborative partnership between social workers and clients
- Presents a practice example to illustrate the initial steps of developing a working partnership
- Examines essential qualities of social work relationships that promote effective partnerships
- Presents methods for initiating collaborative partnerships with clients, including those clients who feel powerless
- Explores the ethical and legal issues of confidentiality

Practitioners who apply these concepts will build partnerships with clients that encourage openness and collaboration in all phases of the professional relationship.

Collaboration and Partnership

To actualize the strengths perspective and encourage empowerment, social workers and clients must collaborate as partners. This collaboration requires adherence "to the profession's long-standing commitment to client self-determination. Working together, worker and client define an area of interest and establish a set of measurable and achievable goals to guide practice" (Sullivan, 1992, p. 207). Empowerment-based social workers respect what client systems already know and can do (Evans, 1992). In short, they recognize client strengths and competence.

The phrase, "begin where the client is," expresses a fundamental social work practice imperative. Strengths-focused social workers interpret "begin where the client is" as a charge to discover potential strengths and resources, support developing competencies, and base constructive solutions on what already works for the client. This view has profound implications for relationships between social workers and clients.

The Dilemma of Social Workers as Experts

Reverence toward social workers as experts fabricates a hierarchy of haves and have nots. In this view, proficient social work experts have the knowledge, insight, and ideas to bestow on inept clients who lack these qualities. Proactive professionals take charge of passive clients. Masterful social workers commence action and ineffectual client systems are acted upon. Interpreted bluntly, the expert professionals are the champs and the clients are the chumps!

Social workers beware! There are traps in this definition of social workers as experts and clients as passive recipients. In fact, there is no successful way out. If clients don't improve, then, of course, social workers are to blame. If clients get better, then social workers get the credit along with the responsibility of being the champion of keeping clients' lives on track. Ultimately, when expert social workers win, passive clients lose their sense of competence and independence. Weick (1983) further describes the insidious nature of this dependency or process of "giving over":

> The process of human judgment has been radically overturned, and, as a consequence, knowledge that is naturally accessible to people because it is personal knowledge is no longer admitted or accepted by them. The result is that their knowledge about themselves becomes partially or wholly hidden. In addition, whatever information they give to the professional is without meaning until the professional confers meaning on it. What is seen, therefore, at the base of the giving over process, is a willingness to give someone else power to define one's personal reality. (p. 468)

This configuration depicts a hierarchy of power and authority. The worker is the expert authority with decision-making power, and the client comes to depend solely on the power resources of the social worker or struggles with the worker to gain a share of the power. This one-sided perspective on expertise is the antithesis of empowerment!

The Rewards of Clients as Experts

Social workers who empower recognize the value of the experiences and competence of clients. Libassi and Maluccio (1986) say:

> Clients are explicitly viewed as partners in the helping process, as persons with assets and potentialities, as resources rather than carriers and/or sources of pathology. Social workers are defined primarily as enabling or change agents who

play diverse roles and use varying approaches in order to provide the conditions and the information necessary for clients to achieve their purposes, engage in their developmental processes, and carry out their adaptive tasks. (p. 171)

Empowerment-based practitioners emphasize a client's active participation and promote self-determination in all aspects of the change effort. Social workers do bring professional expertise to the relationship, but they are not the *sole experts*.

Clients and social workers offer complementary resources to facilitate change. Clients bring expertise about the content of their experiences and social workers bring expertise about the processes of professional intervention. In an empowerment orientation to practice, clients "are viewed as the best experts on and resources for their problems" (Parsons, Hernandez, & Jorgensen, 1988, p. 420). Clients simply know their situations and capabilities best. This view summons social workers to suspend any tendency to disbelieve clients and to acknowledge clients' expertise. It places social workers in the roles of process facilitators, constructing an environment in which a client's power emerges.

The Social Worker's Role

Viewing clients as experts on their own situations directs workers to redefine their roles in more egalitarian or consultative terms (Cox & Parsons, 1992). The egalitarian stance places the worker in the role of partner, while the consultative stance defines the worker more as a mentor in the relationship. Social work clients in Cohen's (1998) study varied in their preferences for partnerships and mentorships. Some liked more of a *client-directed* approach as reflected by the partnership agreement. Others preferred a *client-centered* approach "with workers using their expert knowledge and skills to provide clients with advice and guidance" (p. 438). Significantly, all clients in Cohen's study expressed dissatisfaction with authoritarian workers. Clients clearly wanted to be in charge of what happened in the relationship even when that meant they could decide when they wanted workers to be in charge.

Key to an empowerment approach is the client's sense of power in defining the relationship. To this end, workers continually monitor their behavior for paternalistic tendencies by asking:

1. *With what degree of concentration do I listen to and consider the explicit and implicit communications of the clients or constituents to whom I am responsible?*
2. *Do I silently discount the opinions of any client, client group, or constituent? If so, why so? And what can I do to exchange my silence for dialogue with that person or group?*
3. *When I recommend a particular course of action to a client, do I take ample care and time to elicit from him or her alternative proposals before seeking agreement on the nature and sequence of steps to be taken?*
4. *Has any client given me feedback that I have been remote, intimidating, or inaccessible? If so, what more can I learn from that person about the basis for her or his impression of my unavailability?*
5. *Do I use acronyms, abbreviations, proper names, or specialized language that are foreign to clients in their presence without defining these terms?*
6. *When circumstances force me to rush a client or constituent or to keep him or her waiting, in what ways do I make amends?*

7. *When my professional duty requires me to violate a client's preferences, do I explain my actions and reasoning to that client in as open, direct, and respectful a manner as possible?*

8. *When I feel protective of a client, do I inspect the situation with special care to make sure that I am not underestimating the client or exaggerating my own importance or capability?*

9. *When I find myself thinking primarily about the problems that a client faces, do I make a conscious effort in my contemplation to pay closer attention to his or her strengths and imagination? (Simon, 1994, pp. 188–189)*

Empowerment demands the centrality of the perspectives of client systems in all aspects of social work practice. Collaborative social workers not only begin where the client is, they continue to stay with the client system's perspective throughout all phases of the change process.

Agency Influences on Worker–Client Relationships

The organizational context influences the degree to which social workers and clients can achieve a true partnership. "The question remains as to whether social work practice can fully realize the goals of shared power, mutuality, and collaboration associated with feminist and empowerment-oriented practice models when client/worker relationships are embedded in a hierarchical power structure that simultaneously transcends and impacts on power relationships within the dyad" (Cohen, 1998, p.441). Workers may need to intervene within their own agencies to ensure that they have the necessary power to share with clients. Agencies can provide support through policies favoring collaborative methods and training initiatives designed to equip workers with partnership skills (Marsh & Fisher, 1992). Only empowered social workers can implement an empowering approach.

Making Initial Contacts

Effective social workers begin immediately to promote a client's hopes and active participation. Workers do not wait until implementing action plans to facilitate empowerment. Instead, they consistently act in empowering ways from the outset. Practitioners encourage clients to become full partners by responding to clients with reflective listening skills, offering clients assistance that corresponds to their perceived needs, and encouraging their active participation in all facets of decision-making (Dunst, 1993). Even in the apparently routine tasks of beginning the relationship, workers and clients are already setting patterns that will influence the success of their work.

Recognizing What Clients Bring

Clients experience a variety of thoughts and feelings as they enter working relationships with social workers. Perhaps clients have had previous relationships with helping professionals. Maybe they have specific knowledge about the agency, social workers, or the type of service, predisposing them to trust or resist services. Many clients are directed to social workers by others. The way that clients feel about these referral sources also influences their preconceptions. Each of us approaches new relationships based on our previous experiences. With clients, whatever stories precede their entry into a professional social work relationship inevitably define that partnership.

Maluccio's (1979) research examined clients' perceptions at the time they initiated contact with a family service agency. As might be expected, these new clients reported feelings of distress, discomfort, and confusion. Additionally, they described feelings of hope for finding a solution in comments such as "straighten things out," "get quick answers," and "find a snappy solution" (p. 5). Interestingly, clients also reported they received encouragement from other professionals or family friends who prompted their contact with the worker. Clients' initial expectations reflect discouragement about their own abilities to overcome their problems combined with optimism and encouragement about working with social workers.

Social workers should take heart as many clients do enter professional relationships with seeds of trust and hope. Even clients whose lives have predisposed them to distrust and suspicion often remain alert to clues that this professional relationship may hold promise. The fact is that ambivalence characterizes the approach of most people to any new relationship. It makes sense that we should begin with a "maybe yes" and "maybe no," or a "wait and see" attitude. Social workers cannot predetermine the expectations of clients or head off their feelings of ambivalence; however, social workers can influence first impressions either reinforcing hope or inadvertently accentuating negative feelings. Workers must examine their own predisposition toward clients and construct productive assumptions about client potential if they wish to reveal optimism and confidence from the moment of the first contact.

Initiating Collaboration

Early interactions reveal more than a worker's expectations for success. How the worker organizes the meeting around the client's experience and what the worker discusses about the client's responsibility in the process also begins to shape the degree to which the client collaborates. A worker who commandeers the early phases of the relationship may initiate a cycle of dependency throughout the work. In contrast, a worker who openly discusses the need for the client's active participation, invites a client's expertise, and elicits a client's perspective set a pattern for partnership. Practitioners launch empowering relationships within the first meeting when they communicate positive expectations about success and accentuate the need for client participation.

Beginning Steps: A Practice Example

During their first meeting with a client, workers have much to accomplish. Tasks include making a personal connection, clarifying the purpose of the meeting, describing the worker's role, exploring the client's issues, and wrapping up the meeting with a clear direction that defines the next step (Benjamin, 1987; Kadushin & Kadushin, 1997; Shulman, 1999). Shulman (1999) also stresses the need for workers and clients to discuss issues related to power and authority. Workers use their natural abilities to implement these processes flexibly to match the unique characteristics of each client system. As an example of this beginning process, Karen McBride, a Case Manager at the Northside Hospital Outreach Program, goes through the steps of initiating a relationship with the Fuentes family, her newest client.

The Referral

The medical social worker in the emergency room at Northside Hospital referred the Fuentes family to Karen only a few days before. Doctors there had treated Juanita Fuentes for a broken leg—injured while Juanita was helping her mother, Rosa Hernandez, down from their second floor apartment to a taxi waiting below. Mrs. Hernandez, herself, was not injured. But Juanita, even while being treated for her own injuries, talked about her concern for how she would manage to take care of her mother while her leg mended. Her own daughter Nora was not that helpful. And her husband? Well, Humberto had to work; sometimes he was away from home for days at a time. Karen's job as case manager would be to discover with the Fuentes family how best to meet the needs of Mrs. Hernandez and ensure the well-being of the family while Juanita's leg was healing.

Thinking Ahead

As Karen walks up the street to the Fuentes family's apartment, she can feel her anxiety rise. The relative quiet she left in her office has given way to throngs of people, aromas of spicy food, and the sounds of Latin music—it's all a bit strange to Karen. Her pace quickens. Her eyes focus straight ahead. Karen realizes that she is clutching her briefcase tightly. She has to admit it. She feels uncomfortable, out of her culture so to speak. It only makes sense that she would feel this way in a place so different from her own suburban home and even different from the quiet city street where her office is located.

Karen recognizes that her feelings of strangeness might approximate the feelings of the Fuentes family members when she, a 28-year-old white, suburban social worker arrives at their door. Logically, they might be uncomfortable or have doubts about whether someone who is so young and from a different culture can really understand and respect their situation. Karen will have to work quickly to help the family feel comfortable with her as a person and a professional. Karen's own feelings will help her empathize with the family's response to her.

Karen also contemplates the purpose of her visit and the family's potential reactions. Even though the intent of the outreach program is to help families cope effectively with their medical difficulties, not all clients begin as eager participants. Karen wonders if Juanita will see this visit as an intrusion into her private affairs or as a threat to her way of caring for her mother. Karen doesn't yet know what previous experiences this family may have had with outside assistance, but this will certainly affect their initial comfort with her, too.

As a case manager, Karen has initiated relationships with many clients before. All are strangers to her at first, but they soon become people that she likes, respects, and often admires. But bridging that initial distance between having no relationship and forming a working partnership characterized by mutual respect, trust, and effective communication is no small leap, especially across a cultural gap. Working together with the Fuentes family will again test Karen's abilities to clarify the boundaries of the professional relationship, accept views and lifestyles other than her own, and give clients the freedom to move in directions that work best for them.

Telephone Work

The receptionist in the Northside Hospital's Outreach Program scheduled this appointment. The hospital social worker referred Juanita while she was still at the emergency room since the Fuentes family had no phone and subsequent contact would be difficult. When Karen schedules appointments herself, she directly and succinctly identifies who she is, where she works, and why she is calling. She states her purpose and clearly outlines the client's privileges of how to respond.

With the Fuentes family, Karen would have described her purpose to assist the family to discover ways to care for Mrs. Hernandez while Juanita recovered. She would have assured the family they were in control. For example, she would have told them that setting an appointment with her was completely their choice and, even if they met with her once, they were under no obligation to continue to see her or do what she might suggest. Karen attends to power issues with each client from the first phone call to the last contact. She treats clients as partners from the beginning to the end of their work together.

Meeting and Greeting Clients

Without the advantage of an initial phone contact, Karen will have to work quickly to orient the Fuentes family to the purpose of her visit. This family needs to know who she is and what she is doing there. When Juanita Fuentes opens the door, Karen is direct: "Mrs. Fuentes? I'm Karen McBride from the Northside Hospital Outreach Program. We have an appointment, arranged the day you were at the hospital." Juanita obviously is expecting her. Karen follows as Juanita maneuvers on crutches through the kitchen to the living room where Mrs. Hernandez is waiting. As Juanita introduces Karen to her mother, Karen again explains her presence to the older woman. If Karen expects Mrs. Hernandez to be a contributing partner to their discussion, she has to include her in the conversation from the outset.

Within this brief introductory interchange Karen learns two important aspects of relating to this family. She notes that Mrs. Hernandez speaks halting English. Karen will need to speak clearly and concretely to facilitate Mrs. Hernandez's participation. Karen also learns to call Juanita by her first name after Juanita requests that she do so. A respectful relationship always begins by addressing people in the ways they prefer.

Physical Arrangements

Juanita's choice to meet in the living room is a good one. Everyone seems comfortable and Karen can easily interact directly with either Juanita or Mrs. Hernandez. If this had not been the case, Karen would have requested a rearrangement. Building relationships with a family or group requires direct interactions with each member. When conducting a meeting in a client's home, Karen balances her respect for the family's style, property, and privacy with her own preferences for an arrangement which facilitates family involvement. Karen wants all relevant family members in the room and actively participating. She finds it more empowering to talk *with* people than about them.

When Karen asks Juanita's permission to turn off the television, she completes her physical preparation for the session. Karen's comment—"I want to make sure I can hear everything you have to say and the TV may be distracting. Would you mind if we turned it off?"—shows her respect for the family. Karen consistently defines the meeting as work that requires a client's full attention. In her own office, she doesn't take phone calls or interact with other staff when meeting with clients. Families have her full attention and, likewise, she wants theirs. In home visits, Karen also wants the meeting to be focused and productive. When phone calls or visitors interrupt home meetings, Karen lets clients handle the interruption, but then discusses the need to control interruptions and focus on the meeting, or reschedule if necessary.

Karen accepts the cup of coffee that Juanita offers. Her agency's previous policy restricted workers from accepting gifts of any kind from clients. Now there is flexibility to accept gifts of hospitality in culturally appropriate and friendly ways. Clients have their own traditions of initiating relationships with workers and Karen is sensitive to defining relationships mutually rather that rigidly structuring the visit to meet her own needs. With the Fuentes family, Karen briefly socializes, describing her trip over from the office and inquiring about Juanita's leg before getting down to business. Her experience has taught her that it is culturally appropriate with most Latino clients to establish social contact first.

Getting Down to Business

After the brief social exchange, Karen proceeds with the task at hand. Karen never assumes that clients know all about the social service network. Even from an insider's view, Karen still finds it confusing. For Juanita and Mrs. Hernandez, the connections between Karen's visit, Juanita's trip to the hospital, and her need for assistance in caring for Mrs. Hernandez may be hazy. Again, Karen repeats her name as she hands each of the women one of her business cards. She describes her role and the purpose of the agency for which she works. She clearly traces how she comes to be with them on this day. She recounts Juanita's conversation with the hospital social worker, the worker's call to the Northside Hospital Outreach Program, the appointment made by the receptionist, the information being passed on to Karen, and her arrival at their door. Karen wants to demystify the social work world for this family, a world she hopes they will learn to activate for themselves.

When both women indicate they understand who Karen is, she hands them each a brochure describing her program's services. Karen is pleased that the pamphlet is multilingual. She notices that Mrs. Hernandez follows along in the Spanish language section as Karen highlights important features of the program. Karen stresses that participating in these services is voluntary and has no direct costs to clients. She also talks about confidentiality, assuring the family that she keeps their information private as long as no one in the home is in danger. Karen points out the guarantee of confidentiality and the exceptions as stated in the program brochure. When she completes her explanations, she asks the women if they have questions. Both agree they understand. Karen notices that their nonverbal messages also indicate they are clear on what she is saying.

Respecting the Client's Perspective

Having completed this general business, it's time to get down to specifics and that means Karen turns over the dialogue to Juanita and Mrs. Hernandez. Her simple statement of "Now, it's your turn" immediately activates both women, who relate their own parts of the story of Juanita's injury and the difficulties they are having. Karen is careful to respond to each woman, validating their different views and encouraging their continued sharing. Karen has dual goals to understand the specifics of this family's situation and, simultaneously, to initiate a supportive relationship. To do so, she responds with warmth, acceptance, respect, and empathy.

Karen even attends to building relationships with family members who are not present in the room. When Juanita defends Humberto as hard working and caring, yet unable to help with her mother, Karen accepts her view. When Juanita describes her 17-year-old daughter Nora, who still lives at home, as unwilling to help, Karen's neutral response, "So Nora doesn't think that her help is the answer here," reveals a nonjudgmental acceptance of the choices that Nora is making while indicating to Juanita that she is listening. Karen knows that families work in the ways they do for good reasons. When building relationships with new clients, Karen accepts their current functioning as workable under the present circumstances. She also makes sure that she allies herself with every family member—even those not in the room—since a working relationship with each member of the client system will most likely elicit everyone's best cooperation and contributions.

Continuing the Relationship Work

The initial interchange between Karen and the Fuentes family focuses on launching and defining the social worker–client relationship. However, the dialogue of the first few minutes does not complete the work of building the relationship. Within this first meeting, Karen will continue to shape the partnership as she talks with them to understand their challenges, identify their existing resources and strengths, and clarify the purpose of their work together. In subsequent meetings, Karen will maintain her focus on the quality of the relationship so that the family continues to feel comfortable enough to share their thoughts, express their feelings, and assert their priorities. No matter what phase of the work, Karen will integrate her professional skills with her personal qualities to ensure that her relationship with the Fuentes family remains a resource for its members.

Qualities of Professional Partnerships

With whom do you find yourself talking freely, sharing your innermost thoughts, and revealing the depth of your feelings? Whom do you trust? What characteristics draw you to others? What makes some people approachable and others not? Personal qualities and communication styles can enhance or detract from interpersonal relationships. Likewise, social workers' personal qualities either support or inhibit their success in developing and maintaining empowering relationships with clients.

Research validates the importance of personal qualities in building professional relationships. In his book *Learning from Clients,* Maluccio (1979) reports that "the worker's human qualities are emphasized by clients more than his or her technical skills" (p. 125). Those personal qualities most valued by clients include empathy, genuineness, acceptance, objectivity, and concreteness. Other studies agree that the absence of qualities in workers such as warmth and acceptance directly correlates with intervention failures (Strupp, Fox, & Lessler, 1969). Results of a study by Hopps, Pinderhughes, and Shankar (1995) indicate that workers' attributes of caring and flexibility supported positive outcomes with clients. Competent social workers successfully blend their personal characteristics with professional skills when they respond with genuineness, acceptance, respect, trustworthiness, empathy, sensitivity to diversity, and purposefulness.

Genuineness

Social workers seek to create a comfortable atmosphere in which clients can "be themselves." Certainly, clients are most likely to do so if workers are doing the same. When workers are genuine they initiate authentic relationships with their clients. Drawing on the definitive works of Truax, Mitchell, Carkhuff, and Rogers, Fischer (1978) describes genuineness as a characteristic which facilitates communication and builds open relationships. Genuineness refers to social workers "being 'real.' This means, simply, that at any given moment, workers really are whatever their responses denote.... In fact, genuineness may be best understood as the absence of phoniness, as nondefensiveness, as congruence, and as spontaneity" (p. 199). Who social workers are as people shows through and enhances their professional roles.

On the other hand, workers who lack genuineness fail to connect with clients in productive ways. Clients in Maluccio's (1979) study described such workers as "too nice, phony, put on. Too low key. Too calm and collected. Doing [a] job as a job. Above it all, almighty. Mechanical. Businesslike" (p. 124). These comments depict ingenuine social workers as distant, indifferent, and contrived. In contrast, genuineness liberates social work practitioners to "comfortably be themselves in all their interactions" (Egan, 1998, p. 50).

When Karen McBride interacts with Juanita Fuentes and Mrs. Hernandez, she does so honestly as a concerned person rather than a mechanical professional. When Mrs. Hernandez remarks, "Well, you know, that's the Mexican way," Karen responds with "I'm not really sure—could you explain it to me?" Karen is aware of herself, her similarities and differences from her clients, and her clients' reactions to her. She openly acknowledges these differences rather than distancing herself from the interaction to appear "professional."

Genuineness is different from total honesty. Being genuine does not mean that workers disclose everything they are thinking and feeling about clients. Instead, it means that what workers share is "a real aspect of themselves, not a response growing out of defensiveness or a merely 'professional' response that has been learned and repeated" (Fischer, 1978, p. 199). Being genuine also is not the same as being personal. Professional relationships differ from social relationships. While social workers are friendly and genuinely interested in their clients, they find other ways to expand their networks of friends. In responding genuinely to clients, social workers maintain the qualities of purpose and standards of ethics that define relationships as professional.

Acceptance and Respect

Social workers draw upon their personal qualities of acceptance and respect in building relationships with clients. Workers who demonstrate acceptance affirm the worth of others as "human being[s] without necessarily condoning [their] actions" (Barker, 1999, p. 2). Respectful social workers regard clients as partners, listen to their opinions, communicate cordially, honor cultural differences, and credit clients as having strengths and potential.

Social workers also manifest acceptance through behaviors that communicate unconditional positive regard and nonpossessive warmth. Nonpossessive warmth involves:

> *communication of respect, acceptance, liking, caring and concern for the client in a nondominating way...Thus, the client is accepted as a person with human potentialities: nonpossessive warmth involves valuing the client as a person, separate from any evaluation of his or her behavior and thoughts.... Rather [than approving or sanctioning behavior], it means that despite such thoughts and behaviors, workers are able to communicate, in both the form and content of what they say and how they act, that they appreciate the meaning of such thoughts and behavior to their clients and deeply prize their clients as individuals. (Fischer, 1973, pp. 196–197)*

Unconditional positive regard and nonpossessive warmth are one-way expressions. Social workers demonstrate them without expecting anything in return. However, experience confirms that when social workers consistently treat clients in accepting and respectful ways, clients respond in kind.

A positive view of humankind makes it easier to accept and respect others. The ecosystems perspective offers such a view. As you will recall from Chapter 2, this framework explains all human behavior as evolutionary, adaptive, and functional in context. As Compton and Galaway (1999) suggest, acceptance presumes that "People act as they must in the complexity of their particular human situation; they are what their nature and their environment—coupled with their vision—permit them to be" (p. 178). Social workers appreciate and even admire the unique and creative ways clients match their particular resources with the demands of their environments.

The ways that social workers communicate with clients reveal their acceptance and respect. Accepting workers restrain from asking judgmental "why questions" which critique clients' previous choices. Instead, workers use words such as "what, who, when, where, and how" to arrive at a mutual understanding of events without leaving the impression that clients are doing something wrong. Acceptance means that social workers listen carefully to comprehend rather than critique what they see and hear. Respect means that social workers recognize that clients are doing the best they can under their present circumstances.

Names and Respect

One concrete way of showing respect is in the way that social workers treat clients' names. Some workers address all members of client systems by their first names in an attempt to create a friendly atmosphere. But, Smith (1996) cautions against this approach, especially in cross-cultural relationships based on her observations: "Well-meaning white social work interns sought to convey warmth and concern by addressing their older African American clients on a first-name basis. The clients were often angered and insulted by what was perceived as a lack of respect" (p. 291).

In their study of cross-racial social worker–client relationships, Proctor and Davis (1994) also concluded that workers should "address the client by his or her last name" (p. 317). Only in cases where clients specifically request workers to call them by their first names or nicknames should workers choose to address clients other than in the more formal style of using last names.

Trustworthiness

The presence or absence of trust affects the social worker–client relationship. Trust is the ability to take risks in the context of interpersonal relationships (Johnson, 1997). To reach goals, clients must feel comfortable enough to exchange something that they know for some new way of doing things that has unknown potential. Taking these risks requires trust. Trustworthiness is a multidimensional personal quality based on the client's perception of the worker's reliability, honesty, credibility, sincerity, and integrity. It springs from a non-threatening and open personal approach nestled in the context of professional expertise.

Many factors contribute to developing trust. Trust is reciprocal. In other words, "to get it you must give it." For clients to trust social workers, social workers must trust clients. Social workers trust clients to be experts about their own situations, as open and honest as is currently possible, and motivated to make necessary changes. Each of us knows our own experience best. When others recognize and validate our experience, we begin to trust their value and to see the potential rewards of a relationship with them. Clients who experience a social worker's trust are more likely to trust the resources the worker has to offer.

Interactions influence the movement of trust along a continuum from no trust to complete trust. As social workers follow through on their own commitments, meet a client's expectations, and demonstrate their acceptance of a client's perspectives, trust increases. When social workers violate a client's developing sense of trust through what the client perceives to be distortion, insensitivity, or betrayal, trust plummets and struggles to recover. Trust builds slowly over time through repeated trustworthy acts, but plunges in the blink of an eye. Parents can tell you that it takes a lifetime of relating to build enough trust to give their teenager the keys to the car and only one night of drinking and driving to have to start building trust all over again.

Each social worker–client relationship begins with a different level of trust. Individual differences depend on preconceived notions, personality variables, and cultural norms. A client's previous experience with trusting others is significant for trusting a new relationship with a social worker (Moore-Kirkland, 1981). Perceived similarities and differences between clients and social workers as well as current levels of comfort or stress also affect a client's capability to trust. Wherever on the continuum trust begins, it evolves continuously in the relationship. Trust increases or decreases with respect to the experiences of clients and social workers within and outside of professional relationships. Practitioners develop trusting relationships with clients purposefully, by deliberately behaving in trustworthy ways.

Empathy

Clients experience support and trust when social workers respond with empathy. Empathy is "the helper's ability to perceive and communicate, accurately and with sensitivity, the feelings of the client and the meaning of those feelings" (Fischer, 1973, p. 329). To experience empathy,

> *The worker must perceive the client's gestalt accurately and must also simultaneously feel with the client, understand intellectually how his or her own feelings are different from the client's and hold in abeyance any cognitive distortion such as stereotyping or value judging. (Pinderhughes, 1979, p. 316)*

Empathic communication reflects respect and nonjudgmental acceptance.

Empathy differs significantly from both pity and sympathy. To understand this difference, visualize a response showing pity. Do you see someone patting another on the head while lamenting, "Poor you?" Responses flavored with pity suggest others are helpless and incapable. Feeling sorry for someone clearly indicates pity. Likewise, sympathy grows from viewing others as weak and vulnerable. Showing pity and sympathy defines a hierarchy of those who are competent and capable and those who are unfortunate and needy. When social workers express pity or sympathy, they disempower clients.

In contrast, when social workers respond with empathy, they validate the perspectives of clients. Clients experience the affirmation of having someone join with and understand their thoughts and feelings. Empathy communicates that social workers are *with* clients. Empathic support brings the power of affiliation to clients who are struggling to meet life's challenges. "Empathy is being able to finish a [client's] sentence. Being empathic, though, is *not* finishing that sentence" (Book, 1988, p. 423). Empathy is an "act of loving imagination" (Keith-Lucas, 1972) that empowers clients to work toward goals experiencing their competence, efficacy, and responsibility.

Cultural Sensitivity

With so many systems involved on both sides of this transactional relationship, social workers and clients find much in common as well as much that is different. Successfully responding to both similarities and differences is central to building cross-cultural relationships. Social workers should maintain an openness to cultural similarities and differences "without prejudgment about the inherent rightness of attitudes, values, or behaviors on either side of the equation and with some sensitivity to the fact that the similarities are areas on which relationships can be built" (Nakanishi & Rittner, 1992, p. 33). Perceived similarities lead to a sense of understanding, empathy, and trust. Similarities bond relationships and establish rapport.

Discussing Cultural Differences

Discovering differences is inevitable. The ways workers and clients differ are infinite; possibilities include gender, age, race, ethnicity, lifestyle, socioeconomic status, religion, and values among others. With larger client systems, differences multiply geometrically. These differences affect the dynamics of the helping relationship. Perceived differences may lead to questions about the ability to achieve a mutual understanding. Social workers acknowledge differences directly and respect the client's worldview. Rather than viewing cultural differences as threatening, empowering social workers explore these differences as resources in generating culturally relevant solutions.

Accepting cultural differences is not as easy as we might like it to be. Cultural memberships define the very ways that we view the world. Western thinking tends to value human control over nature, an orientation to the future, individual autonomy, competition, and the work ethic. "Ethnic minorities focus on harmony with the environment, reminiscence about the past and pleasure in the present, collectivity, self-discipline and endurance of suffering, and the extended family" (Lum, 1992, p. 86).

These differences in values, perspectives, and experience are enormous. They make cross-cultural relationships vulnerable to miscommunication and conflicting goals. Bridging cultural gaps requires appreciation of diversity, client-focused responding, and open communication. Research shows that clients respect workers who are able to talk openly about cultural differences. "Fear of offending or of appearing ignorant or incompetent may prevent practitioners from asking direct questions of clients from different cultural backgrounds. The participants in this study interpreted such questions as a sign of interest and respect" (Smith, 1996, p. 296).

In their research, Proctor and Davis (1994) also discovered that "acknowledging misunderstanding or failure to comprehend, the worker is likely to enhance the level of rapport with the client" (p. 319). Rogers (1995) concludes that "it is necessary to raise subject matter and openly discuss taboo topics. Racial identity and sexual orientation are examples of such topics" (p. 64).

Purposefulness

In her classic book, *Social Casework: A Problem Solving Process,* Perlman (1957) defines the benchmark of a professional relationship as "its conscious purposefulness." "What makes the social work relationship special is that its purpose and goal are conscious and fall within the overall purpose and value system of the profession" (Compton & Galaway, 1999, p. 173). In general, social work relationships strive to fulfill the profession's mission to improve quality of life by achieving a goodness of fit between persons and their physical and social environments. In particular, each unique client guides the direction and defines the parameters of the relationship with the social worker.

Constructing Empowering Relationships

To the extent that social workers and clients are able to achieve a true partnership, the relationship empowers. True partnerships develop when both partners have control over their own lives. Each can choose to behave in ways that are congruent with their own particular beliefs and intent at any given time. This freedom springs from mutual respect, acceptance, and a constant sense of permission to "be who you are." Achieving this openness ensures equality and leads to an unguarded dialogue in which new perspectives, options, and choices surface continually.

Recognizing Rights

Being partners guarantees certain rights and privileges. Partners have permission to view situations in their own ways along with the privilege to cooperate with or resist others' viewpoints or requests. For example, considering a client's point of view does not require social workers to sacrifice their own integrity, value base, or professional roles. In other words, social workers' acceptance, respect, and nonjudgmentalism does not signify their approval of a client's behavior. Neither is the client under any mandate to accept the view of the social worker as anything but information on how someone else sees things.

All clients have rights (Table 6.1). Even clients coerced into social work services maintain their privileges to think the way they think, feel the way they feel, and, to the extent that their behavior doesn't hurt themselves or others, behave the way they choose. Inside

---

TABLE 6.1   Clients' Rights

Clients have rights:

- To be treated with dignity and respect
- To privacy through confidentiality
- To participate as collaborative partners in the change process
- To receive culturally sensitive treatment
- To have an equitable share of societal resources
- To view their challenges from their own perspective
- To participate in gathering and analyzing information
- To set their own goals
- To resist what social workers want
- To choose from among the various alternative interventions
- To negotiate the distribution of roles and responsibilities for themselves and the social worker
- To collaborate on evaluation processes
- To help determine time frames and know costs involved

---

empowering social worker and client relationships is a shared belief in equality and common goals, yet freedom to hold differences in perspective.

Taking Responsibilities

Responsibilities accompany privileges. Credible social workers bring professional ethics, knowledge, and skills to their partnerships with clients. They take care of their own needs and wants outside the context of professional relationships. Within professional relationships, they work in an efficient and goal-directed manner, using practice-tested, research-based, and ethically sound strategies.

Clients, too, take responsibility. They are responsible for deciding what goals to select and for approving what strategies to employ. When clients have control, then the choices they make belong to them along with credit for their success. Clients' active involvement in decision-making not only leaves them accountable but promotes their sense of competence as well (Dunst, 1993).

Dual Relationships

Serious problems and ethical issues arise when social workers assume secondary roles or dual relationships with clients such as a personal friendship, business partnership, or sexual relationship (Kagle & Gielbelhausen, 1994; Houston-Vega, Nuehring, & Daguio, 1997; Reamer, 1998). Dual relationships extend beyond relationships with individual clients. Social workers who work with macrosystem clients as consultants, grant writers, board members, and volunteers also need to attend to issues of conflict of interest.

The NASW *Code of Ethics* (National, 2000) explicitly condemns dual relationships and places the responsibility for setting clear boundaries on social workers: "Social workers—not their clients, their clients' relatives or other individuals with whom the client maintains a personal relationship—assume the full burden for setting clear, appropriate and culturally sensitive boundaries" (Section 1.09b).

Practitioners who engage in dual relationships risk disciplinary hearings and sanctions by the NASW and state licensing boards. Practitioners who commit sexual misconduct may find themselves subject to criminal action or a civil suit for malpractice. Moreover, since insurance companies consider sexual misconduct a flagrant breach of professional conduct, these practitioners may find themselves without the benefits of liability insurance coverage (Kurzman, 1995). In any form, dual relationships have the potential to exploit clients, cloud the judgments of professionals, and result in charges of professional misconduct.

Discussing Rights and Responsibilities

When social workers openly take their own responsibilities and privileges seriously and leave space for clients to do the same, they begin to balance and distribute power in the relationship. Empowering social workers directly state their philosophy of practice, clarify their perceptions about the corollary roles of social workers and clients, and talk specifically about their confidence in clients' abilities to reach their own goals. Discussing approaches and roles enlightens clients as to the expectations of the relationship and frees them to contribute to the process.

All social workers make conscious and deliberate choices about how to practice; however, these theories and principles are not their private domain. Clients have the right to know the approach of the particular professional with whom they're working. Practitioners should prepare an understandable explanation of their practice philosophy to share directly with clients. If workers' approaches and clients' preferences are a "mismatch," clients can seek to work with other professionals who practice in ways clients prefer.

When social workers formulate a clear picture of what they do, their blueprint clarifies the roles of "worker" and "client." In the example that follows, note how one social worker explains the collaborative process of an empowering practice approach:

Client: I'm here to find out what you think I should do.

Worker: Okay, but I need your help. The way I see things, you have a lot to offer to what we are going to be doing. In fact, you know your situation best. I count on you to let me know what's happening in your life outside of this relationship, where you want to end up, and make choices about what you think might work best.

Client: Sounds like I'm doing all the work. What will you be doing?

Worker: We both have responsibilities. You can count on me to help you make sense out of what we discover and locate resources that you might need. You bring the expert knowledge about your life. I'll be a guide who, hopefully, can work with you to put it together in a way that will get you where you want to go. Does that make sense to you?

Empowerment-based, strengths-focused social workers convey the expectation that client systems are active participants. When clients indicate that they want to sit back and let social workers do all the work, empowering social workers take time to explain the logical impossibility of this approach. Workers openly discuss the implications of dependency, reveal their belief in client strengths, and candidly admit that they are unable to implement the social work process without the client's contribution.

Augmenting Power

Collaborative partnerships evolve. Many clients enter social work relationships humbled by their perceived inability to handle challenges on their own. Some clients initially expect to give over their power to social workers. Experienced social workers report that clients often request "answers" to their dilemmas even before the social workers have any realistic possibility of understanding their difficulties. Developing solutions takes work, not magic.

"Social worker as magician" is a fictitious role that has no roots in empowering social work practice. Social workers resist the temptation to take over clients' situations by offering quick fixes, standard cures, or free-flowing advice. Only when clients explore and discover their own power and options does the social work relationship engender maximum benefits. Even when clients enter the relationship relinquishing their power, social workers move quickly to shift the locus of power from worker-centered to client-controlled. Ultimately, successful clients conclude their work with practitioners with both the responsibility and the credit for the choices they made. The best preparation for enhancing competence is a growing pattern of control by clients that increases over the duration of the professional relationship.

Ethical social workers actively guard against the temptation to take over the process. Social workers who seek to empower rather than dazzle client systems restrain themselves from trying to solve clients' problems, be experts, and perform extraordinary feats. Amundson, Stewart, and Valentine (1993) describe the "temptations of power and certainty" to which helping professionals fall prey based on their role and status and the needs of clients for the quick relief of a "pat answer." Being obsessed with expert knowledge blocks social workers from comprehending clients' actual real life experiences. "As an antidote to undue emphasis upon power and certainty," Amundson, Stewart, and Valentine suggest "embracing curiosity and the desire to empower" (p. 117). The resulting approach frees social workers from imposing their own standards of what they consider "best" in favor of respecting and appreciating diverse solutions.

Balancing Power through Self-Disclosure

One way to help clients experience equality within the social work relationship is with the worker's selective use of self-disclosure. Workers who expect clients to be trusting and open may need to risk demonstrating these qualities first. "Appropriate self-disclosure can produce a mutual, rather than imbalanced, expectation of information sharing and contribute to a sense of good will toward the client" (Proctor & Davis, 1994, p. 317). Workers seeking to share power should "engage in the reciprocal self-disclosure expected by clients from particular cultural groups—for example, American Indians, some Puerto Ricans, and African Americans" (Pinderhughes, 1995, p. 138).

When Clients Feel Powerless

Rarely do clients engage social work services with the sense that they are in charge of their environments. Their feelings and thoughts are evident when clients say things like, "The world is getting me down" or "Nothing I do seems to make a difference." The research by Hopps, Pinderhughes, and Shankar (1995) found many clients felt overwhelmed by persistent, intractable powerlessness in the face of "poverty and other circumstances—drugs, violence, physical abuse, joblessness" (p. 8). Admittedly, in the early phases, the power dynamics of clients and their situations are often skewed against clients. Clients exhibit feelings of powerlessness in various ways including anger, guardedness, self-hatred, aggression, passivity, humor, or manipulation (Pinderhughes, 1995).

Clients may perceive themselves as being carried along by external events rather than actively shaping their futures. Social workers accept the challenge of reversing this trend. They strive to build relationships in which clients recognize and use strengths to take charge of themselves and change their situations.

Clients view their roles in the social worker–client relationship in different ways. Some may be ready to operate as full partners in the process; others feel beaten down and dependent and look for social workers to lead the way. Research helps us understand why some clients feel helpless and disempowered when they enter relationships with social workers (Seligman, 1975; Abramson, Seligman, & Teasdale, 1978). Simply, experience has taught them to be helpless because their previous attempts have failed. People who learn that their efforts make little or no difference lose motivation. They give up and turn over the responsibility for decision-making to someone else or to chance. When social workers yield to the temptation to rescue those who appear dependent and helpless, they often create harmful effects in their attempts to be helpful (Dunst & Trivette, 1988). In fact, they add to clients' experiences of helplessness.

Many times clients approach social workers dependently because their previous experiences with other helping professionals have convinced them that their role is one of passive acceptance of assistance. There are four ways that help can backfire and set up clients to be helpless (Coates, Renzaglia, & Embree, 1983):

- Help undermines clients' competence when it lessens their control over their lives.
- "Help may foster helpless recipients by directly hindering the acquisition and maintenance of important and useful skills" (p. 254).
- Help seekers often lower their opinions of themselves and their capabilities in response to receiving help since needing to "have help" intimates incompetence.
- "Recipients may have their problem solved by the help, but still become helpless, convinced they could not succeed on their own" (p. 255).

To be "helpful," workers guide clients to their power to help themselves.

Collaborating with Oppressed Clients

Many social work clients enter the relationship burdened by the experience of oppression. When oppression denies people their own dignity and access to the resources of society, they feel disempowered. These feelings interfere with the development of a working partnership especially when clients view workers as similar to their oppressors. According to Pinderhughes (1979):

> *The cross-racial and cross-ethnic helping encounter compounds the consequences of the power differential. For the client, intervention by a member of a group he or she regards as the oppressor may reinforce the powerlessness experienced in a*

moment of need. Intervention by a worker whom the client sees as inferior may also reinforce the client's sense of helplessness. Power issues related to differences in ethnicity, class, sex, age, and other social markers may exaggerate the power inherent in the helping role in a way that causes the worker to misperceive the client. (p. 315)

Ultimately social workers and clients may choose to work on oppression as a goal of the relationship, but what can workers do to get over this initial hurdle? Dean (1993) advises that there is no way for social workers to ignore the power that they hold in these situations even if it is subtle and implied in dominant cultural values and prejudices. Rather than denying them, workers do best to "acknowledge these issues and differences, making them part of the conversation" (p. 131).

The goal of any social work relationship is simple—it's for clients and social workers to resolve difficult situations. Clients are supposed to take charge of their own worlds in enlightened and fruitful ways. Social workers should be proficient in networking resources, advocating clients' rights, and creating macrolevel changes. Establishing an equal partnership is challenging for workers relating to clients who feel helpless, coerced, or oppressed. However, effective collaboration helps clients realize their goals.

Voluntary and Involuntary Clients

The client system's status as voluntary or involuntary profoundly affects the relationship dynamics of power and closeness. Voluntary clients choose to participate freely, based on their perceived notion that social work assistance will help. Involuntary clients are forced by others who hold enough power over them to insist on involvement in social work services (Rooney, 1992; Ivanoff, Blythe, & Tripodi, 1994). Examples of involuntary clients include persons convicted of crimes, parents ordered to receive services to regain custody of their children, and those whose use of substances necessitates mandated treatment. In some ways, all clients are involuntary. Would people decide to seek social work assistance if they weren't stuck on something that they would have preferred to solve on their own?

While clients who are voluntary may choose social work services in desperation, nevertheless they participate with the power of choice to address their challenges in their own ways. They can choose to work with this particular social worker, shop for another, or try a totally different approach. They have choices to remain or to leave the relationship, and they are free to behave in openly powerful ways. Collaborative partnerships are easier to form with clients who are voluntary, as their voluntary status places them on more equal footing as partners from the outset.

In contrast, consider those clients coerced into social work services because they have infringed on the rights of others. In these instances, social workers function as agents of social control as well as advocates for clients' rights. Clients begin the relationship in a "one-down" position, feeling more like prisoners than partners. To develop partnerships with involuntary clients, social workers quickly move to offer them honest and direct information about the structure of the helping relationship and their privileges within it.

Owning up to the reality of the coercive nature of the relationship reflects the social worker's genuineness and trustworthiness. Acknowledging that mandated clients still maintain rights shows the worker's acceptance, objectivity, and respect. This open discussion about limits and privileges is a beginning step toward ensuring equal footing for clients. Chapter 8 provides more extensive information about how workers develop and maintain collaborative relationships with mandated clients.

Partnerships with Larger Systems

Forming empowering relationships with larger client systems—such as groups, organizations, and communities—draws on all the skills already described and more. Workers assist client systems to maximize power by encouraging cohesive development and distribution of leadership. This means that workers facilitate feelings of power in as many members of the system as possible, including those members who may initially feel that their contributions are insignificant. Workers can accomplish this "through helping them to assume useful roles in the group, coaching them to be more assertive in the group, and supporting their contributions during groups meetings" (Garvin, 1997, p. 86).

Workers guide group interactions so that a particularly powerful member does not overshadow the worker's efforts to form working partnerships with other members of the client system. Similar to when a social worker's directive approach inhibits the contributions of clients, dictatorial members of larger group systems are likely to stifle the contributions of other group members. Workers "try to keep the leadership structure fluid by emphasizing temporary assignment to group tasks and rotation of any influential positions" (Garvin, 1997, p. 1997). Therefore, with multiperson client systems, workers make direct connections to each group member, seek and accept the contributions of both active and less active members, and encourage each member to take part.

Respecting Confidentiality

Workers promote a client's power when they maintain confidentiality. Many describe confidentiality as the cornerstone of the social worker–client relationship (Kagle, 1990; Kopels & Kagle, 1994; Dickson, 1998; Reamer, 1998). Generally, confidential information is information deemed private. To maintain confidentiality, workers restrain from disclosing information about clients to others. Fulfilling the ethical obligations of confidentiality demonstrates respect for clients and builds trust.

Ethical codes and legal requirements prescribe the nature of confidentiality in professional social work practice. The NASW *Code of Ethics* (National, 2000) obliges social workers to "respect clients' right to privacy. Social workers should not solicit private information from clients unless it is essential to providing service or conducting social work evaluation or research. Once private information is shared, standards of confidentiality apply" (Section 1.07a). Furthermore, laws at the federal, state, and local levels regulate professional responsibility for confidentiality. The following section explores differences between absolute and relative confidentiality, consents for releasing confidential information, and instances and implications of violating confidentiality.

Absolute and Relative Confidentiality

Given the significance of privacy for the sanctity of professional relationships, many conclude that confidentiality is unconditional, yet there are usually limits to confidentiality in social work practice.

We can distinguish two types of confidentiality, absolute and relative (Wilson, 1978; Barker, 1999; Gelman, Pollack, & Weiner, 1999). With absolute confidentiality professionals never share information in any form with anyone. Workers neither record information about clients in any type of report nor orally share information about clients with supervisors, agency-based colleagues, or any other professional. Few circumstances afford absolute confidentiality. More likely, the principle of relative confidentiality guides practice. Relative confidentiality allows sharing of information within agencies such as in supervision, case conferences, and team meetings. However, relative confidentiality still presumes that, with some exceptions, workers do not share information outside the agency context without the explicit permission of the client (Table 6.2).

Violating Confidentiality

Some workers unwittingly violate confidences (Wilson, 1978; Houston-Vega, Nuehring, & Daguio, 1997). One common violation is *discussing client or work setting situations with their own family and friends* under the guise that not using names or identifying detail protects confidentiality. Family and friends are under no constraint to keep shared information confidential. *Informal sharing with colleagues* in public settings such as social gatherings, coffee break rooms, or the shopping mall also presents serious problems. Additionally, *inappropriate remarks,* such as judgmental commentary about another client or an agency, may irrevocably damage working relationships. *Phone calls taken during sessions* with clients, while not necessarily revealing confidential information, distract and send messages about the potential for divulging private information. Finally, *accidental or careless revelation of records* or identities occurs in numerous ways including leaving confidential records unattended on a desk or in an unlocked file; working on records in public places; greeting a client by name in a public place; discarding unshredded records and notes, or even taking work home. Additionally, using *unprotected means of communication* such as cellular phones, answering machines, fax machines, or e-mail can result in breaches of confidentiality.

If social workers break confidentiality, they seriously violate standards of professional ethics. In fact, in many states, if social workers violate confidentiality, they break the law.

TABLE 6.2   Exceptions to Confidentiality

- Evidence of child abuse or neglect
- Legal mandates for reporting elder abuse or neglect
- Threats by clients to harm themselves or others
- Clients' needs for emergency services
- Guardianship hearings or committal procedures requiring information
- Quality assurance procedures, internal audits, or peer reviews of nonidentifiable case records
- Consultation with colleagues, consultants, and attorneys
- Lawsuits filed against social workers by clients
- Other exceptions, as prescribed by laws and regulations

Possible consequences include professional sanctions and disciplinary actions, loss of professional licenses and certifications, misdemeanor charges, and civil lawsuits (Nye, 1989).

Informed Consent for Releasing Information

Clients can grant a worker permission to release confidential information through a process called informed consent. For a client's consent to be "informed," the worker must fully reveal the conditions, risks, and alternatives of sharing information. However, obtaining consents for the release of information is not without controversy. Questions arise, such as: What constitutes a valid consent? Is it ever appropriate to use a blanket consent? Is it appropriate to respond to a client's request for immediate disclosure if time constraints preclude having a written consent in hand? Are there ever circumstances that do not require social workers to obtain informed consent?

What is proper procedure when a third party and not the client requests information? Is a social worker obligated to inform clients of the results of a request for information or of the potential consequences of not agreeing to sign the form? Can clients withdraw their consent? (Perlman, 1988; Reamer, 1998). State and federal statutes, regulations, and policies, as well as court decisions and case law, stipulate the parameters for disclosing information (Dickson, 1998).

Consent forms clearly detail the nature of the information exchange. Workers should make copies of the completed and signed consent form for the client's case file, the client, and the professional requesting the information. Specific steps social workers take in obtaining informed consent include:

1. Determining client competence
2. Providing service information
3. Ensuring client understanding
4. Documenting informed consent (Houston-Vega, Nuehring, & Daguio, 1997, p. 53)

Privileged Communication

Privileged communication provides the legal ground for confidentiality (Gothard, 1995; Dickson, 1998). Simply put, clients claim legal privilege and ethical social workers maintain confidentiality. Legal privilege protects a client's private communication with a social worker by prohibiting the professional from divulging information in court. Establishing privilege often involves the following elements:

- The client invokes privilege to prevent the social worker's testimony or records from being used as evidence in a court of law.
- The social worker asserts privilege at the client's request. When a client waives this right, the social worker is not legally bound to maintain silence in court.
- The judge considers Wigmore's Principles, relevant statutory and case laws, and client waiver and entitlement to determine whether privilege applies.

By invoking privilege, clients restrict professionals from revealing confidential information in courts of law. In the absence of privilege, court officials compel social workers to testify and document their evidence with written records. Because it holds communication sacrosanct, the legal right of privilege enhances the effect of confidentiality in the social worker–client relationship (Kagle, 1990; Watkins, 1989; Schroeder, 1995).

Wigmore's Principles

In determining whether clients have privilege, legal specialists consider conditions summarized by Wigmore (1961, as cited in Reamer, 1994b). These principles include:

1. *The communication must originate in a* confidence *that it will not be disclosed;*
2. *The element of* confidentiality must be essential *to the full and satisfactory maintenance of the relationship between the parties;*
3. *The* relation *must be one which in the opinion of the community ought to be sedulously fostered; and*
4. *The* injury *that would incur to the relation by the disclosure of the communication must be* greater than the benefit *thereby gained for the correct disposal of litigation. Only if these four conditions are present should a privilege be recognized. (p. 34)*

Safeguarding confidentiality conscientiously protects a client's legal right to privilege. However, privileged communication does not afford the absolute protection of privacy, as numerous exceptions exist, even in states that grant the status of privilege to clients of social workers.

Statutory Provisions

Federal, state and local laws, which may or may not agree, stipulate conditions of privilege. In regard to federal cases, a U.S. Supreme Court ruling on *Jaffee v. Redmond* indicates that clients can now claim protection from disclosure of confidential exchanges with licensed social workers in federal courts (Therapy, 1996). "Jaffee prevents an attorney for the plaintiff from using the discovery process to invade a social worker's privacy and prevents harassment" (Alexander, 1997, p. 388). It also offers full protection to social workers who practice on Native American reservations whose clients face lawsuits or charges in federal courts.

All states and the District of Columbia grant some form of testimonial privilege to psychotherapist–client communications; many states include clinical or licensed social workers in the definition of "psychotherapist" (Alexander, 1997). However, most states do not grant social workers the right to absolute confidentiality. Typically, for clients to establish privilege, the social worker involved must either be licensed or registered or be supervised by someone who is. In some states, privilege extends to social work students; in other states, it does not. Since laws stipulate conditions required for privilege to apply, social workers should learn the implications of the laws governing their specific area of practice. The serious legal implications of these issues press social workers to familiarize themselves with situations where privilege applies, as well as with the exceptions.

Various laws regarding licensure, professional regulation, and human service activities designate conditions for confidentiality and privileged communication. "There are a number of federal and state laws that impose different confidentiality requirements depending on the practice setting" (Saltzman & Furman, 1999, p. 451). In general, stipulations for federal funding restrict social workers from disseminating records and other information in such practice areas as education, medical and health care, criminal justice, and other public services. More specifically, in the public service arena, restrictions apply to child abuse, foster care, adoption, family preservation, Temporary Assistance to Needy Families (TANF), child support, and child custody. Other areas protected by privilege often include work in parole and probation, services to persons with developmental disabilities, practice in home health agencies, and services for persons with AIDS and HIV-related disorders. Federal laws regulating substance abuse treatment stipulate strict confidentiality, forbidding staff from even revealing whether someone is a client and mandating a secure record-keeping system.

Exceptions to Privilege

Like other laws, privilege laws contain exceptions. Based on the NASW model licensure law, social workers are obligated to testify about confidential communications with clients when:

> 1. *The client, or someone acting on the client's behalf, waives privilege, giving written consent for disclosure.*
> 2. *The client brings charges against the social worker.*
> 3. *The client reveals in confidence the contemplation of a crime or harmful act.*
> 4. *The client is a minor who may have been the victim of a crime. (Kagle, 1990, p. 56)*

Certain types of court proceedings, such as commitment hearings, child abuse cases, and trials for serious crimes, abrogate or, in other words, invalidate privilege (Saltzman & Furman, 1999). Subpoenas for records or court appearances require responses. Saltzman and Furman (1999) advise that "one may respond by claiming confidentiality or privilege. If the claim is contested, there will be a court hearing, and a judge will decide if the claim is valid or if the records must be turned over" (p. 461). Search warrants require immediate compliance, although there may be ways to persuade law enforcement officers to wait for a court ruling.

In addition, privilege does not apply when clients know from the outset that social workers may be called upon to testify. Frequently, this is the case with involuntary clients. For example, various situations—such as family violence, child custody disputes, criminal activity, or mental health issues—where social workers gather information on behalf of the court exclude privilege. The presence of another person when private information is shared, called the "third-party rule," may also limit the legal right to privilege (Dickson, 1998).

Balancing Accountability and Privacy

Numerous factors influence the extent to which social workers maintain confidentiality. Codes of ethics and standards for professional practice emphasize confidentiality is necessary to create the atmosphere of trust in which clients are free to reveal their situations. Statutory regulations, case law, judicial interpretations, and agency policies and procedures provide guidelines which support confidentiality. However, these same guidelines demand that professionals balance matters of privacy with the requisites of accountability and the rights of others.

Particularly difficult ethical dilemmas and legal quandaries emerge with the trend toward managed care, the reliance on computer technology, and challenging social issues (Polowy & Gorenberg, 1997; Congress, 1999). For example, managed care officials demand "confidential" information about cases as a requisite to funding (Strom-Gottfried, 1998; Watt & Kallmann, 1998; Rock & Congress, 1999). Increased utilization of technology, computerized databases, and computer networks creates the potential for breaching confidentiality (Davidson & Davidson, 1995, 1996; Gellman, Pollack, & Weiner, 1999). The press of "duty to warn" and "informed consent" in an age of pandemic disease and violence increases social workers' risks of violating confidentiality (Regehr & Antle, 1997; Dickson, 1998). And finally, circumstances under which social workers breach confidentiality may further discriminate against clients from various oppressed population groups (Kopels & Kagle, 1994).

Reflecting Back

Social work values mandate that people be treated with acceptance and respect. The shift toward a more egalitarian partnership between social worker and client system actualizes this value in the professional relationship. But in relinquishing the role of expert, workers are placed in the quandary of who to be. How do practitioners collaborate with clients in ways that liberate client strengths and resources without neutralizing their own power to benefit clients? How does client self-determination apply here? Defining a mutual relationship with clients may not be as simple as it sounds. Visualize yourself in the worker role and then in the client role to consider what kind of professional relationship might work for you.

Looking Forward

The social worker–client relationship sits at the intersection of many influences and opportunities. Empowering social workers recognize these possibilities and work directly to take full advantage of their potential. To do so workers carefully construct partnerships with clients that encourage open sharing, collaboration, and active participation. Workers use their personal qualities and professional expertise in the process of developing this relationship. They also maintain the integrity of the relationship by orienting it to the goals that clients seek and by maintaining clients' rights to confidentiality.

Although social workers define the professional partnership in direct ways, clients experience the relationship most profoundly when discussing their situations. Chapter 7 details the processes that social workers use to talk with clients about the challenges they face. Workers consider both clients' thoughts and feelings in this process. The ways that social workers gather information can contribute to clients' feelings of competence and hope as well as activate clients to continue to invest in the relationship.

C h a p t e r 7

Articulating Situations

While articulating situations, clients and social workers develop a mutual understanding of what they are getting together to do. Until clients begin to explain what purposes bring them to social workers, practitioners have only general ideas of where to begin. An open and respectful dialogue identifies the issues clients confront and elucidates the contexts in which these difficulties occur. During this mutual exchange, clients and social workers define and strengthen their working partnership.

Some clients come with clear ideas about what is going on and what they would like to be doing when the work is done. Others enter with vague feelings of discontent and no clear direction. Many clients feel mired in multiple problems that seem inescapable and unchangeable. All clients bring their own unique constructions of the realities they face. The experiences that clients present are as varied and diverse as clients themselves. So, how does a social worker begin? It's really very simple. Let clients lead the way.

It is a mistake, however, to think that social workers have no responsibility in conversations with clients. Although clients take the lead in defining their stories, social workers are more than passive followers. By choosing responses to determine goals and to locate resources for change, social workers infuse purpose into the dialogue while demonstrating respect for the clients' expertise, freedom, and privilege of self-definition. This exchange requires a delicate power balance between social worker and client, made more complex in the context of social work with larger systems such as organizations and communities.

An effective social worker focuses conversations to describe what is currently happening, to determine goals, and to locate resources for change. This chapter describes how social workers respond to access clients' perspectives. Specifically, this chapter:

- Suggests empowering frames from which to examine client situations
- Explores the process of communication, both verbal and nonverbal, and the influences of culture, emotion, and other experiences on communication
- Presents a continuum of responses for social workers to clarify clients' situations
- Delineates skills for workers to help clients identify and express feelings
- Offers suggestions for social workers as they respond to anger, silence, questions, and feedback
- Considers the special dialogue skills necessary to work effectively with larger client systems

Workers implementing these client-focused responding skills are able to initiate and maintain empowering relationships with diverse clients.

Empowering Dialogue

A man, recently paroled and saddled with a felony record, can't find a job. A girl refuses to return to school after her fight with a teacher. A downtown redevelopment group wants to attract customers to its revitalized town center, an area that has become a gathering place for people who are homeless. A public housing project's reputation for crime and drug traffic complicates a cycle of low occupancy rates, reduced income, and spotty maintenance, further decreasing the attractiveness to potential residents. Each of these client systems faces very different situations that challenge their capabilities to respond.

In articulating the significant dimensions of any of these situations, social workers face choices of how to respond. What information is most relevant? Which avenues of exploration will be productive in leading toward desired goals? What kind of conversation will work best to guide the change process and to establish a working partnership that merges social worker and client expertise?

Listening and Responding

Social workers are active participants in conversations with clients, focusing their attention to understand and articulate the meanings clients intend. Workers listen carefully and then respond directly to access a clear image of the client's world and to communicate interest, appreciation, and concern. The best comments by social workers build on and validate what clients have shared. Clients experience a worker's empathy and respect if the worker can describe the situation as the client sees it. Practitioners learn how to respond to clients by listening to them first.

Social workers demonstrate their acceptance of clients and foster collaboration when they emphasize responding. Using responding skills, workers hold their own views in check in favor of eliciting the client's perspective. Responding in a client-focused dialogue is a "culturally responsive" way to interact, leaving to the client the role of cultural expert. When clients take the lead, they set a cultural tone for the work by revealing their language, style, hopes, and beliefs. Encouraged by a social worker's responses, clients disclose their own theories about events as well as their motivations and priorities.

Professional Responding

A social work professional has a responsibility to maintain the defined purpose of any relationship with a client. Professional practice is client-focused and goal-directed. In conversations with clients, social workers maintain this purpose through thoughtful responses to what clients are saying. Workers deliberately choose responses that are useful in meeting the purposes of the relationship.

All human communication is difficult to punctuate so as to determine who initiates and who follows (Watzlawick, Bavelas, & Jackson, 1967). The reciprocal nature of communication means that communicators influence each other and the direction of their conversation. When social workers respond to clients, clients likewise receive signals from social workers about what to discuss next.

Workers inevitably influence the direction of conversations. Choices made by workers in how to respond to clients are pivot points in the dialogue. Even an apparently "neutral" response by the worker is one choice among several possible responses. Each chosen response contributes to define the direction of the conversation. No doubt about it! Responding is initiating. Helpful responses by social workers guide clients to useful information about their situations without inhibiting the clients' freedom to share their own perspectives.

Proactive Responding

To assist workers in choosing productive responses, O'Melia (1998) introduces the concept of *proactive responding*. Proactive responding weaves three related dialogue skills:

1. *Responses to articulate the current situation and its impact from the client's perspective*
2. *Responses to define a positive outcome to direct the work, and*
3. *Responses to identify strengths and resources available for goal achievement. (p. 2)*

These proactive responses maintain the client's central position as expert on the situation while allowing the worker to infuse a strengths orientation into the process. These responding skills assist clients in describing their current situations, orienting toward the future, and searching for strengths and resources.

Describing the Current Situation

Situations make the most sense when we view them from the client's point of view and in their environmental contexts. A social worker's responses to access the client's unique perspective and relevant contextual information reflect the integration of two theoretical views—social constructivism and the ecosystems perspective. A social worker's best responses validate clients' experiences and expand their views of the world.

Eliciting the Client's Reality

We have already discussed the difficulty of anticipating another's experience. Inevitable differences in perspectives arise, generated by cultural group memberships and individual uniqueness. The differing realities between social workers and clients press workers to withhold their views in favor of eliciting the client's perspective. The worker takes on the role of student to be educated rather than informed cultural expert (Leigh, 1998). As a student of the client's construction of reality, the worker responds reflectively with interest and curiosity until a mutual understanding of the client's situation is achieved.

Discussing Transactions

The social justice imperative directs workers to explore the social, institutional, and political contexts of client situations. All client situations are transactional, so workers examine the goodness-of-fit of persons and their environments rather than investigate failures in the functioning of client systems themselves. When clients say they have failed, a worker immediately responds to link this "failure" to its context where other explanations of the client's experience become evident.

Placing a situation in its systemic context has two major advantages. First, this view assumes no fault or inadequacy on the part of clients. There is simply a gap between what client systems currently need and what their environments presently offer. Removing the need to pinpoint blame frees clients to cooperate rather than fend off the perception of judgment and blame. Second, when we describe situations transactionally, we scan the entire ecosystem in developing resources for change.

Examining the contextual features of situations reveals targets for solutions. Consider a girl who refuses to return to school after a fight with her teacher. A linear view looks first to the child and second to the teacher to see what and who is wrong. In contrast, the transactional view explores other elements of the ecosystem that may be supporting the transaction. Perhaps the girl has concerns about her elderly grandmother's health. Maybe she is reluctant to admit that she is having difficulty reading. Possibly her teacher is succumbing to pressures of increased class size and decreased student support services. Maybe racial and ethnic bias is predisposing other children in the class to pick on her. Events happening within the ecosystem provide clues for assessment and focus for solutions.

Situations involving larger client systems also have transactional dimensions to explore. For example, the task group seeking to revitalize the downtown area needs to look beyond the immediate concern of a few businesses and a few customers to understand the issue more fully. A social worker would guide group members to examine the impact of the city's investment in a new shopping mall on the other side of town, the loss of jobs created when the area's major employer consolidated and moved its operations to another state, the influx of people who are homeless into the downtown area drawn by the empty buildings, and the shifts in population from the town center to suburban areas. Haley (1976) offers this advice: never diagnose a problem that you can't solve. When social workers respond to describe situations in concrete transactional terms, the area in which they search for solvable problems expands.

Orienting toward the Future

The second important response by a social worker is one that shifts the conversation to refine the direction of the work. When clients present what they see as problems, social workers respond by asking how this problem gets in the way. This takes a first step toward defining where clients would like to go (see Chapter 8, Defining Directions).

To shift the focus toward the future, social workers frame clients' situations in terms of challenges, rather than problems. Challenges differ significantly from problems; challenges orient us toward the future. Consider Zeb, a client recently paroled and looking for employment. The problem Zeb presents is his felony record. This fact about his past is unalterable. Focusing on this problem engenders feelings of guilt and powerlessness. However, Zeb's challenge is getting a job. Notice the perspective shift toward the future. Despite Zeb's past, finding a job is still a future option. Similar to how you would assist any recent college graduate seeking a job, the task is to assess Zeb's motivation and interest, define his current capabilities, and determine his needs for additional job skills to increase Zeb's marketability in the eyes of potential employers. There may be no way to expunge the problem of a criminal record, but there are multiple approaches to the challenge of securing employment.

The concept of challenge steers workers away from the notion of eliminating a problem fixed in the past toward overcoming or avoiding hurdles in the pathway leading to a future goal. Previous problems are significant only if they interfere with achieving a desired future. Examine this shift in perspective: the concept of challenge reorients workers to move quickly beyond talking about what is wrong. Instead of dwelling on past problems, social workers encourage clients to articulate where they are going (goals) and what might help them get there (strengths and resources).

Searching for Strengths and Resources

A third effective response by social workers pivots toward a discussion of client strengths and environmental resources available to achieve goals. Social workers consistently choose responses that direct attention to what clients are doing right, what they have accomplished, and what resources may contribute to the effort (see Chapter 9, Identifying Strengths, and Chapter 10, Assessing Resource Capabilities).

Consider the example of a deteriorating public housing project. The social worker's conversation with residents identifies their sense of helplessness about their situation—a reality of substandard living conditions, neglect by the housing authority, and periodic incidents of violence. But as the worker responds to reorient the conversation to how residents cope with their situation, a new picture emerges. Through this shift in direction, the social worker learns that the difficult conditions have contributed to a strong sense of community, some residents have researched their rights as tenants and are poised to assert themselves at the next meeting of the housing authority, and other residents have organized a neighborhood watch program. These newly articulated strengths of the neighborhood are the seeds of the solutions that residents seek.

Human system behavior is adaptive in context. It's likely that something is right in each client's situation. It is always more empowering to validate and improve than to denigrate and redirect. Social workers respond to clients with positive possibilities in mind. What's good about what clients are doing? The answer is "probably a lot."

Sizing Up Situations

Despite their professional knowledge, social workers are basically uninformed when they begin with a new client. Even practitioners who have received extensive referral information lack up-to-the-minute, in-depth information from the experts—the clients themselves. Only clients can tell the stories of their situations. Workers respond to more fully articulate the client's perspective and structure the dialogue for success. Social workers respond proactively to access clients' thoughts and feelings, consider the impact of issues with respect to goals, and locate strengths and resources for solution development (Table 7.1). Articulating situations means responding in ways that respect and inform rather than control and monopolize the conversation.

Exchanging Information

By definition, all communication processes involve exchanges of information between senders and receivers (Figure 7.1). Senders *encode* messages. In this process, senders consider their thoughts and feelings and symbolically represent them in words and actions. The actual verbal and nonverbal delivery of these words and actions transmits a message to the receiver. Receivers, in turn, *decode* or interpret the messages they receive based on their perception of the message. When receivers respond to a sender's message with messages of their own, a dialogue begins. As conversations unfold, receivers become senders and senders become receivers, trading roles as they respectively encode, transmit, and decode messages. Communication is effective to the extent that senders clearly transmit and receiv-

TABLE 7.1   Proactive Responding

Proactive responses maintain the client's central position as an expert on the situation while allowing the worker to infuse a strengths orientation into the conversation. Proactive responding weaves three related dialogue skills, including:

Responses to articulate the current situation

- What is happening from your point of view?
- What else is also happening?
- Who else is involved?
- What impact are those events having?
- How do you make sense out of what is happening?

Responses to define a positive direction

- How would you like it to be instead?
- What would it look like if things were working this way?
- What might indicate that things are beginning to improve?

Responses to identify strengths and locate available resources

- Have things ever worked the way you would like? I'd like to hear about those times.
- When are things working best?
- What are you best at? How might that help us here?
- What's available in the environment that would be a resource?
- Who else might contribute to the effort? What could they do?
- How have you been able to cope with such a situation?
- What do you think other people in your situation might do?

Adapted with permission of the author from "Proactive Responding: Paths Toward Diverse Strengths," M. O'Melia, 1998. All rights reserved.

ers accurately understand messages. Successful communication depends on the active participation and cooperation of both senders and receivers.

Verbal Communication

When we talk, we tell other people about the events in our lives—what has happened in the past, what we are thinking and feeling, and what we anticipate will happen. Typically, clients recount such events as they begin their dialogue with social workers. But, what exactly is the nature of the verbal communication by which clients inform social workers? How do clients remember, reconstruct, interpret, and talk about their situations?

Several theorists contribute to our understanding of the human experience of remembering and reporting events (Bandler & Grinder, 1975; Johnson, 1997). When something happens, we perceive it and tuck it away in our minds for future reference. But, already the event that actually occurred and the representation we store in our memory differ, as our attention is selective. The complexity of events defies our capabilities to absorb all the details. We see

Dialogue Information Loop

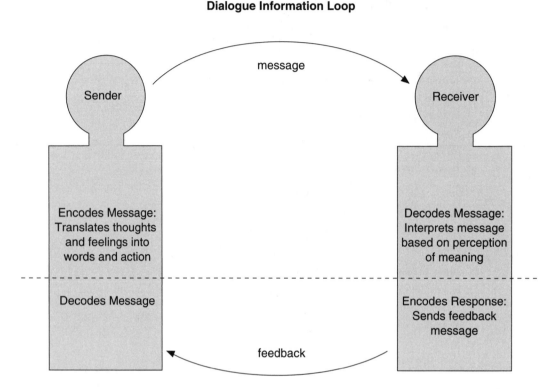

FIGURE 7.1   Communication Processes

what we see, hear what we hear, feel what we feel, and we remember it selectively. Others witnessing identical events do the same, resulting in a different perception of the event. Each of us constructs our own idiosyncratic memories, unique compilations of events as we perceive them.

Memory stores general information rather than precise, meticulous details. Then, when we retrieve information we fill in the gaps to reconstruct events logically, as we expect they would have happened (Loftus, 1979). In other words, when we report these events from memory, we are likely to leave out significant features or even embellish the details. Moreover, we can't possibly share everything we are thinking; there wouldn't be enough time. Most likely, we tailor our remarks to the requisites of specific conversations. Our motives for presenting information, the effect we seek, and our feelings further influence the choices we make in what and how to share. Rather than report our entire memory of events, we selectively delete, generalize, and distort information as we pass it along (Bandler & Grinder, 1975).

When clients express their thoughts about events, naturally, they share only bits and pieces of their stories. Social workers respond to help clients "fill in the blanks." When social workers listen and communicate in ways that encourage clients to rediscover events in fuller, more productive detail, they broaden the view of challenges and empower clients with options. As a result, both social workers and clients achieve a clearer understanding of clients' situations, goals, and resources.

Words Are Ambiguous

In talking with clients about their situations, workers choose their words carefully, as words either facilitate partnerships or block communication processes. For example, when social workers use jargon, technical terms, and vocabulary unfamiliar to clients, these esoteric words elevate social workers into expert roles and leave clients feeling like they have nothing to offer. When social workers use complex, enigmatic terminology, they puzzle clients. One client who participated in a focus group for a child welfare research project talked about the importance of communicating on a level with clients this way: "I mean being personal and friendly and just being down on our level or whatever. It's just really the most important thing they can do" (Drake, 1994, p. 598).

Even when clients and social workers use the very same words they may not mean the same thing (Kadushin & Kadushin, 1997). For example, the words, "eligibility," "referral," and "privacy" can invoke disparate meanings and reactions. And, even common words such as "soon," "later," "possibility," and "likely" leave room for alternative interpretations. Sensitive social workers choose words with an ear for what fits naturally with the world of the client system and continually check in with clients to ensure mutual understanding.

Nonverbal Communication

Words are only part of the messages we communicate. When we talk, we also send nonverbal messages. Humans rely heavily on nonverbal communication to convey and interpret meaning (Burgoon, Buller, & Woodall, 1996). Nonverbal messages accompany every verbal expression and sometimes stand on their own. Body posture, facial expressions, eye contact, head and body movements, and other attending behaviors as well as voice tone, inflection, and intensity all contain nonverbal messages.

Nonverbal communication can be purposeful and practiced, but generally it is spontaneous and continuous. Nonverbal messages often communicate information that would otherwise go unsaid. Longstanding research indicates that nonverbal behavior influences communication processes more prominently than do verbal messages, generating about two-thirds of any communication's meaning (Birdwhistell, 1955). What you think and how you feel shows through in how you behave.

Social workers encourage or inhibit clients by their nonverbal responses to them. Nonverbal messages qualify otherwise neutral information. How we say words conveys information about our attitudes making nonverbal messages particularly important in cross-cultural work. "Minority clients are likely to be particularly sensitive to the degree of congruence between a worker's verbal and nonverbal messages" (Proctor & Davis, 1994, p. 317). When there's a mismatch between verbal and nonverbal messages, we tend to believe the nonverbal ones.

Influences on Communication Processes

A number of factors influence communication processes and create lenses through which we view and interpret messages. These include culture, assumptions, expectations, emotions, and distractors.

Culture

Culture is one of the strongest influences on communication processes. Consider the example of a social worker asking a client the simple question, "What does your family think about this?" Who pops into your mind as you consider your family's reaction? If you are Latino, it is likely that you would think of your extended family as including your godparents (Falicov, 1996). If you are Asian American, you probably consider your extended family with an emphasis on your husband's or father's side (Nakanishi & Rittner, 1996). If you are Native American, you may have thought about a multi-household, extended kinship network with tribal connections, including those in areas far away (Weaver & White, 1997). If you are African American, you might have included blood relatives and long-time friends in the community network as part of your family (Hines & Boyd-Franklin, 1996). If you are European American, you probably flashed on an image of your nuclear family (McGoldrick, 1989). Cultural backgrounds trigger differences in meaning that confound social workers in their attempts to communicate effectively with clients, and they create communication gaps among members of multiperson client systems.

Culture influences some facets of nonverbal communication, while other facets are universally expressed and understood. For example, cross-cultural research discovered that people from different cultures usually interpret certain facial indicators of emotion—surprise, disgust, anger, fear, sadness, and happiness—similarly (Ekman & Friesen, 1975). This research reported remarkable agreement across cultures about communicating and interpreting these facial expressions of emotion. However, cultural differences prescribe variations in the meaning of other types of nonverbal behaviors.

People from different cultures attribute different meanings to gestures, eye contact, and even voice intonation. For example, many North American cultural groups interpret direct eye contact as a sign of support, interest, and respect, yet some Native Americans and Asian Americans interpret direct eye contact as rude and intrusive (Lewis & Ho, 1975). However, be cautious in overgeneralizing, because in a changing and assimilating society, cultural "rules" have exceptions. For example, it is a misconception that Native Americans do not make eye contact. Although this "may have been true for a few tribal cultures (but not all), most American Indian children in urban areas are far removed from such traditions" (Franklin, Waukechon, & Larney, 1995, p. 187).

Additionally, some cultural groups are more sensitive to contextual features of communication, including nonverbal elements:

> *High context cultures, such as traditional Chinese and Japanese, pay great attention to the surrounding circumstances or context of an event; thus, in interpersonal communication, the elements of phrasing, tone, gestures, posture, social status, history, and social setting are all crucial to the meaning of the message. (Chung, 1992, p. 29)*

Given this variability in cultural meaning, social workers must decipher what verbal communications and nonverbal behaviors will work with each client system.

Assumptions

When social workers assume they know the meaning of a client's message, they create a significant barrier to communication (Compton & Galaway, 1999). For example, a practitioner working in foster care observed sparse interaction between a mother and her children during a supervised visit and assumed that the mother's behavior was aloof and disinterested. Talking with the mother after the visit, the social worker learned that the mother wanted to be "a good mom" so she let the kids play video games, but was disappointed in her lack of opportunity to interact with them. "There's always the danger when we don't check things out, that we may think we understand a client's meaning and act as if we do, when we are actually not at all in accord" (Dean, 1993, p. 137). Careful clarification circumvents the pitfalls of assuming meanings.

Expectations

Past experiences create expectations that filter perceptions of here-and-now situations. For example, both workers and clients have expectations for the helping encounter. A client may negatively interpret a social worker's message, "we'll work together," in light of past disappointments with "the system" (Imber-Black, 1988). Or, a social worker who observes particular patterns of communication in a single-parent family may presume that these patterns apply to all single-parent families, overlooking individual differences. Bits and pieces of past experiences influence how people send, receive, and interpret messages. Unchecked, categorical generalizations distort information and severely restrict the ability to communicate effectively.

When social workers mentally forecast what clients will say and do, they create expectations for clients' behaviors (Compton & Galaway, 1999). These predictions even ring louder than clients' actual words. "Our expectations increase the possibility that we will distort the communication we receive. Thus we ask for what we expect to hear—whether the person said it or not" (Kadushin & Kadushin, 1997, p. 59). Clients may expect workers to look down on them for their failures or blame them for their difficulties. To counteract the effect of negative expectations, social workers listen carefully and consciously send messages of acceptance and respect.

Emotions

Communication also involves emotional elements. Frequently, emotions affect how we send, receive, and remember information. For example, stress narrows our focus, distracts our attention, limits our ability to recognize alternatives, and increases our inaccuracies and misinterpretations (Baradell & Klein, 1993). Other research indicates that our moods may even influence our ability to recall information. For example, in a well-known experiment on emotions and memory, Bower (1981) found participants remembered more words when their mood during "input" matched their mood during "retrieval."

On the receiving end, strong emotions may blur our ability to listen accurately. Overidentifying with emotions confuses our own stories with those of the message sender. We project our own circumstances into our understanding of the messages we receive. In other words, caught up with personal emotions, we may interpret information through the masks of our own emotions. Most communications convey emotion, but strong emotions held by either senders or receivers can undermine the effective sharing of information. Social workers take extra caution to communicate effectively in emotionally charged interchanges.

Distractors

Distractors confound communication processes. For example, background noise interrupts concentration, covers up softly spoken messages, and hinders communication with persons who have a hearing loss. Repetitive sounds, such as the ticking of a clock, accentuate silence. Odors, too, may distract us. Certain odors evoke deeply imbedded memories and shift our attention away from the present to the past of our own personal associations. Interruptions such as telephone calls, intercom messages, and requests to step outside suggest to clients that they are of secondary importance. In home visits, distractors, such as radios and televisions, neighbors dropping by, or other household activities, may interrupt the flow of communication. When social workers feel the press of their own agenda or environmental distractions interfere, they take steps to remove the distractions in order to facilitate productive conversations.

Describing Situations

Central to success in any social work endeavor is the ability to describe the client's situation in a useful way. This requires an exchange of information between workers and clients. With individual, family, and small group clients, this exchange is likely to be some form of conversation. Social workers and clients talk directly with each other. With formal systems, organizations, and communities, other methods are necessary to articulate the situation. Dialogue with larger systems may involve formal meetings, public forums, focus groups, or written surveys.

No matter what form this exchange of information takes, two key purposes orient the conversation. First, workers seek to articulate the situation as the client sees it. The idea is to access the client's perspective untainted by the worker's biases. Secondly, workers nudge the conversation toward a broader view, broad enough to place situations in environmental context and to reveal strengths and resources for change.

Accessing the Client's Perspective

Clients know something that workers don't. They know what is happening in their lives and the impact of these events, and they have developed theories about what is going on. The worker's task is to learn what the client knows and in the process help clients organize and understand this information in a useful way. To accomplish this workers listen carefully to what clients say and encourage them to say more.

Clients constantly communicate verbally and behaviorally, telling and showing workers how they think and feel. This abundance of information forces social workers to respond selectively. Empowering social workers choose responses that demonstrate acceptance and respect while encouraging clients to more fully articulate their situations. Through their responses, social workers send their own messages, explore what clients are thinking, and reflect what clients are feeling.

Beginning the Dialogue

Experience this dilemma: You've introduced yourself and greeted the client. What now? The axiom to "begin where the client is" prompts workers to turn over the control of the conversation to clients. Some clients begin on their own, rescuing social workers from the dilemma of initiating the dialogue. Others wait for social workers to lead.

Successful openings require social workers to proceed cautiously so as not to commandeer conversations. Workers who control the dialogue from the beginning may set a pattern that encourages clients to be passive throughout the entire process. Clients, themselves, should direct the initial dialogue rather than being interrogated by social workers. If clients start, let them. If clients wait for you to begin, give up this "in-charge" role as soon as possible.

There may be no single beginning question or phrase that accomplishes this power shift. Some workers use nonverbal prompts such as looking at the client or gesturing their hand in the client's direction. Others experiment with different openings to elicit beginning information. Possibilities include:

- What brings you here?
- OK, I think we can start now.
- Where do we begin?
- Please tell me about your situation.
- I only know a little about what's going on, so you're going to have to fill me in.

Workers find ways to get clients talking. Then, as the dialogue continues, workers relax into a pattern of responding, recognizing clients' privileges to tell their stories in their own ways.

The degree to which social workers are successful in turning the initial dialogue over to clients depends on the client's cultural background. For example, American Indians, Asian Americans, and Latino clients may hesitate to initiate the discussion, trusting instead that the worker will be more direct and active (Sue & Sue, 1999). In keeping with culturally sensitive practice, workers need to match the client's style and balance a direct approach with a response mode that respects the centrality of the client's perspective.

Responding to Thoughts

Workers and clients need a mutual understanding of the client's current situation. In our everyday conversations, we may share our thoughts freely, trying to get others to understand our points of view. In professional conversations, the client's experience is the significant one. Social workers deliberately offer responses to guide clients to describe their situations in concrete and transactional terms. A social worker's purposeful selection of responses:

- Helps workers clearly comprehend clients' challenges
- Promotes clients' understanding of their own situations

- Pursues information relevant to clients' goals
- Develops and maintains a respectful partnership that gives clients control over their own directions
- Encourages all members of multiperson client systems to share their views

Many contributors describe ways for social workers to access a client's perspective (Rogers, 1951; Garrett, 1982; Epstein, 1985; Benjamin, 1987; Satir, 1988; Nunnally & Moy, 1989; Hepworth, Rooney, & Larsen, 1997; Kadushin & Kadushin, 1997; Johnson, 1997; Egan, 1998; Ivey & Ivey, 1999). Workers can choose from a continuum of responses that range from nondirective to focused questions. As a general rule, social workers use the least intrusive responses when clients concretely describe events in context and consider them in the light of their goals. Social workers employ more direct strategies for responding when clients remain ambiguous or repeat information.

A suggested range of responses that elicit the client's perspective without imposing the worker's view include: allowing space, nonverbal behaviors, verbal utterances, restatements, clarifications, summary clarifications, requests to continue, and questions (Figure 7.2). These responding skills are useful for in-person interaction with all levels of client systems, and they provide structure for designing other tools to exchange information with larger client systems.

Allowing Space

If you want to hear what clients have to say, give them the space to talk. The dialogue between social workers and clients includes moments of silence. Quiet spaces give clients chances to formulate words to express their thoughts and feelings. Quiet spaces provide opportunities for clients to participate in conversations as collaborative partners.

Allowing space is not as easy as it sounds. Most of us are socialized to fill the gaps in conversations. Add these personal tendencies to our pride in professional expertise and we may feel the pressure to have answers. To allow space, social workers resist the temptation to describe what they see or what they can guess in favor of giving clients opportunities to express their own thoughts and feelings.

Multiperson Client Systems
Allowing space has special significance in working with multiperson client systems. Here, social workers do more than control their own contributions in ways that leave individual

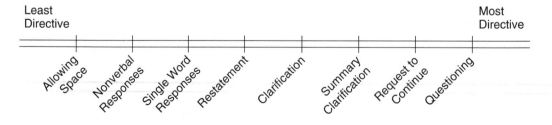

FIGURE 7.2 Response Continuum for Generalist Social Work

clients with opportunities to talk. Workers actually temper the contributions of actively verbal members to create space for more cautious members to contribute. Frequently, silent members of a system have the greatest impact. People who aren't talking have opportunities to observe and think. People who participate less frequently have the most new information to offer. Recognizing the potential resources of all members of a multiperson client system, practitioners work to create space to ensure that all members have chances to contribute.

Nonverbal Responses

Just as social workers observe clients carefully to see what they are saying nonverbally, clients pay attention to social workers' faces, hands, and bodies. The ways workers sit, the looks they give, and how they express themselves are received by clients as full of meaning. Workers can show empathy, support, and comprehension through nonverbal responses while clients talk.

Nonverbal responses send powerful, yet ambiguous messages. Each of us may interpret them differently. For example, an attentive posture with good eye contact and an occasional nod may encourage clients to continue to articulate their views. But as described earlier, there are substantial variations in the way people in various cultures view these attending behaviors (Kadushin & Kadushin, 1997). A hand gesture in the direction of a member of a client system who is not contributing may invite their participation. However, members of some cultural groups view this gesture as threatening or demanding. To discover whether a client receives the message they intend, social workers screen their nonverbal behavior for cross-cultural meanings and observe how clients react.

Single Word Responses

Sometimes, it doesn't take much for social workers to keep people talking about their situations informatively. Simple, one-word responses or even verbal utterances convey an attentive and accepting tone and keep clients talking. Examples include:

- Mmhmm…
- OK
- Yes!
- All right
- Aaah…

When social workers use simple phrases with positive connotations, they nonjudgmentally validate what clients are saying and encourage clients to continue sharing.

Restatement

Social workers can respond by repeating a client's last few words or a significant phrase. This *restatement* functions as a perception check, verifying that workers have listened. Even when social workers do not yet understand what clients are talking about, restatements encourage clients to modify their messages, clarify, and continue to add more information.

Sometimes, restatements cast information in a new light. In offering restatements, social workers select certain parts of the client's message. In this way workers use restatements purposefully to highlight information that offers a transactional view, provide glimpses of strengths, forge a sense of direction toward goals, and uncover potential solutions.

Client: I don't know what to do. Seems like every time I take him to the store, he throws a fit.

Worker: Every time you take him to the store…

* * *

Client: Sometimes I can handle it, sometimes I can't.

Worker: Sometimes you can handle it.

With restatements workers can also guide the focus of the conversation by emphasizing parts of the response with voice inflections or by adding an inquisitive tone.

Client: My mom always complains, nags, and picks on me.

Worker: Your mom *always* picks on you?

* * *

Client: I've been thinking about what I need to do to make a career change.

Worker: You're thinking about a career change?

Social workers use restatements sparingly. This type of response may fail to move conversations forward. Stringing together several restatements parrots the client and may be irritating or even sound sarcastic. Social workers select restatements when they want to emphasize clients' conclusions and ensure they have heard what clients are saying.

Restating what clients say is particularly important with multiperson client systems. This response inserts conversation breaks and discourages any one member from monopolizing exchanges, especially when the worker looks around at other members while restating the contribution. Restating what one member says emphasizes information clearly for other members of the client system to consider. When social workers use restatements, they demonstrate respect, model effective listening skills, and give other members of the client system the opportunity to respond.

Clarification

Clarifying is a more active way for social workers to check their understanding. Kadushin and Kadushin (1997) describe this as "paraphrasing" (p. 128). Here social workers may say, "So, what I hear you saying is…" followed by their best attempt to paraphrase and simplify what the client has just shared.

Client: You can't imagine the burden I feel caring for my father who has Alzheimer's. I never get out anymore. He needs around-the-clock care, can't find his way around the house, repeats the same question again and again, and doesn't sleep much. I'm afraid he's going to get out when I'm not looking, but I just can't keep my eyes on him 24 hours a day.

Worker: So, what I hear you saying is that you are having a tough time caring for your father 24 hours a day.

Clarifying what clients say has positive effects. If clients believe that social workers are on the right track, it means that social workers are listening and understanding. Clarification adds to clients' understanding of their situations.

On the other hand, a client may think the clarification off-base. This challenges clients to try again to convey their point.

Client: Men just always want to be in charge.

Worker: So, men are controlling your life.

Client: Not really. I do what I want. But my husband never listens to my opinions about how he should handle the kids even though what I do works better.

Worker: Oh, I see. You're talking about your husband and how he relates to the kids. You would like him to handle them the way you do.

Client: That's right.

Clearly there are benefits when clients discover new ways to comprehend and explain their situations. When social workers respond by clarifying, they keep clients focused and working even when workers are not completely correct in clients' eyes.

Summary Clarification

When social workers begin to notice important themes or clusters of information, they pull this content together to summarize as well as clarify. To use the summary clarification technique, social workers say things like:

- Let me see if I'm getting this all right. There seem to be three common issues that the residents are most concerned about.

Or, in keeping with a strengths-oriented perspective:

- So, it seems like each time your boss confronts you, you find ways to respond assertively yet respectfully.

In each response, the worker does two things—groups information in a logical way and uses words other than the client's to frame the situation. This response "clears the agenda of items that they have adequately discussed so that [they] can devote attention to items that [they] have not" (Kadushin & Kadushin, 1997, p. 150). Summary clarifications organize the work, prioritize the activity, and develop a focus on goals.

Request to Continue

Sometimes the best response is simply to ask clients to keep talking. Politely, many clients pause for the worker to talk, to make a contribution. When social workers sense that it's their turn to talk, they do so without interrupting clients' thinking. When needed, workers can unobtrusively request clients to continue by using short prompts like:

- Go on…
- Tell me more…
- Please, continue…
- So…
- And, then…
- Comments by others…

When clients are doing a good job of expressing and organizing their own content, social workers encourage rather than interfere with what clients are saying.

Workers sometimes respond with requests for more specific information, such as:

- Tell me more about the time when things were getting better.
- I'd like to talk about parts of your life other than school.
- It does seem like the move to the new neighborhood was significant. Please talk more about that.
- Let's explore the economic and political ramifications of the policy proposal.

Note that when asking for specific information, social workers guide clients to focus on either important issues or areas which seem confusing:

- I'd like to understand better about what you were doing differently.
- Please help me understand specifically what is happening at work.
- I want to hear more about the recreation resources for community youths.
- Help me clear up my confusion about the task force's definition of homelessness.

Requests to continue also give workers direct opportunities to highlight strengths and help clients consider areas of resources which may lead to solutions:

- Could you go over that part again about the new approach you tried?
- So, you're a successful student. Tell me more.
- Let's focus on the steps the neighborhood watch has taken that seem to be working.

Additionally, social workers broaden descriptions by requesting that clients discuss contextual elements:

- I'd like you to tell me what else is happening in your life at this time.
- So, could you list for me who else attended the public forum?
- Tell me more about the new policies your agency developed.

Emphasizing certain topics as important makes these requests for specific information powerful responses. When social workers choose this type of response early in their work with a client, they strive to focus on issues the client presents, rather than leap away from the client's agenda.

Questioning

Questioning is a directive response style which social workers use to pursue more specific, detailed information. As responses, questions merely follow up on what clients have already said. Well-framed questions invite clients to survey what they know rather than confess how they have failed. Specific questions can focus clients directly on their strengths. When social workers construct their questions carefully, they can elicit important information and still let clients lead the way.

Well-trained social workers know that respecting clients' power while asking questions is a practice skill requiring extensive preparation. Envision what it's like to be questioned. Do hot lights and smoke-filled rooms spring to mind as you are being interrogated and forced to justify yourself to the uniformed figures circling around you? Certainly, this is not the atmosphere that social workers want to create as they gather information from clients. Experienced practitioners use questions selectively and phrase them carefully!

Phrasing Questions Is Important

Depending on how social workers ask questions, clients experience them as intrusive and confrontive or as interested and supportive. Questions that seek descriptive information begin with words such as "who," "what," "when," "how often," and "in what way." These questions lead to important concrete and contextual information. In contrast to the judgmental message of "why" questions, "who," "what," "when," "how often," and "in what way" questions are objective and seek information that is readily available.

Social workers avoid questions beginning with "why." "Why" questions force respondents to rationally account for their behavior, although often people do not know "why" they've acted as they have (Kadushin & Kadushin, 1997). Additionally, the word "why" insinuates disapproval and displeasure (Benjamin, 1987). When social workers use "why" questions, they cast doubts on the choices clients have made and produce defensive postures. Consider how the following questions elicit a greater understanding of what clients are saying. When a client says, "He always lets me down," social workers can respond by asking:

- Who is the "he" that you're talking about?
- In what way does he let you down?
- How does this interfere with what you are trying to accomplish?
- What do you think is getting in his way?
- Always? Is there ever a time when he doesn't?

Notice the common elements of these questions. Each question follows up directly on the client's assertion. Each seeks to elicit concrete information about the client's thinking and the events that are occurring. The worker doesn't search for whom to blame, look for why the behavior occurs, or question whether the representation of the event is "really" true. Each question demonstrates acceptance of the client's experience and the associated feelings. Questions work best when they relate directly to what clients say and when answers will add new information to what the partners are exploring.

Combining Responses

In practice, social workers weave combinations of these responses together to facilitate a clear articulation of a client's thoughts. Some clients offer considerable information with little prompting. Others need more direct approaches to explain their situations in concrete and helpful ways. Empowering social workers choose the least directive responses possible that still keep the partners on track. The more clients do on their own, the less directive social workers become.

Practice Example

Understanding the nature of challenges and learning responding skills prepares practitioners to talk with clients. Review the following dialogue to discover the orientation to the future, transactional focus, positive tone, and variety of responses with which Alex Anderson, a practitioner from Northside Prevention Services, responds to Don who calls their telephone hotline.

Alex: Hello. This is the Listening Line. I'm Alex.

Don: Hi. I'm Don.

Alex: Hi, Don. (allows space for client to continue)

Don: You probably want to know why I'm calling.

Alex: Whatever you'd like to tell me.

Don: Well, I've got this problem.

Alex: OK.

Don: You see, I'm the child of an alcoholic.

Alex: Uh huh.

Don: And my life is a mess.

Alex: In what way, a mess?

Don: I can't seem to get anywhere.

Alex: Some place specific in mind?

Don: Yes, a place that's not so lonely.

Alex: A place that's not so lonely. Who might be there?

Don: Friends, family…mostly family.

Alex: Mostly family.

Don: My parents and my sister.

Alex: Seems like you're missing your parents and your sister.

Don: Sometimes.

Alex: I'd like to hear more about your parents and sister.

Don: What do you what to know?

Alex: I guess I'd like to hear the things you think are most important.

Don: Well, I haven't seen them for a while.

Alex: A while?

Don: About six months.

Alex: So, it's been about six months, since…

Don: The big fight.

Alex: The big fight?

Don: Yes, my fight with Dad.

Alex: (waits for client to continue)

Don: The fight where he kicked me out…or I left…I'm not real sure.

Alex: Kind of a mutual thing, huh?

Don: Yes. I guess I just needed some space, but I really wasn't ready for quite this much. Besides, I get concerned about Anna.

Alex: Anna?

Don: My sister.

Alex: So you're concerned about your sister Anna?

Don: Yes, having to deal with my parents and their drinking. It's a lot for a 13 year old.

Alex: So, tell me more.

Don: Well, you probably know the story. Mom and dad go out and drink and then come home and pick on us kids. I used to take most of the heat, but since I moved out I'm sure they're doing it to Anna.

Alex: So let me get this straight. You are calling with a couple of concerns. First, you are kind of missing contact with your family since you haven't seen them for six months. And secondly, you are wondering how your sister is coping with your parents' drinking since you left.

Don: You got it.

Alex: Anything else?

Don: I guess not.

Alex: Seems like you are thinking about changing this situation.

Don: I'm not liking the way things are.

Alex: So is this call the beginning of changing things or are you also doing other things to change this situation?

Don: Well, I wrote my folks a letter, but I didn't mail it.

Alex: You wrote your folks a letter?

Don: Yes, I worked on it a long time.

Alex: What do you think you'll do with it?

Don: I might mail it. I might deliver it in person. I might throw it away.

Alex: You do have a lot of options.

Don: I do, don't I?

Alex: Seems like it.

Don: You know, now that I have written it out, I could probably even talk to them directly about it.

Alex: You do have a lot of options.

Don: I'll have to think about it.

Alex: Well, you seem like a thoughtful person. I have a sense that you'll figure out what to do next.

Don: Well, it's time to do something. I'll just have to decide what.

Alex: Is that something that you want my help with?

Don: Not right now I don't think.

Alex: OK? Sounds like you're on the way to solving this one.

Don: I think maybe you're right.

Alex: Anything else to talk about with me?

Don: Not right now.

Alex: Feel free to call back if you want to keep thinking out loud, if you're looking for a referral someplace, or whatever.

Don: Thanks. I will.

Alex: Good luck, Don.

Alex gently steers Don toward a positive, transactional, and forward-looking orientation. To do this, Alex uses deliberate responses that maintain the centrality of Don's message while organizing and making his presenting challenge more concrete. An effective social worker learns communication and listening skills to respond to clients in ways that balance respect for their views while moving them forward toward resolutions.

Responding to Feelings

The human experience of feeling differs from the experience of thinking. We acknowledge this difference by contrasting what is in our hearts with that which is in our heads. Both information from our heads and from our hearts fuel positive growth and change. All events have associated feelings. As social workers, we encourage clients to identify and articulate feelings by responding to feelings that we observe.

Identifying and expressing feelings benefits everyone. Feelings provide clues about where we stand on things, directions to take, and information about what works. Defining and describing our emotions gives us a sense of control over who we are and how we react. Expressing feelings allows us to be close to and validated by others. The consequences of not expressing feelings include loss of information, sense of isolation, projection of emotions into situations where they don't fit, and even physical and emotional illnesses (Johnson, 1997). When social workers assist clients in accessing their feelings, they empower clients with new information, acceptance, and a sense of control.

The Experience of Feelings

Sharing our thoughts and describing our feelings are very different experiences. For example, running into an old friend at a conference is an observable event that may engender an entire constellation of feelings from surprise to joy to awkwardness. We can readily share our thoughts about the event by remembering and reporting. But when describing the associated feelings, we may be plagued by their ambiguity. For some of us, feelings may be more difficult than thoughts to identify, define, and express. As we try to articulate how we feel about the event of running into an old friend, we may struggle with the task.

Feelings are associated with events occurring within us or outside of us. Feelings are not the events themselves but the emotional associations we have with these events. Feelings may be ambiguous and sometimes surprising or contradictory. Clients may struggle with expressing their feelings, and social workers, likewise, may have difficulty reading the emotions clients express. Social workers and clients work together as partners to identify, verbalize, and validate feelings.

Identifying Feelings

Clients have abundant feelings—about themselves and their situations and about themselves as clients and their social workers. All of these feelings are important in guiding the social work process. Social workers prepare to respond to a client's affect by learning to identify the multiple ways people express feelings and by understanding the cultural implications of such expressions.

With some people, talking about feelings is easy. They relate comfortably on the affective level, expressing feelings directly, articulately, and automatically. But more consistently, clients express feelings nonverbally through facial expressions, voice tone, body posture, and choices of words. Observant social workers select responses to clarify verbal and nonverbal expressions of emotion.

Verbalizing Feelings

As clients describe the events in their lives, the associated feelings show up, either tumbling out verbally as part of the reporting of events or surfacing in nonverbal behaviors. Feelings vary in intensity—from mild to strong, barely noticeable to preoccupying. When social workers see clients express feelings, they respond with verbal reflections which attempt to match both the feeling and its intensity. Social workers make educated guesses about a client's feelings and actively engage the client as an expert to either validate or correct their perceptions.

Following a simple strategy, social workers use reflective skills to identify feelings (Table 7.2). First, workers scan the client's information and behavior for the feeling. Second, they tentatively attach a descriptive label to the feeling. Third, they enhance the client's understanding of the feeling by connecting it with the precipitating event or behavior. Clients benefit from information that links feelings to thoughts. For example, a social worker may say:

- It seems like you're feeling proud of things you've accomplished to this point, especially your success in parenting.
- I may be detecting a note of sarcasm when you talk about the possibility of your promotion.
- I'm sensing a glimmer of hope when you describe your new approach.
- Look's like you're really angry that the state cut back your funding.
- Seems hopeless since each time you complain to the police, nothing seems to change.

As workers offer hunches about what feelings clients may be experiencing, they make their suggestions tentatively. Workers are actually guessing when they reflect a client's feel-

TABLE 7.2   Constructing a Reflection of Feelings

Step #1	Observe for feelings in verbal and nonverbal expression.
Step #2	Tentatively identify the feeling in words.
Step #3	Connect the feeling expressed to the associated events or thoughts.
Step #4	Reflect the feeling to the client verbally using some variation of the formula: It seems that you are feeling _____(the feeling)_____, when you talk about _____(the event or thought)_____.
Step #5	Wait for the client's response to agree or disagree with the reflection.
Step #6	If the client agrees, accept and validate the feeling. If the client disagrees, go through the steps to try again.
Step #7	Remember that feelings are always correct. You need not approve or disapprove of them. Simply, accept them.

ings. Only clients know for sure whether the worker's hunch accurately reflects their emotional experiences. Social workers must check out their perceptions. In the subjective world of feelings, only clients can know for sure!

Notice that nowhere in the process of accessing and expressing feelings do workers directly ask "How do you feel?" Experienced social workers will tell you that the most likely response to "How do you feel?" is an honest "I don't know." Right now, ask yourself the question, "How do I feel?" There is nothing like direct questioning about feelings to send every concept in your mind running for cover. Many of us just go blank or struggle to defend our positions. Pursuing feelings directly from clients often obscures them, rather than bringing them out. Social workers nurture feelings forward with hunches and observations rather than chase them with probing questions.

Validating Feelings

Clients are always right about their feelings. Each and every human being is the one and only expert about how he or she feels. Feelings don't have to make sense; they are entirely personal and subjective experiences. And importantly, feelings do not mandate behavior. Consider this dramatic example. Even when a father reveals to his social worker that he has sexual feelings toward his daughter, he has done nothing wrong unless he acts on those feelings. In fact, by expressing this feeling he is actually doing something right. In doing so, he creates the opportunity to take charge of his feelings rather than have his feelings lead him toward problematic behavior. Social workers acknowledge even this feeling, reinforce the client's trust in sharing, and work quickly to enable the client with the capability to make other choices.

Partnerships grow stronger as clients articulate feelings and social workers accept them. Clients bring with them abundant information about feelings associated with past events as well as their immediate situations. As social workers build professional relationships with diverse clients, they implement cross-cultural skills for communicating about feelings appropriately with diverse clients.

Special Issues in Responding

Certain actions by clients deserve special consideration; they call for thoughtful responses by social workers. Experienced social workers learn successful ways to respond to clients' anger, silence, questions, and feedback while still maintaining openness and equality in the relationship.

Responding to Anger

Naturally, anger is an emotion expressed in many social work encounters. Challenging situations can lead to frustration, disappointment, pain, and sadness—all feelings closely associated with and sometimes expressed by anger. When we hurt, we lash out. When clients hurt, social workers are frequently the targets. Self-confident social workers encourage and validate clients' expression of anger even when it volleys directly toward them. Additionally, workers respond to expressions of anger as opportunities to look for other associated feelings and information.

Each of us has our own degree of comfort with expressing and responding to anger. When clients express anger, social workers respond as they respond to any other feeling they observe: they reflect the feeling to heighten clients' awareness and invite them to clarify their responses.

- You seem angry…
- I can see you are upset…
- Makes you mad, huh?

Practitioners connect the feeling to the associated events, in ways such as:

- You seem angry, when you talk about the way the media puts down your neighborhood.
- When I mention Child Protective Services, I can see your anger.
- Seems to me that you're upset about my suggestion to get information from your probation officer.

Finally, social workers recognize, accept, and validate feelings of anger. They accept the feeling as okay, even good to express, with phrases such as:

- I can understand how this makes you angry. I appreciate that you trusted me enough to share that.
- Feels good to get angry sometimes.
- Go ahead, talk about it. It's okay to be mad.

Generally, when people express anger, this outward expression reflects internal pain. Often, people respond to their own experience of pain by defending their vulnerability with anger. Social workers reach beyond the expression of anger to identify and reflect a client's internal turmoil and pain rather than simply leaving this emotion at the surface level:

- You look angry, but it seems to me you feel sad.
- Makes you mad to feel so helpless, doesn't it?
- I'd probably be fighting back too, if I felt so vulnerable.

As more emotions surface, sensitive social workers maintain an accepting and supportive atmosphere. Workers respond with the same empathetic, reflective, and informative style used to respond to all feelings.

Sometimes, when clients express anger toward social workers, their anger contains a specific message. In other words, the anger is not misplaced or symbolic of internal pain, but the client is actually upset at something the worker is or is not doing. Maybe the social worker is crowding the client, trying to get too close too fast. Maybe, the worker is missing the point or not responding in ways that show understanding and empathy. Maybe, the worker is falling prey to prejudices and stereotypes and not seeing clients for who they really are. Here too, nondefensive responses clarify feedback:

- So, you're upset with my questions?
- You're angry because I interrupted you?
- In your view, I'm just another white person who can't understand a black man?

Anger communicates important information. Workers strive to extract this information for the feedback it provides to guide the relationship productively.

Responding to Silence

In responding to silence, remember the rule in communication: "one cannot not communicate" (Watzlawick, Bavelas, & Jackson, 1967, p. 49). Even silent clients tell us things about themselves. "One of the most significant sounds that requires listening to is the sound of silence and the associated messages of omission. What interviewees avoid saying is as important as what they do say. Not talking is a special way of talking" (Kadushin & Kadushin, 1997, p. 214).

Consider these possible meanings of silence: "I don't want to be here." "It's hopeless." "Leave me alone." "I don't trust you." "I don't trust words." "You might think you are in control, but you can't make me talk." "I don't understand a thing you're saying." According to Laird (1993):

> *Meanings and forms vary cross-culturally, in the ways that silence is used linguistically to foster talk, display anger, suppress or hide difference, maintain control, achieve certain ends, manage emotions, or as part of culturally institutionalized rituals. Silence can spring from fear, from loneliness, from resistance, from the will to survive, from the effort to escape stigmatization, from choice, from strength, from the desire to manipulate others. Silence is as powerful if not more powerful in intersubjective discourses as talk. (p. 248)*

Silence is ambiguous, so, in responding, the worker's empathy and imagination come into play. Social workers formulate hunches about what clients mean by considering contextual elements, nonverbal cues, and the client's characteristics. If a client is involuntary, a lack of trust and the need for some control is likely. If a client is adolescent, withdrawal from and resistance to adults is age appropriate. If the client smiles blankly, a polite lack of understanding may be evident. If the client is Japanese American, silence may show respect for the social worker (Sue & Sue, 1999). If clients have been victimized by severe oppression or abuse, their poverty of words may reveal the void in their sense of self (Belenky, Clinchy, Goldberger, & Tarule, 1986). If the client is a recent immigrant, language and cultural differences may show up in silence. Workers make their best determination about what clients are saying with their silence, verbalize it, and wait for clients to modify the guess to a more accurate view.

Social workers respond verbally to a client's silence. Workers have conversations with clients as if the clients themselves were talking, as in their own way they are. Social workers phrase their responses in ways that invite clients to talk, rather than chase them with probing questions. Social workers may say:

- Must be tough for you to be here just because someone told you you had to come.
- Kind of seems hopeless to try again on something that you've been trying to deal with for so long.
- I can understand how it might be hard to trust a stranger, especially an older person like me. Take your time. Only tell me things when you are ready.
- Is this making sense to you? Could I ask you to explain what you hear me saying?
- ¿Comprende usted? ¿Habla usted inglés?

Whether clients respond verbally or nonverbally, workers continue to converse, providing clients with ample opportunities to talk.

Responding to Questions

Clients ask questions too. Frequently, clients have questions about the social worker's credentials, the agency's procedures, or what the worker is saying. Questions are good signs. They often indicate a developing partnership in which clients feel free to assert their needs and express their curiosity. When clients actively take charge of eliciting information, they exercise their power. Workers encourage clients' power by acknowledging their rights to information and by providing appropriately direct and honest answers.

Certain questions require cautious responses. Frequently, clients seek advice with questions: "What would you do if you were in my situation?" "So which one of us is right?" "What should I do?" Social workers who fall prey to this invitation to be experts find themselves trapped by the dependencies they create in clients. An empowering response is one that recognizes the client's need for assistance evident in the advice-seeking question, yet returns the responsibility for solutions to the partnership. Social workers can say:

- I know you'd like me to give you the answer. Trouble is I don't have it.
- I appreciate your confidence in me, but this must be a tough issue or you would have solved it without me.
- Maybe when I know you and your situation better I can let you know what I think, but right now you know a lot more than I do about what is going on.
- I don't know who's right. Probably you both have valid points.

Social workers always respond to questions, but choose responses that respect the client's expertise.

Responding to Feedback from Clients

As social workers, we benefit from candid appraisals by clients. Clients know best what helps and what does not. We accept, respect, and even encourage clients to make comments concerning both us and the practice process. This means accepting clients' positive commentaries as well as their negative perceptions of who we are as people and professionals.

Social workers learn skills to accept feedback. They prepare themselves for nondefensive listening. They respond with appreciation and enthusiasm to feedback from clients.

- I appreciate your honesty in telling me when I'm off base.
- Thanks for trusting me enough to share that with me.
- I appreciate your telling me how much you enjoy coming here. I think we make a good team, too.
- So, you think I'm not understanding your point of view. I'm glad you let me know. What's the piece you think I'm missing?
- I can understand how it might be difficult to talk to a man about this. How can we make it easier?

Informed social workers incorporate client feedback into the professional relationship and the direction of the work.

Responding to Larger Client Systems

Generalist social workers respond to client systems of all sizes—clients with whom it is necessary to have a continuing dialogue. At all levels of practice workers will respond to clients to elicit their views and to validate their feelings. Practice with any size client requires a worker's "one-with-one" conversational ability. Dialogue with larger client systems places workers in a matrix of conversations.

When practitioners work with larger client systems, they must balance the rights of individuals with the rights of others. This ethical challenge raises numerous questions. For example, is it acceptable for one person within the client group to be the spokesperson? Does everyone need to contribute equally? What if people disagree? How does the social worker respond to each individual member of a system, yet respect the functioning of the group? Two skills—facilitating discussion and respecting existing functioning—provide answers to these questions.

Facilitating Discussion

Social workers coordinate traffic when responding to multiperson client systems (Henry, 1992). They actively involve themselves with the client group to influence "who talks when about what." Social workers guide the interaction so that only one person talks at a time, members listen and respond to one another, all members have opportunities to express their views, and the contributions of all members receive validation and respect. To accomplish this, social workers use a variety of methods.

Workers model effective communication by responding in ways that make the thoughts and feelings of all participants more concrete. Workers frequently summarize the group's discussion, highlighting areas of agreement and clarifying options. When others interrupt, contradict, or let one person monopolize, social workers take more active roles. When more than one member talks at once, social workers may say:

- I love people who talk, but I need it one at a time so I can take it all in.
- I see you both have information. Who wants to start?
- Whoa. There is a lot of enthusiasm here. Good! I want to hear what each of you has to say.

Or social workers may respond nonverbally and:

- Attend to the person who was first talking through eye contact and body posture; then, immediately turn to elicit the view of the person who was interrupting at the first available pause.
- Acknowledge the member's desire to contribute with a hand gesture that holds back the person's contribution temporarily; then, wave them on to share when possible.

When people's different views lead to conflict, workers may say:

- You both have interesting views. I guess there's more than one way to look at this situation.
- You know, no two people see the same thing the same way. I'm sure you're both right.
- Well, that's two ways to look at it. Anyone have another way?
- I love it when people disagree. It always gives you more options.

When one member monopolizes, workers recognize the mutual responsibility of the talking and the silent members by responding:

- Thanks for all the information. You're really working hard here. Maybe somebody else should take it for a while.
- Well, I think I understand your views. I'm going to need everyone's for this to work. Who's up next?
- You really have a good grasp of the situation. What can the rest of you tell me?
- That was a bold move to go first, and now you get to relax and listen while the others talk.

Social workers respond in ways that appreciate contributions yet redirect interactions. Workers validate contributions, encourage participation, and organize the flow of information.

Respecting Existing Functioning

When one member says more or less than another, this does not mean that social workers must intervene. Workers trust that systems have their own style of presenting information and working on issues. How each system member contributes may actually draw on the strengths of the system. Some client systems work best with a combination of talkers and listeners, up-front doers and behind-the-scenes planners. For example, within a given family, a parent who spends more time with the child concerned logically has more to contribute to describing events.

Formal client systems such as organizations are likely to have prescribed interactional processes. With such clients, workers show respect for the organization's structure and practices. For example, if an organization decides through a consensus process that a certain committee will speak for the group, rights of individuals are still assured.

As long as the system operates in a way that respects the contributions of all its members, workers have no reason to interfere. Even when the interaction inhibits the contributions of some members and overburdens others, social workers respect the strength of the client system to operate in a way that suits it best at this time. Sometimes systems correct themselves in ways that facilitate the process. At other times, workers may gradually take more direct approaches to redistribute the control of the conversation.

Reflecting Back

Articulating situations means detailing the core presenting issues from the client's perspective and placing these events in environmental context. The temptation in this process is for social workers to become overly directive in their efforts to frame this information in a useful way. How much power can a social worker leverage in this exchange without derailing collaboration and undermining client empowerment? How might this power balance be affected by culture, worker and client assumptions, or agency expectations? Consider ways to monitor the dialogue between social worker and client to achieve an effective balance of control.

Looking Forward

Articulating issues using a challenge model adds future, transactional, and positive dimensions to the problems clients face. This process is one piece of what practitioners do in order to "begin where the client is." But "where clients are" is not exclusively a place of problems. Even when things look bleak, not everything is going wrong. Clients have resources even in the most difficult times.

For workers to discover available strengths within clients and their environments, they must first help clients define a positive direction. Chapter 8 presents processes that workers implement to assist clients in describing positive directions for their work. In the context of these preliminary goals, workers are then able to initiate a focused search for relevant resources.

Chapter 8

Defining Directions

It's the second Tuesday of the month and members of the Northside Network are gathering for their monthly brown bag luncheon. Established less than three months ago, the Northside Network is a consortium of human service agencies with representatives from all over the Northside community. Network members are quickly discovering that, in spite of the differences in the services that each provides, they really have much in common. As part of the same community, they confront similar community problems and draw from the same selection of resources and opportunities for the clients each serves.

During the first two meetings, members of the group spent time getting to know one another and organizing a structure to guide the functioning of the group. Now it is time to look ahead. Beyond a consensus on working together, members have yet to decide a specific purpose for the Network. Miriam Andovich calls the meeting to order, part of her role as facilitator and the beginning of her work to guide the group to develop a coherent direction for action.

Miriam works in the AIDS prevention project at the Northside Alliance for Family Health. And, today she is the facilitator for the Northside Network—a role that rotates among the group's members. Miriam shifts her focus to the group as a whole and uses many of the same generalist practice skills to facilitate its functioning as she uses with clients in the AIDS prevention project. Miriam suggests the group begin today's work with a brief structured experience she calls "the Network News." She asks that each member take two minutes to update the others about newsworthy events at their agencies. Miriam believes that for the group to decide where they are going they should first establish where they are.

One by one, workers describe current issues affecting the agencies they represent. Tony Marelli announces that the Addictions Recovery Center has new funds for in-school prevention programming, but so far no schools have applied. Mark Nogales describes his organization's concerns about a reduction in participation by county residents in the programs of the County Mental Health Center. Kay Landon notes that the Family Support Program is seeking funds to hire interpreters and bilingual staff. Andrea Barry describes the frustration workers in the Family Preservation Program are experiencing in helping clients locate low-cost housing. The waiting lists for public assistance housing are growing and low-cost private rentals are virtually nonexistent. All Network members contribute their own perspectives on what's happening in the Northside community.

As members report, Miriam writes their comments on large sheets of paper mounted on the wall behind her. Next, she poses the questions: What are our common concerns? What themes are evident that might begin to define our purpose? As members offer their ideas, Miriam responds in ways to encourage interaction, to summarize and clarify what members say, and to guide members to synthesize ideas. Soon, similar opinions about "getting rid of so many restrictions to services" and "simplifying intake processes" lead the members to identify the umbrella issue of accessibility of services as an apparent unifying theme. Miriam sums up the group's direction by saying, "So, our purpose will be to increase the accessibility of our services for the urban and rural county residents." A quick check of members confirms this common purpose. The members act to make their consensus an official agreement or "contract" by proposing it as a formal motion, approving it with a unanimous vote, and recording the transaction in the minutes.

Identifying accessibility as the central issue focuses the group's discussion. Ideas surface concerning community education about available services, services at no cost to clients or based on the clients' abilities to pay, better transportation for clients to reach agencies, staff and community training on cultural sensitivity, more in-home services, and the need to examine restrictive guidelines and eligibility requirements for various programs. Members acknowledge each idea's merit but agree that choosing specific "solutions" right now is premature. No one can say with certainty what poses significant barriers or what actions will have the greatest influence on service accessibility. Members will need a more detailed assessment to focus their efforts on activities that will do the most good.

Before adjourning, several members volunteer to participate on a committee to develop a community resource assessment plan. Implementing this assessment, members will discover which factors currently enhance accessibility and which create obstacles. The more complete assessment information will then contribute to the members' efforts to develop a workable and concrete plan of action.

Miriam's interaction with the Northside Network illustrates how a practitioner assists a community-based organization to define a direction for its work. The same processes apply to practice at other system levels. Both clients and social workers participate in developing a mutual direction. Clients bring their own motivations, sense of destination, and rights to self-determination. Social workers balance their respect for client privileges with their own vision of what could be. Clients benefit from this early effort to define a mutual purpose. "Only when people start creating scenarios of possibility do they move in directions more satisfying to them and the problems become lost or much less influential" (Saleebey, 1994, p. 357).

This chapter describes how social workers and clients define a direction for their work. It also examines priority issues that may arise requiring an immediate response. In detail, this chapter:

- Considers the importance of determining an initial direction
- Outlines processes for envisioning positive outcomes
- Presents ways for workers to activate the motivations of clients
- Discusses how to work collaboratively with clients who are involuntary and those who resist
- Explores preemptive actions for responding to crisis situations including recent trauma, self-destructive behaviors, abuse, potential violence, and threats to survival

Agreeing to a common purpose for the relationship constructs an achievable vision of the future, activates clients to participate in the change process, and directs the search for available resources.

Transforming Challenges into Directions

Defining a direction is the process of negotiating a mutually agreeable purpose or preliminary goal. It logically precedes other actions taken by workers and clients to assess resources or develop an intervention plan (Figure 8.1). In other words, workers and clients postpone setting very specific goals at this early juncture in lieu of establishing a more global initial direction for the work. This beginning agreement about the purpose of the relationship guides the dialogue until gathering enough information to frame a concrete

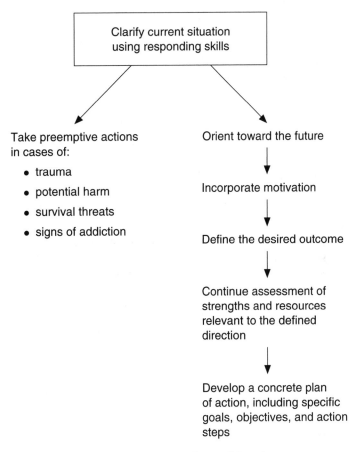

FIGURE 8.1   The Process of Defining Directions

intervention plan with more specific goals and objectives—a plan informed by a goal-focused assessment.

Strength-oriented social workers recognize the benefit of a vision of the future, so they move quickly to "define directions" with their clients. Consequently, this exchange about setting a preliminary direction may occur early in the conversation between a worker and a client system. Oftentimes, clients begin the dialogue at intake by describing what they hope to achieve. In the case of an individual or family client, a practitioner might come to an agreement with the client within a few short minutes of beginning the initial interchange. In contrast, the diversity of perspectives in larger client systems will likely require more dialogue before participants can negotiate a common direction. With client systems at any level, workers may need to nudge clients beyond describing only their present difficulties toward considering future possibilities and constructing their visions of how things should be.

Reshaping a report of a challenging situation into a clear direction empowers and informs social workers and their clients in several ways. First, clients are most likely to achieve outcomes that they can clearly envision (Walter & Peller, 1992). Second, workers learn what clients want, an important context in which to view the information clients offer. For example, understanding a client's overall purpose helps to determine the significance of problematic events and also to identify resources for building a solution. And finally, pausing to consider a preliminary sense of direction gives a generalist social worker time to explore the transactional dimensions of the situation, thereby broadening the field of potential solutions to all system levels.

Orienting Forward, Not Back

Clients invariably know the reasons they seek services from social work professionals. Most often, they want some change in their present situations. For the most positive impact, solution-oriented workers urge clients to go beyond simply identifying what they want to change to describing in detail how they would like it to be. Workers invite clients to "construct a vision of an alternative future that concretely identifies what will be present in a more satisfying future and that focuses on what clients might do differently to make that future happen" (Berg & De Jong, 1996, p. 381). So, logically, in empowerment-based social work practice, social workers ask some variation of the question, "What is your goal in coming here?" (Walter & Peller, 1992). This question directs helping relationships away from describing problems toward constructing solutions, from *what is* to *what will be.*

Social workers assist clients in visualizing what they want. This transforms the conversation from what is not working to the more empowering view of an outcome that could actually happen as the partners work together. Observe the dialogue in which Vanessa, a social worker in the State's Child Protective Unit, responds to focus Kim toward the future.

Vanessa: I understand that you are here to talk about ways to stop hitting your son when he talks back.

Kim: That's right. He'll report me for child abuse if I do it again.

Vanessa: OK. If you're not going to hit your son when he talks back, what do you see yourself doing instead?

Kim: I guess I'll do nothing.

Vanessa: By doing nothing, do you mean that you will allow him to talk back while you just stand there and ignore him or will you just walk away? What exactly are you hoping to do?

Kim: I'm not really sure. I know I can't hit him. I'll get in trouble. He's getting too big and it doesn't help anyway. I really wish he just wouldn't talk back. Then I wouldn't have to do anything.

Vanessa: Seems like you're telling me that the first step will be to ignore your son or walk away when he talks back, but in the long run you'd really like to have him talk with you more respectfully.

Kim: That's right. How can I do that?

Vanessa: I'm not sure right now, but it does give us a general direction to move in. We probably need to start by getting more information about what's going on with you, your son, and your situation before we can figure out specific ways to help you and your son talk together more respectfully.

In this example, Vanessa and Kim quickly determine a positive direction for their work. Notice how Vanessa facilitates this task by responding in ways that enable Kim to maintain control of the general purpose of the relationship while, at the same time, gently reorienting Kim away from describing current dilemmas and forward to look at future solutions.

Framing the Search for Resources

Outcomes that clients can imagine and describe are necessary for success. A view of where you are going gives perspective to the situations that challenge you and guides your exploration for available resources which may be relevant. The role of solution-focused practitioners is "to invite clients to explore and define two matters: (1) what it is they want different in their lives (goals) and (2) what strengths and resources they can bring to bear on making these desired differences a reality" (Berg & De Jong, 1996, p. 377). Social workers know where to steer assessment processes after the desired outcome is clear.

You can see how helpful defining a concrete outcome can be in framing an assessment process if you apply it to the previous example of Kim and Vanessa. Knowing what Kim wants leads Vanessa to focus directly on those resources Kim has to help her talk with her son more respectfully. Vanessa can now orient the dialogue toward times when Kim either walked away before hitting her son or was able to discuss issues with him in a calm manner. Both partners will consider what strengths Kim has drawn on in these times when she felt most effective. Vanessa and Kim can also look for exceptions to the occurrence of the problem, a promising area to explore that may hold clues about resources for a workable solution. Knowing what might be an exception or a relevant strength is only possible in the context of how Kim wants things to be. The agreement about the purpose of the relationship brings specificity to the process and is a necessary prerequisite to discovering useful resources. Chapters 9 and 10 outline specific strategies and suggest tools for assessing client strengths and environmental resources in the context of a clearly defined direction. Chapter 11 details the process of analysis and planning.

Integrating Transactional Dimensions

Setting goals without first developing an ecosystemic understanding is premature from the point of view of generalist practice. When a social worker and client set concrete goals quickly in a brief conversation that stops short of exploring the environmental context, they may miss significant associated issues. Planning too quickly can overemphasize the responsibility of clients to make changes within their own systems while underestimating the potential of their social and physical environments to hold solutions. In other words, we may be asking clients to change themselves (since that is now what we know most about) while ignoring the possible benefits of modifying the world to enhance their well-being.

Reconsider the previous example. What if Kim's unemployment adds stress or fears for her son's safety in the neighborhood and a sense of desperation to her parenting? What if the community's discrimination against Vietnamese immigrants or the housing authority's policy of refusing housing to families without credit histories contributes to a simmering tension in the household which triggers aggression in any difficult interaction? If, early on, a social worker and client set goals which narrowly focus on changing the client's behavior, significant transactional elements may go undetected as possible paths to solutions. Developing an ecosystemic perspective through a broader assessment prior to establishing more concrete goals and plans of action gives flexibility and adds a generalist focus to the process.

Considering Client Motivation

Some social workers summarily dismiss unsuccessful outcomes with a simple, "this client isn't sufficiently motivated." This attitude fails to consider the notion that all behavior is motivated, including such "unmotivated" behaviors as disinterest in service plans, resistance to change, or withdrawal from service. Simply, client behavior, like all human behavior, is motivated toward some end, even if it is not in the direction social workers anticipate.

Clients go where they are motivated to go within the boundaries of resources and constraints. Directions toward goals that will enhance motivation are those that clients believe will result in better conditions, more satisfying situations, and enhanced competence. Clients would be foolhardy indeed to pursue goals they think will do more harm than good or that lead in directions that are unrewarding. Logically, their motives would direct their energies elsewhere. Workers help clients envision desirable outcomes that will motivate their participation and provide a continuing incentive for following through.

A Transactional View of Motivation

Social work has traditionally defined motivation as an individual attribute, something that clients either have or do not have, bring or fail to bring. Motivation is not a characteristic trait of personality or individual functioning, but rather motivation is a product of interactions (Moore-Kirkland, 1981). When understanding motivation as a transactional concept rather than a personal trait, social workers move beyond the tendency to assess behavior as unmotivated or resistive. Instead, they examine the interactions among the client system, the social worker, and the environment for clues to understand the underlying motivation of behavior.

Social workers share responsibilities for incorporating and maintaining clients' motivation to participate in and continue the work. To mobilize motivation, workers employ strategies such as intensifying emotions, enhancing goal states, and altering environmental constraints (Moore-Kirkland, 1981). Early in the process, workers attempt to sustain excitement for engaging in change activities, reduce anxiety that can inhibit a client's actions, and activate emotional arousal by acknowledging the possibility of change.

Motivating Clients Who Have Given Up

Many clients need a motivational boost before they are ready to search for and activate dormant resources. These clients have learned that despite their best efforts, they have been unable to achieve successes. Life has convinced them they are helpless. Researchers have observed this phenomenon, documenting that a chronic lack of success results in a lack of motivation to continue to try (Seligman, 1975; Abramson, Seligman, & Teasdale, 1978).

Clients in oppressive situations may find themselves in this state of learned helplessness. Social structures continue to disenfranchise these clients and keep them from their rightful share of societal resources. Workers can address this situation in four steps by:

- Listening to and validating the client's frustrating experiences
- Framing an achievable direction
- Expressing belief in the worker's and client's abilities to reach the desired outcome
- Searching for resources to effect sociopolitical change

Recognizing Feelings of Hopelessness

Oppression is a real event in the everyday lives of many people. To begin a motivational process with clients who experience oppression, social workers must first recognize and validate the reality of oppression as clients tell their stories. A generalist social worker will likely have similar stories from others to share in the current dialogue to let clients know that they are not alone in their feelings of frustration. Workers should also share how other clients were able to overcome their hopelessness and achieve their goals. For example, Saleebey (1994) describes the efforts of social work students placed in public housing to spread "tales of survival under difficult conditions; stories about compassion, about 'grace under pressure'; tales of accomplishment; and word pictures of people acting effectively with dignity" (p. 356).

Visualizing Positive Outcomes

Workers help clients who feel hopeless define a positive direction. Clients benefit from looking ahead, as looking ahead provides an optimistic context in which to view their present difficulties. Research documents that setting goals increases motivation. Bandura and Cervone (1983) describe a relationship between feelings of self-efficacy, motivation to achieve a self-prescribed goal, and gains in performance. In other words, people made the most progress when they had clear visions of where they were going, participated in defining the direction, and believed that they could achieve their goal. For clients to maintain motivation and keep working in the here-and-now, they need a sense that the end product is in sight. Together, workers and clients can co-construct a new vision for the future and work concretely to achieve it.

Expressing Hope and Optimism

To motivate a client who feels hopeless, workers must bring hope to the situation. Underlying the worker's efforts to instill hope is the worker's belief that the client can achieve. Assumptions that all clients have strengths and recognition of the transactional and transitory nature of challenges contribute to a new understanding that positive changes can occur even for clients who initially view their situations as hopeless. A worker's optimism that a client can achieve is contagious. It begins to construct a reality of alternatives and options that previously seemed unavailable to clients.

Aligning Worker and Client Motivations

Since all human behavior is motivated, we can conclude that clients and workers alike bring motivations to the professional relationship. When workers and clients unite to move in the same direction, this alliance itself becomes a powerful resource in the process. Each validates the sense of purpose in the other. Each contemplates and initiates actions toward the desired outcome. Each has an investment in reaching a common destination. But when workers and clients are heading in different directions, even the most vigorous efforts of one can be neutralized by the energetic efforts of the other. Before clients and workers forge a path ahead, they need to talk enough about where they are going to agree on a mutual direction.

Motivating Larger Systems

Work with larger systems builds on the motivation of individual members. In large client systems, the key is to activate maximum involvement by as many members as possible. In the example of the Northside Network which opens this chapter, all members will report the group's activities to their own colleagues to generate enthusiasm and receive additional input. They will also update their supervisors, administrators, and boards of directors about the Network's activities in order to retain their agencies' official sanctions. Each agency will want assurances that the goals of the Network mesh with its own particular mission. A good fit in terms of goals will motivate agencies to support the Network's efforts.

Nominal Group Technique

Sometimes, workers define directions with large client systems without the time or resources to first develop the group into a consensus decision-making body. Nominal group technique is a formal technique which motivates participants and combines their efforts in setting directions. This quick and efficient process works best with six to nine people (Toseland & Rivas, 1998). However, it can easily be adapted to work with larger organizational and community groups by running the process several times and combining the results.

In general, nominal group technique is a way of generating information about a specified issue, eliciting responses from participants using a round-robin strategy, discussing the ideas participants contribute, and, finally, establishing priorities through a mathematical rank-ordering process. The steps for using this technique include:

1. Before the process begins, prepare a clear statement of the issue or problem to which the group will respond.
2. Provide a copy of the statement for participants and ask them to list their responses without conferring with each other.
3. Have participants share their responses one at a time. Record each response so that all participants can view the list of responses. This is a brainstorming strategy in which participants simply report their responses without discussing them or evaluating them. Participants may add new ideas which occur to them during this process.
4. Beginning with the first item on the list and proceeding in order, discuss each item to eliminate the overlap among ideas and to clarify the meanings of the responses.
5. Ask participants to select a predetermined number of items from the list that they consider most important. This step reduces the number of items from which participants select their "top priorities."
6. Finally, ask participants to rank-order the items they consider in the "top five," using 5 for the highest ranked item and 1 for the lowest. Record the ratings for each item and

calculate the total points assigned to each. Ideas receiving the highest point totals are the ones the group identifies as most important.

Nominal group technique has important advantages as a decision-making process in that it always reaches a conclusion, considers several alternatives, and encourages participation and discussion. As a planning tool, nominal group process assesses needs while increasing collaboration between the worker and the group members (Gerdes & Benson, 1995). It accommodates the motivation of each individual member and, thereby, activates a widespread commitment to the group's direction.

Collaborating with Clients Who Resist

Considering the motivations of clients leads us to look at resistance. When social workers see resistant behaviors in clients, they explore them for the messages they contain. Clients may be sending messages that they want to change direction or that they are discovering environmental obstacles to their participation. Behaviors that look uncooperative on the surface merit careful attention. They indicate important information about clients, social workers, and the environments in which they operate.

Resistance Is Motivated

Resistance from clients is expected. "Resistance to change in general and resistance to being influenced in particular always occurs when individuals, groups, and systems are required by circumstances to alter their established behaviors" (Anderson & Stewart, 1983, p. 1). Certainly, this description makes sense in terms of ecosystems theory. Human systems evolve in ways that represent their best attempts to master their current situations. Why would clients readily change behaviors that have logically developed and provided them with stability and equilibrium? "However great the distress people feel, they resist asking for help, and having asked for help, they resist being influenced by the professionals they have employed to help them" (p. 1).

Look more closely at the assumptions inherent in the assertion that clients always resist. Do we mean that clients are resisting changes or do we mean that clients are resisting what social workers want them to do? If social workers want to go in one direction and clients want to go in another, who is resisting whom? In his work as a family therapist, de Shazer (1989) talks about resistance when he says: "Attributing blame to either party of an interaction is theoretically unsound. Such a split between members of a system inevitably creates imaginary opposition. But clinically, both therapists and clients are in it together" (p. 231). Resistance indicates that clients and social workers are not synchronized. It may reveal a client's motivation to move in a different direction.

Resistance is communication. It often communicates a message that social workers are overstepping their partnership agreements. In other words, at times, clients may rebel against the directions that workers propose simply because they don't want to be told what to do. Any parent experiences those periods in children's lives—the "terrible twos" and adolescence—where no matter how right parents are, they're wrong. Social workers are not parents to clients. Rather, they are partners with them. When clients respond with resistance, social workers cooperate by clarifying just where clients are leading them.

Cooperating with Resistance

Reconsider the framing of social work relationships as collaborative partnerships, incorporate the assumption of client expertise, and then the notion of client resistance melts away. Replace the idea of resistance with the concept of "cooperation" (de Shazer, 1982) . When clients want to go in directions other than those which workers choose, empowering practitioners yield and let clients lead the way. Clients have the privilege to resist. Social workers respect and cooperate with clients who resist. Resistance clearly demonstrates that clients have power! Why would empowering social workers want to invalidate such an expression? Astute practitioners acknowledge that clients have control over the direction of their change and go with the flow rather than fight to be in charge.

Social workers respond to a client's expression of resistance in ways that clarify, organize, and encourage. Workers may say:

- I have the sense that you are not agreeing with me. Please help me understand where I'm off base.
- I keep trying to pull the discussion back to our prepared agenda; however, it seems like this group wants to move in a different direction. I'd like to understand more clearly where you're headed.
- I'm confused. Earlier, I understood that you wanted to protest how the worker at the public aid office is treating you, and now I'm hearing you say that you want to leave well enough alone. In which direction are we going?

Each response acknowledges that social workers have a part in creating resistance. Each response also demonstrates how workers "go with the flow" by turning the responsibility for defining the direction back to the client.

Overcoming Environmental Resistance

Even when clients have a high level of investment and see their outcomes as very desirable, their investments may falter under the burden of environmental constraints. Social workers may misread clients' behaviors as resistance in these situations. Instead, others may be trying to thwart clients' efforts; their access to resources needed for their successful achievement of goals may be limited or nonexistent; or the practicalities of service delivery such as transportation, costs, and location may be prohibitive. Social workers and clients maintain creativity and flexibility in aligning interpersonal and service delivery resources to overcome these very real barriers. They may need to target social or environmental impediments to motivation to clear the way for the clients to fully invest in the process.

Consider the example of Twyla, who attends a mother's support group sporadically. The worker's initial impulse is to confront Twyla for her lack of commitment to the group. However, assessing more closely reveals the nature of Twyla's "resistance." In discussing the issue, Twyla describes her husband's anger over her attendance, her difficulty in locating child care, and the undependable car that she drives. Each one of these environmental factors influences her attendance at group meetings. In fact, in view of these obstacles, even Twyla's sporadic attendance demonstrates a great deal of motivation to participate. To increase Twyla's attendance, the worker needs to target the issues of child care, transportation, and her husband's attitude.

Cooperating with Mandated Clients

Clients who are mandated to receive services are involuntary participants in social worker–client relationships. They are pressured by legal authorities to work with a practitioner they haven't chosen in order to deal with problems they may not believe are important, real, or anybody's business but their own. The majority of clients served in child welfare agencies, probation offices, delinquency intervention programs, and many types of mental health services approach these services involuntarily.

Equalizing power within the helping relationship is a major challenge for social workers in forming partnerships with involuntary clients. The client's sense of powerlessness generated by the specific mandate is often complicated by a life-long experience of oppression since "members of oppressed groups are disproportionately represented among involuntary clients" (Rooney, 1992, p. 21). Seeking to increase an involuntary client's experience of power in a context where someone else is in charge requires the worker to take direct actions that restore the client's feelings of control. So, practitioners move quickly to frame a positive experience, to reconfigure the relationship for collaboration, and to define a mutual direction in which the client's goals are primary.

Constructing Workers' Expectations

Previously, we have discussed the powerful role that expectations play in human interaction. Without reflective consideration, three damaging presuppositions are likely to invade a worker's thinking about mandated clients: (1) "they are 'bad' people," (2) "they won't cooperate no matter what I do," and (3) "they will be unsuccessful." In working with mandated clients, workers must carefully prepare their assumptions to construct an atmosphere conducive to collaboration.

Regarding clients who are mandated to receive services as "bad" people clearly violates the social work principles of nonjudgmentalism and acceptance. It also fails to apply the core ecosystemic concept that orients workers to examine not just the person but the person in the situation as the focus of inquiry. This vision of where the problem is located—in the person or in the situation—is a key element in encouraging clients to cooperate with services. Rooney (1992) describes this as the contrast between the deviant/pathological perspective (the problem is within the individual) versus the structural perspective (the problem is within how the individual relates to the environment). Workers must demonstrate their belief in the structural perspective to join with clients who are involuntary.

Research has also shown that mandated clients, in fact, can achieve success equal to or greater than the outcomes of voluntary clients (Rooney, 1992). Mandates to change may actually act as powerful motivators for clients to confront issues that they have ignored or been unable to face without assistance. Workers must recognize the feasibility of a success-ful outcome, communicate this expectation to clients, and anticipate clients' cooperation to set the helping relationship on a positive course.

Structuring a Working Partnership

Mandated clients enter social work relationships convinced that the practitioner and referral source are functioning as one. Consequently, the feelings of powerlessness and resentment that often accompany the mandate are transferred immediately to the worker. The client is likely to perceive the initial structure of the helping relationship as one-sided—with the cli-ent on one side of the relationship and the worker and mandating authority on the other. For workers to convert this obstacle into a collaborative relationship, they must take direct ac-tion to restructure this initial configuration by joining with the client to develop a productive working relationship.

In many respects, working with mandated clients makes social workers involuntary par-ticipants as well. Workers acknowledge this reality and discuss it openly with their clients. The purpose of this discourse is to shift how the client perceives the role of the worker in re-lation to the referral agency—the "common" outside force. Social workers must draw bound-aries between themselves and the coercive referral source to find the common ground on which to build partnerships with clients. To this end, workers carefully articulate their own roles in relation to the client (as differentiated from the referral source), clearly define the cli-ent's privileges in the newly established relationship, and ascertain the client's motivation and goals in order to place these identified outcomes at the center of their work together.

Distinguishing Worker Roles

To structure the relationship for collaboration, the worker finds ways to ally with the client's perspective. Consider the example of a men's support group, one component of a Batterer's Education Program. These men, ordered to the group by the courts, differ from each other in many ways, yet they share a common desire not to be there. They are frequently resentful of the judge's order and sometimes angry at those whom they perceive have contributed to their predicament. Workers who attempt to partner with this group by placing themselves in a similar social control role discover closed boundaries when trying to build relationships with group members.

Workers can expect a certain amount of resistance from involuntary clients, initially in terms of acknowledging that a problem exists and then in response to worker-initiated change attempts (Slonim-Nevo, 1996). Workers with nonvoluntary clients must weigh the use of the legal authority to force cooperation against the risk of increasing the client's sense of powerlessness.

Articulating Client Roles

Recently stripped of power, involuntary clients are likely to withhold information to gain some sense of control. This secrecy interferes with creating an open atmosphere that facili-tates change. When initiating relationships with involuntary clients, social workers move quickly to identify just what power clients do hold by providing answers to questions such as:

- What realistically do clients control?
- Within the boundaries of the relationship, what privileges do clients have?

- What are the potential sanctions clients may experience for self-disclosure?
- What are the consequences for clients who resist cooperation?

This discussion of the client's legal situation clarifies the boundaries within which both worker and client must work. But, within these boundaries, social workers and clients still enjoy freedom in regard to methods for removing the mandate. In defining what the worker and client will do, mandated clients benefit from direct descriptions of how the work will proceed, from the generation of a realistic array of options and choices that may work under the circumstances, and from active participation in defining objectives and tasks (Rooney, 1992).

Defining a Motivating Direction

Involuntary clients enter professional relationships compelled by someone else's decision—the motivation to participate can be seen as external. But, even these clients are not without their own motivation. At a minimum, mandated clients want to get someone off their backs, regain control over their lives, or prove that they don't need anybody's help. Social workers openly accept these underlying goals of mandated clients as reasonable and focus on what clients can do that will result in their freedom and independence.

Motivational congruence between clients and workers is a key factor in successful outcomes (Rooney, 1992). When clients assert that they don't want to be involved, social workers respond by helping clients define directions that will work for both partners. Social workers may say:

- I believe it when you say that you don't need to be here. What do you think you need to do to convince the Child Protective Unit that you can handle things?
- You're absolutely right. No one can tell you what to do. I certainly don't intend to. What is it that you think we need to be doing?
- It looks like we're stuck together for at least five sessions. Is there something you would like to work on since you're here anyway or do you just want to wait it out?

When appropriate, as part of defining a mutual direction, practitioners work with clients to change the response of the legal authority to the client system. Consider a simple example. When parents are forced to use social work services to prevent their daughter's further truancy, the worker initially accepts the family's goals of getting court and school officials off their backs. When the social worker explores what might happen, the family's roles and responsibilities become apparent. Defining an initial direction in terms of how others will change may motivate an involuntary client. As the work continues, the social worker refines this direction by incorporating what clients will do. In this way, the social worker gradually leads clients to goals that are more client-centered and, therefore, within their power to reach.

Taking Priority Actions

In defining preliminary direction, certain situations demand immediate action by social workers (see Table 8.1). When clients' safety is uncertain, others are at risk, basic survival needs are unmet, or clients are emotionally overwhelmed by recent events, social workers

TABLE 8.1   Situations Requiring Priority Actions

Trauma

Threat of Suicide

Threats toward Others

Child Abuse

Domestic Violence

Survival Needs

Signs of Addiction

---

may choose to take charge. This doesn't mean that social workers strip clients of their control; however, it does mean that social workers ensure the welfare of everyone concerned. Recent trauma, self-destructive behaviors, abuse, threats toward others, needs for food or shelter—these are all situations that direct social workers to seek guidance from their colleagues and supervisors and take definitive actions.

Responding to Trauma

Trauma is a sudden occurrence that requires specialized and immediate attention. When environments are overwhelming, people need help quickly. Traumatic events temporarily overload their abilities to cope. Experiencing violence, unexpected death, or dramatic loss can leave people floundering and in need of immediate support. To respond to trauma, social workers play transitional roles, lending their support, guidance, strengths, and skills until clients can reconnect with their own abilities to take charge.

In dealing with the aftermath of trauma, social workers acknowledge they are unable to alter the actual occurrence itself. Instead, workers focus on clients' responses to the traumatic event. Unloading visual images, hearing stories again and again, encouraging the outpouring of thoughts and memories, accepting and validating feelings—social workers use responding skills to help clients work through trauma. Workers reassure clients that their intense feelings of vulnerability, fears of loss of control, and emotional overload are natural responses in their situation.

Social workers play active roles in responding to crises and trauma. They take the lead in decision-making, offer facts and information to counteract misconceptions arising from the intensity of the experience, activate natural support networks on the client's behalf, and break down the issues facing the client into discrete units to dispel the overwhelming nature of the problem (Sheafor, Horejsi, & Horejsi, 1997). Workers also access concrete resources such as food, shelter, or clothing to supplement any that the client may have lost. Social workers take direct actions to stabilize clients who are experiencing crises; however, workers also strive to return control to these clients as the urgency of their crises subsides.

Larger System Considerations

When a natural tragedy such as a tornado, hurricane, earthquake, flood, or fire strikes, communities may call on social workers to respond. When an organization suffers the dramatic loss of a member or members, many system members may need assistance at once. In general, the same responses used with individuals are also appropriate in responding to trauma in mid- or macrosystems. Community or organization members need to unload the trauma, describe their personal experience with the events, release their feelings, and receive tangible support. But, the number of members affected by such events is likely to exceed the number of social workers available. When workers are unable to respond to each affected system member directly on an individual basis, they use the existing structures and functions of the client system to offer crisis services.

To help a community system respond to trauma, workers activate the existing strengths of the community. Workers locate key community members in the various subsystems of the community—churches, schools, social agencies, clubs, businesses, and neighborhood organizations—that are already functioning to support community members. Having identified key leaders, workers quickly educate these members about the dynamics of the trauma and the locations of necessary resources. These community members, in turn, provide support in the various contexts in which they are already operating.

Imagine how the Northside Network might respond to a severe storm causing extensive damage and injury in the Northside community. The group would recognize that many people would require immediate assistance to alleviate the impact of such a crisis—people unfamiliar with what services are available. The Network could respond by creating an emergency services information and referral committee from among its members. This new committee would have experienced and knowledgeable social workers who could function as a central clearinghouse for information about specialized disaster services as well as coordinate the work of the many agencies involved. Working with local media on an aggressive public information campaign about available services could also be part of the Network's response. To cope with a community level crisis situation, social workers first work on facilitating connections among service providers and then extend these connections to those in need.

Consider another example of responding to a crisis in an organization. When all members of a family perish in a tragic house fire, the principal of the local elementary school where the three children attended calls the trauma team from the County Mental Health Center for assistance. The social worker, Georgia Betts, immediately convenes a meeting of school personnel including administrators, teachers, counselors, cafeteria workers, maintenance workers, and bus drivers. Each of these people already plays an important role in the everyday functioning of the school and directly interacts with students. At this meeting, Georgia begins by processing the trauma with those assembled, recognizing that everyone gathered has experienced this loss. Next, she provides information about various direct and indirect ways that students may demonstrate their grief. Georgia further describes how to encourage students to express themselves and how school personnel can respond to students in ways that accept and validate the students' feelings. Finally, she arranges a referral process for students who need individualized attention. Using the existing resources of the organizational system, the worker effectively responds to this trauma within the context of a larger system.

Responding to the Threat of Suicide

At some time in their careers, most practitioners will work with a client who considers committing or actually commits suicide (Ivanoff & Riedel, 1995). Statistics show that about

30,000 persons commit suicide each year. Many experts believe this figure underestimates the actual incidence (Ginsberg, 1995). Research further suggests that as many as a million people attempt suicide each year and even more contemplate or threaten suicide (Ivanoff & Riedel, 1995).

Although suicide is not confined to any one particular group, a statistical analysis does show certain trends with respect to race, gender, and age. Typically, rates of suicide among whites are higher than most nonwhite groups (Frankel, 1992). Further, a review of U.S. Bureau of Census (1995) data confirms a gender difference, showing suicide rates to be higher among white men when compared to white women. These data also reveal that for whites, the highest rate of suicide is among those 65 years of age and older; whereas for African Americans, suicide rates peak in the young adult years.

Ivanoff and Riedel (1995) also note a trend toward an increased incidence of suicide in persons age 15 to 24; suicide is a leading cause of death in this age group. Data gathered by the U.S. Department of Health and Human Services indicate "gay and lesbian youth are two to three times more likely to attempt suicide than other youths" (Proctor & Groze, 1994, p. 504). Proctor and Groze's research discovered that this risk could be mitigated by positive functioning in the areas of self-perception, family interactions, and social relationships. Their research demonstrates that it is not a homosexual identity, itself, but the social response to it that places gay and lesbian youths at risk.

Recognizing Signals

Competent practitioners learn to recognize the signals that suicidal clients send. Sometimes these signals are direct; at other times, messages are subtle and require careful attention to detect. Types of suicidal messages include:

Verbal direct:	"I will shoot myself if you leave me."
Verbal indirect:	"A life without love is a life without meaning."
Behavioral direct:	Hoarding pills by a chronically ill, severely disabled person.
Behavioral indirect:	Giving away prized possessions, loss of appetite, insomnia. (Evans & Farberow, 1988, p. 63)

Reports of clustering events such as a history of previous attempts or even a recent attempt by a friend or family member may also signal an increased risk for suicide (Evans & Farberow, 1988). Aggressive thoughts toward themselves or others, family dysfunction, lack of social support, parental ambivalence, neighborhood violence, and history of sexual and psychological abuse are possible correlates with suicidal tendencies in preadolescents (Jackson, Hess, & van Dolen, 1995).

Certain changes in functioning may indicate that clients are contemplating suicide (Lamb, 1990; Bloch, 1999). Sudden changes in personal care habits, appetite, or sleeping patterns; increased use of alcohol or drugs; lethargy or agitation; risk-taking behavior; or school failure are all possible indicators. Preoccupation with ideas about death, getting personal affairs in order, describing how the world would be a better place without them, or giving away personal belongings are also clues to suicidal intent. Finally, Lamb cautions that the sudden elevation in mood of a previously depressed person may reveal a feeling of resolution at having made the decision to commit suicide.

Social workers must sort out facts from misconceptions in assessing a client's risk of suicide (Evans & Farberow, 1988). People who frequently talk about suicide may carry through and, having attempted suicide unsuccessfully, may try again. Talking directly to people about their suicidal thoughts is important. Direct talk does not precipitate suicidal behavior, and it may help prevent it. Mistakenly, people assume that only the wealthy and those in families where others have made this choice attempt suicide. Trapped in a web of circumstances, anyone of any socioeconomic status could be at risk.

Although any of these signs may alert social workers to possible suicidal thinking, no one sign is definitive. In fact, many of these behaviors correlate with other issues as well, and some may indicate no problem at all. Studies about suicide inform practitioners about trends and signs, but only clients are experts on what they are really thinking. When workers suspect suicidal thinking in clients, they consult with their supervisors and get further information from clients to assess the actual risk.

Taking Action

When social workers sense that a client is contemplating suicide, they directly discuss their concerns with the client. Workers may say:

- Are you thinking about harming yourself?
- Are you telling me that you're considering suicide?
- I heard you mention killing yourself. Are you really thinking about that?
- I'm noticing several changes in the way you are handling things, sort of like you are giving up. What are you trying to tell me?

Many workers hesitate to pose these questions, fearing that such direct discussion will foster suicidal behavior; however, this is not the case. By directly talking with clients about what they are hearing and seeing, a social worker gives clients permission to talk openly about any self-destructive thoughts.

In discussing suicidal thinking with a client, social workers strive to assess the seriousness of the client's threats. The most important factor for determining the potential of a suicide threat is the individual's plan (Aguilera & Messick, 1982). Workers should consider three important elements:

- Is it a relatively lethal method?
- Does the individual have the means available?
- Is the plan specific? (pp. 116–117)

Risk of suicide is greater when plans are detailed and specific, and when the methods chosen are lethal and readily available. In response to a client who is seriously contemplating suicide, social workers quickly involve support systems for themselves and for the client. Within their own professional support systems, workers seek the advice and counsel of their supervisors, colleagues, or consultants to gain outside perspectives and receive emotional support. Social workers consider whether the client requires hospitalization or, as an alternative, whether to activate the client's natural support system to prevent the suicidal act. Sometimes, the worker and the client enlist friends or family members to accompany the client at all times until the client's self-destructive feelings pass. This strategy is sometimes referred to as putting the person "on watch." Whatever choices social workers make, they ensure that clients are not left alone with their suicidal thoughts and feelings of hopelessness.

Responding to Threats toward Others

Sometimes, social workers learn that clients are planning violent actions toward others. Clearly, when clients threaten violence, they reveal their frustration, stress, and sense of limited options. Ultimately, practitioners will work to help clients alleviate their anger and expand their vision of possible solutions. But, first, workers must intervene to prevent the potential harm.

Violence is not in the best interests of clients or society. "The protection of human life applies to all persons, that is, both to the life of a client and to the lives of others. This principle takes precedence over every other obligation" (Loewenberg & Dolgoff, 1996, p. 62). If social workers truly believe that clients will leave the session and commit violent acts, they are ethically and legally bound to prevent clients from carrying out their plans. Workers strictly adhere to the agency's procedures for reporting the potential harm.

Discussing violent thoughts and feelings with a client tests a social worker's ability to remain nonjudgmental. This is not to say that social workers maintain a permissive attitude toward violent acts. Instead workers discuss the client's thinking openly and neutrally. In this way, workers can encourage continued sharing, relieve pressure, and introduce other less dangerous options for coping. Even if a client persists in planning violence, this open discussion of violent impulses allows workers to assess the reality of what the client may do and supplies information on which to build preventative responses. Similar to dealing with potential suicide by clients, workers seek supervisory support and consider using in-patient services.

Duty to Warn

Under most circumstances, social workers keep what they hear from clients confidential, but in the case of potential violence, social workers function as agents of social control. In these situations, confidentiality is abridged. When clients threaten others, workers take charge and document their actions carefully (Kopels & Kagle, 1993). A landmark court decision made in California, *Tarasoff v. the Regents of the University of California* (1976), set the stage for legislative initiatives and court decisions in other states. This decision stipulates that:

> *When a therapist determines, or pursuant to the standards of his profession should determine, that his patient presents a serious danger of violence to another, he incurs an obligation to use reasonable care to protect the intended victim against such danger. The discharge of this duty may require the therapist to take one or more of various steps, depending upon the nature of the case. Thus it may call for*

him to warn the intended victim or others likely to apprise the victim of the danger,
to notify the police, or to take whatever other steps are reasonably necessary under
the circumstances. (in Ca. 3d 425, 431 (1976) cited in Dickson, 1998, pp. 148–149)

Three criteria invoke duty to warn under *Tarasoff:* (1) a client seriously threatening to do
bodily harm, (2) the client's ability to carry out the threat, and (3) an identified victim
(Gothard, 1995). However, legal obligations vary from state to state. Many states have enacted specific duty-to-warn laws:

> *These statutes create a duty for certain professionals to warn or protect third par-*
> *ties and establish liability for the professionals' failure to do so in specific, limited*
> *circumstances. At the same time these statutes limit liability; if the professional*
> *follows the steps provided by the statutes, no monetary liability or other action can*
> *be taken against the professional. These statutes vary as to which professionals*
> *are subject to the duty, which threats will activate the duty, which victims are owed*
> *the duty, and how the duty can be discharged. (Kopels & Kagle, 1993, p. 109)*

Duty-to-warn laws differ in their definitions of foreseeable threats, stipulations of obligatory actions, requirements to notify law enforcement officials, and mandates for involuntary
hospitalization (Houston-Vega, Nuehring, & Daguio, 1997). Proceeding under duty to warn
"does not mean that social workers need to immediately warn all potential victims of any
threat to danger" (Kagle & Kopels, 1994, p. 220). However, it does compel social workers
to act legally and ethically and proceed according to the principles of standard practice:
"assessing the client situation, with particular attention to factors that indicate imminent
danger; fully documenting decisions and actions; and, where indicated, developing and implementing a plan of action that protects identifiable third parties" (p. 220). Thorough documentation of the assessment and actions that details facts, observations, and verbatim
accounts of interactions offers some protection against malpractice (Houston-Vega, Nuehring, & Daguio, 1997). Prudent responses include such actions as obtaining the client's
consent to warn potential victims, consulting an attorney who is familiar with state laws,
disclosing only enough information to substantiate the warning, and/or asking the client to
consider a voluntary hospitalization (Reamer, 1994b). At first glance, duty to warn may
seem contrary to principles of empowerment. However, consider the consequences of allowing clients to commit acts of violence. Ultimately, if clients harm others, both clients
and those they harm lose power to determine the courses of their lives.

Responding to Child Abuse

When social workers suspect that children in families are being abused, they take appropriate
actions to ensure children's safety and prevent further harm. Child maltreatment takes on
many forms, including physical abuse, neglect, emotional abuse, and sexual abuse. The National Committee to Prevent Child Abuse (NCPCA) estimates that each year child protection

agencies receive reports on over 3 million children who are alleged to have experienced maltreatment. Incidence rates have increased by 45 percent since 1987 (Daro & Wang, 1997). Social workers most likely to deal with these issues are those in child protective services working under mandates to investigate reports of potential abuse or those working in hospital settings. But, even social workers in other practice settings encounter clients in situations where abuse is occurring. Therefore, all practitioners need to know about how to identify abusive situations and how to respond.

Recognizing Signs of Abuse

There are several ways that social workers become aware of child abuse. Sometimes, workers hear reports of events directly from children or parents that describe harsh discipline, events, or "accidents" which prompt workers to obtain further details to assess the child's safety. At other times, social workers observe physical evidence of abuse in the form of bruises, scratches, burns, or other injuries. Many times they hear about abusive events from people outside of the client's family such as friends, extended family members, or neighbors.

Some evidence of abuse is more subtle. Research provides assistance in identifying risk factors, including spousal abuse, unemployment, single parenthood, illness or developmental disabilities, pre-term birth, history of intergenerational abuse or family violence, and addiction (Houston-Vega, Nuehring, & Daguio, 1997; Bethea, 1999).

Children may show behavioral signs that indicate they are being abused, including such diverse personal actions as aggression, self-destructive behaviors, retreat, or withdrawal. How children relate to adults also provides clues to abuse. Children may demonstrate fear of physical contact or affection, extreme dependence and attachment, and excessive attention to parental needs. Children who are abused sometimes reveal problems in social functioning, such as difficulties in learning even though they have no apparent learning deficits, lack of concentration and low energy at school, depression, impulsive behavior, or noncompliance (Lowenthal, 1999). Sexual acting out and evidence of parental neglect are other possible signs of abuse.

Taking Action

Social workers do not immediately assume that families with these characteristics are experiencing family violence. Yet, workers are cautious about not overlooking signals of abuse. When practitioners fail to notice abuse, they unknowingly contribute to it. When social workers detect issues of abuse, the safety of the person being abused takes priority.

Social workers seek more information when they suspect abuse. In some instances, they may need to see members separately to encourage family members to speak openly and freely, and to protect vulnerable family members from reprisals by abusive members. Workers proceed cautiously when persons who are abused and perpetrators are present at the same interview, since revealing information could precipitate retaliation. Children need reassurance about what will happen next to them and their family members. And, workers carefully refrain from making judgmental comments about perpetrators, since the child may have ambivalent emotions of anger and affection about the person involved. As workers respond to information about abuse, they recognize their important role in comforting and protecting those threatened.

Reporting Suspected Child Abuse

Although all states have mandatory reporting laws that require social workers and other designated professionals to report instances of child maltreatment, these laws offer general guidelines rather than specifying those conditions that warrant reports (Houston-Vega, Nuehring, & Daguio, 1997). Some states require actual signs of child maltreatment, others require the presence of parent or child behavioral indicators, while yet others mandate reporting "based on hearsay or reasonable suspicion" (p. 117). States also differ on the actual reporting process—whether reports are by phone or written document and with whom reports are filed. Typically, a state department is charged to provide child welfare services, including prompt investigation and follow-up services with families as their situations require.

Responding to Elder Abuse

Results of the National Center on Elder Abuse's first national incidence study estimate that nearly one-half million older adults living in domestic settings experienced abuse, neglect, or self-neglect in 1996 (Administration on Aging, 1998). Of this number, an estimated 400,000 incidents occur each year that are not reported to adult protective service agencies. This study confirms the "iceberg effect." Reported cases of elder abuse represent the "tip of the iceberg," while the majority of incidents are "hidden" or not disclosed to authorities. A disproportionately large number of these situations involve people over 80 years old. Those who are physically or cognitively frail are particularly vulnerable. Relatives, including spouses and adult children, are the most likely perpetrators of domestic elder abuse.

Most states have enacted reporting laws that designate certain professionals as mandatory reporters of the abuse of adults who are dependent, as defined by age, mental, or physical disabilities (U.S. Department of Justice, 1999). Only some reporting laws designate penalties for noncompliance. States vary as to which agencies take responsibility for receiving and investigating reports of elder abuse and the abuse of other dependent adults. Designated agencies include units of state human service departments, local social service agencies, and law enforcement officials (National Center for Elder Abuse, 1997).

Several factors complicate both identifying and reporting elder abuse. Many older adults, particularly those who are frail, are homebound and away from public scrutiny. Additionally, older adults may be reluctant to bring charges when a family member or loved one on whom they rely has committed the abuse. They may believe they themselves are to blame, or they may be concerned that reporting will ultimately lead to a nursing home placement. Social workers may also experience dilemmas in weighing an older adult's competency for self-determined decision-making, and their own duty to protect a client's safety and well-being.

Responding to Intimate Partner Violence

Violence within marital or couple relationships also requires priority action. Abuse may be physical, psychological, sexual, or economic (Davis, 1995). Practitioners are cautious in working toward any changes in families where such violence is happening for fear that changes in any part of the family system may escalate the occurrence of violence. Therefore, alert social workers watch for signs of violence and, when detected, deal with safety issues first, before addressing other concerns.

Research identifies a number of factors that increase the risk for couple violence (Davis, 1995). Rates of violence are greater among cohabiting couples than among married couples. Younger couples are more at risk than older couples. Experiencing abuse as a child is a clear predictor of becoming involved in domestic violence, either as a victim or a perpetrator. Partner abuse occurs in all socioeconomic groups; however, prevalence is greater in situations of poverty, unemployment, or underemployment. Finally, substance abuse is involved in a majority of battering incidents.

When workers believe that violence is occurring, they may need to meet separately with those at risk in order to elicit honest information in a secure setting and take immediate action to prevent further harm. Social workers need extensive knowledge of community service networks to ensure the safety of persons threatened by domestic violence. A major role for social workers is connecting men and women to appropriate resources. Many communities have domestic violence programs that coordinate multilevel services. A comprehensive approach is necessary, since these clients are likely to require legal assistance, court protection, transitional housing, financial resources, and counseling support.

Responding to Survival Needs

All human beings have universal needs for food, shelter, warmth, and sleep. When these basic needs are unmet, people are unable to accomplish anything else. Maslow (1970) describes this as a hierarchy of needs. This hierarchy has implications for prioritizing actions. For example, to work on helping a client return to school to achieve the goal of obtaining a GED is inappropriate if the client is homeless and in need of food and shelter. When social workers recognize that a client is lacking the necessities for survival, they focus on stabilizing essential supports before working on other issues. "Advocacy/empowerment and primary relationship building alone cannot compensate for homelessness, malnutrition, lack of medical care, and social isolation" (Klein & Cnaan, 1995, p. 210). All social workers need to know about the support services in their communities that provide immediate shelter, food, and financial assistance in order to network clients for life-sustaining assistance.

Responding to Signs of Addiction

Substance abuse and addiction accompany many situations that challenge clients' abilities to cope and frequently preempt their capabilities to address other concerns. Sometimes, mood-altering substance use springs from dissatisfactions with life. At other times, addiction may have physiological roots and create a wave of associated issues blocking abilities to function effectively.

Not all people who use substances are addicted. A probability study of adults in the United States indicates that 14 percent of all adults report alcohol dependence at some time during their lives and 7 percent report alcohol dependence within the last year (American Psychiatric Association, 1994). Other statistics suggest that about 25 percent of the families in the United States will experience the effects of alcoholism at some time (Anderson, 1987).

Typically, for males, alcohol dependence begins in their late teens or early 20s. Oftentimes, they do not recognize their problems with alcohol until almost a decade later. Demographic data suggest that men are most likely to seek help for dealing with alcohol problems in their 30s or 40s. Studies indicate that, for women, the course of alcohol dependence varies greatly and typically onsets later than for men (American Psychiatric Association, 1987).

Characteristically, involvement with alcohol and drugs takes on three different forms: use, abuse, and dependency. Persons who are users likely use alcohol and drugs for pleasure and an enhanced sense of well-being (Griffin, 1991). Users become abusers when "the drug and its effects interfere with the individual's ability to carry out expected responsibilities" (p. 88). Drug dependency occurs when the "individual persists in using drugs, disregarding any negative consequences and exhibiting tolerance to the drug and withdrawal symptoms when he or she cannot have the drug" (p. 88). A worker who discovers that clients are using drugs and alcohol discusses this openly to determine the extent of the involvement and the impact of use. If clients show signs of abuse or dependency, they will probably need assistance from drug treatment programs before continuing to work toward other goals.

When confronting issues of substance abuse, social workers fully respect a client's right to self-determination (Logan, McRoy, & Freeman, 1987). Social workers seek the client's cooperation in making referrals for drug and alcohol assessment and treatment. All treatment for substance abuse requires motivation and participation by clients to be successful. Although social workers may support a client through the process of seeking treatment for substance abuse, as much as possible, workers activate the client's capabilities for accessing treatment services. Exceptions are situations in which social workers recognize that the dependence is disabling and the client is unable to acknowledge the need or activate personal resources for change. At these times, social workers contact members of a client's natural support network to arrange treatment.

Reflecting Back

Trauma, violence toward self or others, threats to survival, and addiction—each of these issues requires that social workers take immediate action to support clients and protect them or others around them from harm. But in doing so, it appears that workers skew the power dynamics of an empowering partnership. In carrying out their mandate to balance the rights of individuals with the rights of others, how can workers enlist clients as partners? Consider how social workers can provide genuine options for clients and maintain an atmosphere of empowerment while taking priority actions to ensure the safety of clients and others.

Looking Forward

Defining directions represents a turning point in the partnership of clients and workers. They now agree on which way they are going. Setting preliminary goals focuses the partners on what to do next. It answers the question of whether workers and clients need to take priority actions to prevent immediate harm or cope with crisis situations. If the current situation allows, the partners can now proceed to look for strengths, resources that may be available to work toward desired outcomes. Articulating situations and defining directions clarify "where the client is" and predict where the partnership is going.

The dialogue phase sets the stage for implementing the discovery processes of identifying strengths, assessing resource capabilities, and planning possible solutions. In the discovery phase, social workers and clients will combine their expertise to generate new information, consider resources available within clients and their environments, and frame possible solutions. Practitioners and clients conduct an organized search for opportunities to overcome restraints and work to recognize strengths and resources to meet defined needs. Identifying strengths, the topic of Chapter 9, initiates these discovery processes.

Part 3

The Discovery Phase: Assessing Resources and Planning Change

Consistent with the strengths perspective, competence-focused assessment searches for capabilities. "Assessment connotes the investigation of positive strengths, healthy functioning, and support systems that can be mobilized for goal planning and problem solving" (Lum, 1986, p. 155). A strengths-oriented assessment offers a forum "for an examination of realizable alternatives, for the mobilization of competencies that can make things different, and for the building of self-confidence that stimulates hope" (Cowger, 1994, p. 265). In the *discovery phase,* workers go beyond the traditional assessment style of diagnosing what is wrong to a more empowering assessment style of locating resources that might be valuable in developing solutions.

Part 3 examines the processes that social workers and clients implement to identify client system strengths and discover resources in their environments. To accomplish this, practitioners use strength-focused dialogue skills and an array of assessment techniques and tools. Information about available resources informs workers and clients as they collaborate to develop coherent and effective plans of action.

C h a p t e r 9

Identifying Strengths

The dialogue between clients and social workers is rich with information. Social workers continually search this dialogue to discover client strengths. However, the process of identifying strengths in clients is not simple. So accustomed are we to detecting problems, we may overlook indicators of client strengths as they pass right before us. Read the following excerpt about Chad as he describes what prompted him to seek assistance at the Northside Addictions Recovery Center. Assess your ability to identify Chad's strengths.

> *"Two weeks ago, I felt like I couldn't go on—that's when I decided to call you. I'd just been laid off and the kids were driving me crazy. I could feel it creeping in— that craving for a drink. I've been sober for 18 months now, but I still think about it every day. Both of my parents had the same problem and at Alcoholics Anonymous they say it's hereditary. Maybe there's no escaping it and I'll die young just like they did. I've needed a drink so bad that I can't stay home, especially with the kids getting on my nerves. I called my friend in to take care of the kids and I hit the pavement, putting in applications all over town—14 to be exact. I don't think any of them will pay what my accounting job paid, but I still can go back and be a mechanic or even be a waiter again, at least temporarily. I don't know what I'll be doing, but I have to do something. I just can't sit around. I'll go crazy. My brother tells me I'm running away from my problems. What do you think?"*

If you are a problem-focused practitioner, you might agree with Chad's brother. You even might think that Chad fits the description of a multi-problem client. After all, he is the adult child of two alcoholics, a recovering alcoholic himself who is craving a drink, recently unemployed, and frustrated with his children.

Switch your focus to recognize Chad's strengths. Do you notice the fact that he lost his job two full weeks ago and still hasn't had a drink? Do you realize that he is already on the move to getting another job, has actually put in applications, and has a wide range of skills to draw on including abilities as an accountant, a mechanic, and a waiter? Do you recognize his social support—a friend to take care of his children and a brother to talk with about his issues? Do you acknowledge that he has overcome the adversity of growing up in an alcoholic family? This is only the beginning of the list of strengths that Chad reveals in these few statements.

If you can recognize Chad's strengths, congratulate yourself on your own strengths. You are well on the way to becoming an empowering practitioner. Recognizing and validating client strengths is fundamental to empowering social work practice—in constructing relationships and in building solutions. This chapter equips practitioners with the knowledge and skills to identify and utilize client strengths in the practice process. In detail, this chapter:

- Defines strengths and emphasizes the importance of incorporating client strengths early in the process
- Overviews what strengths may be present in the functioning of individuals, groups, families, organizations, and communities
- Explains how workers can orient their dialogue with clients to discover existing strengths and in them, the seeds of solutions

- Offers information for workers to increase their abilities to recognize the cultural strengths of African American, Latino American, Asian American, and Native American clients
- Describes strengths with respect to various population group memberships, including women, gays and lesbians, older adults, religious affiliations, and persons with disabilities
- Highlights possible strengths present in clients with histories of adversity including clients who are survivors of oppression, violence, or family disruption

Infusing a Strengths Perspective

The strengths orientation shifts the way social workers view and respond to clients. Strength-focused workers assume client competence and acknowledge client system strengths. To infuse a focus on strengths, practitioners must understand the diverse and contextual nature of strengths, know where to look for strengths in client systems, and know how to provide strength-oriented feedback throughout the process.

What Are Strengths?

In some ways, it seems obvious to each of us where our own individual strengths lie. We recognize some strengths easily and use them to decide how to present ourselves, what activities to pursue, and which career choices to make. Strengths are those things that we are good at—our natural abilities, our acquired talents, and the skills we have developed. But how many times have we received a compliment from someone who has noticed something about us that we have overlooked? Sometimes we are nearsighted in recognizing our own capacity for growth and change. Strengths do involve characteristics, abilities, and behaviors that are obvious to us, but they also include more subtle successes and less apparent capabilities. Whether prominent or elusive, client strengths supply the seeds for developing solutions.

Strengths-oriented social workers develop skills in identifying strengths that are relevant for each level of client system—individual, family, group, organization, neighborhood, or community. Enhancing client systems' views of their own resources means looking diligently and creatively for anything about their functioning that may be useful in activating confidence and achieving goals. Workers locate client strengths "in the context of clients' personal history, their immediate social environment, the larger societal matrix, the mix of individual characteristics, and the meanings clients ascribe to their experiences" (McAuaide & Ehrenreich, 1997, p. 201).

The Contextual Nature of Strengths

What may be an asset for you may be a deficit for others; conversely, what may be an asset for others may be a deficit for you. For example, the ability to bring patience, persistence, and a sense of accomplishment to a repetitive task may benefit a person with retardation who assembles nuts and bolts in a developmental training program, but these same talents may constrain a worker with a temporary employment agency which demands quick adaptation and flexibility to learn new tasks on a daily basis. Strengths are relative; "they cannot be isolated from the situation in which they are expressed" (McAuaide & Ehrenreich,

1997, p. 203). To identify strengths, social workers maintain a transactional view to evaluate how client systems' abilities mesh with their situations.

Consider the example of African American families. Several writers describe the extended family network present in many African American families as a source of strength and support (Boyd-Franklin, 1989, 1993; Bilingsley, 1992; Hill, 1997; Wright & Anderson, 1998). When working with African American clients, culturally sensitive workers consider possible resources in their extended families. However, whether or not the extended family is functioning supportively is specific to each African American client. To understand the resources of a particular client's situation, workers consider questions such as:

- What is actually happening in this client's situation?
- Are extended family members present?
- Are they involved with the client's family?
- Does the client believe that involvement of extended family members helps or interferes?

Workers bring their awareness of potential strengths to each encounter, but only clients can define whether potential strengths are realities for them.

Why Identify Strengths?

Identifying client strengths has many advantages. Most importantly, accentuating strengths highlights possible resources for achieving goals. It also contributes to the process in other important ways. Specifically, identifying strengths solidifies the client–social worker partnership, functions as a generally enhancing intervention, and increases clients' motivation to invest in the process.

Acknowledging Strengths to Build Partnerships

Examine the relationships in your own life. In which of these relationships do you sense control or equality? Of course, you've probably identified those relationships in which you feel that you have something to offer, in which others recognize the potential of your contributions. To engage clients as contributing partners, workers communicate their understanding that clients have resources to offer to the process. "Drawing on the clients' resources in a complimentary manner refutes their position that they are powerless to bring about change, and helps to lead to a sense of autonomy as they realize they are capable of finding solutions to their problems" (Wall, Kleckner, Amendt, & Bryant, 1989, p. 161). Identifying and acknowledging their strengths invites clients into professional relationships as partners.

Building productive relationships requires a degree of openness as well as a sense of equality. Clients often withdraw when social workers narrowly focus on their problems and ignore things they're doing right. Revealing more and more of what is going wrong increases clients' feelings of vulnerability and heightens their defensiveness. And, when the defensive walls go up, exchanges of information dry up. A worker who balances gentle and accepting explorations of challenges with a recognition of strengths encourages clients to bring along feelings of success and power as they explore areas of vulnerability.

Acknowledging a client's strengths early in the developing partnership is especially important in cross-cultural relationships. Obvious cultural differences cast doubts on the abilities of clients and workers to relate successfully to one another. Typically, clients wonder about the effects of these differences on their relationships with social workers. For example, questions include: Will the worker operate from a value base that devalues the client's world view, choices, or lifestyle? Will the worker see cultural differences as threatening or something to change to move the client into the mainstream? Is the worker informed about the client's culture in a general way that allows the worker to place information in a cultural context?

Identifying strengths liberates clients to reveal more about themselves, particularly those aspects of their functioning about which they feel good. Common perceptions about social workers lead clients to tell workers what they believe workers are interested in hearing—their problems. When workers search for and respond to the strengths they detect, they give clients permission to think and share more broadly about their lives. In this way, workers reorient clients toward strengths from the beginning of the overall process.

Recognizing Strengths as a General Intervention

The perfect solution for a particular issue requires a carefully tailored, specifically designed strategy that fits the unique circumstance of each client system. Although there may be several potential solutions to any one dilemma, there is no universal strategy to fit every situation. However, there are certain things that social workers can do that seem to give any client system a general boost. Recognizing client system strengths is one of those things.

Assuming that client systems have resources postures attention toward strengths. It means that social workers enter each working relationship wearing magnifying glasses to accentuate strengths. This creates an empowering atmosphere where good things exist and other good things are possible. A sense of hope and optimism facilitates workers' and clients' beliefs that change and success are possible—a thought that can become a reality in the context of their work together.

Self-esteem is a popular concept that receives much attention in education and parenting. Teachers and parents are supposed to behave in ways that enhance children's positive self-esteem, feelings of self-worth, and belief in their abilities. The theory says that children who feel better about themselves demonstrate higher achievement, feel more secure in experimenting with growth and change, and experience greater success—all qualities that social workers would like to facilitate with clients. Self-esteem accrues based on one's accomplishments, self-affirmation that one is doing something right, and outside recognition of one's achievements, resources, and abilities. Identifying what clients are doing right enhances their feelings of esteem and amplifies their sense of power.

Identifying Strengths as a Motivational Tool

People change when they are motivated to change and when they believe they have the capabilities and resources to do so. This axiom leads us to incorporate client motivation and confidence as a cornerstone of the working relationship. "Adopting a strength-oriented perspective and conveying expectations of responsible, independent behavior also foster hope, self-respect, and commitment to implement strategies for change" (Hepworth, Rooney, & Larsen, 1997, p. 63). Complimenting a client's strengths "helps to point the client in the direction of change...by instilling hope of choice in a situation which appears masterable, by attributing some mystical competency to the client in need" (Wall, Kleckner, Amendt, & Bryant, 1989, p. 161). Identifying strengths and resources heightens clients' motivation and stimulates connections to their capabilities.

Responsible social workers show enthusiasm, hope, interest, and confidence. In the up-front recognition and positive connection with client strengths, workers do their part to motivate clients to continue the work. Experienced practitioners indicate that people stretch to prove the truth of compliments but recoil to defend against criticisms. Workers who keep their eyes and ears open to expressions of strengths and incremental solutions keep clients stretching toward success.

Balancing Strengths and Challenges

Talking about strengths does not mean that workers blatantly ignore the information clients provide about problems. Clients need to unload their difficulties before opening their eyes to more positive views. Interestingly, information clustered around clients' challenges frequently reveals strengths and potential solutions. "To find solutions you must talk about the problem in a solvable way" (Durrant & Kowalski, 1992, p. 111).

Typically, clients let social workers know if they move too quickly to identify strengths and look for solutions. Clients question the shift in direction and work harder to convince the worker that their problems are difficult. They have not yet said all they have come to say; they think the worker hasn't heard enough about the situation to lead toward the way out. When clients have exhausted their stories about their problems and begin to repeat information, workers move on. Workers redirect the focus of conversation by summarizing and clarifying what they understand of the client's perspective, ask if there is anything else, and seek permission to move in a more positive direction. Social workers may say:

- I'm hearing that this marriage has changed in the last few months, that you don't seem to find much time to be together, and when you are together, you don't seem to have much to talk about. Is there anything else? If not, I'd like to find out more about those times before when your marriage was working the way you wanted.
- I guess "support group" isn't a very accurate name for what seems to be happening in the group right now. You all seem to agree that you are beginning to pull back, share less about what you are really thinking and feeling, and you don't know clearly what you want out of it yet. Am I hearing you right? Well, that's one good thing—we seem to have consensus about that. What else do we have that we might build on?
- We all agree that the Council is getting bogged down on defining homelessness. However, several agency representatives to the Community Housing Council have clearly outlined the problems associated with lack of affordable housing, limited shelter space, and the complex referral process. Is this the common ground we're looking for to move our efforts forward?

When workers move too quickly to accentuate strengths, they force clients to respond by working harder to convince workers about the difficulty of their problems. Clients think workers are missing the point or minimizing their issues. Durrant and Kowalski (1992) say:

We do not believe that talking about the problem ("working it through") leads to change; however, we are clear that not talking about it sometimes leads to clients

> *feeling unheard. Therefore…we are alert to our clients' lead and to signs that they need to know that their situation has been understood and their experience validated. (p. 110)*

Research about clients who drop out after only one session confirms this contention (Presley, 1987). The accuracy with which workers identified both client strengths and concerns contributed to making the first session most meaningful. Effective social workers weave their acknowledgment of strengths into their acceptance of the significance of difficulties.

Looking for Strengths

Social workers find client strengths when they are prepared to look for them. Familiarity with research about human resiliency provides workers with information about what studies demonstrate is helpful to people in both general and particular situations. Knowledge about the unique capabilities of specific cultural groups also puts workers on alert for identifying strengths.

Simply, in order to build collaborative relationships on a foundation of strengths, social workers need to know where and how to look for strengths. The rest of this chapter details knowledge and skills essential for detecting and accentuating client strengths. Specifically, sections address looking for strengths in general functioning, in the context of challenges, in cultural contexts, and in adversity.

Highlighting Strengths in General Functioning

Alert social workers notice client strengths from the initial to the final phases of the social work process. It is more empowering for clients to perceive what they have to work with than to notice what is missing. Recognizing clients' capabilities builds confidence, motivation, and feelings of power.

To identify general strengths, workers keep many questions in mind, such as:

- What are the outstanding qualities of this client?
- In what ways does the client demonstrate power?
- How and with whom does the client successfully build alliances?
- What special or unique characteristics distinguish this client from others?
- What skills does this client system have to connect to its environment?
- What resources support the client?
- In what ways does the client contribute to the social and physical environments?
- How has the client been able to adapt to changes?

These questions consider the qualities which characterize competence of any human system in its environmental context. Clients—including individuals, families, groups, organizations, and communities—draw on internal and environmental resources to adapt and progress through their development.

Strengths in Individuals

Workers can locate an individual's personal strengths by exploring cognitive, affective, physical, and cultural attributes. Intelligence, problem-solving skills, and creativity are important cognitive resources. Affective strengths may include positive feelings of self-worth, abilities to identify and express emotions, optimism, and sensitivity. Special physical talents, athletic skills, an attractive appearance, endurance, and good health are all physical qualities that benefit individual functioning. And one's cultural identities may be a source of pride contributing to a positive sense of self and belonging. Each of these personal strengths also enhances an individual's successful interpersonal interactions.

Interpersonal strengths are evident in an individual's natural support network. They include rewarding relationships with immediate family members and extended family support. Friends, neighbors, employers, teachers, ministers, rabbis, and other spiritual leaders—all may provide important resources for individual well-being. An individual's abilities in building social alliances such as good communication skills, warmth, trustworthiness, and commitment are significant strengths for successful interpersonal relationships.

Rewarding connections to community, institutional, and recreational resources can also be sources of strength. When people are aware of available resources, have privileges to access them, and believe they have rights to benefit from what society offers, they are positioned well to build productive connections to the environment—an important source of sustenance for individual functioning.

Strengths in Families

There is no one single formula for a family success. Families have different styles depending on their structure, membership, cultural influences, ethnic heritage, and a host of other environmental variables. However, twenty-five years of research by Beavers and Hampson (1990, 1993) shows trends in family interaction that generally function as strengths:

> *These families show consistently high degrees of capable negotiation, clarity of individual expression, respect for individual choices and ambivalence, and affiliative attitudes towards one another. Each member appears competent, acknowledged, and assured; the resultant product is a group of individuals who are spontaneous, enjoy each other, and are allowed clear and direct expression of feelings, attitudes, and beliefs. (1990, pp. 30–31)*

Notice that no where in this description of family competence is it necessary for there to be two, heterosexual, married, or biological parents or even children, for that matter. Families representing many structures and lifestyles can function competently. The nature of its interaction and the support that each member gives to and receives from their family defines its health.

Collecting information from over 10,000 family members from every state in the United States and more than 22 countries, Olson and DeFrain (1999) discovered remarkable cross-cultural similarities with respect to family strengths. Factors contributing to family satisfaction and resilience include: appreciation and affection, commitment, positive communication, time together, spiritual well-being, and the ability to cope with stress and crisis.

Strengths in Groups

Successful groups are those in which each member contributes to the overall functioning of the group and, in return, receives the benefits of group membership. To accomplish this balance, groups require the strengths of clearly understood goals, effective communication among members, distributed power, appropriate decision-making procedures, conflict resolution skills, and cohesiveness (Johnson & Johnson, 1997). Competently functioning groups also have similar relationships with their environments, accessing and contributing resources in reciprocal exchanges.

Other qualities of group interaction that constitute strengths depend on the group's specific purpose. For example, a task group draws on particular skills of its members that are most relevant to the task at hand. A support group benefits from members' abilities to articulate feelings and demonstrate empathy. A social action group depends on members' feelings of power and their connections to powerful resources in the community at large. A successful committee finds strengths in efficient operating procedures and diversity among members to stimulate creativity. Social workers discover group strengths by examining the individual qualities of members, the dynamic interaction among members, and the group's relationship to its environment.

Strengths in Organizations

There are many possibilities for identifying strengths in larger systems including human services agencies and other organizations. For example, in a social service agency, we may discover talented employees, a good training program, a dedicated volunteer pool, supportive and active clientele, a motivated and dedicated board of directors, a sound program evaluation system, or lucrative relationships with community foundations.

Organizations draw on the strengths of their mission, reputation in the community, family-friendly personnel policies and practices, sound financial management, well-maintained facilities, and receptive administrators. When faced with critical issues such as corporate expansion or downsizing, organizations can rely on their strengths to see them through difficult periods of change.

Strengths in Communities

A community's strengths include an appreciation of its diverse population, shared community values and standards, timely and deliberate response to community problems and needs, and availability of resources. Strengths are also found in well-maintained infrastructures, adequate transportation systems, affordable housing, equitable tax levies, committed office holders, and a sound economy. A community that provides resources and services to meet residents' needs and activates its citizens to participate in city government, community projects, and long-range planning has the fundamental resources it needs to meet upcoming issues.

Assessing strengths of a community is similar to exploring resources of other systems. Social workers inventory the community's assets and audit its capacity for development. To respect diversity, workers remain open to culturally specific clues to community strengths. For example, murals in Latino communities are social indicators of community strengths, both in terms of the content they present and the process by which they develop (Delgado & Barton, 1998). Workers focus concurrently on what the community gives to its members and how members contribute to the community in return.

Solution-Focused Dialogue

Seeking information about what is working, in addition to fleshing out what is not, provides pathways for locating strength while discovering the client's situation. Social workers may say:

- So what have you been doing to try to solve this?
- What works, even for a little while?
- What are you learning about your situation?
- Is there anyone who seems able to cope with what's going on? What are they doing?
- Are there ever times when things just seem to be going better for no apparent reason?
- What have you discovered about yourself as you work on this issue?
- Do you remember a time when this problem didn't exist?
- Tell me what was going on then.

Each of these questions moves problems away from the center of the focus and toward helpful information and possible solutions. Empowering social workers lead clients beyond ruminating about problems by expanding the focus of the dialogue toward solutions.

For the last 15 years, many social workers have shifted from problem-centered to solution-centered dialogue with clients. In fact, focusing on solutions, particularly in interventions with individual, couple, and family system clients, is the subject of numerous books and articles (de Shazer & Molnar, 1984; de Shazer, 1985, 1988; Molnar & de Shazer, 1987; O'Hanlon & Weiner-Davis, 1989; Walter & Peller, 1992; Furman & Ahola, 1992; Berg, 1994; De Jong & Miller, 1995; Berg & De Jong, 1996; Rudes, Shilts, & Berg, 1997; De Jong & Berg, 1998; Greene, et al., 1998; Kadushin, 1998; O'Hanlon & Bertolino, 1998; Campbell, et al., 1999). In addition, Berg and Miller (1992) have been working in the area of substance abuse, Kok and Leskela (1996) in a psychiatric hospital, and Clark (1997a, 1997b, 1998) in corrections, demonstrating that these solution-focused approaches can be effective with even the most difficult issues. Solution-centered dialogue has potential in work with macrolevel systems as well. Sparks (1989) presents such an application to work in organizations.

Similarities exist among the approaches of various writers about specific conversational strategies to elicit client strengths and potential solutions. Each approach compels workers to: (1) create an atmosphere conducive to possibilities; (2) look for exceptions to the occurrence of the problem; (3) survey clients' information for incremental steps in the direction of goals; and (4) search for transferable skills and solutions.

Creating a Solution-Saturated Atmosphere

Myriad influences affect the atmosphere and tone of the transactions between clients and social workers. Solution-focused social workers consciously tend to the climate of their working relationships to instill confidence, optimism, and the idea that success is inevitable. Assumptions influence this atmosphere significantly. When practitioners assume that clients have competence, that challenges are transitory, and that clients have coping skills that they have demonstrated in the past and will do so again in the present and the future, workers promote hope and orient clients toward strengths and solutions.

Specific skills ensure a success-saturated climate. Social workers use language carefully to reveal the presuppositions that clients can and will overcome their challenges (O'Hanlon & Weiner-Davis, 1989). Creating a positive atmosphere is possible when workers show emotional support, use supportive gestures, and speak in tones that convey excitement and hope (Walter & Peller, 1992). Giving compliments also contributes to a solution-saturated atmosphere. Finally, workers can remain alert "for positive changes or for things that are working" (p. 5).

Searching for Exceptions

Sometimes problems entrench clients; it seems like everything is going wrong and nothing is going right. However, "nothing always happens; nothing is always the same" (de Shazer, 1985, pp. 161–162). This concise statement alerts social workers to look for exceptions, for indicators of when things are going well or when difficulties abate, even if only briefly. "Solutions can be unearthed by examining the differences between times when the problem has occurred and times when it has not. Clients often simply need to do more of what is already working until the problem no longer exists" (O'Hanlon & Weiner-Davis, 1989, p. 82). To search for exceptions, workers may say:

- What is happening on those days when things seem less impossible?
- So, most of the time you feel down. What about the other times?
- The residents raise a number of concerns about the recent deterioration of the neighborhood. What continues to be positive about the neighborhood?
- So, these signs of worker burnout have been going on for almost six months. What was different at the agency before things started going wrong?

The way the "exceptions question" works is simple. It "directs the client to search in the present and the past...focusing on those times when clients do not or have not had their problems even though they expected they would" (O'Hanlon & Weiner-Davis, 1989, p. 24). In this way, workers

> *focus on the who, what, when, and where of exception times instead of the who, what, when, and where of problems. The consequence is a growing awareness in both workers and clients of the clients' strengths relative to their goals, rather than the clients' deficiencies relative to their problems. Once these strengths are brought to awareness and thereby made available, clients can mobilize them to create solutions tailor-made for their lives. (De Jong & Miller, 1995, p. 731)*

Detecting Incremental Steps

Probably the strengths most often missed by workers and clients alike are resources that are just developing. Often, clients in challenging situations are experimenting, analyzing, and trying out new behaviors to overcome their current problems. Workers explore these attempts to discover times when clients feel hopeful and identify those that hold even a glimmer of success for the information and possibilities they contain.

Success builds one step at a time. Clients may be capable of accomplishments that are not in and of themselves enough to resolve the current difficulties, but which, nevertheless, may be steps in the right direction. For example, in trying to overcome an early rift that has divided it into subgroups, members of a support group may demonstrate excellent listening skills. Although the worker understands that the support group is not fully accomplished in resolving conflicts, the worker helps members notice that their abilities to listen are strengths that are prerequisites for negotiating resolutions.

If workers and clients can decide where they are going, they can survey clients' current situations for signs that they are moving in the right direction. "When there is evidence of progress, even if it is meager, talking about it allows the conversation to move naturally towards such constructive subjects as what made the improvement possible and who did what to bring it about" (Furman & Ahola, 1992, p. 110). To discover incremental steps, workers first help clients define a direction toward goals (a process presented in Chapter 8). Second, workers direct clients to search their situations for times when they are inching in that direction. Workers may say:

- What is the first thing you will notice when things are getting better? Does that ever happen now?
- If this problem disappeared overnight, what would clue you in when you woke up in the morning? Do you remember a time when that thing was happening?
- So you want everybody on both sides of this blended family to talk openly about how they think things should be organized. I've noticed that everyone has done that here today. Could we talk about how that happened so that we might help it continue?
- When the community and school linkage project began, only a few parents were actively involved. Since that time, the project staff has worked to increase the roster of parents. How can we maximize on this effort?

Sometimes clients cannot describe where they want to go or even what the first step might be. They need opportunities to observe themselves in action to discover if they are making any progress or having any success. De Shazer and Molnar (1984) recommend the "formula first session task," a standardized observation for clients to complete before returning for a second session. They say to clients, "Between now and the next time we meet, I want you to observe, so that you can tell me next time, what happens in your life that you want to continue to have happen" (p. 298). Research on the effect of clients receiving this assignment shows that it correlates positively with cooperation, clarity of goals, and short-term improvement in functioning with respect to the initial challenge (Adams, Piercy, & Jurich, 1991).

Searching for Transferable Skills

Clients often demonstrate abilities in other areas that they can generalize to the situations at hand. Consider the mother who is short-tempered with her child but who shows great patience and restraint in caring for her aging father. Clearly, the skills and tolerance in both caregiving situations have similarities. Recognizing the success in one situation may help generate solutions in the other.

Or, at another system level, consider the example of a community that quickly activates considerable resources in times of natural disaster such as a flood, tornado, or hurricane, but isn't drawing upon those same assets to resolve the ongoing crisis in a public housing project which is deteriorating because of poor maintenance, low occupancy, and high crime. Strengths in one aspect of functioning hold promise for resolving other areas of need.

Recognizing Cultural Strengths

Each of us draws strength from a variety of internal and external resources. We feel strong when we have a clear sense of who we are and where we fit into our world. Likewise, we feel our strength when we are secure that others support the ways we think and believe and we can count on the backing of others around us. All these elements are present in the various cultural identities we hold.

Recall that culture is an aspect of all groups, but is most specifically applied to describe membership in a particular racial or ethnic group. Culture is "a vital bridge between the ethnic community and the dominate society. It contains ethnic customs and beliefs, interdependent family networks, behavioral survival skills, and other distinguishing features" (Lum, 1986, p. 2). Recognizing cultural strengths in clients has potential to activate powerful internal and external resources. It also reveals the worker's acceptance of diversity and bonds cross-cultural relationships.

The influence of culture is pervasive and fundamental to human strength and survival:

Cultural belief systems and behavioral outlook influence people's ideas, customs, and skills. For people of color, the cultural element reinforces positive functioning through family support systems, self identity and self-esteem, and ethnic philosophy of living. These cultural resources are coping mechanisms during stress and crisis. (Lum, 1996, p. 13)

Incorporating cultural strengths is a vital component of empowering social work practice. Unfortunately, "cultural resources are probably those least used by professional social workers in their encounters with clients" (Green, 1999, p. 95).

Strengths in Diversity

What is it that makes us overlook valuable cultural resources? Is it our discomfort with differences that encourages us to emphasize how we are similar to our clients and ignore those differences that we sense may threaten the bond of professional relationships? Is it that we are so accustomed to looking at cultural identities as the roots of prejudice, stereotypes, and oppression that we choose instead to minimize and gloss over rather than accentuate and celebrate our cultural and ethnic diversity? Whatever the reasons, it's time to recognize that ethnicity can function as "a source of cohesion, identity, and strength as well as a source of strain, discordance, and strife—the family, rituals and celebrations, language, and ethnic institutions all provide a source of comfort for many members of ethnic groups" (Devore, 1987, p. 95).

A logical explanation for the lack of attention to cultural strengths is the difficulty of building a knowledge base to detect them. Studies, such as one offered in the *Harvard Encyclopedia of American Ethnic Groups,* list as many as 106 separate ethnic groups in the

United States alone (Devore, 1987). How could any of us possibly know the unique strengths and capacities which characterize each of these distinct groups? Add to that the individual differences among clients even in the same ethnic groups and the task of recognizing cultural resources stymies even the most competent and motivated among us.

Of particular importance for culturally sensitive social workers are strengths present in the characteristics of diverse cultural groups. By definition, the dominant culture enjoys the privilege of defining predominant cultural values and beliefs. Therefore, it is members of diverse cultures who are likely to be judged most harshly and whose strengths are most likely obscured or underestimated.

What workers perceive as right or wrong, health or dysfunction, strength or weakness carries the imprints of their own cultural and ethnic backgrounds. With this restricted view, practitioners may actually interpret something that functions as a strength for a particular client as a deficit instead. Consider the Euro-American social worker who determines that the 24-year-old Puerto Rican woman who stays home to assist with her family is having a problem growing up and leaving home. The worker's value of individual autonomy contrasts sharply with the Puerto Rican view of family interdependence (Ramos-McKay, Comas-Diaz, & Rivera, 1988). In this situation, the worker sees this cultural characteristic as a problem to be solved rather than as a resource for this client and her family and totally misses the point. Learning about various cultures and ethnic groups alerts workers to possibilities, but workers should maintain caution in zealously applying general information to any client's specific situation to avoid stereotyping.

Ethnic Group Strengths

There are common resources among many ethnic groups in the United States, including African Americans, Latinos, Asian Americans, and Native Americans (Lum, 1996). These attributes include the centrality of family, support of the extended family and kinship network, clear vertical hierarchy in families, and the importance of religion and spirituality. Many of these qualities differ from the predominant Euro-American characteristics of independence, autonomy, egalitarianism, and rationality. This contrast demonstrates the need for learning about various racial, ethnic, and cultural groups, but workers should refrain from adopting the simplicity of this overgeneralization. Detecting cultural strengths is not a simple exercise in categorical thinking, but rather arises from careful study of nuances, of the similarities and differences within and among various groups. The sections that follow highlight some of the strengths the cross-cultural literature reveals about ethnic groups.

African Americans

African Americans currently comprise the largest racial minority group in the United States, accounting for approximately 12.8 percent of the total population (U.S. Census, 1999). Previous attention to African Americans focused on "pathology" and judgmentally defined how they differed in their functioning from the cultural majority. The current focus considers these same differences as potential sources of strength (Wright & Anderson, 1998). For example, Boyd-Franklin (1992) lists eight major strengths that social workers are likely to discover when working with African Americans, including: (1) extended family support; (2) the centrality of religion or spirituality; (3) the high value placed on children; (4) adaptability of family roles in response to changing circumstances; (5) informal adoption; (6) cultural loyalty; (7) high priority on education coupled with a strong work orientation; and (8) strong females. Additional strengths include achievement orientation, work orientation, flexible family roles, kinship bonds, self-help and mutual aid, political empowerment tradition, and adaptability in coping (Billingsley, 1992; Hill, 1997).

Strengths in African American clients are more visible through an Africentric worldview that reflects values different from Eurocentric culture.

> *These beliefs are manifested in behaviors such as sharing a communal orientation; living in harmony with nature; demonstrating cooperativeness and avoiding competitiveness, control, and confrontation; being flexible about time and not bound to exact time units; and using spiritual faith in daily activities. (Jackson & Sears, 1992, p. 186)*

The Africentric view places high value on interdependence of individuals with their environment. This fact orients practitioners working with African Americans to be on special alert for resources available within the context of family, social, and community networks.

Appropriate assessments of African American clients go beyond nuclear families, since the community context is basic to "identity, defense, and development" (Sullivan, 1993, p. 7). For example, the strong religious orientation indicates the central institutional role of the church in the African American community, defining churches and, usually, ministers as essential community resources in the ecosystem of many African American individuals and families. Working effectively with African American clients means appreciating their cultural values and traditions and broadly viewing individual functioning in the wider extended family and community contexts.

Latino Americans

Latino and Hispanic American are broad terms applied to many cultures of Spanish descent. Latinos trace their ancestors to places such as Mexico, Cuba, Puerto Rico, other Central and South American countries, and even parts of the Southwestern United States that were formerly Mexican territory. The common Spanish language heritage and categorical grouping by the U.S. government links these cultures, but in other ways comparisons reveal numerous cultural differences (Castex, 1994b). The size of this population group will more than double by 2050, when projections indicate people of Hispanic-Latino origin will constitute 24.5 percent of the U.S. population (U.S. Census, 1996).

Mexican Americans
Mexican Americans are the largest Latino group and the second largest ethnic group in the United States. Mexican American families are embedded in extended family networks that can include godparents and members of other families (Falicov, 1996; Morales & Salcido, 1998). These extended family members share such family functions as "nurturing and disciplining of children, financial responsibility, companionship for lonely and isolated members,

and problem solving" (Falicov, 1996, p. 175). In contrast to more assimilated ethnic groups, Mexican Americans continue to maintain much evidence of biculturalism and bilingualism. Mexican Americans resist assimilation into the U.S. cultural mainstream because of their proximity to Mexico, which provides "a constant infusion of persons and culture" (Martinez, 1988, p. 183).

One of the major strengths of Mexican American families is a quantitative rather than a qualitative difference from other ethnic groups (Martinez, 1988). There are simply more family members available to provide support and resources. The tendency toward having many children, including extended family members as active participants in family activities, events, and decisions, and adding non-related individuals to the family in the form of godparents establishes a natural support network that actively functions as a resource in any individual's development.

Observable differences occur between the "public view" and "private reality" of Mexican American families (Falicov, 1996). For example, many Mexican Americans have a more egalitarian distribution of power in marital relationships than the male-dominated cultural stereotype indicates. The strong value placed on children coupled with the mother's role in child rearing frequently sets up an in-home reality of an in-charge woman while the family maintains a public image that the man is in charge. This observation again alerts culturally sensitive social workers to the need to particularize any general cultural information with concrete information from each unique client system.

Mexican Americans frequently show the same high degree of spirituality that is present in other Latino cultures, such as Cuban and Puerto Rican. "Catholicism provides an order to social behavior that has a stabilizing and adaptive effect on individuals and families, and ...it also offers a source of explanation and control in an inchoate world" (Martinez, 1988, p. 190). Moreover, there are intricate interconnections and interdependencies among the personal physical, mental, and spiritual domains. Knowledge of this connectedness offers spirituality as a strength and as one of many pathways to change for Latino clients.

Other Latino Cultures

Attributes similar to Mexican Americans are also present in other Hispanic cultures. Puerto Rican and Cuban Americans show strengths in extended family support, respect for older family members, and a tendency toward cooperation over competition (Bernal & Shapiro, 1996; Weaver & Wodarski, 1996; Garcia-Preto, 1998). Regardless of similarities, sensitive practitioners avoid grouping all Latino cultures together, just as much as they exercise care in applying general conclusions about the tendencies of any cultural group to particular individuals. For example, Cuban Americans show greater tendencies toward autonomy and individuality than other Latino cultures (Bernal & Gutiérrez, 1988). Since music plays a more prominent role in the lives of Puerto Ricans, some suggest that interventions using music are very appropriate when working with Puerto Rican clients (Ramos-McKay, Comas-Diaz, & Rivera, 1988).

Asian Americans

The ethnically and culturally diverse groups described together as Asian Americans are, proportionately, one of the fastest growing ethnic groups in the United States (Fong &

Mokuau, 1994). Demographic projections indicate that Asian Americans will comprise 8.7 percent of the population in the United States by 2050, as compared to 3.8 percent in 1997 (U.S. Census, 1996; Hooper & Bennet, 1998). Like those ethnic groups clustered as Latino, the description "Asian American" represents various people who trace their origins to countries such as the Philippines, China, Vietnam, Korea, Japan, India, Laos, Cambodia, other Asian countries and the Pacific Islands. Unlike other ethnic groups in the United States, many Asian Americans do not suffer from negative stereotypes of dysfunction. Rather, they are stereotyped as a "model minority," an overgeneralized myth of unilateral brilliance and success. "According to this 'model minority' image, Asian Americans' cultural traits—diligence, frugality, and willingness to sacrifice—propel their upward mobility and win them public accolades" (Crystal, 1989, p. 405).

The "model minority" image has its drawbacks, as does any group stereotyping. It obscures individual differences and diminishes assistance to Asian Americans whose lives do not mirror the myth. And the minority status peripheralizes members of this group from the societal mainstream (Oyserman & Sakamoto, 1997). However, the model minority image does reflect a general awareness that there are strengths present in Asian cultures. Family unity, support for family members, particularly in times of crisis, and strong informal support networks such as churches, clubs, and family associations are strengths common among Asian Americans. A review of the social work literature by Fong and Mokuau (1994) shows general agreement that Asian American and Pacific Islanders hold respect and concern for others in higher regard than individual self-concerns. Considering this cultural emphasis on natural support networks, social workers may seek solutions through the resources of "priests, doctors, indigenous healers, and elders in their work with Asian clients" (p. 412).

The centrality of the family emphasized in many ethnic cultures is perhaps strongest among Asian Americans. Core family values among Asian Americans include family loyalty, unquestioning respect for parents, and "the unspoken obligatory reciprocity that arises out of human relationship, such as kindness and helpfulness" (Ho, 1987, p. 25). Other Asian values include preserving family honor and avoiding shame (Nakanishi & Rittner, 1996; McLaughlin & Braun, 1998). The quest for harmony in all human relationships is an essential value that can function as a powerful resource which compels Asian American clients toward cooperative resolutions (Browne & Broderick, 1994). Social workers must withhold their tendency to push clients toward self-assertion in a cultural context where group interest supersedes individual action and solutions lie in collaborative endeavors.

Native Americans

Although difficult to classify, Native Americans or American Indians comprise about 2 million, less than 1 percent of the population of the United States (U.S. Census, 1996). There are over 500 Native nations. Four of these nations have populations of over 100,000: the Cherokee, Navajo, Chippewa/Ojibway, and Sioux (Weaver & White, 1997).

There are many differences among the Native groups; however, one can identify common values and strengths. Within traditional Native American families, "closeness, collective problem solving, equal responsibility for young children, sharing of resources and of labor are all a way of life evolving out of the clan system in which the family was the core and the clan the extension" (Blount, Thyer, & Frye, 1996, p. 269). The extended family is integral to Native groups' sense of family and community. Family members value generosity, sharing, and giving, and respect the wisdom and leadership of elders (Weaver & White, 1997). Social workers who overlook extended family resources among Native Americans miss opportunities to provide culturally appropriate services. Red Horse (1982) describes a case example in which a child protection unit proceeded to place an "at-risk" child in a foster home forty miles away from the child's natural mother without ever discovering the extended family resources available less than five miles away. These resources included many family members who "offered their homes for foster placement services, guaranteed transportation for visits between mother and child during a period of family therapy, and provided ongoing assistance with parenting" (p. 19).

Many American Indians also find strength in tribal traditions. Garrett (1993–1994) says that tradition embedded in myths and "stories shared by the Indian elders teach culturally related values for learning and encourage that we all get along with each other" (p. 21). In these stories the emphasis is on cooperation and respect over personal achievement and "the interdependence of the family, clan, and tribes, rather than on personal gain or wealth" (p. 20). Encouraging the relating of these stories meets an identified need in Native American children to acquire information about cultural heritage (Franklin, Waukechon, & Larney, 1995). Social workers can ask Native American clients to relate stories about their heritage to discover strengths in tribal and familial histories.

As in other diverse cultures in the United States, spirituality functions as a guiding force. "Spirituality sets the tone for seeking harmony and congruence among mind, body, and spirit" (Red Horse, 1982, p. 18). Peaceful coexistence with natural forces is a key component of Native American spirituality (Yellow Bird, et al., 1995). Spiritual leaders have a significant influence on tribal members and are resources for Native American clients and for professional practitioners. Culturally sensitive social workers recognize that although these leaders may not be professionally trained helpers, they nevertheless, "are trained in very rigorous cultural ways and are quite adept in working with Indian clientele" (Red Horse, p. 18).

Again, workers cautiously apply any overall conclusions about Native Americans to specific clients since "researchers emphasize that there are large intragroup differences among American Indians and intergroup differences among tribes" (Franklin, Waukechon, & Larney, 1995, p. 183). Two major factors influence cultural differences among people described as Native American (Grimm, 1992; Dykeman, Nelson, & Appleton, 1995). First, there are distinctive differences in values and traditions associated with various tribes. This "diversity among indigenous people may be best expressed in the relationship that each nation has with its natural environment" (Yellow Bird, et al., 1995, p. 131). Second, Native Americans show much variation in degree of assimilation into the Euro-American culture. Ethnically sensitive social workers maintain a respectful, alert, and accepting posture to listen for clues as to the possible values and resources in their work with Native Americans.

Strengths in Cultural Group Memberships

Variations in ethnicity are not the only qualities that distinguish cultural groups. Gender, sexual orientation, age, religion, abilities, and other characteristics also lead to groupings which classify and possibly even stereotype cultural group members. Culturally competent social workers learn to identify the unique strengths potentially present in people of many different cultures including women, gays and lesbians, older adults, people with religious affiliations, and people with disabilities.

Women

Slightly more than half of the U.S. population is female. The proportion of women in the labor force has expanded dramatically over the last several decades. Yet, women are short-changed in the market place. Even though their wages have increased, women still earn about 30 percent less than men. More than one-third of all female-headed households have incomes below the poverty level. Older women are particularly vulnerable to poverty. Issues affecting women, such as poverty, homelessness, domestic violence, inadequate child care provisions, and depression, have at their core social and economic inequities. Women show strengths in their abilities to face this social injustice.

Feminism adds a perspective on the strengths of women as survivors of patriarchy, inequalities, and oppression (Simon, 1994). Hanmer and Statham, two feminist social work scholars from Great Britain, urge a view of women "as active, resilient, and enduring actors in their own behalf rather than as sorry objects of other people's words or actions" (as cited in Simon, p. 171). Women discover self-worth and self-identity in their abilities to survive. "Survival involves more than perseverance of living a life of quiet desperation; it means assertion, however unobtrusively this may be expressed. Survival means taking on what has to be confronted, preferably in your time, on your grounds, around your issue" (p. 172).

Categorical definitions of what it means to be feminine or masculine separate women and men. To be feminine is to be interdependent, peaceful, egalitarian, emotional, nurturant, and concerned about others in contrast to masculine tendencies to be independent, rational, decisive, achievement-oriented, aggressive, and concerned about rights and responsibilities. These "appropriate" characteristics demonstrating femininity and masculinity are socially defined, yet they are often assumed to be biologically determined. Gender stereotypes are value-based and have negative effects. They define what "should be manifest for one gender but not the other. Distinctions between the sexes, rather than commonalities, are emphasized, and the isolation of individuals is reinforced" (VanDenBergh & Cooper, 1986, p. 4).

Western culture has traditionally assigned characteristics associated with masculinity a superior status. While masculine characteristics may support the patriarchal values of rugged individualism, competition, and the work ethic, masculine characteristics fall short in promoting cooperation, communication, and interpersonal relationships. This brand of sexism devalues feminine traits and masks the feminine strengths of both women and men. Nurturance, emotional investments in others, cooperation, and communication abilities that respect and honor others are the very elements that support self-growth, strengthen families, enhance interpersonal relationships, and promote "caring" structures within neighborhoods, organizations, communities, and society. These qualities are strengths for social workers to acknowledge in women and in men.

Women of Color

Women of color experience disproportionate rates of poverty and homelessness. From their perspective, these injustices are more likely related to racism, classism, and ethnocentrism than to sexism, factors ignored by traditional feminist perspectives (Gutiérrez & Lewis, 1998). For women of color, "gender oppression is secondary to institutional racism" (Lum, 1996, p. 31). Strengths abound in their abilities to survive oppression and "leverage political power" (p. 111). An exploratory study by Aguilar and Williams (1993, as cited in Lum) revealed "strengths of women of color that derive from their personal, family, and community traits" (p. 30), including hard work, pride in accomplishments, significant support systems, spirituality, optimism, self-motivation, and persistence. Factors identified in the research that contributed to the success of these women were "the achievement of goals, job satisfaction, self-esteem, education and skills, family support and stability, personal strengths, ethnic/racial pride, and community and professional commitment" (p. 31).

Gays and Lesbians

All social work practitioners will interact with clients and colleagues who are gay or lesbian. Compiling results from several studies, Newman (1989) estimates that more than 10 percent of the U.S. population are gay men or lesbian women. Social work requires a broad-based acceptance of sexual diversity with an openness to recognize the strengths of gay and lesbian clients.

In many ways, the strengths of gays and lesbians mirror those of other people. They derive strengths from personal qualities, interpersonal relationships, and connections within their communities. But acknowledging and asserting a homosexual orientation in a homophobic society requires unique struggles, creative adaptations, and the ability to take risks. To function successfully in the heterosexual and gay and lesbian communities, gays and lesbians inevitably learn to be bicultural (Lukes & Land, 1990).

Many gays and lesbians demonstrate considerable strengths in achieving developmental milestones. Developmental processes are complex for gays and lesbians since they must grow into an identity that is not socially sanctioned, a process not faced by heterosexuals (Sullivan, 1994). Gays and lesbians show strengths in recognizing and accepting a sexual identity that varies from the dominant norm, in coming out to others, in maintaining committed partnerships without legal sanction, and in asserting their identities in their social environments. At each developmental phase, gays and lesbians must resolve their own personal ambivalence and risk social rejection—unjust dilemmas imposed by a homophobic society but, nevertheless, situations that elicit assertion, creative adaptation, and personal strength.

The abilities of gays and lesbians to create families outside of the traditional family models is another significant strength. Ainslie and Feltey (1998) note that lesbian couples tend to be independent, self-reliant, assertive, and more flexible in defining gender role expectations suggesting "the possibility of a very positive childrearing environment in lesbian families" (p. 329). Their study concludes that children in lesbian families are accepting of differences and express a high degree of social consciousness about issues such as racism, sexism, and non-violence.

Besieged by misunderstanding, discrimination, and oppression, gays and lesbians have initiated numerous activities to redress these injustices. "The gay and lesbian community shows extraordinary strength and courage in its ability to initiate social action, educational, and advocacy activities in response to AIDS as well as to issues related to violence, and discrimination" (Newman, 1994). Culturally competent social workers recognize the wealth of resources present within gay and lesbian communities and the power of their community organizing skills.

To successfully recognize the strengths of gay and lesbian clients, workers reject negative value judgments rooted in dominant cultural norms, explore their own biases and homophobic tendencies, and openly dialogue with others about sexuality. This is an important aspect of social work practice because "the issues surrounding the gay population exemplify the core social work principles of self-determination and the basic need of full social and civil rights for all oppressed people" (Newman, 1989, p. 209).

Older Adults

Recent census studies in the United States predict that the number of adults 65 years and older will increase from the present 35 million (12 percent of the population) to 39.4 million by 2010, to 69 million by 2039, and 79 million (20 percent of the population) by 2050 (Administration, 1999). Those in the United States over 85 will increase from the present 3.2 million to 18 million by the year 2040. With respect to the world population, projections indicate that more than 60 percent of the population will be over 60 by 2050 (Current state, 1999). By force of sheer numbers, social workers need to understand the strengths related to aging.

People often associate growing older with sensory loss and changes in mobility; however, for most older adults, these changes are neither as cumbersome nor as apparent as many imagine. Successfully coping with a lifetime of events, older adults show signs of resilience physically and emotionally. This realization is enculturated in beliefs by Asian and Pacific Islanders who see older adults "as family decision makers and the keepers of family and cultural wisdom" (Browne & Broderick, 1994, p. 254). As people grow older, they accumulate life experiences, gain perspective, and amass the knowledge of a lifetime.

To discover strengths within older adults, social workers encourage them to talk about their lives including current events and those from the past. Reminiscing provides older adults with opportunities to retell their life stories. Kivnick (1988) says: "Sifting through these newly revealed old treasures allows interrelated parts of the whole that has been the one and only life cycle" (p. 64). The perspective of age lends a new understanding to identity in the context of the life cycle. Since developmental processes build upon each other, older adults have become seasoned experts about each phase of the life cycle.

Religious Affiliations and Spirituality

While there is a loud public outcry about the decline of values in contemporary culture, religious culture is flourishing in the United States. Recent studies conducted by the Princeton Religion Research Center found 9 in 10 Americans indicate they pray and that 3 out of 4 engage in prayer on a daily basis (Gallup, 1999). Studies also conclude that 94 percent of Americans believe in a Higher Power, and 84 percent of Americans have little or no doubt about the existence of God (Religion, 1997). Even of those saying religion is not important to them, 23 percent said they have experienced the presence of God in their lives. For many people in the United States, religion and spirituality are significant influences and potential sources of strength, resilience, and meaning in life (Billingsley, 1992; Jacobs, 1997; Bullis,

1996; Angell, Dennis, & Dumain, 1998; Canda, 1998; Graham, Kaiser, & Garrett, 1998; Haight, 1998; Walsh, 1999; Canda & Furman, 1999; Pellebon & Anderson, 1999).

Although specific beliefs and practices vary considerably, religious affiliation and spirituality have resources to offer. Affiliating with a community of faith provides a network of personal relationships and concrete support in times of need. Common beliefs, stories of the faith, holy days, and ritual celebrations forge a sense of communal identity and purpose. In African American churches, research reveals a "haven which children can learn about their heritage from other African Americans who valued and nurtured them" (Haight, 1998). Compassion, love, and forgiveness—themes in most religions—contribute to personal and interpersonal healing. Commitment to a faith can initiate a sense of meaning, renewal, and hope for the future. Religious commitment may encourage concern for the welfare of others and, for some, foster a zeal for redressing social injustices.

Persons with Disabilities

The U.S. Census Bureau estimates 49 million people in the United States not living in institutions, or about one in five, have a disability. Nearly half that number have a disability classified as severe. Many of these persons with disabilities face a number of challenges in accomplishing life tasks. Not only do their own physical or mental conditions affect their abilities, but, according to the social model of disability, the social context imposes restrictions that limit their capabilities as well (Fine & Asch, 1988; Mullender, 1992–93; Oliver, 1992, 1996; Black, 1994; Beresford, 1994; Goodley, 1997). Stigma, interpersonal degradation, and social marginality lead others to underestimate the capabilities of persons with disabilities as they strive to fulfill meaningful social roles.

The challenge for social workers is to recognize that people with physical, cognitive, and psychological disabilities are also people with abilities. "A collaborative approach to practice with people with disabilities must be founded on the fact that they are people first and disabled second" (Gilson, Bricout, & Baskind, 1998, p. 194). Individuals draw strengths from their own personal resolve, positive self-images, aspirations, priorities, creativity, supportive relationships with family members and friends, successful rehabilitation, and use of adaptive devices. Progressive legislative mandates—such as the Americans with Disabilities Act to remove architectural, transportation, and communication barriers—further ensure the full participation of persons with disabilities in community life.

Clients as Resources for Understanding Cultures

A general knowledge of culture and ethnicity sensitizes practitioners to the diversity of potential resources within special populations. But, even among people with similar cultural identities, workers remain cautious about overgeneralizing. "The capacity for individualizing the client within a specific cultural matrix is the genius and the challenge of effective cross-cultural social work" (Green, 1999, p. 92).

Luckily, as practitioners work to incorporate clients' cultural strengths, they have key respondents with them in the same room. Clients themselves are the best sources of information about their cultural strengths and resources. When social workers bring general cultural awareness, openness to differences, and good listening skills, along with permission for clients to be themselves in a cultural sense, workers learn how to relate to clients in their ethnic and cultural contexts.

Uncovering Strengths in Adversity

Since the advent of psychoanalysis, helping professionals have searched the past to account for why things have gone wrong in the present. In this view, the scars of adversity and dysfunction accumulate to overwhelming proportions. But, strengths-oriented social workers acknowledge that, in spite of the adversity, somehow people continue on their way. Clients who experience victimization are also, by definition, survivors.

"The view that past traumatic experiences are a source of problems in later life is certainly plausible—at least here in the West. The opposite view that past ordeals are valuable learning experiences is equally sensible" (Furman & Ahola, 1992, p. 23). Surviving trauma such as is the case in oppression, victimization, or family disruptions takes strength, courage, and resources. Practitioners working with survivors of any sort have opportunities to explore their clients' success in making it this far.

Surviving Oppression

Groups described as cultural minorities above all share similar histories and experiences with respect to oppression. Oppression is "the systematic, institutionalized mistreatment of one group of people by another for whatever reason" (Yamato, 1993, p. 207). Racism, sexism, ageism, ableism, heterosexism, regionalism, and classism are all various forms of oppression. Each form of prejudice and discrimination denies a particular group access to their fair share of society's resources, violating human rights and principles of social justice.

Certainly, social workers strive to overcome such social injustice, working at the macrolevel to create changes in social policy to increase universal access to resources and opportunities. They also work on their own professional styles to identify and eradicate tendencies to perpetuate oppressive practices in their relationships with clients. Prevention of oppression is the preferred approach. But, the simple fact is that social work practitioners deal with many clients who have already been affected by oppressive forces. On a client-by-client basis, social workers must look beyond the damage that oppression may have caused to applaud the strengths that these same clients have brought to bear in handling injustice.

Successful Coping Skills

Did you notice the predominance of strengths present in family, informal, and natural support networks as you read about various ethnic and cultural groups? Persons denied access to the benefits of society at large learn to cope in other ways. They group together. They help each other out. To meet their own needs, they set up their own informal institutions to circumvent the discriminatory formal institutional processes. The informal adoption practices of African Americans exemplify one such informal "child welfare system."

The "victim system" significantly impacts racial and ethnic minorities (Pinderhughes, 1982). Victimization can impose a trap; however, surviving victimization requires adaptability, flexibility, and strength. Social workers acknowledge the magnitude of the impact of oppression and, at the same time, do not neglect the possibilities of positive adaptation.

One such positive adaptation is the strong extended family network present in African American families, which has roots in their African heritage and developed in response to slavery, threat, and oppression (Boyd-Franklin, 1992). Another adaptive coping skill is the example of "vibes." African Americans, because of the often extremely subtle ways in which racism manifests itself socially, are particularly attuned to very fine distinctions among such variables in interactions. Because of this, many African Americans have been socialized to pay attention to all the nuances of behavior and not to just the verbal message.

Strengths develop in response to oppression. "We African Americans have a history of drawing upon inner and extended family resources to survive from one generation to the next, no matter what the obstacles and indignities" (Franklin, 1993, p. 37). Franklin suggests ways to draw out these strengths in working with African American clients. For example, ask clients to describe the survivors known to them in their own family histories and guide them to search for these same qualities in themselves. A strong connection to history and legacy by African American clients draws on the support of their cultural identity and their success even in the face of the past abuse of slavery.

Responding to Oppressed Clients

All oppressed groups have overcome difficult odds. Clients benefit from exploring the ways they accomplished this. To do so, workers acknowledge and empathize with clients' feelings of oppression, yet urge them on toward the ways they have been able to handle this unfair treatment. Workers may say:

- I know you're right that it's not easy to be an African American in a racist community, but somehow you seem able to cope. How is it that you manage so well?
- It does seem like the school picks on you because you're different. Are there other Mexican American students that you know that seem to get by? What are they doing to cope?
- I agree that this neighborhood doesn't seem to get the same services that the rest of the city gets. I'm so impressed with the way all of you work together, pool your resources, and find ways to cope in spite of their neglect. Maybe, we can use some of the resources this group has already developed here to advocate with city officials for better treatment.

In each example the worker does not underestimate the devastating impact of social injustice, but neither does the worker ignore that clients are making it in spite of the adversity.

Surviving Violence

Many social work clients have experienced various forms of violence including physical, sexual, or emotional abuse. Such trauma can be devastating. But each survivor of such an event has gone on and found ways to get through each day in spite of the difficult circumstances. Social workers can assist these clients by helping them unload their pain, but workers can also help direct clients' attention back to their capabilities, areas of power, and residual abilities to choose their own direction.

Recent immigrants have many times lived through political upheaval resulting in torture, forced evacuation from their homelands, and harrowing experiences in immigration to the United States. The following case study represents a poignant example of such a survivor, a female immigrant from Cambodia who was:

> *actively suicidal at the refugee camp two years after being raped by a Khmer Rouge soldier, because she felt that she could no longer live with the shame. All treatment approaches failed until her reason for what she saw as succumbing to the rape was recognized as a strength—it enabled her to fulfill her responsibility of protecting her younger brother. By reinforcing the worth of her decision to protect her brother, the young woman's sense of self-esteem was strengthened. (Bromley, 1987, p. 238)*

Being violated by abuse or rape tests personal strength. Clients who have survived incidents of such violence in the near or distant past have already passed the test.

Social workers need to be alert to the different ways that people from various cultures cope. "Too often, the active coping strategies of clients who have little social power are misinterpreted as passivity and giving up" (Holzman, 1994, p. 95). Workers acknowledge there is no right way to respond to violence, but recognize that survivors draw on their own developed strengths as they cope.

While workers clearly maintain an orientation toward strengths in viewing clients who are survivors, not all clients are ready to openly acknowledge that they have gone on. On a cautionary note, workers should not move too quickly to point out the successful ways clients are coping. Rather they may need "to incorporate a different kind of gentleness and patience into their clinical repertoires" (Markowitz, 1992, p. 18). Although workers should not move too quickly to highlight survivorship strengths, they nevertheless should remember clients' inner strengths and their own "faith in people's potential to recover and find joy in life" (p. 24).

Surviving Family Disruption

The impact on children of families that experience disruption is a contemporary issue which receives much attention, giving rise to such support groups as Adult Children of Alcoholics (ACOA) or Adult Children of Dysfunctional Families. Many helping professionals trace the difficulties adults experience to origins in problematic family dynamics. In some ways, we are all affected by the dynamics of our families of origin (Carter & McGoldrick, 1989). Each of us develops in unique familial and other social contexts. Each of us carries the impact of these interpersonal systems with us. Each of us also makes choices about how we respond and incorporate these influences. Think about your own life, the ways your family has affected and is affecting you, and the choices that you make to respond.

Strength-oriented social workers acknowledge the inevitable power that families have over children yet also realize that all persons develop their own way to cope. "Care should be taken not to assume that each person who was abused as a child will necessarily be under extreme distress as an adult" (Busby, et al., 1993, p. 338). In fact, "strength can emerge from adversity" and result in resiliencies that promote well-being (Wolin & Wolin, 1993, p. 15). Workers certainly empathize with difficult family experiences, but also focus on the client's response to this history. Workers may say:

- Growing up in an alcoholic family does leave its mark, and I see that you have a good job, a nice home, and people who care about you. How have you managed all of this?
- It must have been terrifying to know that your father was determined to commit suicide. What did you do to overcome that fear and anxiety?
- Growing up in your family meant that you had to grow up fast, almost like you never really got to be a kid. Have you found ways to relax and have fun now that you are in charge of your own life?

Workers do not underestimate the difficulty of childhood abandonment, neglect, or trauma but they also keep an eye toward the future and how clients can incorporate what they have learned into where they want to go.

Reflecting Back

People become social work clients for many reasons, at times because of actions deemed unacceptable by societal standards. These clients often bear labels such as child abuser, batterer, or perpetrator, descriptions that stir negative feelings in the most accepting social worker. Implementing a strengths perspective means that workers shift their focus even with these clients to acknowledge their capabilities and successes. What is your ability to suspend judgment and work to identify strengths in clients who have done "bad" things? How do you do this? Should you do this? Consider your stance in regard to identifying the strengths of clients identified as deviant.

Looking Forward

Identifying strengths is a companion process to articulating situations and defining directions. Social workers simultaneously elicit information about what brings clients to them while also constantly searching to discover the resources available to lead clients toward solutions. A social worker's ability to identify strengths springs from preparation to recognize client strengths in general functioning, in specific responses to the challenging situations, in cultural memberships, and in historical adversity.

Clients are not alone in mustering their capabilities to meet their challenges. They also have the resources of their social and physical environments. Chapter 10 describes additional assessment processes for social workers to implement to discover what else clients and environments have to offer.

C h a p t e r **10**

Assessing Resource Capabilities

When you consider moving into a house, you want to see more than one room. No matter how impressed you are with that one room, you still want to explore the entire house—the other rooms, the attic, the basement, the yard. You may even want to stroll around the neighborhood. Because you know that the ambience of one room alone does not define the experience of living in the whole house, you ask to see it all. Life in one room responds to and affects the rest of the house, the yard, and the neighborhood, just as life in the entire house, yard, and neighborhood responds to and affects life in one room.

Clients may not lead social workers around to the "other rooms, yards, or neighborhoods" of their lives unless workers ask for a tour. A generalist assessment does more than articulate clients' situations and identify their strengths. Regardless of the level of the client system, an assessment of resources at all system levels broadens the area of potential solutions. When social workers guide clients to look beyond their immediate situations to explore contextual systems more thoroughly, they discover new information, resources, and opportunities. Discoveries enable social workers and clients to decipher the relationships among events and identify untapped, yet accessible, resources.

An empowering generalist assessment does more than simply list client and environmental resources. The inquiry of assessment, itself, creates change. As a result, social workers move cautiously to explore and respond productively. The choices clients and social workers make about what to explore begin to shape the possibilities for the solutions they will frame. The processes used in exploring set expectations for clients' involvement in change. Collaboration in this process activates clients to take charge of their own inquiry and builds momentum in their support networks to sustain the change effort.

This chapter discusses ways that clients and workers assess resources available to clients in their environments. Specifically, this chapter:

- Outlines ways to actively involve clients in discovering and assessing available resources
- Offers ways to assess human system functioning using an ecosystems framework, including a five-point schema and a series of assessment questions
- Describes several assessment tools that apply to generalist practice and maintain an orientation toward strengths
- Presents information about recordkeeping

An astute assessment of available resources leads practitioners and clients to distribute their change efforts wisely, selecting strategies that draw on client strengths and activate environmental resources.

Exploring Resource Systems

Social workers and clients assess resource systems to discover gold, not causes or reasons. They work to clarify areas of competence in client:environment transactions. In assessment:

> *The worker is, therefore, guided by these specific purposes: (1) clarifying the unique capacities, skills, motivations, and potentialities of the person; (2) clarifying the characteristics of the impinging environment that influence his or her coping and*

adaptive patterns; and (3) clarifying what needs to be changed in the person and/or the environment, so as to make their transaction more mutually satisfying and growth-producing. (Libassi & Maluccio, 1986, p. 171)

Empowering assessment means looking for resources. Like strengths, resources are relative, identifiable only in context. The actual ways clients interact with their social and physical environments determine what functions as resources for them. To complete an empowering assessment, the partners explore broadly for resources that may be present in the environment, in the interactions of clients with others, and even in other challenges that clients are facing.

Recognizing Environmental Resources

Social workers often locate resources in a client system's physical and social environments. For individuals, environmental resource systems may include family, friends, neighbors, co-workers, supervisors, classmates, teachers, social groups, school, church, social agencies, organizations, and the community. For a non-profit organization, contextual resource systems may include consumers, funding bodies, foundations, professional organizations, local colleges, and other agencies in the service delivery network. For any human system, regardless of size, environmental resources are essential for survival and well-being.

Every part of our lives contributes to or hinders our ability to maneuver successfully through life. Consider your situation as an example. What in your environment facilitates your work? Likely you are reading this book as part of a social work class. Does the instructor frame this information in such a way that enhances your understanding? Do you have classmates with whom you will discuss this material to augment your comprehension? Do you have children for whom your spouse, partner, or friends provide child care so that you can study? Do you have a quiet place to read—the school library, your own room, or a picnic table in the park? The presence or absence of these supportive resources has a lot to do with your success in completing your studies.

Look further and you will also discover other systems that provide resources. How is it that you find yourself in this classroom? Is your family providing financial support? Are you receiving government loans or grants to pay expenses? Are you getting scholarships from community organizations, your church, or the college to defray your costs? Are you working to pay your own way, so that your place of employment is a resource to guarantee your education? Does your ethnic or cultural identity place a high value on educational achievement? The presence or absence of these environmental resources influences whether you have the opportunity for academic success and a career as a social worker. Resource systems—from personal support networks to institutional systems—contribute to even the simplest transaction. Recognizing resources requires awareness of environmental contexts, sensitivity to cultural differences, and openness to a broad range of possibilities.

Turning Challenging Situations into Resources

Certainly, not all aspects of ecosystems are resources per se. A comprehensive assessment frequently leads to a different kind of discovery—the discovery of other problems or challenges.

But, challenges can actually be resources rather than additional constraints. The key is how workers respond. Disempowering responses stack the newly found problems on the others already described. Visualize how this leads to stigmatizing clients with labels such as "multi-problem" or to ascribing blame for "who is causing what." Contrast this response with a more empowering perspective that suggests that recognizing common links among challenging events provides new insights about situations and expands options for change.

Notice in the example that follows how an ecological assessment uncovers additional challenges yet enlarges the arena of potential solutions. An African American woman, Latasha, consults with a social worker about her feelings of depression. Latasha shares her frustration and disappointment in not securing a job in law enforcement despite her obvious qualifications and credentials. Broadening the search for resources to local law enforcement agencies reveals a new challenge—a pattern of discriminatory hiring and promotion practices with respect to women and people of color. Discovering this additional challenge of institutional sexism and racism links Latasha's depression, her unemployment, and the discriminatory hiring practices. Latasha's options for change now expand beyond the personal realm to include political and legal strategies for confronting the discrimination. Latasha's exercise of political power is now an option—an avenue to restore her sense of personal control and relieve her depression.

Collaborating to Search for Resources

Social workers guide clients through an exploration of resource systems, but who or what guides social workers? Ecosystems are enormous. A thorough examination of inside realms, outside environments, and the relationships between systems and their contexts literally goes on forever. After all, while you are examining any ecosystem, it remains dynamic, ever-changing, and constantly evolving even in response to the discovery process itself.

In assessment, empowerment-based social workers don't fall prey to the trap of certainty that classic diagnosis or categorical labels invite. Merely labeling behavior oversimplifies complex dynamics of human interactions and tends to limit options. Amundson, Stewart, and Valentine (1993) advocate a questioning and tentative attitude rather than a precise and expert posture in order to maintain an empowering frame during assessment. They say: "Our certainties about the world may also restrict and constrain us.... In trying to be helpful there is the temptation to enact our privilege, to impose upon others normalizing standards or to be blinded to diversity by the 'professional' certainties of our practice" (p. 111).

Effective social workers offer their reflections in tentative and thought-provoking ways and encourage clients to do the same. Workers purposefully share their thoughts to stimulate new interpretations, develop usable theories, and suggest possible directions in ways that encourage mutual discourse. However, rather than stating the certainties, social workers offer hunches and possibilities with phrases such as:

- I wonder if…
- Is it fair to say that at this time…
- I have a hunch that I'd like your opinion about. Have you ever considered…
- I'm noticing that Hector's legal problems started at the same time your father died. From your point of view, does it look like…

- As I've listened to the Task Force's discussion, I believe that at this time you've identified three major areas to consider for action...
- There may be more, but I seem to hear two different ways of interpreting this situation.

Social workers' insights may, indeed, "unstick" client systems. However, for clients to remain in charge of meaning, social workers phrase their comments in ways that level authority and invite a client to support or disagree with their hypotheses. In recognizing a client's expertise, social workers do not abandon their theoretical knowledge and practice wisdom. Instead, reflective practitioners recognize that the authority of their knowledge has potential to disempower clients. As Hartman (1992) advises: "We need not discard our knowledge, but we must be open to local knowledge, to the narratives and the truths of our clients...to honor and validate our clients' expertise" (p. 484).

To define the scope of an ecosystemic assessment, practitioners rely on clues from clients. Through dialogue, workers and clients maintain an informed perspective on what to assess and the ability to screen for what else they need to know. To assist clients in this exploratory process, workers implement assessment processes that include applying theoretical frameworks, using tools, adding new viewpoints, and conducting observations.

Applying Theoretical Frameworks

Social workers use frameworks drawn from theories about human system behavior and theories of change to organize the search for resources. Some assessment frameworks apply to human systems at all levels, while others are specific to particular situations. The ecosystems framework introduced in Chapter 2 is an example appropriate for generalist practice since it flexibly applies to any system level.

Organizing Assessment Using a Five-Point Ecosystemic Schema

The ecosystems framework can organize the search for resources into a simple five-point schema. Applying this strategy, practitioners begin by clearly identifying the focal system. From there, the framework guides workers and clients to explore what happens inside this system, what happens outside this system, how the inside and the outside of the system connect, and what happens as the system progresses through time. Applying this framework to any client system produces a dynamic explanation of its functioning in context and uncovers available resources (Table 10.1).

Practice Example: Franklin Courts

The following example demonstrates how applying the ecosystems framework organizes the activities of Damon Edwards and the residents of Franklin Courts to assess the situation in the housing complex.

TABLE 10.1   Ecosystems Framework: Assessment Questions

Identify the focal system

- Who are the system's members?
- What characteristics define their membership in the system?

Inside the System

Structural Dimensions: Closeness

- What are the subsystems?
- Who supports whom?
- Are members close to one another or isolated?

Structural Dimensions: Power

- What is the system's hierarchy?
- Who is in charge?
- Who makes decisions?
- Who enforces decisions?
- Do members function autonomously or interdependently?

Interactional Dimensions

- How do members communicate?
- Do members talk directly to one another or do they route messages through third parties?
- Do members offer constructive feedback to one another?
- What are the rules and norms for behavior?
- Does everyone share responsibility?

Biopsychosocial Dimensions

- Are members physically healthy?
- What are the special physical abilities and needs of members?
- How do issues of development and maturation affect the functioning of the system?
- How do members feel?
- Do members share their feelings openly?
- How do members think?
- Do members share their own thoughts and respect the contributions of others?
- What are the individual strengths of various members?

Cultural Dimensions

- What are the various cultural influences?
- What are the cultural strengths of members?
- Do common cultural identities bind members together?
- How do cultural differences influence the relationships within the system?
- What are the predominant beliefs and values of members?
- Are there cultural influences on communication?

Outside the System

- What systems are influential in the environment of the focal system? Consider from among the following depending on the level of the system:
  - Family and extended family members
  - Friends, neighbors, natural support networks
  - Neighborhood, community
  - Organizations, groups

TABLE 10.1   *Continued*

Outside the System

- • Social agencies
- • Social institutions
- • Economic systems
- • Government bodies
- • Policies, laws, regulations
- • How are these influential systems connected to one another?
- • What are the influences of the physical environment?
- • What potential resources exist that the system currently does not access?

Inside and Outside Connections

- • Does the focal system's boundary tend to be open or closed?
- • What information flows across this boundary?
- • Does the system acquire necessary resources from the environment?
- • What does the system contribute to the environment?
- • Are some members more connected to the outside than others?
- • Does the system have power in relationship to outside systems or is it overpowered by environmental demands?
- • What outside systems provide stability?
- • What outside influences tend to disrupt the system's functioning?
- • What is the system's view of the larger environment? Does it see it as threatening or friendly?
- • How is the system's cultural identity viewed in the larger environment?
- • Is the system at risk of discrimination or oppression?

Movement through Time

- • What is the expected development of the system?
- • What physical, psychological, emotional, cognitive, moral, and systemic transitions are occurring at this time?
- • How is the system handling these transitions?
- • What nodal events characterize the system's development?
- • How did the system respond to these nodal events?
- • Does the system flexibly adapt to meet the needs of members?
- • Does the system flexibly adapt to changing environmental demands?
- • Were there times in the past when the system worked the way members would like?
- • What development changes are expected in the near future?

The Referral

The residents of Franklin Courts are angry. During a routine preschool screening, six children living at the low-income housing complex tested positive for lead contamination. The media reports that parents demand action! The Housing Authority says only that "they will look into it." Damon Edwards, a social worker in the outreach and advocacy services division of the Neighbors United Neighborhood Development Program, is also "looking into it."

Fiona Grant, the grandmother of one of the six children, called Damon about the situation. Damon already knows Mrs. Grant from his work with the youth recreation program. She is a powerful and energetic resident of Franklin Courts. Damon is pleased that Mrs.

Grant sees him as a resource. Damon doesn't know what he will find in his meeting with the residents that Mrs. Grant promises to gather. However, he has a way to look at the situation that will give him a sense of what's going on and direction for ways he might contribute. Damon applies an ecosystems framework to ensure a generalist approach to assessment.

What's the Focal System?

As always, Damon first identifies the focal system. In this situation, he knows that he will work with a group system. Mrs. Grant was acting on behalf of all the concerned residents. This, coupled with the urgency of the issue at hand, the common goal of the residents, and the fact that residents are already beginning to function in a collective manner, indicates that group action will be a likely strategy for success.

Identifying the group of residents as his client allows Damon to continue to frame his approach. He will need to look inside the group, at its membership, to discover its resources. He will also need to look outside the group to understand environmental opportunities and constraints. Damon doesn't yet know the kinds of linkages this particular group of residents has to resources in the community, but, certainly, exploring these connections will be important. Finally, Damon will examine the group's process and organizational structure. Theory informs him about effective group development. Damon's task will be as much to encourage the growth of the group itself as it will be to work toward the group's goals.

What's Inside the System?

At the first meeting of the Franklin Courts group, Damon discovers that the crisis of the high lead levels in the children and the potential for further lead contamination has indeed activated the residents of Franklin Courts. Twenty-four adults attend the meeting; three other residents are babysitting so other parents can attend. Much is happening inside the group. Certain members have taken leadership roles. Mrs. Grant is obviously the spokesperson. She convenes the meeting and seems to be in charge of the agenda. When the group adjourns, Mrs. Grant along with three other influential group members volunteer to meet with Damon to plan and bring back recommendations to the group's next meeting. Also, smaller groups are beginning to form around specific issues of concern. The parents of the six children need to arrange immediate specialized assessment of their children's health. Several other residents want to press for an investigation into the source of the contamination and prevent further exposure. Damon quickly sees the possibility for task-oriented subcommittees to work concurrently in multiple directions rather than having the whole group continue its debate over what specific outcome to seek first.

What's Outside the System?

Outside of the group, not too much is happening yet to address the concerns of the Franklin Courts residents. Despite the Housing Authority's promise to look into the lead contamination, the residents have heard nothing from them. The media have expressed interest but have not yet provided extensive reports. On a positive note, the doctor who discovered the problem is sympathetic and willing to support the group's action. And, of course, since the group called Damon, the resources of Neighbors United are accessible to them.

How Does the Inside Connect to the Outside?

Damon sees the group's relationship to the community as a resource to develop. Certainly, the group's connections with other systems need strengthening. For example, somewhere in the city's administration, the Housing Authority is accountable to a higher office; the Franklin Courts' group would benefit from a strong relationship with whomever this might be. Making this important link will increase the group's power in working with the Housing Authority. Damon also considers the doctor and the media as resources the group should continue to activate.

How Does the System Move through Time?

Observing the group's developmental progress shows that it is maturing naturally in a productive way. The way the group itself organized child care during group meetings concretely demonstrates its positive development. Damon can build on the group's robust beginning. He will strive to clarify and cultivate the evolving structure and interaction of the group to maximize collaboration among members. Damon is beginning to understand the group's potential and direction.

Focusing on the residents' group as the client system, looking at its resources inside and out, assessing the group's transactions with its environment, and tracing the group's progress as it develops through time—all facets of an ecosystems assessment—contribute to Damon's broad view of what is happening with this particular group. The ecosystems framework offers a way to conceptualize the group throughout the entire process from assessing the situation to implementing strategies for change.

Organizing Assessment: Applying Ecosystemic Questions

Questions arising from an ecosystemic perspective elucidate client system functioning in context, including information about the structural elements, interactions, psychosocial dimensions, cultural influences, and physical environments of the client system. The following sections list these questions and relate them to an ecosystems perspective.

Assessing Structures

Recall that the structural perspective on human systems examines the configuration of the ecosystem—the arrangement of interactions between the client system and its physical and social environments. The two most important structural elements are power and closeness or, in systemic terminology, hierarchies and boundaries. Assessing the hierarchies and boundaries of the client's ecosystem leads social workers and clients to understand which components may constrain the client and which hold resources for change.

Who Has the Power?

By definition, the success of an empowering social work process depends on clients gaining a sense of power and control. Identifying where the power currently lies is essential to this effort. Even when clients temporarily feel powerless, those persons or systems that contribute to powerlessness are potential sources of power. In other words, if you know where the power is, you know where client systems can get it. An assessment of the ecosystem identifies sources of power.

Consider the following example. A homeless family temporarily stays with a distant relative while waiting for an opening in a rent-subsidized housing complex. But policies at the city's housing authority require that families living in public shelters receive priority in renting available units. Although this policy has merit, it holds this homeless family hostage, leaving them only the alternative of moving from their temporary living arrangement into an overcrowded and understaffed shelter to become eligible for placement. Clearly, the housing authority and its policies have the power. Assessing this power distribution helps the worker and the family generate new strategies, which range from advocacy with the department to political strategies to initiate policy changes at the state level.

Another place to look for power is in the client system itself. Sometimes, clients do exercise power and competence in certain areas of functioning, but feel inadequate in others. For example, the neighborhood group that can organize a neighborhood watch program likely has many of the resource capabilities necessary to lobby a school board to institute cultural sensitivity training for teachers to meet the challenge of discriminatory educational practices and harsh discipline of ethnic minority students. When the answer to "where is the power?" is "with the client," the emphasis shifts from using the identified power in one area to meet the challenge in another. Workers and clients contemplate the following questions to discover power resources:

- Who or what has power?
- How does the client access it?
- Who or what can help the client gain power?
- What might get in the way?
- What power resources does the client already possess?
- What will the client do with the power?

What Connections Are Working?

Alliances within and between systems are important sources of support and assistance. Assessing who is close to whom, what resources clients use successfully, and what supports are already available to clients defines areas of the client's functioning to maintain, strengthen, and develop. For example, the existence of a supportive extended family is a resource for an individual client seeking a job. Extended family members may be willing to increase their support and provide child care, financial assistance for specialized training, transportation to fill out job applications, or encouragement during the stressful time of applying, interviewing, and waiting for a job offer. Existing connections are likely to be resources that social workers and clients can expand.

Assessing existing connections may also reveal that the client's boundaries are currently too open to other forces but, if redefined, have potential to become resources. For example, consider Craig, a divorced father who has custody of his three children. Acknowledging the importance to his children of a strong relationship with their mother, Karen, Craig agrees to an open visitation policy whereby Karen can visit the children in his home whenever she chooses. When Craig and his social worker review the assessment information, they find that Craig has trouble establishing rules and enforcing discipline with the children, and Karen's unpredictable visits complicate this difficulty. Assessing this information identifies the need to renegotiate this boundary—to close it up somewhat—in order to maintain the relationship with the children's mother as a resource, yet fit her visits into an effective routine for the household.

A boundary assessment identifies how connections are working for the client. The answers to questions about boundaries supply information about the client's alliances with people and resources. Questions to consider include:

- What significant connections does the client have?
- Are these relationships functioning effectively?
- Could these connections serve as resources to address the client's current situation?
- What connections might need to be changed in order for them to function as resources?
- What might prevent the client from renegotiating these connections?

What Connections Are Missing?

When assessing how clients connect with others, the connections they lack also become evident. Just as open boundaries allow access to resources, closed boundaries block clients from obtaining resources. A lack of connections to interpersonal and community resources forces clients to meet all their needs on their own, a situation that is likely to deplete their energies rather than sustain their sense of power. Factors preventing a client from connecting to resources include insufficient information, inaccessible resources, financial constraints, ineligibility, transportation needs, suspicion, and fear.

Consider the example of Marian, a woman who feels powerless to have friends, spend time alone away from home, or buy anything for herself without permission. Marian feels trapped by the rigid control and physical power exerted by her husband, Doug. However, a comprehensive exploration of her ecosystem also reveals that Marian is unaware of the Domestic Violence Center, believes that she is not eligible for the woman's support group at her church, and no longer maintains contact with her own family of origin because they don't like Doug. All these components of Marian's ecosystem—her husband Doug, the domestic violence program, the church group, and her own family of origin—have potential to be resources of power.

Think about the options created by identifying the missing connections. The worker recognizes that Doug is pivotal in this issue. He is disconnected from the social work endeavor and possibly from understanding Marian's situation. Obviously, if Doug changes his behavior toward Marian in ways that respect her freedom, she will gain a sense of power. The worker can connect Doug to Marian by inviting him to participate in the social work process. Even if the dynamics of this marriage are such that Doug chooses not to change or refuses to join the effort, the outside sources of support including the domestic violence program, the church, and her family may function to give Marian resources for survival should she decide to confront or leave Doug. Assessing Marian's world locates disconnections from these sources of power and identifies options for initiating empowering connections.

Questions that uncover missing connections include:

- Who is significant to the client system but uninvolved who might be invited to join the effort?
- What potential resources are present that the client might consider in new ways?
- What resources does the worker know about that the client doesn't?
- What is blocking the client from connecting to resources which might help?

Assessing Interactions

An assessment of interactions examines how people and their environments relate and evolve. Remember that human systems behave in ways that seek harmony and balance. What happens in a client system somehow is adaptive in its context. The interactional perspective leads us to contemplate just how things make sense.

Is This the Way Things Should Be?

Some difficulties are inevitable. Pittman (1987) describes developmental crises as universal and expected, saying "they may represent permanent changes in status and function, rather than just temporary phases. They arise from the nature of biology and society" (p. 9). Many times changes that seem unnatural are actually naturally occurring events and transitions in human system development. Examples of life-stage changes are Erikson's (1963) stages of psychosocial development, Carter and McGoldrick's (1989) family life cycle, Papernow's (1993) stages of stepfamily development, and the natural evolution of groups reported by many authors (Henry, 1992; Johnson & Johnson, 1997; Garvin & Tropman, 1998; Schriver, 1998). Knowledge that these changes are expected and, in fact, desirable is a resource that social workers have available to share with clients.

Consider the example of the social worker hired to consult with a delinquency prevention agency. The agency recently received funds to develop a case management system to coordinate services for first-time offenders and attempt to divert them from prosecution by the juvenile justice system. Assessment reveals that for two months, the four-member team worked cooperatively. But, just when they seemed to be getting comfortable with each other, their meetings began to erupt with conflict. The social worker assesses the conflict and recognizes the disequilibrium that naturally evolves in a group as it forms. By helping the team learn conflict-resolution skills to continue its natural development, the worker assists team members to translate their differences into creative resources for developing the new program. To recognize natural transitions, workers and clients consider questions such as:

- What physical, cognitive, and psychological transitions are occurring in members of the client system?
- Do family life cycle transitions apply? Group development transitions? Organizational development transitions?
- Is the event or behavior expected based on the client system's stage of development?
- What changes need to occur to facilitate a smooth transition?

What Have We Got to Lose?

The question, "What have we got to lose?," considers the consequences of change. Recall the ecosystems view of dysfunction: even apparently problematic behavior may be working adaptively somewhere else in the client's ecosystem. As an example, consider the boy whose academic failure at school activates his parents to sit with him in the evening to help with homework, to visit his teacher to confer about his learning difficulties, and to advocate with the school board to hire a reading specialist for the district. Clearly, the boy's behavior is a resource in connecting him to his parents and connecting his parents to the school system.

What would happen if the boy's behavior suddenly improved? These resources might be lost, leaving him isolated and unnoticed. Cowger (1992) recommends considering what life will be like if the problem is resolved. Papp (1983) guides workers to explore the negative consequences of change. She says the worker "should obtain a slow-motion picture leading up to, during, and after the occurrence of the problem" (p. 20). In this way, workers can assess the potential effects problems have in the system. This information provides insight into how the system is balanced and what changes might occur as solutions develop. To consider how difficulties affect a client's situation, workers contemplate:

- How is the system responding to the situation?
- Is there anything good that happens as a result?
- What solutions has the client attempted?
- What else will change when the client overcomes the difficulty?

Assessing Thinking and Feeling

Human beings think and feel. We not only respond to the structure and functioning of the social systems in which we participate, but also to the ways we interpret what happens in these various contexts. An assessment of thinking and feeling results in a clearer understanding of the cognitive and affective factors that influence human behavior.

What Do You Think?

Assessing how the client system functions in its ecosystemic context offers new ways to think about events. Typically, clients bring a particular theory about what is going on to the social work relationship. An assessment of thinking processes sheds new light on these previously fixed notions and theories. When social workers and clients reframe and reconceptualize, they generate many new ways to explain situations. Generating alternative ideas and hypotheses leads to multiple options for change. Questions that disclose aspects of thinking include:

- What explanations does the client system offer? Do all members of the client system hold the same view?
- Does the client hold notions that, if reframed, would incorporate new possibilities?
- How might changes in thinking lead to changes in behavior?

How Does It Feel?

Assessing feelings supplies intuitive hunches about whether social workers and clients are on the right track. Feelings are prominent, as "people have feelings about themselves and their plight, about making decisions, and taking definitive action. People have feelings about having feelings, and all of these are inextricably bound to definition and resolution of the problems they are facing" (Middleman & Wood, 1990, p. 59). Feelings can be a source of energy for change; unattended "they become obstacles to the work" (p. 59). Accessing affective responses taps into clients' motivations, comfort, and spontaneity. Questions that uncover dimensions of feelings include:

- What clues do verbal and nonverbal messages offer about the feelings the client is experiencing?
- In the case of multiperson client systems, are the emotions members express similar or different from one another?

- In what ways are feelings affecting thinking?
- How does the synergy of emotions amplify or diminish the energy available to invest in solutions?

Assessing Cultural Influences

The cultural identities of any particular system influence the way it interacts with other systems. The cultural influences internalized by various system members contribute to diversity within a given social system. A complete assessment of an ecosystem requires an exploration of cultural elements.

What About the Big Picture?

One aspect to consider in assessing cultural influences is how clients fit into the larger picture. Since not all racial, ethnic, gender, or other cultural groups currently receive equal access to the resources of society, the relationship of the culture of the client system to the macrosystem deserves special consideration. Social workers overlook powerful influences when they fail to recognize oppression and discrimination. Helping clients adapt to an environment marked by prejudice and injustice disempowers. Instead, ethical practitioners craft macrosystem interventions to redress injustice. Assessing cultural influences raises the critical consciousness of social workers and clients to the impact of discrimination and oppression and serves as a catalyst for social action and social change. To understand the sociopolitical influences on client systems, workers and clients consider questions such as:

- In what ways do prejudicial attitudes such as racism, sexism, ageism, classism, ableism, heterosexism, and regionalism affect the client's circumstances?
- What roles do discriminatory practices, procedures, and policies play in the client system's situation?
- How has oppression directly and indirectly blocked the client's access to the power?
- What strengths can the worker and client discover in the ways the client adapts to experiences of discrimination and oppression?

How Does the System Fit Together?

Assessing cultural dimensions enlightens the partners in another way. Each member of a client system may be responding to different cultural influences. For example, consider the circumstances of an immigrant family in cultural transition: "Many Spanish-heritage immigrant families in the United States are seeking therapy because of family problems resulting from transitional conflicts specific to their status as immigrants and because their different subsystems adapt to the new country at different rates" (Baptiste, 1987, p. 250). In other words, a cultural assessment reveals that the family conflict is actually a cross-cultural relationship issue. The stress ethnic group members experience as the result of living in two cultures is sociocultural dissonance (Chau, 1989). A similar dynamic occurs in the blending of stepfamilies with conflicting lifestyles (Visher & Visher, 1996). And, certainly, cultural differences are likely to exist among members of larger group, organizational, and community systems. Cultural information is a resource to clients and workers in externalizing the issues rather than personalizing the conflicts. To understand the role of culture, workers consider answers to questions such as:

- What different cultural perspectives are operating?
- Do these cultural perspectives agree or conflict with one another?
- Are factors such as the reasons for and experiences of immigration involved?
- In what ways are intergenerational perspectives a factor?
- To what extent does the experience of living in two cultures result in sociocultural dissonance?

Assessing Physical Environments

The final piece to consider in assessing human systems is the influence of physical environments on client functioning. Workers may not have opportunities to personally view their clients' homes, places of work, or neighborhoods and, furthermore, may neglect to inquire about what these settings are like (Gutheil, 1992). "Yet not knowing how or if clients are able to meet such needs as privacy and personal space leaves workers poorly equipped to evaluate the full meaning of clients' behavior" (p. 391). Deficiencies, obstructions, lack of privacy, and other environmental factors can all contribute to the stress clients experience. The physical environment plays an important role in group dynamics, too. Arrangement of physical space, lighting, and ventilation all make a difference in how group members interact. Physical environments can augment or restrict client functioning and, therefore, are important factors to assess.

Have You Looked Around This Place?

Consider the situation of Deanna, a client with retardation, who seeks assistance to balance her budget. Deanna's caseworker carefully evaluates Deanna's competencies in budgeting and is pleased to see that Deanna has appropriate math skills, demonstrates a good awareness of frugality, and organizes her bills effectively. But when the worker visits Deanna at home, the major issues are much clearer. The old apartment building in which Deanna lives clearly needs maintenance. The windows are not sealed properly, the thermostat is broken, and nearly every faucet leaks. The assessment of Deanna's physical environment leads the social worker to the resources of the city building inspector, the apartment owner, and the utility company in helping Deanna with her budgeting problems.

In assessing physical environments, workers and clients can discover resources and constraints. To weigh the effects of the client system's physical environment, workers ask questions such as:

- In what ways does the client system's physical environment enhance or curtail its ability to function?
- How does the client system respond to the stress that results from factors in the physical environment?
- What modifications to the physical environment would be helpful to the client system? Which are most realistic to pursue?
- Who has the decision-making authority to ensure that these modifications will be made?

Putting the Pieces Together

Answers to these assessment questions construct an ecosystemic vision of a client system's situation. Considering these various dimensions offers a comprehensive view of human system functioning—structure, interaction, psychosocial elements, and cultural influences in the context of the social and physical environments.

Using Assessment Tools

Assessment tools are also useful in structuring the search for resources. Specifically tailored to the purposes and characteristics of client systems, they include such diverse instruments as written questionnaires, standardized psychological tests, visual diagrams, behavioral checklists, role plays, games, toys, dolls, and community resource assessment instruments.

Assessment tools help to describe situations and identify strengths, stimulate discussion, and facilitate sharing of diverse viewpoints in multiperson systems. By employing assessment instruments, workers can screen for issues requiring immediate attention, establish baseline information against which to measure subsequent change, and meet agency record keeping requirements.

Since assessment tools mediate conversations between clients and social workers, they are particularly useful for clients who experience difficulty expressing their thoughts and feelings directly. For example, children who have been sexually abused frequently find it easier to express their experiences by drawing pictures, playing with dolls, or telling stories rather than candidly speaking about their personal experiences with sexual abuse. Shy adolescents may readily complete written forms describing their family relationships rather than struggle to articulate their thoughts and feelings directly. And, recent studies suggest computerized assessments prompt clients to disclose more candid information (Ferriter, 1993). Assessment tools provide an intermediate step—a way to be close in a mode that allows a safe distance.

Assessment tools may be essential with larger systems to ensure that all those involved have a voice. Formalized procedures such as surveys, polls, and forums can access a broad base of information for assessment. The following section describes assessment tools that may fit a client's situation, including social histories, genograms, eco-maps, culturally sensitive assessment, social network maps, and group, organizational, and neighborhood and community assessment frameworks.

Social Histories

A social history organizes information about the history and current social functioning of individuals and families. Additionally, this standardized report describes the congruence between a client's needs and the formal and informal resources currently available (Sheafor, Horejsi, & Horejsi, 1997). The exact format varies with the requirements of the practice setting. Some agencies use outlines to structure detailed narrative reports (Table 10.2). Others use fill-in-the-blank forms that require brief comments in each of several categories. In general, social histories organize demographic data as well as information about personal his-

TABLE 10.2   Social History Outline, Individual Client

Client:

Worker:

Date of Report:

   I. Identifying information: (preferred name, address, phone, date of birth)

  II. Referral information: (source of referral; reason for contact, including challenges faced and previous attempts to resolve; other professional or indigenous helpers currently involved)

 III. Individual functioning: (developmental status; current physical, cognitive, emotional, psychological, and interpersonal capabilities; areas of need)

 IV. Cultural functioning: (race/ethnicity; primary language and languages spoken; significance of cultural identity, cultural strengths, experience of discrimination or oppression)

  V. Family information (names, ages, involvement with client, including spouse/partner, parents, siblings, children, and extended family members)

 VI. Family interaction: (extent of support, family perspective on client, client perspective on family, and relevant family issues)

 VII. Natural support network: (significant relationships—names and nature of involvement)

VIII. Physical environment: (housing situation, financial stability, transportation resources, neighborhood)

 IX. Nodal events: (situation and client's response to deaths of significant others, serious losses or traumas, significant life achievements, other events)

  X. Education: (dates, places, and years of education completed; accomplishments, degrees, and credentials)

 XI. Employment: (current job, type of work, lengths of employment, previous experience, skills, and special training)

 XII. Medical history: (birth information, illnesses/accidents/surgery, medications used, family medical and genetic issues, physical limitations, diet, alcohol and drug use)

XIII. Religion: (denomination, church membership, extent of involvement, spiritual perspective, special observances)

XIV. Social activities: (interests, clubs/organizations, preferred recreation, travels)

 XV. Future plans: (client's perspective on current situation, goals, personal and environmental resources to meet goals, constraints to goal attainment)

tory and life events. Social histories include information about: (1) the client system; (2) the client's concerns, needs, and associated problems; and (3) strengths and limitations of the client in context (Johnson, 1998).

To complete a social history workers may choose to structure interviews to match the social history format. Other times, they facilitate conversations with clients that permit the information to flow naturally. Here, the social history outline serves as a checklist to ensure that all necessary information has been included. Either way, workers inform clients that they are completing a social history and detail how the information will be used.

Social histories, as completed written products, are invaluable resources. For example, in a nursing home, various members of the staff including the social worker, activity director, dietician, physician, or family liaison may use the social history as a reference in planning or coordinating services with the resident. Clearly, this indicates the need for accuracy and clarity in the finished product. Sheafor, Horejsi, and Horejsi (1997) say that good social history reports are brief, simple, useful, organized, confidential, and objective. In addition they should be relevant and should focus on client strengths.

Genograms

Genograms visually represent family chronology (Hartman, 1978, reprinted in 1995; McGoldrick & Gerson, 1985, 1989). As schematic diagrams, genograms provide summaries of information about family history, marriages, deaths, geographic locations of family members, structure, and demographics (Figure 10.1). Completed genograms look somewhat like family trees, especially when they include information about several generations (Hartman, 1978, reprinted in 1995). Workers and clients annotate genograms to communicate information about "the sources of nurturance, stimulation, and support that must be available in the intimate and extended environment to make possible growth and survival" (p. 113).

By highlighting familial information, genograms aid our understanding of relationship patterns, transitional issues, and life cycle changes. To gather information for genograms, workers ask clients to share family stories and traditions. Adding chronological information about nodal family events furnishes additional information about family transitions and identifies points where families have coped with change over the course of time. To incorporate a multicultural perspective, one can add dimensions of diversity to genograms by including "stories of generation, gender, ethnicity, race, class, and migration" (McGill, 1992, p. 344). Genograms are also useful to identify multiple cultural influences, trace intercultural blending through the generations, and emphasize the unique cultural history of any family (Hardy & Laszloffy, 1995; Congress, 1994).

Numerous areas of practice consider genograms essential for assessment. Constructing genograms with older adults affords them opportunities for life review. Practitioners working in medical settings use genograms to trace patterns of health and wellness. And, genograms adapt to many aspects of child welfare as they can be used to trace adoption histories or record foster care placements. Genograms offer clues about intergenerational relationships and propose sources for family support. Consistent with the strengths perspective, genograms can also reveal the patterns of family strengths over time and highlight exceptions to family legacies considered problematic (Kuehl, 1995).

Eco-maps

Eco-maps graphically picture the ecological context of the client system (Hartman, 1978, reprinted in 1995; Hartman & Laird, 1983). Eco-maps focus specifically on the major systems with which clients are involved to visually depict their relationships with these systems. In other words, eco-maps portray transactions between the client and other systems: the exchange of resources, the nature of system relationships, the permeability of boundaries, and connections to the social service delivery system and other contextual supports (Hartman &

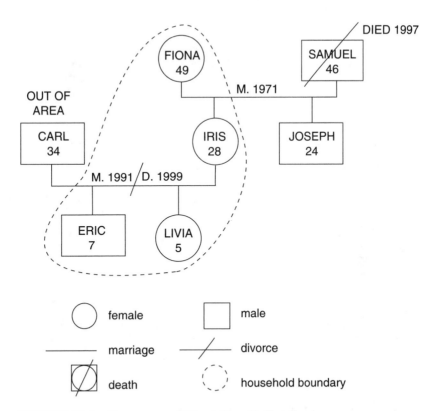

FIGURE 10.1 **Genogram of Fiona Grant's Family. A genogram illustrates family structure and relationships. Genograms list family members in at least two generations, including their names, ages, and dates of marriages and divorces. Workers and clients can also annotate genograms with other information to meet their specific purposes.**

Laird, 1983). To construct an eco-map, Hartman recommends placing the client's household in the middle of the eco-map and adding systems with which the client interacts to the parameters of the map. Lines connecting the systems portray the nature of the relationship and the direction in which energy flows (Figure 10.2). In this way, eco-maps provide information about available resources, existing constraints, and potential new connections.

The eco-map is a tool that encourages collaboration in the worker–client relationship (Hartman & Laird, 1983). Using eco-maps also instigates interaction among family members. "The process of mapping invites lively, active discussion. After all, it is the family's map, and no one knows their world quite the way they do" (p. 185). Furthermore, visual representations accentuate information, offering clients new perspectives. For example, "an eco-map full of stressful relationships showing all of the arrows pointing away from the family may lead a client to say, 'No wonder I feel drained—everything is going out and

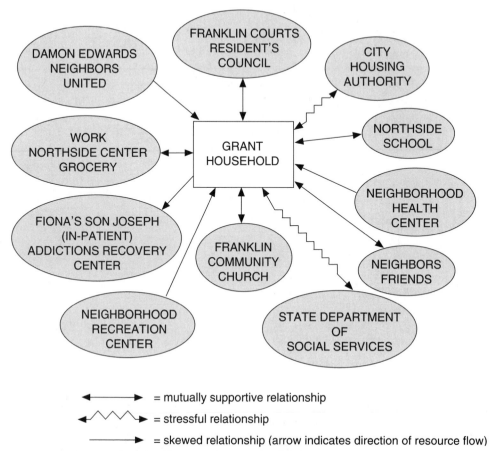

= mutually supportive relationship

= stressful relationship

= skewed relationship (arrow indicates direction of resource flow)

FIGURE 10.2   **Eco-map of Fiona Grant's Household. An eco-map illustrates a human system in context. It identifies significant environmental systems and describes the nature of the relationships. Constructing an eco-map helps clients to clarify environmental resources and constraints.**

nothing is coming in!' " (p. 185). Comparing the eco-maps of family members can offer insight into the differing experiences and perceptions of the various family members (Harold, Mercier, & Colaross, 1997).

Since eco-maps frequently identify changes to make and resources to develop, workers and clients can use them to set goals and construct plans of action. Eco-maps can graphically illustrate change by contrasting a client's initial and concluding eco-maps. Workers also note how eco-maps externalize problems and diminish a client's sense of blame. Eco-maps demonstrate that social workers want to understand clients' unique circumstances and resources rather than search for their inner faults (Hartman & Laird, 1983). A generalist application of the eco-map places a group, organizational, or community client system at the center and maps its transactions with related systems (Mattaini, 1993).

Culturally Sensitive Assessment

For individual and family assessment that is sensitive to cultural differences, social workers augment traditional models of assessment that are more individualistically focused with collectively focused models that begin by exploring the influences and resources in the macroenvironment. One such model is the "Person-In-Family-In-Community Model" (Fong, 1997). This model emphasizes "look[ing] at the person in the context of both the family and the larger society" (p. 42).

To apply this model, social workers assess cultural influences in six areas. They:

1. Identify the family's place of origin and the continued influence of their societal background
2. Explore the family's affiliations with their ethnic community and their attitudes towards social services
3. Determine in which community and family organizations, including ethnic social organizations, the family holds memberships
4. Detail the family's formal and informal roles, expectations for family members' behaviors, decision-making and power structures, and change agents
5. Analyze the subgroup structures in the extended family and their influence on family dynamics and family members.
6. Examine how individual family members are influenced by family roles, obligations, and responsibilities (Fong, 1997)

Social Network Maps

Social network mapping is a tool for assessing social support that pictures a client's social support networks and quantifies the nature of support from the client's point of view (Tracy & Whittaker, 1990). To implement this technique, clients first identify members in their support network, including immediate family or household members, extended family, friends, and neighbors, as well as more formal organizations such as work, school, clubs, church, and other services (Figure 10.3). Then, by using a sorting technique and responding to specific questions, clients describe how they perceive the support they receive from others (Figures 10.4 and 10.5). Social network mapping assesses:

- Who provides social support
- Kind of support available
- Gaps in relationship resources
- Opportunities for reciprocal exchanges
- Presence of negativism and stress that produces criticism
- Barriers to using available resources
- Priority of social support in relation to other challenges

Group Assessment

The defining element of any group is its purpose. Group assessment, therefore, focuses on the "fit" between a group's functioning and its purpose. The purposes of client groups vary

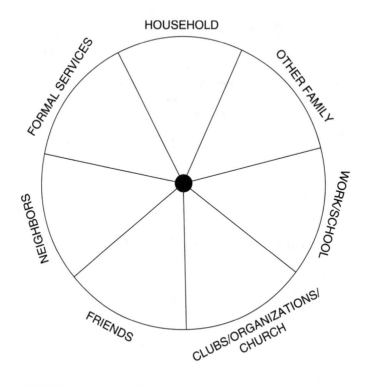

FIGURE 10.3   Social Network Map

Reproduced with permission of the publisher, Families International, Inc., from "The Social Support Network Map: Assessing Social Support in Clinical Practice," by E. M. Tracy and J. K. Whittaker, *Families in Society,* October, 1990.

from those focused on support or therapeutic treatment to those organized for skill development, task completion, or social change. Areas of group functioning to explore include group culture, cohesion, norms, communication, leadership, decision making, controversy, and conflict.

Framework for Group Assessment

Effective groups share common qualities, such as productive communication, good listening skills, appreciation of member diversity, distributed leadership, participatory decision-making procedures, and skills for managing controversy. Similar to other human systems, a group's interaction must be assessed in its context to create a comprehensive view, including the group's goals and resources, interaction patterns, and relationships with various environmental systems.

Group Goals and Resources

- Identify the purposes of the group
- Determine members' motivation to meet the group's purposes

Name	#	Area of life 1. Household 2. Other family 3. Work/school 4. Organizations 5. Other friends 6. Neighbors 7. Professionals 8. Other	Concrete support 1. Hardly ever 2. Sometimes 3. Almost always	Emotional support 1. Hardly ever 2. Sometimes 3. Almost always	Information/ advice 1. Hardly ever 2. Sometimes 3. Almost always	Critical 1. Hardly ever 2. Sometimes 3. Almost always	Direction of help 1. Goes both ways 2. You to them 3. They to you	Closeness 1. Not very close 2. Sort of close 3. Very close	How often seen 0. Does not see 1. Few times/yr. 2. Monthly 3. Weekly 4. Daily	How long known 1. Less than 1 yr. 2. 1–5 yrs 3. More than 5 yrs.
	01									
	02									
	03									
	04									
	05									
	06									
	07									
	08									
	09									
	10									
	11									
	12									
	13									
	14									
	15									
1–6		7	8	9	10	11	12	13	14	15

ID _____
Respondent _____

FIGURE 10.4 Social Network Grid

Reproduced with permission of the publisher, Families International, Inc., from "The Social Support Network Map:
Assessing Social Support in Clinical Practice," by E. M. Tracy and J. K. Whittaker, *Families in Society*, October, 1990.

Instructions/script for social network map.

Step One: Developing a Social Network Map

Let's take a look at who is in your social network by putting together a network map. (Show network map.) We can use first names or initials because I'm not that interested in knowing the particular people and I wouldn't necessarily be contacting any of the people we talk about.

Think back to this past month, say since [date]. What people have been important to you? They may have been people you saw, talked with, or wrote letters to. This includes people who made you feel good, people who made you feel bad, and others who just played a part in your life. They may be people who had an influence on the way you made decisions during this time.

There is no right or wrong number of people to identify on your map. Right now, just list as many people as you come up with. Do you want me to write, or do you want to do the writing?

First, think of people in your *household*—whom does that include?

Now, going around the map, what *other family members* would you include in your network?

How about people from *work or school?*

People from *clubs, organizations, or religious groups*—whom should we include here?

What *other friends* haven't been listed in the other categories?

Neighbors—local shopkeepers may be included here.

Finally, list professional people or people from formal agencies whom you have contact with.

Look over your network. Are these the people you would consider part of your social network this past month? (Add or delete names as needed.)

Step Two: Completing the Social Network Grid

(If more than 15 people are in the network, ask the client to select the "top fifteen" and then ask the questions about only those network members. For each of the questions use the appropriate sorting guide card. Once the client has divided up the cards, put the appropriate code number for each person listed on the network grid.)

Now, I'd like to learn more about the people in your network. I'm going to write their names on this network grid, put a code number for the area of life, and then ask a few questions about the ways in which they help you. Let's also write their names on these slips of paper too; this will make answering the questions a lot easier. These are the questions I'll be asking (show list of social network questions), and we'll check off the names on this grid as we go through each question.

The first three questions have to do with the types of *support* people give you.

Who would be available to help you out in *concrete* ways—for example, would give you a ride if you needed one or would pitch in to help you with a big chore or would look after your belongings for a while if you were away? Divide your cards into three piles—those people you can hardly ever rely on for concrete help, those you can rely on sometimes, and those you'd almost always rely on for this type of help.

Now, who would be available to give you *emotional support*—for example, to comfort you if you were upset, to be right there with you in a stressful situation, to listen to you talk about your feelings? Again, divide your cards into three piles—those people you can hardly ever rely on for emotional support, those you can rely on sometimes, and those you almost always can rely on for this type of help.

Finally, whom do you rely on for *advice*—for example, who would give you information on how to do something, help you make a big decision, or teach you how to do something? Divide your cards into the three piles—hardly ever, sometimes, and almost always—for this type of support.

Look through your cards and this time select those people, if any, in your network who you feel are *critical* of you (either critical of you or your lifestyle or of your skill as a parent). When I say "critical," I mean critical of you in a way that makes you feel bad or inadequate. Divide the cards into three piles—those people who are hardly ever critical of you, sometimes critical of you, and almost always critical of you. Again we'll put the code numbers next to their names.

Now look over your cards and think about the *direction of help*. Divide your cards into three piles—those people with whom help goes both ways (you help them just as much as they help you), those whom you help more, and those who help you more. OK, let's get their code numbers on the grid.

Now think about how *close* you are to the people in your network. Divide the cards into three piles—those people you are not very close to, those you are sort of close to, and those you are very close to—and then we'll put a code number for them.

Finally, just a few questions about *how often* you see people and *how long* you've known the people in your network. Divide the cards into four piles—people you see just a few times a year, people you see daily (if you see someone twice or more than twice a week, count that as "daily"). OK, we'll put their numbers on the grid.

This is the last question. Divide the cards into three piles—those people you have known less than a year, from 1 to 5 years, and more than 5 years.

Now we have a pretty complete picture of who is in your social network.

FIGURE 10.5   Social Network Instructions

Reproduced with permission of the publisher, Families International, Inc., from "The Social Support Network Map: Assessing Social Support in Clinical Practice," by E. M. Tracy and J. K. Whittaker, *Families in Society*, October, 1990.

- Inventory group members' resources to achieve purposes
- Explicate the values, beliefs, and cultural affiliations of group members
- Characterize group consciousness about relevant issues

Group Interaction

- Measure group cohesion and communication effectiveness
- Assess members' respect for differences in perspectives and opinions
- Identify prevailing group norms
- Describe the group's decision-making processes
- Assess the distribution of power and leadership within the group
- Consider the group's ability to manage conflict and controversy

Group–Environment Relations

- Describe the matrix of environmental systems that influences the group and individual members
- Determine the accessibility of environmental resources
- Analyze the impact of race, class, gender, and other cultural identities on group interaction

Organizational Assessment

An organization is a formal group that joins together to make use of collective resources and skills to achieve a common purpose or goal. Social workers implementing organization assessments may consider an organization as a client, as a context for social service delivery, or as a target for change.

Framework for Organizational Assessment

Like any social system, organizations may be assessed by considering their internal characteristics and the demands and resources of their environments.

Organizational Goals and Structures

- Identify the mission, purpose, goals, and the history of the organization
- Describe the organizational governance and decision-making structures
- Define the perspectives or principles that guide leadership and managerial staff
- Characterize the organizational culture and membership and/or constituencies

Organization–Environment Relations

- Detail the economic, political, demographic, fiscal, cultural, legal/governmental, and technological environments of the organization
- Characterize the fit between organizational purpose with tasks and the needs and resources of the environment
- Describe the opportunities and threats posed in the environment
- Identify relevant policy issues that have an impact on organizational functioning

Organizational Competence

- Describe how the organization evaluates its achievement of its purpose and goals, and how the organization uses that feedback to enhance effectiveness
- Assess the organizational capacity for innovation or change
- Identify mechanisms for strategic planning and continuous quality improvement
- Characterize the organizational strengths and weaknesses

Force Field Analysis

Force field analysis, a creative problem-solving technique developed by Lewin (1951), applies to organizational assessment and strategic planning. This strategy is based on the theory that forces within a system either drive toward or restrain change. Either removing restraints or enhancing those forces currently driving toward solutions fuels change (Brager & Holloway, 1992; Hurt, 1998; Hoekstra, Vink, & Fa, n.d.). Steps in force field analysis include:

1. Developing the statement of the problem and session objective by using a brainstorming technique to delineate "what is" and "what should be"
2. List the forces currently driving toward the solution
3. List the forces that obstruct progress
4. Review the driving and obstructing forces and determine which are most significant
5. Reformulate the forces rated "significant" into problems that need to be addressed
6. Generate creative ideas that can be applied as solutions
7. Review and modify strategies for change
8. Detail required actions
9. Identify necessary resources and determine "who will do what when"
10. Delineate specific outcomes that serve as indicators of change (Hurt 1998)

Neighborhood and Community Assessment

Needs assessment differs from asset mapping. Social workers and planners conduct needs assessments to document problems, identify unmet needs, and establish priorities for service and resource development. Asset mapping in a community or neighborhood, on the other hand, involves assessing capacities, resources, and assets. This includes taking an inventory of the individual, associational, and institutional capacities (Kretzmann & McKnight, 1993). In contrast to the traditional community "needs" assessment, a community asset inventory focuses more on what a community has than on what is missing. This shift in emphasis from community problem solving to community capacity building positions localities for implementing asset-based community development strategies.

A comprehensive neighborhood or community assessment includes information gathered through a variety of methods (Kettner, Daley, & Nichols, 1985). *Community surveys* include questionnaires administered face-to-face or mailed to a representative sample of the community population to solicit opinions and collect data about community life. *Key informant studies* involve structured interviews, surveys, or focus groups with individuals identified as having expertise on the subject under study. *Community forums* are open scheduled meetings held to solicit the views of a broad representation of community members. *Telephone poll surveys* are conducted over the phone with members of representative households. *Statistical indicators* profile the community using a collation of census data, demographic and population statistics, and social and economic indicators.

Framework for Community and Neighborhood Assessment

Social workers find community studies useful for inventorying sources of strengths and assessing community competence. A community assessment is also useful for assessing distinct neighborhoods within a larger community. The assessment includes such elements as a community or neighborhood profile, an inventory of assets, and an audit of the capacity for development.

Community Profile

- Summarize the history of the community
- Describe the geographical and jurisdictional boundaries of the community
- Explicate the dominant values, traditions, beliefs, and standards of the community
- Characterize the relationships among community members

Community Inventory of Assets

- Prepare a demographic profile of the community population
- Describe the political/power, economic, religious, education, social welfare, and criminal justice institutions
- Inventory the talent and resource pool of community members
- Inventory the resources in the health and human services delivery system including its agencies, programs, and volunteer initiatives
- Describe the housing, transportation, and recreational resources of the community

Community Audit of Capacity for Development

- Delineate the strengths of the community
- Identify the major community problems
- Evaluate sources of oppression and discrimination
- Evaluate the degree to which the community resources meet the needs of its members
- Assess community competence: How well does the community respond to resident needs? In what ways do community members contribute to the well-being of the community? How does the community relate to other communities and the region?

Focus Groups

Focus groups have been widely used in qualitative research activities that emphasize incorporating respondents' voices (Oesterheld & Haber, 1997; Williams, Abbott, & Taylor, 1997; Bush & Kraft, 1998; Rogers, Meyer, Walker, & Fisk, 1998; Marcenko & Samost, 1999). They also have utility as strategy for macrolevel assessment and as a basis for strategic planning (Butterfoss, Houseman, Morrow, & Rosenthal, 1997). Several features distinguish the focus group strategy, including the characteristics of participants and the processes involved in expediting the strategy (Quible, 1998). Focus groups ideally involve 6 to 12 participants in a 1- to 2-hour discussion session that is recorded. Participants share an interest or affiliation; however, they may or may not know each other. Focus group phases include (1) *planning,* to define the objective, identifying and recruiting participants, and developing general interview guidelines; (2) *conducting,* to design the setting to enhance participation and to facilitate the process in a way that builds trust and elicits different points of view; and (3) *analyzing and reporting,* to transcribe the sessions, conduct a content analysis, and write the final report.

Tools as Resources for Empowerment

Empowerment-based assessment uses tools to discover resources. These tools do not produce products that diagnose or categorize clients and herd them into particular intervention initiatives. Instead, workers employ assessment tools to enrich, motivate, and inform clients. Prior to implementing any tool, practitioners fully explain it, including its administration and purpose. They also share results and discuss implications with clients (Table 10.3).

Adding Viewpoints

All clients enter social work services with their own particular views of their situations. No matter how openly social workers and clients talk, what clients know and report, and what social workers hear and deduce is but a small part of the available information. Soliciting the viewpoints of others provides fresh perspectives and adds indispensable heterogeneity to the information base. Clients and social workers access alternative views by bringing in significant others and collecting information from other professionals.

Bringing in Significant Others

Rather than just talking about what happens in particular environments, social workers and clients have options for inviting others from that environment to present their views. For

---

TABLE 10.3   Considerations in Using Assessment Tools

- What is the purpose of the tool?
- Is the tool a good fit for the unique circumstances of the client system?
- What is the cost in terms of time, effort, and money?
- Are clients fully informed about the tool's purpose and procedure? Do they give their consent to participate?
- Does the tool require special training or certification to administer?
- What is the client's role?
- Will clients see and discuss the results?
- Will the proposed tool provide useful information or does it merely attach a label to the client's behavior?
- How will the results be used?
- Does the tool provide reliable and valid information?

---

example, if an adolescent girl has trouble leaving home for a job training position, her parents' views may enlighten. If a parolee has one last chance to avoid a return to jail, a joint meeting with the parole officer may clarify expectations and impending repercussions of the legal system. If a state legislature is considering welfare reform, the views of constituents presented in legislative testimony are influential.

Certain situations lead logically to involving others within the client's ecosystem. When practitioners work with young children, elderly clients who are frail, or persons with severe developmental disabilities or chronic illnesses, it makes sense to include persons most intensively involved in caregiving roles. A client's cultural background also may provide practitioners with clues about other significant people to involve. As an example, with Native American clients, extended family members are a source of strength whose perspectives may be helpful (Dykeman, Nelson, & Appleton, 1995).

Accessing information directly from collateral resource systems has several advantages. More than simply contributing alternative views, it provides clients with direct access to new information within the supportive atmosphere of the social work relationship and affords social workers a clear view of clients in transaction with significant others. Bringing in others begins the process of activating the natural support network on behalf of clients and involves those who are likely to experience effects as client systems change. Involving others affords clients opportunities to witness the motivations, resources, and strengths of social supports. This information will be important as clients and social workers attempt to shift the functioning of the ecosystem into patterns that help clients reach desired goals.

Contacting Other Professionals

Many clients are involved with more than one type of formal system. So, additional perspectives may be available from psychiatrists, psychologists, physicians, nurses, teachers, ministers, and other helping professionals. Choosing which of these perspectives to access depends on several factors. Those resources clients consider most significant and acceptable clearly direct these choices, since clients themselves control the flow of information between professionals. If the social worker and client anticipate that a particular helping system may be a future target for change, this may be a particularly good time to initiate contact, assess, and involve that system.

Often, social workers and clients discover needs for more information or additional evaluations. No one professional has expertise in every aspect of human behavior. Instead, each profession makes its own particular contribution. Depending on the client's situation, it may be appropriate to consult with physicians, psychologists, occupational therapists, addiction specialists, urban planners, or a myriad of other professionals and organizations. Rather than limit their views of situations, social workers expertly open doors to new perspectives.

The way practitioners access information from other professionals makes a difference. Without exception social workers must obtain a client's permission, as documented by a signed release of information, to legitimate communication with others about the client. This means clients themselves decide whether to give social workers permission to gather information from significant others, records, or other professionals. Clients need to know who is being contacted, what information is sought, why the information is required, and what consequences result if they refuse to permit the contact. Although social workers have a clear responsibility to gather information from other professionals, they share this task with clients as much as possible. Practitioners mutually discuss possible sources of information or consultation with clients and, when feasible, encourage clients to handle the arrangements. When clients discuss, arrange, and follow through on gathering additional information from other professionals, they assume their rightful roles and responsibilities in this process.

Assessing through Observation

The client system, itself, is an important resource for generating new information. Think about it. Any client system's functioning is a dynamic demonstration of its ability to draw on internal and environmental resources. Clients and workers can use this to their advantage by designing ways to observe clients in action.

Observations by Clients

Significant issues warrant observation. Frequently, social workers and clients are operating on vague generalities that require "all or nothing" solutions rather than concrete data that can lead to a more client-specific approach. Social workers and clients construct observations to objectify and update assessment information.

Consider the following example. Tanya confides to Kennedy Brown, the social worker at OPTIONS—an agency providing services for older adults—that her elderly father, Reginald, has lost his ability to take care of himself. This "all or nothing" kind of thinking leads Tanya directly to the single option of placing her father in a nursing home. A new understanding emerges when Tanya observes and charts what Reginald still does for himself as well as what she does for him. With the all-or-nothing thinking, nursing home placement was a fait accompli. Considering more objective observations leads Tanya and Kennedy to redefine the situation and select viable options from community-based services to promote Reginald's independence by maintaining him in his home.

Deciding What to Observe

Notice, in the example above, how Tanya observes not only what Reginald is unable to do but also what he can still do for himself. Strengths-oriented workers check their tendencies to suggest that clients go out and observe only their problems. What kind of effect can you predict if clients observe "the problem" and learn everything that they can about it? Instead, imagine asking clients to review their situations for times when things are going well. Which is the more productive observation, the focus on problems or the focus on exceptions? What do clients discover as they watch the successful parts of their experiences? Consider these examples:

- When a neighborhood group believes the city council is not listening to them, selected group members can attend council meetings to see who the council does heed and what approaches these other people use.
- When domestic partners who are both employed disagree on who is doing more housekeeping, a structured observation not only provides objective data but also clarifies the extent of household tasks necessary if the couple chooses to renegotiate their distribution.

Involving Others in Observing Clients

Some clients—including infants, people with advanced Alzheimer's disease, or those with profound developmental disabilities—are unable to conduct observations themselves. In these cases, social workers may coordinate such observations with other professionals or members of the client's natural support network. When workers involve others in observing, they obtain the client's consent and carefully include the client in the planning process.

Observations by Workers

Observing our own reactions to clients and observing how clients interact with others provides additional assessment information. Workers monitor their own responses, clients' interactions with others, and the interactions within multiperson client systems.

Observing Our Own Reactions to Clients

As social workers, we learn what responses to expect in ourselves as we relate to clients. To learn about clients, we ask ourselves about our thoughts, feelings, and reactions. For example, do we look forward to meetings with clients? Do we feel hopeful or invigorated? Do we distance ourselves or become angry? Do we feel an urge to "take care" of clients? Do we call clients to remind them of appointments, give them rides back and forth, or tell them what to do rather than discuss possibilities? Social workers who are self-aware identify the dynamics of their own responses in order to differentiate those provoked by personal issues from those triggered by clients. Objective social workers strive to keep personal responses separate and share their observations about clients constructively.

Observing How Clients Interact with Others

The potentially rich information embedded within direct interactions prompts social workers to invite significant others to meetings with clients. Consider Robert, a client in the community integrated employment program of the Area Association for People with Disabilities. Robert complains to his case manager that his sister, Barbara, always rifles through his personal belongings. Robert agrees to the worker's suggestion that they invite Barbara to talk with them together. When Barbara explains that she is only separating the laundry, a clearer picture emerges. By observing the interaction between Robert and his sister, the worker discovers a pattern of caretaking in which Barbara seems to assume Robert isn't capable—Barbara leads Robert into the office, tells him where to sit, and answers all questions directed to her brother. The worker also notes that Robert's passive response validates his sister's view and encourages her controlling behavior. These observations provide resources for developing a plan for working out the conflict between the siblings.

Observing Multiperson Client Systems

Working with multiperson client systems offers a firsthand view of how the system functions. Systems reveal their structures and interactional patterns both subtly and directly. Observing who initiates conversations, who contributes the most, who has the last word, and toward whom members look when it's time to respond discloses clues about who's in charge. Observing who supports whom and who sits by whom indicates the subsystem arrangement and closeness among members. These patterns provide direct information about group structure, process, and development.

Reconsider the earlier example of Damon Edwards and the residents of Franklin Courts. Much of what Damon was able to assess came from the transactions that he observed rather than from the questions that he asked. He discovered the group's power structure by noting the nods of agreement when Mrs. Grant spoke. When he asked for volunteers to form a steering committee, indigenous leaders came forward, prodded by those around them who recognized these members as natural choices. Damon also identified existing subgroups by observing how members were seated, who came to the meeting together, and who shared common issues and concerns. Finally, Damon was able to assess the group's development by their abilities to function as a team in planning child-care arrangements, the respectful ways members listened to one another, and the clear sense of direction that the group had already developed. Clients are always telling workers about themselves. Alert practitioners observe these messages for the assessment information they convey.

Recordkeeping

In many ways, records are resources for clients, social workers, agencies, and even the social work profession. Records provide a coherent and organized data base for assessment. Records, like maps, are resource guides. It's hard for people to know how far they've come, unless there's a record of where they started. Likewise, it's hard for people to know which turn to take if they don't have some sense of their destination. A well-constructed record provides concrete evidence of change, information for assessment, and indications for future action.

Records serve as the basis for individual reflection, supervisory discussion, and peer consultation. Agency administrators aggregate data from records to evaluate current programs and plan for the future. Usually, agencies are accountable to funding bodies for grant-funded service provisions. Accurate records support statistical documentation and provide measures of quality assurance. Finally, effective social work records facilitate practice and program evaluation research. This section examines several facets of recordkeeping including the role of recording, types of recording techniques, and ethical and legal issues associated with recordkeeping.

Recording

Recording assists social workers and clients in numerous ways. By keeping track of contacts, activities, and plans, records aid memory. By organizing relevant information and arranging priorities, records ensure continuity. By carefully documenting case activities, records detail productivity and provide an essential component of professional liability risk management. When their clients give permission or when legal constraints mandate, records enhance a worker's ability to share accurate information with other professionals. Finally, records offer legal protection to workers because they concretely document professional activities.

Rather than being a mundane, tedious activity, effective recordkeeping is a useful analytic tool. "Recording provides evidence of the quality of thought and action that have gone into the delivery of service" (Kagle, 1987, p. 463). Writing reports requires us to cluster ideas, develop themes, and organize our thoughts. Writing clarifies our thinking. Whereas statistical records document case activities, descriptive case records individualize accounts of process, impressions, and plans. Records form a baseline against which to measure change.

Valuable records contain objective facts and relevant case-related information and documents, such as letters and releases of information (Maluccio, Fein, & Olmstead, 1986; Ames, 1999). To avoid malpractice suits, social workers should never record anything derogatory about a client (Barker & Branson, 1992).

When we communicate with others via written documents, our documents make a significant impression. Poorly prepared documents detract from their content and may not be taken seriously. People evaluate our ideas by scrutinizing the document's format, presentation of ideas, grammar, and style. Some social service administrators consider written communication skills a top priority in their list of qualifications for prospective employees (Miley, 1989). Factors such as a pleasing format, clear and effective presentation of ideas, correct grammar, and a style which is ethnically sensitive and nonsexist establish credibility (Table 10.4). Effective social workers prepare records carefully.

Types of Recording Formats

Social work records are prepared for a diverse audience, including colleagues, supervisors, third party payers, clients, and court officials (Kagle, 1993). Some records summarize information about goals, objectives, activities, and outcomes; others narrate a detailed account of progress toward goals. Some records are abbreviated, using outlines, checklists, or abridged forms; others incorporate extensive documentation details. Some records are written to comply with court mandates and/or contractual stipulations; others are kept to meet agency standards. The purposes of the record dictate its format, content, and style. "No single method of recording can meet all the needs of social work practice" (Tebb, 1991, p. 428).

Note Taking

Good records begin with gathering accurate information. Some circumstances require note taking. For example, factual data such as names of family members, committee members, birth dates, meeting times, or specific follow-up tasks may be difficult to remember without

---

TABLE 10.4   Tips for an Appropriate Writing Style

- Avoid all derogatory labels (for example, ethnic or racial slurs)
- Demonstrate gender sensitivity
  - Use generic terms to describe people including words such as mail carrier, service person, chairperson, etc.
  - Use the phrases "he or she," "his or her," or "them"
- Maintain nonjudgmentalism
- Refrain from using jargon or slang
- Use concrete descriptions rather than diagnostic labels, generalizations, or subjective wording
- Use active voice
- Proofread your final draft by reading aloud

---

a written record. Typically, asking clients for permission to take even limited notes reduces their defensiveness. Effective requests include:

- I'd like to keep these details straight. Is it all right with you if I take a few notes?
- Does anyone object to my taking notes during our discussion so that we have a record of our decisions?
- This is a pretty long form to fill out. Do you want me to read the questions to you? Do you want to read along with me? I could give you a blank form and you could just tell me the answers and I'll write them down. What do you think would work best?

There is pressure to remember detail, yet a need to take notes in ways that have minimal effect on the process (Kadushin & Kadushin, 1997). By involving clients, social workers convert note taking from a display of expert authority into an empowering strategy. Taking only selective notes during actual meetings with clients requires conscientious social workers to record notes soon after. Noting even a few details will enhance the accuracy of recollection in completing formal reports.

Activity Logs

Probably, the most widely used style of record is a simple and organized log of contacts between workers and clients. This type of record is most useful in keeping the worker and client focused on relevant tasks and forms a data base for worker and agency accountability. Although the content of these records varies across practice settings, most include information about client goals, activities completed, future plans, people involved, and time invested. Examine the activity log of Rita Garcia, a social worker with the state's Child Protective Unit, who uses this record to document her work with Opal Zander (Table 10.5).

TABLE 10.5   Worker: Rita Garcia   Client: Zander Family

Date	Time	Contact	Task/Activity	Action Required
6/19	.25	Call from Smith/DCS	Requested emergency placement for Zander children—4 siblings	Find home for sibling group
6/19	.25	L. Jones	Confirmed Jones will provide foster placement for all four kids	
6/19	.50	Smith/DCS	Discussed disposition of case	Smith will pursue court action
6/19	1.50	Zander children	Provided transport to Jones' home	Call Jones 6/20
6/20	1.75	Opal Zander	Intake: Discussed procedures and requirements. Set goals for family reunification	Schedule joint meeting with team 6/21 (Families United office, 10:30)
6/21	2.25	Team meeting	Set visitation and determined plan of action including (1) moving out of boyfriend's house into transitional housing, (2) secure employment to achieve financial independence	Zander will contact Northside Shelter and the Women's Resource Center

While not offering detailed accounts of her activities, Rita's logs keep her on task and remind her of the sequence of important events when she presents court testimony. She also uses her logs to organize follow-up details.

Process Recording

Process recordings review contacts with clients by including descriptive, specific details. More often found in educational than paid employment settings, process recording applies to any system level, builds self-awareness, refines assessment skills, and supports learning to work effectively with clients (Kagle, 1991). Process recordings support social workers in becoming reflective practitioners and enhances their conscious use of self (Graybeal & Ruff, 1995; Neuman & Friedman, 1997). A number of innovative options for process recording go beyond formal written reports. These include audio- and videotaping, verbal descriptions, role plays, drawings, and in-session and one-way mirror observations by others (Graybeal & Ruff).

Content for properly prepared written process recordings includes the verbatim dialogue, comments on the social worker's reactions and feelings, analyses and interpretations of the transactions, and the supervisor's comments (Neuman & Friedman, 1997). Process recordings need to be written immediately. To organize process recording, one can divide legal-size paper into three or four columns or on a computer, format recording columns using a "landscape" setting to align the paper horizontally. Practitioners evaluate their experiences in the interviewer's column; supervisors provide constructive feedback in the instructor's comments column. Examine the process recording completed by Rita Garcia as she works with Opal Zander toward the goal of increasing Opal's employability (Table 10.6).

Summary Recording

Summary recordings such as progress notes, intake summaries, and referral reports are more typical of the recordkeeping requirements of day-to-day social work practice. Frequency and format depends on agency policy, stipulations of accrediting bodies, government regulations, and grant requirements. Typically, effective summary recordings include:

- Identifying data such as the client's name and identifying number, date of the interview, date the summary is being written, and social worker's name
- Reason for the meeting
- Summary account
- Description of the salient issues
- Worker's impressions
- Follow-up plans and/or goals (Wilson, 1980)

Content focuses exclusively on the client rather than on the worker's responses and reactions. Summary content describes outcomes thematically rather than in step-by-step details.

Ethical and Legal Issues in Recordkeeping

Records document courses of action. However, sharing this information with clients and other professionals raises numerous ethical and legal issues as does the use of computers for recordkeeping.

TABLE 10.6   Excerpts from a Processs Recording

Client: Opal Zander   Date: 7/12   (Individual Session # 8)   Interviewer: R. Garcia

Verbatim Account	Interviewer's Response	Analysis
I called the GED center.	Oh?	Opal's taking the initiative. Want to keep my responses minimal while supporting her efforts.
I can start anytime. They call it "study at your own pace."	Good!	
Not going to cost me any money. They've even got a bus token deal.	Mmhmm . . .	
And, something called a resource center for women like me.	For women like you . . .	Emphasizing Opal's connection with other women in program to increase its appeal.
I think so. I said, "I'm nervous and I've been having some hard times." And, then the lady I was talking to said, well I could try it out. So, I've been thinking . . .(pauses a bit)	Yes?	
Well, I've been thinking about whether I should wait until I get the kids back or start now. I even made this list to decide (list shows lots of pluses).	Looks like you're thinking about starting pretty soon.	Emphasizing Opal's efforts in thinking this through. But did I jump in too soon with this?
The way I see it, I've got some time on my hands right now. And, this GED program gives me a chance to do something positive. I sure need that. And, maybe I can make some friends, like we talked about last time, at that women's center.	I'm really impressed with how you're taking charge.	Opal sees she's making a difference, can build on this for parenting, too. How could we connect this with reunification goals?

Computerized Records

Although computers streamline the processing and sharing of information and facilitate the collection of data, ethical issues abound (Davidson & Davidson, 1995, 1996; Reamer, 1998; Gelman, Pollack, & Weiner, 1999). Since the computerized data bases maintained in social work practice are likely to contain an abundance of confidential information, safeguards to maintain security and to preserve confidentiality are vital. Security measures regulate access to data bases through the use of passwords and other "locked file systems," monitor the access to information afforded by computer networks, and rigorously protect the privacy of information on the computer screen. Principled professionals ensure that storage of computerized information is as safe as the records stored in their locked filing cabinets and that records on their computer screens are as private as the records in their files.

Clients' Access to Records

The NASW *Code of Ethics* (National, 2000) indicates that clients should have reasonable access to their records. Specifically, the code indicates that social workers should provide reasonable access to official records that concern them and, when sharing this information with clients, should protect the confidentiality of other persons noted in the records. Clearly, this code upholds clients' rights to access their records.

Several pieces of federal legislation also champion clients' rights to access their records. For example, the Federal Privacy Act of 1974 (Public Law 93-579), the Freedom of Information Act, and the Family Educational Rights legislation of 1974 (known as the Buckley Amendment) specify guidelines with respect to accessing records from educational institutions or from other federally funded or administered programs. These laws set a precedence that carries over into the private sector (Kagle, 1990, 1991). Both Family Service America and the Child Welfare League of America encourage member agencies to "permit client access to records as part of the counseling process" (Gelman, 1992, p. 75). These codes, laws, and guidelines prescribe the principle; agency policies and procedures furnish detailed directions as to how clients proceed to access their records.

Social workers need to keep in mind the effect of reading the written reports as they prepare clients' records. Workers always write records with the understanding that the records could be read by clients or various third parties (Saltzman & Furman, 1999). Although some professionals struggle with the implications of fully sharing their written impression with clients, research findings indicate "that there is a qualitative improvement in both recording practices and relationships as a result of client participation" (Gelman, 1992, p. 76).

Reflecting Back

Assessment processes infuse professional theory and expertise into the work of social workers and clients. Such processes are empowering to the extent that they contextualize the issues that clients face and locate resources to achieve goals. In contrast, assessment processes that elevate the social worker's expertise or reduce client situations to stigmatizing labels undermine a client's progress. Consider which frameworks and tools are the best fit for empowerment-oriented practice. How would you implement these assessment processes in the most empowering way? Differentiate between client and worker expertise in assessing resource capabilities.

Looking Forward

Assessment requires social workers and clients to think about what they are doing in theoretical and practical ways in order to organize their information into a usable format for planning. Clients contribute to this process by offering their theories, interpretations, and feelings to the assessment. Social workers contribute by integrating theoretical understanding, professional supports, and research information. Social workers can enhance the assessment by keeping written records.

The organized description of client needs and resources that comes from assessment begins to frame the options that the partners have for development and change. Framing solutions, the subject of Chapter 11, takes planning further. To frame solutions, the partners articulate goals, focus on change, consider multiple levels of intervention, and concentrate their energies toward the outcomes they seek.

Chapter *11*

Framing Solutions

During assessment, generalist social workers discover abundant information about what is available, what enhances, and what constrains client systems. In fact, these processes often generate such a wealth of information that workers and clients must pause to sift through and organize these discoveries into a coherent plan before taking action. To plan solutions, social workers and clients work collaboratively to address such questions as: What exactly are we trying to accomplish? Who needs to be involved? What are we going to do? These are questions that have many answers. Even when we know exactly where we want to go, we can probably plan many routes to get there.

Framing solutions means planning, that is, transforming assessment material into manageable strategies for change. From a generalist social work perspective, planning can be complex since a generalist sees multiple options for solutions at each system level. However, when approached in a thoughtful and organized fashion, generalist planning is never a "dead end." There are always other possible approaches or other aspects of the situation that are amenable to change.

This chapter describes how social workers and clients develop comprehensive plans of action. Specifically, this chapter:

- Presents collaborative planning roles for workers and clients
- Considers the impact of the characteristics of client systems on the planning process
- Defines goals and objectives and their importance in planning
- Advocates a generalist focus on planning to encourage an expansive view of potential solutions
- Delineates a step-by-step approach for constructing action plans
- Describes the concept of contracting and how workers and clients establish a contract for change

Successful completion of a comprehensive plan of action prepares social workers and clients with an explicit guide for their intervention efforts.

Collaborative Planning Processes

A plan of action describes what social workers and clients hope to accomplish and how they intend to do it. A complete plan contains several components. It has goals and objectives, possible targets for change, various strategies designed to reach those goals and objectives, a timeline, and evaluation guidelines (Johnson, 1998). Action plans delineate activities which specify what social workers and clients will do, with whom, in what locations, and when. The more concrete the plan the greater the likelihood of accomplishing its purpose. The more flexible the plan the more the partners can tailor it to changes that occur during its implementation.

The ecosystems perspective naturally leads workers and clients to construct multidimensional plans. Siporin (1975) sums this up succinctly, saying that a comprehensive action plan is "multitarget, multilevel, and multiphasic in its design" (p. 259). Siporin elaborates, describing a plan's many component parts, including:

- Broad goals and concrete, measurable objectives
- A prioritization of objectives into immediate, intermediate, and long-term

- Strategies to use and actions to take to meet objectives
- Time frames for implementation
- Identified targets for change
- An inventory of necessary resources such as financial, programs, or staff
- Clear division of responsibility for actions among the client system, social worker, and others
- Evaluation criteria and procedures
- Processes for altering the plan
- A defined point of resolution

Pulling together such a detailed plan of action requires the full participation of both clients and social workers. They openly discuss the information they have discovered, reexamine their goals, and mutually generate ideas about how to accomplish them. Both clients and social workers actively invest in planning processes, but each brings different expertise and plays a different role. Clients are experts on what they want and on what they are willing to do. Social workers contribute technical skills for constructing plans and knowledge of the resources available for implementing them.

Client Expertise in Planning

Clients bring significant expertise to the planning process. They are *content experts*—they know what they want. They are *motivation experts*—they can describe what they are willing to do. They are *skill experts*—they can demonstrate their own capabilities.

Clients have ultimate power over a plan's acceptability. Social workers may suggest, but clients have the right and the responsibility to say what they can and will do. They can give the "thumbs up" or "thumbs down" on the proposed plan. Clients maintain the privilege of selecting the outcomes and strategies they desire. Collaboration guarantees that plans are relevant to what clients want, and the involvement of clients ensures that the very process of constructing a plan activates clients toward its achievement.

Plans as Motivators for Action

Good plans motivate clients. They incorporate client-centered goals—statements of outcomes desired by clients. To respect self-determination and activate clients' participation, goals and strategies must naturally emerge from the collaborative efforts of workers and clients. Workers help clients clarify and operationalize their chosen goals in ways that retain the motivational quality of these goals (Gold, 1990). Goals and plans motivate clients when clients assume their ownership. To "own" their plans, clients need to see them as relevant and participate in their construction.

Worker Expertise in Planning

Workers are both technical and resource experts in the planning process. As technical experts, practitioners apply planning models to organize goals and ideas for change into coherent action plans. To do so, workers listen carefully to what clients want and help break down these goals into workable units. In other words, workers translate vague, abstract goals into measurable and attainable objectives. Practitioners also guide clients to fully articulate specific strategies in ways which clarify the roles of clients and workers, determine who else should be involved, set time frames, determine evaluation criteria, and specify a schedule to review progress. In planning, workers are technical experts who design a framework with clients to flesh out with the content of clients' situations and aspirations.

Workers are also resource experts in the planning process. Practitioners keep informed about what resources might be available beyond the social work relationship. In essence, effective social workers are resource directories, vital links to other resources in the community. Informed social workers help clients consider possible options available in other programs, other persons to access who have relevant skills, and even indigenous community resources which are outside of the formal network of social services.

Issues Affecting Collaborative Planning

As much as possible, workers strive to develop action plans that reflect what clients themselves want to do and are hoping to accomplish. However, three issues affect a worker's ability to collaborate in this way with all clients. These factors include the participatory ability of the client, powerful forces outside of the social work relationship system, and other people who will be affected by the plan.

Participatory Abilities of Clients

Sometimes, the particular challenges of clients limit their abilities to participate fully in planning. Those with overwhelming physical, cognitive, or emotional challenges may be currently unable to define where they are going, what they are willing to do, or what skills and abilities they can contribute. When this is the case, workers use their best judgment to makes choices based on their awareness of the client's situation and what they believe to be the client's best interest. Workers also call on others in the client's life to assist with this process. If the client has a significant natural support system of family and friends, it is likely that they have already been involved in other parts of the process and can continue to participate in planning.

Even when involving other persons in planning, workers strive to ascertain what the client wants. For example, if the planning concerns medical treatment for a hospice patient who is physically unable to participate, any advance directives previously expressed to workers, family members, and friends should be in the forefront of the planning process. For clients who are developmentally disabled or too young to fully comprehend the process, workers still include them and encourage them to express their views.

Outside Influences on Involuntary Clients

Not all clients are free to plan changes that they want. Involuntary clients frequently come encumbered with predetermined goals and limits on their options. For example, a client may be participating in an alternative counseling program to avoid prosecution. Or, a parent may want to regain custody of children placed in foster care and be court-ordered to resolve personal issues and acquire parenting skills. In these cases, the social worker and client must consider the mandates of others. The participation of those representing such outside forces can be direct such as ordering specific activities or treatments; or it may be indirect, allowing workers and clients to develop their own plans subject to review and approval. In either case, workers accept the responsibility of incorporating into the plan the view of whatever authority is requiring the social work intervention.

When social workers accept involuntary clients, they agree to work within the boundaries set by the mandating agent. That does not necessarily mean that clients and social workers have no influence. Social workers should not ignore their implicit power. Those in authority have shown their trust in the worker enough to believe that social work expertise is what is necessary to facilitate change. Why else would they have ordered the client to work with the social work practitioner? If workers believe that clients would benefit from a different strategy or a plan, they may choose to advocate new orders. In this way, social workers balance the desires of the client with the orders of authorities in developing plans that are compatible and agreeable to both.

Considering Significant Others

Social workers consider the perspectives of others even when clients are voluntary. If the client is a 15-year-old youth who wants to move out of the house, the views of the legal guardian are pivotal. If the client is one partner in a committed relationship, social workers use their expertise to anticipate the impact of the proposed plans on the other partner and discuss this view with the client. With the client's permission, workers may even go so far as to invite the partner's direct commentary on the developing plan. Changes in the client will inevitably affect people in relationships with the client. The success of the plan ultimately depends on the cooperation that clients receive from those around them.

Planning with larger systems also considers the potential effect of the plan on others. For example, if the client system is a task group in the community, the foresighted worker encourages group members to seek the opinions of their constituents before implementing the plan. If the client is a social agency, the practitioner encourages agency staff to explore the impact of their proposed changes on the social service delivery system in the community network. Generalist social workers always keep in mind that they do not work with clients in isolation. Effective plans meet the client's goals, but good planning also anticipates and accounts for the responses of others.

Planning in Multiperson Systems

Planning means reaching agreement on what clients and social workers will do to accomplish their goals. This may not be such a difficult task for social workers and individual clients who each have defined roles and clear areas of expertise for the process. But, for client systems with two or more members, planning takes on the new dimension of negotiation. In other words, members of the client system must agree on what they seek and the methods they are willing to use. Dealing with differences, resolving conflicts, and facilitating decision-making are additional skills necessary for planning with multiperson client systems.

Social workers function as facilitators in group planning to ensure the best efforts of the client system and, as much as possible, give each member a voice in the plan. Practitioners facilitate planning in groups of many sizes and types—couples, families, support groups, task groups, case management teams, program units in organizations, boards of directors, and community planning councils, to name just a few. Each group may benefit from a different kind of decision-making process depending on its particular needs, goals, and characteristics.

Decision-Making in Groups

Group planning has advantages. It has profound effects on members including encouraging higher motivation to achieve, increasing commitment to implement the decision, and initiating changes in behavior and attitudes (Johnson & Johnson, 1997). Groups have more resources than any one individual and can actually generate new perspectives and possibilities as members interact with one another. But combining the resources of individual group members also has drawbacks. Effective group decision-making takes more time, requires a significant level of group development and maturity, and depends on effective and respectful interpersonal communication among members. Workers facilitating group planning processes may need to help groups develop and learn decision-making before actually formulating action plans.

Johnson and Johnson (1997) classify group decision-making into several types. Some types ultimately leave decisions in the hands of a single powerful group member. Three examples of individual members tapped to make decisions include members who are in designated authority roles, those respected as experts on the particular issues at hand, or those nominated to poll other members and make decisions based on the input they receive. Sometimes, groups vest this same kind of decision-making power in a subgroup such as an executive planning committee or a team of experts chosen from among the group's membership. At other times, the whole group makes decisions democratically by averaging the opinions of all members or by voting, thereby leaving the decision to the majority. Each of these styles—decision-making by single members, subgroups, or the group as a whole—may be appropriate depending on the unique qualities of the group and the decision to be made.

Consensus

When group members have the time and necessary skills, consensus decision-making may be the most productive (Johnson & Johnson, 1997). Consensus decision-making draws on the concept of the group as a social system. It activates all members to contribute to a mutual decision that reflects the consideration of each member's views and ideas. Henry (1992) says:

> *Consensus does not necessarily represent 100 percent agreement of all the members on one position; it allows for accommodation to minority opinion which is appropriated into the consensual agreement. Individual members' positions are heard, people accommodate to each other's positions, and a consensus emerges. People recognize that their individual good is best realized through the common good and they are willing to give up some of their individual desires for the sake of the whole. (p. 168)*

Though at times difficult to achieve, consensus results in creative decisions that garner participants' support for implementation, draw upon their collective resources, and enhance future decision-making effectiveness (Johnson & Johnson, 1997).

Goals and Objectives

All social work practice is purposeful, directed toward clients' goals. Early in their dialogue with social workers, clients describe a preliminary direction for the work. This sense of purpose guides the assessment process and defines what may function as resources. Now, in planning, workers and clients reconsider this original purpose in light of the assessment information; they translate this initial purpose into a concrete set of realistic goals and objectives. Therefore, as a beginning step in their planning tasks, clients stop, reflect on where they are, and focus clearly on a point in the future where they would like to be. This point of focus is the goal toward which clients and social workers plan a path of objectives and related activities.

Differentiating Goals and Objectives

Articulating goals is the prelude to preparing objectives and designing specific intervention activities. Goal setting prepares clients to "clarify and define the objectives they hope to achieve in the helping relationship and…establish the steps that must be taken and the time needed to reach those objectives" (Barker, 1999, p. 196). Many people, including social workers, often use the terms "goals" and "objectives" interchangeably. Goals and objectives are contextually defined.

For simplicity, we define goals and objectives as having distinct meanings. Goals are broad, general statements of what clients want to accomplish. They express the desired outcomes, ideal conditions, or long-term aims of the helping relationship. *Goals* are not necessarily measurable. In contrast, *objectives* are explicit statements of concrete changes desired by clients in their behaviors or situations. Objectives are readily observable and measurable. Objectives are the smaller, incremental achievements required to reach goals. Workers and clients may set many objectives to achieve a single outcome goal.

Considering Goals

A goal is a simple concept, but how do social workers and clients actually develop goals? When there are a variety of issues, which one gets attention first? Can practitioners and clients work on several goals at once? What steps translate current difficulties into attainable outcomes? Should goals be long-term or immediate? Specific or global? Practitioners answer these questions differently depending on their own practice philosophies and the characteristics of their clients.

What Goals Should Clients Set?
Goals that client systems pursue vary greatly. Goldstein (1973) overviews five types of goals, including:

1. Obtaining some concrete goods or services, or needed resources such as financial assistance, employment, health care, or housing
2. Making important life decisions, resolving crises, relieving immediate distress, or removing barriers to change
3. Modifying structures in social systems, such as a family, an organization, or a community by changing communication patterns, interactional behaviors, or roles and rules
4. Pursuing "foresight goals" or fulfilling some future aspiration through rational planning
5. Recognizing the basic value of growth and change, and seeking social work services to realize their fullest potential

Social workers maintain flexibility to match their strategies and styles of work with the goals for which clients strive.

How Far Ahead?

Goals describe what we hope will happen in the future, but how far ahead do we look? Kisthardt (1992) cautions against goals that reach too far into the future. Social workers maintain flexibility between a long-term outlook as a general guide and a short-term view which clearly defines achievable tasks. A balance of long-term goals with discrete short-term steps keeps the relationship moving successfully forward while ensuring that each step leads in a productive direction.

Reflect for a moment on how you set goals for yourself. Do you have some general ideas about where you would like to be in the future? A 5-year plan? A 10-year plan? As you make daily decisions, do you take small steps in the general direction of your aspirations? Are you a social work student looking ahead to professional practice? What intermediate goals and objectives will you be accomplishing as you move toward your professional career? Likely, you have a clear goal to pass the final exam in this class, but your choice of a field of social work practice may remain vague until you explore the possibilities revealed in further course work and field experiences.

As we progress through a series of accomplishments, we assess, reassess, and decide where to go next. And, sometimes we change direction. This same process works for clients too. Clients benefit from the long-distance look ahead that long term goals provide, but they also need a clear sense of interim steps.

How Many Goals?

Clients may desire many goals simultaneously. However, setting too many diverse goals may give the partners no direction at all. "To begin working on several goals simultaneously is to invite confusion and failure" (Simons & Aigner, 1985, p. 71). When clients have a lot they want to accomplish, social workers facilitate a sequential approach to help clients to organize and set priorities for issues and goals. Focusing on a reasonable number of goals facilitates their attainment. "Both research and practice wisdom show that, in order to be effective, the helping process must concentrate available time and energy on just one, two, or three problems at a time" (Sheafor, Horejsi, & Horejsi, 1997, p. 420). Social workers encourage clients to think broadly and optimistically about the future but guide them to move in one direction at a time.

Translating Goals into Objectives

Goal setting, as part of the planning process, functions as the initial step toward specifying concrete objectives. A number of recent works describe objectives in social work practice (McMahon, 1996; Hepworth, Rooney, & Larsen, 1997; Sheafor, Horejsi, & Horejsi, 1997; Johnson, 1998; Compton & Galaway, 1999). Earlier writing by Siporin (1975) lays a foundation for understanding objectives and articulating their use for social work practice. According to Siporin:

> *Objectives express our values and intentions, and they also give direction and meaning to behavior. Objectives that are clear and explicit evoke investment and*

commitment. When accepted by the individual, there is also an acceptance of re-sponsibility for action to implement them. They give to the individual a conscious sense of purpose and hope. They stimulate awareness of the interrelationships be-tween purpose, choice, and activity and provide a standard against which to judge performance and progress. When shared with others, objectives provide means for communication, identification, and relationship with others. (p. 258)

Practitioners should formulate objectives in meaningful and realistic ways by considering objectives from many perspectives. According to Siporin (1975), effective objectives are:

- Steps toward goals
- Explicit and operational
- Realistic and attainable
- Discrete and time-limited
- Observable and measurable
- Acceptable to both clients and workers

The following paragraphs describe these attributes of objectives in further detail.

Steps toward Goals

How can client systems achieve their goals? Each objective provides a part of the answer to this question. Although possible objectives are numerous and far ranging, those chosen as part of an action plan have one thing in common—each has the specific intent of moving client systems closer to their eventual goals. Objectives are not set to achieve random successes. Instead, they are focused attempts to chip away at the space between where clients are and their goals of where they would like to be. Workers and clients consider two general kinds of objectives:

1. Small positive steps in the direction of goals
2. Removal of obstacles in the path toward goals

By continuing to achieve one step at a time and to remove each obstacle encountered, clients ultimately arrive at their desired goals.

Consider the example of a social worker facilitating a community task group whose members seek the goal of economic development for their deteriorating neighborhood. After a comprehensive assessment of the neighborhood, the social worker and task group are able to specify several objectives to work toward this goal. They set objectives to accomplish small positive steps, including obtaining the designation of "free enterprise zone" for the neighborhood, negotiating with the city council for property tax relief for new businesses, and accessing low-interest loans for neighborhood businesses from a local bank. But, other objectives are also necessary to remove identified barriers, including the negative image of the neighborhood and the high rate of crime. Setting additional objectives to enhance the neighborhood's image as an historic district through a public relations campaign, to increase police patrols, and to institute a neighborhood watch program will take steps toward removing these obstacles. Overall, achieving each of these objectives either takes a direct step or clears the way for the task group to continue toward the goal of neighborhood economic development.

Explicit and Operational

A comprehensive set of objectives that considers changes in clients and their environments may involve many persons and projects. Therefore, stating objectives in as precise and exact a manner as possible is essential. Clearly stated and mutually understood, objectives are prerequisites to establishing a common understanding and building consensus about courses of action. Frequently, failures to achieve objectives result from miscommunication. Making objectives explicit and understandable from the beginning effectively reduces this margin of error.

Objectives function as bridges from goals to the activities implemented in order to reach goals. In other words, objectives break down broad goals into small enough achievements that it begins to be obvious what actions social workers, clients, and others will take to accomplish their purposes. In the previous example of the community task group, the concrete objective to receive low-interest bank loans for neighborhood businesses already implies specific tasks. Obviously, the group will need to designate certain members to contact banks, business owners, and interested entrepreneurs about this project. Explicit objectives state the desired change and the direction of change in terms of specific target behaviors—*who will accomplish what.* In this example, the task group members will convince local banks to grant low-interest loans to neighborhood businesses. Workers and clients can quickly operationalize well-formed objectives into clearly defined strategies and action steps.

Realistic and Attainable

Success builds on success. Clients need objectives that are realistic given their present capabilities, opportunities readily available, and resources potentially accessible. This does not imply that clients should settle for less than they desire. It simply means that workers and clients should construct and prioritize objectives in such a way that each is possible to achieve and each achievement makes the next objective easier to accomplish. Objectives that, under present circumstances, require too big a leap or too much change set up clients for failure and disillusionment. For example, when a client who is unable to read sets an objective to pass a high school equivalency exam, disappointment is likely. Instead, when the worker helps this client set realistic, incremental objectives of enrolling in an alternative high school and beginning work with a tutor, the objective to pass the equivalency test becomes more realistic.

Structuring success into a plan of action is essential for maintaining client motivation and facilitating empowerment. Experiences with success lead to feelings of self-efficacy and beliefs in competence to achieve certain levels of performance (Bandura, 1984). And, clients who perceive themselves as competent are likely to persist and exert greater efforts in their pursuit of goals. On the other hand, clients who perceive themselves as ineffective may be reluctant to engage in change, may expect failure, and may view failures as evidence of personal deficiencies. Workers have responsibilities to work with clients to set attainable objectives, thereby instilling a sense of confidence and control to effect desired outcomes.

When clients experience success and view themselves as causal agents of the outcome, they approach future events with feelings of hopefulness. In other words, accomplishments empower clients with confidence and hope. Zimmerman (1990) states that "learned hopefulness suggests that experiences that provide opportunities to enhance perceived control will help individuals cope with stress and solve problems in their personal lives" (pp. 72–73). On the other hand, experiencing or perceiving a lack of control over events or outcomes may evoke expectations that events in the future are out of reach and beyond control, resulting in symptoms of helplessness (Seligman, 1975). Setting and accomplishing realistic and attainable objectives initiates a chain of success that leads to hope, increased competence, and feelings of power and control.

Discrete and Time-Limited

Setting realistic objectives means taking small steps. Continuing success means dividing goals into discrete enough objective units to accomplish one step after another. For example, Sean, a client with profound developmental disabilities, may be overwhelmed by the singular objective of learning to brush his teeth. But when the worker breaks this objective into the discrete accomplishments of Sean picking up his toothbrush, applying toothpaste, wetting the brush, placing it in his mouth, and moving the brush across his teeth, success is now within reach. Sean and the worker can now focus on one objective at a time and celebrate each success as it occurs.

Redefining objectives as mini-objectives also opens up options of working on objectives sequentially—achieving one objective after another, or concurrently—attempting several objectives at one time. Sean, in the previous example, will likely benefit from a sequential approach. A task group, such as the one in the example working on economic development, has members that can work simultaneously and efficiently in several directions at once and therefore can use a concurrent approach. Achieving each small step, whether sequentially or concurrently, leads to quantum leaps as clients see results, experience success, and gain confidence. Research supports that "self motivation can be best created and sustained by attainable subgoals that lead to larger future ones" (Bandura & Schunk, 1981, p. 587). Feeling satisfied with their achievements of one objective, clients gain a sense of mastery and tend to persist in their change efforts.

Workers and clients also incorporate time considerations when formulating discrete objectives, usually by selecting objectives that can be achieved within a few weeks (Sheafor, Horejsi, & Horejsi, 1997). If clients cannot accomplish an objective quickly, the objective is too broad or too long-term. Workers and clients should break it into smaller, sequential objectives. When meeting at designated intervals, such as once a week, workers and clients can easily consider what can be completed by the next time they meet in deciding what objectives to set. Quick accomplishments relieve immediate pressures and posture client systems toward further advancements.

Observable and Measurable

In response to the press for accountability and for the evaluation of practice effectiveness, objectives serve an important function in assessing goal achievement. "When goals are stated in terms of specific behaviors or events, both the client systems and social worker can observe the extent to which the intervention plan is working" (Simons & Aigner, 1985, p. 74). Objectives concretely articulate the path toward goals. Reaching various objectives provides a series of interim markers for checking progress and affirming success on the way to desired goals.

Well-formed objectives express desired outcomes in both behavioral and quantitative terms. To imagine an objective that is behavioral, envision what the outcome will look like.

Ask yourself whether you and someone with you would agree on what you are seeing. If both you and the other observer would be likely to describe what you are observing in a similar way, then this observation could be set as a behaviorally observable outcome. If you can "see" when an objective is achieved, it is behavioral.

Objectives are measurable when they state specifically to what extent and how often the events or behaviors will occur. For example, when a family sets the objective to resolve differences through negotiation rather than conflict, they could evaluate the achievement of this objective by noting each time differences arise and recording the interaction which follows. Behaviorally observable and measurable objectives lead to the concrete evaluation of outcomes.

Acceptable to Client and Worker

To be effective, any objective must relate to a particular client system, reflecting its strengths, distinct capabilities, current situation, and goals. Too often, workers clone somewhat standard objectives from one case plan to another without considering how a specific client would like to proceed. Rubber-stamp objectives do not account for a particular client's goals and values. They cannot replace objectives developed collaboratively and tailored to address a client's unique needs.

Effective objectives directly relate to changes that clients believe will improve their situations. Even when workers envision social or environmental changes as beneficial for clients, ethical social workers recognize the client's privilege to select goals. Social justice cannot be achieved at the expense of people who are oppressed. Consider the example of the worker who wants to change the state's policy on distributing public assistance, knowing that it will help a specific client who is a single mother receiving welfare benefits. To set this objective, the client needs to clearly understand the implications of this macrolevel approach for her own situation to determine whether she wants to address her individual goals in this way. The product and process of this strategy must be something that this client truly believes is "new, improved, or enhanced" in her own life. Ethical social workers do not use a client as a springboard to larger issues that are of more concern to them than to the client.

Workers also consider whether clients can achieve their objectives without infringing on the rights of others or without coercing change in nonconsenting players. From a generalist perspective, implementing change activities usually involves others in addition to the client system. Even if people are not directly involved in the work, changes in the client system will likely affect others around the client. Social workers maintain professional ethics when they evaluate the potential impact of achieving the client system's objectives on the rights of the client and the rights of others.

Constructing Action Plans

Understanding goals and objectives prepares social workers to develop action plans. Designing action plans with clients at any system level is a deliberate and careful process involving sequential steps. For example, Figure 11.1 illustrates this process in planning with organizations. Plans build on the assessment information gathered and outline procedures

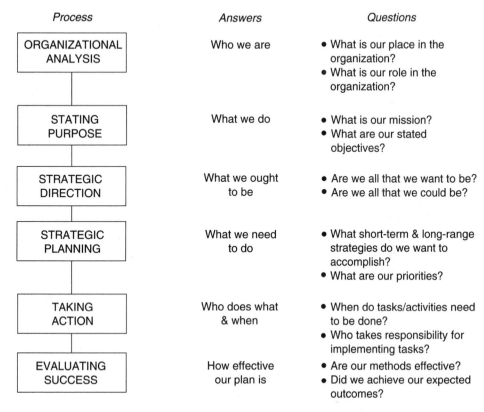

Process	Answers	Questions
ORGANIZATIONAL ANALYSIS	Who we are	• What is our place in the organization? • What is our role in the organization?
STATING PURPOSE	What we do	• What is our mission? • What are our stated objectives?
STRATEGIC DIRECTION	What we ought to be	• Are we all that we want to be? • Are we all that we could be?
STRATEGIC PLANNING	What we need to do	• What short-term & long-range strategies do we want to accomplish? • What are our priorities?
TAKING ACTION	Who does what & when	• When do tasks/activities need to be done? • Who takes responsibility for implementing tasks?
EVALUATING SUCCESS	How effective our plan is	• Are our methods effective? • Did we achieve our expected outcomes?

FIGURE 11.1   **Organizational Planning Process. Strategic planning exemplifies one planning process used with organizational clients. This type of planning is a systematic and interactive process used to realize long-term organizational objectives through the construction of short-term action plans. The process involves broad-base participation to examine organizational potential, set goals and priorities, and create a detailed plan of action for implementing the organization's vision for the future.**

From *Visioning the Future: Organizational Strategic Planning* by B. L. DuBois (April, 1993). Used with permission of the author.

for accomplishing purposes. To develop a relevant and workable plan of action, workers and clients complete the following steps:

1. Set positive and clear outcome goals that fit what clients want and that draw on assessment information
2. Write concrete and achievable objectives
3. Prioritize objectives

4. Generate possible intervention strategies using the broad perspective of generalist practice
5. Specify tasks, responsibilities, and actions necessary to meet objectives
6. Determine intervals and methods to review and modify the plan

Crystallizing Outcome Goals

As the beginning step in constructing action plans, workers and clients clarify goals. They consider what they have learned about clients' situations and capabilities during the assessment process in preparation for framing clear goals. Workers ensure that clients formulate goals in positive terms, stating what clients want and will be doing rather than what they don't want or will be avoiding.

Reorienting Problems to Outcomes

Social workers often help clients reorient their self-described problems into a vision of a desired outcome or solution. In other words, workers help turn clients around from looking back at their problems to facing forward and describing what their lives will be like when they have reached the solution. Social workers guide clients to state goals "in a linguistically positive form, that is in terms of what the client will be doing or thinking, rather than what they will not be doing or thinking" (Walter & Peller, 1992, p. 53).

Stated in positive language, goals reflect aims to enhance or strengthen, not to remediate or reduce. For example, an individual experiencing stress about a recent job loss may state a goal of obtaining other employment. Likewise, a family that seeks counseling because of concern about the constant yelling and bickering among family members may state a goal of finding new ways to resolve differences. Or, neighborhood residents distressed about gang activity may state the broad goal of creating a safe neighborhood. In each example, the worker helps the client system transform what has been into what will be.

Consider the example of Nate Hardy, a social worker with the Northside Development Association. Nate's primary client system is the Northside community itself. He works with various formal and informal groups in the community to meet his agency's mission of improving the quality of life in Northside. In the process of setting positive goals with a neighborhood group, Nate Hardy does two things. He strives for concreteness to describe the current concerns of the neighborhood residents and he works to reorient residents to consider the future.

To understand concerns concretely, Nate uses responding skills:

- When a resident says "I'm unhappy," Nate may respond by inquiring "With whom?" or "About what?"
- When another member of the neighborhood group says they are "falling apart," Nate can respond with, "What are you noticing that leads you to this conclusion?"
- When a neighborhood leader says things can't go on this way, Nate can ask, "What things? In what way?"

As the residents answer Nate's questions each will begin to offer a clearer view of what they are seeking. But these concrete views of the present are likely to be replete with visions of what is wrong or what should stop. Nate is likely to learn:

- The first resident wants others to stop ignoring his opinion.
- The second resident of the neighborhood group wants group members to stop arguing among themselves.
- The indigenous leader hopes to change the way the city budgets its money.

Each of these assertions begins to hint at goals, but they all stop short of defining them concretely and positively. On the contrary, each goal indicates what clients want to get rid of, not specifically what they would like to have happen instead. In other words, these tentative goals focus on negative outcomes—what needs to change, rather than positive ones—what will occur instead. Social workers encourage clients to positively frame their desired outcomes by describing what will be happening rather than what will be missing.

In order to set positive directions, Nate responds to each resident's negatively expressed goal to convert it to a positive statement by saying:

- So, if people stop ignoring you, how would you like them to respond instead? What will they be doing?
- You would like the group to stop arguing. Can you describe for me how it will be when group members handle their disagreements differently?
- What differences in the way the city allocates funds would you like to see?

Nate's continued prodding to consider the future leads each resident to visualize a positive outcome:

- I want this group to include my ideas in their neighborhood development plan.
- I want the group to negotiate decisions cooperatively.
- I would like to see the city adopt new procedures that access citizen's views at each step of the budgeting process.

Notice how Nate helps these residents construct visual descriptions of what they would like in their futures. Walter and Peller (1992) call this process "movie making." Many other contributors agree that positive visions of goals are most effective.

Building on Positive Momentum

Not all client systems who seek social work services experience situations characterized as problematic. And many others, after a strength-oriented assessment process, may see their situations in a new light. In these cases, goals set in planning may be to encourage something to occur more often or to stabilize an already improving situation. For instance, a newly formed stepfamily may discover that their increased expressions of negative feelings is actually a good sign. It indicates that the family is becoming closer, blending together in a more intimate way. They may set goals to learn more about common transitions in stepfamilies in order to anticipate and resolve challenges likely to arise as the new family blends two distinct lifestyles and traditions into one.

Setting positive directions for goals is a straightforward affair when clients are optimistic and recognize existing strengths or recent improvements.

- When a woman says "Things have gotten better since I called you," the worker responds to identify what is working by asking, "What have you noticed that is better?"

- When a couple agrees they "feel hopeful," the worker asks for more details with the question, "What is happening that contributes to this feeling?"
- When the liaison from the agency says "We want to continue to make consensus decisions," the worker reflects and highlights the goal by saying, "I hear you saying that I am here to help you stabilize your abilities to make consensus decisions."

In each of these examples, the worker continues to clarify what works in order to set definitive goals which maintain and strengthen current productive functioning.

Sorting Out Possibilities

Translating problems into positive goals for the future is only one part of an effective goal setting process. To ensure coherent goals, social workers also help clarify information by ordering it logically. Since too many goals may confuse the direction of the work, social workers assist clients in articulating what is most important to them. Helpful ways for social workers to organize information include two seemingly opposite skills. The first involves arranging complex and integrated information into separate compartments. The second involves grouping similar information around common themes.

Creating Discrete Units.   Fant and Ross (1983) describe the analytic technique of "breaking it down." This technique of creating discrete units means taking issues that are complex and separating them into component parts to consider them one piece at a time. In contrast to the approach of clustering which works to resolve several related issues at once, partializing takes seemingly insurmountable challenges and breaks them down into achievable units. "Partializing helps the client gain mastery over a situation because the situation becomes more manageable; it is not an all-encompassing fog that hangs over an entire life" (Hoffman & Sallee, 1994, p. 91). Partializing relieves pressure on client systems and sets the stage for deciding which first step is likely to have the greatest impact on subsequent successes.

Grouping by Similarity.   In contrast, social workers can look for similarities among various issues. By finding the threads that run through several issues, social workers ascertain themes that have multiple ramifications. Clustering these issues leads to setting selective and efficient goals, the achievement of which can have multiple benefits. A mother's overprotectiveness, a son's anxious withdrawal, and a father's depression may all spring from the threat of the surrounding neighborhood. Identifying this central theme may lead to neighborhood change strategies or the family's move to a new location. Addressing this common issue brings relief to each of the family's members. Organizing issues coherently facilitates the planning process.

Writing Effective Objectives

Writing effective objectives is the heart of a good case plan. Well-formed objectives embody the realistic hopes of what clients will accomplish. Good objectives are rooted in concrete information about what clients need and the strengths and resources with which they have to work. Outcome objectives clearly lay out "who will achieve what when." They function as guides and give us markers to indicate if we are getting somewhere or if we need to reevaluate what we are doing and try another way.

Measurable objectives include a number of components. According to Sheafor, Horejsi, and Horejsi (1997), a good intervention objective answers a five-part question:

1. Who...
2. will do what...
3. to what extent...
4. under what condition...
5. by when? (p. 425)

This simple formula provides a useful tool for conceptualizing objectives. Applying it results in objectives that are specific, achievable, and measurable. Consider the following examples of objectives:

- Denise will receive a passing grade in math by the end of the semester.
- Fernando will secure a teaching job within the next month.
- The Patterson family will resolve each disagreement that arises in the next week by using the *stop, listen, and compliment* approach.
- Each administrative staff member of Neighbors United will access a community action grant within the next fiscal year.
- The task group will successfully persuade the city council to implement gang prevention activities within three months.

Notice how each objective offers complete information, yet does so simply and clearly. To ensure they are writing objectives in a meaningful way, workers can evaluate each objective using the following criteria:

1. Is it active? Does it say what someone will achieve?
2. Does it specify one discrete accomplishment rather than many?
3. Does it include a time frame for completion?
4. Can you observe, measure, and evaluate it?
5. Do the social worker, client, and other participants understand it and what their particular part of it is?
6. Is it easy enough to accomplish yet significant enough to make it worth the effort?
7. Are both client and worker comfortable with it?
8. Does it fit with agency practices and social work ethics? (Sheafor, Horejsi, & Horejsi, 1997)

Clearly written objectives lead clients directly to the goals they seek.

Determining Measures
The true test of whether an objective is a concrete enough outcome to guide actions is whether the partners can measure its achievement. Realistically, if clients and workers are to know that they have been successful, they must be able to concretely identify achievement criteria for each objective in the action plan.

For example, consider the efforts of the Child Welfare Division of Northside Prevention Services. The Division has set an objective to increase child safety within the community during the next year. Measurable criteria for achieving this objective include:

- The reported incidence of child abuse will decrease by 25 percent over the same time period from last year.
- Fifty percent of residents responding to a random telephone survey will indicate they would report child abuse if they suspect it.
- The Public Health Department will report a 50 percent reduction in child injuries from poisoning and household accidents in the three months following the home safety campaign.

Determining ways to measure the attainment of objectives focuses the efforts of all involved in implementing the plan.

Prioritizing Objectives

After articulating objectives, clients and social workers examine them to establish priorities. This process assigns preference to certain objectives in light of critical needs and resource availability (Pincus & Minahan, 1973). Clearly, protecting a client's safety, relieving distress, and meeting basic human needs are always priority actions. But, beyond addressing these immediate needs, setting priorities poses a number of value decisions. Social workers and clients develop priorities by considering motivational factors, the likelihood of success, and the work that might have the greatest or most widespread effect. Logical sequencing may be inherent in the objectives themselves, since some things have a natural order. Questions that may help clients rank priorities include:

- Which objectives are most motivating to the client?
- Which will most likely lead to success?
- Which issues are most pressing?
- What does the client want to do first?
- Is there a logical order in which to proceed?
- Is anyone at risk?
- Are priority actions necessary?

Clients have privileges to define the priorities. Social workers have responsibilities to identify risks and take necessary actions to ensure the safety of clients and others.

Screening Generalist Intervention Strategies

Generalist social workers think broadly. Even though workers encourage clients to focus narrowly on concrete outcomes, they broaden clients' perspectives to recognize multiple strategies to achieve these goals and objectives. Systemically oriented social workers acknowledge and act on the principle that changes in one part of the system create changes in other parts of the system. This means that workers and clients can aim anywhere in their related ecosystems—inside or outside of the social work relationship system—to create changes in the direction of desired outcomes.

Considering multiple system levels as targets for change adds the generalist perspective to the planning process. During assessment, workers and clients trace the transactional nature of issues. As a result, they discover numerous locations toward which to direct their efforts, specifically, toward client systems, related environmental systems, or the transactions between systems. Interventions at any level may produce the desired change. Synchronizing actions at many system levels, sequentially or in concert, may have the greatest impact.

Relating Outcomes to Locations for Change

Deciding on goals and objectives and locating places to direct attempts at change are companion processes. Considering what you want to accomplish has implications for where you need to work. Considering the places to which you have access to work has implications for the kinds of activities that are possible. Once clients articulate the outcomes they desire, planning how to reach those goals can begin in either place. In other words, workers and clients consider two general questions: What resource systems are available and how might they contribute to reaching the goal? Or, conversely, what are the steps to take and what locations are possible for achieving those steps? Each question starts from a different place but ends up with a realistic plan.

Monkman (1991) presents a framework of broad outcome categories for both persons and their environments which illustrates the relationship between outcomes desired and locations for attempting changes. Each outcome category correlates with a specific system level or possible target for change.

Outcomes for Persons

Survival Outcomes	Obtaining and using resources defined as basic necessities for life activities
Affiliation outcomes	Forming close personal relationships or support systems
Growth and achievement	Expanding contributions to one's self and others
Information and skills	Increase knowledge to acquire proficiency to deal effectively with life situations

Environmental Outcomes

Informal resources	Accessing extended kin and friendship networks for support, affection, advice, and services
Formal resources	Accessing services from membership organizations and associations
Societal resources	Accessing resources found in social institutions
Expectations	Seeking redefinition of normative behavior and changing role expectations by persons or institutions in the social environment
Laws, policies, customs, and rules	Seeking change by governing and legislative bodies and in administrative rules

The particular goals that clients seek lead workers and clients around the ecosystem to gather resources, forge new connections, or make necessary changes. Since clients' problems do not arise in isolation of their situations, solutions also are contextually based. As clients focus in on the objectives necessary to achieve their goals, the places they must direct their efforts become more obvious. For example, a teenage girl who wants to improve her academic performance may choose strategies that lead her to school to learn what teachers are wanting from her, to her family to negotiate a quiet space and time away from chores in which to complete homework, to her social group to locate a study partner, and to her own self to increase her persistence in completing tasks. Each one of these systems influences her current functioning and can contribute to her goal of improved academic performance. The goals and objectives that clients set lead logically to the locations to consider for solutions.

Choosing Targets for Change

For each client system there are four general locations to consider as targets for change (Figure 11.2). These areas include:

- The client system
- Subsystems of the client system
- Environmental systems in the context of the client
- Transactional systems or the connections between clients and their environments

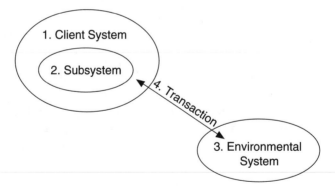

FIGURE 11.2   Locations for Change. Social workers applying an ecosystems perspective see many possible targets for change. Specifically, the worker and client can choose to intervene with the client system, a subsystem of the client system, an environmental system in the client's context, and/or the transactions between client and environment.

A change in any one of these areas of functioning may result in the achievement of clients' goals. Generalist social workers and their clients frequently use a multifaceted strategy by selecting and combining many targets for change into a unified approach.

Reconsider the example of Nate Hardy and his client system, the Northside community. In open forums, the community has set an objective to increase the availability of low-cost housing. Now, in beginning to formulate strategies, Nate and interested community members are scanning the resource systems of the neighborhood to determine where to direct their efforts at change. To facilitate this effort, Nate charts out the following ideas and locations for change to present for the citizens' review:

Client System

- Create a community newsletter which lists and compares costs of available rentals to encourage competition and lower rents
- Establish an annual festival to celebrate the history of the neighborhood and its current cultural diversity as a way to increase cohesion and affiliation among residents

Subsystems

- Organize a new group of community members with home building and repair skills to volunteer to fix up currently uninhabited homes
- Initiate a program with the Northside Vocational High School to remodel abandoned homes as educational projects and sell them at cost to neighborhood residents

Environmental Systems

- Modify the local banking practices of lending only for new construction projects
- Change city ordinances which limit the number of "unrelated" persons in the same household to allow friends to live together and reduce housing costs through sharing

Transactional Systems

- Organize a tenant's rights group to attend city council meetings and advocate for new rent control ordinances
- Obtain a federal grant to build scattered subsidized housing units throughout the neighborhood

All the options Nate lists are strategies involving different parts of the Northside community and its environment. Any one strategy works toward the goal of increasing available low-cost housing in the neighborhood. Choosing a combination of these approaches offers even greater possibilities for achieving a broad-based impact.

All client systems have component parts and environments that offer possible locations for change. Consider a family system. A worker could facilitate changes in the ways the family makes decisions. Another possible change could be in how the parents relate which, in turn, would affect the rest of the family. How much extended family support the family uses, how parents and children relate to jobs and school, how society views this family in terms of culture, race, socioeconomic status, and lifestyle—all contribute to what is happening with this family and all also hold potential for how this family might change. When considering the places to intervene, clients and social workers look broadly to consider changes at many system levels.

Choosing Effective Strategies

To determine what strategies to implement requires a careful organization of available information and options. There are many methods workers can employ to generate options. Frequently, workers compile written lists with clients in order to ensure that they comprehensively consider everything that is necessary. Some recordkeeping procedures require such lists of identified strengths, needs, and possibilities for change.

Brainstorming

A helpful strategy to employ in considering strategies is *brainstorming,* which "produces a wide range of possibilities through a freewheeling discussion aimed at generating many possible solutions" (Hepworth, Rooney, & Larsen, 1997, p. 417). In brainstorming, workers and clients list as many ideas as they can imagine without any evaluation of which would be best. The free-flowing nature of this process unleashes creativity and cooperation. This strategy is especially useful in planning with multiperson client systems since it encourages all to participate in the planning process with no fear that their ideas will be criticized.

Matching Resources and Needs

Matching resources available to client needs is another effective approach for developing intervention strategies. For example, Cowger (1992) recommends charting information to include client system strengths and needs on one side and environmental system resources and obstacles on the other. In this way, the partners delineate the strengths and resources available with respect to the challenges presented. Note how this charting emphasizes the transactional nature of client issues, highlighting possible strategies in the environment as well as those targeting changes in the client system itself.

Cowger's (1992) framework illustrates how the organizational processes chosen influence the planning that follows. This charting method focuses on both clients and environments and builds on strengths in the process. Consider the differences in the plan that would result from a procedure focusing only on a client's failures or inadequacies. How the partners organize the information makes a difference. Social workers help clients organize information in ways that motivate, encourage, and predict success. The questions to ask when matching challenges with resources include:

- What strengths and abilities does the client demonstrate in one area of functioning that might transfer to dealing with the challenge?
- What untapped resources are present in the environment to meet the client's defined needs?
- What does the client need that the worker can provide directly or access for the client?
- What resources need to be expanded or developed?

Answering all these questions orients workers and clients to the resources they currently have to meet objectives and what other resources might be necessary. Social workers also evaluate the usefulness of potential social service resources to choose effective strategies (see Table 11.1).

Emphasizing Client Strengths

The most empowering plans build on client strengths. To discover strength-oriented options, workers and clients ask themselves two questions:

- What are clients doing right that they should continue to do? In other words, what should they reinforce and strengthen?
- What strengths and resources of clients or their social and physical environments apply to the current situation?

Enhancing existing strengths and matching resources to needs are steps toward building action plans that clients can approach with feelings of confidence and expectations of success.

Incorporating Resources of Social Workers

Good action plans also anticipate what workers can bring to the process. What do workers know? What can workers do? To what resources do workers have connections? Some needs that clients bring may require these types of resources for successful resolutions, but be cautious here. Empowering social workers recognize the need to hold their own resources in check so as not to encourage dependency on the part of clients. Workers do not develop strategies that place themselves in central roles and leave the clients as passive observers.

TABLE 11.1   Schema for Assessing Resources

Criteria	Description
Relevance	Does the resource offer services that are congruent with the client system's identified needs? Will the resource meet the client system's goals?
Availability	Will the resource be available when the client system requires it? Is there a waiting list? Do certain circumstances qualify for a quick response?
Accessibility	Is the office located on convenient travel routes? Does the resource offer services in the client's language? Sign language? Are the facilities accessible to those with disabilities?
Eligibility	What are the guidelines for receiving this service? Are there income, location, age, or other qualifiers?
Applications	Is there a formal application process? Who needs to fill out what form? What time frame is imposed on the application process? Are supporting documents required?
Fee	Is there a sliding fee scale? If fees are involved, has the client system been informed of the fee schedule? Will the client realistically be able to pay for the service? Under what circumstances can the fee be waived?
Feasibility	Considering all of the aforementioned factors, is this a viable resource?

The best strategies place clients in charge and use workers' resources and skills as supplemental. Clients need as many opportunities as possible to experience their own effectiveness and affirm their expertise.

Weighing Costs and Benefits

Not all available strategies are equal. It is likely that there is no perfect solution; there are pros and cons to each possibility. Before composing definitive objectives, workers and clients weigh the costs and benefits of each proposed strategy. Pertinent questions include:

- Is there an advantage to using one resource rather than another?
- What are the costs of each approach in terms of time and money?
- Are there possible hidden costs?
- Are some strategies easier to implement than others?
- What are the potential risks or consequences?
- Do certain combinations work better than others?
- Is there a logical order for proceeding? Should one approach be implemented first and another held back and used only if necessary?
- Should accessing multiple resources be gradual or simultaneous?
- Do clients think that certain strategies will work better for them than others?
- Which options are best based on the worker's practice experience?
- Does practice evaluation research offer suggestions about approaches?

The answers to these questions lead clients and workers to choose strategies that have the greatest likelihood of success.

Delineating Tasks and Responsibilities

Some strategies are so simple and direct that the way to achieve them may be obvious. At other times, additional specification is necessary so that all people involved know their roles and responsibilities in completing the task. Consider the example of a task group on gang prevention. To achieve their objective of influencing the city council to adopt their recommendations, the task group needs to complete more detailed planning. Tasks and responsibilities assigned may include: One member will call the city clerk to reserve a place on the council meeting's agenda. Another member will arrive at the meeting early to save a block of chairs so that task group members can sit together and be seen as a cohesive political unit. Someone will call the local newspaper to guarantee news coverage. And, the social worker will write a news release incorporating the group's recommendations to distribute to the representatives of the media. Delineating these specific roles and responsibilities ensures a coordinated effort in implementing the objective. Using a format similar to Figure 11.3, clients and practitioners can prepare a detailed implementation plan.

Setting Reviews and Evaluations

Effectively written objectives define intervals for reviewing progress. Since they specify time frames, workers and clients naturally will stop to review how they are doing at those

Worksheet: Implementation		Calendar												
Task	Who is Responsible	J	F	M	A	M	J	J	A	S	O	N	D	

FIGURE 11.3 Taking Action. The organizational action plan lists the tasks, specifies responsibilities for carrying out specific action steps, and provides a timetable for completion.

From *Visioning the Future: Organizational Strategic Planning* by B. L. DuBois (April, 1993). Used with permission of the author.

times. Each review offers workers and clients an opportunity to proceed as planned or to make modifications. Figure 11.4 presents a useful tool for recording the effectiveness of strategies and the level of outcome achievement.

Some social delivery systems structure intervals for review in their program procedures. For example, school social workers are very familiar with the Individual Education Plan (IEP), which is an annually updated plan outlining the program tailored for a student with special educational needs. To accommodate unanticipated events, rapid improvements, or changing needs, each IEP also offers opportunities to reconvene the planning body if necessary. Good planning requires periodic reviews and flexibility to modify plans as necessary.

Contracting

The concept of contract underlies all phases of the social work process. Simply, a contract is "an agreement between the consumer and the provider of service" (Fox, 1987, p. 494). Although formal contracts usually refer to the explicit agreements that social workers and clients forge to operationalize action plans, an implied contract secures the social worker–client relationship from the initial contact to the last. Contractual agreements vary from "assumed" to explicit. The operating contract "may merely be an understanding between worker and client; or it may be a formal, written, signed agreement" (Johnson, 1998, p. 325). The formality of the contract varies depending on the preferences of the worker, the client, and agency policy.

Clarity is essential for a contract's success. Workers ensure that all parties involved in the contract clearly understand what they are agreeing to do and hoping to achieve. The most

Worksheet: Evaluating Success				
Objectives	Strategies	Expected Outcomes	Achievement Level	
			Met	Unmet

FIGURE 11.4   **Evaluating Organizational Planning. Evaluation considers the level of achievement of objectives and reviews the utility of strategies used in the change process.**

From *Visioning the Future: Organizational Strategic Planning* by B. L. DuBois (April, 1993). Used with permission of the author.

effective contracts have flexibility, incorporate the views of clients, and concretely define the next step.

The Evolving Contract

Describing the contract between social workers and clients as evolutionary makes sense in terms of the developmental nature of the social work process. The social work contract evolves through phases of agreeing to work together to agreeing to assess the situation to agreeing to the plan for change. "Contracting and recontracting as integral parts of the helping process are flexible, dynamic and continuous processes that must remain sensitive to changes that occur" (Germain & Gitterman, 1980, pp. 60–61). Henry (1992) explains how the contract evolves to keep pace with the development of a group client. Members originally contract with themselves and the worker for their own individual purposes, but they change this contract to incorporate more group-centered content as they begin to function as part of the group. What members are working on, how they view themselves, and what seems possible changes as the work continues.

The contract changes as the professional relationship and focus of the work progresses over time (Table 11.2). Initially, workers and clients agree to meet and form a working alliance—the *contract for the relationship*. The initial dialogue leads to clarity about purpose and defines a direction for the partners to explore the situation further—the *contract for assessment*. Discovering available resources leads to an explicit plan to accomplish the concrete goals defined—the *contract for change*. When social workers and clients achieve

TABLE 11.2   **The Evolving Contract**

Phase	Type of Contract	Description
Dialogue Phase	Contract for Relationship	Agreement to form a working partnership to define direction
	Contract for Assessment	Agreement to further explore the situation and assess the resources available
Discovery Phase	Contract for Change	Agreement to a plan of action to activate and expand resources and opportunities
Development Phase	Contract for Resolution	Agreement to conclude the client–social worker relationship

their desired outcomes, they agree to dissolve the relationship—the *contract for resolution.* At each point of contracting and recontracting for their work together, social workers and clients have opportunities to redefine their collaboration.

Contracting for Change
When social workers and clients agree to a comprehensive plan of action, this constitutes a contract for change. Contracting for change refers to "the explicit agreement between the worker and the client concerning the target problems, the goals, and the strategies of social work intervention, and the roles and tasks of the participants" (Maluccio & Marlow, 1974, p. 30). Creating an action plan clearly lays out the work that a client system and social worker will do. Forging an agreement to proceed with the plan is a contract for change.

There is evidence that social work contracts for change, especially those that state objectives explicitly, enhance practice effectiveness. "Contracting promotes focus and avoids ambiguity. It necessitates an explicit partialization of the problems and goals. It avoids games and hidden-agenda items that frequently accompany the helping process" (Fox, 1987, p. 498). Contracts also give practitioners measurable criteria on which to base their evaluations of success.

Contracting as an Empowering Process

Contracting with clients has benefits beyond a simple clarification of current status and future direction. Contracts emphasize client participation, facilitate communication, improve commitment, and foster a sense of autonomy and self-determination (Fox, 1987). Contracting "reduces some of the power discrepancy between client and worker at a time when the client is under stress and vulnerable to manipulation" (Germain & Gitterman, 1980, p. 53).

Each time that social workers and clients renegotiate their working agreement, clients experience their power in the relationship. They have an opportunity to control what happens next. Renegotiating the contract also explicitly gives clients permission to change the direction of their work. It can rebalance the power when a social worker's expertise has encouraged the client to settle into a dependent pattern in their relationship. Explicitly discussing the evolving contract continues to share power with clients over the course of the relationship.

Reflecting Back

Goal-directed planning focuses on outcomes. The ultimate measure of success is goal achievement. Some people question whether this emphasis on goals and endpoints represents a culturally biased view. Are concreteness and goal achievement Western precepts that ignore significant intangibles, such as relationship and process variables? Can purposeful change be guided by a process vision of relating the way you want to relate and approaching challenges in a deliberately ethical and proactive way? Consider the path of change that works most effectively for you. Do you succeed best when you have an outcome vision in mind, or do things work best when you interact in a preferred way and let the future take care of itself?

Looking Forward

Framing solutions means planning how client systems and workers intend to reach their goals. Planning accomplishes important tasks. It clarifies what the client is seeking, considers what aspects of the client system's functioning and context hold possibilities for solutions, and determines strategies necessary to succeed. The culmination of the planning process is a concrete action plan. Mutual planning produces a synergistic solution that reflects the expertise of both clients and workers. In the upcoming development phase, clients and workers implement the plan, evaluate its effectiveness, and wrap up their work together in a way that maintains progress.

Part 4

The Development Phase: Implementing, Evaluating, and Stabilizing Change

Intervening with clients and their environments tests the versatility of generalist social workers. What workers actually do depends on the client system's capabilities, the responses of the impinging environment, and the accessibility of essential resources. Sensitive social workers do what is necessary, but they balance their involvement so as not to undermine the developing power of their clients. As workers collaborate with clients to implement action plans, they facilitate an ongoing evaluation of the progress toward goals and prepare to conclude their work.

Part 4 describes the *development phase* of social work practice, in which clients and social workers carry out the plans they have constructed. Chapters in this section explain how the partners activate existing resources in clients and their environments, create empowering alliances, and expand available opportunities. Within the development phase, workers and clients also evaluate their efforts and wrap up their work in ways that stabilize the progress achieved.

Chapter *12*

Activating Resources

Donna Lester is the mother of 8-year-old twin boys who the Child Protective Unit at the State Department of Social Services recently determined were beyond Donna's control. Donna herself initiated the chain reaction that led to the removal of her children by asking the local police department for help. The police then called in the Child Protective Unit. Donna's boys were placed in foster care, activating Jon Allen's role as a Case Advocate in the Foster Care Program at Northside Family Services.

Jon understands why some people see Donna as having little potential, as her challenges are considerable. Her moderate level of mental retardation, desperate financial situation, and recent separation from an abusive and alcoholic boyfriend on whom she still periodically depends for assistance could label Donna as "chronic" or "multiproblem." But Jon's strengths-oriented assessment has revealed Donna to be "multi-talented" as well. Donna is good at recognizing her need for help. The call to the police is clear evidence of that. She succeeded in getting her boyfriend to move out and is no longer subsidizing his alcoholism, something she learned through her participation with Al-Anon. Donna is also extremely nurturant to her children, emotionally expressive, and loving. Besides, she's an excellent cook with a good sense of nutrition. Donna's needs are significant, but she is not without resources.

Donna is definite about her goal of having her sons return home. With this goal in mind, Jon and Donna develop a plan of action that targets three key objectives: Donna sets objectives to use effective and positive parenting methods, to stabilize her financial situation through public assistance and part-time employment, and to increase her abilities to function independently of her abusive boyfriend. These concrete objectives frame the work ahead.

Jon meets with Donna twice a week. At one meeting, Jon spends time with Donna alone to review her situation, discuss her options, encourage her progress, and plan activities for the week—small steps toward the outcomes she desires. He finds himself working directly to boost Donna's self-esteem, develop her sense of power, and maintain her motivation by listening to her story, highlighting her successes, congratulating her on progress, and designing readily achievable tasks.

During the second meeting each week, Jon monitors Donna's regular visit with the boys. Prior to visits he and Donna collaborate to develop a plan for how she will handle the boys. During the visits, Jon sits back, creating space for Donna to test her parenting skills. Jon records his observations, particularly those parenting skills that he sees as effective so that he and Donna can review and discuss them after the visit. Once, Jon arranges for the visit to occur in the office so he can videotape the family's interaction. Watching the tape, Donna realizes how much of the time she is actually effective in handling her sons' behaviors.

Working with Donna alone is not enough. To increase productive transactions with others in her social environment, Jon works with Donna "to fill in her eco-map," as he and Donna name this activity. During assessment, they had drawn Donna's social and community support network as it existed. Now, during their meetings, they pull this eco-map out and target various connections to reinforce or change.

At Jon's suggestion, Donna meets with her public assistance worker to determine the extent to which her sons' foster care placement lowers her benefits and to find out when, after her sons return home, her benefits will increase. Donna obtains a copy of the rules describing how a part-time job will affect her assistance. In addition, Jon links Donna to the local community college's program for screening interests and skills to determine possible employment options. When the inventory reveals Donna's expertise in food preparation,

Jon refers her to the State Employment Service where Donna locates a part-time job in the cafeteria of the local middle school—an opportunity which fits her skills and involves hours that will not require her to arrange for child care.

Jon also connects Donna to parenting classes at his own agency. When Donna's difficulty with reading interferes with her ability to keep up with the other parents in the class, Jon advocates within his agency to provide Donna with an individualized approach. He proposes to the agency's board of directors that they allocate funds to purchase videotapes on parenting skills. Jon's assertion that Donna has a right to access these educational services in a way that she can understand, as guaranteed under the American with Disabilities Act, strengthens his recommendation that the board approve the purchase.

Jon encourages Donna to maintain her attendance at Al-Anon meetings and participate in some of the family social events the program offers. He also coaches Donna on how to build on her work relationships at the school cafeteria to develop them into social relationships for her own enjoyment and to provide support in times of stress. This expanding social network gives Donna options other than her old boyfriend when she feels the need for friends or recreation.

Each of these activities contributes to Donna's successful achievement of her objectives. Jon's observations and suggestions about parenting, the newly acquired educational videotapes, and Donna's persistence in learning new parenting skills increase her effectiveness as a parent. Donna's meetings with public assistance workers and her new job stabilize her financial situation. Jon's nurturance, respect, and activities to build Donna's self-esteem along with Donna's newly developed network of friends increase her confidence to function independently of her previously abusive boyfriend. With these objectives accomplished, the goal of the boys' return home is within reach.

Jon's work with Donna activates her to develop her potential and attain her goals. To activate means to mobilize, energize, charge, stimulate, excite, arouse, start, trigger, and prompt. Notice the unifying thread of meaning in these words. Activating is a beginning, a "jump start," not a lifelong commitment. Activating resources means to take what is available within clients and their ecosystems and get it going. It does not mean to take care of, do for, drag to, control, fix, or treat. Both partners get things moving and keep things going in the direction of goals.

This chapter explores how social workers and clients intervene to activate resources to help clients reach their goals. It describes the processes and skills workers use to implement action plans in ways that respect, motivate, and empower clients. Specifically, this chapter:

- Outlines interventions for activating resources within clients and their environments
- Details how workers help to sustain progress during the development phase
- Describes how workers recognize and enhance a client's experience of power
- Provides strategies for broadening options through changing people's views and behaviors
- Explains various aspects of effective resource management
- Discusses educational processes that respect client systems

By employing these processes, a social worker can increase clients' experience of power and efficient use of available resources and develop their skills for resolving their own situations.

Applying Generalist Intervention Skills

Various authors describe the activities in this part of the social work process as interventions (Compton & Galaway, 1999), strategies for change (Hepworth, Rooney & Larsen, 1997), or direct and indirect actions (Johnson, 1998). Although these terms place a different emphasis on who is doing what, each describes this as a phase for development—the time when social workers and clients put their plans into action.

Implementing plans requires generalist social workers to draw on an array of skills for working with both client systems and their environments. Workers employ strategies to accentuate and develop client system strengths, experiment with changes in the ways clients do things, renegotiate the transactions of client systems with their environments, and modify environmental systems. These are mutual tasks in which clients and social workers play complementary roles.

Intervention across System Levels

Generalist social workers, regardless of their practice setting, interweave generic practice skills with intervention skills specific to the level of client system. Since a client system may be an individual, couple, family, group, organization, neighborhood, or community, generalists must be adept at those skills that apply to the identified client system. In addition, regardless of the level of the client system, workers also intervene at other system levels on behalf of the current client. This chapter's opening example details how a worker collaborates directly with a client while also activating other resources in the client's environment to achieve the direction of the desired change. Generalist social work intervention is an endeavor that involves work at multiple system levels.

Despite the diversity of human systems, certain social work practice skills are universal. All clients, from individuals to communities, benefit from a social worker's interest, encouragement, and organized approach. Clients at all levels respond to an increased sense of power and new ways to look at their situations. And all clients benefit from productive connections to resources, relevant information, and newly acquired skills. Generalist social workers can facilitate these benefits throughout the development phase as they carry out their roles associated with consultancy, resource management, and education. Throughout their work practitioners employ strategies for maintaining progress, developing power, changing perspectives, managing resources, and educating (Table 12.1).

Maintaining Progress in the Action Plan

During the development phase, social workers consult to keep moving as directly as possible in the directions that clients desire. Workers maintain a positive, yet objective, stance on progress in order to monitor the structure and facilitate the process of the work. To efficiently structure activities during this phase, practitioners draw on the plan that workers and clients have previously framed. To promote effective processes, workers intervene in ways

TABLE 12.1 Generalist Skills for Activating Resources

Maintaining Progress
- Implementing Action Plans: facilitating a productive, goal-seeking process; reviewing and updating plans as necessary
- Enhancing Interactions: encouraging participation; responding to clarify situations, refine goals, and locate resources; building alliances among participants
- Sustaining Motivation: validating client's views and feelings; providing nurturance; expressing optimism

Developing Power
- Promoting Leadership: asserting client privileges in the relationship; acknowledging leadership abilities
- Recognizing Choices: enhancing agency by recognizing existing options; locating areas of client's control
- Locating Genuine Options: expanding resource networks; overcoming oppressive conditions
- Magnifying Strengths: responding to highlight strengths; recognizing incremental steps

Changing Perspectives
- Offering Feedback: reflecting client actions; examining behavior with respect to goals
- Creating New Concepts: reframing; offering metaphors
- Reconstructing Narratives: externalizing; co-constructing; generating multiple interpretations
- Changing Behaviors: considering new ways to do things; experimenting with behavior change

Managing Resources
- Linking Clients with Resources: locating resources; maximizing client administration of resource network
- Case Advocacy: developing power within the service network; using professional influence on client's behalf
- Maximizing Clients' Rights: implementing a social justice agenda; ensuring clients' due process rights

Educating
- Teaching: modeling; role-playing; structuring educational experiences
- Sharing Information: sharing professional expertise; self-disclosing

to enhance the interactions of the client system and continue to maintain the client's motivation toward the goal.

Implementing Action Plans

Social workers keep the plan in the forefront of the development phase. The action plan prescribes what social workers and clients do when they are together and frames activities to accomplish between meetings. In those instances when the work gets somewhat off-track, social workers use the plan to review progress and redefine directions. Social workers need not rigidly enforce previous agreements. Plans are flexible, yet they structure coordinated efforts for approaching challenges in ways that lead to the achievement of goals.

Collaborating on Actions

The combination of in-meeting activities and between-meeting tasks keeps clients and workers actively moving toward goals. Each meeting provides direct opportunities to activate client resources. Social workers and clients generate new perspectives, reinforce effective behavior, and create additional options for change. Clients and workers use meetings to plan additional activities for each to implement. Between meetings, clients may experiment with new behaviors, observe the impact of change attempts, or connect to necessary resources in the environment. Social workers may investigate untapped community resources for their potential use, advocate with other systems, or consult with supervisors on a client's progress.

Over the course of time, as clients demonstrate their abilities to do more, social workers do less. In fact, as client systems become proficient in organizing and activating their own resources, workers modulate from being active interveners to becoming more reflective and encouraging facilitators. Enduring solutions are ones that clients discover within themselves and in the ways they manage their own worlds.

Enhancing Interactions

Workers encourage client systems to identify and express what they are thinking, feeling, and doing. Even as clients and social workers implement plans, dialogue and discovery skills remain important. Most of what social workers and clients are actually doing throughout the generalist social work process is communicating, exploring new perspectives, sharing observations, and gaining a mutual, concrete understanding of what is happening. Clients continue to benefit from articulating thoughts and feelings. Workers enhance interactions through their skills to maintain focus, encourage participation, and handle differences.

Maintaining Focus

In the development phase, workers and clients already have agreed to a plan, complete with concrete objectives and definitive activities. With this information in mind, workers help clients "stay on course." For example, workers may say:

- I'm pleased to hear that your job is going well—I'm wondering if you had a chance to call your ex-wife like we talked about last week.
- I thought we were here to talk about your marriage and whether or not you wanted me to refer you to a marriage counselor. So far all we're talking about today is problems with the kids. Are you ready to talk about the referral or have you changed your mind?
- We certainly do have fun whenever this group gets together and now we have some work to do. Who wants to report on their committee assignment first?

Notice how these practitioners encourage clients to talk about relevant issues and report on activities that are current. Social workers facilitate communication by focusing conversations on the tasks at hand.

In addition to maintaining a consistent focus on current tasks, workers also encourage clients to talk about one relevant issue in depth before moving on to another. Shifting from issue to issue often evades dealing intensively with feelings associated with a particular issue

(Shulman, 1999). *"Holding to focus* sends the message to the client that the worker means to discuss the tougher feelings and concerns" (p. 173). When workers allow clients to skip around, they inadvertently conspire with clients to avoid troublesome issues. Clients may sense that workers are either uncomfortable or don't feel competent to handle what they need to discuss. Workers cannot force clients to talk about particular issues; nevertheless, they should demonstrate that they can handle tough issues if clients choose to do so.

Larger systems multiply the difficulties that practitioners may experience in keeping the work on track. To focus many people at once, workers rely less on their interactional skills and more on structured processes. Examples include using written agendas, handouts, questionnaires, audiovisual materials, structured experiences, minutes of previous meetings, and mailings between meetings. Initiating more formal meeting procedures and using tangible materials can keep large groups focused on current issues.

Encouraging Participation

Client systems activate more resources when they function in ways that allow all members to give what they have to give. This does not mean that every member must contribute equally to each interaction, but instead each member's expertise is used as appropriate to the various issues and actions of the group (Toseland & Rivas, 1998). People need assurance that they have the right to their views, the privilege to express them, and the trust that others will listen and accept their ideas even when they disagree. In structural terms, members require some degree of power within the system's hierarchy and enough space to feel free to assert their opinions. Facilitative social workers interact directly with client systems to work toward this differentiated and respectful type of structure.

Social workers have many ways to ensure that all group members have opportunities to contribute. To coordinate conversational traffic, one might comment:

- Well, I've heard three opinions. Just two more to go. Who's next?

To ensure that group members hear each contribution, one might inquire:

- Could I ask you to tell me what you just heard Ryan say? Seems like you might have missed it.

To help members accept and appreciate divergent opinions, practitioners can point out the potential contributions of differences with comments such as:

- I really don't think that one of you has to be right and the other wrong. You're probably both right. You're two different people. You're bound to see things differently and that's okay; it gives us more to work with.

In each of these responses, workers encourage the participation of all group members.

Additionally, social workers can use more formal approaches to encourage participation. Situations such as conversations dominated by only one subgroup or members talking only with the worker hamper the full participation by other group members and require direct action by the worker (Toseland & Rivas, 1998). Implementing a structured experience disrupts this uneven pattern of participation. For example, the social worker could begin a meeting by individually asking each group member what to discuss. Dividing the time available into equal blocks safeguards time for exploring each member's issues. Structuring interactions to encourage participation activates previously untapped resources.

Stimulating Support within Client Systems

Workers can encourage alliances among group members with simple responses. For example, highlighting similarities among members builds alliances:

- I guess the adults in this family see things in the same way.
- I noticed the three of you were nodding in agreement when Geena was talking.

Additionally, articulating underlying expressions of affection solidifies connections between group members:

- I'm seeing you express a strong commitment to working things out with Sharon when you say that.
- All this worry, concern, and nagging seems like love to me!

Recognizing alliances contributes to clients' feelings of support and power, encourages self-confidence, and increases abilities to risk changes.

Physical arrangements develop alliances, as well. Within a meeting, workers can purposefully arrange seating to encourage closeness. For example, perceptive practitioners create seating arrangements that remove physical barriers to interactions. Commonly, social workers intervening with family systems place parents together and children separately to facilitate the cooperative development of a parenting team and a supportive sibling subsystem.

Assignments of tasks and activities can also be used to create alliances. For example, to develop new subsystems of previously disconnected members, group leaders can implement exercises requiring subgroup activities. Likewise, community workers organize various task groups to involve individual members with each other more intensively.

Paradoxically, holding a separate meeting for selected subgroups within a client system is a powerful strategy for creating alliances. At the community level, consider the impact when the worker convenes a meeting between leaders of four different factions within a neighborhood organization. The effective alliance among leaders of these conflicting factions increases the respective power of each subgroup and of the entire neighborhood. In working with families, weigh the benefit of conducting a separate interview with parents when working with a family on issues of parental authority. A separate session with parents draws a clear generational boundary and gives the parents a chance to discuss parenting strategies as well as their own relationship issues.

Handling Differences

Differences of opinion are inevitable when systems have more than one member. When topics spark heated debate and divisive conflicts, workers can maintain collaboration among group members by asking each to represent the opposing view or summarize what others are saying (Johnson & Johnson, 1997). Rather than narrowly repeating singular viewpoints, this exercise facilitates listening to alternative views and builds on the unique contributions.

For example, consider this interaction at an interdisciplinary staffing. The facilitator intervenes in a potentially antagonistic disagreement by saying:

> *I'm hearing several interesting and different perspectives. I guess that's the beauty of bringing people from different disciplines together. To make progress toward some kind of agreement though, we need to make sure that we are listening to everyone's input. It would probably help if we stopped for a minute and summarized the views we're hearing from each other to make sure that we're all on the same wavelength before we move on.*

Notice how this social worker facilitates the way the team members communicate rather than simply adding information which could fuel the debate.

Sustaining Motivation

Social workers enter clients' lives at vulnerable times—times when clients need support. While experimenting with growth and change, clients are even more likely to be unsure of themselves. Although empowering social workers do not foster dependency in clients, neither do they abandon clients. Instead they motivate clients with support, acceptance, and caring. Workers encourage clients as they risk new behaviors, experience setbacks, and celebrate successes. To encourage clients to keep working during times of change, workers strive to validate clients' experiences, reassure them about the uneven nature and the sometimes slow pace of change, respect their uniqueness, and provide emotional support.

Validating the Client's Reality

To maintain their change efforts, clients need to know that someone else understands their experiences. This validation is especially important when clients are oppressed and see workers as unfamiliar with their particular stressors. For example, "openly identifying and discussing institutionalized racism, discrimination, or economic disparities, can minimize clients' feelings of self-blame and helplessness and foster racial pride and identity" (Gibson, 1993, p. 391). This discussion cements the working relationship and energizes the client's participation.

Another way that workers can validate clients is to normalize their experiences. "A normalized approach suggests that behavior cannot be viewed objectively, but must be viewed in terms of a person's intentions, motives, and reasons" (Parsons, Hernandez, & Jorgensen, 1988, p. 419). Considering a behavior in its environmental context means that workers convey their belief that, in these particular circumstances, most people would respond similarly. In other words, the client's behavior makes sense in context, especially in terms of the gender, life style, and ethnic identity of the client. "Normalizing allows clients to stop blaming themselves, or someone else, and then to do something different" (Walter & Peller, 1992, p. 119).

Accepting the Nature of Change

Change occurs erratically. "Complex systems…do not change in a smooth, unbroken line but in discontinuous leaps" (Hoffman, 1989, p. 92). Sometimes clients leap forward. At other times they stabilize or return to old ways. Resistance to change is a natural part of development; all human systems tend to maintain the comfort of habitual patterns in the face of changing situations. When things do change, humans take breaks to restabilize and see what things are like before they continue on. It's natural for clients to slow down progress that is occurring, back up, and do it the old way again to find a sense of security before moving ahead.

Introducing the notion of "setbacks" normalizes the process of change:

> *We tell clients that for every three steps forward there are two steps back. While we tell clients that the two steps backward are normal, we also tell them that we are concerned that they will mistakenly see the normal two steps back as failure and possibly give up on what is working. Often, after this type of normalizing, we give clients the assignment to notice how they get themselves back on track when the setback occurs. (Walter & Peller, 1992, p. 152)*

Some client systems require particular patience with respect to accepting the pace and pattern of their change. For example, discussing their work with persons who are homeless and mentally ill, Sheridan, Gowen, and Halpin (1993) say that:

> *Because service delivery to the homeless mentally ill is often a long, slow process, workers must be able to maintain a positive attitude about clients' progress even when it occurs in small but significant increments. In other words, workers must be patient, persistent, flexible, sincere, respectful, and, most important, committed to the well-being of their clients. (p. 417)*

Clients are sensitive to views about how they are doing. Effective social workers demonstrate patience and enthusiasm for even the smallest incremental changes and remain optimistic when change is slow.

Respecting Uniqueness

No two client systems change in the same way, have the same set of resources or constraints, or magically respond to the exact same strategy. Social workers take caution in applying "standard techniques" or "cookbook interventions" which fail to acknowledge the unique qualities of a particular client system. Certainly, social workers' general practice wisdom and knowledge of special populations contributes to their thinking. But even the most tried and true, research-supported strategies need modifications to suit specific situations.

Respecting uniqueness means that social workers acknowledge their differences from clients as well. Saying, "I know exactly how you feel," denies the reality of differences. To ask the client, "I guess I'm not really sure. How do potential employers in this area respond to someone who has recently immigrated?" shows respect by recognizing the client's first-hand expertise. Openly discussing and accepting differences transforms potential barriers into working alliances.

Providing Emotional Support

Workers provide emotional support in two basic ways. First, they comment enthusiastically on a client's progress. Walter and Peller (1992) describe this as cheerleading, "emotional support that comes across through raised voice tones, gestures, excited expressions, or the choice of words" (p. 106). Workers also provide emotional support by using compliments which reflect on the changes that clients have made and give them credit for these changes.

Workers can also provide powerful emotional support by sharing feelings about their experience of working with clients. Sharing these feelings works in two important ways: "[It] effectively strengthens the working relationship (the process), while contributing important ideas for the client's work (the content)" (Shulman, 1999, p. 168). However, rather than serving the worker's own personal needs, Shulman cautions that the worker's "feelings should be shared in pursuit of professional purposes as the worker implements the professional function" (p. 199).

Developing Power

People feel their own power when they become aware of their expertise, resources, and gifts. People have a sense of control when others allow and respect their views. People feel powerful when they connect to the power of others. Empowerment-based strategies provide clients with information, offer options and opportunities to make decisions, and help to build social support networks (Gibson, 1993). Empowerment requires that workers help clients develop leadership, recognize choices, locate genuine options for solutions, and cultivate strengths and abilities.

Promoting Leadership

All human systems benefit from capable leadership. Workers can help client systems activate power by encouraging the evolution of effective leadership patterns. Consider social work practice with a community. To achieve a broad-based participation in community change, an effective strategy develops leadership among diverse community constituents. For example, social workers facilitate the involvement of indigenous leaders to work efficiently toward the community's goals. Practitioners recognize and work with those leaders who have expertise for the task and who represent the views of their constituents.

Practitioners can also work to support leadership in a family system. An example of this is the worker in a shelter for homeless families. Ziefert and Brown (1991) describe how:

> *The parenting role disintegrates quickly when a family becomes homeless. A primary task for shelter advocates is to reconnect family members to one another by strengthening their adaptive social role behaviors. Family boundaries are often fragmented and parent roles abdicated. (p. 217)*

To empower these families, Ziefert and Brown (1991) suggest that workers support parental authority with rules that leave parents in charge but protect children from being hurt. Workers can also offer information on parenting skills such as the benefits of giving positive feedback to their children, using time outs, and modeling negotiation. Furthermore, they suggest that agencies budget money for workers to give parents so parents can take their children out for recreation and celebrate birthdays—activities that enhance parents in their children's eyes. Supporting the parenting role contributes to the whole family's sense of power and well-being.

Recognizing Choices

Since it is impossible to change things that are beyond control, articulating what clients realistically control is an important strategy for developing power. Remember that the ecosystems view describes behavior as mutually determined rather than linearly caused. Even though people may feel somewhat powerless in a situation, they may somehow participate in its continuation. Social workers look for and point out the choices people make. When clients see what elements of a situation they can control, they can also identify what they can change.

Walter and Peller (1992) describe this process as "enhancing agency." They say:

> We ask questions that reflect our assumption that clients are capable, that they are already solving the problem, that they are responsible for solving the problem, that they have the freedom to do what they want, and that they are the experts on what they want and will do. (p. 160)

Select phrases such as "so you chose to" and "you decided that you would" when responding to what clients report. Clients experience their own power when they see elements of their choices in situations rather than viewing them as beyond control.

Locating Genuine Options

Assuming that clients share responsibility for their choices does not mean that workers blame clients for the actions of others. Rather, workers direct attention to the ways in which clients choose to participate and respond. Without question, a woman physically abused by her husband is not responsible for this violence and cannot be expected to change her spouse's behavior. No one has that kind of control over another person. However, the client does have choices about her own behavior and the way in which she responds to violence. The social worker's role is to help this client discover and access realistic choices—temporary shelter, an order of protection, an arrest warrant, referral for therapy—and to assure her freedom to choose among available options. "Empowerment and self-determination are dependent not only on people making choices, but also on people having available choices to make" (Cowger, 1994, p. 263).

Where exactly do workers and clients locate viable alternatives to submitting to oppressive relationships? There are two ways that systems can gain power in relationships where they feel powerless (Simons & Aigner, 1985). The first strategy is to find out the source of the dominant system's power and then help the client system find another way to meet those needs, circumventing the need for the powerful system and undermining its power base. For example, in abusive relationships, women may depend on their partners for financial support and shelter for themselves and their children. The availability of resources such as public assistance and transitional housing diminishes the abusive partner's power and control.

The second way to deal with oppressive power is to find out who else is oppressed by the powerful system and join them to form a united front (Simons & Aigner, 1985). For example, when a resident of an apartment complex is unable to get the owner to make necessary repairs, teaming with others in the same building may produce results. When all residents announce that they will withhold their rent, the financial incentive may work to rearrange the power between the residents and the owner and stimulate the owner to make the repairs. Limiting the owner's options enhances the residents' power base.

Magnifying Strengths

Magnifying strengths activates resources and enhances a client's experience of power. No matter what roles practitioners are playing with clients, workers survey the situation for evidence of strengths and positive changes that are already occurring. Practitioners maintain attention to three areas to detect strengths, including clients' behaviors and accomplishments, distinguishing characteristics, and their base of tangible resources and support networks (Kirst-Ashman & Hull, 1999). Practitioners need to be constantly alert to clues about resources. The strategy of a "positive asset search" highlights this continual scanning for resources (Ivey & Ivey, 1999).

Even in apparently desperate circumstances, people demonstrate adaptive behavior and coping skills. For example, people who are homeless "display a remarkable capacity to cope and adapt to conditions that most of us would find intolerable" (Sheridan, Gowen, & Halpin, 1993, p. 413). Specifically, they have unique abilities, skills, and competence in

> *learning how to eat any kind of food (from meal programs or garbage dumpsters), sleep anywhere (on a door stoop, in a park, or in a noisy, frightening shelter), and meet basic needs (through panhandling, recycling aluminum cans, or accepting a stranger's kindness).... (p. 413)*

Social workers build their own abilities to recognize and activate clients' skills in the diverse forms in which clients demonstrate them.

Highlighting Solutions

Social workers discover strengths in clients by using focused listening, which "involves attempting to concentrate on a specific part of the client's message" (Shulman, 1999, p. 151). For example, when the social worker notices that a mother's efforts to gather updated information about her child's behavior at school accompanies her child's increased attendance, the social worker stops, analyzes, and reflects on what is working. Possibly, the mother's involvement with school shifted the child's attention in the same direction. Maybe, the mother's attention to the child rather than her recent job loss relieved the child's anxiety about the family. Perhaps, the mother's obvious commitment to the child's success in school is affecting the ways that teachers interact with the child, altering the school environment and learning experience for the child. Identifying what's working offers options with which to experiment to maintain the child's progress in attending school more consistently.

Shaping Competence

Workers are more effective in assisting clients to function consistently with their goals when they modify existing interactions rather than intervene as if clients are doing nothing right. This skill as it is used in family therapy is "shaping competence" (Nichols & Schwartz, 1998). "Shaping competence is like altering the direction of the flow. By high-lighting and shaping the positive, structural therapists help family members use functional alternatives that are already in the repertoire" (p. 261).

This strategy is easily adapted to other types of client systems. Place yourself in the position of a worker facilitating a support group and observing the responses of various members to one member's crisis. Your comment that you are impressed with a particular group member's ability to empathize without giving advice will likely influence other members to follow suit. In this way, you are able to guide the group toward a pattern of supporting each other's strengths without undermining their competence. Shaping competence acknowledges client systems' existing expertise and activates their resources in the direction of desired changes.

Changing Perspectives

Interventions to change perspectives involve broadening the available base of information by examining, reframing, or reinterpreting behavior and circumstances. Workers may assist clients to step outside of their situations and look at them in new and more productive ways. Clients and social workers may also select strategies that offer opportunities for changing perspectives through behavioral change. Set in the context of trying new options, small-scale "experiments" investigate the effects of different behaviors.

Offering Feedback

The simplest way for workers to help clients reflect on and change their behaviors is by us-ing behaviorally phrased feedback. Practitioners witness how clients interact in the context of professional relationships. Through this type of observation, social workers can assess:

- How client systems approach challenging situations
- What skills clients bring that work for them
- The ways clients involve others in building relationships and seeking solutions
- Which parts of the ecosystem help or hinder the progress

Additionally, workers observe a client's level of trust, ability to articulate ideas, awareness of feelings, patience, persistence, sense of humor, and creativity. Social workers are in positions to disclose their perceptions about clients by offering carefully constructed feedback.

Constructing Feedback

Examine the following examples of feedback:

- Could I give you some feedback? I just observed you talk to your daughter about her curfew for a full five minutes without yelling. I wonder what's working?
- I have an observation if you are ready for it. It seems to me that each time this agency has a funding crisis, the response is to expect workers to do more for less. It just hap-

pened this week when the board of directors decided to eliminate two positions, redistribute the workload, and freeze salaries.

- It's so encouraging to work with someone who takes risks like you. Just now, when I suggested we try something new, you immediately thought of three possibilities.

Notice how carefully these social workers frame feedback. Drawing on works by Benjamin (1987), Johnson and Johnson (1997), Egan (1998), Johnson (1998), and Ivey and Ivey (1999), constructive feedback:

- Describes rather than evaluates behavior.
- Shares perceptions rather than offers advice.
- Identifies specific current behaviors rather than recalls incidents from the past.
- Reports positive behaviors as well as points to improve.
- Keeps pace with the client's readiness.

When workers offer feedback neutrally, clients can attach their own evaluations to the information. Since workers give feedback about specific behaviors rather than about the "person" of the client, clients have opportunities to behave in new ways that more clearly match their intent.

Confronting in a Supportive Way

Social workers give clients feedback to enhance their interpersonal effectiveness, or the congruence between their intent and the behavioral outcome (Johnson, 1997). In other words, can you decide what you want, do something to obtain it, and end up getting it? If you can, you are, at least in this one instance, interpersonally effective. When clients articulate the intent of their behaviors, workers can observe and determine which behaviors net intended results and which miss their marks. Workers use this approach to highlight successful behaviors as well as those that may need changing.

To confront effectively, workers help clients articulate their actions in three parts—intent, behavior, and outcome. As workers carefully trace with clients the sequence of intent to behavior to outcome, clients often see things differently and choose new behaviors. Consider the following example. Support group member Tom has grown tired of the way that John monopolizes the conversation. Tom responds by disagreeing with everything that John offers, leaving other group members withdrawn and disinterested. When Tom complains that nothing seems to work to stifle John, the worker can lead Tom to see his own involvement by analyzing his behavior.

- The *intent*—Tom wants John to be less active and other group members to say more.
- The *behavior*—Tom argues with what John says.
- The *outcome*—the whole group revolves around John's issues and Tom's disagreement with John.

So, is Tom getting what he wants?

Workers use a confronting strategy selectively, usually after establishing a significant, respectful relationship and in an atmosphere of support (Compton & Galaway, 1999). In observing and reporting their observations of clients' social effectiveness, workers do not need to blame or accuse but simply to lay out patterns for clients to review and take action.

Confronting works best when it fits the situation. It is particularly effective when confronting value issues. This helps clients "by making them aware they more or less chronically hold certain values and attitudes or behave in ways that are counter to their own expectations of competence or morality" (Grube, Mayton, & Ball-Rokeach, 1994, p. 157). Cultural factors also determine whether to use this strategy. Culturally competent social workers recognize that, for traditional Asian American clients, confrontation and conflict "may violate their cultural rules. Asian culture says, 'It is good to have harmony and to be in sync with your environment.' Harmony is what Asians consciously or unconsciously seek and is evidenced by their behaviors" (Chung, 1992, p. 31).

Creating New Concepts

The way that we respond to a situation may have more to do with the way we interpret it than the actual event itself. Cox, Parsons, and Kimboko (1988) report a study of cross-generational caregivers and their experience with the "burden of caregiving." These researchers discovered that, among these caregivers, "no significant relationship was found between perceived burden and objective burden" (p. 433). Further, this study showed that caregivers who perceived their burden as light showed higher levels of affection toward and greater communication with those receiving care regardless of the actual objective burden of the caregiving. Clearly, this demonstrates the potential of positive views for creating positive responses. It points to the possibility that workers can help clients by offering options for interpreting events in empowering rather than stifling ways.

Reframing

"Look on the bright side" may sound like a naive approach; however, a positive outlook energizes clients. Clients who feel like they are not getting anywhere benefit from views that they may, after all, be up to something constructive. Reframing examines a situation previously perceived as negative and takes a new look, describing it as somehow positive, functional, or useful (Watzlawick, Weakland, & Fisch, 1974). Toseland and Rivas (1998) describe the effect of using this strategy with group clients: "Once a member experiences a problem from a new perspective, the positive aspects of the situation are highlighted and the negative aspects of the situation have a better chance of being changed" (p. 266).

One way to reinterpret behavior is to consider the view that *the response determines the meaning* (Walter & Peller, 1992). Even apparently problematic behavior may be up to something good. Consider the following examples. The group member who monopolizes is helping other members to avoid dealing with difficult issues. The boy who constantly tests his Dad's authority is succeeding in getting his Dad closely involved. The depressed adolescent has discovered ways to elicit the support and nurturance of family and friends. The employee who files grievance after grievance is clarifying and developing the agency's policies and procedures.

Reframing also works to prevent problems from developing. Ben-Ari's (1995) study of coming out demonstrates that the way parents perceive a son's or daughter's disclosure of homosexuality makes a difference in their response. When social workers can lead parents to frame this disclosure as a means to gain intimacy rather than to shock or blame parents, parents adjust more easily to the information. When social workers consider the question, "What's good about it?," they give clients new perspectives on positive things that are already happening.

Using Metaphors

Another way to reframe situations is to describe them in the form of a story or metaphor. Consider the parents frustrated over their child's slow progress in learning to read. When the social worker places this situation in the context of the traditional fable, "The Tortoise and the Hare," it transforms the behavior from lagging behind to steadily improving. The previous description stimulates feelings of anxiety and impatience. The new description recognizes success and leaves room for confidence and encouragement.

Metaphors are necessarily ambiguous, letting clients make their own interpretations. This ambiguity makes metaphors particularly suitable for describing and working with feelings. When social workers and clients seek to articulate feelings, workers use phrases like:

- You feel like you are out on a limb.
- So it's kind of like you're just drifting in the middle of a lake, not really getting anywhere.
- Seems like you've hit rock bottom.

Using these same metaphors social workers offer hopeful directions, such as:

- Well, maybe, it's time to edge back toward the trunk.
- So as you are drifting, what do you see that catches your interest?
- Now that you're at the bottom, at least there's only one way to go—what's the first thing that needs to happen to pick yourself back up?

In activating client system resources, social workers introduce stimulating new perspectives, options, and interpretations to affect the way clients think, feel, and behave.

Using Narrative Strategies

"Reality is never experienced directly but is always filtered through human processes of knowing and creating meaning" (Laird, 1995, p. 151). People behave in ways consistent with what they believe is true rather than in keeping with some concrete reality to which we all ascribe. Such is the view of the social constructivist. We each have our own story to tell. These stories are resources that "need to be explored, to become valued, and to be rendered employable" (Saleebey, 1994, p. 352). Workers help clients take charge of their stories in ways that emphasize client strengths, experience their pride, and prepare them to narrate their way into a more desirable future.

To work with clients' narratives, social workers "serve as skillful facilitators, as editors searching for an undiscovered subtext, as conveners of groupings in search of problem-solving conversations, or as advocates for the inclusion of new characters and new resources" (Dyche & Zayas, 1995, p. 389). Social workers withhold any professional commentary to encourage clients to tell the stories of their lives. "By being too quick to translate a client's story into a theoretical construct, we may miss the nuances and unique qualities a particular client brings as well as the client's own creative efforts at problem solving" (Dean, 1993, p. 133).

Implementing a narrative strategy requires social workers to facilitate three activities during assessment and intervention—collaboration, reflexivity, and multiplicity (Laird, 1995). *Collaboration* is a familiar process in all empowering practice, requiring a specific focus on and respect for a client's experience rather than an externally accepted reality. *Reflexivity* means that social workers use responding skills that allow clients to view their stories more objectively—skills that separate stories out for joint reflection by both clients and workers. *Multiplicity* is accomplished by simply generating multiple ideas and interpretations. Both clients and workers can contribute to this "brainstorming." The use of reframing and metaphors described previously can be applied to this process. The more options clients have for viewing and interpreting their current story, the more opportunities they have for choosing empowering meanings to guide its future development.

Several techniques support a narrative approach. With individuals and families, workers can draw genograms to identify the "cast of characters" over the generations, and have clients narrate significant tales about the various family members. Workers respond by identifying dominant themes and strengths demonstrated over the years. Groups can construct their stories by using journaling (Brower, 1996). In this approach each group member keeps independent logs of their responses to the group and reads them to each other at group meetings to contribute to "a narrative that gives their group experience coherence, history, rules, myths, and meaning" (p. 342). Considering even larger systems, Saleebey (1994) says that we must project individual client narratives toward agencies and institutions for mid- and macrolevel interventions. Techniques which encourage positive interpretations and increase a client's experience of power and importance are central to a narrative strategy.

Externalizing

Narrative strategies have the advantage of separating the story of someone's life from the actual person. In other words, the story is external to the person and can be modified or directed by the person. This is especially significant when people tell stories replete with problems, since the person and the problem become separate. Social work has already adopted this concept as evidenced in the politically correct description of a "person with a disability" rather than a "disabled person."

The process of separating people from their problems is "externalization" (White, 1989). First, help people talk about their problems as a separate entity—as something external to themselves. Then, look for "unique outcomes"—those times when people felt most in control of their problems. As clients describe these exceptions to problematic times, they simultaneously experience a sense of control and identify possible ways that they can repeat this success.

Trying Out New Behaviors

In many ways, action plans are carefully designed "experiments" for change. They are hunches for clients and workers to test out to see if they work to achieve goals. Experimentation always yields productive results. A "success" moves clients toward desired outcomes and a "failure" provides valuable information to guide future actions. Small-scale experiments, designed by workers and clients and implemented between meetings, can inform and change. To derive maximum benefit, each activity is mutually constructed, carefully implemented, and comprehensively evaluated (Table 12.2).

TABLE 12.2   Guidelines for Between-Meeting Activities

Types of Activities
- Information gathering through observation
- Connecting to and disconnecting from persons, groups, services, and situations
- Maintaining and repeating productive behaviors
- Taking small steps in the direction of goals

Construction
- Determine client's willingness to participate
- Generate possible activities in mutual discussion
- Select activities based on:
  —Relevance to goals
  —Likelihood of success
  —Client's motivation to complete

Implementation
- Define as experimental
- Keep it clear, concrete, and simple
- Define roles of all participants
- Secure agreements to follow through
- Repeat agreement to ensure understanding

Follow-up
- When activity is completed:
  —Discuss outcomes
  —Access information from all members involved
  —Accept differences in perspectives
  —Validate each participant's perceptions
  —Highlight specific strengths and skills clients demonstrated in the activity
  —Note variations in expected outcome to detect unanticipated solutions
  —Construct follow-up activity
  —Encourage increased responsibility by client in constructing the next activity
- When activity is not completed:
  —Discuss obstacles
  —Determine how to overcome obstacles
  —Consider taking a smaller step
  —Implement the same activity
- If client chose not to complete activity:
  —Determine source of resistance
  —Change activity to match client's current motivation
  —Update client's outcome goals to ensure that worker and client are moving in the same direction

Constructing Experimental Activities

Social workers and clients have an array of possible activities to choose from in constructing experiments. Four options include conducting observations, connecting and disconnecting, maintaining productive actions, and taking small steps toward goals.

Observations.   Observations are cautious experiments used to gather additional information. They ask for no direct change by the client system but often produce change since observing one's own or someone else's behavior frequently has impact. Clients observe when good things are happening or those times when problems are not occurring to decipher what might contribute to these successful events (Walter & Peller, 1992). For example, managers in an organization might observe those times when employees show regular attendance and positive attitudes. The understanding developed helps to repeat those transactions that relieve stress and burnout.

Connecting and Disconnecting.   Situational challenges are transactional in nature, involving clients and others. Clients can experiment with change by connecting to new people and resources or by disconnecting from previous relationships. For example, members of an adolescent group working to disassociate from gang membership may agree to keep away from areas of gang activity and refrain from talking with known gang members. These same group members may each also agree to choose a new person to eat lunch with in the school cafeteria in order to begin new peer relationships to replace their previous gang associations.

Maintaining Productive Actions.   Encouraging clients to experiment with repeating productive actions is a powerful technique. Consider the example of Nancy and her client Jerome. Jerome is a social worker, questioning his choice of profession since he frequently feels depressed and burned out. Recently, Jerome told Nancy about his angry outburst in an interdisciplinary team meeting when the group refused to consider changing the case plan of a client with whom he was working. Knowing that Jerome shows incredible patience and acceptance in his work with his clients, Nancy suggested an experiment whereby Jerome would imagine that the interdisciplinary team members were his clients rather than professional colleagues. In other words, Nancy asked Jerome to experiment with transferring his skills in a successful area of functioning to test their benefits in another.

Taking Small Steps.   Taking a small step toward the goal is an experiment worth trying. Well-defined objectives in a comprehensive action plan will clearly indicate the options for these small steps. However, taking direct steps toward goals is risky and may activate a client's resistance to change. Social workers encourage clients to take these risks by reassuring them that this step is indeed only experimental. Once clients experience the results, they can continue in the direction of the change or they can return to previous ways of behaving if they choose.

Implementing Activities

Some refer to these experiments as homework assignments or directives. But, imagine your response to someone assigning or directing you to do something. Social workers circumvent resistance by framing these activities clearly as experiments and collaborating with clients to develop them. The social worker might say, "Are you interested in trying a little experiment?" "So those are my ideas, what do you think?" Clients are more likely to implement experiments that they help construct and agree to complete. "So we agree. You'll try this out and let me know what happened next week."

A well-designed experiment has several components. It describes "who will do what when." The best experiments are concrete, simple, and easily understood by clients and workers. With multiperson systems, all members need to understand what they are agreeing to do and know what their particular responsibilities are. Useful experiments also specify the time frame for completion and describe how the social worker and client will evaluate the impact. When experiments are relevant, clear, and collaboratively constructed, they are likely to produce the most positive results.

Following Up

To complete a successful experiment, workers lead clients through a step-by-step process that evaluates the results. Workers may ask the following questions:

- Tell me the details. How did you carry it out?
- Did you implement the experiment as constructed or did you vary it? What led you to make these changes?
- What happened? Did it turn out like you expected? Did something unexpected happen?
- What did you learn that might help us decide what to do next?

When clients fail to follow through on completing assignments, workers also pursue additional information, by asking:

- So what got in the way? Was there no opportunity or did you decide it wasn't something you wanted to do? Did you understand what you were supposed to do?
- Are you willing to try to complete it again or do you think we're off base here?
- What would you like to do instead?

Even when clients do not follow through, workers use their responses as information for constructing additional activities. Well-designed experiments actively involve clients in the change process. Experimenting leaves clients in control and builds their confidence. When workers sequence experiments one after the other, they gradually pull back from the task in ways that increase clients' responsibilities for their development and implementation. Activating resources in this way prepares clients to function independently of the social worker.

Managing Resources

All human systems from individuals to communities need environmental resources to sustain their functioning. During assessment, workers explore the various connections that clients have with their environments to see what works and should be reinforced, to detect what is not working and should be modified, and also to recognize what is missing and should be established. To manage resources, social workers and clients collaborate to locate realistic options, make appropriate connections, and take steps to ensure that clients are successful in accessing resources.

Linking clients to necessary resources casts generalist social workers in the roles of brokers and advocates, mediators, activists, and catalysts. To play these roles effectively requires workers to know what the social delivery system has to offer, to learn current eligibility requirements for supportive services, to be open to indigenous resources that communities may possess, and to participate in resource development projects. Chapters 13 and 14 further explore managing resources at the mid- and macrolevel client system levels and in the context of professional relationships.

Linking Clients with Resources

Accessing resources confronts social workers with a common question. How much help do they give to clients in this process? The empowering answer is "as much as is necessary and as little as needed to be effective." Workers are supplemental in helping clients make connections. The immediate goal of any connection of client to resource system is to turn the management of the connection over to the client. "Linking clients to resources is not empowering, but education about resources is" (Parsons, Hernandez, & Jorgensen, 1988, p. 421). Whether workers simply inform clients about resources or take more direct actions, they consistently work for clients to understand the process and how clients might activate these same resources without direct intervention by workers.

In linking clients with other services, social workers choose their methods based on the current capabilities of client systems with an eye toward how they might increase clients' own resource management skills. For example, consider Denise VanDeViere, an aftercare worker for Northside Hospital, and her client Cassie Carter, who is recovering from a serious head injury. Denise and Cassie have determined that Cassie will apply for Social Security Disability Income (SSDI), supplemental financial assistance administered through the State Office of Public Assistance. To assist Cassie in this endeavor, Denise has a continuum of options varying from most supportive to least involved. These options, from most to least involved, include:

- Denise will call Louise Campbell, a caseworker she knows at Public Assistance (PA) to arrange an appointment. She will also gather the appropriate medical documentation to demonstrate Cassie's eligibility, pick up Cassie, and accompany her to the appointment.
- Cassie will call Louise, mention that Denise has suggested the call, and arrange the appointment. Denise will gather the necessary medical records, pick up Cassie, and accompany her to the appointment.
- Cassie will arrange the appointment, sign appropriate forms for release for information, gather up her medical records, and meet Denise at the PA office. Denise will guide Cassie through the application process and advocate only as necessary.
- Denise will give information to Cassie about SSDI and the procedures for application through PA. Cassie will make the necessary arrangements to go to PA, apply for the assistance, and report the results of her efforts to Denise at the next meeting.

Each option leads to the same outcome—Cassie applies for SSDI. But each option draws differently on the resources of the client and social worker. The best choice is the one in which clients feel confident in their abilities to succeed, use as much of their own capabilities as possible, and learn additional skills for the future. Considering these issues, Denise and Cassie decide that Cassie will make the necessary arrangements, that both will ride the bus together so that Denise can help Cassie learn to use the public transportation system, and that Cassie will do the talking at PA unless she directly seeks the assistance of Denise.

Case Advocacy

Sometimes, clients are unable to make successful connections to necessary resources. Even when informed about access to other services, clients may experience unexpected obstacles or a lack of responsiveness. In these cases social workers may choose to add their professional power to ensure a successful connection. Although ideally designed to respond to clients' needs, the social delivery network is in reality economically strapped, short of staff, and bureaucratically complex. Frequently, social workers need to support clients through a maze of bureaucratic red tape to access the services for which they are eligible.

Advocacy means that social workers collaborate with clients to influence the way other systems respond to a client's attempts to gather resources. A research study questioning social workers about their advocacy activities found that 90 percent of these workers do case advocacy on a regular basis (Ezell, 1994). Activities with which social workers were most likely involved include educating clients on their rights, pushing for clients' rights in agencies, arguing for more effective services for clients, teaching advocacy skills to clients, educating the general public on an issue, and negotiating with agencies on behalf of clients.

The way in which social workers advocate for their clients makes a difference, particularly with high-risk clients who have multiple challenges such as chronic mental illnesses, developmental disabilities, substance addictions, or major health issues such as AIDS. A client with multiple challenges needs to "personally witness the worker's advocacy on his or her behalf. There can be no empowerment without participation or, at least, presence and observation. By modeling this behavior, the client learns to become an active consumer/participant" (Klein & Cnaan, 1995, p. 205). All clients benefit more from working with rather than by being worked on by social workers.

Seasoned social workers begin to see patterns in the experiences of clients who are similarly frustrated in their need to connect with certain resources. For example, a worker may notice that all clients receiving public assistance are unable to take entry-level positions in the workforce because of the threat of considerable loss of health care benefits, leaving them worse off than before. Obviously, case-by-case advocacy leads workers to realize the need to focus their efforts toward policy change. Social workers recognize the need to expand their efforts from case advocacy to cause advocacy when recurrent themes emerge in their direct practice experiences (Barber, 1995). Chapter 14 describes how workers implement efforts to change restrictive and counter-productive social policies.

Maximizing Clients' Rights

Maximizing clients' rights expands their opportunities within the social service delivery system by increasing their access to programs, services, and other benefits. However, sometimes restrictive policies, guidelines, or procedures block clients' attempts to obtain services to which they are rightfully entitled. When interpretations of rules and regulations deny clients access to programs and services, they have rights to fair hearings, appeals, and due process.

Fair Hearings and Appeals

Clients' rights include their right to fair hearings. Fair hearings provide the mechanism for appealing decisions which have negatively affected clients' benefits or services (Chambers, 1993). Common to many types of programs and services, the Social Security Act stipulates the process for fair hearings and appeals as a mandated component of service delivery. As Chambers describes:

> *A fair-hearing procedure is one in which a client or applicant is given the opportunity to appeal to an administrative tribunal or a judge (or a panel of judges) who hears arguments of both sides. This tribunal reviews agency policy, practices, and enabling legislation and then renders a decision for or against the agency or the complainant. The administrative judge is duty-bound to hold the agency to decisions and actions that are consistent with agency policy, tradition, or legislative mandate. The judge can require the agency to reverse its prior actions or decisions and/or change its policies and procedures. (p. 206)*

Hearing procedures differ with respect to the independence of the hearing officer. In some instances, judges are subject to their peers' review of their actions. In other instances, the hearing officer is simply an administrator in charge of the program subject to the appeal. Social workers need to be familiar with their own employers' fair hearing and appeals policies and procedures as well as those in agencies to which they refer clients. Ethical workers inform clients of their options and rights. When a client decides to appeal decisions about benefits and services, the worker advocates directly or links the client to a concerned professional who can advocate the client's position.

Due Process

Due process of law protects individuals' rights in dealings with the government. Whether rules provide strict guidelines for implementation or whether they allow for discretionary decision-making, the U.S. Supreme Court regards constitutional due process as a central facet of welfare benefits (Chambers, 1993). Key features of due process involve clients' rights to:

- Be informed in a timely manner about the specifics of administrative actions, including the basis for these actions.
- Argue their point of view at the hearing in writing or in person.
- Be represented by legal counsel.
- Face witnesses directly and question them in the context of cross examination.
- Participate in an open or public hearing.
- Have their appeal heard by an impartial, unbiased hearing officer or judge.
- Have the facts of their record form the basis for the decision and obtain a written report which details the facts of their case and applicable laws. (Handler cited in Chambers, 1993)

Social workers are not lawyers, but the practice of social work requires knowledge about laws affecting services to clients and legal resources within their professional support networks.

Educating

Clients and social workers sometimes select educational strategies to expand the knowledge base of clients and other relevant systems. New information often leads to novel solutions. To educate clients, workers can choose among various teaching strategies including role-playing, implementing structured curriculums, and modeling. Workers also share information with clients by offering relevant professional knowledge and appropriately disclosing personal information.

Teaching

Learning expands knowledge and skills and, therefore, the interpersonal resources upon which to build empowerment. Like all effective social work practice, educational endeavors "begin where the client is." With respect to teaching, this means identifying the learner's objectives and learning style. Collaborative educational efforts involve both the facilitator and learners in the joint process of "assessing needs, setting objectives, selecting appropriate methodologies and materials, and developing evaluation procedures as well as actively participating in the facilitation of the learning" (Galbraith, 1991, p. 3). Collaborative teaching transforms educational processes so that learners become users rather than simply recipients of education. Various types of educational experiences activate resources for clients, including role-playing and structured training experiences.

Role-playing

Role-playing is an option for developing interpersonal skills. For example, when a client complains that an employer never listens, the worker may suggest a role-play. First, the client describes the behaviors of the employer to guide the worker's portrayal. Then, the partners play out the scenario, discovering information about the client's approach and hypothesizing possible responses and feelings the employer may be having and exploring the client's perspective. Role-playing provides an arena for trying out new behaviors without risking the consequences of failure (Johnson & Johnson, 1997).

Role-playing is also useful in working with groups (Toseland & Rivas, 1998). There are numerous variations from structured experiences using scripts to unstructured experiences selecting various members for roles and facilitating extemporaneous interaction, observation, and feedback. Group members may play themselves to practice new behaviors or play another person's role in order to increase their empathy and understanding for the other person's position. Playing roles that require group members to represent views they themselves do not hold is particularly useful in developing skills in task groups, in teaching them to elucidate alternatives, and in reaching consensus in group decisions.

Structured Training Experiences

There are many other ways to teach clients communication and relationship skills. Many agencies have brochures, manuals, or do-it-yourself skill development books for clients to use. Detailed skill development programs are packaged and offered commercially for nearly every kind of interpersonal development. Examples include training in parenting such as The STEP program, Parent Effectiveness Training (PET), and Tough Love. Many social work groups focus on developing interpersonal skills such as assertiveness, job interview skills, or expressing emotions. Examples of other educational topics include managing stress, dealing with caregiving issues, developing a strategic plan, working on a team, negotiating, and effective decision-making.

As with any educational experience, material should be culturally sensitive and geared to identified learning objectives, levels, and learning styles of the participants (Table 12.3). Cultural variations do exist in learning styles. For example: "A large proportion of European-Americans learn easily from details, a greater percentage of Native Americans learn most easily when watching, imagining, and reflecting" (Gilliland, 1992, as cited in Dykeman, Nelson, & Appleton, 1995, p. 153). Successful educational programs also consider participants' schedules to determine the best time frames and build in supports for attendance such as child care and transportation.

Technical supports for educational programming are expanding rapidly. For example, microwave interconnects multiple learning sites. Interactive teleconferences allow participants to interact with well-known experts. Camcorder technology allows participants to record activities, play back the video, and evaluate their responses. And, computer-based programmed learning takes advantage of individualized instruction and immediate feedback. Effective social workers keep current on technological developments to offer educational opportunities for their clients.

Modeling

How many of us have heard a parent say, "Do as I say, not as I do"? How many of us have followed this advice? Unavoidably, social workers find themselves as models to clients on how to cope, communicate, and relate. It only makes sense that clients should look to social workers and their expertise about human behavior for this kind of example. Social workers acknowledge their responsibility as role models by monitoring their own behaviors to check for consistency with what they are saying.

Based on the social learning model developed by Bandura (1986), modeling promotes behavioral changes through the observation, imitation, and vicarious experience of the

---

TABLE 12.3 Developing Training Modules

Collaboratively, educators and learners:
- Assess the learning needs
- Identify the learning outcomes, that is, what knowledge or skills or attitudes will be achieved through the training
- Identify various types of learning experiences necessary to achieve learning outcomes such as existing curricula, role plays, films, speakers, lectures, or simulations
- Screen proposed learning strategies for cultural appropriateness
- Sequence the training agenda for a single session or schedule for multiple sessions
- Implement the training sessions
- Evaluate the learning outcomes and the methods used

gains the modeled behavior attains. In social work practice, modeling occurs "when the client has an opportunity to observe the worker perform or when the worker encourages the client to observe the behavior of someone else" (Garvin & Tropman, 1998, p. 119). Being chosen as a model depends on perceived similarities between the model and the observer (Bandura). In other words, in the context of social work, the more clients identify with workers, the greater the likelihood they will learn through modeling.

Examples of modeling are endless. If social workers want clients to listen to one another, workers must first demonstrate their own abilities to listen to what clients are saying. If a social workers wants clients to assert themselves, the practitioner responds enthusiastically when clients disagree with the worker's view. If social workers want clients to show patience, workers demonstrate how they expect change at a realistic and incremental rate. If practitioners discover they themselves are unable to do what they are asking from clients, workers re-examine their own expectations.

Sharing Information

One of the most important resources all clients have is the social worker. Many writers describe the ways in which social workers develop their abilities to influence clients. "Studies have shown three characteristics to be important: expertise, trustworthiness, and likability" (Simons & Aigner, 1985, p. 117). Additional characteristics include the worker's legitimate authority, reputation, and control over resources, services, and the flow of information (Pincus & Minahan, 1973). Practitioners have influence with clients when:

> 1. *They are knowledgeable about the topic under consideration and will use that knowledge for the client's benefit.*
> 2. *They have been granted the authority by some legitimate organization or licensing body to offer services, and will live up to the limits on their legitimate areas of influence included in the client–worker contract for intervention goals.*
> 3. *They are warm and caring individuals who respect the client. (Feld & Radin, 1982, p. 195).*

To effectively employ influence as an intervention, social workers develop their professional reputations and their skills in sharing expertise and self-disclosing.

Offering Professional Knowledge

Clients are experts, but acknowledging client expertise does not strip practitioners of their own. Empowering social workers often offer clients theoretical information, practice wisdom, and research knowledge. Shulman (1999) says:

> *The client looks to the worker as a source of help in difficult areas. If the client senses that the worker is withholding data (facts, ideas, values, and beliefs), for whatever reason, the withholding can be experienced as a form of rejection. (p. 186)*

The information shared should be consistent with the agreed upon contract, connected to the client's immediate concerns, and within the area of the worker's expertise.

Workers are cautious about using their own expertise, so as not to undermine clients' expertise. The most empowering way to share expertise is by responding to the client's request. Notice the style and kinds of expertise workers offer in the following examples:

- So, you're interested in what I know about stepfamilies. I did just read some research the other day that said parenting works best when both parent and stepparent discuss together what to do with children, but then the biological parent actually implements what they decide. The research reports that children are much more likely to accept the authority of the biological parent.
- It might help you decide what to do if I shared some information about what we generally see happen when someone first moves into our facility. Are you interested in that?
- I'm impressed with your interest in what we've learned about how foster children adjust to placement. Our observations support your experience as a foster parent; frequently, children do have difficulty eating and sleeping for the first few days.
- I've completed the research you requested and I have located six foundations that are possible sources of funds for transitional housing.

Each example draws on some piece of the social worker's knowledge base—practice experiences, knowledge of human behavior, theoretical frameworks, or research outcomes. Each comment either responds to what the client seeks or asks permission from the client to continue. None of these examples presents the worker's expertise as absolute, but instead as a piece of information that *might* be helpful or *might* somehow explain. Clients can glean from it what they will. When these workers share their knowledge, they do so as participants in the process rather than as all-knowing and all-seeing expert professionals. Social workers selectively use their expertise to inform and normalize, not to impress or undermine.

Sharing expertise requires cultural competence. Cultural awareness gives clues to how workers should present information, since people from different cultures tend to differ in their styles of learning. Varying cultural attitudes toward authority also have implications for the approach that workers might choose in sharing expertise. Finally, workers carefully screen the information they offer to ensure that the content is a "cultural fit."

Self-Disclosing

Social workers are people, too. They have lives, relationships, families, jobs, successes, setbacks, embarrassments, and dreams. Sometimes, social workers carefully choose from among their own personal experiences to share something of benefit to clients. Note that this is a selective process. Workers screen personal information to ensure that it is relevant to clients' situations. For example, workers may share:

- I remember what a difficult time I had when my father died.
- I overcame my fear of talking in front of people by taking a speech class at a community college.
- I remember feeling so inadequate my first day on this job. I even got lost in the parking building that day.
- My husband and I fight sometimes, but we've learned what works for us is to take breaks, think about it, and come back to talk again in an hour or two.

Workers differentiate between self-disclosing and giving advice. Advice says, "This is how you ought to do it." Self-disclosure says, "This is what it is like for me. I don't know whether this is helpful to you or not. You'll have to decide for yourself." Workers can self-disclose information most effectively by identifying what they share as a personal experience and acknowledging that the information may or may not be useful to the client. This lets clients respond in whatever ways they choose (Table 12.4).

Reflecting Back

Activating resources again tests the worker's ability to do enough, but not too much, for a client. Empowerment-oriented social workers temper their expertise out of respect for client self-direction and determination. But, recent research shows that experienced social workers in many fields of practice actually implement a whole range of interventions that vary from nondirective reflection to determinative action taken without the knowledge or agreement of the client system (Rothman, Smith, Nakashima, Paterson, & Mustin, 1996). What circumstances are most appropriate for a nondirective approach? What conditions warrant a social worker's direct authoritative actions? Consider how you will respond in actual practice.

Looking Forward

To enhance a client's experience of power and competence, workers use strategies to build confidence within client systems and encourage clients to take over their own development.

TABLE 12.4   Checklist for Self-Disclosure

Before self-disclosing, workers carefully screen information to keep their personal sharing professional by asking themselves the following questions:

1. What experiences have I had that may offer new information, a different perspective, or demonstrate empathy?
2. Is this information relevant to the client's situation at this particular time?
3. Do I have a close enough relationship with the client to share personal information? Will personal sharing confuse or inhibit the client?
4. Is it culturally appropriate to disclose this information?
5. What is my motivation in sharing this information? To build the relationship? To inform? To impress?
6. In what way do I expect the client to respond to this information? To see new possibilities? To understand that we have similar experiences?
7. What is the best way to offer this information neutrally? Will the client experience this as advice, contributing to feelings of inadequacy or failure?
8. Can I share this information briefly enough to maintain the focus on the client's issues rather than my own personal life?

Practitioners work consistently for clients to recognize their own power to affect events in their current transactions, become aware of choices and options for continued development and change, increase knowledge about and use of available resources and opportunities, and strengthen skills for reaching goals and developing solutions. Social workers and clients collaborate to activate existing resources as they implement plans of action.

In an ideal world, efficiently and creatively working with what is available would be enough. Clients would get where they want to go. Social workers would freely consult, manage resources, and educate. But, all social workers and clients confront situations where they wish there were other options. Activating resources sometimes reveals gaps in service delivery and limited opportunities for clients. Simply dealing with existing resources is not adequate for meeting current and changing needs.

To respond to this resource scarcity, social workers strive to enrich environments. Chapter 13 describes how workers increase the available pool of resources by creating new alliances among clients, within the service delivery network, and in clients' natural support networks. Chapter 14 extends the view of possible interventions by describing the social worker's responsibilities for expanding opportunities in the environment. Workers may implement community development strategies, influence social policy, advocate legislative change, and initiate social action. Generalist social workers do not limit their intervention activities to changing clients themselves; they also modify the environment to enhance clients' choices and opportunities.

Chapter *13*

Creating Alliances

When the social work team of Consuela Diaz and Darrell Foster arrives at the community center, they feel like they are late. The members of the Community Action Council are already talking among themselves, handing out various task group reports, and compiling an agenda for the official meeting. Marvella Harvey, chairperson of the Council, is talking to some members about the Council's new advocacy program, through which the Council represents the interests of citizens in their dealings with city officials, law enforcement officers, and state political representatives. Other members talk excitedly in small groups, pull out additional chairs from the storeroom to accommodate the overflow crowd, or snack on the coffee and cookies that someone has supplied. The workers see that the group has taken on a life of its own.

As social workers for the Northside Development Association, Consuela and Darrell worked with the Community Action Council from its inception as an informal group of interested citizens. Earlier in their work with the Council, Consuela and Darrell played facilitative roles in the group's operation, guiding the Council through various phases of organization, assessment, and analysis in order to create a comprehensive plan of action. But now, the plan is in motion and so are the members of the Council. Both Consuela and Darrell recognize the signs. This group is sensing its power and learning to wield it. It's time for the two workers to take another step back. They greet the members of the Council and take seats on the side of the room.

After Marvella calls the meeting to order, Consuela and Darrell observe firsthand the abilities the group has developed. The members organize their interaction productively, actively seek each other's views, listen closely to one another, welcome differences of opinions as stimulating options rather than threats to unity, and focus on their goals. They even wrap up the meeting by posting a concrete list of the activities that each task group will complete by the next meeting. The members of the Community Action Council can see where they are, plan where they are going next, and know they have the capabilities to get there.

Clearly, the Community Action Council is activated—keeping in touch with its resources, feeling its power to make changes, and demonstrating the skills to do so. Do you sense the momentum building in this group? Do you notice how the group seems to be taking over the process of reaching its own goals? This client system is on the move! It is this kind of movement that social workers seek as they work to create and activate alliances.

This chapter discusses the activities of social workers and clients in building productive alliances in their respective environments. Specifically this chapter:

- Describes how alliances empower clients and social workers
- Discusses the use of group alliances for mutual aid and social action
- Explores options for strengthening natural support networks
- Examines case management as an effective strategy for coordinating services
- Considers the role of organizational alliances in service delivery and resource development
- Surveys opportunities for social workers to gain support through professional alliances

Social workers who create and facilitate alliances for their clients and for themselves will generate resources for service delivery and construct supportive environments for practice.

The Power of Alliances

When you add 1 + 1, what do you get? In the world of math, the answer is obviously 2. But in the world of empowering social work, 1 + 1 = 3! Think about the social worker–client system relationship as an example to understand this "new math." When you add the resources of the social worker to the resources of the client, you have two resources with which to begin. But as the social worker and client work together, a third resource emerges—the synergistic resource created through a collaborative alliance.

The possibilities for resource-generating alliances exist beyond the social worker–client relationship (see Figure 13.1). Social workers support clients' efforts to build productive connections with others. Alliances are possible among clients sharing the same issues and interests such as those that develop when social workers facilitate client groups. Alliances are available within clients' natural support networks. And importantly, as in the example of case management, practitioners can cement collaborative partnerships among clients and their various service providers.

Even beyond the immediate context of the client, social workers build professional alliances that will have indirect benefits for clients. The organization-to-organization connections forged within interagency coalitions strengthen working relationships among service providers, reveal areas that require resource development, and provide muscle to influence political and legislative action. Finally, the connections that social workers make with each other and other professionals provide support and stimulation which will ultimately benefit clients through workers' feelings of support, increased motivation, and fresh ideas.

Developing Alliances through Groups

All people benefit from supportive relationships with others. Such relationships contribute to feelings of confidence and security. Good relationships have *synergy;* they actually become resources—stimulating ideas, feelings, and experiences impossible for any individual to create independently. Moreover, "group work embodies social work's belief in the transaction between the individual and the environment" (Birnbaum & Auerbach, 1994, p. 333). Social workers encourage the development of empowering alliances through their effective use of groups.

Groups and Empowerment

Social work groups are vehicles for personal growth, skill development, and environmental change. Groups provide "new perspectives, awareness that others have similar problems and concerns, role models for learning new behaviors, and opportunities to be helpful to others" (Sheafor, Horejsi, & Horejsi, 1997, p. 435). In fact, "group methods may be the key client system in empowerment-based practice" (Parsons, Jorgensen, & Hernandez, 1994, p. 113). Groups provide the forum for people to develop skills in critical thinking, receive information and validation, and organize a power base from which to advocate change in larger social systems.

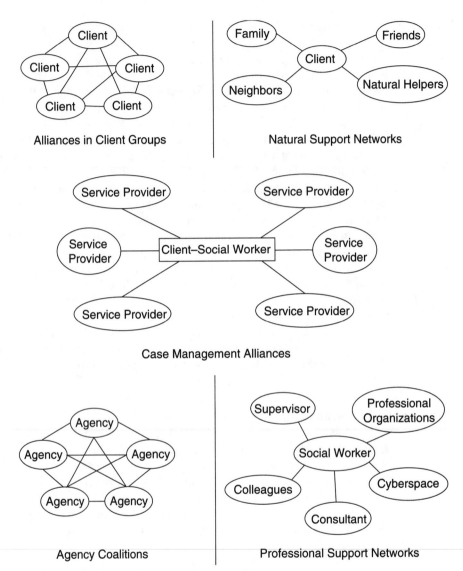

FIGURE 13.1   Types of Alliances. Clients can benefit from many types of alliances including those with other clients who have similar concerns, supportive relationships within their natural support networks, alliances between clients and their service providers, organizational coalitions among agencies providing services, and the worker's own alliances within the professional network of support.

Group work characterizes the social work profession's tradition of empowerment with those persons who are oppressed. "The roots of group work are in social reform, democratic participation, social action, mutual aid, and concern with vulnerable and oppressed populations" (Birnbaum & Auerbach, 1994, p. 333). Drawing on the work of Garvin, Schriver (1998) describes five types of empowerment-oriented groups that are particularly applicable with clients who are members of oppressed cultural groups. These groups include:

- *Consciousness-raising groups* in which members share experiences and explore feelings
- *Treatment groups* to deal with the impact of social oppression on the behaviors and attitudes of members
- *Social action groups* to target systems in the environment for change
- *Network and support groups* to reduce feelings of isolation and increase members' awareness of their strengths
- *Skill groups* to develop abilities in communication, leadership, and social change strategies.

In all these groups, members share resources with each other rather than depend primarily on the social worker's skills and expertise.

Mutual Aid in Groups

Small groups provide opportunities for enhancing mutual aid among clients, a setting in which clients help themselves by helping each other. "The group is an enterprise in mutual aid, an alliance of individuals who need each other, in varying degrees, to work on certain common problems" (Shulman & Gitterman 1994, p. 14). Workers facilitate interactions among members and stimulate processes which activate members' contributions to each other.

Mutual Aid Processes

Nine qualities of mutual aid processes empower group members (Shulman & Gitterman, 1994). *Sharing data* provides group members with opportunities to benefit from the knowledge and resources each member contributes. The *dialectical process* involves point and counterpoint discussions in which members articulate and synthesize divergent views. The abilities of some members to begin to talk about *"taboo subjects"* lend courage to others to do the same. Importantly, mutual exchanges also foster the sense of *"all being in the same boat."* There is solace in knowing that others have similar experiences. *Mutual support* flows through individual members as well as the group as a whole and has reciprocal effects. Lending support to others benefits both the givers and the receivers. However, caring in and of itself is not enough to facilitate change. *Mutual demand* confronts the need to make changes and holds members accountable for taking action. *Individual problem solving* occurs when work in the group moves back and forth between specific cases and general issues. *Rehearsal* is a role play strategy for practicing new behaviors in a context where support and feedback can increase members' confidence in their abilities to change. Finally, there is *strength in numbers.* United with others, people will take actions that they dare not or cannot do alone.

Facilitating Group Functioning

Social workers have responsibilities to ensure that groups function in ways that maximize the benefits of mutual aid. Workers use skills to: (1) conceptualize and initiate the group, (2) develop the system of mutual aid essential to the group's success, and (3) mediate the interactions among group members and between the group and its environment to maintain and achieve the group's purpose.

Social workers complete many tasks to initiate an effective group. Often, workers decide on a group approach based on contacts with several individual clients who are expressing similar needs. At other times, the ideas for groups come from social issues identified by the worker or as suggestions from indigenous community leaders. Once the group is envisioned, workers complete other pre-group activities, including steps in launching a group. This includes developing the proposal, receiving sanction for the group from the sponsoring organization, accessing and screening potential members, and orienting members selected to the purpose and process of the group (Corey & Corey, 1997).

As the group begins, facilitators develop the system of mutual aid which characterizes the group approach. To accomplish this, workers direct members' interactions toward one another, help members respond to what other members are saying, foster the development of respectful and functional group norms, and highlight members' common characteristics and concerns (Germain & Gitterman, 1996). This phase of group work is the formation stage, a time when the group takes on its own unique identity. During this time, members begin to sense the power of the group alliance and recognize their place in the structure of the group.

Finally, to achieve the purposes of the group, social workers keep members on task, network appropriate resources and information to members, and help members implement goal-directed activities. Key skills for social workers during this phase of group operation include resolving conflicts, facilitating decision-making, and stimulating creativity. For groups to be empowering, workers teach and model these skills so that members themselves can take responsibility for the group's interaction and success.

A Group Example

Irizarry and Appel (1994) describe their group work with inner city youths—African American and Puerto Rican girls from ten to thirteen years of age. The authors describe these girls as experiencing a double marginality—coping with the developmental transitions to adolescence in the context of ethnic identity issues and poverty. The specific incident occurred on a subway trip to Coney Island. "The restraint of space and apparent scrutiny by passengers led to noisy behavior by the girls" (p. 129), which eventually led to their being ejected from the train. The worker indicated that the girls treated the event as a joke, even though their plans were ruined and they had to return home. An excerpt from the case illustrates the girls' movement toward autonomy through their experience of mutual aid while discussing their experiences:

> *The next day while we were eating cookies at the center, the whole episode was spontaneously reviewed. Judy remarked quite somberly, that she imagined passengers thought they were girls on a trip from a "loony house." Nilda added, without laughter, "We all looked crazy—no wonder people stared." Comments ensued*

about various crazy people from the neighborhood and how they acted. I asked if they wanted people to think that about them. Carmen instantly replied no but that it was my fault because I hadn't screamed at them and made them stop.

I said I hadn't thought I was a policewoman to go around watching how they behaved, and that they were always telling me how much they didn't like their teachers bossing them around so much. Nilda said I could be in some ways like a teacher. Judy agreed—to tell them to sit down. I said that I was willing to remind them to sit down if they wanted me to, but also asked them if they thought it would really stop them. Tata led the general response that no one could stop them when they got going "like that." I said that I thought one of the hardest things for anyone to learn in life was to act the way they really wanted. (pp. 129–130)

Demonstrating an important skill in group facilitation, the social worker in the example does not control the process or evaluate what the group members have done, but instead she encourages the members themselves to interact and reflect on their own experiences.

Social Action in Groups

Whereas mutual aid in groups supports individual change, social action in groups generates activities which aim toward mid- and macrolevel changes. Sometimes workers and clients initiate social action groups for the sole purpose of mid- and macrolevel change. At other times, social action emerges from the processes of mutual aid through which group participants identify the interconnections between personal difficulties and public issues.

Gutiérrez (1991) describes her experiences of moving from mutual aid to advocacy and resource mobilization in her work with Latino and African American mothers in a community mental health center setting. The center ran a series of groups over a nine-month period. The initial group was a *support group* to address the concrete issues the women identified—"family stress, dangerous neighborhoods, and an inadequate school system" (p. 209). Gutiérrez observes that "for most of the women, this engagement toward changing concrete issues worked toward the resolution of personal problems as well" (p. 209). The second group was a *skills-building group,* primarily concerned with issues related to parenting. The group was designed to deal with issues the women identified in a supportive group atmosphere. At the group members' request for continued involvement, the graduates of the first skills building group became *mentors* for women who joined an open-membership parenting group. From this experience, the fourth group, a client-led *social support and social action group,* evolved. Topics for discussion included "how to budget their welfare allotment, how to make toys and gifts for children, understanding their children's behavior, and sex education" (p. 210). When educational concerns were a recurrent theme, the group took action to invite a representative from the local school board to their meeting. When the results of this conversation did not address their concerns, they initiated discussions with an attorney who spearheaded a class action directed at the lack of special education services in the community. "This example indicates how in less than a year, these women moved from feeling overwhelmed by their young children to feeling capable of confronting the city board of education" (Gutiérrez, p. 210).

Liddie (1991) also describes her work with a group for mothers whose children were enrolled in a day care program. Liddie and her colleagues used strategies "to increase the women's sense of self and their autonomous actions" (p. 140). Their intentional orientation toward empowerment placed the group members in charge of decisions about the group's activities—the agenda, guest speakers, meal preparation and clean-up, social and educational events, attendance at day care board meetings, and discussions with local politicians. Several interesting projects resulted from their increased self-confidence and their collaborative efforts in identifying common issues and strategizing action plans. They successfully organized a contingent of 500 community members to demonstrate at city hall about their objections to cuts in day care funding. The group also arranged meetings with the day care staff to express their desires to develop more mutually beneficial working relationships.

What began as a support group for mothers developed into a vehicle for addressing issues in the community and with the day care center. What began as women questioning their own worth and even denying their own strengths evolved to circumstances where women experienced firsthand their individual and collective accomplishments.

Self-Help Groups

Workers are not always pivotal in constructing empowering groups. Self-help groups develop when individuals with similar concerns or problems join together to be helpful resources for one another. The caring that occurs in self-help or mutual support groups creates an empathic environment for exchanging ideas and providing relevant information, offers strategies for coping and problem resolution, and empowers group members to confront troubling issues (Powell, 1995). Interestingly, research demonstrated that the effectiveness of peer-led groups for caregivers is similar to that of groups led by professionals (Toseland, Rossiter, & Labrecque, 1989).

Typically, peers (who are participating as group members) rather than social service professionals facilitate mutual support groups. These groups usually form around common concerns or problem areas such as substance abuse, intimate violence, grief issues, divorce, stepparenting, and health and wellness concerns. Examples of nationally organized self-help groups include Alcoholics Anonymous, Parents without Partners, and the National Alliance for the Mentally Ill. Not only do these groups provide mutual exchange and support, but they often have a political agenda as well, seeking to change public attitudes and laws that affect their constituencies.

Working with Self-Help Groups

Because of their potential role for providing clients with support and connections to others with similar difficulties, social workers develop skills for linking clients with self-help groups. To draw on these resources, social workers:

- Develop a file that contains descriptions of the self-help resources
- Identify the key participants in local self-help groups
- Discuss the benefits of self-help groups with clients
- Give clients up-to-date information or brochures about the self-help group
- Provide clients with specific and accurate information about meeting times, locations, and contact persons

Self-help groups are part of a natural helping system within any community that supports the well-being of its members. When social workers draw on the resources of self-help groups, they help strengthen the client's sense of belonging to a community.

Empowerment and Self-Help

Empowerment-oriented practitioners view self-help as integral to clients' experiences of empowerment (Parsons, 1991; Gutiérrez, 1994; Lee, 1994; Simon, 1994; Powell, 1995). Self-help groups provide emotional and social support, concrete assistance, a forum for learning new skills, and a base of power for collective action (Dodd & Gutierrez, 1990). The self-help group members, by definition, help each other. Sullivan and Rapp describe the empowering nature of peers helping peers as a process in which an individual "is no longer simply a passive object of services who hopes to recover, survive, or regain health, but an active member of a synergistic group" (1994, p. 95).

Participating in experiences where peers help peers has indirect effects as well. Cox and Parsons (1993) report the comments of a grandmother who describes the synergistic effect of her participation in a peer counseling program for older adults:

> *You know, one never knows what is in store for them. You just cannot plan things. I am taking care of my two granddaughters, one is 16 and one 20. Their mother, my daughter, is an alcoholic, and refuses to deal with them. I really have tried my best, but just haven't been able to reach them. They feel that I'm too old and re- moved from their world. The kids never shared their thoughts or feelings with me nor their doings in school. However, since I joined the peer counseling program, I started to apply some of the things I learned on my own grandkids. Do you know that now we sit around the table at suppertime and talk! The kids are now inter- ested in what I'm doing and learning. They think it's great! Imagine at my age go- ing to school and learning new things! I believe they think grandma is not so stupid after all. They even told their friends about me. Believe it or not, they have started thinking of aging and the attitudes that surround aging, including their own. Isn't it great! This program is my salvation! (pp. 132–133)*

Strengthening Natural Support Alliances

People may overlook the significant support they receive from social ties such as their re- lationships with family members, friends, colleagues, and their associations with churches, schools, or clubs (Table 13.1). However, support networks play an essential role in social functioning and are a potential resource in the social service delivery network.

Social Support

Social support includes those exchanges in our social networks that provide "emotional en- couragement, concrete assistance or tangible aid, and advice and information" (Kemp, Whit- taker, & Tracy, 1997, p. 73). Family members, friends, neighbors, acquaintances, colleagues, self-help group members, and professionals are all potential sources of social support.

Numerous research findings underscore the significance of social support in protect- ing, moderating, and buffering the effects of crises and in contributing to peoples' resiliency

TABLE 13.1   Social Support Networks

Informal Systems	Membership Systems	Professional Systems
Spouses	Churches and Synagogues	Social Workers
Partners	Informal Social Clubs	Mental Health Practitioners
Children	Clubs	Educators
Parents	Associations	Clergy
Siblings	Civic Organizations	Lawyers
Extended Family	Fraternities and Sororities	Doctors and Nurses
Friends	Athletic Teams	Dieticians
Neighbors	Parent Teacher Associations	Speech Therapists
Classmates	Unions	Psychologists
Co-workers	Fraternal and Social Organizations	Elected Officials
	Recreational Memberships	
	Art and Music Groups	
	Hangouts (Bars, the Mall, Supper Clubs)	
	Mutual Aid Groups	

in the face of ongoing stress (Feiring, Taska, & Lewis, 1998; Ma, 1998; Salgado de Snyder, de Jesus Diaz-Perez, Maldonado, & Bautista, 1998; Pugliesi & Shook, 1998; White, Bruce, Farrell, & Kliewer, 1998). Conversely, a lack of social support and a sense of social isolation often magnify the difficulties people experience and reduce the pool of resources that contributes to solutions.

Social support, by definition, involves connections with others. However, connections with others alone do not guarantee experiences of social support (Whittaker & Tracy, 1991; Beeman, 1997; Kemp, Whittaker, & Tracy, 1997; El-Bassel, Chen, & Cooper, 1998). The quality of these relationships makes a difference. Support occurs when relationships are based on reciprocity, mutuality, and shared power in an atmosphere where people can offer what they have to offer and receive the resources they seek.

Social support may provide resources for clients, yet workers should not expect naturally supportive networks to solve all dilemmas. Cautioning against viewing social support as a panacea, experts recommend defining social support as " a necessary but not sufficient component of a comprehensive service plan which likely will include family treatment, parent education, case management, and related services" (Whittaker & Tracy, 1991, p. 176). Social support networks play a significant role; however, they are best considered as complementary to rather than a substitute for professional social services. The strength of social support may be culturally based. Culturally responsive social workers recognize that extended family and community networks play a significant role in some cultures and geographic regions.

Workers' Roles in Encouraging Social Support

A person's social support network usually develops naturally. But, workers can also encourage these networks to develop purposefully. Workers can participate in designing physical environments that create opportunities for interaction. They can also teach clients social skills to prepare them for new relationships. Finally, workers can access natural helpers in the community directly to ally them with clients who need support.

Designing Environments

Our physical surroundings either enhance or inhibit the potential for developing social relationships. Research in social psychology shows that: "Just as it is possible to build oppressive environments that stifle social activity, it is also possible to design them to promote social activity and support" (Fleming, Baum, & Singer, 1985, p. 327). Research upon which these authors draw indicates that the opportunities for social contact, the proximity of people to each other, and the appropriateness of space for group interaction all influence the formation of groups and other social networks.

The physical design of space—whether homes, offices, meeting rooms, apartment complexes, residential facilities, neighborhoods, or communities—influences the number of social exchanges people make, and likewise, the chances they have for becoming friends. Social workers can participate in designing spaces that support the development of social relationships and also in modifying the existing environments to promote social interactions.

Enhancing Interactional Skills

The advantage of physical environments that support social interactions is lost if people have not had an opportunity to develop their skills in relating to others. In the context of professional relationships, social workers have opportunities to observe clients in action in an "up-front and personal way." Workers' experiences with client systems offer information about how clients interact. Social workers draw selectively from this reservoir to provide feedback to clients about their skills.

When social workers notice a client's interpersonal skills, they mention them for the client's benefit. Giving compliments to clients about what social workers see has proven positive effects (Wall, Kleckner, Amendt, & Bryant, 1989). Clients who recognize their own interpersonal skills and abilities carry confidence into relationships with others. Workers say things like:

- It's always good to talk with you. You have such a good sense of humor and we all appreciate a good laugh.
- That's what I like about you! You listen so carefully when people talk and you are so good at understanding how they feel.
- I appreciate your honesty about your feelings toward the child protective unit. It is so much easier to relate to people who are up front about their views.
- I admire the way you follow through. People can always count on you to keep your commitments to them.

Friendships are based on mutuality and exchange. Friendships are most likely to flourish in the context of shared interests, activities, and projects rather than concentrated efforts at "being friends." Enabling the development of social support networks requires creative use of clients' interests and existing connections. For example, social workers could encourage clients interested in the outdoors to join a hiking club or group interested in environmental causes, clients with school-age children to volunteer to assist with school activities or participate actively in school-based organizations, or clients who, by their age, qualify, to take part in their community's programs for "seniors."

Activating Natural Helpers

All communities contain natural helpers, people known in their neighborhoods, workplaces, schools, or churches who function effectively on their own and who provide resources and support to others around them (Germain & Gitterman, 1996). Practitioners who focus their work in a particular community gradually become aware of people who play central roles as indigenous helpers. Indigenous leaders may reveal themselves through their community leadership and voluntarism. Or social workers can discover their presence gradually as they hear about their activities in conversations with community members.

Many people are able to link themselves to natural helpers through their existing relationships or the community grapevine. For those clients who have been unable to establish this kind of natural support, social workers can play important roles. Linking clients with appropriate natural helpers

> requires the motivation, interest, and agreement of both parties. Helpers should be evaluated on the basis of how helpful they are, not on whether their values and attitudes are congruent with professional ones. Ethnic, racial, or religious matches may be desirable depending on the needs and circumstances. (Germain & Gitterman, 1996, p. 357)

Linking people to naturally occurring resources has advantages. These solutions are embedded within the client's environment and are likely to have enduring results. They are also free from the limitations of more formal helping systems such as shortages in funding, changes in programs, and bureaucratic red tape.

Case Management: Client–Service Alliances

Case management creates and strengthens alliances among service providers and with clients. A popular, contemporary approach for networking health care and social services, case management coordinates relevant resources involved with a particular client system. The shift to social policies and funding protocols that endorse case management strategies ensures that case management will retain its pivotal role in the delivery of services (Rose & Moore, 1995). This section defines case management, describes its purpose, presents a case example, details case management activities, and examines key issues associated with the urgency to contain costs and the propensity to "manage cases" rather than provide effective service.

Case Management Defined

Case management services are delivered by an individual or team "who organizes, coordinates, and sustains a network of formal and informal supports and activities designed to optimize the functioning and well-being of people with multiple needs" (Moxley, 1989, p. 21).

Case managers work with clients who need access to several types of resources. They also work with the members of interdisciplinary teams who are working with particular clients. Case managers seek "to assure that clients of human services systems receive the services, treatment, care, and opportunities to which they are entitled" (Weil & Karls, 1989, p. 1).

Origins of Case Management

One can trace the impetus for case management to six factors: deinstitutionalization, decentralization of services, clients with multiple needs, fragmentation of services, the nature of informal social supports, and the press to contain costs in the face of limited funds and scarce resources (Moxley, 1989).

- *Deinstitutionalization* is the trend to provide community-based rather than institution-based services. This means that clients with multiple challenges must sustain their ability to live independently by locating appropriate services among the complicated array of community-based programs.
- The trend toward *decentralization* intensifies the need for coordinating services among multiple community-based service providers. "From the perspective of many clients and their families, accessing and using community services can be as difficult as untangling a Gordian knot" (p. 13).
- Without the benefits of case management, clients with *complex issues and multiple needs* must somehow piece together a "patchwork" of resources for themselves. Often they must access services from multiple providers, many of whom have never communicated with one another.
- The *constraints of the requirements* for services—including geographic boundaries, age restrictions, income guidelines, and categorical eligibility stipulation—fragment the delivery of social services. This fragmentation complicates the tasks of coordinating services and determining for which services clients are eligible.
- *Social support networks* can either enhance or reduce the positive effect of formal services. Case managers can play a unique role to ensure that formal and informal resources reinforce each other, maximizing the benefits of each.
- The *press to contain costs* and conserve scarce resources yet still meet the needs of clients requires the efficient processes that case management offers.

Expanding Role for Case Management

Largely as a result of these trends, case management is rapidly acquiring a reputation as a major social work practice strategy with clients who have multiple needs. In fact, case management is used extensively in the fields of mental health, addictions, developmental disabilities, health care, rehabilitation, corrections, public welfare, child welfare, and family-based and aging services (see Table 13.2). Within this array of fields, public, private not-for-profit, and private for-profit agencies provide case management services. Case management is the exclusive domain of some of the agencies; whereas, others offer case management services as one of several programs and services. Increasing numbers of generalist social workers will be employed as case managers or, at least, in practice settings that use case management for the delivery of programs and services. "Case management is a pragmatic response to the realities of today's service delivery" (Austin & McClelland, 1996, p. 1).

TABLE 13.2   Policies Establishing Case Management

P. L. 91–517	Developmental Disabilities Act of 1970
P. L. 92–603	Medicare waivers and Medicaid, Social Security Amendments of 1972
P. L. 95–478	Older Americans Act, revisions of 1978
P. L. 94–142	Education for All Handicapped Children Act of 1975
P. L. 96–272	Federal Adoption Assistance and Child Welfare Act of 1980
P. L. 96–499	Community and Home Based Waiver provision of the Omnibus Budget Reconciliation Act of 1981
P. L. 98–459	Revisions to the Older Americans Act of 1984
P. L. 100–79	Stuart B. McKinney Homeless Assistance Act of 1987
P. L. 100–485	Family Support Act of 1988
P. L. 100–381	Ryan White Comprehensive AIDS Resources Emergency Act of 1990

The Purpose of Case Management

Effective case management links clients to services, connects service providers with each other, and redresses shortcomings in service delivery. Based on the work of Applebaum and Austin, Quinn (1995) specifies a broad range of client-oriented and system-oriented objectives as an example of the purpose of case management in the field of case management in long-term care:

Client-Oriented Objectives

- To assure that services given are appropriate to client needs.
- To monitor appropriateness of long-term care services.
- To improve client access to the continuum of long-term care services.
- To support the client's caregivers.
- To serve as a bridge between institutional and community-based care systems.

System-Oriented Objectives

- To facilitate the development of noninstitutional services.
- To promote quality in long-term care service delivery.
- To enhance the coordination of long-term care service delivery.
- To target individuals most at-risk of nursing home placement in order to prevent inappropriate institutionalization.
- To contain cost by controlling client access to services. (pp. 237–238)

Scan these objectives to note their general themes. Some of the objectives relate to initiating, planning, implementing, and evaluating services with a particular client. Others relate to the service delivery system itself—coordinating, evaluating, and containing costs, as well as revamping existing services and creating new ones. Although this list focuses on case management in long-term care, these same objectives readily adapt to other settings.

Case Management in Action: A Practice Example

Like other case managers, Kennedy Brown finds he is dealing with issues at all system levels. His responsibilities lead him to work with service providers, as well as clients and their families.

When Sarah Martin calls to inquire about the availability of community-based services for her parents, Kennedy Brown hears a familiar story. As a case manager for OPTIONS, a Northside agency that provides services and programming for older adults, Kennedy recognizes the need for environmental supports as people become frail. Sarah's parents, Ida and George Palmer, are both 75. Until recently, they were able to maintain their normal routine, living in their own home, tending their yard, enjoying the neighborhood children, watching television, and reading. However, when Sarah had visited with her parents the day before, her mother confided that she had been keeping a nightly vigil for several weeks, guarding against George's wandering off during the night. Sarah was shocked to learn that her father, who always seemed so chipper when she visited, had been declining for some time and that her mother had been protecting their "secret." Sarah reports that Ida, although sick with exhaustion herself, is committed to caring for George. After all, they've been married for 55 years.

Sarah feels torn. Both she and her husband work full-time and their children have numerous work, school, and family commitments; however, she knows she must do something. The question Sarah poses to Kennedy Brown says it all: "Are there any services in our community that can help my parents?" Kennedy Brown sets up a meeting with Sarah and her parents to discuss their situation more fully and determine a course of action that will support the Palmers.

Kennedy Brown's meeting with his new clients uncovers multiple concerns. Sarah and her parents concur that for George and Ida to remain in their own home they require supportive services as soon as possible to meet George's physical needs and to assist Ida in her caregiving role. Together they begin to generate some options:

- Medical evaluation at Northside Hospital's specialized program for older adults
- Meals on wheels
- Homemaker services for assistance with household chores
- "Afternoon Out" respite program

Additional issues may surface after addressing the Palmer's immediate needs. Long-term goals will likely include expanding the family's understanding about disease processes and aging as well as coping with their grief over George's declining health. For example, Sarah and her mother may want to join a caregiver support group or enroll George in the OPTIONS' Adult Care Center. Kennedy knows that depending on their assessment, the interdisciplinary medical team might recommend that George participate in the university-based research project to test the effectiveness of a new drug used to treat Alzheimer's disease.

Kennedy's work with the Palmers also means working with the resource network. Kennedy will convene meetings of service providers who will work with the Palmers as well as attend meetings of providers that focus on general issues of the client population he serves. Case managers are generalists, simultaneously working with microlevel clients and operating at the midlevel to coordinate service provisions, enhance interagency cooperation, identify gaps in services and problems with delivery, and increase the efficient use of scarce resources.

Three factors are essential for productive case management, including "an accurate assessment and recurring re-evaluation with the client of what is needed; the existence of the needed services; and the power to ensure that the services are in fact delivered in a timely fashion" (Dinerman, 1992, p. 4). Case managers coordinate the delivery of services, provide for continuity in their provision, seek fiscal accountability, and ensure service effectiveness. Their activities encompass work with case management clients and with various aspects of the delivery system itself.

Case Management Activities with Clients

Case managers rely on generic social work processes to carry out their case management activities. Core functions include outreach, assessment, planning, linking, advocacy, monitoring, and evaluation (Moxley, 1989; Greene, 1992; Rubin, 1992; Abramson & Rosenthal, 1995; Austin & McClelland, 1996). This section highlights four major case management activities—outreach, planning in case staffings, linking clients with resources, and advocacy.

Outreach
The intent of outreach is to heighten the visibility of programs and services by educating the general public and other service providers about available programs. A more focused activity, case finding, directs outreach efforts toward those who are likely to need the services the information is promoting. Case managers hope that through the early identification made possible by outreach, their work with clients can prevent problems of a greater magnitude.

Community education initiatives include public speaking engagements, newspaper articles, brochures and pamphlets, and fund raising campaigns. Contacts with key people in the community, such as indigenous leaders, clergy, visiting nurses, teachers, day care providers, lawyers, and physicians, often play a key role in outreach work, too. The client's first contact for assistance is often not with a social worker but, instead, with a community member or professional who is in a position of acting as a "bridge" to appropriate programs and services.

Planning in Case Staffings
Interdisciplinary staffings, a common planning strategy among service providers, coordinate work with client systems. Joint planning efforts synchronize services and avoid unnecessary duplications.

For empowerment-oriented social workers, the key issue in case staffings is ensuring an active role for clients. Many times, staffings exclude clients, ostensibly so professionals can "talk more openly." Carefully examine what this position reveals about professionals' communication with clients and the long-range effect of denying clients direct access to key information about their own situations. Decision-making processes that exclude clients usurp informed consent. Empowerment-based social work practice places clients genuinely in control over what happens in their lives by guaranteeing their participation in case staffings!

Social workers play various roles at case staffings. Sometimes they function as information givers, talking directly about their views of the client's situation. They may also be facilitators, guiding the group's interaction in such a way that clients have opportunities to offer their perspectives and other participants hear and respect what clients say. At other times, staffings require workers to switch their level of focus from their client to the interdisciplinary helping system itself. When focusing on the way the helping system functions, social workers support the effective development of the team. For example, a worker can facilitate a sense of rapport, nonjudgmental openness, and equal distribution of power by listening carefully and by encouraging participants to voice their opinions.

Linking Clients with Resources

Case managers are consummate information specialists. They offer technical assistance with respect to availability, benefits, eligibility requirements, application procedures, and other vital information about resources. In discussing the linking activities of her work with pregnant teens, Davis (1992) indicates she must weave "together people in agencies and programs dealing with adoption, dropouts, genetic counseling, job training, health, day care, equity, women's issues, fathers, family planning, child abuse issues, human growth and development, nutrition, parenting, and career planning" (p. 29).

By providing relevant information, case managers guide clients through the maze of the service network to assist them in acquiring suitable resources. Kaplan (1992) suggests several strategies for linking clients with resources. Effective case managers need to:

- Be familiar with the resources, having, in so far as possible, firsthand information to draw upon
- Plan ahead for emergency situations, anticipating, for example, the types of crises clients are likely to experience
- Create new resources when none exist
- Coordinate the services of multiple providers
- Modify the linkages with resources as the client's circumstances change

Advocacy

Advocates use their influence to compel the social service delivery system "to be more responsive to the unmet needs of clients" (Kisthardt & Rapp, 1992, p. 121). Questions to evaluate the necessity for initiating advocacy activities include:

- Is the resource *available*?
- Is the resource *accessible*?
- Is the provider willing to make the necessary *accommodations*?
- Will the resource be *adequate*? (Kisthardt & Rapp)

To be culturally competent, case managers raise "awareness of discriminatory and oppressive practices and institutionalized forms of racism, sexism, ageism, ableism, and homophobia that create barriers to access" (Rogers, 1995, p. 65).

Rather than directing the advocacy process, case managers are most empowering when they support clients to advocate for themselves. Client-driven advocacy places clients in roles that control advocacy activities, leaving corollary roles for social workers to support clients' actions (Moxley & Freddolino, 1994). As initiators, clients define their own needs and select activities to address them. To facilitate this role, social workers as mentors model ways to solve problems, teach skills for dealing with institutions and bureaucracies, and suggest ways to network with others. Clients as implementors act on their own behalf, while social workers as coaches guide clients in their advocacy activities. Clients determine whether they should continue, modify, or halt their advocacy activities. Through their support role, social workers bolster clients' advocacy efforts and back their decisions. Clients as educators inform professionals about what they want to achieve, how they want to achieve it, and what they are willing to accept from a provider, telling the social worker when to act as the client's representative "to resolve disputes through mediation and negotiation, or through more assertive actions such as administrative hearings or formal legal action" (p. 99).

This client-driven model of advocacy does more than help clients gain access to services. It also "promotes the values of self-determination and client control over intervention activities" and "addresses the basic needs and resources of clients from the perspectives of clients themselves" (Moxley & Freddolino, 1994, p. 104).

Case Management Activities with the Delivery System

Case managers also work with other professionals in the delivery system itself, both to coordinate the work of various programs and professionals involved with particular clients and to build a more responsive social service delivery network.

Coordinating Services

The purpose of coordinating services is to ensure "that services are being implemented in harmonious and compatible ways by the human service providers and social network members who have been organized by the case manager to respond to client needs" (Moxley, 1989, p. 101). In coordinating services, the case manager reviews the service provisions to ensure that their goals are congruous, that the services delivered correspond with the agreed-upon plan, and that opportunities for service providers to communicate exist. Factors that impede coordination include turf issues, competition among service providers, disagreements about priorities and intervention strategies, and the lack of a common vision for the plan.

Collaboration reaps the same benefits with service providers as it does with clients. Sheridan, Gowen, and Halpin (1993) indicate cooperating with service providers "is most challenging for workers who tend to perceive the system as unresponsive, unworkable, or even as 'the enemy.' For various reasons, barriers exist in the service delivery system and agencies differ in their responsiveness to client needs" (p. 416). These authors describe their case management efforts with homeless clients and the success they experience with providers by beginning "with the assumption that personnel wanted to be helpful, that they knew their jobs, and that they cared about client service" (p. 416).

Relating to Other Professionals

Sometimes connections between clients and potential resource systems need to be modified. In these situations, workers use skills to enhance the relationships of clients with resource systems. This requires a sorting out of responsibilities between family systems and larger system helpers: "The simplest and most direct form of intervention with families and larger systems is that which delineates and/or redistributes tasks among the larger system represen- tatives" (Imber-Black, 1988, p. 136). Clarifying roles reduces conflicting messages to the client, prevents overlaps in service delivery, and alleviates turf battles among various service providers. When clients renegotiate their connections to larger systems, they can shift the distribution of power—getting larger systems to work for them rather than on them.

The way in which social workers approach other systems has an impact on the ensuing success. Workers should use "language and tone that communicates a sense of appreciation to the various participants in the macrosystem. Contributions that have worked should be selected out and confirmed" (Imber-Black, 1988, p. 135). Representatives of resource sys- tems are people, too. They respond to the same respectful treatment, appreciate the same consideration, and need the same validation as clients. Effective social workers empower environmental systems as well as clients in their work to reach clients' goals.

Building Responsive Networks of Services

Even the best plans are inadequate when resources are unavailable or inaccessible. A prime function of case managers is to advocate changes within the delivery system to make its ser- vices more appropriate, adequate, and accessible:

> *Put somewhat differently, if there were comprehensive service planning coupled with adequate and appropriate resources; if there were integration of diverse ser- vice system components; if there were highly responsive provider systems with both facility of access and appropriate modes of intervention; and if there were client- driven supportive services tied to adequate material resources such as safe, afford- able housing, there would be no need for case management. (Rose, 1992, p. 271)*

Case managers are in key positions for building more responsive networks of social ser- vices. "The daily practice of case management provides ample opportunity to identify and document service delivery effects, barriers, and obstacles originating at the system level, es- pecially in fiscal and operational policies" (Austin, 1993, p. 457). Case managers can ad- dress service delivery issues by:

- Creating changes in organizations or the networks of service delivery providers.
- Participating in capacity building or "strengthening the network of community re- sources so that it will be responsive to other clients in the future" (Moxley, 1989, p. 94).
- Finding ways to "influence the development of new resources and programs" (p. 94).

However, case management is no panacea for an inadequate social service delivery system that is badly in need of structural reform and financial investment. "By itself, case management services cannot alter biases and shortages in the delivery system.... In the absence of adequate funding, case managers cannot create services that do not exist" (Austin, 1992, p. 64).

Workers' Resources for Case Management

Social work knowledge and skills support case management activities. Effective case manage- ment builds on a sound base of knowledge about the consumers such as key developmental issues, cultural backgrounds, and the community context. A resourceful case manager also knows about relevant programs and services—their eligibility requirements, costs, restrictions, application procedures, and availability. Being prepared with information helps workers coach clients to deal more successfully with service providers.

Case managers employ skills to build relationships, exchange information, use the telephone productively, and manage time (Quinn, 1995). Skills in listening are important for relating to both clients and colleagues. Gathering and conveying information to clients and around the helping system is also pivotal to competent case management. When communicating over the phone, case managers have "facts in hand," respond to messages in a timely fashion, inquire about the best time to return a call, and craft succinct, yet informative, messages. Time management skills help case managers balance countless demands such as responding to crises, coordinating the activities of multiple service providers, and meeting deadlines. Effective organization is the key. Marking appointments, meetings, forms to fill out, calls to make, deadlines, and follow-up work on a daily calendar effectively organizes a workload.

Computer Skills

Contemporary case managers operate computers to facilitate communication and record-keeping (Kraus & Pillsbury, 1994; Fancett & Hughes, 1996). Computer skills can streamline tasks such as writing reports, networking information, and keeping records, assessing risks, and tracking progress (Butterfield, 1995; Oyserman & Benbenishty, 1997; Miller & DiGuseppe, 1998; Schoeh, et al., 1998). Computers also enhance communication capabilities through e-mail. Computers assist clients and social workers in identifying potential sources of support and are even becoming significant venues for self-help and professionally facilitated groups (Finn, 1995, 1996; Galinsky, Schopler, & Abell, 1997; Schopler, Abell, & Galinsky, 1998). The information accessible through the World Wide Web (WWW) includes web sites with countless resources for learning about such topics as aging, health concerns, and Alzheimer's disease. With a computer and a modem, social workers can access research reports and demographic data, obtain program information, converse with others about social issues, and register their opinions on Capitol Hill.

Critical Issues and Ethical Dilemmas

Although many clients benefit from case management services, this area of practice is also laden with critical issues and ethical dilemmas. Among them are:

- Who's in charge of decision-making?
- What are the implications of managed care for the delivery of social services?
- Who needs to know and who actually has permission to receive information about a particular client?
- Can clients access the services they want or do they have to settle for what they can get?

Who's in Charge of Case Management?

Who is responsible for making decisions? The client? The client's family? The case manager? The team of service providers? The representative of the funding body? The case monitor?

The empowering answer to these questions is that workers and clients collaborate as "co-managers" in assessing what they need and agreeing on what is to be done (Dinerman, 1992).

Dinerman (1992) warns workers against the seduction of "management" in case management positions, particularly when working with clients whom society labels as dependent—such as those who are frail, in ill health, or have chronic mental illness. This type of case management is control that is disguised as care, "not from malevolence but simply from the dynamic of powerful and resourceful professionals interacting with vulnerable and resource-weak clients.... Precisely when care is beneficent, intrusions upon autonomy can go unchecked, unscrutinized, even unobserved behind the curtain of good intentions" (Collopy, 1992, p. 56). The more case managers manage decisions for clients, the less involved clients are likely to be. "Non-compliance is one likely response to such situations. Effectiveness in case management in any event requires joint and participatory planning by clients and case managers" (Dinerman, 1992, p. 7).

An ethical dilemma occurs when the client's choice is dramatically different from that of the case manager, and it is the case manager's opinion that the client's choice will create problematic risks for the client:

> *Clearly, case managers should not impose their own views of acceptable risk on clients and families. But what are a case manager's rights when he or she cannot in good conscience accede to the plan the client prefers? Does the case manager have a duty to refer the case to another case manager? If several case managers and their supervisors agree that the client's choices are dangerous to self or society, is this a test of truth? (Kane, 1992, p. 224)*

In this instance, the case manager must balance the benefits of supporting the client's autonomous decision-making against the risks of harming the client through passive neglect (Austin, 1996). An open discussion with the client about the worker's views maintains the collaborative relationship and helps to inform the client's and the worker's choice.

Issues of autonomy become more complicated when individuals rely on the support of others to exercise their chosen options. In the case of older adults who are frail, self-determination may be limited by the abilities of their life partners, adult children, friends, and neighbors to support their decisions (Kane, 1992). Furthermore, the "right" decision for the client may not be the best decision for family members or, for that matter, the taxpayers. An ecosystemic perspective considering the client in social context helps case managers and clients generate solutions that fit their circumstances.

Service Users' Involvement. Ensuring that clients remain in charge of case management and, therefore, their lives, is a major impetus for the empowerment-oriented service user's movement in England that includes mental health system survivors, older adults, persons with learning difficulties, and persons with disabilities (Beresford, 1994, 1997, 1999; Oliver, 1994, 1996; Aspis, 1997; Barnes & Shardlow, 1997; Bott, 1997; Morris, 1997; Barnes & Bennett, 1998). One example of an organization in this movement is "Shaping Our Lives," an influential organization for persons with disabilities that draws upon the expertise of service users to influence policy and program research, planning, and evaluation (Turner, 1997). Goals include empowering service users by advocating personal decision-making and control, creating responsive programs and services, redressing discrimination and social injustice, and promoting social change. Fisher's (1994) extensive research on social work and partnership indicates that the most effective way to ensure that empowerment theory is translated into day-to-day practice is "by establishing an active and prominent role for users in policy and practice development" (p. 289).

Managed Care

Managed care is a means for determining the type of behavioral, health, and mental health services provided and for regulating the costs of these services. Lauded by some as a strategic way of controlling costs, managed care is criticized by others as provider-driven care regulated by restrictive cost-controlled policies rather than by concern for health care consumers.

For the most part, services controlled by care management organizations have been located in the private sector, particularly those services reimbursed by private health insurance carriers. As more government entities strive to contain costs, public sector services are contracting with managed care groups to oversee the allocation of entitlements. People question whether the safety net historically provided by public sector services will be lost when for-profit managed care companies restrict or deny service claims. In some cases, already over-burdened voluntary agencies are called upon to provide services without remuneration for those clients denied access to public sector services. Managed care has widespread implications for service delivery. For example, Hopps, Pinderhughes, and Shankar (1995) observe that "multilevel, multisystem intervention is becoming less and less feasible in this day of managed care, which reinforces the segmenting of problems and the achievement of limited goals" (p. 138).

Many raise issues regarding the appropriateness of a managed care environment for social work professionals and their clients (Davidson & Davidson, 1995, 1996; Strom-Gottfried, 1998; Watt & Kallmann, 1998; Rock & Congress, 1999). Legal, professional, and fiscal dilemmas include:

Legal Issues

- *Is a social worker's cooperation with a managed care company inherently in conflict with his or her fiduciary responsibilities related to confidentiality, truth-telling, and loyalty to clients?*
- *Are social workers colluding with managed care personnel to violate clients' civil rights?*
- *Because it may not be possible to have a clear understanding or accurate knowledge of the accessibility and distribution potential of information related to a managed care entity, are the customary consent to release information forms valid?*
- *To what degree is the social worker liable should an unforeseen outcome occur about which the client was given no warning?*
- *Is it always in the client's best interests for social workers to attempt to explain the limits of confidentiality in a managed care environment (what about the very fragile client?), and if not, how will the social worker justify ignoring the duty to tell clients the truth? (Davidson & Davidson, 1996, p. 212)*

Social Work Purpose

- *Does the social worker's primary duty shift from the client to the managed care company?*
- *In a bureaucracy where individual rights have been supplanted by principles of group management, are social workers moving subtly into a role in which they will function as agents of social control?*
- *Is the relationship with managed care a slippery slope, wherein the social worker initially discloses benign information but may be called on later to reveal information that could be used to discriminate against vulnerable individuals (for instance, to identify clients in gay relationships, who may be considered high risk for insurance purposes)?*
- *What are the ethical obligations of social workers to clients as a collective group who appear to have little freedom to challenge this loss of rights to confidentiality or otherwise influence their situation as an organized group? (Davidson & Davidson, 1996, p. 213)*

Fiscal Matters

- *Because of the need to be paid for services by third-party payers, are social workers and social services agencies forced to sacrifice clients' rights in order to be recompensed?*
- *How far does the social worker's duty to aid go when there is an "inconvenience" to the self (for example, "punishment" by exclusion from managed care provider lists if designated "uncooperative")? (Davidson & Davidson, 1996, p. 213)*

Preserving Confidentiality

Confidentiality issues abound in case management. Even when clients have signed release of information forms, the basic quandary is "Who exactly has permission to know what when?" For example:

- To what extent does the release of information detail the precise circumstances of sharing information?
- How much information must the case manager share to initially secure service provisions?
- Are all service providers privy to all of the confidential details or is sharing of information selective, based on relevance and the desires of the client?
- If the client chooses to limit disclosure, will providers, likewise, limit or even refuse to provide services?
- If a client signs releases early in the case management process, does this cover new information revealed during the course of service delivery or is it necessary to secure updated releases?
- What are the implications for confidentiality if case managers enter confidential information into the managed care data base?

- Can we assume confidentiality if case management services are provided under mandated auspices such as an entitlement program, medicaid, public child welfare, or the criminal justice system?
- What confidentiality issues are raised if case management team members who are present during a case review are not involved with the particular client?
- Does sharing information with multiple providers negate the client's right to claim legal privilege?

Case managers and clients should clarify the rules of confidentiality before clients choose to disclose sensitive information and revisit issues about disclosure periodically to keep pace with the changing base of information.

Accessing Services

In the face of limited funds and rising costs, case managers must be ingenious financial managers to stretch their budgets to meet clients' needs. Caps on spending drive case managers to create plans that work effectively for the least amount of money. "The case manager is expected to contain program costs by controlling clients' access to services, particularly high-cost services" (Kane, 1992, p. 223). Gatekeeping secures the road to fiscal accountability, but does it guarantee clients' rights? Denying access to services often means that clients have to settle for services that are least expensive and available rather than being able to secure the best fit for what they want and need.

To resolve the ethical dilemma posed by being gatekeepers as well as advocates, case managers must define their role as serving a population group rather than an individual client (Kane, 1992). "The case manager becomes an advocate for identifying and meeting the needs of the entire group fairly and well, as well as for meeting the needs of any given individual" (p. 221). The perspective of the case manager is "to allocate services appropriately in a community, use resources wisely for those most in need, document inadequacies of total resources for planning purposes, and introduce system-wide incentives to improve the quality of all care providers in the community" (p. 220). Case managers also participate in social and political actions to enlarge the pool of resources available to potential consumers.

Organizational Alliances for Service Delivery

Federal programs, state bureaucracies, community service networks, and multiservice agencies are all locations where social workers and clients might find necessary resources. But for the uninformed, these potential resource networks can be tangled webs that frustrate, disappoint, and disempower. To avoid this tangle and to function effectively as service brokers, social workers educate themselves about resource systems. They learn policies, eligibility requirements, referral procedures, and appeal processes of the systems which may be important to their clients.

An effective way to learn about other programs and to increase the effectiveness of the network itself is through creating service delivery alliances. Social workers use a variety of strategies to connect with other service organizations. These strategies include building interagency coalitions, developing effective working relationships with other professionals, working on teams, and leading meetings.

Building Interagency Coalitions

"A coalition of agencies is a relatively short-term agreement between agencies to work together on specific issues" (McInnis-Ditrich, 1994, p. 53). Representatives of the agencies come to some agreement about how they can work on a joint initiative to address a particular community issue or an aspect of social service delivery. These ventures are "characterized by mutual benefit, interdependence, reciprocity, concerted action, and joint production" (Abramson & Rosenthal, 1995, p. 1479). McInnis-Dittrich lists several conditions necessary for building successful coalitions among agencies. Each agency must:

- Participate on a voluntary basis
- Retain its autonomy
- Share common goals with other potential coalition members
- Discern the benefits of participating in the coalition

Those leading the effort toward interagency collaboration draw upon numerous skills for the outcome to be successful. Leaders take roles in "setting the tone, assessing and managing the group process, keeping the activity on target, and handling administrative details" (Abramson & Rosenthal, 1995, p. 1485). They also create an appropriate climate, forge members' commitment to the purpose of the collaboration, envision a positive outcome, mediate conflicts effectively, and build consensus among members. An effective leader simultaneously maintains a vision of the whole alliance while understanding the intricacies of the constituent parts.

An interagency coalition includes "multiple perspectives and stakeholders [and] assures that the product, program, or solution will reflect an informed and thorough vision" (Abramson & Rosenthal, 1995, p. 1482). Each project benefits from a broad base of ownership and a diverse pool of expertise. Working with other agencies distributes the costs and responsibilities of new ventures among the coalition members. Successful collaborative efforts are likely to improve the overall communication and linkages between and among agencies. Coalitions also present a united front, with more power to influence decision-makers, legislators, the media, and the general public. "Collaboration is a highly effective approach to service delivery, capable of resolving previously intractable problems and creating innovative and comprehensive interventions" (p. 1486).

Working on Teams

Social workers implement teamwork skills to activate professional alliances and to collaborate effectively with other professionals. When the various components of a service delivery system are working as a team, clients benefit from the harmonious operation of helping systems. A team is:

> *a group of people, each of whom possesses particular expertise and each of whom is responsible for individual decisions and action; team members share a common*

purpose, and meet together to pool knowledge, ideas, and meanings, from which interaction plans are made, actions taken, and future plans influenced. (Brill, 1998, p. 193)

Professionals often work in teams to design programs and services, plan community action efforts, and develop social action strategies. Teams also convene to coordinate work with individual clients or families when several professionals are involved. Efficient team meetings require responsible preparation, effective organization, economical use of time, and respectful participation by team members. Characteristics of effective team members include interpersonal knowledge, values, and skills such as conflict resolution, collaborative problem solving, and communication; and self-management knowledge, values, and skills, such as goal-setting, program management, and planning and task coordination (Stevens & Campion, 1994). Steps for efficient team work include:

- Identifying the problem, including its dimensions and boundaries
- Stating the team's purpose with respect to the defined problem
- Agreeing on goals
- Delineating tasks and specifying which team member "will do what when" for each of these tasks
- Evaluating the outcome, including the achievement of goals as well as the process of work as a team (Brill, 1998)

Leading Effective Meetings

Well-conducted meetings begin with a stated purpose, follow an agenda, and complete business within the specified time. Effective meeting facilitators help participants articulate short- and long-term objectives and delineate clear expectations for the tasks to be accomplished between meetings by individuals, officers, standing committees, ad hoc committees, or staff members. The person leading the meeting also takes responsibility for focusing discussions, encouraging participants to contribute their perspectives, and guiding the discussion toward decisions and actions.

Agendas structure meetings by listing the order of business and specifying items for discussion and action. An agenda serves as a physical reminder of the purpose of the meeting. Typically, it identifies the date and time of the meeting and lists items of business including committee reports, carry-over or "unfinished business," and topics under "new business," and specifies points the group will need to act on through discussion, consensus, or a formal vote.

Wrapping up a meeting is critical for maintaining motivation and progress toward goals. Several activities end meetings effectively:

- Reviewing decisions and plans to help participants reflect on the actions taken and the plans made during the meeting, offering an opportunity to ensure that those who have committed to follow-up tasks know what they are to do
- Agreeing on a date and time for the next meeting and requesting members' input in regard to the agenda

- Incorporating the successes of the present meeting into the future work of the group by encouraging participants to critique accomplishments and suggest areas for improvement (Schwartz, 1994)

To the extent that formal meetings are conducted effectively, participants are likely to continue to invest their time and effort. Conducting effective meetings requires the leader to prepare carefully (see Table 13.3).

Professional Support Networks

Social workers frequently ally themselves with other professionals for support. Supportive professional relationships are usually available within the worker's immediate organizational environment. These relationships are a worker's best ally to avoid burnout. Beyond the agency setting, the resources of professional memberships and connections via computers can also stimulate a worker's professional development and provide a web of support.

Alliances within Organizations

Work settings provide important alliances to support social workers as people and as practitioners. A "one-step removed" perspective offers a fresh look when workers are stumped. Sometimes, the client–social worker relationship falls into unproductive patterns, failing to work efficiently toward goals or to envision a broad range of solutions. In these situations the social worker has several options for assistance. Supervisors provide seasoned expertise and a more objective look at the information workers bring. A review by a team of peers offers a synergistic resource created by group interaction. Consultants can provide a technical view and offer specific information that is unavailable in the worker's knowledge base or particular practice setting.

Supervision

Most social workers, especially beginning practitioners, function in settings that provide ongoing supervision. "When properly used, supervision is part of the profession's responsibility

---

TABLE 13.3　Tips for Leading an Effective Meeting

- Develop an orderly agenda
- Send out timely meeting notices including minutes from the last meeting and the agenda for the upcoming meeting
- Arrange the meeting space to ensure comfort and participation
- Review the agenda before the meeting begins
- Welcome participants as they arrive
- Pace the meeting to complete tasks within the agreed upon time
- Draw upon listening and skills to facilitate discussion
- Thank participants for their involvement in the group's activities and acknowledge the group's accomplishments

---

to monitor its own practice by having the most competent social workers share their knowledge and skills with those who are working toward higher levels of competence" (Konle, 1982, p. 44). At a minimum, supervision requires the worker to be accountable. In its most effective form, supervision accomplishes three purposes: (1) to structure practice by asking the worker to report and reflect on the work with the client system, (2) to provide a support system to reinforce and encourage the work, and (3) to create a forum to identify the worker's strengths and set goals for professional development.

Supervisors employ a variety of helpful analytic tools with workers. Supervisors use techniques such as: modeling, role-playing, concept identification, and forecasting (Fant & Ross, 1983). *Modeling* draws on the similarities of the supervisor–worker relationship with the worker–client relationship. Workers become more sensitive to a client's perspective when having experiences which parallel those of the client. *Role plays* function in a similar way with supervisors taking the roles of workers and workers acting out specific aspects of the client's situation, experientially increasing the worker's empathy and awareness. This also allows the worker to observe the more experienced supervisor in action. Moreover, supervisors integrate the theory and knowledge base of the profession into the unique client information brought by the worker. Using *concept identification,* the supervisors connect their specific observations to the theory which supports them. "This kind of knowledge helps the worker to become creative, use his or her own ideas to demonstrate these principles, and generalize the learning" (p. 243). Finally, supervisors use a technique called *forecasting* to alert workers to what might be coming up by drawing on the supervisor's knowledge of human system behavior and practice experience.

Peer Review

Frequently, social workers participate as members of teams that provide professional support. There are many advantages to peer review. Presenting a client's situation to the team compels the worker to organize information coherently. The questions that team members ask often reveal information gaps for the worker and client to fill. Team members may also notice similarities between the situation presented and experiences with clients of their own and offer suggestions on what they have tried with success in these other situations. Finally, the careful review afforded by the peer consultation process accentuates for clients the importance of their situations.

Consultation

The complexity of human behavior extends beyond the knowledge base of any single professional. Sometimes, workers and clients need more information for a comprehensive assessment, or they need specific expertise to implement an intervention strategy. In these cases, workers seek the assistance of consulting specialists. Useful outside perspectives may include consultants who are psychologists, neurologists, dieticians, attorneys, indigenous healers, and clergy. For macrosystem clients these specialists may be economists, demographers, urban planners, engineers, or sociologists. Consultation usually moves beyond the worker's organizational setting and requires the worker to gain the client's explicit approval and written permission to do so.

Job Stress and Burnout

Empowerment-based social workers function best when their work environments empower them as professionals, support a focus on strengths, and encourage their efforts to collaborate with clients as partners. Work settings designed to cushion stress involve employees in decision making, compliment their success, and enhance their self-efficacy, competence, and sense of professional empowerment. In contrast, when workers lack a sense of control, experience insufficient collegial and supervisory support, and receive little recognition for their accomplishments, such work environments become hotbeds of burnout. High job stress combined with few rewards and scanty involvement in decision-making have profound repercussions for professionals (Arches, 1991; McNeely, 1992; Burnished, 1994; Soderfeldt, Soderfeldt, & Warg, 1995; Barber & Iwai, 1996; Guterman & Bargal, 1996; Brown & O'Brian, 1998; Wharton, 1999). Research studies demonstrate that over-involvement in one's job also leads to burnout (Koeske & Kelly, 1995; Acker, 1999). Furthermore, practitioners who work with persons who have experienced trauma are vulnerable to compassion fatigue (Figley, 1995).

Strict rules and regulations, unreasonable amounts of paperwork, overbearing workloads, and unfavorable physical work environments all increase pressures that can disempower social workers. These work conditions are likely to intensify workers' feelings of immersion in the physical, social, financial, and psychological problems of their clients (Maslach, 1976; Cole, 1999; Maslach & Leiter, 1999). When accumulating demands exceed a worker's tolerance, the likelihood of job burnout increases dramatically. When social workers experience burnout, their personal and professional sense of power dwindles along with their practice competence. Research indicates that workers experiencing burnout are more likely to apply coercive and expert influence strategies (McCarthy & Frieze, 1999).

Burnout takes its toll on workers, clients, and the delivery of social services. Among its serious symptoms is "an orientation to clients characterized by (1) negativism, cynicism, distancing and objectification, (2) inflexibility and rigid adherence to rules, and (3) blaming the victim" (Arches, 1985, p. 16). Practitioners experiencing burnout become less objective, less positive, and less concerned about their clients. Moreover, burnout curtails creativity. The aftermath includes petty and dogmatic thinking as well as oppressive, rigidly bureaucratic behavior (Maslach, 1976). Burnout can also lead to a worker's "loss of idealism, feelings of hopelessness, lowered morale, lack of initiative, absenteeism, alcohol and drug use, and physical and emotional exhaustion" (Dressel, 1992, p. 216). All these consequences are polar opposites to empowerment-based practice.

Responses to Job Stress and Burnout

Workers can counter the effects of work stress and the tendency toward burnout. Social workers can learn to work effectively within bureaucracies, using skills "to capitalize on the possibilities of organizational life" as well as "to neutralize its stresses and dangers" (Pruger, 1978, p. 154). A feminist orientation considers the political context of the worker's practice: "When workers act on a political understanding of their client's problems, they are also more likely to make a political analysis of their own workplace and personal situations and are less prone to self-blame" (Gottlieb, 1992, p. 316). Taking an active role in shaping the work environment is an antidote to burnout.

Stress management experts also recommend numerous personal strategies to counter the effects of stress, including relaxation exercises, guided imagery, meditation, exercise, hobbies, recreational activities, and supportive relationships with family and friends. Cognitive strategies include reframing one's understanding of stressful circumstances as challenges, maintaining a perspective of optimism and hope, and sustaining a keen sense of humor. Studies indicate resiliency-enhancing factors include such characteristics as personal self-efficacy and sense of mission, social support, and recognition for job-related capabilities (Zunz, 1998).

Professional Memberships

Social workers augment their immediate networks of support through their affiliations with professional associations, such as the National Association of Social Workers (NASW) and other special interest organizations. These affiliations enhance professional identity, provide opportunities to exchange ideas, and encourage professional growth through conferences, publications, newsletters, and funding for research. Professional organizations also create opportunities for interdisciplinary coalitions and alliances solidifying a united force for policy and legislative advocacy at the local, state, and federal levels.

More than 153,500 social work professionals hold membership in the NASW, one of the world's largest professional associations (Goldstein & Beebe, 1995). Full membership in the NASW is contingent on graduation from a baccalaureate or master's degree program accredited by the Council on Social Work Education (CSWE). Students in these programs also qualify for membership at a reduced rate. Associate membership is available to human service providers with other educational backgrounds.

The NASW has 56 chapters, one in each state and in Washington, DC, New York City, Puerto Rico, the Virgin Islands, Guam, and an international chapter that serves members in Europe and other parts of the world. Special interest groups within the NASW, such as the National Committees on Minority Affairs, Lesbian, Gay, and Bisexual Issues, and Women's Issues provide opportunities to emphasize the diverse views of the Association's members. To support its membership, the NASW develops standards for various fields of practice, endorses a code of ethics, sponsors local and national conferences and workshops, publishes numerous books and journals, and advocates on Capitol Hill and in state legislatures.

In addition to the NASW, there are numerous other professional organizations and special interest groups that provide support to social workers (Tourse, 1995). Like the NASW, these groups shape professional identity, set standards and monitor practice, provide opportunities for exchanges of ideas and collective endeavors, and foster interdisciplinary relationships. Many publish journals and newsletters (see Table 13.4).

Colleague Assistance

Collegial support cushions the effects of stress, provides a reduction of isolation along with a sense of connection with others, and assuages the effects of burnout. In addition to providing for collegial exchange, professional social support networks offer a safety net for professionals who experience difficulty with stress, drug addiction, or alcohol abuse

TABLE 13.4   Examples of Professional Organizations

American Association of Industrial Social Workers
Baccalaureate Program Directors (BPD)
Child Welfare League of America (CWLA)
Commission on Gay Men/Lesbian Women
Council on Social Work Education (CSWE)
International Association of Schools of Social Work
International Federation of Social Workers (IFSW)
International Council on Social Welfare
National Network for Social Work Managers
National Federation of Societies of Clinical Social Work
National Association of Puerto Rican/Hispanic Social Workers
National Association of Oncology Social Workers (NAOSW)
National Indian Social Workers Association
National Association of Black Social Workers
National Association of Social Workers (NASW)
North American Association of Christians in Social Work
The Society for Social Work Administrators in Health Care

(Reamer, 1992, 1994b). National statistics indicate that at least 10 percent of social work practitioners experience drug addiction or alcohol abuse. Psychological stress and psychiatric disorders create difficulties for others.

The NASW policy statement on "Professional Impairment" recommends lending assistance through programs organized by local NASW chapters (Professional, 1999). Colleague assistance programs offer peer support and encourage workers troubled by psychological stress or chemical dependency to seek professional assistance.

Connections in Cyberspace

There are alliances to support social workers beyond the macrosystem level. A rising global consciousness coupled with advances in communication technology give social workers stimulating new alliances to explore in the "megasystem." The concept of the megasystem expands our consciousness to consider accessing and sharing resources in the international community. It also begins to explore the relevance of the "person:global social and physical environment" realm.

New computer technology broadens the possibilities for social workers to create alliances with other professionals around the world. Social workers can take advantage of this technology to correspond with others via e-mail or participate in listserv discussion groups or other bulletin board systems on the Internet or commercial online services. Accessing information on the World Wide Web is another advantage of computer technology. Web sites contain a wealth of material—U.S. Census Bureau data, financial information, online electronic libraries with full-text articles, directories of local programs and services, notices of conferences and workshops, and information about various colleges and universities. Table 13.5 lists a few examples of WWW sites of interest to social workers.

TABLE 13.5   Examples of World Wide Web Sites

SWAN   http://www.sc.edu/swan/   Social work access network of web connections of interest to social workers

National Institute for Social Work   http://www.nisw.org.uk/   Focuses on international aspects of social work and social care

The New Social Worker   http://www.socialworker.com/   For social work students and recent graduates, features previews of the magazine, tips on job searches, and links to related web sites

Minnesota Center Against Violence and Abuse   http://www.mincava.umn.edu/   Links to bibliographies, papers, video resources, and related web sites

Web of Addictions   http://www.well.com/user/woa/#return_point   Information about drug and alcohol addictions, including facts, resources, and conferences

Institute for Research on Poverty   http://www.ssc.wisc.edu/irp/   Provides links to poverty data, on-line articles, and papers

Reflecting Back

The impetus for managed care has moved from promoting cost-effectiveness in the case plan, to imposing cost-containment criteria on the service package, to restricting service provisions to the least costly service. The effect of managed care on case planning raises a number of concerns. How should social workers respond to the reliance on off-site managed care consultants to approve intervention strategies, to prescribe the term of service, and to require labeling of client behavior for third-party reimbursement? As you contemplate these issues, consider professional ethics and standards of care as explicated by the NASW Code of Ethics (National, 2000), underlying issues of oppression and discrimination, and constraints of agency budgets and their reliance on third-party reimbursement.

Looking Forward

To be empowering, social workers themselves must experience empowerment in the context of their workplace, relationships with colleagues, and everyday professional practice. Workers apply their understanding of power and powerlessness to their own agency system, the service delivery network, and social institutions. In this way, they model effective behaviors for clients, encourage empowerment of staff through worker-led peer-support groups, create innovative programs and a more responsive system for the delivery of services, and engage in social and political action.

Working within the context of the delivery system reveals gaps in service delivery and limited opportunities for clients. Simply dealing with existing resources does not adequately meet current and changing needs. To respond to this scarcity in resources and opportunities, social workers strive to redress social injustices and oppression and enrich the pool of environmental resources. Chapter 14 describes these macrolevel strategies to change policy and legislation, neighborhoods and communities, and social institutions.

C h a p t e r *14*

Expanding Opportunities

All human systems—individuals, families, groups, organizations, and communities—depend on internal resources and environmental opportunities to survive, develop, and change. The interconnections among micro-, mid-, and macrosystems give generalist social workers many intervention options to expand opportunities and work for social change. Sometimes, practitioners and clients develop individually oriented solutions to address the effects of social problems of a particular client system. However, an orientation toward empowerment calls for integrating the profession's social adaptation and social change methodologies into one coherent strategy (Franklin, 1990). Regardless of the system level of the client, generalist practitioners initiate change at multiple system levels. They incorporate macrolevel change strategies which strengthen social policies and enhance community competence into their day-to-day practice of social work.

Think back on some of the practice examples presented in earlier chapters. Damon Edwards and Nate Hardy are two social workers who operate principally with larger systems in ways that ultimately benefit individuals. Damon Edwards facilitates changes in community policy through his work with the residents of Franklin Courts. By successfully changing the city's response to the crisis of lead contamination, Damon and the residents' group will improve the quality of life for the people of Franklin Courts. These policy changes at the community level will benefit other public housing residents in the city as well. Also, consider the example of Nate Hardy of the Northside Development Association. His work to increase the availability of low-cost housing has far reaching benefits for the entire Northside community. Typical of larger system interventions, many people draw from changes made and resources developed at the macrolevel.

Even those workers whose practice focuses primarily on microlevel clients demonstrate concern for expanding opportunities at other system levels. For example, Andrea Barry, who works in family preservation services, is active in the child welfare lobby in her state. Mark Nogales, who works in the field of mental health, represents his agency on a panel of providers who are planning a more coordinated service network for persons with chronic mental illness. Paul Quillin, a social worker in a family agency, is writing a grant to fund a family life education project to implement in the local school district. Kay Landon and Karen McBride, both outreach health care providers, serve on their state NASW chapter's political task force. Each of these generalist social workers puts ecosystemic principles into action by working simultaneously on issues in personal and public domains.

This chapter identifies options for environmental change and offers concrete strategies for social workers and clients to work together to expand opportunities. Specifically, this chapter:

- Clarifies the relationship of opportunities to empowerment
- Explains methods for expanding opportunities through resource mobilization, public education, and grant writing
- Explicates strategies for community organization and development
- Discusses how to formulate and analyze social policy to create more responsive social institutions
- Describes social action and advocacy interventions
- Delineates processes for legislative advocacy including lobbying and legislative testimony
- Presents suggestions for expanding professional resources

All generalist social workers may draw on these methods and strategies whether they work directly with mid- or macrolevel client systems or they look broadly for options to assist microlevel client systems.

Opportunities: Keys to Empowerment

Expanding opportunities in the social structures of society is both ethical and effective social work practice. The profession's mandate for social justice and the NASW *Code of Ethics* (National, 2000) charges social workers to extend opportunities and resources to all citizens, particularly those who are disenfranchised and oppressed. The Code says:

> *Social workers should promote the general welfare of society, from local to global levels, and the development of people, their communities, and their environment. Social workers should advocate for living conditions conducive to the fulfillment of basic human needs and promote social, economic, political, and cultural values and institutions that are compatible with the realization of social justice. (Section 6.01)*

To meet these ethical responsibilities in the broader society, practitioners develop expertise for modifying social and physical environments, drawing upon existing community resources, linking clients with natural helping networks, and creating new resources (Maluccio & Whittaker, 1989; Kemp, Whittaker, & Tracy, 1997). Social workers remain faithful to the core purposes of the social work profession when they return to their social function of linking people with needed resources, solidifying the network of available resources, and involving themselves in community education and community development (Specht & Courtney, 1994). Recognizing that human systems acquire resources through ecosystemic transactions, generalist workers develop the opportunity structures of society.

In empowerment-based practice, the social worker's role is "to open up options, to help clients expand their choices, or to help them become free to consider multiple paths" (Hartman, 1993, p. 504). However, many obstacles exist to locating resources for clients. Among these are constraints in social institutions, economic policies, political practices, ideologies, and the legacy of history. Social workers strive to overcome the risks of these environmental obstacles to enhance environmental opportunities for clients.

Environmental Opportunities

Expanding opportunities means creating new resources for client systems in their social and physical environments. Those ideologies and social institutions that foster individual and societal well-being are *environmental opportunities* (Garbarino, 1983). Examples of such macrosystem opportunities include public support in times of crisis, political support for child welfare, and economic support for residential environments that, in addition to shelter, provide for social and physical needs. These opportunities promise hope in times of challenge and sustain development in everyday adaptations.

Responsive environments enrich social functioning. Access to health care, adequate education, technical training, child care, civil rights, jobs, transportation, and comprehensive community-based services—all enhance the abilities of individual citizens to function effectively and contribute to the general well-being of society. To facilitate empowerment, practitioners create resources in natural helping systems and other mediating structures such as churches and the work place, and influence social policy and social change in political and economic institutions (Zimmerman & Rappaport, 1988). Social workers depend on the opportunities of resource-rich environments to contribute to their clients' sense of power.

Environmental Risks

For some systems, the rainbow of opportunity leads to an empty pot of gold. Oppression, discrimination, and dehumanization disenfranchise many from society's opportunity structures. Shortages and barriers in resource provisions, social inequities, and lack of opportunities create social problems and pose *environmental risks* (Garbarino, 1983). Environmental risks are ideologies or cultural alignments that work against the well-being of individuals and society. Examples of such risks include national economic policies that create inequities and increase poverty for some, social policies that aggravate role strain such as conflicts between work roles and parenting roles, and social patterns that magnify racism, sexism, or other discriminatory practices. In short, a "macrosystem risk is a social event or a pattern that disrupts and impedes the caring community" (p. 15). Limiting environmental risks while expanding environmental opportunities promotes social justice and actualizes empowerment.

Empowerment and Opportunities

Expanding opportunities means promoting client self-sufficiency through social, economic, educational, and political change. It also means eliminating discriminatory barriers that deny access to resources. The NASW *Code of Ethics* (National, 2000) stipulates that: "Social workers should act to expand choice and opportunity for all persons, with special regard for vulnerable, disadvantaged, oppressed, and exploited persons and groups" (Section 6.04b). To expand opportunities in ways that facilitate empowerment, workers and clients implement strategies that enhance clients' sense of mastery as well as their participatory or political competence. This includes activities that expedite clients' access to services by maximizing their rights and removing obstacles in social service delivery. Likewise, at the community level, workers team with clients to expand public services such as transportation, affordable housing, social service outreach, and community education. Most importantly, social workers assertively advocate social change to provide institutional supports in the sociopolitical environment.

An economically and socially stratified society distributes its wealth unequally and systematically denies opportunities for some people to participate in decisions about resource allocations. Breton (1994) explores this disempowering cycle—the lack of resources coupled with the lack of power to affect decisions about resource distribution, describes how this perpetuates oppression, and offers ideas for change:

> There would be no need for empowerment work if there was a just distribution of power and resources in the society, and a just distribution of the opportunities to

participate in the allocation of existing resources and the creation of needed resources, in other words, if we lived in a just society. In a just society, by definition, power and resources would be shared equitably. People who did not know how to exercise their power or were psychologically unable to exercise it, would be taught and/or helped to do so; people who did not access the resources they need or participate in decisions as to their creation and allocation would be encouraged and helped to access these resources, or would be educated to participate in the democratic process whereby decisions are taken by citizens on the creation and allocation of resources. (p. 32)

For those persons who are powerless or oppressed, choices are limited and, too often, control over opportunities and resources rests with the actions of "others" (Barber, 1995). Social workers must be cautious to avoid being one of those "others" who are limiting their clients' choices. Empowerment-oriented social workers maximize clients' involvement in efforts to influence social policy decisions. Clients take their rightful place in controlling their own opportunities through:

- Collective action to achieve a just balance of power targeting socioeconomic, political, and structural systems change.
- Awareness of political responsibilities, recognizing that socioeconomic and political forces shape people's lives and a class-stratified society creates problems for members of marginalized classes.
- Consciousness of the right to have a voice and to exercise that voice.
- Recognition of their own competence, trust in their knowledge and abilities and, in turn, acknowledgment of their competence by others.
- Use of different sources of power—personal, collective, and political—to produce desired results. (Breton, 1994)

Empowerment in Groups and Communities

Group and community methods are particularly important for addressing issues of powerlessness with those who have experienced oppression (Breton, 1994; Lee, 1994; DuBois & Miley, 1999; Miley & DuBois, 1999). The group is "the instrument through which members can develop that sense of community and mutual support which is needed in the process of social change" (Lewis, 1991, p. 32). Social change:

requires the active engagement of members of the vulnerable population, as well as "helpers," professionals, religious, and educators, in this exploration and action. It necessitates a critical mass of adherents working toward a reconstruction of the social fabric, a praxis for change. Member participants in social work groups are a vital part of the praxis for change, and may have the greatest stake in defining and working toward that change. (p. 28)

Group work is key to social action: "Concepts such as 'empowerment' and 'advocacy' suggest lines of development towards a more central role for group work and for social action in group work" (Shapiro, 1991, p. 17).

Group intervention is a prelude to critical consciousness. Developing a critical consciousness is a process of learning to perceive and question social, economic, and political contradictions and take action against oppression. For Freire (1993, 1997), the development of critical awareness, or conscientization, transforms people from a naïve state to critical consciousness. Freire views critical education as a form of networking knowledge. Praxis, or the combination of reflection and action, is a central theme. Critical learning and thinking generate power within individuals; whereas, the process of critical education—reflecting on one's reality, critically examining the world, and engaging in dialogue with others—leads to collective action for social change.

Consciousness-raising is the process of developing a heightened sense of awareness and increased knowledge about oppression and its effects. Consciousness-raising and self-awareness are key components of empowerment at the individual and the interpersonal levels. Individuals who experience similar issues can join together, develop a critical consciousness about their status, and believe that their collective voice can influence change. This same critical consciousness is a prerequisite to collective action and social change (Gutiérrez, 1995). Thus, empowerment-based practice through work with groups and communities addresses issues of oppression at the personal or interpersonal level and institutes corrective actions at the collective or social policy level.

Resource Expansion

Social workers wield their power and encourage clients to do the same in accessing necessary services to meet clients' needs. However, "all the power in the world is useless if the requisite services do not exist" (Dinerman, 1992, p. 4). Sometimes, what people require is simply not there. But, needs must be met one way or another!

Identifying Resource Shortages

The network of social service delivery agencies, organizations, and private practitioners offers significant resources for its clientele. However, given the diversity of human problems and social issues, the ever changing needs of human systems, and the complexities of organizational structures, it is no surprise to discover that gaps and barriers exist in the panorama of services and resources in most communities. Table 14.1 offers guidelines for analyzing a community's human service delivery system.

Many issues contribute to the gaps and barriers in service delivery. DuBois and Miley (1999) detail them as follows:

- *Fragmentation of services* results from ineffective or inefficient planning for programs and services. Clients frequently experience fragmentation when they are involved with multiple providers. Lack of coordination, conflicting recommendations, and differing rules, regulations, and procedures are confusing and create unnecessary burdens with which clients must contend.
- *Agency turf* battles ensue when agencies mark their territories and exert their domains of authority. Competition for clients and funding, and therefore survival, complicates

TABLE 14.1   Framework for Human Service Delivery System Analysis

PART I   CONTINUUM OF NEEDS

1. Identify health and human service needs
2. Delineate the service needs of special populations and ethnic minorities
3. Describe the patterns of needs among various population groups

PART II   CONTINUUM OF SERVICES

1. Inventory informal and formal support services
2. Describe the program parameters and eligibility requirements for each service
3. Describe the structures and opportunities for interagency planning and collaboration
4. Characterize the service delivery network as comprehensive or fragmented; driven by client needs or resource availability

PART III   GAPS AND BARRIERS IN THE SERVICE DELIVERY SYSTEM

1. Assess unmet needs of target population groups in the service delivery system
2. Identify gaps in service delivery
3. Assess physical and social barriers to accessing services
4. Evaluate the effectiveness of the service delivery network as a coordinated system

---

cooperative working relationships and coordinated planning in the overall delivery of services.

- *Bureaucratic disentitlement* is a covert process that curtails public sector programs and services, without the benefit of public hearings, by using policy retrenchments and procedural changes rather than overt budget reductions (Lipsky, 1984).
- *Social triage* classifies clients as "treatable" or "untreatable" and, therefore, judges clients as qualified or unqualified for particular programs and services. Triage responds to the pressures of insufficient funding by attempting to sift out those who would be least likely to benefit from the provision of services (Jenkins, 1983).
- *Privatization* is the trend toward decreasing the spectrum of public sector social services, encouraging instead the development of services in the private sector. At issue is the likelihood of differential services—those for the rich and those for the poor, those for persons with adequate health insurance and those for persons without insurance benefits (Ostrander, 1985; Abramovitz, 1986).
- *Accessibility of services* is fundamental. Transportation and child care constraints, fees for services, limited times for appointments, waiting lists, and the lack of multilingual professionals seriously limit resource accessibility.

Mobilizing Resources

To fill gaps and overcome service delivery barriers, workers mobilize resources in the private and public arenas. Social workers exercising the role of mobilizer assemble people and organizations and marshall their combined energies to achieve mutual goals. As partisans in social conflict, mobilizers act "to animate one's client group to advocate for itself collectively and, at the same time, to advocate as vigorously as possible for that group's interest" (Simon, 1994, p. 164).

In social work practice, "it is not the resource but the resource holder—individual, group, or organization—that one has to act on to gain access to needed services. Therefore, the problem becomes not one of technical manipulation but of interpersonal influence" (Murdach, 1987, p. 503). Mobilization tasks include:

- Knowing the setup
- Dramatizing the issues
- Devising strategies
- Building support
- Maintaining momentum (p. 504)

These tasks are accomplished by bringing together diverse constituencies, opening lines of communication, developing a common agenda, clarifying the direction of goals, and outlining strategies for action. Through mobilizer activities, clients become influential political forces (Simon, 1994).

Educating the Public

Mindful of the importance of educating citizens about a wide range of subjects—including social issues, social policy development, and the availability of social service resources—social workers disseminate information through community education. Community education includes such diverse outreach activities as media promotions, television and radio appearances, public service announcements, newsletter mailings, educational brochures, staffing information booths at community fairs, speaking engagements, and video productions. Even responding to newspaper editorials through opinion editorials provides an opportunity for educating the general public about key issues (Stoesz, 1993). Community education promotes a broader usage of social services and raises community consciousness about issues of concern to social workers and the population groups with whom they work.

Writing Grants

Often the burning question with respect to creating opportunities through innovative social service programs is, "Where will we get the money?" Agencies face tough choices in expanding service delivery. They can either economize within the current budget, switch the program's emphasis from established programs to new services, or expand the agency's funding base. While any of these financial strategies can yield money for new programs, acquiring new sources of funding through grants frequently gains top priority. When agencies receive grants for new programs, they expand resources rather than simply shift them around.

Writing grants requires the same kind of thinking social workers apply to working with client systems, including conducting assessments, developing plans that incorporate measurable objectives, implementing strategies, and evaluating outcomes. Five sections typical of various types of grant applications are:

- The *statement of the problem and needs assessment* section details the identified problem. It answers questions such as who is involved, the extent of the problem, and its financial implications at the federal, state, and local levels. This section of the application also describes the problem as addressed in professional journals, reports, and other relevant documents and discusses what other programs have already tried.

- Grant applications incorporate a section on measurable *goals and objectives* or outcomes the proposed program aims to achieve. The proposal also establishes a baseline from which to measure change.
- The third section specifies the *program activities* designed to meet the stated goals and objectives. In other words, it delineates the "who, what, when, where, and how" for implementing the program.
- The *evaluation plan* typically includes a timeline; describes data collection procedures, names those responsible for collecting the data, and details the methods to be used for analyzing the data; and specifies who will receive the report.
- Grant applications explicate a *budget* for the program proposal, noting sources of additional revenue and "in kind" matches, as well as line item expenditures. (Wolk, 1994)

Successful grant writers follow the instructions for the grant application "to the letter" and consult with designated staff from the funding organization for clarifications.

Community Change

All of us live and work within communities. As community residents, we draw upon the opportunities that our community offers and, in turn, contribute to its economic, political, educational, social, and cultural resources. How well a community supports family life and the extent that its members enrich community life attests to the competence of the community. The nature of this reciprocal exchange between a community and its members determines its need for change and further development:

> *By framing the issue in this way, community becomes an active, rather than passive, concept. Instead of functioning as a shell within which families exist, community becomes a life-giving, resource-rich membrane that sustains and nourishes its members. The primary purpose of a community must be to provide the best possible environment for promoting the well-being of its members. (Weick & Saleebey, 1995, p. 146)*

At times, forces such as a weak economy, restrictive federal and state policies, prejudice and discrimination toward special population groups, and limited health and social service resources mitigate the competence of a community with respect to its total population (Felin, 1995). These external and internal forces become targets of change as social workers focus their efforts to enhance community competence.

Community Theories

Two broad social science perspectives frame social workers' understanding of "community" (Martinez-Brawley, 1995). The *structural perspective* considers the spatial, geographic, and political identities of a community. It views the community as a structure—such as a city, village, or neighborhood—that carries out political or social functions and mediates between individuals and other social structures. The *sociopsychological perspective* regards a community as a network of social bonds, emphasizing the degree of member belongingness. From this point of view, the way people relate to one another and their sense of "we-ness," rather than place or function, define community.

Both perspectives influence social work practice at the community level. From the structural perspective, community change involves realigning social and political structures—a community organizing function. From the sociopsychological perspective, community change enhances relationships and solidarity among community members—a community development function.

Community Organizing

Community organizing is a method social workers use "to help individuals, groups, and collectives of people with common interests or from the same geographic areas to deal with social problems and to enhance social well-being through planned collective action" (Barker, 1999, pp. 90–91).

Empowerment-based social workers tailor the same generalist processes with individuals, families, and groups to structure their community change efforts. These processes, detailed throughout this text, are easily applied to community work, including:

- *Forming partnerships* with community residents, local governmental officials, and other community leaders.
- *Articulating situations* that interfere with the competence of the community.
- *Defining* the purpose and *direction* of the community change strategies.
- *Identifying* relevant community *strengths.*
- *Assessing* community *resource capabilities.*
- *Framing solutions* to address community challenges and unmet needs by planning strategies to facilitate change.
- *Activating* and mobilizing existing community *resources*—people, services, support base.
- *Creating alliances* among and between formal and informal community structures
- *Expanding opportunities* in community institutions through advocacy, policy changes, and resource development.
- *Recognizing* and measuring the *successes* of the community involvement in the organizing effort.
- *Integrating* and stabilizing the *gains* made within the social networks and sociopolitical structures of the community.

Models of Community Organizing

Three classic models of community organizing typify the community-level practice of social work—locality development, social planning, and social action (Rothman & Tropman, 1987). Building on the three traditional modalities of community work, new community practice paradigms feature asset-based community development or community capacity building (Kretzmann & McKnight, 1993), community development corporations (Krumholz, 1999; Clavel & Deppe, 1999), and grassroots organizing (Pilisuk, McAllister, & Roth-man, 1996; Couto, 1998). Local participation and informal support networks are hallmarks of contemporary community-oriented social work.

- *Locality development model*—building a sense of community solidarity among diverse groups and constituencies of citizens so that, collectively, they can resolve community or neighborhood concerns.
- *Social planning model*—researching community needs and developing plans for long-term solutions to substantive community problems.
- *Social action model*—using confrontational tactics to advocate changes that promote social justice and shifts in power structures.
- *Asset-based community development*—drawing upon the capabilities and assets in a neighborhood or community to fuel change through responding to needs, defining social services, and managing resources at the local level.
- *Community development corporations*—assisting families in low-income neighbor-hoods to develop local organizations to redress economic, social, and environmental problems within the catchment area.
- *Grassroots organizing*—generating action from within neighborhoods and communi-ties through the efforts of indigenous local leaders and their neighborhood or commu-nity constituents.

The Role of the Community Organizer

As community organizers, social workers promote the interpersonal and political develop-ment of constituency groups and facilitate change at the neighborhood, community, and so-cietal levels. Practitioners "work as consultants, planners, grant developers, or active leaders, and they usually seek to help community members achieve social justice, economic or social development, or other improvement" (Barker, 1999, p. 91).

Community organizers today initiate many of the same activities they have in the past: they bring diverse constituencies together to dialogue about issues they have in common; they bridge differing agendas; they promote grassroots leadership development; they use empowering strategies to develop a critical consciousness; and they encourage collective action. "Among the organizer's most valuable skills remains the ability to challenge the ac-cepted vision of things" (Fisher & Kling, 1994, p. 19). In other words, community organiz-ers in the new social movement arena, like their historical counterparts, question the status quo. They call for re-examining the assumptions that stabilize social structures and the so-cietal values that perpetuate them.

Community Development

In contrast to community organization, which focuses on community structures and func-tions, community development focuses on the sociopsycholgical functioning of a commu-nity. Community development activities are "efforts made by professionals and community residents to enhance the social bonds among members of the community, motivate citizens for self-help, develop responsible local leadership, and create or revitalize local institutions"

(Barker, 1999, p. 90). Community development enhances community competence by increasing the involvement of citizens in community life.

People Require Opportunities: A Practice Example

As a way to understand the impact of community development, consider the two very different scenarios that explore how Raymond meets his needs in ways that match what the community environment has to offer. First, think of Raymond as a young man who is really moving up in the world. His success in working security has led to his position in sales. His skill in sales has shown the top brass his growing abilities in management. Clearly, Raymond is a natural leader who has opportunities to exercise and develop his potential. Less than a year ago, Raymond was just another poor kid from the wrong part of town. Fifteen years old, confined by poverty, and intimidated by the roving gangs in his Northside neighborhood, Raymond's life looked like it had no future. There seemed to be no way out. But, then, "opportunity" fell into his lap when Terrence introduced him to the War Lords.

Raymond knew about the War Lords before he became acquainted with Terrence. The War Lords were one of three gangs that roamed and ruled Raymond's neighborhood. Raymond thought that the gangs had always been a part of his neighborhood, but his mother told him that the gangs showed up recently, just when people thought things couldn't get any worse. But, the gangs made it worse, or so Raymond's mother said.

Raymond had his own ideas about the War Lords; they were his ticket out. Before the War Lords, Raymond felt trapped. Now, Raymond felt a sense of belonging and some control over his life. Running with the War Lords, he was enjoying money from illegal ventures, the safety of tough and loyal friends, and the power of gang membership. Raymond believed his mother didn't really understand the realities of life when she said that she trusted her faith, hard work, and the family to get her "somewhere." After all, that "somewhere" was a cramped unit of public housing in a neighborhood that was under siege each time the sun went down.

From the outside looking in, joining a gang doesn't make much sense. But, Raymond's view of life holds little promise elsewhere. Like all human beings, Raymond seeks emotional and economic security, the freedom to develop his abilities, and the chance to be a success. And, the way Raymond sees it, the War Lords provide the only path to those goals. While gangs are certainly antisocial and threatening, viewed from another perspective, they provide what their members perceive as plausible opportunities for security and success. Given other genuine choices, Raymond may be able to avoid the lure of gang membership. Social workers have responsibilities to create those choices. The press for social justice compels workers to develop opportunities, particularly for those who, like Raymond, are disenfranchised and oppressed.

Now, imagine a different scenario for Raymond's story, one in which other opportunities are available, where Raymond has choices, and the neighbors have hope. Here, too, Raymond is really moving up in the world. His good work as a cashier at Northside Center Grocery has led to his new position as the night manager. His position as night manager pays more than running the register and gives Raymond opportunities to show the store manager his talents in public relations and the quick way he masters new responsibilities. He is developing marketable skills, building a good job record, and making money, too. In fact, Raymond is beginning to feel like he has some control over his life. Just one short year ago, Raymond didn't see a future for himself. Stuck in a deteriorating Northside neighborhood with no money and no plans—even joining a gang had started to seem like his only real option. But, that was before Northside Center opened and Raymond discovered he has some real choices.

A community development effort generated the original idea for Northside Center. After receiving a parcel of land, city leaders polled residents in Raymond's neighborhood for ideas about what to do with the property. Results revealed an overwhelming need for convenient neighborhood businesses and services, as families had to travel long distances just to take care of basic needs—like buying groceries, filling prescriptions, and doing laundry. Community groups, social agencies, and city leaders combined their efforts to make the neighborhood's dream a reality in the opening of Northside Center, a small mall with a grocery store, a pharmacy, and a laundromat.

These early businesses were just the beginning. Last summer, business expanded to include a farmer's market. A startling success, the market drew customers and vendors from all parts of the city and the surrounding rural areas, bringing together people who otherwise would be leading totally separate lives. Northside Center also added a community service agency which coordinates neighborhood social services and recreational activities and provides local residents with information and referral services. It was at the drop-in center that a group of neighbors initiated plans for a watch program to deter gang activity.

Developed as a partnership of local businesses, city leaders, social service agencies, and community members, Northside Center does more than bring the convenience of groceries, medicine, and laundry back to the neighborhood. It expands opportunities for employment, builds relationships among neighbors, and reconnects the Northside neighborhood to the larger community. And, Raymond is reaping the benefits of this new opportunity, too. He has a job and plans for the future.

Empowerment and Community Development

Empowerment-oriented community development incorporates two core strategies: "promoting the participation of community members in the change process with a focus on self-initiative and providing technical assistance to enable leadership development" (Zippay, 1995, p. 263). Clearly, it is important to organize *with* members of a community in a collaborative sense, rather than *for* them in a patriarchal sense. Community members participating in development efforts acquire a critical consciousness about the needs of the community as a whole and the benefits of collective action. Community organizers promote indigenous leadership, provide leadership development training, and offer a range of proven organizing strategies.

Community Organizing in Minority Communities

Minority communities have a long history of activating informal supports of families and neighbors as well as formal networks of churches and fraternal organizations to meet individual and community needs through self-help programs (Austin & Lowe, 1994). To redress institutional racism, confront oppression, and secure civil rights, professional organizers build upon the self-help traditions in minority communities.

The community development worker establishes legitimacy by joining with the community through invitations or endorsements (Pantoja & Perry, 1998). Rivera and Erlich (1998) summarize important qualities for the success of organizers in racially and culturally diverse communities. In addition to sharing similar cultural and racial characteristics with the community with which they are working, organizers:

- Are familiar with the culture of the community including its values, belief systems, and traditions
- Possess linguistic competence in language style and subgroup slang of the ethnic community members
- Convey collaborative leadership styles
- Are adept in analyzing the power dynamics, mediating influences, and the economic relationship between the ethnic community and the wider community
- Bring practice wisdom and professional knowledge about the record of success and failures of organizing activities
- Are skillful in using concientization and empowerment strategies in disenfranchised communities
- Are capable of analyzing the psychological makeup of the community
- Understand the dynamics of organizational functioning and decision-making
- Are adept at evaluating community problems and trends and involving community members in participatory research
- Are skillful administrators in planning, developing, and managing programs
- Recognize their own abilities, intentions, and limits

Policy Development

Throughout their careers, social work professionals discuss policy issues, and social workers, on their own and collectively through professional associations like the NASW, are in positions to frame public policy and debate the consequences of policy directives. Direct service practitioners have at their fingertips key information about social problems gleaned from their front-line experiences. They also have ideas about causes of and solutions to those problems. Because of their close proximity to consumers of social services, workers witness the intentional and unintentional effects of policies on social service delivery in general and their clients in particular. In committing to social justice and expanding opportunities, social workers use the information they accrue to make policy concerns an integral aspect of their professional practice.

Policy Analysis and Change

Social policy analysis involves studying and evaluating those public policies which are intended to address citizens' needs or to redress identified social problems. Social workers monitor legislation or other forms of policy during its development to analyze its intent and anticipate its potential consequences. During the phase of policy development, workers can offer critical data to shape the direction of the policy. After the implementation of a policy, social workers can assess its actual impact on targeted populations, measure the degree to which it achieves its goals, examine its short- and long-term consequences, evaluate its social implications, and determine its cost-effectiveness.

As policy analysts, social workers examine the social, economic, and political variables evident in the process of formulating policies, study the values and preferences that those policies reflect, and analyze the legalities as well as the costs and benefits of implementing the policies (Gilbert & Terrell, 1998; Barker, 1999). Many authors propose comprehensive models for policy analysis (Prigmore & Atherton, 1986; Martin, 1990; Karger & Stoesz, 1998; Gilbert & Terrell, 1998; Chambers, 1993; DiNitto & Dye, 1999). Table 14.2 highlights the major components of a policy analysis.

Consumer Participation in Policy Development

As identified stakeholders in social welfare policy and agency services, social workers *and their clients* must find meaningful ways to participate in the policy process—from clarifying issues to setting priorities to formulating, implementing, and evaluating policies. Meaningful citizen participation requires "the active, voluntary engagement of individuals and groups to change problematic conditions and to influence policies and programs that affect the quality of their lives or the lives of others" (Gamble & Weil, 1995, p. 483). Empowerment-based practice presupposes that consumers will be directly involved in developing policies at all levels—from those of local agencies to those of national organizations and the federal government.

> *The responsibility of social workers to see that clients' voices are heard and understood by policymakers and to work for inclusion of clients in policy-making becomes*

TABLE 14.2   Framework for Policy Analysis

PART I   POLICY SPECIFICATIONS

1. Detail the history of the policy under study and related policies
2. Describe the problems that the policy will redress
3. Identify the social values and ideological beliefs embedded in the policy
4. State the goals of the policy
5. Summarize the details of the policy regarding implementation, funding, eligibility criteria, and other stipulations

PART II   POLICY FEASIBILITY

1. Identify projected outcomes of the policy
2. Discuss the political and economic feasibility of the policy
3. Characterize the support or dissent for the policy
4. Assess the ramifications of the policy for the existing health and human service delivery structures

PART III   POLICY MERITS

1. Assess the effectiveness and efficiency of the implementation of the policy
2. Weigh the social costs and consequences of the policy
3. Evaluate the differential effects of the policy on diverse population groups
4. Judge the merits of the policy

clear when the focus is put on the strengths rather than the deficits of the people for whom the policies and programs are developed. (Chapin, 1995, p. 509)

Many opportunities exist for active citizen participation. Broad-based constituent involvement in strategic planning, community forums, brainstorming sessions, and consumer advisory groups are all mechanisms for involving a variety of interested parties, including clients, in policymaking. Interested individuals and public interest groups contact political leaders to share information and experiences about a policy issue. Issues networks form in particular policy arenas, bringing different sets of players together as issues change or attention shifts from one policy to another (White, 1994).

Agency Policy and Consumer Participation

When consumers participate in developing agency policy, it safeguards their rights as clients, secures the relevancy of program services, and holds agencies accountable to their constituencies. Consumer participation may "curb the career and professional self-interest of staff members" and "constrain policy decisions toward the needs of clients rather than the needs of the community or the service delivery staff" (Chambers, 1993, p. 209). Also, including client–consumers on advisory committees and boards of directors increases the congruence of agency goals with those of social service consumers (Turner, 1994).

Individual consumers who participate in policy development benefit from the self-growth, increased feelings of personal control, and networks of cooperative relationships that develop. Factors that increase the likelihood of consumers' successful participation include a clear mandate for their participation, a power base from which to assert their right to participate, and recognition of their legitimacy as spokespersons.

Social service consumers can be involved in several aspects of organizational development, including:

- Defining service delivery procedures and setting agency policies
- Participating in program evaluation
- Influencing the direction of strategic planning
- Presenting testimony on proposed social policy and legislative changes
- Helping in fundraising activities
- Identifying new areas for service initiatives
- Participating on staff and administrative hiring committees
- Serving on advisory committees and boards of directors

Involving clients in making policy decisions requires that social workers provide technical knowledge rather than direct the process as rational experts (O'Donnell, 1993). For example, workers support effective group decision-making to analyze the situation, refine goals and objectives, and develop plans of action. Workers and clients function as partners, recognizing that the authority for decision-making in this process rests with clients.

Social Activism and Social Advocacy

Accessible and equitable resources in the social, economic, educational, and political institutions of society directly affect persons' ability to achieve an optimal level of social functioning. Social activism is a strategy to redress the inequities that result from differential social status, resource distribution, and power. The NASW *Code of Ethics* (National, 2000) makes clear the expectation that social workers will utilize social and political action as a means to guarantee access to resources and opportunities for all persons. To ensure fair access to existing rights, entitlements, and resources, generalist practitioners work toward creating opportunities in macrolevel systems through social action and advocacy.

A Heritage of Social Reform

Social action and social advocacy permeate the early history of the social work profession. Seeking to address social problems associated with industrialization, urban overcrowding, and immigration, settlement house workers utilized their research and community organizing skills to initiate social change.

> *By the turn of the century, the South End Settlement House in Boston, Henry Street in New York, and university settlements in both New York and Chicago had become centers for research, discussion, and political agitation to improve urban conditions. They led fights for better housing laws, shorter work hours, and improved working conditions. They also conducted surveys and distributed research reports that became the intellectual basis for some of the period's social legislation. (Franklin, 1990, p. 62)*

Even the micro-oriented Charity Organization Society recognized the effects of environmental conditions and focused attention on public issues such as unemployment and housing and their effect on individuals.

Throughout the twentieth century, many professionals carried on this tradition of social action and social reform. Among the most noteworthy is Bertha Capen Reynolds, a social activist and advocate who instilled in her students and colleagues the necessity for political activity, social advocacy, and other pursuits of social justice. Writing about social casework, Reynolds (1951) described it as helping "people to test and understand their reality, physical, social and emotional, to mobilize resources within themselves and in their social environment to meet their reality or change it" (p. 131).

With the recent trend toward privatization, some people question whether activism remains central to social work practice. Many social workers say "Yes!" A study of activism among social work professionals found that "participation in the profession and commitment to values of professionalism were associated with activism" (Reeser, 1991, p. 1). Social workers who identify strongly with their profession are likely to reflect social work's heritage of social action.

Promoting Social Action

A strong commitment to social justice, egalitarian values, and the ability to take risks are professional ingredients that prompt social workers to social action. Successful advocates:

- Build a consensus among stakeholders regarding the need for change
- Develop agreement among stakeholders as to the nature of the desired outcome

- Explore issues in the context of the whole community system
- Recognize that community problems are interrelated, and that solutions in one arena may lead to solutions in others
- Find pathways for working outside of adversarial systems
- Adopt a strengths-focused perspective that identifies assets, capacities, and opportunities, rather than a problem-focused perspective that restricts its vision to liabilities, issues, and limitations (Flower, 1998)

Advocacy Role

Advocates work to achieve social justice by empowering people to speak out and exercise their influence to correct inequity. "In matters of social injustice, the realm of public affairs should become a political domain where people can be enabled to represent their own interests" (Rees, 1991, p. 145). Achieving social change through advocacy that empowers requires the active partnership of citizens who are vulnerable or disenfranchised with professionals who recognize the public issues inherent in personal troubles. This banding together to advance social purpose of the profession "provides the opportunity for empowerment, for active, responsible participation in the social or public realm" (Lewis, 1991, p. 28). Advocates speak on behalf of clients and encourage clients to speak for themselves when situations deny them rights and entitlements. Ezell (1994) conducted research on social workers' use of advocacy activities in their practice. Included among those identified as frequently used are informing clients of their rights, advocating improvements in service delivery, empowering clients to advocate on their own behalf, promoting agency policies that respect clients' rights, and engaging in public education on social issues.

Advocacy efforts can focus either on protecting the interests of individual clients or on the general issues of collective causes. As you recall from Chapter 12, case or client advocacy refers to working on behalf of one's client or client group to obtain needed services or social welfare entitlements. In contrast, class or cause advocacy seeks to redress collective issues through championing social reform and developing responsive social policies.

On the surface, these two types of advocacy seem separate and distinct in purpose and action. Indeed, case advocacy is usually associated with microlevel practice, while cause advocacy is an important component of macrolevel practice. Yet it is often the experience of microlevel work that provides the impetus for macrolevel change. There is an essential relationship between micro- and macrolevel practitioners in successful advocacy efforts:

> *The class advocate cannot bring about change without needed data from case advocates who have a clear understanding of the effect of social policy on individual clients. Changing policy is time consuming and slow. The micro social worker does not always have the time to address policy change and therefore must rely on the macro practitioner to work for social justice. (Mickelson, 1995, p. 97)*

Significant interconnections exist between case and cause advocacy. Practitioners play important roles in teaming with clients to intervene at the mid- and macrolevel (Wood & Middleman, 1991). To involve clients in advocacy efforts, workers provide them with pertinent information, use consciousness-raising strategies to help clients understand the impact of the sociopolitical and economic systems on their situations, ensure client access to existing agency services and entitlements, and argue with decision makers for expanded client entitlements and new services. Importantly, workers help them organize into groups to push for their rights and entitlements en masse, since supportive alliances of people with similar concerns provide a sense of power.

Designing Advocacy Interventions

Whether case or cause advocacy, the process begins by identifying the particulars of the injustice:

> *The decision to pursue the advocacy of a case or a cause, or a combination of both, will usually have been preceded by the identification of an injustice which it is felt cannot be rectified simply by efficient administration or negotiation. The identification of an injustice and the sense of conviction that the removal of this injustice should become a priority, even in a congested workload, goes hand in hand with the advocacy process. It is not sufficient merely to recognize an injustice. You have to believe that this issue should be fought for, and if necessary over a long period of time. (Rees, 1991, p. 146)*

The knowledge, skills, values, and processes of generalist practice apply to a social worker's advocacy efforts regardless of the particular system targeted for change. In designing advocacy interventions, social workers consider numerous variables, including:

- At what social system level do advocates *define the problem*? For instance, does the problem reflect a personal need, a relationship difficulty, a social service delivery gap, an interorganizatonal conflict, or an inequitable social policy?
- What is the *objective* of the intervention? For example, is the purpose of the advocacy effort to entitle clients to available services or to expand the pool of resources?
- What is the *target system* for the advocacy intervention? In some situations, this may be the advocate's own agency, another organization, or a social institution. Advocates evaluate the positive or negative nature of their relationship with decisionmakers in the system targeted for change.
- What *sanction,* right, or authority does the worker have to intervene in a targeted system? Legal rights, judicial decisions, and client entitlements all provide leverage for advocacy efforts.
- What *resources* are available? Sound advocacy requires resources such as the worker's professional expertise, political influence, credibility, and negotiating skills as well as clients' expertise and supports.
- How likely will the target system be *receptive* to the advocacy effort? Typically, when target systems consider the advocacy "legitimate," reasonable, or lawful, they are more receptive to negotiating change.
- What *level of intervention* is necessary to achieve the desired outcome? Different levels include policy changes, procedural or administrative modifications, and alterations in discretionary actions taken by management or staff.

- Who is the *object of the advocacy* intervention? Depending on the cause, individuals with whom the advocate intervenes may range from the direct service worker, to an agency administrator, to a regional organization, to a legislative body.
- What *strategies or modes of intervention* are appropriate to achieve the desired objectives? Advocates may assume roles as adversaries, negotiators, or collaborators. They employ a variety of intervention techniques such as mediating disputes, building coalitions, negotiating differences, and exchanging information.
- What can advocates learn from the *outcomes of prior advocacy efforts*? Advocates glean information from both their successes and failures. (McGowan, 1987)

Political Awareness

Social work by nature is a political profession (McInnis-Dittrich, 1994). Social workers use the political strategies of consensus-building, compromise, negotiation, and even conflict to resolve inequities in the allocation of social welfare services and to achieve social justice.

Our perception of problems as either personal or public, how we assign blame and responsibility, and our preferences for change strategies all depend on our political ideals. At the societal level, social welfare policy and social change activities are shaped by the tension among factions representing the liberal, conservative, and radical perspectives.

Liberal

Liberals vigorously campaign for social policies that champion fundamental human rights and social equality. Key priorities include safeguarding political and civil liberties through economic freedom and democratic participation. Liberals believe that all citizens should have opportunities to participate fully in society but also recognize how social problems that disrupt personal social functioning sometimes curtail citizen participation. Advocating public responsibility for addressing root causes of social injustice, liberal ideology promotes governmental solutions. Thus, liberals view social welfare programs as a citizen's right and a legitimate function of the government.

Neoliberalism surfaced in response to the resounding defeat of liberal politicians in the 1970s and 1980s. Neoliberalism favors reducing government expenditures and encouraging partnerships with private entrepreneurs to accept increased responsibility for ensuring citizens' welfare (Karger & Stoesz, 1998). Neoliberals advocate privatization or the administration of social welfare programs by private businesses and corporations rather than the government.

Conservative

The conservative position reveals an individualistic perspective based on Western values such as rugged individualism and the work ethic. Conservatism embraces a capitalistic free-market economy and the preservation of social stability through existing institutional structures. This view deems problems as public only when the stability of societal structures is threatened and, even then, offers solutions that foster individual rather than social change. Since conservatives believe problems result from personal failure, they limit governmental support of social welfare to temporary services so as not to destroy individual initiative.

Like the neoliberals, conservatives support privatization of social services through efforts such as voluntary charities, self-help organizations, and business corporations.

Neoconservatives actively oppose welfare programs (Karger & Stoesz, 1998). They propose a needs-based approach which requires workfare, compels familial responsibility for dependents, and switches responsibility for welfare from the federal government to state and local governments and the private sector (Anderson as cited in Karger & Stoesz, 1998). This view faults megastructures, such as big government and big business, for social problems. Neoconservatives want to contain government programs, increase private sector responsibility for the welfare burden, and use mediating structures such as neighborhoods, voluntary associations, and churches as sources of change (Berger & Neuhaus, 1977).

Radical

The radical perspective holds society responsible for social inequities and advocates redressing these inequities through change in the institutional fabrics of society. Radicals believe that problems in living generate from social structures rather than from within individuals themselves. Furthermore, radicalism posits that, instead of contributing to social justice, conventional public social welfare oppresses, stigmatizes, and regulates the poor and disadvantaged (Piven & Cloward, 1971). Changing these oppressive conditions requires sweeping macrostructural reform to construct a noncapitalistic welfare state in which all citizens share societal benefits equally.

Social Work and Political Perspectives

Methods to achieve the profession's mandate for social justice draw from divergent political, economic, and social ideologies. While social workers are not expected to adopt a singular viewpoint, clarifying their particular ideological and political positions is essential to professional practice.

No one political ideology represents the social work position. In fact, social workers' duties of social control often conflict with their pursuits of social reform. Regarding this conflict, workers "need to understand and utilize both control and reform types of strategies, principles, and procedures, as they are appropriate in helping situations. Social work practice needs both conservative and radical contributions" (Siporin, 1980, p. 524). While we may be tempted to forge our ideas about social policy into one political mold, the dialogue that results from various political perspectives generates creative tension, clarifies positions, and revitalizes the social work profession.

Legislative Advocacy

Pressing for change in public policies requires advocacy in the context of legislative activities. In today's political and economic climate, everything social workers and their clients do is affected by legislation and social policies. The dearth of funding, the glut of problems, and the competition among programs make legislative advocacy skills vital to everyday practice. Strategies and skills for legislative advocacy include legislative analysis, lobbying, and legislative testimony.

Legislative Analysis

Numerous pieces of legislation interest social work professionals including diverse laws related to child welfare, health care reform, education, public welfare, mental health, and emergency relief services. Social workers focus on five areas to analyze legislative proposals: substantive issues, committee structure, fiscal requirements, political dimensions, and support and opposition relative to the legislative initiative (Kleinkauf, 1989).

To analyze substantive issues, legislative advocates consider the status of current laws and regulations, extent of proposed changes, constituency affected, potential ramifications, and the inherent social work value issues. Since proposed legislation is assigned to specific *legislative* committees that hold hearings, social workers identify the members of relevant committees and ascertain their positions on social work issues. The *fiscal analysis* of the proposed legislation reviews the results of the findings of the committee on the costs of implementing the sources of funds. Social workers ensure that sound fiscal analysis considers "human" as well as monetary costs. Estimating the likelihood that the bill will gain enough support to pass means scrutinizing its *political status.* This involves reviewing the way in which it was initiated, surveying the position of key legislators, and evaluating plans supporting its passage. Social workers identify which governmental agencies are affected, list those individuals and systems which *support or oppose* the bill, and summarize the major points of their positions. By thoroughly investigating these key areas, workers can evaluate a bill's chances for passage and estimate the impetus for mobilizing political action to support or oppose it.

Lobbying

Lobbying is any political activity that seeks to sway the plans of lawmakers and government officeholders for legislative and public policy. Lobbyists attempt to persuade lawmakers to draft legislation favorable to their special interest positions.

Professional staff lobbyists employed by the NASW carry out many of the lobbying functions for the social work profession. The Educational Legislative Action Network (ELAN) serves as a communication and action network for the congressional districts of the NASW's various chapters. Another NASW-sponsored initiative, Political Action for Candidate Election (PACE), tracks the voting records of legislators and promotes political awareness and lawful action by the NASW membership.

Social workers take five basic steps to prepare for lobbying activities:

1. Assess strengths and limitations with respect to commitment, time, sponsors, alliances, and information regarding the policy context and related strategic processes.
2. Set the action agenda by estimating goals for change, priorities, and fallback positions.
3. Identify target policymakers, including their motivations and the values that underlie their definition of issues.
4. Gather and evaluate evidence by checking the credibility of one's sources.
5. Prepare a case that describes the issue; argues from a definition, cause-effect, or action perspective; and presents a rebuttal. (Richan, 1996)

Successful lobbying encompasses diverse activities and tasks (Mahaffey, 1982). Workers first must keep track of pertinent legislation as well as legislative committee activities, plans, and decisions. Workers may even offer legislators technical assistance and expertise.

Most importantly, lobbyists build coalitions. They cultivate liaisons between organizational sponsors and legislators. To accomplish this connection, lobbyists train and organize a cadre of social workers to become politically involved by writing letters, making phone contacts, and testifying at legislative hearings.

Too often the public policy debate frames issues as struggles between competing interests, pitting the middle class against the poor or care for the aged against care for children. Blecher and Hegar (1991) advocate advancing empowerment-based social welfare by featuring the values that underlie policy options rather than a competing struggle for limited resources. They say: "By emphasizing a collective role in meeting common human needs that cut across class lines, social work can help demonstrate that empowerment for anyone is linked with the empowerment of others" (p. 50).

Legislative Testimony

At public hearings sponsored by legislators or public officials, social workers and their clients can ask questions about newly proposed or adopted policies and express opinions on important social issues. Public hearings are often mandated by law. Additionally, the general public may demand a hearing be held to discuss controversial issues if one has not been scheduled.

When presenting testimony before legislative committees and at public hearings, clients and social workers may share written or oral statements about their own experiences and expertise. More often than not, clients who tell their own stories have the most powerful effect on lawmakers. Speaking in their own voices from their own experiences and on their own behalf, clients can effectively address the merits of particular social service programs and the probable impact of proposed bills.

To maximize the desired impact of legislative testimony, social workers follow these guidelines:

- Conduct substantive and procedural research on pending bills or policy by reviewing existing related statutes, gathering information that refutes or supports it, figuring the costs of its implementation, learning the position taken on the bill by those governmental offices or organizations that will ultimately be affected by its passage, and tracking its passage through committees.
- Analyze the committee's membership, political affiliations, and constituencies for sources of influence and support.
- Prepare factual testimony or a position paper that expresses the general opinion of the group or organization that you represent.
- Testify calmly and with straightforward information.
- Answer questions directly and from an informed knowledge base without claiming more expertise on the issue than you possess.
- Follow up by providing promised additional materials or documentation and continue to track the bill through the various assigned committees. (Kleinkauf, 1981)

When social workers prepare written testimony, their finished documents should be clear and understandable, free of jargon, based on facts and logic rather than use humor or hostility, and focus exclusively on the proposed legislation (Sharwell, 1982).

Successful Legislation: The Americans with Disabilities Act

The results of legislative advocacy can be dramatic. The Americans with Disabilities Act of 1990 (ADA, Public Law 101-596) exemplifies legislation with far-reaching significance for making environmental modifications in areas such as employment, architecture, commercial facilities, and telecommunications.

The ADA, which went into effect on July 25, 1992, expands opportunities for over 43 million citizens in the United States with physical or mental disabilities. The ADA intentionally confronts discrimination experienced by persons with disabilities and is comparable to the nondiscrimination protection afforded by Title VII of the Civil Rights Act of 1964 for race, sex, national origin, and religion (Asch & Mudrick, 1995). As the ADA states:

> *Individuals with disabilities continually encounter various forms of discrimination, including outright intentional exclusion, the discriminatory effects of architectural, transportation, and communication barriers, overprotective rules and policies, failure to make modifications to existing facilities and practices, exclusionary qualification standards and criteria, segregation, and relegation to lesser services, programs, activities, benefits, jobs, or other opportunities. (sec. 2, a 5)*

In response, the ADA elucidates these national goals with respect to the rights of individuals with disabilities: "to assure equality of opportunity, full participation, independent living, and economic self-sufficiency for such individuals" (sec. 2.1, 8).

Legislation and Social Justice

To recognize the impact of beneficial legislation on human rights, consider the ADA's guarantee of equalized access to employment. The employment section of the ADA requires employers to make "reasonable accommodation," which entails:

> *(a) making existing facilities used by employees readily accessible to and usable by individuals with disabilities; and (b) job restructuring, part-time and modified work schedules, reassignment to a vacant position, acquisition or modification of equipment or devices, appropriate adjustment or modifications of examinations, training materials or policies, the provision of qualified readers or interpreters, and other similar accommodations for individuals with disabilities. (sec. 101, 9)*

Furthermore, the law specifically prohibits discrimination against persons with disabilities: "No covered entity shall discriminate against a qualified individual in regard to job application procedures, the hiring, advancement, or discharge of employees, employee compensation, job training, and other terms, conditions, and privileges of employment" (sec. 102, a).

Social Work and the ADA

This public policy provides the foundation for advocating the rights of persons with disabilities. However, ethical social workers carefully distinguish between their role and the role of legal professionals. Woody (1993) differentiates these roles, indicating that the purpose of human service professionals is "to *advance understanding* of the ADA-based rights in the minds of the person with a disability and his or her family members, and it is the purpose of the attorney to *advance the legal interests* of the person with a disability" (p. 76).

Social workers advocate for just social legislation and inform clients of the implications of legislative action. However, practitioners leave the legal protection of clients' rights to those qualified to provide such services.

Social workers with the assistance of community advocates for disability rights can and should encourage their own agencies to

> *audit their physical facilities and evaluate their policies, practices, and procedures to ensure that they do not discriminate against individuals with disabilities in the delivery of services either by denying them services or by failing to provide the service in the most integrated setting. (Orlin, 1995, p. 236)*

Agencies may need to pay particular attention to enhancing the means of communication with persons who have hearing, speech, or vision impairments to ensure that clients with these disabilities can be actively involved in resolving their own situations.

Resources for Professionals

By identifying and filling service delivery gaps, advocating social change, influencing legislative policy, or modifying physical environments, workers themselves function as valuable resources in their clients' environments. Similarly, when workers invest in their own development, they expand their own resourcefulness and indirectly increase opportunities for their clients. Workers develop their own professional resources through staff development, continuing education, and professional reading.

Staff Development Training

Staff development training provides educational opportunities within the context of the agency setting for employees and volunteers. Staff development activities range from initial orientations to the agency's policies, procedures, programs, services, and specific practice modalities to more advanced training sessions. The agenda for staff development activities matches the agency's goals and identified training needs. Training modules sometimes deal with abstract ideas such as the implications of the strengths perspective for practice and, at other times, with concrete instruction such as the use of particular assessment instruments, reporting forms, or practice evaluation tools. To keep pace with developing knowledge and skills, many agencies incorporate ongoing staff development into their normal operations.

Continuing Education

Social work professionals expand their own base of resources by participating in educational experiences. In fact, regulating bodies and professional organizations consider continuing education so vital that they require it for licensure and other accreditation renewals.

Some agencies offer continuing education funding as a part of their employee benefit packages. Opportunities vary including participating in workshops, going to professional conferences, and taking additional academic courses. Each offers the benefits of professional renewal and the support of colleagues with similar interests.

Professional Reading

Complementing the resources of more formal educational opportunities, professional reading expands our knowledge and stimulates innovative practice (Table 14.3). Reading enriches practice with new ideas and scientific research. Bibliographies about specific topics of interest to social work professionals are available through the NASW, CSWE, Families International, Inc., and Child Welfare League of America (CWLA). Computerized searches such as ERIC or Dialogue, the indexed article summaries available in *Social Work Abstracts,* and sources on the World Wide Web also lead to a wealth of current reference materials. Cultivating efficient library skills benefits academic pursuits as well as professional careers.

Reading Research Literature

Reading research literature increases a worker's knowledge of social work practice, an endeavor that will certainly have indirect benefits for clients as well. Educated social workers become familiar with the structure of research articles in order to understand the article and ensure accuracy when they apply the information to their practices.

Research articles follow some type of standardized format, such as that prescribed by the American Psychological Association (APA). Published research articles typically include a/an:

- Abstract that highlights salient research issues and key findings
- Introduction that provides the background or context of the study, a review of the literature, and a statement of the research problem or question and hypotheses
- Methods section that describes the data collection methodologies and sampling procedures
- Results section that explicates the research findings, often accompanied by tables and figures
- Discussion of implications for theory and practice
- Appendices, when included, that contain copies of the measuring instruments or survey forms

Workers critically evaluate research to assess its usefulness for their professional practices. Culturally competent social workers recognize that research reveals general trends that may or may not apply to the unique situations of a particular client system.

Reflecting Back

Some scholars charge that social work practitioners pay little attention to macrosystems change in their practices. Because social work has a dual focus—on both enhancing indi-

TABLE 14.3 Selected Journals and Periodicals

Administration in Social Work
Adolescence
Adoption and Fostering
Adult Foster Care Journal
Advances in Alcohol and Substance Abuse
Affilia
Aging
Alcoholism Treatment Quarterly
American Journal of Community Psychology
American Journal of Drug and Alcohol Abuse
American Journal of Family Therapy
American Journal of Orthopsychiatry
American Journal of Psychiatry
American Journal of Psychotherapy
American Journal of Sociology
Annals of The American Academy of Political
    and Social Science
Arete
Australian Social Work
British Journal of Social Work
California Sociologist
Child and Adolescent Social Work Journal
Child Welfare
Child and Youth Services
Children Today
Clinical Social Work Journal
Community Mental Health Journal
Computers in Human Services
Crime and Delinquency
Daedalus
Ethnic and Racial Studies
Exceptional Children
Families in Society
Family Relations
Family Therapy
Federal Probation
Geriatrics
Gerontologist
Health and Social Work
Hospital and Community Psychiatry
Human Relations

Human Services in the Rural Environment
International Journal of Social Work
Journal of Community Practice
Journal of Continuing Social Work Education
Journal of Elder Abuse and Neglect
Journal of Family Social Work
Journal of Gay and Lesbian Social Services
Journal of Gerontological Social Work
Journal of Marital and Family Therapy
Journal of Ethnic and Cultural Diversity
    in Social Work
Journal of Poverty
Journal of Primary Prevention
Journal of Progressive Human Services
Journal of Rehabilitation
Journal of Social Service Research
Journal of Social Work Education
Journal of Sociology and Social Welfare
Journal of Teaching in Social Work
NASW Legislative Alerts and Updates
NASW News
New Social Worker
Prevention in Human Services
Psychology of Women Quarterly
Public Welfare
Reflections
Research in Social Work Practice
School Social Work Journal
Smith College Studies in Social Work
Social Development Issues
Social Forces
Social Problems
Social Service Review
Social Thought
Social Work
Social Work Abstracts
Social Work in Education
Social Work in Health Care
Social Work Research
Social Work with Groups
The Urban and Social Change Review

vidual functioning and expanding opportunity structures in society—practitioners are well advised to give due regard to facilitating change in social environments. In fact, the empowerment approach to social work practice holds that macrolevel change is integral to client empowerment. Is a philosophy of empowerment sufficient for practitioners, particularly "direct service" or "clinical" practitioners, to fulfill the moral obligation of the purpose of social work? Consider the commitment empowerment-oriented practitioners must make to *social* work.

Looking Forward

Expanding opportunities during the development phase enhances the availability and accessibility of needed resources. Resources in client systems' personal, interpersonal, organizational, and societal domains afford options and accord power for resolving challenges. Social workers and clients join together to activate individual and collective energies to initiate social reform and work toward community development.

But, how effective are the resources, including the professional relationship and social work strategies, in satisfying the client's expressed goals? Chapter 15 explores evaluation and research as empowering processes for assessing the effectiveness of intervention methods and the accomplishment of goals. Only when clients recognize their success and determine what worked do they truly experience their own power.

Chapter *15*

Recognizing Success

Are clients achieving their goals? Is our work with clients making a difference? Are we using the most effective and efficient strategies? These are important questions that social workers and clients ask themselves throughout the development phase of the intervention process. Social work evaluation and research answers these questions and provides information to enrich future attempts. In empowerment-based social work, the purpose of evaluation goes beyond simply measuring outcomes and processes. It also affirms the accomplishments made by clients and confirms the effectiveness of social service programs and social policies. The phrase, "recognizing success," frames evaluation research as a process that empowers by highlighting the positive achievements of clients.

Certainly, the emphasis on recognizing success does not diminish the accountability function of measurement in evaluation research. Social workers do need to acknowledge that not all strategies lead to successful solutions. If social work programs and practices fall short of their stated outcomes, their utility should be questioned. And, if the level of goal achievement does not satisfy their expectations, clients may lose confidence. Monitoring activities during a social work intervention affords opportunities to make necessary changes. Ongoing review and evaluation allow workers to modify their approaches and give clients opportunities to redirect their efforts.

Research is central to all generalist social work practice. Workers evaluate their own practice continuously to increase the effectiveness of their work with clients. Additionally, practitioners participate in more global projects to evaluate programs within their agencies. Some social workers practice as research specialists, evaluating theories, approaches, and methods in order to contribute their scientific findings to the knowledge base of social work.

This chapter examines the methods social workers use to evaluate their own practice and to contribute to the research base of the profession. In detail, this chapter:

- Describes the purposes of social work evaluation and research
- Differentiates among monitoring and evaluating progress, client outcome assessment, and program evaluation
- Explicates the research process, defines research terminology, and presents key ethical issues in research
- Delineates the methods of single-system design
- Summarizes action research as an empowerment-oriented research model

Skills in conducting research and evaluation as well as in applying the results are essential for competent generalist practice.

Social Work Evaluation and Research

Research was paramount to the work of early social work pioneers. At the turn of the century, settlement house workers documented adverse societal conditions through research studies that ultimately led to legislative and social policy reforms in child labor practices, housing, sanitation, and the juvenile court. In that same era, principles of social investigation and "scientific charity" guided the casework of friendly visitors of the charity organization societies. Throughout the remainder of the century, practitioners continued to apply research methods to address social problems and to use evaluation techniques to demonstrate the effectiveness of social work practice.

Today, social workers continue the tradition of integrating research and evaluation into their practice. Consider the various ways that the generalist social workers featured in previous chapters can carry out research and evaluation projects.

- Mark Nogales conducts a needs assessment to determine whether or not there is a need for more community-based services for persons with chronic mental illnesses. Mark gathers information from clients and their families, mental health advocates, human service practitioners, employers, and other key informants to document gaps in services and identify the types of services most needed.
- Kay Landon routinely administers client satisfaction surveys to access clients' perceptions of the quality and usefulness of the home health services they receive.
- Paul Quillin prepares a paper for publication on his empirical research about the relationship between the degree of parental involvement and the level of children's self-esteem.
- Karen McBride, along with four of her clients, participates in a regional study, the purpose of which is to identify the characteristics of practitioners that clients perceive as most empowering. As a research participant, Karen uses process recording to document her actions and behaviors; her clients complete research surveys to evaluate Karen's approach.
- As a "research consumer," Tony Marelli reads professional journals and attends conferences to learn about innovative practice strategies that he can apply to his addictions recovery work.
- Damon Edwards collects data on the incidence and severity of the lead poisoning problem at Franklin Courts and prepares a position paper in order to influence the housing authority's action on lead abatement.
- Rita Garcia uses single-system case monitoring designs to help clients in the family reunification program evaluate their progress and identify areas that require further work.
- OPTIONS, the agency for which Kennedy Brown works, is a lead agency in the State Department of Aging Services case management pilot program. OPTIONS will implement an innovative assessment component that directs workers to seek specific information about clients' preferences for the delivery of home-based services—including how, when, and by whom. Another agency that is not implementing the new component will serve as the control. After a six-month period, researchers will evaluate the data to determine whether increased personal choice results in a lower rate of nursing home admission.
- In his work with the Northside Development Association, Nate Hardy prepares a cost-benefit analysis of a public-private partnership between the city and owners of apartment complexes in the community. His findings lend Nate support to influence the city council to consider his proposal to increase the availability of low-income housing through a viable alternative to costly new construction.

These examples illustrate how generalist social workers participate in a variety of research and evaluation activities in their day-to-day practice. Social work professionals, as active researchers, develop and test the theory base of their practice and contribute to the field through their own research activities.

Integrating Practice and Research

Social work practice and research are interdependent. The practice arena offers many opportunities to engage in research and evaluation. Research, in turn, is an important tool for conducting ethical and effective practice. "There seems little question that the heart of the development of an empirically based approach to practice is the extent to which theory, research, and practice can be integrated" (Fischer, 1993, p. 32).

Social work practice generates social research—a knowledge-building function. Held accountable for their actions by clients, agencies, and funders, social workers evaluate the changes made by clients, the effectiveness of specific intervention strategies, and the overall outcomes of programs and services. To demonstrate accountability, social workers evaluate these various components of their practice to determine whether client systems' situations improve during the course of social work interventions. To generate practice knowledge, social workers use research to ascertain what specific strategies account for clients' improvements (Tolson, 1990; Reid, 1995; Grinnell, 1997). In this way, social work research expands the knowledge base of practice and provides a way to evaluate practice effectiveness.

Similarly, *social research informs social work practice*—a solution-seeking function. Social work requires research-based knowledge to understand human behavior as well as social processes and social problems that differentially affect client systems. Practitioners make numerous professional judgments in their day-to-day practice activities. Research-oriented social workers frame their decisions and actions on knowledge that has been subjected to the rigors of research, rather than on personal hunches and untested assumptions (Powers, Meenaghan, & Toomey, 1985).

Practice Evaluation

Practice evaluation is a method of assessing the outcomes and measuring the effectiveness of social work strategies. In empowerment-based social work practice, the principle function of evaluation is to recognize success. Practitioners and clients monitor *progress*—to assess what clients *achieve* and to evaluate what programs *accomplish* rather than what they fail to do. Recognizing success during evaluation infuses the strengths perspective into practice. It increases the client system's energy and motivation for further change, directs the partners to repeat effective strategies, and acts as a catalyst for improving social services.

Three types of practice evaluation predominate in social work—progress evaluation, outcome assessment or client goal attainment, and program evaluation. *Progress evaluation* refers to continually monitoring and evaluating the success of the action plan. *Outcome assessment* involves measuring a client's achievement of goals and the effectiveness of the methods used in the change process. *Program evaluation* evaluates the effectiveness of a particular program or service in accomplishing programmatic goals. General evaluative criteria apply to each (Table 15.1).

Progress Evaluation

Action plans direct clients' and practitioners' activities during the development phase. These plans include well-defined goals, concrete objectives, and specific activities for social work-

TABLE 15.1 General Evaluative Criteria

Effectiveness	Was the desired outcome attained?
Efficiency	Was the outcome reached in the most direct way?
Equity	Were the client's rights protected? Were the rights of others ensured?

ers and clients to carry out to reach the desired outcomes. However, the most comprehensive plan can only suggest strategies that social workers and clients believe have the best possibility of attaining a successful outcome. No action plan is an absolute, iron-clad, definitive answer. Instead, action plans are dynamic in their implementation; social workers and clients are *experimenting* with a *proposal* for a solution. Throughout the social work intervention, a client and a practitioner periodically take stock of what is happening to determine what is and what is not working. In light of this, the social worker has responsibility for participating in the implementation of the plan and also for monitoring, evaluating, and updating the plan.

Monitoring and Evaluating Action Plans

Workers monitor and evaluate action plans as they are implemented to detect positive movements and steer activities in the direction of the desired outcomes. When workers and clients discover success, they stay the course. If a plan is ineffective or unworkable, the worker stops to discuss the situation with the client in order to revise the plan. As social workers oversee the implementation of the plan, they look for answers to several evaluation questions:

- Are both clients and workers doing what they have contracted to do?
- Are some parts of the plan working and other parts running into roadblocks or dead ends?
- What activities have the greatest impact? What activities take a lot of effort but realize a minimal return?
- Is the plan on the right track or is it falling short of expectations?
- Are clients actively involved in carrying out their part of the plan?
- If they are not, what is getting in the way?
- Do clients understand their roles or do they lack confidence that implementing the plan is worth the effort?
- Have clients' goals and motivations changed?

Updating Plans

After considering this new evaluative information, workers and clients modify action plans to incorporate recent changes and emerging strengths. Before considering a new approach, workers caution clients not to discard previously planned activities until they have had a chance to be successful. Sometimes, progress is slow and requires patience for success. On the other hand, expedient workers and clients do not consistently repeat those strategies that fail to produce any success.

Client Outcome Assessment

In client outcome assessment, workers simultaneously evaluate the degree of goal achievement and the effectiveness of the strategies implemented. In short, social workers apply this type of practice evaluation to gain answers to two basic questions: "Were the desired client outcome goals reached?" and "In what ways did the social work methods employed contribute to the desired change?" The process of assessing client outcomes:

> *involves specifying goals for clients; developing ways of measuring these goals; routinely applying these measurement strategies to determine if clients are attaining the goals; and then using this information to decide whether to continue, discontinue, or revise the intervention plan. The goal or purpose is to monitor client's progress toward the attainment of goals (goals can involve prevention, maintenance, or change) and adjust the intervention plan according. (Blythe, 1990, pp. 29–30)*

Additional information workers and clients can gain from outcome assessments includes the identification of the client's strengths and resources that contribute to goal achievement, the degree of change, the stability of the change, the unintended or unanticipated consequences of the change, and the efficiency of the change effort.

Questions that focus on client outcome assessment include:

- To what extent did the client system accomplish its goals?
- Can the changes be attributed to the intervention?
- Are there other factors that can account for the changes?
- Which client strengths and environmental resources were most significant in achieving results?
- Does the situation warrant further intervention?
- In what ways should workers modify their strategies?
- How does this information apply to follow-up work with this client and to work with future clients?
- To what degree was the client system involved in the evaluation process?

In spite of its name, outcome assessment is not a "tag on" last step in the helping process. Rather, workers conduct this type of evaluation in their earliest contacts with clients and repeat it throughout the process of their work together. Each time clients and social workers meet, they clarify the current situation, discuss goals and objectives, and examine progress. Each discussion involves a "mini" outcome assessment to evaluate progress made and plan the next step. Outcome evaluation is a continuously applied evaluation process that checks the achievement of each activity and objective.

Outcome assessment has four practical uses in social work. First, it provides concrete, continuous feedback on progress toward goals. This information is invaluable as clients and practitioners refine goals and develop further plans. Second, measuring the level of the achievement of goals and objectives documents outcomes and promotes accountability. Third, results of evaluations provide vital information that social workers can incorporate in planning with other clients. Finally, practitioners use the results of outcome assessment for their own professional development. These four benefits—continuous feedback, accountability, transferability, and professional development—make outcome assessment an essential part of every social worker's professional practice.

Goal Attainment Scaling

Goal attainment scaling (GAS) is another type of evaluation design that measures client achievement levels. In this evaluation, practitioners use clients' statements of their goals as the criteria for measurement. Thus, goal attainment scaling is individualized and tailored for each client system. Social workers can apply goal attainment scaling at all client system levels.

Framed around explicit and measurable goal statements rather than problem areas, goal attainment scaling typically uses a five-point scale of predicted levels of attainment. These levels range, for example, from "much less than expected" to "much more than expected," or from "least favorable outcome" to "most favorable outcome." For each point on the scale, the client specifies a behavioral outcome appropriate to the designated levels of outcome achievement. To achieve a quantitative GAS score, social work researchers assign a numeric weight to each point in the scale.

For example, the Northside Community Action Council has identified three goals: (1) to form a Neighborhood Watch Program; (2) to demolish abandoned buildings; and (3) to propose an ordinance to limit on-street parking to residents only. Table 15.2 illustrates the goal attainment scale for this case example.

Program Evaluation

Since many meritorious social programs compete for limited funding, funding agents expect assurances that programs for which they provide money do make a difference. Program evaluations determine the value of the particular program under review. Moreover, the *Code of Ethics* (National, 2000) sets forth standards for accountability: Social workers

TABLE 15.2   Northside Community Action Council: Goal Attainment Scale

Goal Attainment Level	Goal 1: Form a Neighborhood Watch Program	Goal 2: Demolish abandoned buildings	Goal 3: Establish an ordinance to limit on-street parking to residents only
Much less than expected outcome achievement	No neighborhood support for program	Lawsuits ensue over target properties	Residents object to the proposed ordinance
Less than expected outcome achievement	Participation by a few households	Agreement to demolish but postponed two years	Proposed ordinance defeated
Expected level of outcome achievement	Half of the households participate	A scheduled plan for demolition approved	Ordinance considered by city council
More than expected outcome achievement	Household participation and commitment to weekly meetings	Funds for neighborhood rehabilitation and renovation considered	Ordinance passed by city council
Much more than expected outcome achievement	Full neighborhood participation and private security	Full funding for building renovations	Off-street parking lot constructed

should not promise what they cannot deliver. Program evaluation provides the tangible evidence required for fiscal responsibility and ethical accountability. Additionally, program evaluation tracks the achievement of programmatic goals and objectives and identifies gaps to address in services and areas of service delivery.

Program evaluation asks the question: "Is the program accomplishing what it set out to do?" There are a number of methods that social workers use to secure data to discover the answer. Considering each client's outcome and compiling the results helps to determine whether a particular program has met its goals. Agencies may also administer consumer satisfaction surveys to ascertain clients' perspectives on the effectiveness of workers and services. Follow-up surveys of former clients and referral agencies are other sources of valuable information regarding the effectiveness and reputation of a particular program. Periodic reviews of case files by agency staff reveal client progress in relation to the overall program goals and agency mission. Finally, formalized processes such as quality assurance checks by peers and supervisors provide internal mechanisms for program evaluation. Each method of program evaluation examines services from a different angle. A combination of approaches leads to a more comprehensive view of service delivery.

Program evaluation measures the effects that programs have on the clientele served, the agency organization, and the general public. Examples of researchable questions for program evaluation include:

- Does the program cause desired changes for clients?
- Is the program sensitive to diverse populations?
- Did the program meet the expectations of funding organizations?
- Are the program objectives consonant with the agency mission?
- What are the strengths and weaknesses of the program?
- Is staffing for the program adequate?
- How accessible is the program to potential clientele?
- Does the program alter public attitudes or awareness?
- Does this program continue to satisfy a need in the community?
- Is this program viable?

Program Evaluation Design

An evaluation design is a written plan for administering the evaluation study, including ways to obtain the information and report the results. The evaluation design specifies both *when* to collect data and *what* data to collect (Mika, 1996). Specifically, it

- Details the evaluative questions
- Identifies the required informational data
- Describes the data collection instruments
- Delineates data collection procedures, including sampling, who will collect the data, and timeline
- Specifies techniques for analyzing data
- Provides guidelines for interpreting the data and reporting the results (Worthen, Sanders, & Fitzpatrick, 1997)

Evaluators may communicate the results of their program evaluation studies as in-house written reports, as executive summaries, as on-line communications, and as journal articles. Whatever form reports take, evaluators carefully attend to both content and format. With respect to content, well-written reports include the evaluation findings and the implications for the various stakeholders, such as program constituencies, funding bodies, and accrediting agencies. A clear, visually pleasing, and consistent format creates an impression of competence and credibility. Additionally, narrative explanations complement the technical presentation of the data and enhance reports' readability. In writing evaluation reports, evaluators also consider their intended audience. The written report should be understandable and maintain readers' interest. In sum, evaluators should observe four standards in communicating the program evaluation findings—utility, feasibility, propriety, and accuracy (Stufflebeam, 1994).

Agency personnel use program evaluation data to make administrative decisions. These research findings provide information useful for formulating agency policy, especially with respect to planning programs, developing services, setting priorities, and allocating resources. Program managers also use program evaluation research to identify ways to streamline agency procedures and replicate successful strategies in other program areas.

Consumer Satisfaction Surveys

Program evaluators often poll clients to determine their satisfaction with services. Consumer satisfaction surveys assess clients' perceptions or attitudes about an agency's delivery of services (Figure 15.1). These surveys solicit clients' views about the relevance of the services received, the extent to which the services actually resolved their presenting problems, and their satisfaction with the social work process. Although they are valuable sources of information, client satisfaction instruments measure the subjective experiences of clients. Alone, they are not sufficient to evaluate the quality of services. They are important from an empowerment perspective, as client satisfaction surveys ensure that clients have opportunities for feedback that can influence agency policies and program development.

Empowerment Evaluation

Empowerment evaluation is an alternative approach to the more conventional program evaluation methodologies; its purposes are to foster ongoing self-assessments and promote continuous program improvements (Fetterman, 1996; Brown, 1997; Secret, Jordan, & Ford, 1999). In actualizing participants' self-determination, empowerment evaluation emphasizes participant learning and capacity building (Patton, 1997). Empowerment evaluation also uses evaluation to influence policy development (Fetterman, 1994).

In assessing program value, empowerment evaluation employs collaborative, democratic processes of participation by program constituencies and/or staff. Through these processes, "program participants learn to continually assess their progress toward self-determination goals and to reshape their plans and strategies according to the assessment" (Fetterman, 1996, p. 6).

Five facets frame the methodology of empowerment evaluation—training, facilitation, advocacy, illumination, and liberation (Fetterman, 1996). *Training* refers to teaching program participants to internalize evaluation principles and practices, to conduct their own evaluation, and through the process to become more self-sufficient as evaluators and to create

PARTICIPANT SURVEY

RESPITE CARE PROGRAM

CHILD DEVELOPMENT CENTER

We value your comments about your satisfaction with the respite care services offered by the Child Development Center. The information you provide will help us evaluate and improve our services.

1. How many times have you used the respite care services in the past month? _____

2. How satisfied are you with the services you received?
   _____ Completely satisfied
   _____ Satisfied
   _____ Dissatisfied
   _____ Very dissatisfied
   Comments:

3. How dependable is your respite worker?
   _____ All of the time
   _____ Most of the time
   _____ Some of the time
   _____ Not at all
   Comments:

4. Is the respite service available when you need it?
   _____ Always
   _____ Usually
   _____ Sometimes
   _____ Rarely
   Comments:

5. In what ways could the services and respite worker be more helpful to you?

FIGURE 15.1   Example of Client Satisfaction Survey

---

opportunities for capacity building. *Facilitation* characterizes the role of empowerment evaluators "as coaches or facilitators to help others conduct a self-evaluation" (p. 11). As coaches, evaluators offer general direction and guidelines, provide suggestions about process, and help participants create evaluation designs. *Advocacy* refers to assisting disenfranchised people to become empowered through their participation in evaluation processes and subsequent recommendations for program improvements. Advocacy includes both helping others to advocate on their own behalf, and advocating on behalf of disempowered groups. Advocacy extends to advocating policy and legislative change as well as economic development. *Illumination* means promoting insight or framing new understanding "about roles, structures, and program dynamics" (p. 15). In this way, program participants acquire confidence in their abilities to assess problems and frame workable solutions. Finally, *liberation,* which is an outgrowth of illumination, refers to the emancipation of one's self and the corollary action to take charge of one's life. In other words, "empowerment evaluation enables participants to find new opportunities, see existing resources in a new light, and redefine their identities and future roles" (p. 16). Illumination and advocacy are the distinguishing marks of empowerment evaluation that make it truly empowering rather than merely participatory (Patton, 1997).

Empowerment evaluation incorporates several steps for helping program participants learn how to evaluate programs, including:

> *(a) taking stock or determining where the program stands, including strengths and weaknesses; (b) focusing on establishing goals (determining where you want to go in the future with an explicit emphasis on program improvement); (c) developing strategies and helping participants determine their own strategies to accomplish program goals and objectives; and (d) helping program participants determine the type of evidence required to document credibly progress toward their goals. (Fetterman, 1996, p. 18)*

The voices of consumers, customers, or clients may be inadvertently silenced or reinterpreted in the struggle of competing interests of program staff, managers, and external stakeholders to control the evaluation process and interpret the findings. Empowerment evaluation ensures that the voices of service consumers play a prominent role in the evaluation process.

Research

Research is a method of systematic investigation or experimentation. In the context of social work, research both informs practice and adds to the knowledge base of the profession. Social workers conduct research to test theories about human behavior and the social environment and to document evidence of the effectiveness of intervention strategies. To conduct formal research for purposes of practice evaluation, program development, and policy analysis, generalist social workers learn about the research process, research terminology, and related ethical issues.

The Research Process

Research is a meticulous and organized process that follows a logical progression of steps. Most often these interdependent steps include:

1. Specifying the research problem
2. Reviewing the professional literature
3. Relating the research problem to theory
4. Formulating a testable hypothesis
5. Selecting the research design
6. Gathering data
7. Analyzing the data

   8. Interpreting the results
   9. Identifying implications for practice
  10. Preparing the research report

   The research process begins by identifying a problem and formulating a hypothesis. *Problem identification* evolves from a general concern or curiosity. From a general interest, the researcher narrows the field of study to formulate a researchable question. Through a *review of the literature,* the researcher locates and studies research related to the research question to determine the status of knowledge and viewpoints about this and similar problems. The researcher then explores the *relationship of the research problem to theory,* examines alternative theories, and formulates the problem into a testable hypothesis by expressing the problem in precise terms. A *hypothesis* is a tentative statement of the relationship that exists between two variables, such as the social work intervention and the client outcome. Sometimes hypotheses specify the nature of the relationship between the independent and dependent variables.

   Conducting research also involves designing the research plan for collecting, analyzing, and interpreting the data. The *research design* conceptualizes the sequence of strategies necessary to test the hypothesis and details the methods for gathering and analyzing data. *Gathering data* is the process of systematically collecting information pertinent to the research question. A researcher may locate data in existing data or generate original data through observations, surveys, interviews, tests, or experiments. *Data analysis* employs techniques such as scaling, graphical presentations, or statistical manipulations in order to examine and evaluate the data. *Data interpretation* gives meaning and understanding to the research results. The researcher is then in a position to infer or project the *implications* for practice of the research findings and suggest subsequent courses of action. Finally, researchers compile their findings in *research reports* and disseminate the information through publications or presentations. The empowerment-oriented practitioner–researchers must be sensitive to client participation throughout the research process.

Research Terminology

Research has a vocabulary of its own. Explaining all the nuances of social work research and practice evaluation is beyond the scope of this chapter. The following sections briefly highlight fundamental concepts relevant to a beginning understanding of research. For in-depth information, consult a specialized book on social work research and statistics (Rubin & Babie, 1997; Weinbach & Grinnell, 1998; Bloom, Fischer, & Orme, 1999; Royse, 1999; Sirkin, 1999).

Variables
Research variables are concepts that vary in ways that can be observed, recorded, and measured. Examples are variations in behaviors among different client systems or in the behaviors of the same client system at different points in time. Research variables may also be differences among types of social work interventions or variations within a single intervention. Practice evaluation research examines the relationship between the variables of the social work "intervention" and the "client outcomes" in order to monitor and evaluate a client's progress and to guide decisions about a social worker's methodology.

Independent Variables. Social work researchers typically designate the intervention as the *independent variable.* As such, the intervention is the causal or influencing variable that affects change. For example, consider a home visitor prevention program that offers support and child development information to new parents. The home visitor program is the independent variable when evaluating whether the program reduces the incidence of child abuse and neglect in a community. Likewise, the program is the independent variable when measuring participants' increased knowledge of infant care.

Any social work intervention may itself have numerous variations. For instance, an intervention can vary in type, intensity, and length of time. The home visitor program can offer in-home visitation by a trained volunteer twice a week for six months or once a week for a year; or parents may or may not attend parenting skills classes conducted by a child development specialist in conjunction with the visitation component; or the program may involve all new parents or only those defined as at-risk. Consequently, research practitioners make conscious choices about which interventions to select, how to arrange and implement them, and over what period of time to administer them.

Dependent Variables. The outcome of the intervention, that is, changes in the incidence, severity, or degree of the targeted problems, solutions, or changes in the client system's behaviors, attitudes, or feelings *depends* on the intervention. Hence, the problem or behavior being measured is called the *dependent variable.* The primary goals of many home visitor programs are to reduce child abuse and neglect and enhance parenting effectiveness. In this instance two variables—the incidence of abuse and the level of parenting skills—are dependent variables. Carefully formulated research designs accurately measure the changes in the dependent variable. Clearly, positive change in the dependent variable is the goal of social work intervention and is of utmost importance in practice evaluation.

Intervening Variables. Frequently, researchers are unable to conclude that the outcomes are entirely the result of the action of the independent variable. Sometimes other factors interject their influence. These factors are *intervening variables.* An intervening variable is any other variable that inadvertently affects the outcome, either positively or negatively. Suppose, in the home visitor program that the reports of child abuse decrease over time. Evaluators should question whether the home visitor program is solely responsible and consider other possibilities for this positive outcome. Examples of intervening variables may be a lower birth rate, the improvement of the economic climate in the community, or the increased availability of affordable child care. Researchers strive to design research studies in ways that, in so far as possible, control for the effects of intervening variables.

Graphing the Variables. In social work research, the relationship between the influencing and resulting variables are framed in terms of X and Y. X denotes the independent variable or the "influencing" intervention; whereas, Y denotes the dependent variable or the "resulting" change. To represent data pictorially, the researcher locates the independent variable (X) on the horizontal axis of a graph and places the dependent variable (Y) along the vertical axis. The graph plots the relationship between the independent (X) and dependent (Y) variables. Each point on the graph represents the position at which the X and Y variables intersect (Figure 15.2). In this way, the graph portrays the effect of the intervention on the direction of change, either positive or negative.

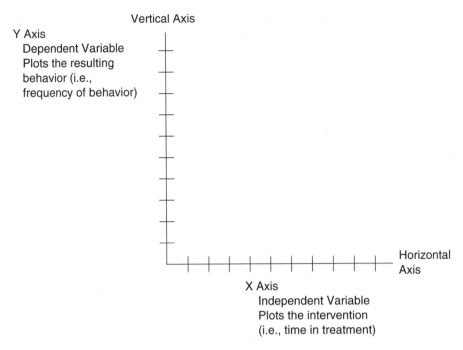

FIGURE 15.2   Example of Graph of X and Y Variables

Hypotheses

Hypotheses state the connection between the independent and dependent variables. An *hypothesis* is a tentative statement of the relationship between these two variables. In practice evaluation, the variables are the intervention variable and the outcome variable. Simply, the research hypothesis in outcome assessment states that if X (the intervention) occurs, then Y (the outcome) results. In the example about the home visitor program, one hypothesis postulates that if a community implements a home visitor program (X), then the incidence of child abuse and neglect (Y) will decrease. Another possible hypothesis states that new parents who participate in the program (X) are likely to follow up with well-baby appointments (Y) and immunization schedules (Y) at a higher rate than nonparticipants. The research process subjects the hypotheses to tests or comparisons to either prove or disprove the supposition that a relationship exists between the intervention and outcome variables. Here are several examples of hypotheses:

- If the Acme company sponsors on-site child care provisions, then workers' absenteeism will decrease.
- Foster parents who complete the intensive training program are less likely to experience placement disruptions.
- The incidence of residential burglary will decrease after implementing the neighborhood watch program.
- Julie's score on the self-esteem scale will increase as she participates in counseling.

Measurement

In evaluating practice effectiveness, researchers assign meaningful labels or numeric values to the observations made and the data collected about client progress and the intervention methods. Measurement is an objective process by which the evaluator collects data. One uses measures to assess the status or the "what is" of the object under study or to evaluate the value of the "what should be." In terms of the relationship between evaluation and measurement, one measures first, then uses the measures to assess or evaluate. For example, researchers can label the degree of achievement of client goals on a continuum from fully achieved to unachieved, or they can calculate actual behaviors into percentages. Likewise, workers can evaluate interventions by classifying successful or unsuccessful attempts or by simply counting the number of sessions. Measurement considerations include asking questions such as:

- What is the purpose of the measurement?
- What is it exactly we want to measure?
- Who will make the measurement?
- What format will be required for collecting the measures?
- Where and when will the measurements be made? (Grinnell & Williams, 1990)

Reliability and Validity

Researchers consider issues of reliability and validity in choosing measuring instruments such as questionnaires, surveys, structured observations, and diagnostic scales. A measuring instrument is *reliable* when its measures are similar or consistent over time or with repeated applications. "Validity is concerned with obtaining operationally what one has defined theoretically" (Sedlack & Stanley, 1992, p. 202). In other words, a measuring instrument has validity when it measures accurately the variable it intends to measure.

To be effective, measuring instruments must be both reliable and valid. Reliability and validity are two distinct yet interrelated issues. It is possible for an instrument to be reliable, that is to consistently result in same measures over time, and not be valid by failing to measure what it's supposed to measure. In short, if a measuring instrument or variable used to represent the concept is not valid, don't bother to test for reliability, as a lack of validity automatically nullifies reliability. On the other hand, if a measuring instrument is valid, that is, it measures what it's supposed to measure, then it may prove reliable. Reputable measurement tools have passed appropriate tests and statistical analyses for reliability and validity. Typically, documentation about reliability and validity accompanies published scales.

All social work practitioners should understand the concepts of reliability and validity. First and foremost, social workers, as research consumers, draw upon the published research findings of others to guide their practice. In this capacity, social workers consider reliability and validity information to critically examine the research for its accuracy and usefulness. Second, in their role as research practitioners, social workers often develop their own tools for use with various clients and routinely collect data from clients to evaluate client outcomes and practice methods. Well-constructed research designs and reliable and valid data collection instruments are necessary for practitioners to have confidence in their research results. And finally, for the research specialist whose primary function is building theories or conducting practice research, measures of reliability and validity are central to designing research instruments, constructing diagnostic scales, and making statistical inferences.

Qualitative and Quantitative Data Analysis

Social workers collect information, or data, about their clientele. *Data* are the facts gathered about the client system's situation. The data collected either describe qualities of the variables being studied, or measure their quantity. For instance, in conducting a community study on the plight of those who are homeless, practitioners may gather qualitative information through verbal descriptions or written accounts by persons who are homeless or from providers of services to these clients. The data collected in this example are qualitative because they *describe* the conditions of homelessness. If, however, a social worker was researching the effectiveness of shelter programs on reducing the number of homeless families in the community, the data gathered are quantitative. In this instance, quantitative data involve a *numerical measurement* of the homeless population before and after the program's implementation. Both qualitative and quantitative data inform social work practice.

Data and research methodologies are interdependent: The nature or type of data—whether qualitative or quantitative—dictates the methodology most applicable for the data analysis. Simply put, if the data consist of words, researchers select qualitative methods; if the data are numeric, researchers select quantitative methods. Qualitative data usually results in descriptive analysis although researchers can still assign numeric representations to the words and apply limited statistical analyses. Examples of qualitative research in social work include case studies, document research, surveys, and key informant studies. On the other hand, researchers may analyze quantitative data mathematically using more powerful statistical applications. Experimental, quasi-experimental, and other studies involving statistical analysis are examples of quantitative research.

The role of hypotheses differs in qualitative and quantitive research. In qualitative studies, researchers can construct hypotheses and make generalizations about the relationship of the independent and dependent variable after collecting and analyzing the data. Quantitative studies are hypothesis-driven studies; in these studies, researchers develop the design to test hypotheses and draw conclusions about specific causal relationships (Grinnell, 1997). Each type of research makes a unique contribution to the research base of social work practice.

Ethics in Research

As with other aspects of social work practice, ethics influences the ways practitioners conduct social work research. Practitioners are responsible for designing and carrying out research and evaluation both knowledgeably and ethically (Gillespie, 1995). This includes considering diversity in each aspect of the research process. Relevant ethical principles include:

- *Informed Consent*—Research subjects give their consent to participate only after researchers fully disclose the purpose of the research, what it entails, and its potential effects or consequences.
- *Confidentiality*—Researchers assure the privacy of clients' responses.
- *Anonymity*—Researchers carefully guard the identity of the respondents.
- *Voluntary Participation*—Clients' involvement in research is strictly by their choice. Researchers never coerce respondents into participating.

- *Objectivity*—Researchers conduct studies and report results impartially.
- *Careful Research Design*—Researchers construct designs that are unobtrusive so as not to conflict with practice priorities.
- *Accurate Reports of Findings*—Researchers report their findings accurately to avoid misrepresenting the data.

Guidelines for ethical research endeavors are set forth clearly in the NASW's *Code of Ethics* (National, 2000):

- Social workers engaged in evaluation or research should obtain voluntary and written informed consent from participants, when appropriate, without any implied or actual deprivation or penalty for refusal to participate, without undue inducement to participate, and with due regard for participants' well-being, privacy, and dignity. Informed consent should include information about the nature, extent, and duration of the participation requested and disclosure of the risks and benefits of participation in the research. (Sec. 5.02e)
- Social workers should inform participants of their rights to withdraw from evaluation and research at any time without penalty. (Sec. 5.02h)
- Social workers engaged in evaluation or research should protect participants from unwarranted physical or mental distress, harm, danger, or deprivation. (Sec. 5.01j)
- Social workers engaged in evaluation or research should ensure the anonymity or confidentiality of participants and the data obtained from them. Social workers should inform participants of any limits of confidentiality, the measures that will be taken to ensure confidentiality, and when any records containing research data will be destroyed. (Sec. 5.01l)

Following ethical guidelines for research not only protects clients' rights, it also ensures the integrity of the results.

Single-System Designs

One of the most practical ways for social workers to assess client change and evaluate practice effectiveness is through the use of single-system evaluation designs. Also called single-subject or single-case designs, this design typically involves evaluating and monitoring the effects of interventions on a client system's target problem. The term "single-system" indicates this design applies the same research principles to evaluating interventions in multiperson systems such as families, groups, organizations, neighborhoods, and communities.

To be implemented successfully, single-system designs must meet three requirements. They must:

- State the change objective in measurable terms.
- Evaluate the achievement with reliable and valid outcome measures (that is, the observations, verbal reports, and physiological measures) that produce quantitative data.
- Display the data graphically (Grinnell, 1997).

For applications of single-system designs to be empowering, clients must be actively involved in all aspects of design, implementation, data analysis, and interpretation. Empowerment-oriented practitioners take caution to avoid the role of "analytical expert" in interpreting behaviorally driven, single-system outcome evaluations. This collaboration may heighten clients' motivation for change and promote self-direction in change activities.

Phases of Single-System Designs

One distinguishing characteristic of single-system designs is the planned comparison of measurements made in a preintervention period with measurements completed during or after the intervention. The periods of time during which observation of the client systems' behavior or evaluation of the client systems' progress occurs are called phases. To compare the "before" and "after," practitioners need to understand the concepts of baseline and intervention phases.

Baseline Phase

To implement a single-system design, practitioners first establish a baseline. Taken in the preintervention period, baseline measurement involves a series of observations of the naturally occurring frequency of the behaviors under study. Workers measure the behavior that reflects the client's problem or observe the client's situation as it presently exists for a specified period of time.

Carefully constructed research establishes a baseline measure prior to introducing intervention strategies. However, ethical researchers consider the detrimental effects of counting adverse behaviors to acquire baseline data with clients who need immediate relief. Sometimes the choice to gather baseline information gives way to the need for immediate intervention.

Intervention Phase

In a single-system research design, an intervention is what practitioners do to affect or change the identified target behaviors. As such, "interventions may be thought of as a single *procedure* (ordinarily one technique), a *package* (a combination of two or more procedures), or a *program* (a combination of packages and or procedures integrated in work with a given client system" (Bloom & Fischer, 1982, p. 245). Possible interventions may include such differing practice techniques as marriage counseling, a twelve-step program, advocacy, mediation, a support group, neighborhood development, or a community action. Recall that, in social work research, the intervention is the independent variable, meaning that it is within the control of the worker and the client. They may apply an intervention, change its intensity, or withdraw it.

Alphabetic Notation

Researchers use alphabetic notation to represent the phases in single-system designs. The letter A denotes the baseline or preintervention phase and subsequent letters designate the intervention phases. So, an AB design indicates a baseline phase (A) followed by an intervention phase (B). Likewise, the ABC design includes a baseline phase (A), followed by an intervention phase (B), which in turn is followed by another, yet different, intervention (C). How the baseline and intervention phases are arranged determines the type of single-system research design being implemented.

Types of Single-System Designs

Single-system designs commonly used in social work include case study or monitor design (B design), the basic baseline-intervention design (AB design) and other variations of the AB design, notably, the successive intervention design (ABC design), the withdrawal or reversal design (ABAB design and the BAB design), and multiple baseline designs.

Using the B design or the AB design answers the *evaluative* question: Did the client's situation improve during the course of treatment? (Grinnell 1997). The reversal designs are *experimental* designs and answer the question of causation: Did the client system improve because of social work intervention? Social workers are more likely to seek answers to evaluative questions in their practice by using the B or AB design, as these designs are more practical to implement than the more ambitious experimental designs which require rigorous controls (Thyer, 1990).

AB Design

The AB design is a useful and popular single-system design that social workers use to observe and measure change in target problems. In fact this basic design meets the needs of most social work practitioners (Corcoran, 1993). It is simple to apply since it includes only one baseline period (A) and one intervention period (B). In many ways, it is one of the least intrusive evaluative measures in terms of preserving social work practice priorities. It naturally fits into an organized practice process—observing first what is and then implementing and evaluating efforts to change.

In the AB design, workers introduce a single independent variable or intervention technique following the baseline phase. Practitioners monitor the shifts in the data from the baseline phase to the intervention phase to determine whether or not the client's situation is improving. From this information, the practitioner can draw only tentative conclusions about whether the intervention led to the improvement or whether changes were caused by some extraneous event, an intervening variable, or by chance. Despite this limitation, the AB design does provide immediate feedback about the direction of change during the intervention phase. As a result, practitioners and clients can discuss the possible explanations for the change and modify their strategies if necessary.

Consider the following case example that uses an AB design:

> *The Millwork Company discontinued Mr. Jones' job position, resulting in termination of his employment. His unemployment benefits are insufficient to meet his family's income needs. He wants to find new employment, but he is hesitant to seek other jobs and lacks confidence in his job seeking and interviewing skills. To feel prepared and confident for a job interview, Mr. Jones role-played a simulated interview with his employment counselor. Together, they analyzed the videotaped interview and noted points of strengths and areas for improvement.*

As depicted in Figure 15.3, during the five-week baseline or preintervention phase, Mr. Jones applied for a total of 7 jobs. Following the role-play intervention, Mr. Jones significantly increased the number of employment applications.

Client System: Individual—Mr. Jones
Target Problem: Hesitancy to apply for jobs
Intervention: Videotaped role play of a job interview

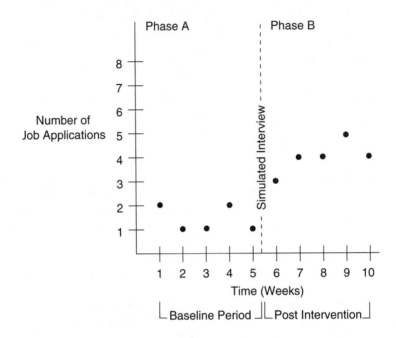

**FIGURE 15.3   AB or Baseline and Intervention Design.
Evaluation: The number of job applications Mr.
Jones placed each week increased after the role
play of the simulated interview.**

B Design

The B design is often referred to as the case study method or the monitoring design. With this design, clients and practitioners apply an intervention and monitor the client's target problem to see if it is changing in the desired direction. This design does not stipulate taking baseline measurements prior to implementing the intervention strategy. However, in some situations, practitioners can ascertain a retroactive baseline from preexisting records or verbal reports from the client system. The lack of a baseline for comparing before and after measures is a significant drawback of this design method as the design offers no way to decipher what accounts for observed changes.

The following case example illustrates the B design:

> *Polly Martin, a 14-year-old, displays symptoms of anorexia, an eating disorder resulting in weight loss. At the start of the intervention phase, she weighs 92 pounds, 20 percent less than her original body weight of 115 pounds. Polly participated in*

an eating disorder program that included self-esteem counseling, nutritional counseling, and self-monitoring of food intake through the use of food cards.

As Figure 15.4 shows, Polly gradually gained a total of 10 pounds over the course of the eating disorder intervention program. In Polly's situation, a baseline period or measurement was inadvisable given the potential seriousness of her eating disorder.

ABC Design

Workers use successive intervention phases following the baseline period when implementing the ABC single-system design. Like the basic AB design, the ABC design establishes a pattern of data in the baseline phase (A), followed by introducing an intervention in the first intervention phase (B), and then adding a different, or perhaps modified, intervention (C). If workers add even more interventions, they would label subsequent intervention phases as D, E, and so on.

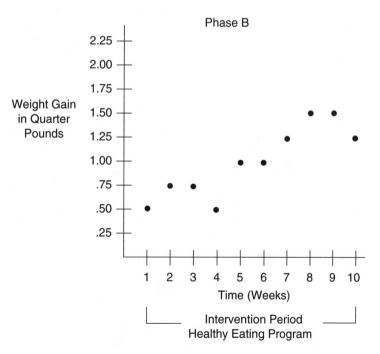

Client System: Individual—Polly Martin
Target Problem: Anorexia
Intervention: Healthy Eating Program

FIGURE 15.4   B or Case Study or Monitor Design. Evaluation: By the 10th week in counseling, Polly gained a total of 10 pounds.

ABC designs apply when practitioners introduce multiple intervention components in sequence, or when they modify one intervention in frequency or intensity because it doesn't appear to be working as planned. Because practitioners introduce several interventions during the change process, they are uncertain which specific intervention created the desired effect.

The ABC design is used in the following case example:

> *For the past 6 months, the Kanton metropolitan community saw a rising unemployment rate, as local industry experienced severe cutbacks, subsequent layoffs, and manufacturing plant closings. The Kanton Economic Development Group recognized a need for a two-part approach to the problem—a job retraining program and a job placement program. The EDG contracted with the W. O. R. K. organization (Work, Opportunities, and Resources for Kanton) to design and implement community-based programming for the displaced workers.*

Figure 15.5 shows the decreasing unemployment rate over the course of the year as each of the programs was being implemented.

ABAB Design

Simply, the ABAB design is a string of AB designs used to evaluate changes in the same client system after reapplying the same intervention technique. Following the initial baseline and intervention phases, the ABAB design adds a second baseline phase after which workers reintroduce the intervention. They establish the second baseline by discontinuing or withdrawing the intervention for a period of time. Social workers and clients may plan this withdrawal or may simply experience an unexpected pause in the intervention.

The ABAB single-system design is a *reversal* or *withdrawal design*. Logically, we presume that if the target behavior improves during the first intervention phase, reverts when the intervention is withdrawn, and improves again during the second intervention phase, the improvement is likely to result from the intervention. Thus, the ABAB design offers more evidence of the causal effects of the intervention on the behavior or target problems.

Clearly, ethical issues emerge with planned withdrawals of interventions, especially when an intervention appears to be helpful. Concerned social workers question whether clients will suffer unnecessarily if their situation reverts to the preintervention level. After all, the well-being of client systems is a priority concern of social work practice. In some cases, social workers and clients purposely discontinue services temporarily to test whether clients can independently sustain the gains. At other times, an unexpected time-out from intervention caused by either clients' or social workers' circumstances offers an opportunity for establishing the second baseline.

BAB Design

The BAB design is also a reversal design, without establishing an initial baseline pattern. Instead, the social worker immediately introduces an intervention (Phase B). Later, the worker withdraws the intervention and observes changes in the behavior, establishing a postintervention baseline (Phase A). Subsequently the worker reapplies the intervention (Phase B).

Client System: Community—Kanton
Target Problem: High unemployment rate
Interventions: 1. Job retraining program
                2. Job placement program

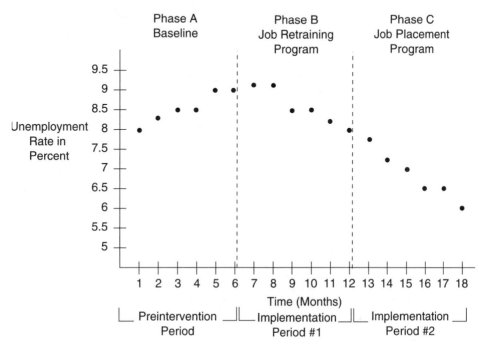

FIGURE 15.5 **ABC or Successive Intervention Design. Evaluation: The community unemployment rate steadily decreased as both the job retraining program and job placement program were being implemented.**

Changes in the patterns of data observed and measured during the first intervention period (B), the withdrawal period (A), and the second intervention period (B) provide valuable information about the effectiveness of the intervention on the target problems. If, after the intervention is withdrawn, the behavior gains are lost during Phase A, and then later improve when reintroducing the intervention, the social worker can make a stronger inference about the causal influence of the intervention. Again, ethical social workers carefully explore the potential consequences of withdrawing services that appear to be working.

Multiple-Baseline Designs
Another variation of the AB design establishes baselines with and observes changes in multiple clients, in multiple settings, and for multiple target problems. This multiple-baseline design allows social workers to monitor three types of situations. Workers can track (1) more than one client system that shares the same problem and utilizes the same intervention, (2) a

client system that experiences the same problem in more than one setting, or (3) a single subject who exhibits more than one problem situation in the same setting.

Evaluating multiple client systems with the same problem allows the practitioner to generalize findings with different clients. Monitoring the effects of the intervention on one client system in two or more settings looks for a generalization of the outcomes within the client's functioning. The multiple-baseline design also allows practitioners to simultaneously evaluate changes in multiple problem situations presented by a single client system.

Limitations of Single-System Designs

Contemporary social work practice and research literature is expansive in describing the application and in questioning the appropriateness of single-system research designs (Thyer & Thyer, 1992). Single-case evaluations and single-system research designs are gaining a degree of acceptance by social work practitioners to evaluate practice effectiveness and to contribute to the knowledge base of practice. However, these designs may not fit all practice situations.

Single-case designs readily adapt to measuring behavioral change. But not all social workers use behavioral or task-centered models that specify problems in the ways necessary to implement single-case designs. Thus, methodological issues arise in applying single-subject research by those practitioners who employ other approaches. To apply single-system designs in these situations, researchers carefully delineate and operationally define client outcome goals in ways that can be measured objectively (Nelsen, 1990, 1993). Researchers should identify intermediate progress indicators to monitor the achievement of short-term objectives in long-term interventions.

Agencies hold direct service practitioners accountable for assessing client outcomes and evaluating the effectiveness of the interventions they use. Practitioners are also in positions to conduct empirical or experimental practice research. Yet, the question of how to accommodate the research role without violating the service role is important (Thomas, 1978). Certainly, research should not intrude on the client–practitioner relationship, nor should research dominate the intervention process. The social work profession needs to continue to develop single-case evaluation techniques that fit more naturally with practice; view evaluation as a process to enhance practice rather than an exercise in accountability; and adopt a variety of formats to accommodate diverse client populations, intervention goals, and practice methodologies (Gingerich, 1990).

Action Research

Through research, we develop theories about social problems, human behavior, and client population groups. From research findings, we acquire information to guide decisions at the levels of policy, programs, and direct practice. These research findings can be tainted by the personal values and biases of researchers, erroneous assumptions in research designs, and the political nature of the research process. Action or advocacy research is especially appropriate with population groups that are in some way disadvantaged or oppressed (Davidson, 1988; Fleming & Ward, 1999). This style of research ensures clients' participation in all aspects of the research design, as it entails:

> *involving the client from start to finish; lending support to the world view of the client or client-group, including cultural, ethnic, linguistic, religious, socioeconomic, or other minority orientation; and devising a research method and issue implications for practice that stand to improve the quality of life of the client group. (Davidson, 1988, p. 115)*

As an empowerment-oriented research method, action research reshapes the relationships between service users and practitioners, giving voice and status to service users (Beresford & Evans, 1999; Evans & Fisher, 1999). With roots in international development initiatives and the work of Freire (1973, 1993), action research originates "with the people," particularly those who are oppressed (Brown, 1994; Brydon-Miller, 1997; Hills, 1998; Fleming & Ward, 1999; McNicoll, 1999). Its goal is to facilitate social change by focusing on "the specific concerns of the community as well as the fundamental causes of the oppression" (p. 660). Action research is also useful in stimulating organizational change, with work *within* rather than *on* the organization (Fisher, 1994). One such study was "designed to show the processes involved in bringing the users' voice to the centre of social services policy and practice, and in producing a staff and policy development programme with the capacity to deliver substantial changes towards the greater participation of users" (p. 279). Action research is particularly relevant to multicultural community organizing, as research, action, and outcomes intertwine in action research processes (Gutiérrez, Alvarez, Nemon, & Lewis, 1996). Thus, one "can expect participant and community empowerment, capacity building, and change to result from these efforts" (p. 506).

By definition, action research is participatory. The relationship of the researcher and community participants provides the foundation for successful implementation. The research itself begins with a community member's request for assistance in conducting research. The researcher and community members come to an agreement on procedural details and work collaboratively throughout the action research process as co-learners, from developing the design, to collecting the data, to implementing plans for change. Whereas the role for the researcher is one of educator (Brown, 1994), participants may have roles as informants, interpreters, planners, implementers, facilitators, researchers, and recipients (Dick, 1997a, 1997b). "Participatory research is an empowering experience for participants, a process that validates their realities and their rights as people to be heard, respected, and recorded as a part of history" (Brown, 1994, p. 295). It gives voice to the participants, reveals their worldviews, affirms their humanity, and leads to a heightened critical consciousness and processes of reflection and action.

The processes of action research incorporate elements of research, education, and action. Action research cycles through a series of recurring steps—plan, act, observe, reflect. Critical reflection, similar to conscientization, plays an integral role in the process, as it lends vision to subsequent cycles of planning–acting–observing–reflecting. "The final stage is one of shared reflection and consolidation of the learning that has taken place, and a reexamination of the political, social, and economic conditions facing the community" (Brydon-Miller, p. 661).

Reflecting Back

The shifting paradigm to participatory evaluation and action research in social work raises a number of issues. Among these issues are the efficacy of moving from the use of external evaluators to internal evaluators, the effects of involvement by community stakeholders and social service consumers in all parts of evaluation or research design, and the changing role of the evaluator from evaluation expert to policy advocate. How can social workers as evaluators and researchers reconcile these innovations with sound evaluation and research design? Consider, for example, the requirements of rigorous quantitative measures, the adaptability of qualitative measures to the stories of consumers, and user involvement in research and evaluation as an empowerment strategy.

Looking Forward

Social work research and evaluation support effective generalist practice. Practitioners and policy makers rely on sound research methods and evaluative processes to identify ways to enhance social service delivery. The evolutionary nature of social work requires practitioners, as clinicians, to contribute to the knowledge and skill base of the profession.

Recognizing client and program successes in social work practice suggests progress, achievement, and accomplishment. Thus, the process of recognizing success cues the client and social worker whether it is time to conclude their work together. If clients are sufficiently satisfied with their level of goal achievement, social workers and clients prepare to bring closure to the professional relationship. Chapter 16 explores how social workers and clients wrap up their work together in ways that credit clients with success and stabilize the progress achieved.

C h a p t e r **16**

Integrating Gains

The rule in personal relationships is that as long as things are going well they will continue to evolve and intensify. The rule in social worker–client relationships is that even when things are going well, relationships will end. Practitioners work themselves out of a job with each successful practice endeavor. Simply, the common goal of all social work is for client systems to operate independently of the social worker, drawing instead on their own competence, support networks, and the resources of a just society.

Social work literature often refers to the final step in the social work process as "termination" (Pincus & Minahan, 1973; Fortune, 1995; Johnson, 1998; Hess & Hess, 1999; Kirst-Ashman & Hull, 1999). To others, like Gutheil (1993), the word "terminate" has nefarious connotations. While "terminate" does mean discontinue or conclude, it also invokes more negative undertones associated with death, dismissal, and being fired. And, who can avoid the "terminator" video image of automatic weapons, violence, and destruction? Other writers offer the alternative description of this phase as "endings," (Maluccio, 1979; Shulman, 1999; Compton & Galaway, 1999; DuBois & Miley, 1999).

Whatever words or phrases practitioners choose, their words should reflect the reality that when workers and clients resolve their professional relationships, they don't encapsulate their work and put it aside. Paradoxically, social work practice "endings" are also beginnings. Wrapping up "signifies both an ending of the working relationship and the beginning of life without the professional helping person" (Gutheil, 1993, p. 163). Clients go on, empowered to incorporate what they have learned into how they continue to cope. Social workers also move on, enriched with yet another professional relationship experience and additional practice wisdom.

Describing this last process as "integrating gains" emphasizes the importance of client growth, development, and change beyond the professional relationship. This last step in empowering social work ventures is crucial for the success of the process as a whole. Within the context of each successful social work endeavor, clients have discovered the power available in the strengths within themselves and in the resources of their environments. A social worker's task in wrapping up the relationship is to sustain the client's ability to draw upon and amplify this power independently. This last step is crucial for the success of the process as a whole. Adept endings help client systems integrate the work of earlier phases, recognize achievements, build a sense of mastery, consolidate gains, and provide a springboard into the future.

This chapter describes what social workers and clients do to resolve their work together in ways that integrate and apply what each has gained from the experience. Specifically, this chapter:

- Describes social work endings
- Details endings that involve completing contracts
- Specifies circumstances leading to referrals and specifies effective procedures for making referrals as closure
- Guides social workers on how to respond when clients prematurely withdraw from services
- Discusses special ending issues associated with clients who die
- Considers closure processes used with group-, organization-, and community-level client systems

Social workers end their work with clients in ways that stabilize desired changes and empower client systems to continue functioning competently.

Social Work Endings

Generally, three situations define exit points for most client systems (Table 16.1). Workers celebrate with clients who reach their goals and wish clients well when they decide instead to continue on their own, refer clients to other professionals when necessary; or acknowledge the rights of clients to withdraw from services as they see fit. Each type of resolution requires a unique process to wrap up the work in a way that benefits clients and leaves workers with information to fuel their continuing professional development.

The actions a worker takes at closure vary, depending on the preferences and behaviors of clients and the specific situation. In planning effective closure processes, workers consider many issues, among them:

- The degree of success that has been achieved so far
- The potential benefits of continuing the work
- The duration and intensity of the relationship with the client system
- The resources available to continue the work in this particular setting
- Whether the client is voluntary or mandated
- The client's plans
- The role the social worker may play in the client's life after the closure

The scenarios for concluding work with client systems vary to meet each particular client's needs. Endings also differ depending on the level of client system. Work with individuals and families has a degree of intimacy that may reveal itself in the intensity of feelings during the closure process. In group work, individuals are likely to be facing the loss of relationships

TABLE 16.1 Types of Closure

Categories	Description	Social Work Processes
Completing Contracts	Clients made significant progress or achieved success in the plan of action and no longer need social work services	Preparing for resolution Discussing readiness Reviewing progress Sharing feelings Generalizing outcomes
Closing with Referral	Clients require continued services beyond the contracted work with the practitioner that may involve more specialized provider expertise or agency programming	Acknowledging limited resources Smoothing the transition Tracking clients' progress
Responding to Client Withdrawal	Clients, on their own initiative, conclude the helping relationship	Preparing for early withdrawal Recognizing exiting clues Pursuing mutual resolution

with other group members as well as the discontinuation of the relationship with the social worker. Work within organizations and communities may be ongoing rather than short-term, redefining the closure process as a transition to the next task or project rather than signaling the end of the professional relationship itself. Generalist practitioners acknowledge the variability of social work closures and fit the closure process to the unique characteristics of the client system and the situation.

Completing Contracts

The first and most preferred resolution is when clients have made significant progress toward the goals they have set. Planning for this kind of ending begins early in the relationship with the negotiation of a specific contract for services. Recognizing that it is time to resolve the relationship "according to plan" hinges on the clarity of the observable and measurable outcomes contained in this contract. Resolving a social work relationship by successfully completing the contract is the culmination of a collaborative effort. Both social workers and clients deserve credit. Both benefit from an opportunity to reflect on their work and incorporate what they have learned for their future endeavors. To maximize the benefits of their experience, workers and clients examine where they are, review where they've been, and predict where they are going after their work together ends (Figure 16.1).

Many writers suggest activities that resolve the relationship, consolidate gains, and maintain progress (Feld & Radin, 1982; Henry, 1992; Garvin, 1997; Hepworth, Rooney, &

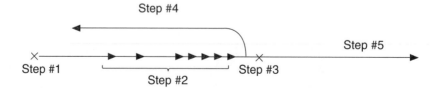

FIGURE 16.1   Endings in Social Work

Step #1   Clarify the time-limited nature of the relationship during the first meeting.

Step #2   Offer periodic reminders of closure throughout the process, increasing their frequency near the end.

Step #3   Determine a specific ending point at which time the client's status will change from "open" to "closed."

Step #4   Facilitate a review of the work. Discuss the client's situation at the beginning, the changes made, the specific activities that led to the changes, and the client's capabilities demonstrated. Also, share the associated feelings about the entire process and the upcoming closure.

Step #5   Discuss the client's future plans, new goals, potential challenges that might arise, any follow-up contacts that may occur, and the process by which clients can reconnect if necessary.

Larsen, 1997; Johnson, 1998; Toseland & Rivas, 1998; Kirst-Ashman & Hull, 1999). Specific steps in successful resolutions include:

- Thorough preparation throughout the entire process, especially in terms of contracting, and periodic reminders of the time-limited nature of the relationship
- Open discussion about the client's readiness for closing, including a concrete evaluation of success, drawing on both client and worker perspectives
- Comprehensive review of the relationship highlighting the client's contributions, significant achievements, and methods used to achieve results
- Mutual sharing of feelings about the relationship and the upcoming closure
- Anticipating the future, projecting upcoming challenges, and predicting the client's continuing success
- Clear agreement on the point of transition from "active" to "closed," description of how the client accesses additional service if necessary, and discussion of possible follow-up contacts

Preparing for Resolution

Effective social workers anticipate the end of the professional relationship even from the beginning of the work. Social workers foreshadow successful resolutions by defining a purposeful and professionally oriented relationship from the outset (Hess & Hess, 1999). They continue to hone the specificity of this purpose as they create action plans with concrete enough outcomes to clearly indicate that the work is complete.

Throughout the entire process, supportive social workers remind clients of the transitory nature of the relationship by using direct and indirect messages. Social workers may say:

- I noticed that this is the end of our third month of working together—halfway through the six-month period that our program permits.
- By my count, this is group meeting number 8 out of 12. Just four meetings left on our agreement. I guess that means if there's anything you've been putting off that you'd like to talk about, this might be the time.
- Six months from now—after we're done—you'll look back and remember this time when you actually beat the system at its own game!
- You always come up with such sound ideas on your own. It gives me confidence that you'll be able to handle things after we're done.

Social workers intersperse these comments selectively early in the process, but interject them more frequently as the ending becomes imminent. By the time only a few meetings are left and clients are clearly finishing up, the discussion of endings becomes central in conversations between clients and workers. Although workers cannot control if clients choose to drop out of service suddenly, ethical social workers never abruptly withdraw service from clients without explanation or direction.

Recall the flexibility of the social work contract and how it keeps pace with the current focus of the work during the course of the relationship. Through this continuous renegotiation of the contract, clients clearly experience their power to continue or end the work.

These discussions offer clients legitimate exit points, acknowledging their rights to self-determination about how they would like to pursue their goals. Choosing to wrap up with the social worker in favor of working toward goals on their own may signal that clients are empowered, feeling their own sense of efficacy to succeed on their own.

Stopping Short of Goals

Sometimes, clients and workers make significant progress yet don't quite attain predetermined goals. Clients have reached a plateau where continued joint efforts are producing no appreciable benefit; the relationship has run its course at this particular time. Perhaps, the goals were overly ambitious. Maybe, the immediate crisis has passed, leaving clients comfortable with where they are and with limited motivation for continuing their change efforts. When workers see few possibilities for productivity in future sessions, they may suggest renegotiating the original goals to those outcomes clients have already achieved. In other words, they ask, "Is this good enough?" If clients agree, social workers proceed with closure activities that celebrate what clients have achieved thus far, and emphasize that clients may return for additional work in the future.

Discussing Readiness

Social workers observe carefully for signs that the work is done. They monitor progress toward goals and assess clients' developing abilities to cope independently of the helping relationship. Workers are not alone in "looking for the end." Although most of the social workers in Maluccio's (1979) study asserted the decision to end the professional relationship was mutual, most of the clients indicated that they themselves initiated the closure.

As clients near their goals, social workers engage them in conversations about their readiness to finish up the work. Periodically evaluating progress in carrying out the action plan is one way that workers measure a client's preparedness for ending the relationship. Workers also keep an eye on other behavioral indicators that clients are moving from interdependent work with the social worker to independent work of their own. Behaviors that signal clients may be outgrowing the need for professional assistance include when clients:

- Use meetings with the worker as a forum to bounce off their ideas about what to do rather passively seeking the worker's suggestions and expertise
- Take the initiative between meetings to modify and improve on plans developed with the social worker
- Begin to manage the process of change by organizing their own assessment, analysis, planning, and intervention activities to modify situations they desire to change
- Acknowledge their own abilities openly, demonstrate confidence, and express optimism

When workers believe that the time for closure is approaching, they share their observations directly with clients. "I'm noticing that you seem to be taking the process over yourself. I'm wondering what you still need from me?" Workers also respond enthusiastically to clients' comments that "we're handling things much better" or "I'm feeling more confident of my ability" with comments like "I see that too!" Workers keep the progress toward goals in the forefront of discussions. If workers let this actual purpose of the relationship recede into the background, then the appropriate time for closure will be difficult to pin-point since the "relationship may become the focus of the work together, rather than a vehicle" (Hess & Hess, 1999, p. 490).

Evaluating

Although evaluation is integral to successful work throughout the entire social work process, it functions in a very important way near the end. As part of the closure process, a comprehensive evaluation identifies what works, clarifies the methods and strategies that the client uses most effectively, empowers the client with information that might be useful in meeting future challenges, and brings a sense of completion. Evaluative questions that facilitate closure include:

> What did you like best about our work together?
> What did you like least about our work together?
> What will you miss about our work together?
> What do you look forward to when we stop working together? (Gutheil, 1993, p. 171)

There are many techniques available to workers and clients for evaluating their success. Chapter 15 provides an overview of these approaches, including single-system design, goal attainment scaling, and qualitative methods. Workers and clients choose evaluation methods that fit their particular situation the best and actively involve clients. For example, with individual and family clients, Gutheil (1993) suggests using comparative eco-maps. Clients compare their support networks at the beginning of the work to their networks as they exist at the end. Imagine the impact on a client of viewing the differences between an earlier eco-map, sparse with connections compared to a subsequent one, rich with community and social supports developed during the course of the social work endeavor.

Responding to Evaluations

Honest appraisals can be empowering. Both workers and clients benefit from evaluating their work nondefensively. Openly considering what worked and what didn't gives concrete information on which to build future solutions. To elicit open evaluations, workers ask directly for feedback about their work and respond nondefensively by thanking clients for information whether it compliments or criticizes.

Social workers should accept appreciation from clients, yet some practitioners are reluctant to acknowledge their good work, fearing that they will take away from a client's sense of achievement. Dunst and associates (1988) underscore the significance of reciprocity since it "minimizes [clients'] sense of indebtedness" (p. 74). Acknowledging mutual accomplishments should represent no problem for collaborative social work partnerships, since both partners have contributed to their success. Social workers accept their part of the credit while continuing to highlight those aspects of the work for which clients deserve praise. Many clients want to express their gratitude as part of "getting their feelings out" before the end; social workers should not let their own humility block any client's needs to express appreciation.

Reviewing Progress

Reviewing progress solidifies changes and reinforces a client's sense of achievement. To do so, social workers reminisce with clients about the work from its inception to it current state, accentuating what clients did to make the positive changes that have occurred. This review should include activities to identify gains, as endings should be a time for adding up what has been learned (Shulman, 1999, p. 213) In other words, social workers and clients retrace their progress to identify and reinforce client strengths and abilities. Feld and Radin (1982) stress the importance of such a strengths-oriented review process, saying that "a sense of competency is a goal applicable to virtually all recipients of social work services, in all contexts, in all settings" (p. 481).

Giving Clients Credit

Clients make two types of attributions regarding their progress—situational and dispositional (Feld & Radin, 1982). Situational attributions are those in which clients credit workers with creating the changes. Dispositional attributions, on the other hand, are those in which clients believe they themselves created the improvement and experience their own competency. You can guess which kind of conclusion works best to empower clients. When clients make situational attributions, workers get the credit and clients do "not expect the behavior to continue when contacts with the worker are ended" (p. 481). By making dispositional attributions, clients acknowledge their part in creating the change and "they are more likely to anticipate the improvement will remain after termination" (p. 481). A review process encouraging dispositional attributions helps clients to believe they can "go it alone."

Social workers draw on their own memories and careful progress notes to credit clients for their contributions. Social workers may say:

- I remember when we first got together how you felt like you would never be able to move out on your own, but then you put your mind to it, got a job, put together a workable budget, and now you're talking about buying a car.
- This group has seen some tough times—like the time that you had the big disagreement and several of you walked out of the room. I was so impressed with your abilities to talk that through, assert your opinions, and still reach consensus on a plan.
- I've seen other people just give up when they lose a child, but that certainly hasn't been my experience with you. You turned your grief into action, used your influence to organize the local chapter of Mothers Against Drunk Drivers, and found out just what you had left even after losing so much. I'd like to bottle your resilience and take it home with me.

Workers who use empowering processes throughout their work with clients discover they have many examples of client capabilities to emphasize in this review process.

Sharing Feelings

To bring closure to the relationship, social workers and clients share their feelings about completing their work. Practitioners can anticipate the possible range of feelings clients may experience by considering the intensity and length of the relationship, content of the work, size of client system, the client's past experiences with transitions, and the reason for ending (Fortune, 1995; Kirst-Ashman & Hull, 1999).

Often, when we think about endings, we think of the feelings related to grief and sadness. Siebold's (1992) review of the literature finds that many writers describe endings as "grim processes" of mourning and separation that pose difficulties for both clients and social workers; however, this is not necessarily the case when workers focus on a client's potential mastery, adaptation, and maturation process. Endings can be positive events: "when clients see themselves as moving on to new possibilities and increased opportunities, termination is a time of celebration as well as loss" (Gutheil, 1993, p. 174). Feelings at this time can include many that are related to success—elation, exhilaration, relief, contentment, affection, confidence, mastery, power, satisfaction, respect, and joy!

Consider the findings of a study by Fortune, Pearlingi, and Rochelle (1992) as evidence of the positive feelings clients and workers may experience as they complete their work. These researchers surveyed 69 respondents (both workers and clients together for at least 10 sessions, having completed their work within 6 months prior to the survey) to gather information about client and practitioner reactions to closure. They report that:

> *Practitioners responding to the questionnaire reported strong positive reactions to termination for both their clients and themselves. Negative reactions were weak or absent. Among clients, the strongest reactions were positive affect (pride, accomplishment, independence), evaluation of success, evaluation of the therapy experience, and positive flight. Least strong were nihilistic flight, regression, denial, recapitulation, and expression of a need for further treatment. Among practitioners, the strongest reactions were pride in the client's success and pride in their own skill; least strong were relief, doubt about their effectiveness, doubt about the client's progress, and reexperiencing of previous losses. (p. 176)*

Research like this reorients workers from merely empathizing with their clients' feelings of loss at closure to joining clients in their celebrations of success.

Our personal experiences with transitions combined with our sense of competence as professionals and our feelings toward clients influence how we respond as the working relationship ends (Hess & Hess, 1999). Questions to spark social workers' self-awareness about endings include:

- What are my experiences with separations and transitions including high school graduation, moving, divorce, death, loss of friendships, job promotion, or leaving home?
- How have I reacted to transitions? Have they been marked by anxiety, ambivalence, optimism, or a sense of challenge?
- What helps me through transitions?
- How do I view myself as a professional? How do I respond to negative evaluations of my work? Can I accept compliments about my work?
- How do I feel about my work with this particular client system?
- What did I do right? What could I have done differently?

Self-awareness helps us to differentiate our own experiences from those of our clients, supports a forthright evaluation of our work, and leads to constructive resolutions of our relationships with client systems.

Generalizing Outcomes

Even though closure means that the work is "winding down," social workers are not quite done yet as there is evidence that the carryover of gains into everyday activities is not automatic. Ways to stabilize progress "have commanded increasing attention as a result of alarming follow-up research findings indicating that many clients do not maintain the gains they achieve during the formal helping process" (Hepworth, Rooney, & Larsen, 1997, p. 611). The most effective closure activities generalize into a client's everyday functioning.

Accomplishments are more likely to generalize when social workers have helped clients continually focus on relevant issues and situations, as well as practice new skills and behaviors in a variety of situations and settings, and when clients have gained confidence in their own abilities rather than in those of the worker (Toseland & Rivas, 1998). The most enduring work is that which is consistently integrated into the client's functioning throughout the entire process. The rise of community-integrated programs, work with natural support networks, in-home treatment, and policies of deinstitutionalization reflect attempts to make and keep social work practice immediately relevant in clients' natural settings.

Changes also endure when clients not only experience the results of the success, but also when they learn the process by which the success has been achieved (Johnson, 1998; Toseland & Rivas, 1998). To teach process, workers openly collaborate with clients to define problems clearly, complete comprehensive assessments, articulate concrete action plans, and actively implement change strategies. At closure, workers can help clients take knowledge of these processes with them by reviewing the processes implemented and discussing how to apply these processes to issues that may arise in the future.

Stabilizing Success

An important activity in closure is for workers and clients to make connections between what they have done together and how clients might approach upcoming issues (Hess & Hess, 1999). Workers should help clients with "appropriate bridging to activities outside of treatment" (Fortune, Pearlingi, & Rochelle, 1992, p. 177). A comprehensive review that emphasizes client strengths facilitates this connection and empowers clients to move on with an objective understanding of their ability to resolve issues on their own.

Clients benefit from an appraisal of their strengths and how they might work in the future, but Shulman (1999) cautions workers to "resist the temptation to reassure the client who expresses doubts about competency" (p. 216). He adds that even though workers can display confidence in clients, they should stop short of minimizing the difficulties that may lie ahead. Clients transition to independent functioning best with an honest view of their competencies and how these abilities might help them in the future.

Firming Up Social Supports

Clients function most effectively after discontinuing their work with practitioners if they have ongoing support from others. Self-help groups, natural helping networks, clubs, neighborhoods, and churches are other places that clients and workers can explore for ongoing support. Diversity-sensitive practice requires that "ethnically appropriate resources [be] identified and used to sustain the achievement of goals following termination" (Leung, Cheung, & Stevenson, 1994, p. 719).

Earlier work in which workers helped clients assess and activate resource systems on the client's behalf may already leave clients closely involved with supports that will help maintain their stability. To facilitate further access to supports, workers can help clients plan what events will require the support of others, determine ways that they will contact supports if necessary, or even invite significant others into closing sessions (Simons & Aigner, 1985).

Celebrations and Ritualized Endings

What traditions does your family have to mark passages, transitions, and achievements? Do you have family gatherings, picnics, suppers, or ceremonies? Do certain family members play particular roles in giving toasts, lighting candles, singing songs, giving gifts, or preparing special food? Are passages recorded in your family albums, books, or other treasures? Individuals and families as well as groups frequently mark normal life passages, milestones, and achievements by rituals and ceremonies. Rituals provide human systems with structured ways to deal with emotions, vehicles for communication, and means to celebrate accomplishments (Laird, 1984; Imber-Black, 1988; Gutheil, 1993; Imber-Black & Roberts, 1998).

There is evidence that rituals function positively for the endings of social worker–client relationships as well (Gutheil, 1993). Rituals provide a definitive transition point for both social workers and clients. "Such procedures, by framing the termination and making it stand out as a special part of the work help underscore the important role of this phase in putting closure on the work and consolidating gains" (p. 167). Rituals mark progress, celebrate strengths, and anticipate the possibilities of the future. By providing structure for communicating thoughts and emotions about endings, ceremonies help us cope with ambiguous and sometimes contradictory feelings.

In designing meaningful ceremonies to resolve relationships, workers and clients create experiences that are symbolic of the achievements of the work. "Graduation" ceremonies with music, processionals, and "diplomas" may successfully signify the end of a training group. Collaborating on creating a mural or collage may signify a stepfamily's successful blending into a cohesively functioning unit. Exchanging photographs between clients and workers may give each something of the other to hold on to as they go their separate ways. Each event integrates the gains of the work completed and clearly indicates the transition in the client system and the professional relationship.

Looking to the Future

Constructive resolutions look to the future. To encourage competent functioning beyond the relationship, social workers and clients envision plans and future successes as well as anticipate upcoming challenges. Workers inquire how clients will approach potential issues, develop plans for follow-up including specifying resources for continued support, possibly suggest the idea of a "check-up" appointment, or simply acknowledge that reincidence does not represent failure.

Social workers are not prophets, but their knowledge of human behavior in general and their experiences with specific clients may allow workers to formulate hunches about what might be coming up. Expected life transitions, particular risk factors in clients' lives, previous patterns likely to resurface—all may be worth mentioning so that clients are not blindsided by their optimism in having accomplished current tasks.

Read the following examples of how social workers help clients anticipate upcoming challenges:

- I have been so impressed with your ability to figure out how to balance giving Hank the freedom to be with his friends with your concerns about the safety of the neighborhood. But I also see that Celia is approaching that age where she will want to do the same. What have you learned from this experience with Hank that you think might help you with Celia's transition to adolescence?
- This neighborhood really did dodge the wrecking ball just in the nick of time. Your abilities to organize, target key people in the city's administration, and generate public support have been amazing. I also recognize that some of the same concerns that prompted the city's actions still exist—the high crime, sporadic maintenance, and abandoned buildings. Have you thought what you might do with the resources you've developed to head off the city's next move before it happens?
- You really do seem set for now. Your skill in managing all of those services to keep Howard at home is nothing short of miraculous. But we both know that Alzheimer's is a progressive disease. What sort of plans are you making for the future?

Each of these comments reflects workers' confidence in their clients yet indicates the reality that things don't stand still; clients will have to continue to cope as time goes on. Workers can guide clients to apply the skills and processes they have learned to each of these upcoming situations.

Following Up

For successful resolution, workers and clients also clarify exactly where the relationship goes from here. The practitioner's posthelping responses can ensure that this process remains empowering (Dunst & Trivette, 1988; Dunst, Trivette, & Deal, 1988; Dunst, Trivette, Davis, & Cornwell, 1988; Dunst, 1993). Will there be additional contacts? Should clients schedule a check-up visit for three months to monitor if they are still on track? Will someone from the agency contact clients to check their continuing progress as part of the agency's outcome evaluation procedure? How will clients access their records if they choose to do so? What if clients really feel the need to contact the worker again—how do they do it? Is it acceptable for clients to get back in touch? Can they call with good news or are contacts limited to those requests for additional assistance? What are clients supposed to do if they coincidentally run into workers in other contexts, at the mall, the grocery store, or the movies?

These questions deserve attention to alleviate clients' concerns about the future. As workers and clients discuss the answers to these issues they modify their working agreement to formulate a "contract for closure" that specifies how clients will continue without workers and the conditions under which clients or workers may reinitiate contact. Clients need information about policies and procedures for reconnecting to the worker. Clarity about these issues gives clients the information they need to make sound decisions about managing their own resources in the future. Social workers should also take steps to ensure that any follow-up contact is noncoercive and voluntary (Houston-Vega, Nuehring, & Daguio, 1997).

Closing with Referral

Sometimes relationships between social workers and clients end before reaching the desired goals. For a variety of reasons, workers identify the need to refer clients elsewhere for continued service. This decision may be prompted by the agency's restrictions on length of service or client eligibility, the worker's move to a new position, or the worker's lack of qualifications to continue working with the client's issues that have surfaced. Changes in clients' needs, crisis events in their lives, or lack of continuing progress may also precipitate a referral and subsequent resolution of the professional relationship.

Previous chapters describe processes for linking clients with available resources while clients continue to work with the current agency and worker. But when referring clients at closure, workers attempt to smooth the transition, maintain client motivation, and incorporate any progress achieved so far into the work of the subsequent helping relationship. In closing with clients by referring to another service, workers are simultaneously ending and beginning—wrapping up a phase of the work and orienting clients toward a successful start somewhere else.

Acknowledging Limited Resources

When practitioners contract with clients for social work services, workers agree to keep up their end of the bargain. In other words, workers guarantee that what clients appear to need is a good fit for what the agency offers. To honor this agreement, workers monitor three systems—the agency, the client, and the worker. Changes in any of these systems may create a gap between what the client seeks and what the agency or worker can provide. Social workers know that it is time to resolve the professional relationship with an appropriate referral when these systems are unable to mesh in ways effective to reach clients' goals.

When Client Needs Exceed Worker Limits

Sometimes, workers discover that their practice abilities or settings can offer nothing further. Workers may recognize this situation in their own inability to respond to what clients want or when updated assessment information reveals that clients need something that workers do not have available. Ethical social workers accept their limits and refer clients when the situation moves beyond the worker's role or expertise.

Discovering the need to refer is not unusual. Some challenges surface more slowly than others. When clients withhold significant information, workers may blame themselves or clients. However, this does not mean that workers are inadequate or that clients have been "lying." Sensitive subjects may require extensive testing of the worker and a trusting, established professional relationship for the client to come forward. Examples where clients are reluctant to quickly share "what is really happening" often involve alcoholism, drug addiction, sexual abuse, or criminal behavior. When clients have developed enough trust to disclose these issues, workers respond in a trustworthy manner by referring clients to the most appropriate service.

Dale Storonski is well acquainted with the constraints that sometimes lead him to end his work with clients by referring them to others for continued assistance. Dale, a delinquency prevention worker at Northside Youth Services, recently closed a case that provides such an example. Todd, a client referred to Dale after his arrest for shoplifting, continued his illegal activity in spite of their work to focus Todd on more productive activities. When Todd finally admitted to Dale that he was using cocaine daily, Dale explained his inability to work with addiction in his particular setting and referred Todd to the Addictions Recovery Center. In this situation, the indications for referral were explicit. The priority actions necessary for the best interests of this client required Dale to close out his work and refer Todd elsewhere for continuing service.

Service Restrictions

At other times, organizational constraints prescribe endings rather than leaving the actual choice to social workers or clients. Agencies may impose time limits based on guidelines from fund sources or policies about the distribution of services. For example, managed care companies often dictate the length of social work services to maintain availability of space (Hess & Hess, 1999). Service restrictions also occur when agency policies target clients in a particular age range, feature time-limited interventions, or emphasize crisis resolution rather than long-term work. Consider a delinquency prevention program that may only work with juveniles under the age of 18, since older clients are no longer at risk of "delinquency" according to the laws of the particular state. As a part of developing a service continuum, the agency can mitigate any disruptions by negotiating "working agreements" with adult-oriented services to accept referrals when the delinquency prevention program's clients turn 18.

Other organizational stipulations affect the nature and duration of service as well. For example, many workers practice in host settings, where social work services are supplementary to the organization's primary mission. Such organizations include hospitals, schools, or private businesses. Organizational factors, including discharge from the hospital, the end of the school year, or termination of employment, can force social workers to finalize their work quickly (Hess & Hess, 1999). Although social workers can anticipate these endings, they may not represent "natural" conclusions or resolutions. For successful closure with these clients, workers clarify the limits of their services at the outset, only negotiate goals that fit the setting, and provide referral options at closure.

Finally, internal changes in an agency's structure or mission may shift a worker's responsibilities and create other personnel and programmatic changes which affect the continuity of services. Fiscal constraints all too often determine parameters for services. Social workers assess what impact these changes will have on clients and apprise them of what they can expect. When agency practices, guidelines, or changes force clients out before they are ready, ethical social workers build bridges to other assistance to sustain client motivation, safety, and progress.

Implementing Legal Mandates

All social workers are mandated to report incidents that threaten clients' safety or the safety of others. High-risk situations including child abuse, elder abuse, intimate violence, and potential suicide or homicide require that workers take immediate steps to secure the safety of those involved. This may entail actions to report concerns to state protective services, local police, or potential victims, or to arrange for clients to be evaluated at community mental health centers. Chapter 8 describes these circumstances and the priority actions that social workers must take to prevent harm.

Moreover, complying with legal mandates may interrupt a practitioner's work with a client. Mandated service providers are likely to have service arrangements that make pre-existing services unnecessary or shift previous goals to a secondary importance in the face of the current crisis. In some cases, clients themselves may respond to the worker's actions negatively, feeling betrayed or undermined and refuse to continue the relationship. As a result, a social worker's contract with a client may be preempted by the mandated report of a dangerous situation.

Social workers cannot be swayed by the potential for service disruption in handling such events. A social worker's ethical responsibility to report harm takes precedence over the preference for service continuance. However, workers should also be careful not to abandon clients at these times of crisis. Clients benefit from workers who stay involved for a sufficient time period to make the necessary transition. A worker's goals at this time are similar to other situations in which the client transfers to a new service provider or withdraws prematurely from service. The worker attempts to consolidate the progress from the work thus far and facilitate the success of the subsequent plan.

As an example consider the case of Linda, a client who reveals to youth worker Dale Storonski that her grandfather has been sexually abusing her. Dale's mandated report to the Child Protective Unit results in Linda's removal from her grandparents' home and emergency placement in a foster home across town. The web of services offered by the child welfare system usurps Dale's role with Linda, requiring that he close out his work and prepare Linda to work successfully within the new service arena. To facilitate this transition, Dale arranges a conjoint meeting with Linda, her new caseworker, and her foster family to discuss his previous work with Linda and participate in updating Linda's case plan for implementation under these new circumstances.

Recognizing Interim Success

Resolving a professional relationship by referring clients elsewhere is not a defeat, but a step on the way to success. Identifying a more appropriate service clearly moves clients toward the solutions they seek. When making the transition to a new service, workers reflect this perspective by reviewing the client's successes so far in a positive way. So, workers guide clients to discuss their readiness to discontinue, highlight achievements, encourage the exchange of feelings, and anticipate future development.

Making Referrals

When workers reach the limit of what they can offer, they have an ethical obligation to discuss this with clients openly and offer clients other resource possibilities (Wells with Masch, 1986). Failure to offer honest information about the worker's or agency's limitations may leave clients with feelings that they are being "dumped." To avoid misunderstandings, workers may say:

- As we discussed when we first got together, the crisis service we offer only allows us thirty days per client. Things seem a little calmer now, but you've told me that you still would like to build on the progress you are making. I have several possibilities about where to go next that I think we should discuss.

- You have been great at figuring out how to deal with the kids and avoid using physical punishment, but now you are asking me for assistance with your marriage and I don't really feel qualified as a marriage therapist. There are, however, several excellent programs that I could recommend to you.
- I need to let you know that I'll be leaving my position in three weeks. I got a promotion, but that moves me out to the regional office. I know we're right in the middle of things here, so I'd like to work quickly to refer you on to the new worker so we don't lose any ground. Is that OK with you?
- I know that we have come a long way together and that you are still facing a big challenge in confronting the school board about some of its discriminatory suspension policies. But guidelines set by my board of directors prevent me from participating in the kind of protest against the school that you are planning. I do know that the Center for Citizens' Rights has dealt with some similar concerns. Would you be interested in contacting them for continued support?

Notice how in each example workers directly acknowledge their limitations, offer honest expectations, reinforce the progress already made, and clearly indicate where clients might go next.

Smoothing the Transition

Workers have a double dilemma in referring clients to others for continuation of the work. If workers have been successful so far, clients have probably developed a sense of confidence in the relationship and will be reluctant to transfer. If the work has run into obstacles, clients may be discouraged about continuing with anyone. Recognizing these potential hazards in closing a case by referral, practitioners work carefully on transitions that keep client systems moving forward.

Imagine yourself in the role of a client for a minute. You finally take a risk of getting some assistance. Things are going pretty well until your social worker starts talking about running out of time—something about eligibility and agency policy. What would help you pick up with a new worker where you left off with the old one? Clearly the transition would be easier if you didn't have to start all over. You would want the new worker to be informed. You would also want the new worker to be someone you could relate to easily. And you might want to circumvent all the red tape that some agencies put you through before you actually get into one of the inner offices or get the direct service worker into your home.

Facilitating Client Control

You can help clients accept referrals to subsequent services by recognizing that clients don't want to start all over. By following a few simple suggestions you can assist clients and new workers to build on the progress already made. For example, it works best to refer clients to another human being with a name, description, and set of qualifications rather than an agency, program, or department. Find out specifically who the new worker will be and inform the client. If possible, give the client alternatives from which to choose (Simons & Aigner, 1985). Let clients decide if they want you to call to facilitate their entry, or whether they should make the first contact and mention your name. Also, learn the new agency's entry procedures so you can prepare clients to expedite those sometimes confusing and uncomfortable beginning processes. Remember that clients have already entered the social service network. They are on the "inside" and you should not throw them back out and leave them to enter all over again.

Collaborate with clients on how to transfer information. Find out exactly what clients want you to say and what information they would like to share in their own way. Consider the possibility of a collective meeting between you, the new worker, and the client system. This has the advantage of launching the new relationship near the same level of intimacy and comfort that was built in the previous professional relationship. Clients will be likely to discuss issues openly in front of the new worker secure in the presence of an established relationship. This kind of referral conference also allows all of the participants to discuss the work already completed in a format that allows for clarification and questioning. When time or organizational restraints prevent this direct type of transfer, social workers and clients still work cooperatively toward a process that sets back the progress as little as possible.

Tracking Progress

As a final step, workers follow up referrals to ensure that clients have made the new connections and to receive feedback on whether clients felt prepared for the changes. In follow-up contacts with clients, workers are cautious not to intrude on the relationship of the client with the new worker. With the client's permission, practitioners may also contact the new worker, acting to cement the referral link between the programs.

Responding to Clients' Discontinuation of Services

Clients conclude their work in different ways, sometimes earlier than social workers would prefer. Many reasons prompt clients to withdraw from services prematurely—reasons that vary widely, from clients' feelings of disillusionment to their feelings of success and empowerment. Regardless of the reason, workers recognize that clients have the privilege to withdraw from services as they see fit. Even involuntary clients can choose to stop and then experience the consequences for their refusal to continue.

Preparing for Early Withdrawal

Practitioners work actively to resolve relationships successfully even with clients who drop out of services. First, workers structure each meeting with clients in such a way that if clients fail to return they have still gained something from the work. Second, workers learn to recognize signs that clients are drifting away in order to invite an open discussion about the direction of the work. Finally, workers follow up with clients who drop out to clarify the status of the relationship, receive feedback on the reasons that clients discontinued the service, and let clients know how to return in the future if they so desire.

The dynamic nature of social work practice demands that workers attend to all facets of the process simultaneously, regardless of the specific phase that time factors may indicate. As social workers, we assess clients as we build partnerships with them; we observe clients change and develop even while we are still discovering what they can do; we continue to build relationships as we implement changes; and we *anticipate the end of the relationship even as we are beginning.* Preparing for the inevitable ending, workers "integrate gains" throughout the entire process. To do so, workers consistently guide clients in the direction of their strengths, their goals, and their power. Clients will then leave the work with greater confidence in their abilities even if they exit prematurely.

"Every session is the first and every session is the last" (Walter & Peller, 1992, p. 140). This phrase depicts a here-and-now style of practice, and also says that social workers help clients best when they function as if each session could be the last. When workers end each meeting with a summary of the progress made and concretely plan the next step to take, clients leave with a sense of accomplishment and direction whether or not they return for their next scheduled meeting.

Recognizing Exit Clues

Alert social workers attend to clients' clues of pending departure. Many times clients reveal their tendency to withdraw in behavioral rather than verbal ways. Clients begin to show up late for meetings, cancel sessions frequently because more important events are occurring, or miss appointments altogether. They neglect to carry out activities as planned in previous sessions. Clients may seem inattentive or fail to present important issues during meetings. All of these behaviors may indicate early withdrawal. However, these signals are ambiguous, leaving workers to share their observations and ask clients about their motivation to continue.

When workers see evidence that client involvement is waning, they bring these observations to the forefront. Workers do not accuse clients of hidden agendas. Instead, they convey acceptance and acknowledge that clients have choices to stop early. In the example that follows, notice the worker's up-front, yet accepting tone in sharing observations with a client showing exiting behaviors:

> *I'm a little unclear about what's going on. This is the second week you've come late to our appointment. You're also telling me that you really don't have much to talk about, haven't gotten around to completing the experiment we designed, and you need to leave early today. Seems like you are handling life fine without me. I'm wondering if you're thinking that we've gone about as far as you want to and you'd like to wrap up or take a break.*

Clarifying what clients are saying with "withdrawing" behaviors works whether or not the worker's hunches are correct. If clients are indeed preparing to depart, workers can initiate processes to wrap up the work more productively. If clients are unaware that they are losing focus, a worker's comments may bring them back to task. If clients are indirectly communicating other issues, such as their dissatisfaction with the worker or the present plan, the worker's feedback invites direct discussion and redirection. When workers share their observations that clients are not keeping their commitments to the process, they remind clients they have the privilege to take charge of where the relationship goes next.

Pursuing Mutual Resolutions

Sometimes, workers miss the clues that indicate clients are leaving. Other clients leave no clues. When clients simply "don't show" or call and cancel not only the next appointment but the work altogether, the professional relationship is left unresolved. The reasons clients withdraw abruptly probably vary. Some may feel angry or hopeless. Some may feel that things are good enough. Others may perceive that the worker isn't really interested. Still others may assess that the effort in time, transportation, and cost does not justify the limited benefits they are receiving. Or, factors totally unrelated may interfere. Regardless of the reasons, effective workers try to accomplish a mutual resolution of the relationship.

Good social work requires that practitioners follow up with clients who make "unplanned" exits (Hepworth, Rooney, & Larsen, 1997). Workers have several purposes in doing so, including:

- Understanding a client's reasons for withdrawing
- Validating a client's right to withdraw
- Inviting the client back for future work if desired
- Reinforcing any client progress thus far
- Evaluating and improving the worker's own skills in "reading" client messages, and resolving relationships effectively
- Clarifying the "open" or "closed" status of clients for agency accountability purposes

Most importantly, this follow-up contact reassures clients they can feel comfortable in pursuing their goals in their own way and at their own pace. Workers should not leave clients with thoughts that they have somehow done something wrong, since "being cast in the role of 'truant'… may make clients reluctant to return later if they need additional help" (Hellenbrand, 1987, p. 767). For the work to remain empowering beyond the resolution of the relationship, workers demonstrate their acceptance and support of a client's decision even to withdraw prematurely (Dunst, Trivette, Davis, & Cornwell, 1988).

Service Discontinuation Can Mean Success

Not every client who drops out is sending messages of hopelessness or rejection. Acknowledge the possibility that clients are making informed choices even when they choose directions that you don't expect. Maluccio's (1979) research offers evidence that some clients get what they are looking for in a brief time. More recently, Presley (1987) reports that clients who withdraw after only one session actually claim they experienced benefits and subsequently moved on to use other natural and professional resources. This study concludes that, after a single session, clients were "able to determine and meet their own needs" (p. 607). Finally, Toseland's (1987) research indicates that discontinuance may be grounds for optimism. These results reframe a client's departure even after only one session as potentially good news, not failure.

When Clients Die

The realm of social work reflects the human seasons of birth through death. Social workers in medical settings and gerontological services are most likely to experience a client's death. But social workers in other settings may also be confronted with the realities of death especially since "the epidemic growth of health and social problems, such as AIDS and crack cocaine addiction, has increased the likelihood of such trauma" (Shulman, 1999,

p. 226). As a result, all social workers need fundamental knowledge about grief and its impact as well as skills to support those who have survived the loss of someone they loved.

Grief

Classic studies of grief by Kübler-Ross (1969) offer a paradigm for understanding the emotional dimensions of our experiences with death and dying. These emotions may include:

Denial	"Not me, this isn't happening."
	"It doesn't really affect me."
Anger	"How could this happen?"
	"This is so unfair."
Bargaining	"If only…"
	"I'd trade places, if I could."
Depression	"It's all so hopeless."
	"I don't know why I even try."
Acceptance	"Even when you expect it, it's tough anyway."
	"It's times like these I really count on the support of those around me to help me through."

More recent research on grief describes the idiosyncratic response of each individual to loss and casts doubt on the abilities of any worker to accurately assess and treat a client's grief by applying a predetermined model. "Emphasis is turning to the concept of co-facilitation of a process with the client's perspective taking the lead" (Humphrey & Zimpfer, 1996). This collaborative approach matches the reality that people may experience only some of the emotions Kübler-Ross identifies, experience these emotions in various sequences, or respond completely differently.

A person's age, gender, health, coping style, cultural background, religious beliefs, previous experiences with death, and availability of familial and social support all contribute to feelings of vulnerability, resiliency, or loss when people die (Harper, 1994). Some people may talk readily about their sorrow; others may feel a greater need for privacy and withhold their feelings from the scrutiny of others. Still others may disavow their loss, separating themselves from consciously considering their feelings, feelings that may emerge in other ways such as physical affliction, anger, depression, or acting out behavior. Being able to anticipate the loss provides opportunities to work on unfinished business prior to death (Zilberfein, 1999).

To respond in a supportive way to those who are grieving, workers accept the diverse methods people use to deal with loss and allow survivors to cope at a pace that fits the person and the situation. Supportive workers extensively employ good listening skills even when clients repeat information, accept both direct and indirect expression of feelings, and encourage adaptive coping strategies. Responsible social workers also update their information on the array of community services available for grief support, including those specialty services such as support groups for parents who have lost children, people losing partners to AIDS, and people who have lost loved ones to violence.

Grieving the Death of a Client

Although experiencing the death of a client certainly differs from enduring the loss of a family member or friend, personal and professional grief have common elements. Emotional responses of workers vary, depending on the unique qualities of the worker, the client, and the nature of the professional relationship. Kramer (1998) articulates four factors influencing the way a social worker copes with a client's death, including the worker's:

- Sense of preparedness to deal with personal losses
- Feelings of competence to assist clients and family members with death and dying
- Perception of confidence in professional knowledge and skills for helping clients with the grieving process
- Degree of cognitive and emotional assimilation of the inevitability of his or her own death

The particular circumstances of the client's death—whether it was sudden, lingering, or marked by suffering, as well as the impact on the client's family and significant others—also influence the worker's experience and response.

The recollections of Emily Carter, a Northside Hospital hospice social worker, convey the emotional experience of working with death and dying:

> *Faces of clients and their stories fill my memory. Knowing them, I've learned about myself. I remember 8-year-old Amanda whose rage was fueled by incurable cancer and fear of loneliness, and her parents whose anguish choked their ability to comfort their daughter. I recall Seth, the plucky 3-year-old boy with leukemia who brought laughter to the hospital unit and bittersweet joy to his parent's heart. And there is Irene, from the skilled care unit, with whom I had worked for several months. We were talking about my going on vacation when she abruptly said, "Let me put on my glasses so I can see your face clearly one more time!" And, then we talked about my leaving and her dying. She thanked me for being someone who did not judge her for being angry, someone who would sit with her in silence, someone who would listen to her reminiscing about her past and musing about the future, someone who helped her to discover hope even in the face of sorrow. I remember crying with Irene that day and later grieving her death. Mostly, I remember the power of her affirmation and the meaningfulness of our work together.*

Self-awareness and support are key components in handling issues of death and dying. Workers who cope successfully with the deaths of clients are honest in their appraisal of impact. It is not "unprofessional" to grieve the loss of a genuine relationship. Practice settings such as hospitals, extended care facilities, hospice programs, and caregiver support programs frequently develop staff support services to deal with the significant effects of working in situations where clients die.

Death by Accident or Intention

One of the most difficult experiences that workers may confront is when clients die in ways that workers believe might have been prevented. When clients die of drug overdoses, are murdered participating in gang activity, or take their own lives, workers may be left with guilt that somehow they could have done more or something different. Shulman (1999) emphasizes the importance of the practice setting in helping workers cope. He offers a three-step model for responding to such events: first, to encourage the worker to grieve; second, to elicit support from other workers with similar experiences or whose positions put them at risk of the same experience; and finally, to refocus the worker toward other clients who still need assistance.

Resolving Relationships with Larger Systems

Closure skills with larger systems incorporate all those processes already discussed. Workers perform tasks to help members express feelings, evaluate progress, function independently, plan for the future, and maintain progress (Garvin, 1997; Toseland & Rivas, 1998). But ending the work with a multiperson client system requires additional actions to stabilize the functioning of the system as a whole and to ensure the continuing well-being of its members. Consider the special circumstances of resolving relationships with groups, organizations, and communities.

Small Group Endings

Social workers facilitate small group clients with many different purposes. The specific purpose affects the interaction, development, intensity, duration, and character of the group. To plan appropriately for closure, workers analyze each group's particular characteristics, examine important events that have transpired during the life of the group, and consider where the group and its members will go next.

Whether the group is closed- or open-ended is a significant feature that affects closure activities. A closed-ended group meets for a predetermined number of meetings or long enough to reach a desired goal. At closure, the group disbands, and all members leave at once. Conversely, an open-ended group continues to meet as some members "graduate." At any given time, a worker may be wrapping up with some group members while simultaneously initiating new members into the group's activities. The different meanings of "ending" in these two types of groups lead workers to facilitate closure activities to fit each situation.

Closed-Ended Groups

Closed-ended groups may work to raise consciousness among people who are oppressed, implement social action strategies in the larger environment, provide mutual aid, or increase members' skills in communication, assertion, parenting, or other areas of functioning. Successful groups of these types progress through sequential or recurring phases of coming together, negotiating structures and communication patterns, completing the group's agenda, and wrapping up the work (Schriver, 1998). By the time the group moves toward closure, all members have worked together to create a shared experience and history with one another. They have convened simultaneously, learned to communicate and relate with one another, worked collaboratively on common tasks, and now face the reality that the group as a resource will soon cease to exist for them.

The similar experiences of members in closed-ended groups allow workers to steer the focus toward shared concerns. All members will benefit from conversations which review and evaluate the work, share feelings, and look ahead toward how the group's benefits can be integrated into each member's functioning outside of the group. Review Figure 16.1 presented earlier in this chapter for a summary of these activities. Adapting closure activities to a group client, workers also recognize the additional complexity that each group member is actually ending multiple relationships at once. Members are resolving their relationships with the worker, with each other, and with the group itself. Workers guide members to express their thoughts and feelings concerning each of these relationships as the work ends. Particularly, members should consider that the group as an entity will not exist past the closure, leaving them without the group as a resource "to fall back on."

Open-Ended Groups

Groups structured in an open-ended style may include treatment groups to modify behaviors, addiction recovery groups, and support groups such as those focused on grief, caregiving stress, or survival from violence. Similar to participation in other groups, members will progress through phases defining their relationship to, comfort in, and work with the group. But because members are entering and leaving the group at different times, each member is constructing an idiosyncratic and unique history with the group—sharing common experiences with some group members but having very little interaction with others. In facilitating closure activities with an open-ended group, workers face a collection of members at various developmental levels with very diverse needs.

Even when only one member leaves an open-ended group, every other group member also experiences the closure, yet this event holds a different significance for each. All group members can benefit from an open exchange of the different perspectives they hold. New members are able to imagine themselves completing their work as they listen to others describe their progress and success. Members who are now leaving can "see" their own progress more vividly through the eyes of new members. When a member leaves, workers simultaneously wrap up with that member while also using this success to activate other members who may be only beginning their work.

Resolving Intermember Relationships

When practitioners complete their work with group clients, the worker–client relationship is not the only one to resolve. Members of larger client systems also have relationships with each other—relationships from which members have benefited and on which they have grown to depend. Workers must also provide opportunities for members of multiperson client systems to wrap up their work with each other in ways that acknowledge and support the benefits of relationships among group members.

If you are a proficient math student, you can readily calculate the incredible number of relationship combinations in a client system with many members. In a small group of 5 people, there are 10 dyadic relationships and many small group combinations. In a group of 10 members there are 45 dyadic relationships and subgroup possibilities enough to boggle the mind. Imagine the complexity of relationships in a large organization or community! Obviously, there is not enough time to individually resolve all of these relationships or even know the significance of each one. To cope with closing these multiple relationships, workers initiate structured processes to meet members' needs in a time-efficient and productive way.

Structured Endings

Workers plan final meetings with larger client systems to provide all members with opportunities to share their thoughts and feelings about the work completed and to consider the future. For example, workers may solicit written feedback from members and present summary information to the group. Practitioners may also use structured experiences in which members take turns responding to similar questions, such as "What was the most important thing you learned?" or "How do you anticipate using what you have learned in the future?" Henry (1992) recommends that workers encourage members to formulate an "independent contract" in which members make agreements with themselves about what they will do on their own after closure.

A rotating dyadic experience in which each group member talks briefly one-on-one with each other group member also offers opportunities for members to wrap up with each other. Workers may leave the topic of these dialogues to the discretion of the members. As an alternative, workers can suggest that members thank each other for the benefits that have accrued based on the relationship or reminisce about positive interactions and events that have occurred in the life of the group.

Endings with Organizations and Communities

Much work with organizations and communities involves face-to-face human interaction working with people in various leadership roles, task groups, or teams. Therefore, resolving relationships with these larger client systems draws on the same skills that workers implement with individuals, families, and small groups. But integrating gains in work with mid- and macrolevel systems additionally requires substantive changes in organizational or community structures, policies, procedures, and operations (Kettner, Daley, & Nichols, 1985). Workers see a larger system's readiness for closure when the system has institutionalized the desired changes by incorporating them into the functioning of the organization or community itself. To wrap up their work, organizational- and community-level workers also strive to support the continuing development of leadership, intrasystem alliances, and widespread collaboration in decision-making.

Institutionalizing Change

To maintain the stability of progress initiated in a larger system client past the point of closure, workers target changes in policies and practices that will endure. "When the change in an organization's purpose, structure, and procedures or service arrangements is no longer perceived as change, but as an integral part of its ongoing activities, the innovation is institutionalized" (Germain & Gitterman, 1996, p. 395). A social system's tendency to maintain equilibrium works in favor of sustaining desired changes that become a routine part of the system's functioning.

Consider the example of Damon Edwards, first presented in Chapter 10, as he wraps up his work with the residents of Franklin Courts. The residents have achieved their goals. The children with lead poisoning are receiving medical treatment, the source of the contamination has been discovered, and city work crews are renovating buildings to ensure their safety. To stabilize these changes, the members have also initiated policy changes in the housing authority's code that ensure monitoring of materials used in public housing work projects. Organizing annual blood screenings is another institutionalized accomplishment that will monitor the health of those children already exposed to lead. These embedded changes in policy and practices are institutional changes that will have enduring benefits after Damon and the residents of Franklin Courts complete their work together.

Sustaining Empowered Functioning

The ultimate goal for any level of client system in empowerment-based social work practice is the sustained empowered functioning of the client after the contracted work is completed. With larger system clients this "may include developing organization or community ability to make decisions based on a representational influence, gaining and maintaining political power, and ensuring the decisions are implemented for the benefit of the organization or community" (Harrigan, Fauri, & Netting, 1998, p. 76). Key elements necessary to sustain this empowered functioning include leadership development, collegial collaboration, and consensus-building skills such as negotiation and mediation.

Drawing on the Franklin Courts example, Damon Edwards can work to enhance the leadership of Fiona Grant. Having identified Mrs. Grant's leadership abilities early in the work, Damon has always found ways to create plenty of space for her to lead, leaving himself in a consulting role. The group's success has activated Mrs. Grant's motivation further, and she has now expanded her activities to focus on other neighborhood issues. At closure, Damon directly states his confidence in Mrs. Grant's abilities and offers honest feedback on her strengths as he sees them.

To encourage powerful alliances within the group, Damon also helps group members establish a resident council that meets regularly to review conditions at Franklin Courts, maintains a presence at city council meetings, and monitors the activities of the housing authority, even after the initial crisis fades. Developing leadership and maintaining effective structures and alliances will empower the residents to continue their efforts without needing Damon's involvement. Through his work with this council Damon has also facilitated the development of decision-making skills. Members work toward consensus by accessing each participant's views, respecting differences of opinion, and creating plans that incorporate the strengths of everyone involved.

Termination or Transition?

An important consideration in closure activities with organizations and communities is the role that the social worker will play with the system after the point of closure. In organizational practice, the worker is often a member of the client system itself and will continue to be so when the project at hand is complete. In community practice the worker is likely to have a long-term, ongoing relationship with the community, wrapping up one project and moving on to the next. In these situations, closure will not mark the end of the relationship with the client system but instead signifies a change in the worker's role.

For such a transition to be successful, the "closure" must be clearly understood and the client system must be able to sustain the desired changes without the continuing efforts of the social worker. "If the practitioner is an on-going member of the organization or community in which the change took place, future activity must be restricted to an on-going, established role and responsibility to ensure that change is fixed with some other individual, position, group, or unit" (Harrigan, Fauri, & Netting, 1998, p. 75). Damon Edwards' successful work in supporting Fiona Grant and the resident council as leaders in Franklin Courts allows him to return to his previous role in the Northside Community. He will still interact with the Franklin Courts residents, but refrain from doing for them what they can now do for themselves.

To increase clarity about the role changes that occur at these points of transition, macrolevel practitioners discuss them openly. Workers may also use symbolic means to mark the turning point in their involvement. Work with groups, task forces, committees, organizations, and communities has long been known for its use of ritualized endings. Parties, ceremonies to recognize accomplishments, certificates of merit, voting approval of the final committee report, and notifications of grant funding all affirm accomplishments, mark endings, and serve as bridges to new beginnings. In planning closure ceremonies, workers seek to offer members opportunities to reflect on their work together and define their future relationships with each other in addition to wrapping up with the social worker.

Endings Are Beginnings

An effective closing process does not end the client's development. Instead, it is a beginning for the client to stabilize the progress achieved, to integrate the skills learned, and to function independently. The success of this transition rests not only on the closing activities, but it also requires a process that encourages client self-direction throughout the entire social work relationship. A collaborative social worker and client partnership that recognizes client strengths, creates productive alliances, and increases opportunities empowers clients with the resources to continue to function competently after the professional relationship is done.

Social workers also move beyond the partnership, enriched by another practice experience. An ending that carefully reviews the process and includes an open exchange of thoughts and feelings offers workers important feedback about their professional skills and interpersonal qualities. The practice wisdom gained by workers from each client stimulates the worker's professional development and becomes a resource on which workers draw for each client system yet to come.

Epilogue

Andrea Barry walked out into the summer evening. She felt energized, enthused, and content all at the same time. The Northside Network's annual conference always seemed to leave her with feelings of confidence, a sense of support, and something new to try. Following each conference of the last two years, Andrea had experienced similar feelings. It felt good to get together with Northside's other social workers.

The idea to start the annual conference had come up at one of the Northside Network's brown bag lunches. With each meeting of the Network, members were seeing more clearly that they were all "in this together." In spite of their differences in agency settings and clientele, all workers used similar practice processes. And, each Northside social worker also drew resources from the Northside community. What benefitted the work of one held potential benefits for them all. It only seemed logical that they should pool their efforts. The annual conference was one way they did that.

The conference was a multidimensional experience. Each member of the Network facilitated a workshop, presentation, or task-oriented session. From Mark Nogales, Andrea had learned about the integration of the strengths perspective into working with clients with mental illnesses. Andrea had also participated in writing a position paper about the need for more low-cost and transitional housing. She had really enjoyed the "Tune In, Don't Burn Out" workshop, where Tony Marelli had taught relaxation skills and stress reduction techniques. She attended a panel discussion of several clients discussing what services, approaches, and workers' styles they felt were most helpful. And, Andrea herself had presented the results of her research on the impact of cultural sensitivity training on worker–client relationships.

But it was the closing ceremony that had left Andrea with the afterglow that she would carry into the evening and back to work tomorrow. Kay Landon was the facilitator. She led those attending through a series of reflections on the work of the past year, an update of current conditions in the Northside community, and a guided fantasy experience of where they could be one year from now. As the experience drew to a close, Kay invited participants to share what being a social worker meant to them. It was Damon Edwards' words that still rang in Andrea's thoughts.

We are in a beautiful place here. We are social workers. We have the opportunity to know people. Some are people similar to others we might have run into anyway. But many are people that we would never know in any other way. They all fascinate us, because each of them brings their own unique way. They are resources to us. They have taught us more about human diversity than we have learned in textbooks.

We are in an important place here. We sit at the crossroads. Because as social workers we connect to people at all different levels. We are the elevators of society's people. We pick them up in one place and go with them to where they want to go. We understand the connections and the connectors.

We are in a challenging place here. We weave science and art. Because social work practice needs spontaneity with precision. Because people aren't simple and neither are we. And all that is gold does not glitter.

We are in a vulnerable place here. People show us their pain. They share their reality and shake our beliefs. They swamp our perspectives as we work for their goals. And just when we get there, we let them go.

We are in the right place here. Somehow we've always been on the way. The world has nurtured us and now we nurture it in return. Just as all universes seek balance, we too work as part of our world's solution. We are naturals. We revel in the opportunities for the world and for us.

Glossary

Absolute confidentiality social worker's guarantee that client information will never be recorded or shared in any form; rarely offered in actual practice

Acceptance social work principle; positive regard for clients transmitted by viewing them as partners, listening to their opinions, communicating cordially, honoring cultural differences, and crediting them with strengths and potential

Access to resources social work principle; guarantees fair access to available alternatives and opportunities; a cornerstone of social justice

Accountability social work principle; involves professional proficiency, integrity, impartiality, responsible use of resources, and utilization of sound protocols in practice and research

Action research empowerment-oriented, participatory research method that incorporates elements of research, education, and action; works toward organizational, community, and social change goals

Activating resources development phase practice process; workers and clients collaborate to put plans into action, mobilizing available resources through consultancy, resource management, and education

Active listening dialogue skill whereby social workers respond in ways that communicate understanding and acceptance of the client's message

Activist role resource management role at the macrolevel; workers identify and rectify detrimental societal conditions and involve the general public in change efforts

Advocacy actions taken to achieve social justice, protect the interests of clients, or champion collective causes

Advocate role resource management role at the microlevel; workers act as intermediaries between clients and other systems to ensure clients' access to resources and to protect clients' rights

Alliances collaborative partnerships among individuals, families, groups, organizations, communities and/or others to achieve support, service coordination, and social change

Articulating situations dialogue phase practice process; workers and clients develop a mutual understanding of the situations that prompt clients to seek social work assistance; places client situations in environmental context

Assessing resource capabilities   discovery phase practice process; surveys available and potential resources within the client's ecosystem; details a positive, broad-based view of the client system in transaction with its environment

Boundary   a structural concept referring to the degree of closeness between two systems in transaction; defined by proximity, intensity, and frequency of interaction

Brainstorming   free-flowing group process to generate, but not evaluate, creative ideas or solutions; frequently used as part of group, organizational, and community planning

Broker role   resource management role at the microlevel; workers assess situations, provide clients with choices among alternative resources, and facilitate clients' connections with referral agencies

Burnout   sense of physical and psychological exhaustion resulting from disempowering work environments or becoming overly responsible for clients

Case management   process of accessing and coordinating an array of services and supports relevant to a specific client's needs and goals

Catalyst role   resource management role targeting action within the social work profession; workers team with colleagues and other professionals to create organizational, policy, and other social change

Client-driven services   a model of service delivery in which clients and their goals determine the nature and direction of services

Client outcome assessment   evaluates the degree of goal achievement and the effectiveness of intervention strategies with a particular client system

Clients' rights   legal and ethical privileges guaranteed to those assuming the client role

Closed-ended group   a group that meets for a predetermined number of meetings, or long enough to reach a desired goal; all members begin and end their participation at the same time

Coalition   cooperative alliance of agencies or individuals; formed by a short-term agreement to address a specific issue or need

Collaboration   working relationship characterized by partnership between clients and social workers working together to understand situations and create change

Colleague role   consultancy role at the professional level; workers provide professional acculturation for other social workers through mentoring, guidance, and support

Competence   the ability of any human system to take care of itself and its members and to contribute to the resources of its environment

Confidentiality   social work principle ensuring privacy of client information

Consciousness-raising   facilitation of an individual's or group's critical awareness and sensitivity to status, privilege, and relative situation; prelude to social action

Constructivism   perspective that says individuals create their own reality through interaction and interpretation of experience

Consultancy   social work function; workers and clients at any system level confer and deliberate together to develop plans for change and seek solutions for challenges to social functioning

Consumer satisfaction survey   instrument that assesses clients' perceptions or attitudes about an agency's delivery of services

Convener role   resource management role at the midlevel; workers promote interagency discussion and planning, mobilize coordinated networks for effective service delivery, and advocate policies that promise equitable funding and just service provisions

Creating alliances   development phase practice process; aligning the efforts of clients in empowerment groups, within their natural support networks, and as partners in the service delivery network; at the midlevel, developing collaboration among colleagues, supervisors, and professional organizations

Critical consciousness   awareness of the interconnections between the personal and political

Cultural competence   a social worker's ability to acquire and utilize extensive knowledge about various cultural groups

Cultural diversity   describes the phenomena of human differences as generated by membership in various identifiable human groups

Cultural responsiveness   the ability to use client-perspective-centered practice skills as a method to achieve multicultural competence

Cultural sensitivity   a worker's attitude of acceptance, respect, and appreciation for each client's cultural uniqueness

Culture   a quality of all communities of people identified by geographic location, common characteristics, or similar interests; includes values, norms, beliefs, language, and traditions

Defining directions   dialogue phase practice process; practitioners and clients articulate a mutual understanding of the purpose of their work together

Development phase   grouping of social work practice processes describing how practitioners and clients activate interpersonal and institutional resources, create alliances with other systems, expand opportunities through resource development, evaluate success, and integrate gains

Dialogue phase   grouping of social work practice processes describing how social workers and clients exchange information to develop a partnership relationship, articulate clients' situations, and agree to a purpose for their work together

Discovery phase   grouping of social work practice processes describing how clients and social workers systematically locate relevant strengths and resources with which to build concrete plans for solutions

Dual relationships   secondary roles of social workers with clients, including friendships, business associations, family relationships, or sexual involvement; dual roles may constitute serious ethical violations

Duty to warn   legal obligation of professionals to inform potential victims of impending danger

Eco-map   a diagram depicting the ecological context of a focal system

Ecosystem   the social and physical environment within which human systems exchange resources in a reciprocal relationship

Ecosystems perspective   a theoretical view of human system behavior that conceptualizes the exchanges between people and their physical and social environments as evolutionary and adaptive in context

Education   social work function that describes the information exchange and educational partnerships of co-learners and co-teachers at all levels of social work practice

Empathy   the experience of sharing another's perspectives and feelings

Empowering approach   social work practice method that links micro and macro practice strategies; builds solutions on the existing and potential capabilities of client systems and their environments to effect personal, interpersonal, social, and political change

Empowerment both an outcome and process in social work practice: as an outcome, empowerment describes the experience of competence—a personal sense of efficacy and control, voice in interpersonal relationships, and privilege to share in societal resources; as a process, empowerment describes the acquisition and amplification of power at the personal, interpersonal, and sociopolitical levels

Empowerment evaluation alternative approach to conventional program evaluation; fosters ongoing self-assessments and promotes continuous program improvements

Enabler role consultancy role at the microlevel; workers engage individuals, families, and small groups in counseling processes

Environment the larger physical and social system that contains a focal system

Environmental opportunities those ideologies, social institutions, and community supports that foster individual and societal well-being

Environmental risks ideologies, institutions, or cultural alignments that work against the well-being of certain individuals and therefore of society as a whole

Equilibrium a state of balance in a human system maintained through feedback; must be disrupted to allow system change

Expanding opportunities development phase practice process describing how social workers join with clients to expand societal resources through program development, community organizing, and social action

Externalizing strategy of separating the person from the problem; introduced in the narrative approach

Facilitator role consultancy role at the midlevel; workers activate the participation of constituents in organizational development efforts

Feedback information that maintains existing system equilibrium or induces change

Feminist perspective a cluster of views that posit gender as a key element of social organization at all levels of interaction; connects personal issues to political and social forces to create individual, interpersonal, and social change

Focal system human social or individual system on which work is focusing

Focus groups qualitative research technique for gathering information about a particular topic from a select group of respondents

Force field analysis planning strategy to identify drives and obstacles for achieving macrolevel change

Forming partnerships dialogue phase practice process describing how a worker and a client system define an empowering relationship to reflect the uniqueness of the client system and fit the purposes and standards of the social work profession

Frame of reference our perceptions of others and expectations of situations that influence how we process information and interpret events

Framing solutions discovery phase practice process describing collaborative, concrete, and generalist methods for workers and clients to develop detailed plans for action

Generalist practice integrated and multileveled approach to social work practice; generalist practitioners work with clients at all system levels, link clients to resources, advocate just social policies and responsive service delivery, and research practice effectiveness

Genograms schematic diagrams that visually represent family structure and chronology

Genuineness personal quality of effective workers characterized by authenticity, nondefensiveness, and spontaneity

Goal attainment scaling (GAS) type of evaluation design that measures client achievement levels

Goals desired outcomes; articulated purposes of the social worker–client relationship

Goodness-of-fit ecosystemic concept describing a mutually beneficial balance between persons and environments

Hierarchy the distribution of power, status, and privilege among individuals and subsystems in a particular system

Holon a quality of all systems; indicates that a system is a part of a larger system and simultaneously composed of smaller systems

Human dignity and worth central social work professional value that holds all people have the right to respect and consideration, regardless of race, ethnicity, gender, sexual orientation, age, ability, or socioeconomic status

Hypotheses a research term describing a tentative statement about the relationship between independent and dependent variables

Identifying strengths discovery phase practice process describing how social workers and clients search for client strengths in interpersonal relationships, community connections, cultural memberships, previous experiences, and current change attempts

Individualization social work principle acknowledging the distinctive qualities and circumstances of each person; key element of multicultural competence

Informed consent a process for ensuring that clients understand alternatives and accept consequences of service decisions

Integrating gains development phase practice process that emphasizes the importance of client growth, development, and change as the professional relationship ends

Interactional view perspective that examines the ways people communicate and relate within a system and in transaction with their environments

Intervention phase in single-system design, what practitioners and clients do to affect or change the identified target behaviors

Involuntary clients people participating in social work services as a result of mandates by others; frequently seen in child welfare, domestic violence, criminal justice, mental health, and substance abuse

Macrolevel intervention social change in neighborhoods, communities, and society, through such activities as neighborhood organizing, community planning, locality development, public education, policy practice, and social action

Measurement process by which a researcher or evaluator collects data

Mediator role resource management role at the midlevel; workers use skills to negotiate differences and resolve conflicts within group and organizational networks

Metaphor ambiguous descriptions that frame situations in new ways, inviting clients to make their own interpretations

Microlevel intervention work with people individually, in families, or in small groups to foster changes within personal functioning, in social relationships, and in the ways people interact with social and institutional resources

Midlevel intervention work to create changes within organizations and formal groups, such as task groups, teams, organizations, and the service delivery network

Monitor role consultancy role at the professional level; workers provide support for colleagues to uphold expectations for ethical conduct

Motivation   the degree of attention and energy within a human system to move in a specific direction

Multicultural competence   the integration of cultural knowledge, values, and skills to relate to clients in culturally relevant and appropriate ways

Mutual aid group   group in which members help themselves by helping each other

Mutual causality   circular causality; ecosystemic principle stating that a person's behavior is mutually determined in interaction with others; does not apply to relationships with significantly skewed power differentials

Natural helpers   people known in their neighborhoods, workplaces, schools, or churches as those who function effectively on their own and who provide resources and support to others around them

Nodal event   expected and unexpected life-changing event that disrupts an individual's or system's equilibrium

Nominal group technique   structured, democratic group process to motivate participants and combine their efforts in determining goals, objectives, and action plans

Nonjudgmentalism   social work principle that requires workers to neither blame nor evaluate others as good or bad, allowing others to make their own value decisions

Nonverbal communication   messages accompanying every verbal expression and sometimes standing on their own, including body posture, facial expressions, eye contact, head and body movements, other attending behaviors, voice tone, inflection, and intensity

Objectives   articulated, small, positive steps toward goals; planned actions to remove obstacles in the path toward goals

Objectivity   social work principle requiring the separation of one's personal feelings from others' situations

Open-ended groups   ongoing group focused on a topic or shared concern; new members enter and other members leave at any time as the group continues to meet

Oppression   the injustice that results from the domination and control of resources by certain groups at the expense of others; practices and policies that entitle favored groups and disenfranchise others

Outreach role   educational role at the macrolevel; workers inform the general public about social problems, describe social injustices, and suggest services and policies to address these issues

Planner role   consultancy role at the macrolevel; workers collect data systematically, explore alternative courses of action, and recommend changes to community leaders

Policy analysis   studying and evaluating policies to assess underlying values and impact on service delivery

Power   having access to information and societal resources; being able to choose actions from many possibilities and act on one's choices

Practice evaluation   method of assessing the outcomes and measuring the effectiveness of social work strategies

Praxis   taking action, pausing to observe the impact, then reflecting on the action and its impact to guide the next action

Privilege   ascribed social status and access to societal resources based on cultural group memberships, such as in the examples of "male privilege" or "white privilege"

Privileged communication   legal stipulation that protects a client's private conversations with a social worker by prohibiting the professional from divulging information in court

Proactive responding   dialogue skills used by strengths-focused social workers to encourage clients to articulate their thoughts and feelings about the current situation, define a positive direction, and locate strengths and resources for change

Process recording   an educational tool; verbatim account of dialogue with clients, comments on the social worker's reactions and feelings, analysis and interpretations of the transactions, and the supervisor's comments

Program evaluation   outcome assessment used to determine the value of a program under review

Progress evaluation   monitoring and evaluation of the implementation of the action plan to identify areas of success and target aspects for change

Qualitative research   research describing and analyzing the qualities of the variables being studied; a descriptive analysis such as a case study or key informant study

Quantitative research   research measuring the quantity of the variables being studied; studies involving statistical analysis, such as in experimental research

Recognizing success   development phase practice process that emphasizes what clients have accomplished and describes the numerous ways to measure the achievement of goals and evaluate service effectiveness

Referral   initiation of a new linkage between a client and a service provider or community resource

Reframing   development phase skill in which workers respond so as to offer new perspectives on clients' situations; usually examines a situation perceived negatively and reinterprets it as positive, functional, or useful

Relative confidentiality   legal and ethical requirement of practice; requires that, with few exceptions, information about clients remains private and confidential within the agency context

Reliability   quality of a measurement tool or process that indicates measures are similar or consistent over time or with repeated applications

Research   a method of systematic investigation or experimentation to enrich theory and refine practice applications

Research process   a meticulous and organized process that follows a logical progression of steps including specifying the research problem, reviewing literature and relating to theory, formulating a hypothesis, selecting a research design, gathering and analyzing data, interpreting the results, and identifying the implications for practice

Researcher role   educational role at the professional level; workers conduct empirical research and practice evaluation to contribute to the knowledge base of the profession

Resistance   traditionally defined as client lack of cooperation with the worker's attempts to change the situation; in empowerment practice, defined as the client's motivation to move in a direction different from the worker's; requires a re-examination of goals to move toward cooperation

Resource management   social work function through which social workers stimulate exchanges with resources that client systems already use to some extent, access available resources that clients systems are not using, and develop resources that are not currently available

Response continuum   variety of responses used by workers to articulate the client's perspective on the current situation; range from nondirective to a question-focused pursuit of information

Scholar role   educational role at the professional level; workers continue to develop knowledge and skills through continuing education, training, and scholarly reading; then share knowledge through professional presentation

Self-determination   social work principle upholding people's rights to make their own decisions

Self-help groups   groups of individuals with similar concerns or problems who join together to be helpful resources for one another

Single-system design   research design for evaluating the effects of interventions on a client system's target problem; usually includes a baseline phase (indicated by A) and one or more intervention phases (indicated by alphabetical notation such as B, C, D, etc.); may include repeating baseline observations, such as in the ABAB design

Social action   venue for sociopolitical empowerment; collective action to reallocate sociopolitical power so that disenfranchised citizens can access the opportunities and resources of society and find meaningful ways to contribute to society as valued citizens

Social action group   a group mobilized around shared concerns to work toward creating mid- and macrolevel changes

Social constructionism   perspective that views reality as a construction of social interaction and language; says we are who we interpret ourselves to be as influenced by the ways in which the world sees and describes us

Social constructivism   newly coined word to describe the synthesis of the constructivist and social constructionist perspectives

Social justice   core social work value stating that society should afford the same rights, opportunities, and benefits to all its members

Social network map   tool for assessing social support, picturing social support networks, and quantifying the nature of the support

Social policy   laws, rules, and values that direct the delivery of health and human services and determine how a society distributes its resources to promote well-being among its members

Social support   networks of personal and professional support that cushion stress, help people to cope, and provide material assistance

Social system   groups of people defined by a pattern of relationship or shared attributes

Solution-focused dialogue   conversation with clients that creates an atmosphere conducive to possibilities, clearly articulates what clients want, and discovers incremental steps in the direction of goals

Strategy   action implemented by workers and clients to achieve desired objectives

Strengths   resources to initiate, energize, and sustain change processes, such as personal abilities, resourcefulness, and creativity, as well as resources in interpersonal relationships, culture, organizational networks, and community connections

Strengths perspective   view of people as resourceful with untapped mental, physical, emotional, social, and spiritual abilities and capacities for continued growth

Structural view   a systemic perspective describing the arrangement of individuals and subsystems within a human system; focuses on power distribution and alliances within a system and between a system and its environment

Subsystem   smaller systems within every system

Teacher role   educational role at the microlevel; workers and clients acquire and use information to resolve current issues

Team   group of people collaborating to achieve a defined mutual purpose

Trainer role   educational role at the midlevel; workers function as resource specialists for formal groups and organizations

Transaction   reciprocal interactions between people and their social and physical environments; may sustain or deplete a system's resources

Trust   the ability to take risks in the context of interpersonal relationships

Validity   quality of a measurement process or tool when it accurately measures the variable it intends to measure

Variable   research term identifying concepts that vary in ways that can be observed, recorded, and measured

Voluntary clients   participants in social work services who have the privilege to participate freely without coercion, based on their perceived notion that social work assistance will help

Wholeness   systemic concept describing the interdependence of relationships within and among systems and their environments; implies that change in one part of the ecosystem will precipitate changes in other parts of the ecosystem as the system seeks a new equilibrium

Appendix *A*

THE NATIONAL ASSOCIATION OF SOCIAL WORKERS

Code of Ethics

(Approved by the 1996 NASW Delegate Assembly and revised by the 1999 NASW Delegate Assembly.)

Overview

The *NASW Code of Ethics* is intended to serve as a guide to the everyday professional conduct of social workers. This *Code* includes four sections. The first section, "Preamble," summarizes the social work profession's mission and core values. The second section, "Purpose of the *NASW Code of Ethics*," provides an overview of the *Code*'s main functions and a brief guide for dealing with ethical issues or dilemmas in social work practice. The third section, "Ethical Principles," presents broad ethical principles, based on social work's core values, that inform social work practice. The final section, "Ethical Standards," includes specific ethical standards to guide social workers' conduct and to provide a basis for adjudication.

Preamble

The primary mission of the social work profession is to enhance human well-being and help meet the basic human needs of all people, with particular attention to the needs and empowerment of people who are vulnerable, oppressed, and living in poverty. A historic and defining feature of social work is the profession's focus on individual well-being in a social context and the well-being of society. Fundamental to social work is attention to the environmental forces that create, contribute to, and address problems in living.

Social workers promote social justice and social change with and on behalf of clients. "Clients" is used inclusively to refer to individuals, families, groups, organizations, and communities. Social workers are sensitive to cultural and ethnic diversity and strive to end discrimination, oppression, poverty, and other forms of social injustice. These activities may be in the form of direct practice, community organizing, supervision, consultation, administration, advocacy, social and political action, policy development and implementation, education, and research and evaluation. Social workers seek to enhance the capacity of people to address their own needs. Social workers also seek to promote the responsiveness of organizations, communities, and other social institutions to individuals' needs and social problems.

The mission of the social work profession is rooted in a set of core values. These core values, embraced by social workers throughout the profession's history, are the foundation of social work's unique purpose and perspective:

- service
- social justice
- dignity and worth of the person
- importance of human relationships
- integrity
- competence.

This constellation of core values reflects what is unique to the social work profession. Core values, and the principles that flow from them, must be balanced within the context and complexity of the human experience.

Purpose of the NASW Code of Ethics

Professional ethics are at the core of social work. The profession has an obligation to articulate its basic values, ethical principles, and ethical standards. The *NASW Code of Ethics* sets forth these values, principles, and standards to guide social workers' conduct. The *Code* is relevant to all social workers and social work students, regardless of their professional functions, the settings in which they work, or the populations they serve.

The *NASW Code of Ethics* serves six purposes:

1. The *Code* identifies core values on which social work's mission is based.
2. The *Code* summarizes broad ethical principles that reflect the profession's core values and establishes a set of specific ethical standards that should be used to guide social work practice.
3. The *Code* is designed to help social workers identify relevant considerations when professional obligations conflict or ethical uncertainties arise.
4. The *Code* provides ethical standards to which the general public can hold the social work profession accountable.
5. The *Code* socializes practitioners new to the field to social work's mission, values, ethical principles, and ethical standards.
6. The *Code* articulates standards that the social work profession itself can use to assess whether social workers have engaged in unethical conduct. NASW has formal procedures to adjudicate ethics complaints filed against its members.[1] In subscribing to this

---

[1]For information on NASW adjudication procedures, see *NASW Procedures for the Adjudication of Grievances.*

Code, social workers are required to cooperate in its implementation, participate in NASW adjudication proceedings, and abide by any NASW disciplinary rulings or sanctions based on it.

The *Code* offers a set of values, principles, and standards to guide decision making and conduct when ethical issues arise. It does not provide a set of rules that prescribe how social workers should act in all situations. Specific applications of the *Code* must take into account the context in which it is being considered and the possibility of conflicts among the *Code*'s values, principles, and standards. Ethical responsibilities flow from all human relationships, from the personal and familial to the social and professional.

Further, the *NASW Code of Ethics* does not specify which values, principles, and standards are most important and ought to outweigh others in instances when they conflict. Reasonable differences of opinion can and do exist among social workers with respect to the ways in which values, ethical principles, and ethical standards should be rank ordered when they conflict. Ethical decision making in a given situation must apply the informed judgment of the individual social worker and should also consider how the issues would be judged in a peer review process where the ethical standards of the profession would be applied.

Ethical decision making is a process. There are many instances in social work where simple answers are not available to resolve complex ethical issues. Social workers should take into consideration all the values, principles, and standards in this *Code* that are relevant to any situation in which ethical judgment is warranted. Social workers' decisions and actions should be consistent with the spirit as well as the letter of this *Code*.

In addition to this *Code,* there are many other sources of information about ethical thinking that may be useful. Social workers should consider ethical theory and principles generally, social work theory and research, laws, regulations, agency policies, and other relevant codes of ethics, recognizing that among codes of ethics social workers should consider the *NASW Code of Ethics* as their primary source. Social workers also should be aware of the impact on ethical decision making of their clients' and their own personal values and cultural and religious beliefs and practices. They should be aware of any conflicts between personal and professional values and deal with them responsibly. For additional guidance social workers should consult the relevant literature on professional ethics and ethical decision making and seek appropriate consultation when faced with ethical dilemmas. This may involve consultation with an agency-based or social work organization's ethics committee, a regulatory body, knowledgeable colleagues, supervisors, or legal counsel.

Instances may arise when social workers' ethical obligations conflict with agency policies or relevant laws or regulations. When such conflicts occur, social workers must make a responsible effort to resolve the conflict in a manner that is consistent with the values, principles, and standards expressed in this *Code*. If a reasonable resolution of the conflict does not appear possible, social workers should seek proper consultation before making a decision.

The *NASW Code of Ethics* is to be used by NASW and by individuals, agencies, organizations, and bodies (such as licensing and regulatory boards, professional liability insurance providers, courts of law, agency boards of directors, government agencies, and other professional groups) that choose to adopt it or use it as a frame of reference. Violation of standards in this *Code* does not automatically imply legal liability or violation of the law.

Such determination can only be made in the context of legal and judicial proceedings. Alleged violations of the *Code* would be subject to a peer review process. Such processes are generally separate from legal or administrative procedures and insulated from legal review or proceedings to allow the profession to counsel and discipline its own members.

A code of ethics cannot guarantee ethical behavior. Moreover, a code of ethics cannot resolve all ethical issues or disputes or capture the richness and complexity involved in striving to make responsible choices within a moral community. Rather, a code of ethics sets forth values, ethical principles, and ethical standards to which professionals aspire and by which their actions can be judged. Social workers' ethical behavior should result from their personal commitment to engage in ethical practice. The *NASW Code of Ethics* reflects the commitment of all social workers to uphold the profession's values and to act ethically. Principles and standards must be applied by individuals of good character who discern moral questions and, in good faith, seek to make reliable ethical judgments.

Ethical Principles

The following broad ethical principles are based on social work's core values of service, social justice, dignity and worth of the person, importance of human relationships, integrity, and competence. These principles set forth ideals to which all social workers should aspire.

Value: *Service*
Ethical Principle: *Social workers' primary goal is to help people in need and to address social problems.*

Social workers elevate service to others above self-interest. Social workers draw on their knowledge, values, and skills to help people in need and to address social problems. Social workers are encouraged to volunteer some portion of their professional skills with no expectation of significant financial return (pro bono service).

Value: *Social Justice*
Ethical Principle: *Social workers challenge social injustice.*

Social workers pursue social change, particularly with and on behalf of vulnerable and oppressed individuals and groups of people. Social workers' social change efforts are focused primarily on issues of poverty, unemployment, discrimination, and other forms of social injustice. These activities seek to promote sensitivity to and knowledge about oppression and cultural and ethnic diversity. Social workers strive to ensure access to needed information, services, and resources; equality of opportunity; and meaningful participation in decision making for all people.

Value: *Dignity and Worth of the Person*
Ethical Principle: *Social workers respect the inherent dignity and worth of the person.*

Social workers treat each person in a caring and respectful fashion, mindful of individual differences and cultural and ethnic diversity. Social workers promote clients' socially responsible self-determination. Social workers seek to enhance clients' capacity and opportunity to change and to address their own needs. Social workers are cognizant of their dual responsibility to clients and to the broader society. They seek to resolve conflicts between clients' interest and the broader society's interests in a socially responsible manner consistent with the values, ethical principles, and ethical standards of the profession.

Value: *Importance of Human Relationships*
Ethical Principle: *Social workers recognize the central importance of human relationships.*

Social workers understand that relationships between and among people are an important vehicle for change. Social workers engage people as partners in the helping process. Social workers seek to strengthen relationships among people in a purposeful effort to promote, restore, maintain, and enhance the well-being of individuals, families, social groups, organizations, and communities.

Value: *Integrity*
Ethical Principle: *Social workers behave in a trustworthy manner.*

Social workers are continually aware of the profession's mission, values, ethical principles, and ethical standards and practice in a manner consistent with them. Social workers act honestly and responsibly and promote ethical practices on the part of the organizations with which they are affiliated.

Value: *Competence*
Ethical Principle: *Social workers practice within their areas of competence and develop and enhance their professional expertise.*

Social workers continually strive to increase their professional knowledge and skills and to apply them in practice. Social workers should aspire to contribute to the knowledge base of the profession.

Ethical Standards

The following ethical standards are relevant to the professional activities of all social workers. These standards concern (1) social workers' ethical responsibilities to clients, (2) social workers' ethical responsibilities to colleagues, (3) social workers' ethical responsibilities in practice settings, (4) social workers' ethical responsibilities as professionals, (5) social workers' ethical responsibilities to the social work profession, and (6) social workers' ethical responsibilities to the broader society.

Some of the standards that follow are enforceable guidelines for professional conduct, and some are aspirational. The extent to which each standard is enforceable is a matter of professional judgment to be exercised by those responsible for reviewing alleged violations of ethical standards.

1. Social Workers' Ethical Responsibilities to Clients

1.01 Commitment to Clients
Social workers' primary responsibility is to promote the well-being of clients. In general, clients' interests are primary. However, social workers' responsibility to the larger society or specific legal obligations may on limited occasions supersede the loyalty owed clients,

and clients should be so advised. (Examples include when a social worker is required by law to report that a client has abused a child or has threatened to harm self or others.)

1.02 Self-Determination

Social workers respect and promote the right of clients to self-determination and assist clients in their efforts to identify and clarify their goals. Social workers may limit clients' right to self-determination when, in the social workers' professional judgment, clients' actions or potential actions pose a serious, foreseeable, and imminent risk to themselves or others.

1.03 Informed Consent

(a) Social workers should provide services to clients only in the context of a professional relationship based, when appropriate, on valid informed consent. Social workers should use clear and understandable language to inform clients of the purpose of the services, risks related to the services, limits to services because of the requirements of a third-party payer, relevant costs, reasonable alternatives, clients' right to refuse or withdraw consent, and the time frame covered by the consent. Social workers should provide clients with an opportunity to ask questions.

(b) In instances when clients are not literate or have difficulty understanding the primary language used in the practice setting, social workers should take steps to ensure clients' comprehension. This may include providing clients with a detailed verbal explanation or arranging for a qualified interpreter or translator whenever possible.

(c) In instances when clients lack the capacity to provide informed consent, social workers should protect clients' interests by seeking permission from an appropriate third party, informing clients consistent with the clients' level of understanding. In such instances social workers should seek to ensure that the third party acts in a manner consistent with clients' wishes and interests. Social workers should take reasonable steps to enhance such clients' ability to give informed consent.

(d) In instances when clients are receiving services involuntarily, social workers should provide information about the nature and extent of services and about the extent of clients' right to refuse service.

(e) Social workers who provide services via electronic media (such as computer, telephone, radio, and television) should inform recipients of the limitations and risks associated with such services.

(f) Social workers should obtain clients' informed consent before audiotaping or videotaping clients or permitting observation of services to clients by a third party.

1.04 Competence

(a) Social workers should provide services and represent themselves as competent only within the boundaries of their education, training, license, certification, consultation received, supervised experience, or other relevant professional experience.

(b) Social workers should provide services in substantive areas or use intervention techniques or approaches that are new to them only after engaging in appropriate study, training, consultation, and supervision from people who are competent in those interventions or techniques.

(c) When generally recognized standards do not exist with respect to an emerging area of practice, social workers should exercise careful judgment and take responsible steps (including appropriate education, research, training, consultation, and supervision) to ensure the competence of their work and to protect clients from harm.

1.05 Cultural Competence and Social Diversity

(a) Social workers should understand culture and its function in human behavior and society, recognizing the strengths that exist in all cultures.

(b) Social workers should have a knowledge base of their clients' cultures and be able to demonstrate competence in the provision of services that are sensitive to clients' cultures and to differences among people and cultural groups.

(c) Social workers should obtain education about and seek to understand the nature of social diversity and oppression with respect to race, ethnicity, national origin, color, sex, sexual orientation, age, marital status, political belief, religion, and mental or physical disability.

1.06 Conflicts of Interest

(a) Social workers should be alert to and avoid conflicts of interest that interfere with the exercise of professional discretion and impartial judgment. Social workers should inform clients when a real or potential conflict of interest arises and take reasonable steps to resolve the issue in a manner that makes the clients' interests primary and protects clients' interests to the greatest extent possible. In some cases, protecting clients' interests may require termination of the professional relationship with proper referral of the client.

(b) Social workers should not take unfair advantage of any professional relationship or exploit others to further their personal, religious, political, or business interests.

(c) Social workers should not engage in dual or multiple relationships with clients or former clients in which there is a risk of exploitation or potential harm to the client. In instances when dual or multiple relationships are unavoidable, social workers should take steps to protect clients and are responsible for setting clear, appropriate, and culturally sensitive boundaries. (Dual or multiple relationships occur when social workers relate to clients in more than one relationship, whether professional, social, or business. Dual or multiple relationships can occur simultaneously or consecutively.)

(d) When social workers provide services to two or more people who have a relationship with each other (for example, couples, family members), social workers should clarify with all parties which individuals will be considered clients and the nature of social workers' professional obligations to the various individuals who are receiving services. Social workers who anticipate a conflict of interest among the individuals receiving services or who anticipate having to perform in potentially conflicting roles (for example, when a social worker is asked to testify in a child custody dispute or divorce proceedings involving clients) should clarify their role with the parties involved and take appropriate action to minimize any conflict of interest.

1.07 Privacy and Confidentiality

(a) Social workers should respect clients' right to privacy. Social workers should not solicit private information from clients unless it is essential to providing services or conducting social work evaluation or research. Once private information is shared, standards of confidentiality apply.

(b) Social workers may disclose confidential information when appropriate with valid consent from a client or a person legally authorized to consent on behalf of a client.

(c) Social workers should protect the confidentiality of all information obtained in the course of professional service, except for compelling professional reasons. The general expectation that social workers will keep information confidential does not apply when disclosure is necessary to prevent serious, foreseeable, and imminent harm to a client or other identifiable person. In all instances, social workers should disclose the least amount of confidential information necessary to achieve the desired purpose; only information that is directly relevant to the purpose for which the disclosure is made should be revealed.

(d) Social workers should inform clients, to the extent possible, about the disclosure of confidential information and the potential consequences, when feasible before the disclosure is made. This applies whether social workers disclose confidential information on the basis of a legal requirement or client consent.

(e) Social workers should discuss with clients and other interested parties the nature of confidentiality and limitations of clients' right to confidentiality. Social workers should review with clients circumstances where confidential information may be requested and where disclosure of confidential information may be legally required. This discussion should occur as soon as possible in the social worker–client relationship and as needed throughout the course of the relationship.

(f) When social workers provide counseling services to families, couples, or groups, social workers should seek agreement among the parties involved concerning each individual's right to confidentiality and obligation to preserve the confidentiality of information shared by others. Social workers should inform participants in family, couples, or group counseling that social workers cannot guarantee that all participants will honor such agreements.

(g) Social workers should inform clients involved in family, couples, marital, or group counseling of the social worker's, employer's, and agency's policy concerning the social worker's disclosure of confidential information among the parties involved in the counseling.

(h) Social workers should not disclose confidential information to third-party payers unless clients have authorized such disclosure.

(i) Social workers should not discuss confidential information in any setting unless privacy can be ensured. Social workers should not discuss confidential information in public or semipublic areas such as hallways, waiting rooms, elevators, and restaurants.

(j) Social workers should protect the confidentiality of clients during legal proceedings to the extent permitted by law. When a court of law or other legally authorized body orders social workers to disclose confidential or privileged information without a client's consent and such disclosure could cause harm to the client, social workers should request that the court withdraw or limit the order as narrowly as possible or maintain the records under seal, unavailable for public inspection.

(k) Social workers should protect the confidentiality of clients when responding to requests from members of the media.

(l) Social workers should protect the confidentiality of clients' written and electronic records and other sensitive information. Social workers should take reasonable steps to ensure that clients' records are stored in a secure location and that clients' records are not available to others who are not authorized to have access.

(m) Social workers should take precautions to ensure and maintain the confidentiality of information transmitted to other parties through the use of computers, electronic mail, facsimile machines, telephones and telephone answering machines, and other electronic or computer technology. Disclosure of identifying information should be avoided whenever possible.

(n) Social workers should transfer or dispose of clients' records in a manner that protects clients' confidentiality and is consistent with state statutes governing records and social work licensure.

(o) Social workers should take reasonable precautions to protect client confidentiality in the event of the social worker's termination of practice, incapacitation, or death.

(p) Social workers should not disclose identifying information when discussing clients for teaching or training purposes unless the client has consented to disclosure of confidential information.

(q) Social workers should not disclose identifying information when discussing clients with consultants unless the client has consented to disclosure of confidential information or there is a compelling need for such disclosure.

(r) Social workers should protect the confidentiality of deceased clients consistent with the preceding standards.

1.08 Access to Records

(a) Social workers should provide clients with reasonable access to records concerning the clients. Social workers who are concerned that clients' access to their records could cause serious misunderstanding or harm to the client should provide assistance in interpreting the records and consultation with the client regarding the records. Social workers should limit clients' access to their records, or portions of their records, only in exceptional circumstances when there is compelling evidence that such access would cause serious harm to the client. Both clients' requests and the rationale for withholding some or all of the record should be documented in clients' files.

(b) When providing clients with access to their records, social workers should take steps to protect the confidentiality of other individuals identified or discussed in such records.

1.09 Sexual Relationships

(a) Social workers should under no circumstances engage in sexual activities or sexual contact with current clients, whether such contact is consensual or forced.

(b) Social workers should not engage in sexual activities or sexual contact with clients' relatives or other individuals with whom clients maintain a close personal relationship when there is a risk of exploitation or potential harm to the client. Sexual activity or sexual contact with clients' relatives or other individuals with whom clients maintain a personal relationship has the potential to be harmful to the client and may make it difficult for the social worker and client to maintain appropriate professional boundaries. Social workers—not their clients, their clients' relatives, or other individuals with whom the client maintains a personal relationship—assume the full burden for setting clear, appropriate, and culturally sensitive boundaries.

(c) Social workers should not engage in sexual activities or sexual contact with former clients because of the potential for harm to the client. If social workers engage in conduct contrary to this prohibition or claim that an exception to this prohibition is warranted due to extraordinary circumstances, it is social workers—not their clients—who assume the full burden of demonstrating that the former client has not been exploited, coerced, or manipulated, intentionally or unintentionally.

(d) Social workers should not provide clinical services to individuals with whom they have had a prior sexual relationship. Providing clinical services to a former sexual partner has the potential to be harmful to the individual and is likely to make it difficult for the social worker and individual to maintain appropriate professional boundaries.

1.10 Physical Contact

Social workers should not engage in physical contact with clients when there is a possibility of psychological harm to the client as a result of the contact (such as cradling or caressing clients). Social workers who engage in appropriate physical contact with clients are responsible for setting clear, appropriate, and culturally sensitive boundaries that govern such physical contact.

1.11 Sexual Harassment

Social workers should not sexually harass clients. Sexual harassment includes sexual advances, sexual solicitation, requests for sexual favors, and other verbal or physical conduct of a sexual nature.

1.12 Derogatory Language

Social workers should not use derogatory language in their written or verbal communications to or about clients. Social workers should use accurate and respectful language in all communications to and about clients.

1.13 Payment for Services

(a) When setting fees, social workers should ensure that the fees are fair, reasonable, and commensurate with the services performed. Consideration should be given to clients' ability to pay.

(b) Social workers should avoid accepting goods or services from clients as payment for professional services. Bartering arrangements, particularly involving services, create the potential for conflicts of interest, exploitation, and inappropriate boundaries in social workers' relationships with clients. Social workers should explore and may participate in bartering only in very limited circumstances when it can be demonstrated that such arrangements are an accepted practice among professionals in the local community, considered to be essential for the provision of services, negotiated without coercion, and entered into at the client's initiative and with the client's informed consent. Social workers who accept goods or services from clients as payment for professional services assume the full burden of demonstrating that this arrangement will not be detrimental to the client or the professional relationship.

(c) Social workers should not solicit a private fee or other remuneration for providing services to clients who are entitled to such available services through the social workers' employer or agency.

1.14 Clients Who Lack Decision-Making Capacity

When social workers act on behalf of clients who lack the capacity to make informed decisions, social workers should take reasonable steps to safeguard the interests and rights of those clients.

1.15 Interruption of Services

Social workers should make reasonable efforts to ensure continuity of services in the event that services are interrupted by factors such as unavailability, relocation, illness, disability, or death.

1.16 Termination of Services

(a) Social workers should terminate services to clients and professional relationships with them when such services and relationships are no longer required or no longer serve the clients' needs or interests.

(b) Social workers should take reasonable steps to avoid abandoning clients who are still in need of services. Social workers should withdraw services precipitously only under unusual circumstances, giving careful consideration to all factors in the situation and taking care to minimize possible adverse effects. Social workers should assist in making appropriate arrangements for continuation of services when necessary.

(c) Social workers in fee-for-service settings may terminate services to clients who are not paying an overdue balance if the financial contractual arrangements have been made clear to the client, if the client does not pose an imminent danger to self or others, and if the clinical and other consequences of the current nonpayment have been addressed and discussed with the client.

(d) Social workers should not terminate services to pursue a social, financial, or sexual relationship with a client.

(e) Social workers who anticipate the termination or interruption of services to clients should notify clients promptly and seek the transfer, referral, or continuation of services in relation to the clients' needs and preferences.

(f) Social workers who are leaving an employment setting should inform clients of appropriate options for the continuation of services and of the benefits and risks of the options.

2.   Social Workers' Ethical Responsibilities to Colleagues

2.01 Respect

(a) Social workers should treat colleagues with respect and should represent accurately and fairly the qualifications, views, and obligations of colleagues.

(b) Social workers should avoid unwarranted negative criticism of colleagues in communications with clients or with other professionals. Unwarranted negative criticism may include demeaning comments that refer to colleagues' level of competence or to individuals' attributes such as race, ethnicity, national origin, color, sex, sexual orientation, age, marital status, political belief, religion, and mental or physical disability.

(c) Social workers should cooperate with social work colleagues and with colleagues of other professions when such cooperation serves the well-being of clients.

2.02 Confidentiality

Social workers should respect confidential information shared by colleagues in the course of their professional relationships and transactions. Social workers should ensure that such colleagues understand social workers' obligation to respect confidentiality and any exceptions related to it.

2.03 Interdisciplinary Collaboration

(a) Social workers who are members of an interdisciplinary team should participate in and contribute to decisions that affect the well-being of clients by drawing on the perspectives, values, and experiences of the social work profession. Professional and ethical obligations of the interdisciplinary team as a whole and of its individual members should be clearly established.

(b) Social workers for whom a team decision raises ethical concerns should attempt to resolve the disagreement through appropriate channels. If the disagreement cannot be resolved, social workers should pursue other avenues to address their concerns consistent with client well-being.

2.04 Disputes Involving Colleagues

(a) Social workers should not take advantage of a dispute between a colleague and employer to obtain a position or otherwise advance the social workers' own interests.

(b) Social workers should not exploit clients in disputes with colleagues or engage clients in any inappropriate discussion of conflicts between social workers and their colleagues.

2.05 Consultation

(a) Social workers should seek the advice and counsel of colleagues whenever such consultation is in the best interests of clients.

(b) Social workers should keep themselves informed about colleagues' areas of expertise and competencies. Social workers should seek consultation only from colleagues who have demonstrated knowledge, expertise, and competence related to the subject of the consultation.

(c) When consulting with colleagues about clients, social workers should disclose the least amount of information necessary to achieve the purposes of the consultation.

2.06 Referral for Services

(a) Social workers should refer clients to other professionals when the other professionals' specialized knowledge or expertise is needed to serve clients fully or when social workers believe that they are not being effective or making reasonable progress with clients and that additional service is required.

(b) Social workers who refer clients to other professionals should take appropriate steps to facilitate an orderly transfer of responsibility. Social workers who refer clients to other professionals should disclose, with clients' consent, all pertinent information to the new service providers.

(c) Social workers are prohibited from giving or receiving payment for a referral when no professional service is provided by the referring social worker.

2.07 Sexual Relationships

(a) Social workers who function as supervisors or educators should not engage in sexual activities or contact with supervisees, students, trainees, or other colleagues over whom they exercise professional authority.

(b) Social workers should avoid engaging in sexual relationships with colleagues when there is potential for a conflict of interest. Social workers who become involved in, or anticipate becoming involved in, a sexual relationship with a colleague have a duty to transfer professional responsibilities, when necessary, to avoid a conflict of interest.

2.08 Sexual Harassment

Social workers should not sexually harass supervisees, students, trainees, or colleagues. Sexual harassment includes sexual advances, sexual solicitation, requests for sexual favors, and other verbal or physical conduct of a sexual nature.

2.09 Impairment of Colleagues

(a) Social workers who have direct knowledge of a social work colleague's impairment that is due to personal problems, psychosocial distress, substance abuse, or mental health difficulties and that interferes with practice effectiveness should consult with that colleague when feasible and assist the colleague in taking remedial action.

(b) Social workers who believe that a social work colleague's impairment interferes with practice effectiveness and that the colleague has not taken adequate steps to address the impairment should take action through appropriate channels established by employers, agencies, NASW, licensing and regulatory bodies, and other professional organizations.

2.10 Incompetence of Colleagues

(a) Social workers who have direct knowledge of a social work colleague's incompetence should consult with that colleague when feasible and assist the colleague in taking remedial action.

(b) Social workers who believe that a social work colleague is incompetent and has not taken adequate steps to address the incompetence should take action through appropriate channels established by employers, agencies, NASW, licensing and regulatory bodies, and other professional organizations.

2.11 Unethical Conduct of Colleagues

(a) Social workers should take adequate measures to discourage, prevent, expose, and correct the unethical conduct of colleagues.

(b) Social workers should be knowledgeable about established policies and procedures for handling concerns about colleagues' unethical behavior. Social workers should be familiar with national, state, and local procedures for handling ethics complaints. These include policies and procedures created by NASW, licensing and regulatory bodies, employers, agencies, and other professional organizations.

(c) Social workers who believe that a colleague has acted unethically should seek resolution by discussing their concerns with the colleague when feasible and when such discussion is likely to be productive.

(d) When necessary, social workers who believe that a colleague has acted unethically should take action through appropiate formal channels (such as contacting a state licensing board or regulatory body, an NASW committee on inquiry, or other professional ethics committees).

(e) Social workers should defend and assist colleagues who are unjustly charged with unethical conduct.

3.   Social Workers' Ethical Responsibilities in Practice Settings

3.01 Supervision and Consultation

(a) Social workers who provide supervision or consultation should have the necessary knowledge and skill to supervise or consult appropriately and should do so only within their areas of knowledge and competence.

(b) Social workers who provide supervision or consultation are responsible for setting clear, appropriate, and culturally sensitive boundaries.

(c) Social workers should not engage in any dual or multiple relationships with supervisees in which there is a risk of exploitation of or potential harm to the supervisee.

(d) Social workers who provide supervision should evaluate supervisees' performance in a manner that is fair and respectful.

3.02 Education and Training

(a) Social workers who function as educators, field instructors for students, or trainers should provide instruction only within their areas of knowledge and competence and should provide instruction based on the most current information and knowledge available in the profession.

(b) Social workers who function as educators or field instructors for students should evaluate students' performance in a manner that is fair and respectful.

(c) Social workers who function as educators or field instructors for students should take reasonable steps to ensure that clients are routinely informed when services are being provided by students.

(d) Social workers who function as educators or field instructors for students should not engage in any dual or multiple relationships with students in which there is a risk of exploitation or potential harm to the student. Social work educators and field instructors are responsible for setting clear, appropriate, and culturally sensitive boundaries.

3.03 Performance Evaluation

Social workers who have responsibility for evaluating the performance of others should fulfill such responsibility in a fair and considerate manner and on the basis of clearly stated criteria.

3.04 Client Records

(a) Social workers should take reasonable steps to ensure that documentation in records is accurate and reflects the services provided.

(b) Social workers should include sufficient and timely documentation in records to facilitate the delivery of services and to ensure continuity of services provided to clients in the future.

(c) Social workers' documentation should protect clients' privacy to the extent that is possible and appropriate and should include only information that is directly relevant to the delivery of services.

(d) Social workers should store records following the termination of services to ensure reasonable future access. Records should be maintained for the number of years required by state statutes or relevant contracts.

3.05 Billing

Social workers should establish and maintain billing practices that accurately reflect the nature and extent of services provided and that identify who provided the service in the practice setting.

3.06 Client Transfer

(a) When an individual who is receiving services from another agency or colleague contacts a social worker for services, the social worker should carefully consider the client's needs before agreeing to provide services. To minimize possible confusion and conflict, social workers should discuss with potential clients the nature of the clients' current relationship with other service providers and the implications, including possible benefits or risks, of entering into a relationship with a new service provider.

(b) If a new client has been served by another agency or colleague, social workers should discuss with the client whether consultation with the previous service provider is in the client's best interest.

3.07 Administration

(a) Social work administrators should advocate within and outside their agencies for adequate resources to meet clients' needs.

(b) Social workers should advocate for resource allocation procedures that are open and fair. When not all clients' needs can be met, an allocation procedure should be developed that is nondiscriminatory and based on appropriate and consistently applied principles.

(c) Social workers who are administrators should take reasonable steps to ensure that adequate agency or organizational resources are available to provide appropriate staff supervision.

(d) Social work administrators should take reasonable steps to ensure that the working environment for which they are responsible is consistent with and encourages compliance with the *NASW Code of Ethics*. Social work administrators should take reasonable steps to eliminate any conditions in their organizations that violate, interfere with, or discourage compliance with the *Code*.

3.08 Continuing Education and Staff Development

Social work administrators and supervisors should take reasonable steps to provide or arrange for continuing education and staff development for all staff for whom they are responsible. Continuing education and staff development should address current knowledge and emerging developments related to social work practice and ethics.

3.09 Commitments to Employers

(a) Social workers generally should adhere to commitments made to employers and employing organizations.

(b) Social workers should work to improve employing agencies' policies and procedures and the efficiency and effectiveness of their services.

(c) Social workers should take reasonable steps to ensure that employers are aware of social workers' ethical obligations as set forth in the *NASW Code of Ethics* and of the implications of those obligations for social work practice.

(d) Social workers should not allow an employing organization's policies, procedures, regulations, or administrative orders to interfere with their ethical practice of social work. Social workers should take reasonable steps to ensure that their employing organizations' practices are consistent with the *NASW Code of Ethics*.

(e) Social workers should act to prevent and eliminate discrimination in the employing organization's work assignments and in its employment policies and practices.

(f) Social workers should accept employment or arrange student field placements only in organizations that exercise fair personnel practices.

(g) Social workers should be diligent stewards of the resources of their employing organizations, wisely conserving funds where appropriate and never misappropriating funds or using them for unintended purposes.

3.10 Labor–Management Disputes

(a) Social workers may engage in organized action, including the formation of and participation in labor unions, to improve services to clients and working conditions.

(b) The actions of social workers who are involved in labor–management disputes, job actions, or labor strikes should be guided by the profession's values, ethical principles, and ethical standards. Reasonable differences of opinion exist among social workers concerning their primary obligation as professionals during an actual or threatened labor strike or job action. Social workers should carefully examine relevant issues and their possible impact on clients before deciding on a course of action.

4.   Social Workers' Ethical Responsibilities as Professionals

4.01 Competence

(a) Social workers should accept responsibility or employment only on the basis of existing competence or the intention to acquire the necessary competence.

(b) Social workers should strive to become and remain proficient in professional practice and the performance of professional functions. Social workers should critically examine and keep current with emerging knowledge relevant to social work. Social workers should routinely review the professional literature and participate in continuing education relevant to social work practice and social work ethics.

(c) Social workers should base practice on recognized knowledge, including empirically based knowledge, relevant to social work and social work ethics.

4.02 Discrimination

Social workers should not practice, condone, facilitate, or collaborate with any form of discrimination on the basis of race, ethnicity, national origin, color, sex, sexual orientation, age, marital status, political belief, religion, or mental or physical disability.

4.03 Private Conduct

Social workers should not permit their private conduct to interfere with their ability to fulfill their professional responsibilities.

4.04 Dishonesty, Fraud, and Deception

Social workers should not participate in, condone, or be associated with dishonesty, fraud, or deception.

4.05 Impairment

(a) Social workers should not allow their own personal problems, psychosocial distress, legal problems, substance abuse, or mental health difficulties to interfere with their professional judgment and performance or to jeopardize the best interests of people for whom they have a professional responsibility.

(b) Social workers whose personal problems, psychosocial distress, legal problems, substance abuse, or mental health difficulties interfere with their professional judgment and performance should immediately seek consultation and take appropriate remedial action by seeking professional help, making adjustments in workload, terminating practice, or taking any other steps necessary to protect clients and others.

4.06 Misrepresentation

(a) Social workers should make clear distinctions between statements made and actions engaged in as a private individual and as a representative of the social work profession, a professional social work organization, or the social worker's employing agency.

(b) Social workers who speak on behalf of professional social work organizations should accurately represent the official and authorized positions of the organizations.

(c) Social workers should ensure that their representations to clients, agencies, and the public of professional qualifications, credentials, education, competence, affiliations, services provided, or results to be achieved are accurate. Social workers should claim only those relevant professional credentials they actually possess and take steps to correct any inaccuracies or misrepresentations of their credentials by others.

4.07 Solicitations

(a) Social workers should not engage in uninvited solicitation of potential clients who, because of their circumstances, are vulnerable to undue influence, manipulation, or coercion.

(b) Social workers should not engage in solicitation of testimonial endorsements (including solicitation of consent to use a client's prior statement as a testimonial endorsement) from current clients or from other people who, because of their particular circumstances, are vulnerable to undue influence.

4.08 Acknowledging Credit

(a) Social workers should take responsibility and credit, including authorship credit, only for work they have actually performed and to which they have contributed.

(b) Social workers should honestly acknowledge the work of and the contributions made by others.

5.   Social Workers' Ethical Responsibilities to the Social Work Profession

5.01 Integrity of the Profession

(a) Social workers should work toward the maintenance and promotion of high standards of practice.

(b) Social workers should uphold and advance the values, ethics, knowledge, and mission of the profession. Social workers should protect, enhance, and improve the integrity of the profession through appropriate study and research, active discussion, and responsible criticism of the profession.

(c) Social workers should contribute time and professional expertise to activities that promote respect for the value, integrity, and competence of the social work profession. These activities may include teaching, research, consultation, service, legislative testimony, presentations in the community, and participation in their professional organizations.

(d) Social workers should contribute to the knowledge base of social work and share with colleagues their knowledge related to practice, research, and ethics. Social workers should seek to contribute to the profession's literature and to share their knowledge at professional meetings and conferences.

(e) Social workers should act to prevent the unauthorized and unqualified practice of social work.

5.02 Evaluation and Research

(a) Social workers should monitor and evaluate policies, the implementation of programs, and practice interventions.

(b) Social workers should promote and facilitate evaluation and research to contribute to the development of knowledge.

(c) Social workers should critically examine and keep current with emerging knowledge relevant to social work and fully use evaluation and research evidence in their professional practice.

(d) Social workers engaged in evaluation or research should carefully consider possible consequences and should follow guidelines developed for the protection of evaluation and research participants. Appropriate institutional review boards should be consulted.

(e) Social workers engaged in evaluation or research should obtain voluntary and written informed consent from participants, when appropriate, without any implied or actual deprivation or penalty for refusal to participate; without undue inducement to participate; and with due regard for participants' well-being, privacy, and dignity. Informed consent should include information about the nature, extent, and duration of the participation requested and disclosure of the risks and benefits of participation in the research.

(f) When evaluation or research participants are incapable of giving informed consent, social workers should provide an appropriate explanation to the participants, obtain the participants' assent to the extent they are able, and obtain written consent from an appropriate proxy.

(g) Social workers should never design or conduct evaluation or research that does not use consent procedures, such as certain forms of naturalistic observation and archival research, unless rigorous and responsible review of the research has found it to be justified because of its prospective scientific, educational, or applied value and unless equally effective alternative procedures that do not involve waiver of consent are not feasible.

(h) Social workers should inform participants of their right to withdraw from evaluation and research at any time without penalty.

(i) Social workers should take appropriate steps to ensure that participants in evaluation and research have access to appropriate supportive services.

(j) Social workers engaged in evaluation for research should protect participants from unwarranted physical or mental distress, harm, danger, or deprivation.

(k) Social workers engaged in the evaluation of services should discuss collected information only for professional purposes and only with people professionally concerned with this information.

(l) Social workers engaged in evaluation or research should ensure the anonymity or confidentiality of participants and of the data obtained from them. Social workers should inform participants of any limits of confidentiality, the measures that will be taken to ensure confidentiality, and when any records containing research data will be destroyed.

(m) Social workers who report evaluation and research results should protect participants' confidentiality by omitting identifying information unless proper consent has been obtained authorizing disclosure.

(n) Social workers should report evaluation and research findings accurately. They should not fabricate or falsify results and should take steps to correct any errors later found in published data using standard publication methods.

(o) Social workers engaged in evaluation or research should be alert to and avoid conflicts of interest and dual relationships with participants, should inform participants when a real or potential conflict of interest arises, and should take steps to resolve the issue in a manner that makes participants' interests primary.

(p) Social workers should educate themselves, their students, and their colleagues about responsible research practices.

6. Social Workers' Ethical Responsibilities to the Broader Society

6.01 Social Welfare

Social workers should promote the general welfare of society, from local to global levels, and the development of people, their communities, and their environments. Social workers should advocate for living conditions conducive to the fulfillment of basic human needs and should promote social, economic, political, and cultural values and institutions that are compatible with the realization of social justice.

6.02 Public Participation

Social workers should facilitate informed participation by the public in shaping social policies and institutions.

6.03 Public Emergencies

Social workers should provide appropriate professional services in public emergencies to the greatest extent possible.

6.04 Social and Political Action

(a) Social workers should engage in social and political action that seeks to ensure that all people have equal access to the resources, employment, services, and opportunities they require to meet their basic human needs and to develop fully. Social workers should be aware of the impact of the political arena on practice and should advocate for changes in policy and legislation to improve social conditions in order to meet basic human needs and promote social justice.

(b) Social workers should act to expand choice and opportunity for all people, with special regard for vulnerable, disadvantaged, oppressed, and exploited people and groups.

(c) Social workers should promote conditions that encourage respect for cultural and social diversity within the United States and globally. Social workers should promote policies and practices that demonstrate respect for difference, support the expansion of cultural knowledge and resources, advocate for programs and institutions that demonstrate cultural competence, and promote policies that safeguard the rights of and confirm equity and social justice for all people.

(d) Social workers should act to prevent and eliminate domination of, exploitation of, and discrimination against any person, group, or class on the basis of race, ethnicity, national origin, color, sex, sexual orientation, age, marital status, political belief, religion, or mental or physical disability.

The Northside Community

The Northside Community Service Delivery System

Generalist Social Work Practice: An Empowering Approach draws examples from the fictitious Northside community. The following list describes the agencies and organizations referred to throughout the book.

- Northside Family Services—a multiprogram family service agency providing family preservation services, foster care, and counseling for individuals, families, and groups
- Families Together—a private agency contracting with the state department of social services to provide a continuum of foster care services including recruiting, screening, and training foster parents. Agency programs include support services for families with children in foster care such as family life education and supervision of visits, and advocacy services for children in the foster care system
- Neighbors United—a community action program sponsoring a variety of neighborhood programs including neighborhood watch, delinquency prevention, social action, outreach, and advocacy services
- Northside Hospital—a large hospital employing social workers in numerous health and community services including outreach, aftercare, hospice, elderly services, and emergency room support
- Coalition for the Homeless—a cooperative network of agencies that provides services for homeless persons, including emergency shelter, transitional housing, meal programs, food pantries, preventive health care, and educational assessment and referral. The coalition pools resources to fund certain staff positions and seek continuing program funding
- Run and Play Day Care Center—a subsidized infant and child day care that provides family support services including parent education and support groups for parents
- Northside Care Center—a continuing care facility that offers residential care, specialized nursing care, and family support services
- Addictions Recovery Center—a comprehensive substance abuse agency providing community education and prevention programs, addiction evaluation, detoxification, in-patient treatment, individual counseling, and support groups

- County Mental Health Center—a community mental health center offering in- and out-patient treatment, community support programs for people with chronic mental illness, day treatment programs, occupational therapy, and counseling for individuals, couples, families, and groups
- Northside Prevention Services—a prevention agency offering in-home family support services to prevent institutional placement of family members with special physical and mental needs, a telephone hotline, coordination of child abuse prevention efforts, and community education about parenting and healthy family functioning
- Northside Human Resource Center—an agency that provides employee assistance programs, staff training, and grant writing services
- Northside Network—a consortium of human service providers with representatives from several Northside social agencies and programs working toward goals of mutual support, service coordination, and resource development
- Northside Alliance for Family Health—an agency offering a full range of health services with emphasis on reproductive health and AIDS prevention
- Area Association for People with Disabilities—a multiservice agency offering a spectrum of service to people with mental and physical challenges including case coordination, employment training, community integrated residential placements, respite, recreational services, and skill development for independent living
- Domestic Violence Center—a specialized program offering crisis services, emergency placement, individual and family counseling, support groups, and legal advocacy
- State Department of Social Services—a comprehensive state government system structured into departments, such as public assistance, the child protective unit, the department of aging, and others, to deliver public social services
- Northside Development Association—a community action agency that uses macro-practice strategies to enhance the well-being of members of the Northside community
- Community Action Council—a citizens' group initiated by the Neighborhood Development Association that has developed community action, neighborhood watch, and advocacy programs
- OPTIONS—an agency that provides community-based services, case management, and programming for older adults to maintain independent functioning and provide support for caregivers
- Northside Center—a community-created service center composed of private businesses including a grocery store, pharmacy, laundromat, and farmer's market as well as a community service center offering information and referral service, recreational activities, and a drop-in center
- Northside Youth Services—an agency working with youth under the age of 18 and their families to address delinquency prevention, court diversion, and family preservation

Practice Examples

The following list highlights major practice examples featured throughout *Generalist Social Work Practice: An Empowering Approach.*

- Andrea Barry of Northside Family Services' Family Preservation Program works with the Clemens family who have been referred by the State Child Protective Unit. The example illustrates the major features of the approach to generalist social work used in the book including the ecosystems perspective, the strengths orientation, empowerment, and the integrated nature of practice, policy, and research. (Chapter 1, pp. 4–5)

- The example of Grady, a man unable to read, illustrates the adaptability of human behavior characteristic of the ecosystems perspective. (Chapter 2, pp. 23–24)
- Tony Marelli of the Addictions Recovery Center experiences burnout in response to changes in his agency's situation. His situation illustrates the interrelatedness of systems in the same ecosystem. (Chapter 2, p. 47)
- Paul Quillin of Northside Family Services prepares to work with a support group for gay and lesbian parents. This example shows how social workers prepare a positive mindset, reflect on value issues, and create positive expectations about the resources that clients will bring. (Chapter 3, pp. 60–63)
- The example of Mark Nogales and Olivia Adams demonstrates how workers can build on clients' strengths in achieving their goals. (Chapter 4, pp. 76–77, 81)
- Kay Landon of Northside Prevention Services' Family Support Program works with Helen and Jack Ingersoll after Jack suffers head and back injuries. This example concretely illustrates each of the 11 empowering processes described in the subsequent chapters as applied at the microlevel of practice. (Chapter 5, pp. 104–107)
- Effie Mako, an employee assistance counselor for the Northside Human Resource Center, works with organizational client Environmental Industries to improve employee relationships and develop teamwork abilities. This example demonstrates this book's empowering approach to change with a midlevel client system. (Chapter 5, pp. 108–111)
- Leon Casey is a community prevention specialist at the Neighborhood Development Association working to reduce racial tension in the Northside Community. This example applies the 11 empowering processes to intervention with a community, demonstrating the applicability of this practice approach at the macrolevel. (Chapter 5, pp. 111–113)
- Karen McBride of Northside Hospital's Outreach Program initiates a relationship with the Fuentes family. A description of her work details concrete steps for forming empowering partnerships, emphasizes cultural influences, and highlights ethical considerations. (Chapter 6, pp. 124–128)
- Alex Anderson of Northside Prevention Services' Listening Line responds to a caller's issues. The dialogue offers at least one concrete example of each response from the response continuum presented in the chapter and shows how to combine responses effectively to help clients articulate challenges, strengths, and possible directions. (Chapter 7, pp. 164–167)
- The Northside Network meets and Miriam Andovich facilitates a group process to set preliminary goals and contract for assessment. (Chapter 8, pp. 177–178)
- Chad, a recovering alcoholic, describes his desire for a drink to Tony Marelli of the Addictions Recovery Center. This example describes how to identify clients' strengths even while discussing their challenges. (Chapter 9, p. 204)
- Damon Edwards of Neighbors United works with residents of Franklin Courts, a public housing project, to resolve the problem of lead contamination. This example demonstrates how to apply an ecosystems perspective to an assessment process. (Chapter 10, pp. 233–237)

- Rita Garcia with the Child Protective Unit records her work with Opal Zander whose children have been placed in foster care. Her work provides examples of different styles of recording. (Chapter 10, pp. 262–264)
- Nate Hardy of the Northside Development Association helps develop a plan for increasing available low-cost housing in the Northside Community. This example, presented in two parts, describes how to respond in ways that assist clients to set positive goals and objectives and highlights the various systems that social workers and clients consider in selecting locations for initiating change. (Chapter 11, pp. 280–281, 287)
- Jon Allen, a case advocate in the Foster Care Program at Northside Family Services, works with client Donna Lester to "activate her resources" to regain custody of her twin boys. Jon's work exemplifies the broad range of activities of generalist social workers, demonstrating the functions of consultancy, resource management, and education. (Chapter 12, pp. 298–299)
- Consuela Diaz and Darrell Foster of the Northside Development Association facilitate the work of the Community Action Council and its chairperson, Marvella Harvey. Their work exemplifies how generalist practitioners work to build empowering alliances among clients with similar concerns in order to initiate social action. (Chapter 13, p. 328)
- Kennedy Brown of OPTIONS brokers services, in collaboration with George and Ida Palmer who are coping with the possibility that George has Alzheimer's Disease, demonstrate case management strategies. (Chapter 13, pp. 341–342)
- Two scenarios depict the contrasting stories of Raymond, a Northside adolescent—growing up in a neighborhood of limited opportunities compared to growing up in a neighborhood with accessible resources. The comparison shows the impact of expanding opportunity structures as a strategy for macrolevel change. (Chapter 14, pp. 370–371)
- A series of short examples offers research options for most of the agencies and social workers already described in the book. A second set of brief examples illustrates various single-system designs. (Chapter 15, p. 389)
- Dale Storonski of Northside Youth Services describes several ways that workers may end their work with clients. His description includes examples of reaching desired outcomes, making referrals, reacting to clients who withdraw from service, and coping with service restrictions. (Chapter 16, pp. 425–427)
- Emily Carter, a social worker in Northside Hospital's Hospice Unit, reflects on her experiences with clients who have died. (Chapter 16, p. 433)
- The closing example describes the Northside Network's annual conference, demonstrating the role that generalist social workers play in developing their own expertise and contributing to the social work profession. (Epilogue, pp. 439–440)

References

Abramovitz, M. (1986). The privatization of the welfare state: A review. *Social Work, 31,* 257–264.

Abramson, J. S., & Rosenthal, B. B. (1995). Interdisciplinary and interorganizational collaboration. In R. L. Edwards (Ed.), *Encyclopedia of social work: Vol 2* (19th ed.) (pp. 1479–1489). Washington, DC: NASW Press.

Abramson, L. Y., Seligman, M. E. P., & Teasdale, J. C. (1978). Learned helplessness in humans: Critique and reformulation. *Journal of Abnormal Psychology, 87,* 49–74.

Abramson, M. (1985). The autonomy-paternalism dilema in social work practice. *Social Casework, 66,* 387–391.

Acker, G. M. (1999). The impact of clients' mental illness on social workers' job satisfaction and burnout. *Health and Social Work, 24*(2), 112–119.

Adams, J. F., Piercy, F. P., & Jurich, J. A. (1991). Effects of solution focused therapy's "formula first session task" on compliance and outcome in family therapy. *Journal of Marital and Family Therapy, 17,* 277–290.

Adams, P., & Krauth, K. (1994). Empowering workers for empowerment based practice. In L. Gutiérrez & P. Nurius (Eds.), *Education and research for empowerment practice* (pp. 183–194). Seattle, WA: University of Washington Press.

Adams, R. (1997). Empowerment, marketization, and social work. In B. Lesnick (Ed.), *Change in social work* (pp. 69–87). Aldershoot, England: Arena.

Administration on Aging (1998). Conclusions—National elder abuse incidence study. Retrieved June 28, 1999 from the World Wide Web: *http://www.aoa.dhhs.gov/abuse/report/H-Conclusions.html*

Administration on Aging (1999). Demographic changes. Retrieved June 8, 1999 from the World Wide Web: http://www.aoa.dhhs.gov/aoa/stats/aging21/demography.html

Aguilera, D. C., & Messick, J. M. (1982). *Crisis intervention: Theory and methodology* (4th ed.). St Louis, MO: The C. V. Mosby Company.

Aho El Nasr, M. (1989). The term "client" in the social work profession. *International Social Work, 32,* 311–318.

Ainslie, J., & Feltey, K. (1998). Definitions and dynamics of motherhood and family in lesbian communities. In J. M. Schriver. *Human behavior and the social environment* (pp. 327–343). Boston: Allyn & Bacon.

Akamatsu, N. (1998). The talking oppression blues: Including the experience of power/powerlessness in the teaching of "cultural sensitivity." In M. McGoldrick (Ed.), *Re-visioning family therapy: Race, culture, and gender in clinical practice* (pp. 129–143). New York: Guilford Press.

Akamatsu, N., Basham, K., & Olson, M. (1998). Teaching a feminist family therapy. *Journal of Feminist Family Therapy, 8*(2), 22–36.

Alexander, R. (1997). Social workers and privileged communication in the federal legal system, *Social Work, 42*(4), 387–391.

American Psychiatric Association. (1987). *Diagnostic and statistical manual of mental disorders* (3rd ed., revised). Washington, DC: Author.

American Psychiatric Association. (1994). *Diagnostic and statistical manual of mental disorders* (4th ed.). Washington, DC: Author.

Ames, N. (1999). Social work recording: A new look at an old issue. *Journal of Social Work Education, 35*(2), 227–237.

Amundson, J., Stewart, K., & Valentine, L. (1993). Temptations of power and certainty. *Journal of Marital and Family Therapy, 19*(2), 111–123.

Anderson, C. M., & Stewart, S. (1983). *Mastering resistance: A practical guide to family therapy.* New York: Guilford Press.

Anderson, R. E., Carter, I., & Lowe, G. (1999). *Human behavior in the social environment: A social systems approach* (5th ed.). New York: Aldine de Gruyter.

Anderson, S. C. (1987). Alcohol use and addiction. In A. Minahan (Ed.), *Encyclopedia of social work: Vol 1* (18th ed.) (pp. 132–142). Silver Spring, MD: National Association of Social Workers.

Angell, G. B., Dennis, B. G., & Dumain, L. E. (1998). Spirituality, resilience, and narrative: Coping with parental death. *Families in Society, 79*(6), 615–630.

Arches, J. (1985). Don't burn, organize: A structural analysis of burnout in the human services. *Catalyst, 5* (17/18), 15–20.

Arches, J. (1991). Social structure, burnout, and job satisfaction. *Social Work, 36,* 202–206.

Asch, A., & Mudrick, N. R. (1995). Disability. In R. L. Edwards (Ed.), *Encyclopedia of social work: Vol 1* (19th ed.) (pp. 752–761). Washington, DC: NASW Press.

Aspis, S. (1997). Power on whose terms? *Community Living, 10*(3), pp. 20–21.

Austin, C. D. (1992). Have we oversold case management? *Journal of Case Management, 1*(2), 61–65.

Austin, C. D. (1993). Case management: A systems perspective. *Families in Society, 74,* 451–458.

Austin, C. D., & McClelland, R. W. (1996). Introduction: Case management—Everybody's doing it. In C. D. Austin & R. W. McClelland (Eds.), *Perspectives on case management practice* (pp. 1–16). Milwaukee, WI: Families International.

Austin, M. J., & Lowe, J. I. (1994). Debate 9: Should only African-American community organizers work in African-American Neighborhoods. In M. J. Austin & J. I. Lowe (Eds.), *Controversial issues in communities and organizations* (pp. 128–129). Boston: Allyn & Bacon.

Bailey, D. (1994). Organizational empowerment from self to interbeing. In L. Gutiérrez & P. Nurius (Eds.), *Education and research for empowerment practice* (pp. 37–42). Seattle, WA: University of Washington Press.

Baines, D. (1997). Feminist social work in the inner-city: The challenges of race, class, and gender. *Affilia, 12*(3), 297–317.

Bandler, R., & Grinder, J. (1975). *The structure of magic I.* Palo Alto, CA: Science and Behavior Books.

Bandura, A. (1984). Recycling misconceptions of perceived self-efficacy. *Cognitive Therapy and Research, 8*(3), 231–255.

Bandura, A. (1986). *Social foundations of thought and action: A social-cognitive theory.* Englewood Cliffs, NJ: Prentice Hall.

Bandura, A., & Cervone, D. (1983). Self-evaluative and self-efficacy mechanisms governing the motivational effects of goals systems. *Journal of Personality and Social Psychology, 45,* 1017–1028.

Bandura, A., & Schunk, D. H. (l981). Cultivating competence, self-efficacy, and intrinsic interest through proximal self-motivation. *Journal of Personality and Social Psychology, 41*(3), 586–598.

Baptiste, D. A. (1987). Family therapy with Spanish-heritage immigrant families in cultural transition. *Contemporary Family Therapy, 9*(4), 229–251.

Baradell, J. G., & Klein, K. (1993). Relationship of life stress and body consciousness to hypervigilant decision making. *Journal of Personality and Social psychology, 64*(2), 267–273.

Barber, C. E., & Iwai, M. (1996). Role conflict and role ambiguity as predictors of burnout among staff caring for elderly dementia patients. *Journal of Gerontological Social Work, 26*(1/2), 101–116.

Barber, J. G. (1995). Politically progressive casework. *Families in Society, 76,* 30–37.

Barker, R. L. (1999). *The social work dictionary* (4th ed.). Washington, DC: NASW Press.

Barker, R. L., & Branson, D. M. (1992). *Forensic social work: Legal aspects of professional practice.* New York: The Haworth Press.

Barnes, M., & Bennett, G. (1998). Frail bodies, courageous voices: Older people influencing community care. *Health and Social Care in the Community, 6*(2), 102–111.

Barnes, M., & Shardlow, P. (1997). From passive recipient to active citizen: Participation in mental health user groups. *Journal of Mental Health, 6*(3), 289–300.

Barnes, M., & Walker, A. (1996). Consumerism versus empowerment: A principled approach to the involvement of older service users. *Policy and Politics, 24*(4), 375–394.

Bartlett, H. (1970). *The common base of social work practice.* New York: National Association of Social Workers, Inc.

Beavers, W. R., & Hampson, R. B. (1990). *Successful families: Assessment and intervention.* New York: W. W. Norton & Company.

Beavers, W. R., & Hampson, R. B. (1993). Measuring family competence: The Beavers Systems Model. In F. Walsh (Ed.), *Normal family processes* (2nd ed.) (pp. 73–103). New York: Guilford Press.

Beeman, S. K. (1997). Reconceptualizing social support and its relationship to child neglect. *Social Service Review, 71*(3), 421–440.

Belcher, J. R., & Hegar, R. L. (1991). Social work and the casualties of capitalism: Empowerment of the urban poor. *Journal of Progressive Human Services, 2*(1), 39–53.

Belenky, M. F., Clinchy, B. M., Goldberger, N. R., & Tarule, J. M. (1986). *Women's ways of knowing: The development of self, voice, and mind.* New York: Basic Books.

Bem, S. L. (1993). *The lenses of gender: Transforming the debate on sexual inequality.* New Haven, CT: Yale University Press.

Ben-Ari, A. (1995). Coming out: A dialectic of intimacy and privacy. *Families in Society, 76,* 306–314.

Benjamin, A. (1987). *The helping interview* (4th ed.). Boston: Houghton Mifflin.

Beresford, P. (1994). *Changing the culture: Involving service users in social work education.* Cambridge: Black Bear Press.

Beresford, P. (1997). Identity, structures, services and user involvement. *Research, Policy, and Planning, 15*(2), 5–9.

Beresford, P. (1999). Towards an empowering social work practice: Learning from service users and their movements. In W. Shera & L. Wells (Eds.), *Empowerment practice in social work: Developing richer conceptual foundations* (pp. 259–277). Toronto, Canada: Canadian Scholars' Press.

Beresford, P., & Evans, C. (1999). Research note: Research and empowerment. *The British Journal of Social Work, 29*(5), 671–677.

Berg, I. K. (1994). *Family based services: A solution-focused approach.* New York: W. W. Norton & Company, Inc.

Berg, I. K., & De Jong, P. (1996). Solution-building conversations: Co-constructing a sense of competence with clients. *Families in Society, 77,* 376–391.

Berg, I. K., & Miller, S. D. (1992). *Working with the problem drinker: A solution-focused approach.* New York: W. W. Norton.

Berger, P., & Neuhaus, J. R. (1977). *To empower people: The role of mediating structures in public policy.* Washington, DC: American Enterprise Institute.

Bernal, G., & Gutiérrez, M. (1988). Cubans. In L. Comas-Diaz & E. E. H. Griffith (Eds.), *Clinical guidelines in cross-cultural mental health* (pp. 233–261). New York: John Wiley & Sons.

Bernal, G., & Shapiro, E. (1996). Cuban families. In M. McGoldrick, J. Giordano, & J. K. Pearce (Eds.). *Ethnicity and family therapy* (2nd ed.) (pp. 155–168). New York: Guilford Press.

Bethea, L. (1999). Primary prevention of child abuse. *American Family Physician, 59*(6), 577+. Retrieved June 27, 1999 from InfoTrac database (Expanded Academic ASAP) on the World Wide Web: http://www5.infotrac.galegroup.com

Biestek, F. P. (1957). *The casework relationship.* Chicago: Loyola University Press.

Bilingsley, A. (1992). *Climbing Jacob's ladder: The enduring legacy of African American families.* New York: Simon & Schuster.

Birdwhistell, R. (1955). Background to kinesics. *Etc., 13,* 10–18.

Birnbaum, M., & Auerbach, C. (1994). Group work in social work education: The price of neglect. *Journal of Social Work Education, 30*(3), 325–335.

Black, R. B. (1994). Diversity and populations at risk: People with disabilities. In F. G. Reamer (Ed.), *The foundations of social work practice* (pp. 393–416). New York: Columbia University Press.

Blecher, J. R., & Hegar, R. L. (1991). Social work and the casualties of capitalism: Empowerment of the urban poor. *Journal of Progressive Human Services, 2*(1), 39–53.

Bloch, D. S. (1999). Adolescent suicide as a public health threat. *Journal of Child and Adolescent*

Psychiatric Nursing, 12(1), 26+. Retrieved June 27, 1999 from the InfoTrac database (Expanded Academic ASAP) on the World Wide Web: http://www5.infotrac.galegroup.com

Bloom, M., & Fischer, J. (1982). *Evaluating practice: Guidelines for the accountable professional.* Englewood Cliffs, NJ: Prentice-Hall, Inc.

Bloom, M., Fischer, J., & Orme, J. G. (1999). *Evaluating practice: Guidelines for the accountable professional* (3rd ed.). Boston: Allyn & Bacon.

Blount, M., Thyer, B. A., & Frye, T. (1996). *Social work practice with Native Americans.* In D. F. Harrison, B. A. Thyer, & J. S. Wodarski (Eds.), *Cultural diversity and social work practice* (2nd ed.) (pp. 257–298). Springfield, IL: Charles C Thomas, Publisher.

Blythe, B. J. (1990). Improving the fit between single subject designs and practice. In L. Videka-Sherman & W. J. Reid (Eds.), *Advances in clinical social work research* (pp. 29–32). Silver Spring, MD: NASW Press.

Boes, M., & VanWormer, K. (1997). Social work with homeless women in emergency rooms: A strengths-feminist perspective. *Affilia, 12*(4), 408–426.

Book, H. E. (1988). Empathy: Misconceptions and misuses in psychotherapy. *American Journal of Psychiatry, 145*(4), 420–424.

Bott, S. (1997). Involving physically disabled users in service planning and delivery: Shropshire as a case study based on two national projects. *Research, Policy, and Planning, 15*(2), 38–42.

Bower, G. H. (1981). Mood and memory. *American Psychologist, 36,* 129–148.

Boyd-Franklin, N. (1989). *Black families in therapy: A multisystems approach.* New York: Guilford Press.

Boyd-Franklin, N. (1992, July). *African American families in therapy.* Presentation for the Illinois Chapter of the National Association of Social Workers. Springfield, IL.

Boyd-Franklin, N. (1993). Race, class, and poverty. In F. Walsh (Ed.), *Normal family processes* (2nd ed.) (pp. 361–376). New York: Guilford Press.

Brager, G., & Holloway, S. (1992). Assessing prospects for organizational change: The uses of force field analysis. *Administration in Social Work, 16*(3/4), 15–28.

Brekke, J. S. (1987). Detecting wife and child abuse in clinical settings. *Social Casework, 68,* 332–338.

Breton, M. (1993). Relating competence-promotion and empowerment. *Journal of Progressive Human Services, 5*(1), 27–44.

Breton, M. (1994). On the meaning of empowerment and empowerment-oriented social work practice. *Social Work with Groups, 17*(3), 23–37.

Breton, M. (1999). Empowerment practice in a post-empowerment era. In W. Shera & L. Wells (Eds.), *Empowerment practice in social work: Developing richer conceptual foundations* (pp. 222–233). Toronto, Canada: Canadian Scholars' Press.

Bricker-Jenkins, M. (1991). The propositions and assumptions of feminist social work practice. In M. Bricker-Jenkins, N. R. Hooyman, & N. Gottlieb (Eds.), *Feminist social work practice in clinical settings* (pp. 271–303). Newbury Park, CA: Sage Publications.

Bricker-Jenkins, M., Hooyman, N., & Gottlieb, N. (Eds.). (1991). *Feminist social work practice in clinical settings.* Newbury Park, CA: Sage Publications.

Brieland, D., Costin, L., & Atherton, C. R. (1985). *Contemporary social work: An introduction to social work and social welfare.* New York: McGraw-Hill.

Brill, N. I. (1998). *Working with people: The helping process* (6th ed.). White Plains, NY: Longman Publishers.

Bromley, M. A. (1987). New beginnings for Cambodian refugees—Or further disruptions? *Social Work, 32,* 236–239.

Brower, A. M. (1988). Can the ecological systems model guide social work practice? *Social Service Review, 62,* 411–429.

Brower, A. M. (1996). Group development as constructed social reality revisited: The constructivism of small groups. *Families in Society, 77,* 336–343.

Brown, C., & O'Brian, K. M. (1998). Understanding stress and burnout in shelter workers. *Professional Psychology Research and Practice, 29*(4), 383–385.

Brown, E. G. (1982). Rationale for a generalist approach to social work practice. In D. S. Sanders, O. Kurren, & J. Fischer (Eds.), *Fundamentals of social work practice* (pp. 119–130). Belmont, CA: Wadsworth.

Brown, J. W. (1997). [Review of the book Empowerment evaluation: Knowledge and tools for self-assessment and accountability]. *Health Education & Behavior, 24*(3), 388–391.

Brown, P. A. (1994). Participatory research: A new paradigm for social work. In L. Gutiérrez & P. Nurius (Eds.), *Education and research for empowerment practice* (pp. 293–303). Seattle, WA: Center for Policy and Practice Research, School of Social Work, University of Washington.

Browne, C., & Broderick, A. (1994). Asian and Pacific Island elders: Issues for social work practice and education. *Social Work, 39,* 252–259.

Brydon-Miller, M. (1997). Participatory action research: Psychology and social change. *Journal of Social Issues, 53*(4), 657–666.

Bullis, R. K. (1996). *Spirituality in social work practice.* Washington, DC: Taylor and Francis.

Burgoon, J. K., Buller, D. B., & Woodall, W. G. (1996). *Nonverbal communication: The unspoken dialogue* (2nd ed.). New York: Harper and Row.

Burnished or burnt out: The delights and dangers of working in health. (1994). *The Lancet, 344*(8937), 1583–1584.

Busby, D. M., Glenn, E., Stegell, G. L., & Adamson, D. W. (1993). Treatment issues for survivors of physical and sexual abuse. *Journal of Marital and Family Therapy, 19,* 377–392.

Bush, I. R., & Kraft, M. K. (1998). The voices of welfare reform. *Public Welfare, 56*(1), 11–21.

Butterfield, W. H. (1995). Computer untilization. In R. L. Edwards (Ed.), *Encyclopedia of social work: Vol 1* (19th ed.) (pp. 594–613). Washington, DC: NASW Press.

Butterfoss, F. D., Houseman, C., Morrow, A. L., & Rosenthal, J. (1997). Use of focus group data for strategic planning by a community-based immunization coalition. *Family and Community Health, 20*(3), 49–59.

Campbell, J., Elder, J., Gallagher, D., Simon, J., & Taylor, A. (1999). Crafting the "tap on the shoulder:" A compliment template for solution-focused therapy. *The American Journal of Family Therapy, 27*(1), 35–44.

Canda, E. R. (1988). Conceptualizing spirituality for social work: Insights from diverse perspectives. *Social Thought, 14*(1), 30–46.

Canda, E. R. (1998). Afterword: Linking spirituality and social work: Five themes for innovation. *Social Thought, 18*(2), 97–106.

Canda, E. R., & Furman, L. (1999). *Spiritual diversity in social work practice: The heart of helping.* New York: The Free Press.

Carter, B., & McGoldrick, M. (1989). Overview: The changing family life cycle—A framework for family therapy. In B. Carter & M. McGoldrick (Eds.), *The changing family life cycle: A framework for family therapy* (2nd ed). Boston: Allyn & Bacon.

Castex, G. (1994a). The function of stereotyping processes: A challenge for practice. In L. G. Gardella, R. Daniel, M. C. Joyner, N. Mokuau, & J. M. Schriver (Eds.), *In memory of Ronald C. Federico: A BPD Festschrift* (pp. 8–16). Springfield, MO.

Castex, G. M. (1994b). Providing services to Hispanic/Latino populations: Profiles in diversity. *Social Work, 39,* 288–297.

Chambers, D. E. (1993). *Social policy and social programs: A method for the practical public policy analyst* (2nd ed.). New York: Macmillan Publishing Company.

Chapin, R. K. (1995). Social policy development: The strengths perspective. *Social Work, 40,* 506–514.

Chau, K. (1989). Sociocultural dissonance among ethnic minority populations. *Social Casework, 70,* 224–239.

Chau, K. L. (1995, March). *An exploratory validation of an index of cross-cultural competency for social work.* Paper presented at the annual program meeting of the Council on Social Work Education, San Diego, CA.

Chung, D. K. (1992). Asian cultural commonalities: A comparison with mainstream American culture. In S. M. Furuto, R. Biswas, D. K. Chung, K. Marase, & F. Ross-Sheriff (Eds.), *Social work practice with Asian Americans* (pp. 27–44). Newbury Park, CA: Sage Publications.

Clark, M. D. (1997a). Strength-based practice: The new paradigm—juvenile offender rehabilitation. *Corrections Today, 59*(2), 110–111.

Clark, M. D. (1997b). Interviewing for solutions: A strength-based method for juvenile justice (part 2). *Corrections Today, 59*(3), 98–101.

Clark, M. D. (1998). Strength-based practice: The ABC's of working with adolescents who don't want to work with you. *Federal Probation, 62*(1), 46+. Retrieved June 4, 1999 from InfoTrac database (Expanded Academic ASAP) on the World Wide Web: http://www5.infotrac.galegroup.com

Clark, P. G. (1989). The philosophical foundation of empowerment. *Journal of Aging and Health, 1*(3), 267–285.

Clavel, P., & Deppe, M. (1999). Innovation in urban policy: Movement and incorporation in city administration and community development. *Policy Studies Journal, 27*(1), 115+. Retrieved October 3, 1999 from Info Trac database (Expanded Academic ASAP) on the World Wide Web: http://www5.infotrac.galegroup.com

Coates, D., Renzaglia, G. J., & Embree, M. C. (1983). When helping backfires: Help and helplessness. In J. D. Fisher, A. Nadler, & B. M. DePaulo (Eds.), *New directions in helping, Vol 1: Recipient reactions to aid* (pp. 251–279). New York: Academic Press.

Cohen, M. B. (1998). Perceptions of power in client/worker relationships. *Families in Society, 79*(4), 433–442.

Cole, J. (1999). An ounce of prevention beats burnout. *HR Focus, 76*(6), 1+. Retrieved October 3, 1999 from InfoTrac database (Expanded Academic ASAP) on the World Wide Web: http://www5.infotrac.galegroup.com

Collopy, B. J. (1992). Autonomy in long term care: Some crucial distinctions. In S. M. Rose (Ed.), *Case management and social work practice* (pp. 56–76). New York: Longman.

Compton, B. R., & Galaway, B. (1999). *Social work processes* (6th ed.). Pacific Grove CA: Brooks/Cole Publishing Company.

Congress, E. (1994). The use of culturagrams to assess and empower culturally diverse families. *Families in Society, 75*, 531–540.

Congress, E. (1999). *Social work values and ethics: Identifying and resolving professional dilemmas.* Chicago: Nelson Hall.

Corcoran, K. J. (1993). Practice evaluation: Problems and promises of single-system designs in clinical practice. *Journal of Social Service Research, 18*(1/2), 147–159.

Corey, M. S., & Corey, G. (1997). *Groups: process and practice* (5th ed.). Pacific Grove, CA: Brooks/Cole Publishing Company.

Council on Social Work Education (1992). *Curriculum policy statement for baccalaureate degree programs in social work education.* Alexandria, VA: Author.

Couto, R. A. (1998). Community coalitions and grassroots policies of empowerment. *Administration & Society, 30*(5), 569–594.

Cowger, C. D. (1992). Assessment of client strengths. In D. Saleebey (Ed.), *The strengths perspective in social work practice* (pp. 139–147). New York: Longman.

Cowger, C. D. (1994). Assessing client strengths: Clinical assessment for client empowerment. *Social Work, 39*, 262–268.

Cox, E. O. (1991). The critical role of social action in empowerment oriented groups. *Social Work with Groups, 14*(3/4), 77–90.

Cox, E. O., & Parsons, R. J. (1992, March). *Building community through empowerment-oriented groups.* Paper prepared for Council on Social Work Education's Annual Program Meeting. Kansas City, MO.

Cox, E. O., & Parsons, R. (1993). *Empowerment-oriented social work practice with the elderly.* Pacific Grove, CA: Brooks/Cole Publishing Company.

Cox, E. O., Parsons, R. J., & Kimboko, P. J. (1988). Social services and intergenerational caregivers: Issues for social work. *Social Work, 33,* 430–434.

Crystal, D. (1989). Asian Americans and the myth of the model minority. *Social Casework, 70,* 405–413.

Current state of the planet (1999, June 6). *Manchester Guardian Weekly, 160*(23), p.7.

Daro, D., & Wang, C. T. (1997). Current trends in child abuse reporting and fatalities: NCPCA's annual fifty state survey. Retrieved August 27, 1997 from the World Wide Web: http://www.childabuse.org/5096sum.html

Davidson, J. R., & Davidson, T. (1996). Confidentiality and managed care: Ethical and legal concerns. *Health and Social Work, 21,* 208–215.

Davidson, M. E. (1988). Advocacy research: Social context of social research. In C. Jacobs, & D. D. Bowles (Eds.), *Ethnicity and race: Critical concepts in social work* (pp. 114–130). Silver Spring, MD: National Association of Social Workers, Inc.

Davidson, T., & Davidson, J. R. (1995). Cost-containment, computers, and confidentiality. *Clinical Social Work Journal, 23,* 453–464.

Davis, I. L. (1992). Client identification and outreach. In B. S. Vourlekis & R. R. Greene (Eds.), *Social work case management* (pp. 27–34). New York: Aldine de Gruyter.

Davis, L. E., & Gelsomino, J. (1994). An assessment of practitioner cross-racial treatment experiences. *Social Work, 39,* 116–123.

Davis, L. V. (1995). Domestic violence. In R. L. Edwards (Ed.), *Encyclopedia of social work: Vol 1* (19th ed.) (pp. 780–789). Washington, DC: NASW Press.

Dean, R. G. (1989). Ways of knowing in clinical practice. *Clinical Social Work Journal, 17*(2), 116–127.

Dean, R. G. (1993). Constructivism: An approach to clinical practice. *Smith College Studies in Social Work, 63*(2), 127–146.

Dean, R. G., & Rhodes, M. L. (1998). Social constructionism and ethics: What makes a "better" story? *Families in Society, 79*(3), 254–262.

De Jong, P., & Berg, I. K. (1998). *Interviewing for solutions.* Pacific Grove, CA: Brooks/Cole Publishing Company.

De Jong, P., & Miller, S. D. (1995). How to interview for client strengths. *Social Work, 40,* 729–736.

Delgado, M., & Barton, K. (1998). Murals in Latino communities: Social indicators of community strengths. *Social Work, 43*(4), 346–356.

Dennis, R. E., & Giangreco, M. F. (1996). Creating conversation: Reflections on cultural sensitivity in family interviewing. *Exceptional Children, 63*(1), 103–116.

de Shazer, S. (1982). *Patterns of brief family therapy: An ecosystemic approach.* New York: Guilford Press.

de Shazer, S. (1985). *Keys to solution in brief therapy.* New York: W. W. Norton.

de Shazer, S. (1988). *Clues: Investigating solutions in brief therapy.* New York: W. W. Norton.

de Shazer, S. (1989). Resistance revisited. *Contemporary Family Therapy, 11*(4), 227–233.

de Shazer, S., & Molnar, A. (1984). Four useful interventions in family therapy. *Journal of Marital and Family Therapy, 10,* 297–304.

Devore, W. (1987). Developing ethnic sensitivity for the counseling process: A social work perspective. In P. Pedersen (Ed.), *Handbook of cross-cultural counseling and therapy* (pp. 93–98). New York: Praeger Publishers.

Devore, W., & Schlesinger E. G. (1999). *Ethnic-sensitive social work practice* (3rd ed.). Boston: Allyn & Bacon.

Dick, B. (1997a). Participative processes. Retrieved June 29, 1999 from the World Wide Web: *http://www.scu.edu.au/schools/sawd/arr/partproc.html*

Dick, B. (1997b). A beginner's guide to action research. Retrieved June 29, 1999 from the World Wide Web: *http://www.scu.edu.au/schools/sawd/arr/guide.html*

Dickson, D. T. (1998). *Confidentiality and privacy in social work: A guide to the law for practitioners and students.* New York: The Free Press.

Dinerman, M. (1992). Managing the maze: Case management and service delivery. *Administration is Social Work, 16*(1), 1–9.

DiNitto, D. M., & Dye, T. R. (1999). *Social welfare politics and public policy.* Boston: Allyn & Bacon.

Dodd, P., & Gutiérrez, L. (1990). Preparing students for the future: A power perspective on community practice. *Administration in Social Work, 14*(2), 63–78.

Drake, B. (1994). Relationship competencies in child welfare services. *Social Work, 39,* 595–602.

Dressel, P. (1992). Patriarchy and social welfare work. In Y. Hasenfeld (Ed.), *Human services as complex organizations* (pp. 205–223). Newbury Park, CA: Sage Publications.

DuBois, B. (1993, April). *Visioning the future: Organizational strategic planning.* Presentation for the National Fraternal Congress of America, Communications Section. Lake Tahoe, NE.

DuBois, B., & Miley, K. K. (1999). *Social work: An empowering profession* (3rd ed.). Boston: Allyn & Bacon.

DuBois, B., Miley, K., & O'Melia, M. (1993, April). *Applying an empowerment process in social work practice.* Paper presented at the Central Midwest Conference on Child Abuse. Moline, IL.

Dungee-Anderson, D., & Beckett, J. O. (1995). A process for multicultural social work practice. *Families in Society, 76,* 459–466.

Dunst, C. J. (1993, April). *Empowerment strategies in human services programs.* Paper presented for the Central Midwest Conference on Child Abuse. Moline, IL.

Dunst, C. J., & Trivette, C. M. (1988). Helping, helplessness, and harm. In J. C. Witt, S. N. Elliot, & F. M. Gresham (Eds.), *Handbook of behavior therapy* (pp. 343–376). New York: Plenum Press.

Dunst, C. J., Trivette, C. M., Davis, M., & Cornwell, J. (1988). Enabling and empowering families of children with health impairments. *Children's Health Care, 17*(2), 71–81.

Dunst, C. J., Trivette, C. M., & Deal, A. G. (1988). *Enabling and empowering families.* Cambridge, MA: Brookline Books.

Dunst, C. J., Trivette, C. M., & Hamby, D. W. (1996). Measuring the helpgiving practices of human services program practitioners. *Human Relations, 49,* 815–835.

Durrant, M., & Kowalski, K. (1992). Enhancing views of competence. In S. Friedman (Ed.), *The new language of change* (pp. 107–137). New York: Guilford Press.

Dyche, L., & Zayas, L. H. (1995). The value of curiosity and naivete for the cross-cultural psychotherapist. *Family Process, 34,* 389–399.

Dykeman, J., Nelson, R., & Appleton, V. (1995). Building strong working alliances with American Indian families. *Social Work in Education, 17*(3), 148–158.

Egan, G. (1998). *The skilled helper: A problem-management approach to helping* (6th ed.). Pacific Grove, CA: Brooks/Cole Publishing Company.

Ekman, P., & Friesen, W. V. (1975). *Unmasking the face.* Englewood Cliffs, NJ: Prentice Hall.

El-Bassel, N., Chen, D-R., & Cooper, D. (1998). Social support and social network profiles among women on methadone. *Social Service Review, 72*(3), 379–401.

Epstein, L. (1985). *Talking and listening: A guide to the helping interview.* St Louis, MO: Times Mirror/Mosby.

Erikson, E. H. (1963). *Childhood and society* (2nd ed.). New York: Norton.

Evans, C., & Fisher, M. (1999). User controlled research and empowerment. In W. Shera & L. Wells (Eds.), *Empowerment practice in social work: Developing richer conceptual foundations* (pp. 348–369). Toronto, Canada: Canadian Scholars' Press.

Evans, E. N. (1992). Liberation theology, empowerment theory and social work practice with the oppressed. *International Social Work, 35,* 135–147.

Evans, G., & Farberow, N. L. (1988). *The encyclopedia of suicide.* New York: Facts on File.

Ezell, M. (1994). Advocacy practice of social workers. *Families in Society, 75,* 36–46.

Falicov, C. J. (1996). Mexican families. In M. McGoldrick, J. Giordano, & J. K. Pearce (Eds.). *Ethnicity and family therapy* (2nd ed.) (pp. 169–182). New York: Guilford Press.

Fancett, S., & Hughes, M. (1996). The development of a client record system within a non-governmental child care organization. *Computers in Human Services, 13*(1), 63–72.

Fant, R. S., & Ross, A. L. (1983). Supervision of child care staff. In H. Weissman, I. Epstein, & A. Savage (Eds.), *Agency-based social work: Neglected aspects of clinical practice* (pp. 238–250). Philadelphia: Temple University Press.

Federico, R. (1983). *The social welfare institutions* (4th ed.). Lexington, MA: D.C. Heath and Company.

Feiring, C., Taska, L. S., & Lewis, M. (1998). Social support and children's and adolescent's adaptation to sexual abuse. *Journal of Interpersonal Violence, 13*(2), 240–260.

Feld, S., & Radin, N. (1982). *Social psychology: For social work and the mental health professions.* New York: Columbia University Press.

Felin, P. (1995). *The community and the social worker.* Itasca, IL: F. E. Peacock Publishers, Inc.

Ferriter, M. (1993). Computer aided interviewing in psychiatric social work. *Computers in Human Services, 9*(1/2), 59–72.

Fetterman, D. M. (1994). Empowerment evaluation: Presidential address. *Evaluation Practice, 15*(1), 1–15.

Fetterman, D. M. (1996). Empowerment evaluation: An introduction to theory and practice. In D. M. Fetterman, S. J. Kaftarian, & A. Wandersman (Eds.), *Empowerment evaluation: Knowledge and tools for self-assessment and accountability* (pp. 3–46). Thousand Oaks, CA: Sage Publications, Inc.

Figley, C. R. (1995). *Compassion fatigue: Coping with secondary traumatic stress disorders in those who treat the traumatized.* New York: Brunner/Mazel.

Fine, M., & Asch, A. (1988). Disability beyond stigma: Social interaction, discrimination, and activism. *Journal of Social Issues, 44,* 3–21.

Finn, J. (1995). Computer-based self-help groups: A new resurce to supplement support groups. *Social Work with Groups, 18*(1), 109–117.

Finn, J. (1996). Computer-based self-help groups: Online recovery for addictions. *Computers in Human Services, 13*(1), 21–41.

Fischer, J. (1973). An eclectic approach to therapeutic casework. In J. Fischer (Ed.), *Interpersonal helping: Emerging approaches for social work practice* (pp. 317–335). Springfield, IL: Charles C Thomas.

Fischer, J. (1978). *Effective casework practice: An eclectic approach.* New York: McGraw Hill.

Fischer, J. (1993). Empirically-based practice: The end of ideology? *Journal of Social Service Research, 18*(1/2), 19–64.

Fisher, D. D. V. (1991). *An introduction to constructivism for social workers.* New York: Praeger.

Fisher, M. (1994). Partnership practice and empowerment. In L. Gutiérrez & P. Nurius (Eds.), *Educa-*

tion and research for empowerment practice (pp. 275–291). Seattle, WA: Center for Policy and Practice Research, School of Social Work, University of Washington.

Fisher, R., & Kling, J. (1994). Community organization and new social movement theory. *Journal of Progressive Human Services, 5*(2), 5–23.

Fleming, J., & Ward, D. (1999). Research as empowerment: The social action approach. In W. Shera & L. Wells (Eds.), *Empowerment practice in social work: Developing richer conceptual foundations* (pp. 370–389). Toronto, Canada: Canadian Scholars' Press.

Fleming, R., Baum, A., & Singer, J. E. (1985). Social support and the physical environment. In S. Cohen, & S. L. Syme (Eds.), *Social support and health* (pp. 327–345). New York: Academic Press.

Flower, J. (1998). A toolkit for building a healthy city. *National Civic Review, 87*(14), 293+. Retrieved June 28, 1999 from InfoTrac database (Expanded Academic ASAP) on the World Wide Web: http://www5.infotrac.galegroup.com

Fong, R. (1997). Child welfare practice with Chinese families: Assessment issues for immigrants from the People's Republic of China. *Journal of Family Social Work, 2*(1), 33–47.

Fong, R., & Mokuau, N. (1994). Not simply "Asian American": Periodical literature review on Asians and Pacific Islanders. *Social Work, 39,* 298–306.

Fortune, A. E. (1995). Termination in practice. In R. L. Edwards (Ed.), *Encyclopedia of social work: Vol 3* (19th ed.) (pp. 2398–2404). Washington, DC: NASW Press.

Fortune, A. E., Pearlingi, B., & Rochelle, C. D. (1991). Criteria for terminating treatment. *Families in Society, 72*(6), 366–370.

Fortune, A. E., Pearlingi, B., & Rochelle, C. D. (1992). Reactions to termination of individual treatment. *Social Work, 37,* 171–178.

Fox, R. (1987). Short-term, goal-oriented family therapy. *Social Casework, 68,* 494–499.

Frankel, M. (1992). Suicide: Highest in wide-open spaces. *American Demographics, 14*(4), 9.

Franklin, A. J. (1993). The invisibility syndrome. *The Family Therapy Networker, 17*(4), 32–39.

Franklin, C., Waukechon, J., & Larney, P. S. (1995). Culturally relevant school programs for American Indian children and families. *Social Work in Education, 17*(3), 183–193.

Franklin, D. L. (1990). The cycles of social work practice: Social action vs. individual interest. *Journal of Progressive Human Services, 1*(2), 59–80.

Freire, P. (1973). *Education for critical consciousness.* New York: Continuum.

Freire, P. (1993). *Pedagogy of the oppressed* (New rev. 20th anniversary ed.). New York: Continuum Publishing Company.

Freire, P. (1997). *Pedagogy of the heart.* New York: Continuum Publishing Company.

Freud, S. (1987). Social workers as community educators: A new identity for the profession. *Journal of Teaching in Social Work, 1,* 111–126.

Furman, B., & Ahola, T. (1992). *Solution talk: Hosting therapeutic conversations.* New York: W. W. Norton.

Galbraith, M. W. (1991). The adult learning transactional process. In M. W. Galbraith (Ed.), *Facilitating adult learning: A transactional process* (pp. 1–32). Malabar, FL: Krieger Publishing Company.

Galinsky, M. J., Schopler, J. H., & Abell, M. D. (1997). Connecting group members through telephone and computer groups. *Health and Social Work, 22*(3), 181–188.

Gallup Organization Princeton. (1999, May 6). Poll releases—As nation observes national day of prayer, 9 in 10 pray—3 in 4 daily. Retrieved June 8, 1999 from the World Wide Web: http://www.gallup.com/poll/releases/pr990506.asp

Gamble, D. N., & Weil, M. O. (1995). Citizen participation. In R. L. Edwards (Ed.), *Encyclopedia of social work: Vol 1* (19th ed.) (pp. 483–494). Washington, DC: NASW Press.

Garbarino, J. (1983). Social support networks: Rx for the helping professions. In J. K. Whittaker & J. Garbarino (Eds.), *Social support networks: Informal helping in the human services* (pp. 3–28). New York: Aldine deGruyter.

Garcia-Preto, N. (1996). Puerto Rican families. In M. McGoldrick, J. Giordano, & J. K. Pearce (Eds.). *Ethnicity and family therapy* (2nd ed.) (pp. 183–199). New York: Guilford Press.

Garcia-Preto, N. (1998). Latinas in the United States: Bridging two worlds. In M. McGoldrick (Ed.), *Revisioning family therapy: Race, culture, and gender in clinical practice* (pp. 330–344). New York: Guilford Press.

Garrett, A. (1982). *Interviewing: Its principles and methods* (3rd ed) New York: Family Service Association of America.

Garrett, J. T. (1993–1994). Understanding Indian children. *Children Today, 22*(4), 18–21, 40.

Garvin, C. D. (1997) *Contemporary group work* (3rd ed.). Boston: Allyn & Bacon.

Garvin, C. D., & Tropman, J. E. (1998). *Social work in contemporary society* (2nd ed.). Boston: Allyn & Bacon.

Gelman, S. R. (1992). Risk management through client access to case records. *Social Work, 37,* 73–79.

Gelman, S. R., Pollack, D., & Weiner, A. (1999). Confidentiality of social work records in the computer age. *Social Work, 44*(3), 243–252.

Gerdes, K. E., & Benson, R. A. (1995). Problems of inner-city schoolchildren: Needs assessment by nominal group process. *Social Work in Education, 17,* 139–147.

Gergen, K. J. (1994). *Realities and relationships: Soundings in social construction.* Cambridge, MA: Harvard University Press.

Germain, C. B. (1979). Ecology and social work. In C. B. Germain (Ed.), *Social work practice: People and environments* (pp. 1–22). New York: Columbia University Press.

Germain, C. B. (1983). Using social and physical environments. In A. Rosenblatt & D. Waldfogel (Eds.), *Handbook of clinical social work* (pp. 110–133). San Francisco: Jossey-Bass Publishers.

Germain, C. B., & Gitterman, A. (1980). *The life model of social work practice.* New York: Columbia University Press.

Germain, C. B., & Gitterman, A. (1995). Ecological perspective. In R. L. Edwards (Ed.), *Encyclopedia of social work: Vol 1* (19th ed.)(pp. 816–824). Washington, DC: NASW Press.

Germain, C. B., & Gitterman, A. (1996). *The life model of social work practice: Advances in theory and practice.* New York: Columbia University Press.

Gibelman, M. (1998). Women's perceptions of the glass ceiling in human service organizations and what to do about it. *Affilia, 13*(2), 147–165.

Gibson, C. M. (1993). Empowerment theory and practice with adolescents of color in the child welfare system. *Families in Society, 74,* 387–396.

Gil, D. G. (1994). Confronting social injustice and oppression. In F. G. Reamer (Ed.), *The foundations of social work knowledge* (pp. 231–263). New York: Columbia University Press.

Gilbert, N., & Terrell, P. (1998). *Dimensions of social welfare policy* (4th ed.). Boston: Allyn & Bacon.

Gillespie, D. F. (1995). Ethical issues in research. In R. L. Edwards (Ed.). *Encyclopedia of social work: Vol 1* (19th ed.) (pp. 884–893). Washington, DC: NASW Press.

Gilson, S. F., Bricout, J. C., & Baskind, F. R. (1998). Listening to the voices of individuals with disabilities. *Families in Society, 79*(2), 188–196.

Gingerich, W. J. (1990). Rethinking single-case evaluation. In L. Videka-Sherman & W. J. Reid (Eds.), *Advances in clinical social work research* (pp. 13–24). Silver Spring, MD: NASW Press.

Ginsberg, L. (1995). *Social work almanac.* Washington, DC: NASW Press.

Gitterman, A. (1991). Introduction: Social work practice with vulnerable populations. In A. Gitterman (Ed.), *Handbook of social work practice with vulnerable populations.* New York: Columbia University Press.

Gold, N. (1990). Motivation: The crucial but unexplored component of social work practice. *Social Work, 35*(1), 49–56.

Goldstein, H. (1973). *Social work practice: A unitary approach.* Columbia, SC: University of South Carolina Press.

Goldstein, H. (1987). The neglected moral link in social work practice. *Social Work, 32,* 181–186.

Goldstein, H. (1990). Strength or pathology: Ethical and rhetorical contrasts in approaches to practice. *Families in Society, 71,* 267–275.

Goldstein, S. R., & Beebe L. (1995). National Association of Social Workers. In R. L. Edwards (Ed.), *Encyclopedia of social work: Vol 2* (19th ed.) (pp. 1747–1764). Washington, DC: NASW Press.

Goodley, D. (1997). Locating self-advocacy in models of disability: Understanding disability in the support of self-advocates with learning difficulties. *Disability and Society, 12*(3), 367–379.

Gothard, S. (1995). Legal issues: Confidentiality and privileged communication. In R. L. Edwards (Ed.), *Encyclopedia of social work: Vol 2* (19th ed.) (pp. 1579–1584). Washington, DC: NASW Press.

Gottlieb, N. (1992). Empowerment, political analyses, and services for women. In Y. Hasenfeld (Ed.), *Human services as complex organizations* (pp. 301–319). Newbury Park, CA: Sage Publications.

Graber, L., & Nice, J. (1991, Fall). The family unity model: The advanced skill of looking for and building on strengths. *The Prevention Report,* pp. 3–4.

Graham, M. A., Kaiser, T., & Garrett, K. J. (1998). Naming the spiritual: The hidden dimension of helping. *Social Thought, 18*(4), 49–61.

Graybeal, C. T., & Ruff, E. (1995). Process recording: It's more than you think. *Journal of Social Work Education, 31,* 169–181.

Green, J. W. (1999). *Cultural awareness in the human services: A multi-ethnic approach* (3rd ed.). Boston: Allyn & Bacon.

Greene, G. J., Jensen, C., & Jones, D. H. (1996). A constructive perspective on clinical social work practice with ethnically diverse clients. *Social Work, 41*(2), 172–180.

Greene, G. J., Lee, M-Y., Mentzer, R. A., Pinnell, S. R., & Niles, D. (1998). Miracles, dreams, and empowerment: A brief therapy practice note. *Families in Society, 79*(4), 395–400.

Greene, R. R. (1992). Case management: An arena for social work practice. In B. S. Vourlekis & R. R. Greene (Eds.), *Social work case management* (pp. 11–25). New York: Aldine de Gruyter.

Greene, R. R., & Ephross, P. H. (1991). *Human behavior theory and social work practice.* New York: Aldine de Gruyter.

Greif, G. L. (1986). The ecosystems perspective "Meets the press". *Social Work, 31,* 225–226.

Griffin, R. E. (1991). Assessing the drug-involved client. *Families in Society, 72,* 87–94.

Grimm, L. L. (1992). The Native American child in school: An ecological perspective. In M. J. Fine & C. Carlson (Eds.), *The handbook of family-school intervention* (pp. 102–118). Boston: Allyn & Bacon.

Grinnell, R. M. (1997). *Social work research and evaluation* (5th ed.). Itasca, IL: F. E. Peacock Publishers, Inc.

Grinnell, R. M., & Williams, M. (1990). *Research in social work: A primer.* Itasca, IL: F. E. Peacock Publishers, Inc.

Grube, J. W., Mayton, D. M., & Ball-Rokeach, S. J. (1994). Inducing change in values, attitudes, and behaviors: Belief system theory and the method of value self-confrontation. *Journal of Social Issues, 50*(4), 153–173.

Gruber, J., & Trickett, E. J. (1987). Can we empower others? The paradox of empowerment in the governing of an alternative school. *American Journal of Community Psychology, 15,* 353–371.

Gummer, B. (1983). Consumerism and clients rights. In A. Rosenblatt & D. Waldfogel (Eds.), *Hand-book of clinical social work* (pp. 920–938). San Francisco: Jossey-Bass Publishers.

Guterman, N. B., & Bargal, D. (1996). Social workers' perceptions of their power and service outcomes. *Administration in Social Work, 20*(3), 1–19.

Gutheil, I. A. (1992). Considering the physical environment: An essential component of good practice. *Social Work, 37,* 391–396.

Gutheil, I. A. (1993). Rituals and termination procedures. *Smith College Studies in Social Work, 63*(2), 163–176.

Gutiérrez, L. M. (1989, March). *Empowerment in social work practice: Considerations for practice and education.* Paper presented at the Council on Social Work Education Annual Program Meeting, Chicago, IL.

Gutiérrez, L. M. (1991). Empowering women of color: A feminist model. In M. Bricker-Jenkins, N. R. Hooyman, & N. Gottlieb (Eds.), *Feminist social work practice in clinical settings* (pp. 199–214). Newbury Park, CA: Sage Publications.

Gutiérrez, L. (1992). Empowering ethnic minorities in the twenty-first century: The role of human service organizations. In Y. Hasenfeld (Ed.), *Human services as complex organizations* (pp. 320–338). Newbury Park, CA: Sage Publications.

Gutiérrez, L. M. (1994), Beyond coping: An empowerment perspective on stressful life events. *Journal of Sociology and Social Welfare, 21*(3), 201–219.

Gutiérrez, L. M. (1995). Understanding the empowerment process: Does consciousness make a difference? *Social Work Research, 19,* 229–237.

Gutiérrez, L., Alvarez, R. A., Nemon, H., & Lewis, E. A. (1996). Multicultural community organizing: A strategy for change. *Social Work, 41*(5), 501–508.

Gutiérrez, L. M., & Lewis, E. A. (1998). A feminist perspective on organizing with women of color. In F. G. Rivera & J. L. Erlich (Eds.), *Community organizing in a diverse society* (pp. 97–115). Boston, MA: Allyn and Bacon.

Gutiérrez, L., & Nagda, B. A. (1996). The multicultural imperative in human services organizations: Issues for the twenty-first century. In P. R. Raffoul & C. A. McNeece (Eds.), *Future issues for social work practice* (pp. 203–213). Boston: Allyn & Bacon.

Gutiérrez, L. M., & Ortega, R. (1991). Developing methods to empower Latinos: The importance of groups. *Social Work with Groups, 14*(2), 23–43.

Haight, W. L. (1998). "Gathering the Spirit" at First Baptist Church: Spirituality as a protective factor in the lives of African American children. *Social Work, 43*(3), 213–221.

Haley, J. (1976). *Problem solving therapy.* New York: Harper.

Hanna, M. G., & Robinson, B. (1994). *Strategies for community empowerment: Direct-action and transformative approaches to social change practice.* Lewiston, NY: The Edwin Mellen Press.

Hardy, K. V., & Laszloffy, T. A. (1995). The cultural genogram: Key to training culturally competent family therapists. *Journal of Marital and Family Therapy, 21,* 227–237.

Harold, R. D., Mercier, L. R., & Colaross, L. G. (1997). Eco maps: A tool to bridge the practice-research gap. *Journal of Sociology and Social Welfare, 24*(4), 29–44.

Harper, J. M. (1994). Variables to your grieving process. Retrieved May 9, 1999 from the World Wide Wed: http://rivendell.org/library.dir/variables.html

Harrigan, M. P., Fauri, D. P., & Netting, F. E. (1998). Termination: Extending the concept for macro social work practice. *Journal of Sociology and Social Welfare, 25*(4), 61–80.

Hartman, A. (1978, reprinted in 1995). Diagrammatic assessment of family relationships. *Families in Society, 76,* 111–122.

Hartman, A. (1992). In search of subjugated knowledge. *Social Work, 37,* 483–484.

Hartman, A. (1993). The professional is political. *Social Work, 38,* 365–366.

Hartman, A., & Laird, J. (1983). *Family centered social work practice.* New York: Free Press.

Hasenfeld, Y. (1987). Power in social work practice. *Social Service Review, 61,* 469–483.

Held, B. J. (1995). The real meaning of constructivism. *Journal of Constructivist Psychology, 8,* 305–315.

Hellenbrand, S. C. (1987). Termination in direct practice. In A. Minahan (Ed.), *Encyclopedia of social work: Vol 2* (18th ed.) (pp. 765–769). Silver Spring, MD: National Association of Social Workers.

Henry, S. (1992). *Group skills in social work: A four dimensional approach.* Pacific Grove, CA: Brooks/Cole Publishing Company.

Hepworth, D. H., Rooney, R. H., & Larsen, J. (1997). *Direct social work practice: Theory and skills* (4th ed.). Pacific Grove, CA: Brooks/Cole Publishing Company.

Hess, H., & Hess, P. M. (1999). Termination in context. In B. R. Compton & B. Galaway, *Social Work Processes* (pp. 489–497). Pacific Grove, CA: Brooks/Cole Publishing Company.

Hill, R. B. (1997). *The strengths of African American families: Twenty-five years later.* Washington, DC: R & B Publishers.

Hills, D. (1998). Engaging new social movements. *Human Relations, 51*(12), 1457+. Retrieved June 29, 1999 from InfoTrac database (Expanded Academic ASAP) on the World Wide Web: http://www5.infotrac.galegroup.com

Hines, P., & Boyd-Franklin, N. (1996). African American families. In M. McGoldrick, J. Giordano, & J. K. Pierce (Eds.), *Ethnicity and family therapy* (pp. 66–84). New York: Guildford Press.

Hingsburger, D. (1990). *i to I: Self concept and people with developmental disabilities.* Mountville, PA: VIDA Publishing.

Hirayama, H. & Hirayama, K. (1988) Empowerment through group participation: Process and goal. In M. Parnes (Ed.), *Innovations in social group work: Feedback from practice to theory, selected proceedings of the 5th Symposium on Social Work with Groups* (pp. 119–131). New York: The Haworth Press.

Ho, M. K. (1987). *Family therapy with ethnic minorities.* Newbury Park, CA: Sage Publications.

Hoekstra, H., Vink, M., & Fa, R. T. A. (undated). Background. Retrieved June 30, 1999 from the World Wide Web: *http://www.univaris.fr/CRINFO/dmrg/MEE98/misop016/node2.html*

Hoffman, K. S., & Sallee, A. L. (1994). *Social work practice: Bridges to Change.* Boston: Allyn & Bacon.

Hoffman, L. (1989). The family life cycle and discontinuous change. In B. Carter & M. McGoldrick (Eds.), *The changing family life cycle: A framework for family therapy* (2nd ed.) (pp. 91–105). Boston: Allyn & Bacon.

Holahan, C. J., Wilcox, B. L., Spearly, J. L., & Campbell, M. D. (1979). The ecological perspective in community mental health. *Community Mental Health Review, 4,* 1–9.

Hollis, F. (1967). Principles and assumptions underlying casework principles. In E. Younghusband (Ed.), *Social work and social values* (pp. 22–38). London: George Allen & Unwin Ltd.

Holzman, C. G. (1994). Multicultural perspectives on counseling survivors of rape. *Journal of Social Distress and the Homeless, 3*(1), 81–97.

Home, A. (1999). Group empowerment. In W. Shera & L. Wells (Eds.), *Empowerment practice in social work: Developing richer conceptual foundations* (pp. 234–245). Toronto, Canada: Canadian Scholars' Press.

Hooper, L. M., & Bennett, C. E. (1998). The Asian and Pacific Islander population in the United States: March 1997 (Update). Retrieved June 8, 1999 from the World Wide Web: *http://www.census.gov/prod/3/98pubs/p20–512pdf*

Hopps, J. G., Pinderhughes, E., & Shankar, R. (1995). *The power to care: Clinical practice effectiveness with overwhelmed clients.* New York: The Free Press.

Houston-Vega, M. K., Neuhring, E. M., & Daguio, E. R. (1997). *Prudent practice: A guide for managing malpractice.* Washington, DC: NASW Press.

Humphrey, G. M., & Zimpfer, D. G. (1996). *Counselling for grief and bereavement.* London: Sage Publications.

Hurt, F. (1998). Implementing great new ideas through the use of force-field analysis. *Direct Marketing, 61*(1), 54–56.

Imber-Black, E. (1988). *Families and larger systems.* New York: The Guilford Press.

Imber-Black, E., & Roberts, J. (1998). *Rituals for our time: Celebrating, healing, and changing our lives and relationships.* Northvale, NJ: Aronson.

Imre, R. W. (1982). *Knowing and caring: Philosophical issues in social work.* Lanham, MD: University Press of America, Inc.

Irizarry, C., & Appel, Y. H. (1994). In double jeopardy: Preadolescents in the inner city. In A. Gitterman & L. Shulman (Eds.), *Mutual aid groups, vulnerable populations, and the life cycle* (2nd ed.) (pp. 119–149). New York: Columbia University Press.

Ivanoff, A. M., Blythe, B. J., & Tripodi, T. (1994). *Involuntary clients in social work practice: A research-based approach.* New York: Aldine de Gruyter.

Ivanoff, A. M., & Reidel, M. (1995). Suicide. In R. L. Edwards (Ed.), *Encyclopedia of social work: Vol 3* (19th ed.) (pp. 2358–2372). Washington, DC: NASW Press.

Ivey, A. E., & Ivey, M. B. (1999). *Intentional interviewing and counseling: Facilitating client development in multicultural society* (4th ed.). Monterey, CA: Brooks /Cole Publishing Company.

Jackson, H., Hess, P. M., & van Dolen, A. (1995). Preadolescent suicide: How to assess and how to respond. *Families in Society, 76,* 267–279.

Jackson, A. P., & Sears, S. J. (1992). Implications of an Africentric worldview in reducing stress for African American women. *Journal of Counseling & Development, 71,* 184–190.

Jacobs, C. (1997). On spirituality and social work practice. *Smith College Studies in Social Work, 67*(2), 171–175.

Janis, I., & Rodin, J. (1980). Attribution, control and decision making: Social psychology and health care. In G. Stone, F. Cohen, & N. Adler (Eds.), *Health Psychology* (pp. 487–521). San Francisco: Jossey-Bass Publishers.

Jenkins, S. (1983). Social service priorities and resource allocation. In A. Rosenblatt, & D. Waldfogel (Eds.), *Handbook of clinical social work* (pp. 814–825). San Francisco: Jossey-Bass.

Johnson, D. W. (1997). *Reaching out: Interpersonal effectiveness* (6th ed.). Boston: Allyn & Bacon.

Johnson, D. W., & Johnson, F. P. (1997). *Joining together: Group theory and group skills* (6th ed.). Boston: Allyn & Bacon.

Johnson, L. (1998). *Social work practice: A generalist approach* (6th ed.). Boston: Allyn & Bacon Publishers.

Kadushin, A., & Kadushin, G. (1997). *The social work interview.* New York: Columbia University Press.

Kadushin, G. (1998). Adaptations of the traditional interview to the brief-treatment context. *Families in Society, 79*(4), 346–357.

Kagle, J. D. (1987). Recording in direct practice. In A. Minahan (Ed.), *Encyclopedia of social work: Vol 2* (18th ed.) (pp. 463–467). Silver Spring, MD: National Association of Social Workers.

Kagle, J. D. (1990). Teaching social work students about privileged communication. *Journal of Teaching in Social Work, 4*(2), 49–65.

Kagle, J. D. (1991). *Social work records* (2nd ed). Belmont, CA: Wadsworth Publishing Company.

Kagle, J. D. (1993). Record keeping: Direction for the 1990s. *Social Work, 38,* 190–196.

Kagle, J. D., & Gielbelhausen, P. N. (1994). Dual relationships and professional boundaries. *Social Work, 39,* 213–220.

Kagle, J. D., & Kopels, S. (1994). Confidentiality after Tarasoff. (*Tarasoff v. Board of Regents of the University of California,* 1976). *Health and Social Work, 19*(3), 217–222.

Kane, R. A. (1992). Case management: Ethical pitfalls on the road to high-quality managed care. In S. M.

Rose (Ed.), *Case management and social work practice* (pp. 219–228). New York: Longman.

Kaplan, K. (1992). Adult protective services case management. In B. S. Vourlekis & R. R. Greene (Eds.), *Social work case management* (pp. 89–105). New York: Aldine de Gruyter.

Karger, H. J., & Stoesz, D. (1998). *American social welfare policy: A pluralist approach,* (3rd ed.). New York: Longman.

Keeney, B. P., & Ross, J. M. (1985). *Mind in therapy.* New York: Basic Books, Inc., Publishers.

Keith-Lucas, A. (1972). *The giving and taking of help.* Chapel Hill, NC: University of North Carolina Press.

Kemp, S. P., Whittaker, J. K., & Tracy, E. M. (1997). *Person-environment practice: The social ecology of interpersonal helping.* New York: Aldine de Gruyter.

Kettner, P. M., Daley, J. M., & Nichols, A. W. (1985). *Initiating change in organizations and communities: A macro practice model.* Monterey, CA: Brooks/Cole Publishing Company.

Kieffer, C. (1984). Citizen empowerment: A developmental perspective. In J. Rappaport, C. Swift, & R. Hess (Eds.), *Studies in empowerment: Toward understanding and action* (pp. 9–36). New York: Haworth Press.

Kirst-Ashman, K. K., & Hull, G. H. (1999). *Understanding generalist practice* (2nd ed.). Chicago: Nelson-Hall Publishers.

Kisthardt, W. E. (1992). A strengths model of case management: The principles and functions of a helping relationship with persons with persistent mental illness. In D. Saleebey (Ed.), *The strengths perspective in social work practice* (pp. 59–83). New York: Longman.

Kisthardt, W. E., & Rapp, C. A. (1992). Bridging the gap between principles and practice: Implementing a strengths perspective in case management. In S. M. Rose (Ed.), *Case management and social work practice* (pp. 112–125). New York: Longman.

Kivnick, H. Q. (1988). Grandparenthood, life review, and psychosocial development. *Journal of Gerontological Social Work, 12*(3/4), 63–81.

Klein, A. R., & Cnaan, R. A. (1995). Practice with high risk clients. *Families in Society, 76,* 203–211.

Kleinkauf, C. (1981). A guide to giving legislative testimony. *Social Work, 26,* 297–303.

Kleinkauf, C. (1989). Analyzing social welfare legislation. *Social Work, 34,* 179–181.

Koeske, G. F., & Kelly, T. (1995). The impact of overinvolvement on burnout and job satisfaction. *American Journal of Orthopsychiatry, 65,* 282–292.

Kok, C. J., & Leskela, J. (1996). Solution-focused therapy in a psychiatric hospital. *The Journal of Marital and Family Therapy, 22*(3), 397–406.

Konle, C. (1982). *Social work day-to-day: The experience of generalist social work practice.* New York: Longman Inc.

Kopels, S., & Kagle, J. D. (1993). Do social workers have a duty to warn? *Social Service Review, 67,* 101–126.

Kopels, S., & Kagle, J. D. (1994). Teaching confidentiality breaches as a form of discrimination. *Arete, 19*(1), 1–9.

Kramer, B. J. (1998). Preparing social workers for the inevitable: A preliminary investigation of a course on grief, death, and loss. *Journal of Social Work Education, 34*(2), 211–227.

Kraus, A., & Pillsbury, J. B. (1994). Streamlining intake and eligibility systems. *Public Welfare, 52*(3), 21–29.

Kretzmann, J. P., & McKnight, J. L. (1993). *Building communities from the inside out: A path toward finding and mobilizing a community's assets.* Chicago: ACTA Publications.

Krill, D. F. (1988). Existential social work. In R. A. Dorfman (Ed.), *Paradigms of clinical social work* (295–316). New York: Brunner/Mazel Publishers.

Krumholz, N. (1999). Equitable approaches to local economic development. *Policy Studies Journal, 27*(1), 83+. Retrieved October 3, 1999 from InfoTrac database (Expanded Academic ASAP) on the World Wide Web: http://www5.infotrac.galegroup.com

Kübler-Ross, E. (1969). *On death and dying.* New York: Macmillan.

Kuehl, B. P. (1995). The solution-oriented genogram: A collaborative approach. *Journal of Marital and Family Therapy, 21,* 239–250.

Kurzman, P. (1995). Professional liability and malpractice. In R. L. Edwards (Ed.), *Encyclopedia of social work: Vol. 1* (19th ed.) (pp. 1921–1927). Washington, DC: NASW Press.

Laird, J. (1984). Sorcerers, shamans, and social workers: The use of ritual in social work practice. *Social Work, 29,* 123–129.

Laird, J. (1990). Creating the world, or, watch your language! *Smith College Studies in Social Work, 60*(3), 213–215.

Laird, J. (1993). Women's secrets—Women's silences. In E. Imber-Black (Ed.), *Secrets in families and family therapy* (pp. 243–267). New York: W. W. Norton & Company.

Laird, J. (1995). Family-centered practice in the postmodern era. *Families in Society, 76*(3), 150–162.

Lamb, J. M. (1990). The suicidal adolescent. *Nursing, 90,* 20(5), 72–76.

Lee, J. A. B. (1994). *The empowerment approach to social work practice.* New York: Columbia University Press.

Lee, J. A. B., et al. (1997). Reflection on empowerment groupwork across racial lines: My sister's place. In T. Mistry & A. Brown (Eds.), *Race and groupwork* (pp. 66–98). London: Whiting & Birch, Ltd.

Lee, M-Y., & Greene, G. J. (1999). A social constructivist framework for integrating cross-cultural issues in teaching clinical social work. *Journal of Social Work Education, 35*(1), 21–37.

Leigh, J. W. (1998). *Communicating for cultural competence.* Boston: Allyn & Bacon.

Lenrow, P. B., & Burch, R. W. (1981). Mutual aid and professional services: Opposing or complementary? In B. H. Gottlieb (Ed.), *Social networks and social supports: Vol. 4, Sage studies in community mental health* (pp. 233–257). Beverly Hills, CA: Sage Publications.

Leung, P., Cheung, K. M., & Stevenson, K. M. (1994). A strengths approach to ethnically sensitve practice for child protective service workers. *Child Welfare, 53,* 707–721.

Levy, C. S. (1976). *Social work ethics.* New York: Human Sciences Press.

Lewin, K. (1951). *Field theory in social science.* Westport, CT: Greenwood Press.

Lewis, E. (1991). Social change and citizen action: A philosophical exploration for modern social group work. *Social Work with Groups, 14*(3/4), 23–34.

Lewis, R. G., & Ho, M. (1975). Social work with Native Americans. *Social Work, 20,* 379–382.

Libassi, M. F., & Maluccio, A. N. (1986). Competence-centered social work: Prevention in action. *Journal of Primary Prevention, 6*(3), 168–180.

Liddie, B. W. (1991). Relearning feminism on the job. In M. Bricker-Jenkins, N. R. Hooyman, & N. Gottlieb (Eds.), *Feminist social work practice in clinical settings* (pp. 131–146). Newbury Park, CA: Sage Publications.

Lipsky, M. (1984). Bureaucratic disentitlement in social welfare programs. *Social Service Review, 58,* 3–27.

Loewenberg, F. M., & Dolgoff, R. (1996). *Ethical decisions for social work practice* (5th ed.). Itasca, IL: F. E. Peacock Publishers, Inc.

Loftus, E. (1979). *Eyewitness testimony.* Cambridge, MA: Harvard University Press.

Logan, S. L., McRoy, R. G., & Freeman, E. M. (1987). Current practice approaches for treating the alcoholic client. *Health and Social Work, 13,* 106–113.

Longres, J. F. (1995). *Human behavior in the social environment.* Itasca, IL: F. E. Peacock.

Lowenthal, B. (1999). Effects of maltreatment and ways to promote children's resiliency. *Childhood Education, 75*(4), 204–209.

Lukes, C. A., & Land, H. (1990). Biculturality and homosexuality. *Social Work, 35,* 155–161.

Lum, D. (1986). *Social work with people of color: A process-stage approach.* Monterey, CA: Brooks/Cole Publishing Company.

Lum, D. (1992). *Social work with people of color: A process-stage approach* (2nd ed.). Pacific Grove, CA: Brooks/Cole Publishing Company.

Lum, D. (1996). *Social work with people of color: A process-stage approach* (3rd ed.). Pacific Grove, CA: Brooks/Cole Publishing Company.

Ma, J. L. C. (1998). Effect of perceived social support on adjustment of patients suffering from nasopharyngeal carcinoma. *Health and Social Work, 23*(3), 167–174.

Mahaffey, M. (1982). Lobbying and social work. In M. Mahaffey, & J. Hanks (eds.), *Practical politics: Social workers and political responsibility* (pp. 69–84). Silver Spring, MD: National Association of Social Workers.

Maluccio, A. N. (1979). *Learning from clients.* New York: The Free Press.

Maluccio, A. N. (1981). Competence-oriented social work practice: An ecological approach. In A. N. Maluccio (Ed.), *Promoting competence in clients: A new/old approach to social work practice* (pp. 1–24). New York: The Free Press.

Maluccio, A. N., Fein, E., & Olmstead, K. A. (1986). *Permanency planning for children: Concepts and methods.* New York: Tavistock Publications.

Maluccio, A. N., & Libassi, M. F. (1984). Competence clarification in social work practice. *Social Thought, 10,* 51–58.

Maluccio, A. N., & Marlow, W. D. (1974). The case for contract. *Social Work, 19*(1), 28–36.

Maluccio, A. N., & Whittaker, J. K. (1989). Therapeutic foster care: Implications for parental involvement. In R. P. Hawkins & J. Breiling (Eds.), *Therapeutic foster care: Critical issues* (pp. 161–181). Washington, DC: Child Welfare League of America.

Marcenko, M. O., & Samost, L. (1999). Living with HIV/AIDS: The voices of HIV-positive mothers. *Social Work, 44*(1), 36–45.

Markowitz, L. M. (1992). Reclaiming the light. *The Family Therapy Networker, 16*(3), 17–25.

Marsh, P., & Fisher, M. (1992). *Good intentions: Developing partnerships in social services.* York, England: Joseph Rowntree Foundation.

Martin, G. T. (1990). *Social policy in the welfare state.* Englewood Cliffs, NJ: Prentice Hall.

Martinez Jr., C. (1988). Mexican-Americans. In L. Comas-Diaz & E. E. H. Griffith (Eds.), *Clinical guidelines in cross-cultural mental health* (pp. 182–203). New York: John Wiley & Sons.

Martinez-Brawley, E. E. (1995). Community. In R. L. Edwards (ed.), *Encyclopedia of social work: Vol. 1* (19th ed.) (pp. 539–548). Washington, DC: NASW Press.

Maslach, C. (1976). Burned out. *Human Behavior, 5*(9), 16–22.

Maslach, C., & Leiter, M. P. (1999). Take this job and…love it! (6 ways to beat burnout). *Psychology Today, 32*(5), 50+. Retrieved October 3, 1999 from InfoTrac database (Expanded Academic ASAP) on the World Wide Web: http://www5.infotrac.galegroup.com

Maslow, A. H. (1970). *Motivation and personality.* New York: Harper & Row.

Mattaini, M. A. (1993). *More than a thousand words: Graphics for clinical practice.* Washington, DC: NASW Press.

May, R. (1972). *Power and innocence: A search for the sources of violence.* New York: W. W. Norton and Company, Inc.

McAuaide, S., & Ehrenreich, J. H. (1997). Assessing client strengths. *Families in Society, 78*(2), 201–212.

McCarthy, W. C., & Frieze, I. H. (1999). Negative aspects of therapy: Client perceptions of therapists' social influence, burnout, and quality of care. (Social influence and social power: Using theory for understanding social issues). *Journal of Social Issues, 55*(1), 33+. Retrieved October 3, 1999 from InfoTrac database (Expanded Academic ASAP)

on the World Wide Web: http://www5.infotrac.galegroup.com

McGill, D. W. (1992). The cultural story in multicultural family therapy. *Families in Society, 73,* 339–349.

McGoldrick, M. (1989). Ethnicity and the family life cycle. In B. Carter & M. McGoldrick (Eds.), *The changing family life cycle: A framework for family therapy* (2nd ed.) (pp. 69–90). Boston: Allyn & Bacon.

McGoldrick, M., & Gerson, R. (1985). *Genograms in family assessment.* New York: Norton.

McGoldrick, M., & Gerson, R. (1989). Genograms and the family life cycle. In B. Carter & M. McGoldrick (Eds.), *The changing family life cycle: A framework for family therapy* (2nd ed.) (pp. 164–189). Boston: Allyn & Bacon.

McGowan, B. G. (1987). Advocacy. In A. Minahan (Ed.), *Encyclopedia of social work: Vol 1* (18th ed.) (pp. 89–95). Silver Spring, MD: National Association of Social Workers.

McInnis-Dittrich, K. (1994). *Integrating social welfare policy and social work practice.* Pacific Grove, CA: Brooks/Cole Publishing Company.

McInnis-Dittrich, K. (1997) An empowerment-oriented mental health intervention with elderly Appalachian women: The women's club. *Journal of Women and Aging, 9*(1/2), 91–105.

McIntosh, P. (1998). White privilege: Unpacking the invisible knapsack. In M. McGoldrick (Ed.), *Revisioning family therapy: Race, culture, and gender in clinical practice* (pp. 147–152). New York: Guilford Press.

McLaughlin, L. A., & Braun, K. L. (1998). Asian and Pacific Islander cultural values: Considerations for health care decision making. *Health and Social Work, 23*(2), 116–126.

McMahon, M. O. (1996). *The general method of social work practice: A problem solving approach* (3rd ed.). Boston: Allyn & Bacon.

McNeely, R. L. (1992). Job satisfaction in the public social services: Perspectives on structure, situational factors, gender, and ethnicity. In Y. Hasenfeld (Ed.), *Human services as complex organizations* (pp. 224–255). Newbury Park, CA: Sage Publications.

McNicoll, P. (1999). Issues in teaching participatory action research. *Journal of Social Work Education, 35*(1), 51–62.

McPhatter, A. R. (1991). Assessment revisited: A comprehensive approach to understanding family dynamics. *Families in Society, 72,* 11–21.

McPhatter, A. R. (1997). Cultural competence in child welfare: What is it? How do we achieve it? What happens without it? *Child Welfare, 76*(1), 255–278.

McPheeters, H. L. (1971). *A core of competence for baccalaureate social welfare.* Atlanta, GA: The Undergraduate Social Welfare Manpower Project.

Meyer, C. (1993). *Assessment in social work practice.* New York: Columbia University Press.

Mickelson, J. S. (1995). Advocacy. In R. L. Edwards (ed.), *Encyclopedia of social work: Vol. 1* (19th ed.) (pp. 95–100). Washington, DC: NASW Press.

Middleman, R. R., & Wood, G. G. (1990). *Skills for direct practice in social work.* New York: Columbia University Press.

Mika, K. L. (1996). *Program outcome evaluation: A step-by-step handbook.* Milwaukee, WI: Families International, Inc.

Miley, K. K. (1989). *Social service employer survey.* Research prepared for Black Hawk College. Moline, IL.

Miley, K., & DuBois, B. (1999). Empowering processes for social work practice. In W. Shera & L. Wells (Eds.), *Empowerment practice in social work: Developing richer conceptual foundations* (pp. 2–12). Toronto, Canada: Canadian Scholars' Press.

Miller, D. B., & DiGuseppe, D. (1998). Fighting social problems with information: The development of a community database—The Violence Information Project. *Computers in Human Services, 15*(1), 21–34.

Molnar, A., & de Shazer, S. (1987). Solution-focused therapy: Toward the identification of therapeutic tasks. *Journal of Marital and Family Therapy, 13,* 349–358.

Monkman, M. M. (1991). Outcome objectives in social work practice: Person and environment. *Social Work, 36*(3), 253–258.

Moore-Kirkland, J. (1981). Mobilizing motivation: From theory to practice. In A. N. Maluccio (Ed.), *Promoting competence in clients: A new/old approach to social work practice* (pp. 27–54). New York: The Free Press.

Morales, A. T., & Salcido, R. (1998). Social work practice with Mexican Americans. In Morales, A. T. & Sheafor, B. W. (Eds.), *Social work: A profession of many faces* (8th ed.) (pp. 513–539). Boston: Allyn & Bacon.

Morales, A., & Sheafor, B. W. (1998). *Social work: A profession of many faces* (8th ed.). Boston: Allyn & Bacon.

Moreau, M. M. (1990). Empowerment through advocacy and consciousness-raising: Implications of a structural approach to social work. *Journal of Sociology and Social Welfare, 17*(2), 53–67.

Morris, J. (1997). Care improvement? A disability rights perspective. *Social Policy and Administration, 31*(1), 54–60.

Moxley, D. P. (1989). *The practice of case management.* Newbury Park, CA: SAGE Publications.

Moxley, D. P., & Freddolino, P. P. (1994). Client-driven advocacy and psychiatric disability: A model for social work practice. *Journal of Sociology and Social Welfare, 21*(2), 91–108.

Mullender, A. (1992–93). Disabled people find a voice: Will it be heard in the move towards community care? *Practice, 6*(1), 5–15.

Mullender, A. (1996a). Groups as a means of empowerment. In P. Parsloe (Ed.), *Pathways to empowerment* (pp. 125–140). Birmingham, England: Venture Press.

Mullender, A. (1996b). The empowerment framework: Bridging the gap between individuals and social structures in health care. In N. Berkowitz (Ed.), *Humanistic approaches to health care: Focus on social work* (pp. 181–200). Birmingham, England: Venture Press.

Murdach, A. D. (1987). Resource mobilization and coordination. In A. Minahan (Ed.), *Encyclopedia of social work: Vol 2* (18th ed.) (pp. 503–507). Silver Spring, MD: National Association of Social Workers.

Murdock, S. H., & Michael, M. (1996). Future demographic trends: The demand for social welfare services in the twenty first century. In P. R. Raffoul & C. A. McNeece (Eds.), *Future issues for social work practice* (pp. 3–18). Boston: Allyn & Bacon.

Nakanishi, M., & Rittner, B. (1992). The inclusionary cultural model. *Journal of Social Work Education, 28,* 27–35.

Nakanishi, M., & Rittner, B. (1996). Social work practice with Asian Americans. In D. F. Harrison, B. A. Thyer, & J. S. Wodarski (Eds.), *Cultural diversity and social work practice* (2nd ed.) (pp. 87–111). Springfield, IL: Charles C Thomas, Publisher.

National Association of Social Workers (1981). *Standards for the classification of social work practice: Policy statement 4.* Silver Spring, MD: Author.

National Association of Social Workers (2000). *Code of ethics of the National Association of Social Workers.* Washington, DC: Author.

National Center for Elder Abuse (1997). Elder abuse information series #2: Elder abuse in domestic settings. Retrieved August 26, 1997 from the World Wide Web: *http://www.interinc.com/NCEA/Statistics/p3.html*

Nelsen, J. C. (1990). Single-case research and traditional practice: Issues and possibilities. In L. Videka-Sherman & W. J. Reid (Eds.), *Advances in clinical social work research* (pp. 37–47). Silver Spring, MD: NASW Press.

Nelsen, J. C. (1993). Testing practice wisdom: Another use for single-system research. *Journal of Social Service Research, 18*(1/2), 65–82.

Neuman, K. M., & Friedman, B. D. (1997). Process recordings: Fine-tuning an old instrument. *Journal of Social Work Education, 33*(2), 237–243.

Newman, B. S. (1989). Including curriculum content on lesbian and gay issues. *Journal of Social Work Education, 25,* 202–211.

Newman, B. S. (1994). Diversity and populations at risk: Gays and lesbians. In F. G. Reamer (Ed.), *The foundations of social work knowledge* (pp. 346–392). New York: Columbia University Press.

Nichols, M. P., & Schwartz, R. C. (1998). *Family therapy: Concepts and methods* (4th ed.). Boston: Allyn & Bacon.

Norlin, J. M., & Chess, W. (1997). *Human behavior and the social environment: A social systems model* (3rd ed.). Boston: Allyn & Bacon.

Nosko, A., & Breton, M. (1997–98). Applying a strengths, competence, and empowerment model. *Groupwork, 10*(1), 55–69.

Nunnally, E., & Moy, C. (1989). *Communication basics for human service professionals.* Newbury Park, CA: Sage Publications.

Nye, S. G. (1989). Since you've asked: Legal issues for social workers. *NASW Illinois Chapter Bulletin, 28*(12), p. 4.

Nystrom, J. F. (1989). Empowerment model for delivery of social work services in public schools. *Social Work in Education, 11,* 160–170.

O'Donnell, S. (1993). Involving clients in welfare policy-making. *Social Work, 38,* 629–635.

Oesterheld, J. R., & Haber, J. (1997). Acceptability of the Conners Parent Rating Scale and Child Behavior Checklist to Dakotan/Lakotan parents. *Journal*

of the American Academy of Child and Adolescent Psychiatry, 36(1), 55–63.

O'Hanlon, B., & Bertolino, R. (1998). *Invitation to possibility land.* New York: Brunner/Mazel.

O'Hanlon, W. H., & Weiner-Davis, M. (1989). *In search of solutions: A new direction in psychotherapy.* New York: W. W. Norton.

Oliver, M. (1992). Changing the social relations of research production. *Disability, Handicap, & Society, 7*(2),101–114.

Oliver, M. (1994). Moving on: From welfare paternalism to welfare citizenship. *Social Action, 2*(1), 12–16.

Oliver, M. (1996). *Understanding disability: From theory to practice.* London: Macmillan Press.

Oliver, M. (1997). The Disability Movement is a new social movement. *Community Development Journal, 32*(3), 244–251.

Olson, D. H., & DeFrain, J. (1999). *Marriage and family diversity and strengths* (3rd ed.). Mountain View, CA: Mayfield Publishing Co.

O'Melia, M. (1991). *Generalist Perspectives in case coordination.* Workshop presentation at The Association for Retarded Citizens of Rock Island County, Rock Island, IL.

O'Melia, M. (1995, May). Skills for protecting children while preserving families. Workshop presentation for New Partnership. Appleton, WI.

O'Melia, M. (October, 1998). *Proactive responding: Paths toward diverse strengths.* Paper presented at BPD 16th Annual Conference, Albuquerque, N.M.

Orlin, M. (1995). The Americans with Disabilities Act: Implications for social services. *Social Work, 40,* 233–239.

Ostrander, S. A. (1985). Voluntary social service agencies in the United States. *Social Service Review, 59,* 435–454.

Oyserman, D., & Benbenishty, R. (1997). Developing and implementing an integrated information system for foster care and adoption. *Computers in Human Services, 14*(1), 1–20.

Oyserman, D., & Sakamoto, I. (1997). Being Asian American: Identity, cultural constructs, and stereotype perception. *Journal of Applied Behavioral Science, 33*(4), 435–453.

Pantoja, A., & Perry, W. (1998). Community development and restoration: A perspective. In F. G. Rivera & J. L. Erlich (Eds.), *Community organizing in a diverse society* (pp. 220–242). Boston: Allyn & Bacon.

Papernow, P. (1993). *Becoming a stepfamily: Patterns of development in remarried families.* San Francisco: Jossey-Bass.

Papp, P. (1983). *The process of change.* New York: The Guilford Press.

Pardeck, J. T. (1988). Social treatment through an ecological Approach. *Clinical Social Work Journal, 16,* 92–104.

Parsons, R. J. (1991). Empowerment: Purpose and practice principle in social work. *Social Work with Groups, 14*(2), 7–21.

Parsons, R. J., Hernandez, S. H., & Jorgensen, J. D. (1988). Integrated practice: A framework for problem solving. *Social Work, 33,* 417–421.

Parsons, R. J., Jorgensen, J. D., & Hernandez, S. H. (1994). *The integration of social work practice.* Belmont, CA: Brooks/Cole Publishing Company.

Patten, S., Gatz, Y. K., Jones, B., & Thomas, D. (1989). Posttraumatic stress disorder and the treatment of sexual abuse. *Social Work, 34,* 197–203.

Patton, M. Q. (1997). Toward distinguishing empowerment evaluation and placing it in a larger context. *Evaluation Practice, 18*(2), 147–163.

Pellebon, D. A., & Anderson, S. C. (1999). Understanding the life issues of spiritually-based clients. *Families in Society, 80*(3), 229–238.

Perlman, G. L. (1988). Mastering the law of privileged communication: A guide for social workers. *Social Work, 33,* 425–429.

Perlman, H. H. (1957). *Social casework: A problem solving process.* Chicago: University of Chicago Press.

Perlman, H. H. (1976). Believing and doing: Values in social work education. *Social Casework, 57,* 381–390.

Piccard, B. J. (1988). *An introduction to social work: A primer* (3rd ed.). Homewood, IL: The Dorsey Press.

Pilisuk, M., McAllister, J., & Rothman, J. (1996). Coming together for action: The challenge of contemporary grassroots community organizing. *Journal of Social Issues, 52*(1), 15–37.

Pincus, A., & Minahan, A. (1973). *Social work practice: Model and method.* Itasca, IL: Peacock Publishers.

Pinderhughes, E. B. (1979). Teaching empathy in cross-cultural social work, *Social Work, 24,* 321–316.

Pinderhughes, E. B. (1982). Afro-American families and the victim system. In M. McGoldrick, J. K.

Pearce, & J. Giordano (Eds.), *Ethnicity and family therapy* (pp. 108–122). New York: Guilford Press.

Pinderhughes, E. B. (1983). Empowerment for our clients and for ourselves. *Social Casework, 64,* 331–338.

Pinderhughes, E. B. (1989). *Understanding race, ethnicity, and power.* New York: The Free Press.

Pinderhughes, E. (1995). Empowering diverse populations: Family practice in the 21st century. *Families in Society, 76,* 131–140.

Pinderhughes, E. B. (1997). The interaction of difference and power as a basic framework for understanding work with African Americans: Family theory, empowerment and educational approaches. *Smith College Studies in Social Work, 67*(3), 323–347.

Ping-Kwong, K. (1997). Towards empowerment and advocacy: Practice and policy in social services for older people in Hong Kong. *Asia Pacific Journal of Social Work, 7*(2), 46–62.

Pittman F. S. (1987). *Turning points: Treating families in transition and crisis.* New York: W. W. Norton.

Piven, F. F., & Cloward, R. A. (1971). *Regulating the poor: The functions of public welfare.* New York: Vintage Books.

Plant, R. (1970). *Social and moral theory in casework.* London: Routledge and Kegan Paul.

Polowy, C. L., & Gorenberg, C. (1997). Legal issues: recent developments in confidentiality and privilege. In R. L. Edwards (Ed.), *Encyclopedia of social work* (19th ed., 1997 supplement) (pp. 179–190). Washington, DC: NASW Press.

Poole, D. L. (1998). Politically correct or culturally competent? (Editorial). *Health and Social Work, 23*(3), 163–166.

Powell, T. J. (1995). Self-help groups. In R. L. Edwards (Ed.), *Encyclopedia of social work: Vol. 3* (19th ed.) (pp. 2116–2123). Washington, DC: NASW Press.

Powers, G. T., Meenaghan, T. M., & Toomey, B. G. (1985). *Practice focused research: Integrating human service practice and research.* Englewood Cliffs, NJ: Prentice-Hall, Inc.

Pray, J. (1991). Respecting the uniqueness of the individual: Social work practice within a reflective model. *Social Work, 36,* 80–85.

Presley, J. H. (1987). The clinical dropout: A view from the client's perspective. *Social Casework, 68*(10), 603–608.

Prigmore, C. S., & Atherton, C. R. (1986). *Social welfare policy: Analysis and formulation*. Lexington, MA: D.C. Heath and Company.

Proctor, C. D., & Groze, V. K. (1994). Risk factors for suicide among gay, lesbian, and bisexual youth. *Social Work, 39,* 504–512.

Proctor, E. K., & Davis, L. E. (1994). The challenge of racial difference: Skills for clinical practice. *Social Work, 39,* 314–323.

Professional impairment. (1999, March). *NASW News, 44*(3), p. 16.

Pruger, R. (1978). Bureaucratic functioning as a social work skill. In B. Baer & R. Federico, *West Virginia undergraduate social worker curriculum development project: Educating the baccalaureate social worker* (pp. 149–168). Cambridge, MA: Ballinger Publishing Company.

Pugliesi, K., & Shook, S. L. (1998). Gender, ethnicity, and network characteristics: Variation in social support resources. *Sex Roles: A Journal of Research, 38*(3–4), 215–238.

Quible, Z. K. (1998). A focus on focus groups. *Business Communication Quarterly, 61*(2), 28–36.

Quinn, J. (1995). Case management in home and community care. *Journal of Gerontological Social Work, 24*(3/4), 233–248.

Ramos-McKay, J. M., Comas-Diaz, L., & Rivera, L. A. (1988). Puerto Ricans. In L. Comas-Diaz & E. E. H. Griffith (Eds.), *Clinical guidelines in cross-cultural mental health* (pp. 204–232). New York: John Wiley & Sons.

Rappaport, J. (1981). In praise of paradox: A social policy or empowerment over prevention. *American Journal of Community Psychology, 9,* 1–25.

Rappaport, J. (1984). Studies in empowerment: Introduction to the issue. *Prevention in Human Services, 3,* 1–7.

Rappaport, J. (1985). The power of empowerment language. *Social Policy, 17,* 15–21.

Rappaport, J. (1987). Terms of empowerment/exemplars of prevention: Toward a theory for community psychology. *American Journal of Community Psychology, 15*(2), 121–144.

Rappaport, J., Reischl, T. M., & Zimmerman, M. A. (1992). Mutual help mechanisms in the empowerment of former mental patients. In D. Saleebey (Ed.), *The strengths perspective in social work practice* (pp. 84–97). New York: Longman Press.

Reamer, F. G. (1987). Values and ethics. In A. Minahan (Ed.), *Encyclopedia of social work: Vol 2* (18th ed.) (pp. 801–809). Silver Spring, MD: National Association of Social Workers, Inc.

Reamer, F. G. (1992). The impaired social worker. *Social Work, 37,* 165–170.

Reamer, F. G. (1993). *The philosophical foundations of social work*. New York: Columbia University Press.

Reamer, F. G. (1994a). Social work values and ethics. In F. G. Reamer (Ed.), *The foundations of social work knowledge* (pp. 195–230). New York: Columbia University Press.

Reamer, F. G. (1994b). *Social work malpractice and strategies for prevention*. New York: Columbia University Press.

Reamer, F. G. (1995). *Social work values and ethics*. New York: Columbia University Press.

Reamer, F. G. (1998). *Ethical standards in social work: A critical review of the NASW Code of Ethics*. Washington, DC: NASW Press.

Red Horse, J. (1982). Clinical strategies for American Indian families in crisis. *Urban and Social Change Review, 15*(2), 17–19.

Rees, S. (1991). *Achieving power: Practice and policy in social welfare*. North Sydney, Australia: Allen & Unwen.

Reeser, L. C. (1991). Professionalization, striving, and social work activism. *Journal of Social Service Research, 14*(3/4), 1–22.

Regehr, C., & Antle, B. (1997). Coercive influences: Informed consent in court-mandated social work practice. *Social Work, 42*(3), 300–306.

Reid, W. J. (1995). Research overview. In R. L. Edwards (Ed.), *Encyclopedia of social work: Vol. 3* (19th ed.) (pp. 2040–2054). Washington, DC: NASW Press.

Religion can answer society's problems has been dominant view since 1957. (1997, October). Emerging trends. Retrieved June 8, 1999 from the World Wide Web: http://www.prrc.com/et.html

Reynolds, B. C. (1951). *Social work and social living*. New York: Citadel Press.

Richan, W. C. (1996). *Lobbying for social change*. New York: Haworth Press.

Rivera, F. G., & Erlich, J. L. (1998). A time of fear: A time of hope. In F. G. Rivera & J. L. Erlich (Eds.), *Community organizing in a diverse society* (pp. 1–24). Boston: Allyn & Bacon.

Rock, B., & Congress, E. (1999). The new confidentiality for the 21st century in a managed care environment. *Social Work, 44*(3), 253–262.

Rogers, C. R. (1951). *Client centered therapy.* Boston: Houghton Mifflin.

Rogers, G. (1995). Educating case managers for culturally competent practice. *Journal of Case Management, 4*(2), 60–65.

Rogers, W. A., Meyer, B., Walker, N., & Fisk, A. D. (1998). Functional limitations to daily living tasks in the aged: A focus-group analysis. *Human Factors, 40*(1), 111–125.

Rooney, R. H. (1992). *Strategies for work with involuntary clients.* New York: Columbia University Press.

Rose, S. M. (1992). Case management: An advocacy/empowerment design. In S. M. Rose (Ed.), *Case management and social work practice.* New York: Longman.

Rose, S. M., & Moore, V. L. (1995). Case management. In R. L. Edwards (Ed.), *Encyclopedia of social work: Vol. 1* (19th ed.) (pp. 335–340). Washington, DC: NASW Press.

Rosenthal, R., & Jacobson, L. (1968). *Pygmalion in the classroom.* New York: Holt, Rinehart and Winston.

Rothman, J., Smith, W., Nakashima, J., Paterson, M. A., & Mustin, J. (1996). Client self-determination and professional intervention: Striking a balance. *Social Work, 41*(4), 396–405.

Rothman, J., & Tropman, J. E. (1987). Models of community organization and macro practice perspective. In F. M. Cox, J. L. Erlich, J. Rothman, & J. E. Tropman (Eds.), *Strategies of community organization: Macro practice* (pp. 3–26). Itasca, IL: F. E. Peacock.

Rounds, K. A., Weil, M., & Bishop, K. K. (1994). Practice with culturally diverse families of young children with disabilities. *Families in Society, 75*(1), 3–14.

Royse, D. (1999). *Research methods in social work* (3rd ed.). Chicago: Nelson-Hall Publishers.

Rubin, A. (1992). Case management. In S. M. Rose (Ed.), *Case management and social work practice* (pp. 5–20). New York: Longman.

Rubin, A., & Babbie, E. (1997). *Research methods for social work* (3rd ed.). Pacific Grove, CA: Brooks/Cole Publishers.

Rudes, J., Shilts, L., & Berg, I. (1997). Focused supervision seen through a recursive frame analysis. *The Journal of Marital and Family Therapy, 23*(2), 203–215.

Ryan, W. (1976). *Blaming the victim* (Rev. ed.). New York: Vintage Books.

Saleebey, D. (1990). Philosophical disputes in social work: Social justice denied. *Journal of Sociology and Social Welfare, 17*(2), 29–40.

Saleebey, D. (1992a). Introduction: Power in the people. In D. Saleebey (Ed.), *The strengths perspective in social work practice* (pp. 3–17). New York: Longman Press.

Saleebey, D. (1992b). Introduction: Beginnings of a strengths approach to practice. In D. Saleebey (Ed.), *The strengths perspective in social work practice* (pp. 41–58). New York: Longman Press.

Saleebey, D. (1992c). Conclusion: Possibilities of and problems with the strengths perspective. In D. Saleebey (Ed.), *The strengths perspective in social work practice* (pp. 169–179). New York: Longman Press.

Saleebey, D. (1994). Culture, theory, and narrative: The intersection of meanings in practice. *Social Work, 39*(4), 351–359.

Salgado de Snyder, V. N., de Jesus Diaz-Perez, M., Maldonado, M., & Bautista, E. M. (1998). Pathways to mental health services among inhabitants of a Mexican village. *Health and Social Work, 23*(4), 249–258.

Saltzman, A. (1986). Reporting child abusers and protecting substance abusers. *Social Work, 31,* 474–476.

Saltzman, A., & Furman, D. M. (1999). *Law in social work practice* (2nd ed.). Chicago, IL: Nelson-Hall.

Satir, V. (1988). *The new peoplemaking.* Mountain View, CA: Science and Behavior Books.

Saulnier, C. F. (1996). *Feminist theories and social work: Approaches and applications.* New York: Haworth Press.

Schafer, C. M. (1969). Teaching social work practice in an integrated course: A general systems approach. In G. Hearn (Ed.), *The general systems approach: Contributions toward an holistic conception of social work* (pp. 26–36). New York: Council on Social Work Education.

Schoeh, D., et al., (1998). Developing and using a community bank. *Computers in Human Services, 15*(1), 35–53.

Schopler, J. H., Abell, M. D., & Galinsky, M. J. (1998). Technology-based groups: A review and conceptual framework for practice. *Social Work, 43*(3), 254–267.

Schorr, A. L. (1985). Professional practice as policy, *Social Service Review, 59,* 178–196.

Schriver, J. M. (1998). *Human behavior and the social environment.* Boston: Allyn & Bacon.

Schroeder, L. O. (1995). *The legal environment of social work.* Washington, DC: NASW Press.

Schwartz, W. (1974). Private troubles and public issues: One social work job or two? In R. W. Klenk & R. M. Ryan (Eds.), *The practice of social work* (2nd ed.) (pp. 82–101). Belmont, CA: Wadsworth Publishing Company, Inc.

Schwarz, R. M. (1994). *The skilled facilitator: Practical wisdom for developing effective groups.* San Francisco: Jossey-Bass Publishers.

Secret, M., Jordan, A., & Ford, J. (1999). Empowerment evaluation as a social work strategy. *Health and Social Work, 24*(2), 120+. Retrieved August 22, 1999 from InfoTrac database (Expanded Academic ASAP) on the World Wide Web: http://www5.infotrac.galegroup.com

Sedlack, R. G., & Stanley, J. (1992). *Social research: Theory and practice.* Boston: Allyn & Bacon.

Seligman, M. E. P. (1975). *Helplessness.* San Francisco, CA: Freeman Press.

Shapiro, B. Z. (1991). Social action, the group and society. *Social Work with Groups, 14*(3/4), 7–21.

Sharwell, G. R. (1982). How to testify before a legislative committee. In M. Mahaffey & J. Hanks (Eds.), *Practical politics: Social workers and political responsibility* (pp. 85–98). Silver Spring, MD: National Association of Social Workers.

Sheafor, B. W., Horejsi, C. R., & Horejsi, G. A. (1997). *Techniques and guidelines for social work practice* (4th ed.). Boston: Allyn & Bacon.

Sheridan, M. J., Gowen, N., & Halpin, S. (1993). Developing a practice model for the homeless mentally ill. *Families in Society, 74,* 410–421.

Shulman, L. (1999). *The skills of helping individuals, families, groups, and communities* (4th ed.). Itasca, IL: F. E. Peacock Publishers, Inc.

Shulman, L., & Gitterman, A. (1994). The life model, mutual aid, oppression, and the mediating function. In A. Gitterman & L. Shulman (Eds.), *Mutual aid groups, vulnerable populations, and the life cycle* (2nd ed.) (pp. 3–28). New York: Columbia University Press.

Siebold, C. (1992). Forced termination: Reconsidering theory and technique. *Smith College Studies in Social Work, 63*(1), 325–341.

Simon, B. L. (1990). Rethinking empowerment. *Journal of Progressive Human Services, 1,* 27–39.

Simon, B. L. (1994). *The empowerment tradition in American social work: A history.* New York: Columbia University Press.

Simons, R. L., & Aigner, S. M. (1985). *Practice principles: A problem solving approach to social work.* New York: Macmillan Publishing Company.

Siporin, M. (1975). *Introduction to social work practice.* New York: MacMillan.

Siporin, M. (1980). Ecological systems theory in social work. *Journal of Sociology and Social Welfare, 7,* 507–532.

Siporin, M. (1983). Morality and immorality in working with clients. *Social Thought, 9*(4), 10–28.

Siporin, M. (1985). Current social work perspectives on clinical practice. *Clinical Social Work Journal, 13,* 198–217.

Sirkin, R. M. (1999). *Statistics for the social sciences.* (2nd ed.). Thousand Oaks, CA: Sage.

Slonim-Nevo, V. (1996). Clinical practice: Treating the non-voluntary client. *International Social Work, 39,* 117–129.

Smalley, R. (1967). *Theory for social work practice.* New York: Columbia University Press.

Smith, L. A. (1996). Unique names and naming practices among African American families. *Families in Society, 77,* 290–297.

Soderfeldt, M., Soderfeldt, B., & Warg, L. E. (1995). Burnout in social work, *Social Work, 40,* 638–646.

Solomon, B. B. (1976). *Black empowerment: Social work in oppressed communities.* New York: Columbia University Press.

Solomon, B. B. (1983). Value issues in working with minority clients. In A. Rosenblatt & D. Waldfogel (Eds.), *Handbook of clinical social work* (pp. 866–887). San Francisco: Jossey-Bass Publishers.

Solomon, B. B. (1987). Human development: Sociocultural perspectives In A. Minahan (Ed.), *Encyclopedia of social work: Vol 1* (18th ed.) (pp. 856–866). Silver Spring, MD: National Association of Social Workers, Inc.

Sparks, P. M. (1989). Organizational tasking: A case report. *Organizational Development Journal, 7,* 51–57.

Specht, H. (1983). Policy issues in clinical practice. In A. Rosenblatt & D. Waldfogel (Eds.), *Handbook of clinical social work* (pp. 721–730). San Francisco: Jossey-Bass Publishers.

Specht, H., & Courtney, M. E. (1994). *Unfaithful angels: How social work has abandoned its mission.* New York: The Free Press.

Stevens, M. J., & Campion, M. A. (1994). The knowledge, skill, and ability requirements for teamwork: Implications for human resource management. *Journal of Management, 20*(2), 503–530.

Stoesz, D. (1993). Communicating with the public. *Social Work, 38,* 367–368.

Strom-Gottfried, K. (1998). Is "ethical managed care" an oxymoron? *Families in Society, 79*(3), 297–307.

Strupp, H., Fox, R., & Lessler, K. (1969). *Patients view their psychotherapy.* Baltimore, MD: Johns Hopkins University Press.

Stufflebeam, D. L. (1994). Recommendations for improving evaluations in U.S. public schools. *Studies in Educational Evaluation, 20,* 3–21.

Sue, D. W., & Sue, D. (1999). *Counseling the culturally different.* New York: John Wiley & Sons.

Sullivan, M. (1993). The Nguzo Saba: African-centered values as tools for family assessment, support, and empowerment. *Family Resource Coalition Report, 12*(1), 6–7.

Sullivan, T. R. (1994). Obstacles to effective child welfare service with gay and lesbian youths. *Child Welfare, 73,* 291–304.

Sullivan, W. P. (1992). Reclaiming the community: The strengths perspective and deinstitutionalization. *Social Work, 37,* 204–209.

Sullivan, W. P., & Rapp, C. A. (1994). Breaking away: The potential and promise of a strengths-based approach to social work practice. In R. G. Meinert, J. T. Pardeck, & W. P. Sullivan (Eds.), *Issues in social work: A critical analysis* (pp. 83–104). Wesport, CT: Auburn House.

Swift, C. (1984). Empowerment: An antidote for folly. *Journal of Prevention in Human Services, 3,* xi–xv.

Swift, C., & Levin, G. (1987). Empowerment: An emerging mental health technology. *Journal of Primary Prevention, 8*(1/2), 71–94.

Tarasoff v. the Regents of the University of California, 551, P.2d 334 (Calif. 1976).

Tebb, S. (1991). Client-focused recording: Linking theory and practice. *Families in Society, 72,* 425–432.

The counter-attack of God. (1995). *The Economist, 336*(7922), 19–21.

Therapy privilege upheld. (1996, July). *NASW News, 41*(7), p. 7.

Thomas, E. (1978). Research and service in single-case experimentation: Conflicts and choices. *Social Work Research and Abstracts, 14*(Winter), 20–31.

Thyer, B. A. (1990). Single-system research designs in social work practice. In L. Videka-Sherman & W. J. Reid (Eds.), *Advances in clinical social work research* (pp. 33–36). Silver Spring, MD: NASW Press.

Thyer, B. A., & Thyer, K. B. (1992). Single-system research designs in social work practice: A bibliography from 1965 to 1990. *Research on Social Work Practice, 2*(1), 99–116.

Tillich, P. (1962). The philosophy of social work. *Social Service Review, 36*(1), 13–16.

Timberlake, E. M., Sabatino, C. A., & Martin, J. A. (1997). Advanced practitioners in clinical social work: A profile. *Social Work, 42*(4), 374–385.

Tolson, E. R. (1990). Why don't practitioners use single-subject designs? In L. Videka-Sherman & W. J. Reid (Eds.), *Advances in clinical social work research* (pp. 58–64). Silver Spring, MD: NASW Press.

Toseland, R. W. (1987). Treatment discontinuance: Grounds for optimism. *Social Casework, 68,* 195–204.

Toseland, R. W., & Rivas, F. F. (1998). *An Introduction to group work practice* (3rd ed.). Boston: Allyn & Bacon.

Toseland, R. W., Rossiter, C. M., & Labrecque, M. S. (1989). The effectiveness of two kinds of support groups for caregivers. *Social Service Review, 63,* 415–432.

Tourse, R. W. (1995). Special-interest professional associations. In R. L. Edwards (Ed.), *Encyclopedia of social work: Vol. 3* (19th ed.) (pp. 2314–2219). Washington, DC: NASW Press.

Tower, K. D. (1994). Consumer-centered social work practice: Restoring client self-determination. *Social Work, 39,* 191–196.

Tracy, B., & DuBois, B. (1987, September). *Information model for generalist social work practice.*

Paper presented at the meeting of the Baccalaureate Program Directors of Social Work Programs, Kansas City, KS.

Tracy, E. M., & Whittaker, J. K. (1990). The social support network map: Assessing social support in clinical practice. *Families in Society, 71,* 461–470.

Trivette, C. M., Dunst, C. J., Boyd, K., & Hamby, D. W. (1995). Family-oriented program models, helpgiving practices, and parental control appraisals. *Exceptional Children, 62*(3), 237–238.

Trivette, C. M., Dunst, C. J., & Hamby, D. (1996). Characteristics and consequences of help-giving practices in contrasting human services programs. *American Journal of Community Psychology, 24*(2), 273–293.

Turner, K. D. (1994). Consumer-centered social work practice: Restoring client self-determination. *Social work, 39,* 191–196.

Turner, M. (1997). Reshaping our lives. *Research, Policy and Planning, 15*(2), 23–25.

U.S. Bureau of the Census. (1995). *Statistical abstract of the United States: 1995* (115th ed.). Washington, DC: U.S. Government Printing Office.

U.S. Bureau of the Census. (1996). Resident population of the United States: Middle series projections, 2035–2050, by sex, race, and Hispanic origin, with median age. Retrieved June 8, 1999 from the World Wide Web: *http://www.census.gov/population/ projections/nation/nsrh/nprh3550.txt*

U.S. Bureau of the Census. (1999). Resident population estimates of the United States by sex, race, and Hispanic origin: April 1, 1990 to April 1, 1999. Retrieved June 8, 1999 from the World Wide Web: *http://www.census.gov/population/ estimates/nation./intfile3-1.txt*

U.S. Department of Justice. (1999). Elder abuse and neglect. Retrieved June 28, 1999 from the World Wide Web: *http://www.ojp.usdoj.gov/ovc/ncvrw/ 1999/elder.htm*

VanDenBergh, N., & Cooper, L. B. (1986). Introduction. In N. VanDenBergh & L. B. Cooper (Eds.), *Feminist visions for social work* (pp. 1–28). Silver Spring, MD: National Association of Social Workers.

Visher, E. B., & Visher, J. S. (1996). *Therapy with stepfamilies.* New York: Brunner/Mazel, Inc.

von Bertalanffy, L. (1968). *General system theory.* New York: George Braziller, Inc.

Wall, M. D., Kleckner, T., Amendt, J. H., & Bryant, r. d. (1989). Therapeutic compliments: Setting the stage for successful therapy. *Journal of Marriage and Family Therapy, 15,* 159–167.

Walsh, F. (1998). Beliefs, spirituality, and transcendence: Keys to family resilience. In M. McGoldrick (Ed.), *Re-visioning family therapy* (pp. 62–77). New York: The Guilford Press.

Walsh, F. (1999). *Spiritual resources in family therapy.* New York: The Guilford Press.

Walter, J. L., & Peller, J. E. (1992). *Becoming solution-focused in brief therapy.* New York: Brunner/Mazel, Inc.

Ward, D., & Mullender, A. (1991). Empowerment and oppression: An indissoluble pairing for contemporary social work. *Critical Social Policy, 11*(2), 21–30.

Watkins, S. A. (1989). Confidentiality and privileged communications: Legal dilemma for family therapists. *Social Work, 34,* 133–136.

Watt, J. W., & Kallmann, G. L. (1998). Managing professional obligations under managed care: A social work perspective. *Family and Communiity Health, 21*(2), 40+. Retrieved March 28, 1999 from InfoTrac database (Expanded Academic ASAP) on the World Wide Web: http://www5. infotrac.galegroup.com

Watzlawick, P., Bavelas, J. M., & Jackson, D. D. (1967). *Pragmatics of human communication.* New York: W. W. Norton.

Watzlawick, P., Weakland, J., & Fisch, R. (1974). *Change: Principles of problem formation and problem resolution.* New York: W. W. Norton & Company.

Weaver, H. N., & White, B. J. (1997). The Native American family cycle: Roots of resiliency. *Journal of Family Social Work, 2*(1), 67–79.

Weaver, H., & Wodarski, J. S. (1996). Social work practice with Latinos. In D. F. Harrison, B. A. Thyer, & J. S. Wodarski (Eds.), *Cultural diversity and social work practice* (2nd ed.) (pp. 52–86). Springfield, IL: Charles C Thomas, Publisher.

Weick, A. (1980). Issues of power in social work practice. In A. Weick & S. T. Vandiver (Eds.), *Women, power, and change* (pp. 173–185). Washington, DC: NASW, Inc.

Weick, A. (1983). Issues in overturning a medical model of social work practice. *Social Work, 28,* 467–471.

Weick, A. (1992). Building a strengths perspective for social work. In D. Saleebey (Ed.), *The strengths perspective in social work practice* (pp. 18–26). New York: Longman Press.

Weick, A., Rapp, C., Sullivan, W. P., & Kisthardt, W. (1989). A strengths perspective for social work practice. *Social Work, 34,* 350–354.

Weick, A., & Saleebey, D. (1995). Supporting family strengths: Orienting policy and practice toward the 21st century. *Families in Society, 76,* 141–149.

Weil, M., & Karls, J. M. (1989). Historical origins and recent developments. In M. Weils & J. M. Karls (Eds.), *Case management in human service practice* (pp. 1–28). San Francisco, CA: Jossey-Bass Publishers.

Weinbach, R. W., & Grinnell, R. M. (1998). *Statistics for social workers* (4th ed.). Boston: Allyn & Bacon.

Weisz, A. N. (1999). Legal advocacy for domestic violence survivors: The power of an informative relationship. *Families in Society, 80*(2), 138–147.

Wells, C. C., with Masch, M. K. (1986). *Social work ethics day to day: Guidelines for professional practice.* New York: Longman.

Wharton, A. S. (1999, January). The psychosocial consequences of emotional labor. *The Annals of the American Academy of Political and Social Science,* pp. 158+. Retrieved June 5, 1999 from InfoTrac database (Expanded Academic ASAP) on the World Wide Web: http://www5.infotrac.galegroup.com

Whipple, V. (1996). Developing an identity as a feminist family therapist: Implications for training. *Journal of Marital and Family Therapy, 22*(3), 381–396.

White, K. S., Bruce, S. E., Farrell, A. D., & Kliewer, W. (1998). Impact of exposure to community violence on anxiety: A longitudinal study of family social support as protective factor for urban children. *Journal of Child and Family Studies, 7*(2), 187–203.

White, L. G. (1994). Policy analysis as discourse. *Journal of Policy Analysis and Management, 13*(3), 506–525.

White, M. (1989). The externalizing of the problem and the re-authoring of lives and relationships. In M. White (Ed.), *Selected papers* (pp. 5–28). Adelaide, Australia: Dulwich Centre Publications.

Whittaker, J. K., & Tracy, E. M. (1991). Social network intervention in intensive family-based preventive services. *Prevention in Human Services, 9*(1), 175–192.

Williams, G. A., Abbott, E. R., & Taylor, D. K. (1997). Using focus group methodology to develop breast cancer screening programs that recruit African American women. *Journal of Community Health, 22*(1), 45–56.

Wilson, M. K., & Anderson, S. C. (1997). Empowering female offenders: Removing barriers to community-based practice. *Affilia, 12*(3), 342–358.

Wilson, S. J. (1978). *Confidentiality in social work.* New York: The Free Press.

Wilson, S. J. (1980). *Recording: Guidelines for social workers.* New York: The Free Press.

Witkin, S. L. (1999). Constructing our future (Social constructionism) (Editorial) *Social Work, 44*(1), 5–8.

Wolin, S. J., & Wolin, S. (1993). *The resilient self: How survivors of troubled families rise above adversity.* New York: Villard Books.

Wolk, J. L. (1994). Grant writing: Linking the social work program to the community. *Journal of Teaching in Social Work, 10*(1/2), 83–97.

Wood, G. G., & Middleman, R. R. (1991). Advocacy and social action: Key elements in the structural approach to direct practice in social work. *Social Work with Groups, 14*(3/4), 53–63.

Woody, R. H. (1993). Americans with Disabilities Act: Implications for family therapy. *The American Journal of Family Therapy, 21*(1), 71–78.

Worthen, B. L., Sanders, J. R., & Fitzpatrick, J. L. (1997). *Program evaluation: Alternative approaches and practical guidelines.* White Plains, NY: Longman Publishers.

Wright, O. L., & Anderson, J. P. (1998). Clinical social work practice with urban African American families. *Families in Society, 79*(2), 197–205.

Wylie, M. S. (1996). Going for the cure. *The Family Therapy Networker, 20*(4), 21–37.

Yamato, G. (1993). Something about the subject makes it hard to name. In V. Cyrus (Ed.), *Experiencing race, class, and gender in the United States* (pp. 206–213). Mountain View, CA: Mayfield Publishing Company.

Yellow Bird, M., Fong, R., Galindo, P., Nowicki, J., & Freeman, E. M. (1995). The multicultural mosaic. *Social Work in Education, 17*(3), 131–138.

Young, I. (1994). Punishment, treatment, empowerment: Three approaches to policy for pregnant addicts. *Feminist Studies, 20,* 33+ retrieved from http://www.elibrary.com

Ziefert, M., & Brown, K. S. (1991). Skill building for effective intervention with homeless families. *Families in Society, 72,* 212–219.

Zilberfein, F. (1999). Coping with death: Anticipatory grief and bereavement. *Generations, 12*(1), 69–74.

Zimmerman, M. A. (1990). Toward a theory of learned hopefulness: A structural model analysis of participation and empowerment. *Journal of Research in Personality, 24,* 71–86.

Zimmerman, M. A., & Rappaport, J. (1988). Citizen participation, perceived control, and psychological empowerment. *American Journal of Community Psychology, 16,* 725–750.

Zippay, A. (1995). The politics of empowerment. *Social Work, 40,* 263–267.

Zunz, S. J. (1998). Resiliency and burnout: Protective factors for human service managers. *Administration in Social Work, 22*(3), 39–54.

Name Index

Subject Index